CHRISTIAN BAPTISM:

IN TWO PARTS.

PART FIRST—INFANT BAPTISM.

PART SECOND—MODE, OBLIGATION, IMPORT, AND RELATIVE ORDER.

BY REV. F. G. HIBBARD,

OF THE GENESEE CONFERENCE.

New-York:

PUBLISHED BY LANE & SCOTT,

200 Mulberry-street.

JOSEPH LONGKING, PRINTER.

1851.

CHRISTIAN BAPTISM.

PART I.—INFANT BAPTISM.

PRO HOC ET ECCLESIA AB APOSTOLIS TRADITIONEM SUSCEPIT, ETIAM PARVULIS BAPTISMUM DARE.—ORIGEN.

THEIR CHILDREN, ALSO, SHALL BE AS AFORETIME.—JEREMIAH.

TO THE

REV. NATHAN BANGS, D. D.

Dear Sir,—I could not do justice to my own feelings should I pass this opportunity afforded by the dedication of this humble volume to you, without bearing my public testimony to the high sense I entertain of your personal worth, the efficiency of your public labours, and of your kindness to me.

Your life has truly been one of labour, responsibility, and care; not, however, unrequited by the gratitude and honourable preferments of that growing church, the champion of whose rights and immunities you may justly be called.

When American Methodism was yet in her infancy,—(and, though of rapid growth, she has scarcely yet attained her full vigour,)—when, as yet, her policy and her characteristic tenets were novel to the age; her institutions, her ministry, and her doctrines, were boldly assailed by men who had little else than a gray antiquity to sanction their pretensions, and whose ignorance of Methodism, and envy at her prosperity, inspirited them in their offensive career, you stood up in her defence.

Your early and long association with these unhappy conflicts, your deep paternal sympathy in the protracted struggle, your fearless and generous devotion to the cause of truth, as connected with these events, are topics of grateful and satisfactory remembrance, and combine to inspire the belief that you will continue to share a liberal solicitude with your worthy compeers in those polemic essays that may, from time to time, be put forth for the defence of truth.

That you may live many days to bless the church and the world in the exalted stations to which the providence of God has called you—that your age may be soothed and sustained by the comforts and hopes of the gospel—that the goodliest allotments of Heaven may fall to your domestic and social inheritance during the remnant of your eventful and useful life—and that the approbation of our Master in heaven may be your memorial in death, is the prayer of, dear sir,

Your obliged friend and servant in the gospel,

F. G. Hibbard.

PREFACE.

1. Some time since a professional friend, being in my study, happened to take up a volume of Mr. Cotton's edition of the celebrated works of Drs. Wall and Gale on Infant Baptism; and perceiving that they contained more than two thousand pages, octavo, mainly on the single argument from church history, laid down the volume, saying, "he was sorry there was anybody in the world so foolish as to write so much on a subject like that of infant baptism." The surprise, and consequent remark of my friend, did not originate in any disrespect for the institutes of Christianity, but simply in not appreciating the just dimensions, and polemic history, of the subject. He felt no surprise at seeing the volumes that have been written with a view to explain the nature and treatment of disease, or the endless Reports that have been made to illustrate the true application of law and evidence, in civil matters. If men would study more the *history* of theology, they would better understand the cost of defending it.

2. The details of argument gone into, in the following pages, may appear to some to be unnecessary; but to such I have only to say, I have not written for the learned, but for the sincere inquirer of humbler capacity, and have aimed to set forth those facts only which are necessary to be taken into account, in order to master the argument, and to feel its force.

Also, the highly controverted state in which every thing is found relating to this subject, as well as the peculiar nature of the argument itself, must be my apology for having said so much. True, the argument might, in its strictest form, have been compressed within a much narrower compass; and to this form it was my first intention to confine it. But, upon further reflection, I could not feel that such a plan would be productive of the greatest good to the reader. Objections to infant baptism are everywhere thrown, from the pulpit and the press, before the minds of young Christians. These they have not learned to meet and obviate; and though they have not yielded to them an assent, still they exert a disturbing influence upon their faith. Without mentioning all these objections and arguments in detail, it has been my constant endeavour to keep them in view, and to hold them, in all their protean shapes, so steadily before the Bible argument, as to furnish the reader with ample means for detecting and refuting their sophistry. But although the work has swelled beyond the limits I had at first assigned it, still I think it will be found the argument has never been abandoned for foreign or irrelevant speculations. Some trifling repetitions have unavoidably occurred, while some other matters, not deemed important, although treated by other authors, have been omitted. In the following pages the reader is presented with all that information which is strictly important to the subject. He is particularly requested to observe the *order* of the argument; a general syllabus of which he will find in the chapter of contents. This he should attentively scan before reading the work.

3. It is a great calamity to the cause of truth, that its professed advocates are so often men of strong party feeling, who indulge in an unguarded, and, I may say, reckless habit of stating both their own doctrine and also that of an opponent. It is hence, that indefensible positions are often assumed, false issues taken, personal feelings enlisted, and a large amount of vituperation and abuse fabricated. I would not appear invidious in my distinctions, but if the reader have ever read a late work on Baptism by Rev. James J. Woolsey, he will have found a melancholy demonstration of all I have stated. To mention but one instance of many, on p. 244 the author opens a section on the *silence* of the New Testament respecting infant baptism, and gives this statement of the Pedobaptist position:—"*The validity of infant baptism is plead for as of divine appointment, because there is no prohibition against it.*" In a former section he has thus stated a kindred position:—"*The validity of infant baptism is urged, and thought to be established, on the ground of its being taken for granted, without any express command in the New Testament.*" In these sections the author has argued to the principle, that *mere* silence, and *mere* absence of prohibition, cannot afford *authority* for a practice. Now, no one but a mad-

man could be his opponent in this case. He has misstated both the position and reasonings of the Pedobaptists. The peculiar point of the argument, as insisted on by the Pedobaptists, is not once developed, or even alluded to, in any way, through the whole course of his remarks. Is it any wonder that men do not understand each other, or that parties are not reconciled?

4. If the reader would be profited by the investigations which are pursued through the following pages, he must have patience to *examine* before he ventures to decide. The subject is of that nature that it cannot be dismissed with a hasty consideration. The force of the argument does not lie imbodied in terse, isolated passages, which require but a single effort of the mind to comprehend them, and which leave upon the mind, with scarcely an effort of its own, the lively images of an intuitive conviction. A process of reasoning must be gone through,—a somewhat extended range of observation must be brought immediately under the eye of the mind,—and then the force of the argument must result from these varied premises,—from the coincidence and focal blaze of these collocated facts, which the mind should group and scan at a single synthetic effort.

If I have any doubt of the ultimate satisfaction of the reader's mind as to the reality of the divine institution of infant baptism, that doubt is the offspring, not of any suspicion that there is a want of evidence in the case, but, of a fear that the reader will be deluded into that mental imbecility which rejects all testimony but the most positive and absolute;—which has not patience or courage adequate to the length, and breadth, and depth of an extended argument;—and which, at last, making virtue of its own folly, professes to be guided only by the specific and positive declarations, in so many words, of the word of God.

5. In the following Treatise I have assumed that infants are in a regenerated state. This, I am fully aware, will be likely to provoke controversy, and many will reject all conclusions based upon this doctrine. But who are those who deny this doctrine? First, there is a class who believe that all infants who are "not elected" will finally perish. Such infants, of course, whether baptized or not, cannot be regenerated. Secondly, there are those who

believe that regeneration, in adults and infants, is a concomitant of baptism. Hence, as there can be no regeneration either *before* or *without* baptism, unbaptized infants cannot be in a regenerated state. Thirdly, there are those who profess no settled or specific view of the regeneration of infants; only they believe that all infants, dying in infancy, will be finally saved.

It is well known to the student in church history, that few, very few, since the days of the apostles, have ever openly held to the damnation of any of those infants who die in infancy. The Calvinistic school forms the largest exception. There have been those who have held that all unbaptized infants, dying in infancy, go to a sort of middle state, between heaven and hell, as the reader will see in the fifth chapter of this work. Others, as St. Austin, (see pp. 209–211,) with more consistency, held that where the want of baptism was not the fruit of any wicked and wilful disposition of the individual, he would be saved without it. The Protestant Episcopal Church, it appears, chooses, in regard to the state of unbaptized infants hereafter, to observe entire silence. (See pp. 270, 271, of this work.)

Now, all I wish here to say is, that I do not insist upon any peculiar sense of the word *regenerate.* The term has been adopted, in the following pages, because it conveniently expresses the doctrine of infant salvation. All I mean by it is, that infants are, whether baptized or not, in a state of grace; that they are embraced in the provisions of the atonement; that, if they die in infancy, they will be saved, and if they live, they will come under the gracious economy of Heaven, and receive the free offer of life. I wish not to contend about a word. I take the words of Christ, Matt. xix, 14, to refer to all infants, *as such,*—not to "elect" infants, or to baptized infants, or to the infants of Christian parents, merely. On this point, "if any man be ignorant, let him be ignorant."

I have only to add, as greater men have said before me, "If I have done well, and what is fitting the [argument,] it is that which I desired; but if slenderly and meanly, it is that which I could attain unto," 2 Mac. xv, 38.

F. G. Hibbard.

Penn Yan, N. Y., Aug. 20, 1842.

CONTENTS.

PART I.

CHAPTER I.—THE CHURCH.

CHAPTER II.

ORDINANCE OF INITIATION.

CHAPTER III.

THE INITIATORY RITE OF THE CHURCH ALTERED.

SECTION I.

SECTION II.

SECTION III.

SECTION IV.

CHAPTER IV.

ADDITIONAL EVIDENCE.

CHAPTER V.

HISTORICAL ARGUMENT.

SECTION I.

SECTION II.

BEFORE THE PELAGIAN CONTROVERSY.

AFTER THE RISE OF THE PELAGIAN CONTROVERSY.

SECTION III.

CHAPTER VI.

OBJECTIONS TO INFANT BAPTISM ANSWERED.

CHAPTER VII.

BENEFITS OF INFANT BAPTISM.

SECTION I.

SECTION II.

CHAPTER VIII.

GROUND OF INFANT BAPTISM.

APPENDIX.

PART II.

A

TREATISE ON INFANT BAPTISM.

CHAPTER I.

THE CHURCH.

ITS ANTIQUITY—ITS PROPER AND ESSENTIAL CHARACTER —DIFFERENCE BETWEEN THE COVENANT AND THE LAW—JEWISH AND CHRISTIAN CHURCHES SUBSTANTIALLY ONE AND IDENTICAL.

SECTION I.

1. First of all, in our reasoning upon the subject before us, we must have enlightened views with respect to the real church of God. We are not about to inquire which of all the existing churches professing to be Christian is the true one; much less are we about to set up a plea of exclusiveness, and say, "The temple of the Lord are *we*." We pass by the different Christian sects,—ascending the stream of time beyond their origin,—and ask, When did the church of God begin to display itself? And here we may admonish the reader, that it will be some time before we shall be prepared to draw our conclusions, and directly urge the force of our arguments. Meantime, he must go with us into details and arguments which may appear dry, but which are necessary to establish our premises. If he have not patience for all this, he had better here abandon the investigation.

When we inquire into the proper antiquity of the church of God, we are led far back in the world's history, to a period remote from the age of Christ and his apostles, and even beyond the prophets and Moses. At an early stage in the history of nations, after the flood, God called Abram, and separated him from his own kindred, and from his own nation, and organized his family into a church proper, bringing them into a visible covenant relation to himself. Jehovah had covenanted with his servants, the patriarchs, at different times, since the days of the first man. These covenants had been distinguished by signs, as that with Noah, by the "token" of the "bow in the clouds;" but never had the covenant of grace and mercy, which was to be ratified by the blood of God's own Son, been so largely revealed to man; and the visible token or mark of this covenant had never before been fixed upon the *persons themselves*, who entered as a second party to participate in its gracious provisions. This covenant, then, which God made with Abraham, differs from all others. The covenant with Noah, alluded to above, related to the perpetual order and harmony of the material world, securing "seed-time and harvest, summer and winter, day and night," &c. But this with Abraham related pre-eminently to spiritual blessings, to be bestowed upon the world through Christ. The *sign* of the covenant made with Noah was a "BOW" set in the clouds; the *sign* of the covenant with Abraham was "CIRCUMCISION,"—a mark set upon the male descendants of that patriarch, and upon all others who voluntarily came under its injunctions. Indeed, in whatever light we view it, we shall find this was the first attempt of Jehovah, on record, to bring man directly into a visible covenant relationship with himself. This transaction forms the first model of a visible church with which the world has ever been acquainted. It is here we date our idea of church. The importance of the subject will justify our detaining the reader a little further on the particular features of this covenant, which we regard as the great charter of the visible church, within whose ample folds are gathered and united both Jews and Gentiles.

2. Let us attend, for a moment, to our just ideas of what constitutes the church of God. We are not now about to bring the test of a *shibboleth* to this stupendous question. We do not propose this inquiry in the spirit of a sectarian. We plant ourselves upon the broad Bible principle, and ask, What is the Bible definition of CHURCH?

The visible church of God, in whatever clime or part of the world it may subsist, is composed of a congregation of persons, who are distinguished by the following particulars :—1. They hold to the cardinal doctrines of the Bible; those doctrines which are necessary to make a person wise unto salvation. I do not say that these doctrines must necessarily be embraced in all cases with an equal degree of clearness :—they must be received in a manner answerable to the light which distinguishes the particular dispensation under which the church may live. 2. They worship God according to his own will and directions, written or otherwise expressed. 3. They must be separated and distinguished from the world at large by a particular mark or sign, appointed by God as a token of their fidelity to him, and of the divine favour to them.

I know not that any one feature distinguishes the church of God that does not properly fall under one or other of these heads. Descriptions may be given more in detail, and many accidents may attach to the true visible church at one given time, that may not characterize it at another; but it is of the primary character of the church that we speak. Now, it is obvious that all these primary characteristics of the church belonged to those who were united to the covenant of Abraham, and were conferred on them by that covenant. Not that the model of the church was in all respects as perfect in the family of Abraham as it was afterward rendered: on the contrary, it was evidently improved under Moses, and still more under Christ. But, I repeat it, in the family of Abraham was the first germ of a visible church; and the covenant of God with that patriarch was the first charter under which men ever formed themselves into a visible church compact, and the first, of which we have any record, that God ever gave to man for that purpose.

3. The state of the argument renders it necessary that we should enter into proof of this position. It has been stoutly denied that the covenant of Abraham conveyed any grant of church privileges, or, indeed, of any spiritual blessings.* It will be our business to show that it imbodied the rudiments of the gospel of Christ, and was the date of church relations. The words of the covenant, as

* See, for instance, Woolsey on Baptism, p. 287; Jewett on Baptism, p. 62, &c.; and Mr. Pengilly's Tract, p. 60.

reiterated and renewed to Abraham, from time to time, run thus:—

"The Lord said unto Abraham ... I will make of thee a great nation, and I will bless thee, and make thy name great; and thou shalt be a blessing: and I will bless them that bless thee, and curse them that curse thee: and in thee shall all families of the earth be blessed. ... Lift up now thine eyes, and look from the place where thou art, northward, and southward, and eastward, and westward; for all the land which thou seest, to thee will I give it, and to thy seed for ever. And I will make thy seed as the dust of the earth. ... Look now toward heaven, and tell the stars if thou be able to number them; and He said unto him, So shall thy seed be. And he believed the Lord, and he counted it to him for righteousness. ... And God talked with Abram, saying, As for me, behold, my covenant is with thee, and thou shalt be a father of many nations. Neither shall thy name be any more called Abram, but Abraham; for a father of many nations have I made thee. And I will make thee exceeding fruitful, and I will make nations of thee; and kings shall come out of thee. And I will establish my covenant between me and thee, and thy seed after thee, in their generations, for an everlasting covenant; to be a God unto thee, and to thy seed after thee. And I will give unto thee, and thy seed after thee, the land wherein thou art a stranger, all the land of Canaan, for an everlasting possession, and I will be their God. ... And thy seed shall possess the gate of his enemies; and in thy seed shall all the nations of the earth be blessed." Gen. xii, 1–3; xiii, 14–17; xv, 1–7; xvii, 1–8; xxii, 15–18; xxvi, 3, 4; xxviii, 14, 15.

Before entering upon a close examination of the several parts of this covenant, it is important that the reader be reminded, first, that it has ever been a prevalent custom among the Orientals to teach by *metaphor* and *allegory*,—by making sensible objects the representatives of spiritual things. It is not needful here to dwell upon the prevalence or the advantages of this mode of teaching; but suffice it to say that, by this means, a twofold sense is attached to almost every part of this covenant,—a *literal* and a *spiritual* sense. This will appear, on Scriptural authority, in the process of our remarks. Secondly, it is chiefly by the light of other parts of Scripture, and particularly of the New Testament, that we are to interpret the true meaning of the words of this covenant. This remark may apply to a very large portion of the Old Testament Scriptures, especially to their types, and allegories, and prophetic sayings. It is evident that Abraham understood this covenant in a higher sense than merely to refer to temporal good; and it is not improbable that he received explanations of its high spiritual import, of which the text of Moses does not give full intimation. The same inspiration that guided Paul's pen in portraying its exalted character, doubtless shed its illuminations upon the mind of the patriarch.

1.) The first item of this covenant which we notice, is God's promise to bless Abraham: "I will bless thee, and make thy name great; and thou shalt be a blessing.... By myself have I sworn, saith the Lord, ... that in blessing I will bless thee;" that is, I will greatly bless thee.

That this promise includes great temporal prosperity will not be doubted. In this feature also it was abundantly fulfilled. But beyond this it looked forward to, and embraced spiritual things. 1. It included the blessing of justification;—Abraham's faith was accounted to him for righteousness. So Paul, speaking of salvation by faith, calls it "the blessing of Abraham." "Christ hath redeemed us from the curse of the law . . . that the blessing of Abraham might come on the Gentiles through Jesus Christ;" and this "blessing" he immediately calls "the promise of the Spirit through faith." "So then, they which are of faith, are blessed [after the same manner] with faithful Abraham." Gal. iii, 9, 13, 14.

2. This blessing, also, included the promise that Abraham should be rewarded as a righteous person. This reward was to be such as was suited to the obedience of faith,—the reward of a holy man in this life, and at the general judgment. The apostle says, "BY FAITH Abraham, when tried, offered up Isaac," &c.; after which memorable act of obedience, God says, "By myself have I sworn, BECAUSE THOU HAST DONE THIS, and hast not withheld thy son, thine only son: that in blessing I will bless thee," &c. But that blessing which is the appropriate reward of moral obedience must not stop short at

temporal things; and thus Abraham viewed it, and "looked for a city which hath foundations, whose builder and maker is God," Heb. xi, 10. Indeed, the whole subject is elevated infinitely above the dignity of a mere commercial or secular transaction.

2.) God promises to Abraham a numerous posterity: "I will make of thee a great nation,—I will make thy seed as the dust of the earth:—thou shalt be a father of many nations," &c.

All admit that these and kindred expressions imply a numerous and powerful natural posterity. But it is the twofold sense of these expressions to which we call attention, and it is in that second and higher sense that they are made to include a promise of gospel blessings. The question is, In what sense was Abraham to become the "father of many nations?" or his seed to be (in the hyperbolical language of the promise) "as the dust of the earth?" The merest tyro in divinity will readily perceive the answer to this question. The New Testament clearly and explicitly establishes the sense of this promise, and proves that, in its grandest import, it looked forward to gospel days, and comprehended gospel blessings. In speaking of the posterity, or "children of Abraham," two kinds are mentioned by Paul,—those who are so by natural descent, and those who are so by imitating, or "walking in the steps" of that patriarch. The true force and meaning of the promise in question are thus clearly established, and the whole matter put to rest by Paul:—"For the promise that he should be the heir of the world, was not to Abraham, or to his seed, through the law, but through the righteousness of faith. . . . Therefore, it is of faith, that it might be by grace; to the end the promise [of justification and life] might be sure to all the seed: not to that only which is of the law, but to that which is of the faith of Abraham, who is the father of us all, as it is written, 'I have made thee a father of many nations.'" "Know ye, therefore, that they which are of faith, *the same are the children of Abraham*. . . . And if ye be Christ's, *then are ye Abraham's seed*, and heirs according to the promise." Rom. iv, 13, 16, 17; Gal. iii, 7, 29.

Nothing further need be added in proof of the twofold sense of this part of the covenant, and that the spiritual was the higher and more important sense. If it be inquired, For what purpose hath God constituted Abraham the father of all believers, and what advantages do they derive from that appointment? we reply: "According to the apostle Paul, Abraham was constituted the father of all believers, for the purpose of receiving, on their behalf, and in their name, the promises of those blessings, which God, of his great goodness, intends to bestow on them.... And in thus constituting Abraham the father of all believers, whether Jews or Gentiles, for the purpose of receiving on their behalf the promises of the covenant, God accommodated himself to the ideas of mankind, who consider what is promised in a covenant as more binding than the simple declaration of one's intention."*

3.) The third promise of this covenant contains a grant of the land of Canaan: "I will give to thee, and to thy seed after thee, the land wherein thou art a stranger, all the land of Canaan, for an everlasting possession."

Here, also, concerning the first and literal meaning of this promise, there can be no dispute, and in this sense also it was faithfully fulfilled to Abraham and his posterity. But it had a higher meaning; namely, that, under the image of Canaan, the possession of a better country, even a heavenly, was promised. This is abundantly proved by the following facts:—When the Israelites had sinned in the wilderness, God solemnly and irreversibly interdicted their admission into the promised land. Num. xiv, 23, 28, 30. Five hundred years after that event, David, the king of Israel, exhorted his countrymen not to harden their hearts like their forefathers, and thus incur a similar judgment. In this exhortation he calls the land of Canaan, in its higher import, a "rest," and exhorts his countrymen not to come short of it. Psa. xcv. Paul, in alluding to this exhortation of David, says: "Again, when speaking by David, so long a time afterward, he [the Spirit of God] designates, or definitely names, a certain day, [in which they should enter into the true rest of faith,] TO-DAY; as it is said, 'To-day, if ye will hear his voice, harden not your hearts,'" Heb. iv, 7. Here, then, we find the psalmist, about four hundred years after the Israelites had been

* See Dr. Macknight on the Covenant with Abraham, whose analysis of the covenant we have mainly adopted.

settled in Canaan, exhorting his countrymen to enter into the promised rest. And Paul justly reasons thus:—"For if Joshua had given them rest, then would he [the Spirit] afterward [by the mouth of David] not have spoken of another time; [when they should enter into the rest which the Scriptures promised.] There remaineth, therefore, a rest to the people of God." Heb. iv, 8, 9. I consider Professor Stewart has hit the true sense:—"In David's time, nearly five hundred years after unbelievers in the wilderness were threatened with exclusion from the promised inheritance, the psalmist makes use of the commination which has been quoted, in order to deter those whom he addressed from hardening their hearts as the ancient Israelites did, and so losing the rest (as they did) which God had proffered to the obedient and the believing. The rest, then, could not be merely the land of Canaan, (as the Jews of Paul's time understood it to be,) for this both believers and unbelievers, living in the time of the psalmist, already enjoyed. Consequently, the rest spoken of by the psalmist was of a spiritual nature, pertaining only to believers."* And it was this spiritual and heavenly rest that was typified and set forth in the promise, under the figure of the earthly Canaan. And thus did Abraham understand it; for Paul afterward declares that, "*by faith*, he sojourned in the land of promise, as in a strange country . . . *for he looked for a city which hath foundations, whose builder and maker is God*," Heb. xi, 9, 10, &c.

4.) The fourth particular in this covenant is thus stated:— "I will establish my covenant between me and thee, and thy seed after thee, in their generations, for an everlasting covenant. And I will be their God."

This promise applies to Abraham and his natural descendants in its literal import. Thus, the chief advantage of being a Jew was summed up in this statement:—"Unto them were committed the oracles of God." "To them," says Paul, more in detail, "pertaineth the adoption, and the glory, and the covenants, and the giving of the law, and the service of God, and the promises." Rom. iii, 1, 2, and ix, 4. All the external blessings of the covenant belonged to the Jew. This was the peculiar privilege of Abraham's natural descendants. The spiritual blessings

* Professor Stewart's Comment. *in loc.*

belonged to them not as *Jews*, but as *believers*. Thus was God's covenant ever with Abraham, and with his seed after him. But this is to be taken also in a higher sense. The covenant of the Lord is with the spiritual seed of Abraham,—with all true believers. In this sense it is truly an "everlasting covenant."

The promise that he would be a God to Abraham and to his seed, implies that they shall know and worship the true God, and that God will protect and save them. This has been fulfilled, in a general sense, in the Jewish nation, but in a higher and more important sense in all genuine believers,—the spiritual descendants of Abraham. In other words, it is the church proper, in all ages, to whom this promise has been, and is to be, in its more eminent sense, fulfilled. The deep meaning, then, of this part of the covenant is sufficiently obvious without further remark.

5.) The last item we shall specify in this covenant is contained in the following words:—"In thy seed shall all the nations of the earth be blessed."

For a full understanding of this part of the covenant we must go, as before, to the New Testament. We are assured by Paul that this refers to Christ, and is a promise that all nations should be blessed through him. His words are: "Now to Abraham and his seed were the promises made. He saith not, And to seeds, as of many; but as of one, And to thy seed, which is Christ." Gal. iii, 16. Here, then, is an end of all controversy respecting the proper evangelical character of this covenant. The authority of inspiration has settled this question, and is against the Baptists in this matter. But furthermore, the apostle would be, if possible, more explicit. He says, "And the scripture, foreseeing that God would justify the heathen (τα εθνη *the nations*) by faith, preached the gospel before unto Abraham, saying, In thee shall all nations be blessed," Gal. iii, 8. Here, then, it is plainly asserted, that when God promised to bless all nations through Abraham and his seed, he preached the gospel to that patriarch; that is, he revealed to him the plan of salvation for all nations through Christ. Our Saviour says to the Jews, "Your father Abraham rejoiced to see my day, and he saw it, and was glad," John viii, 56. It was in the light of this covenant, and especially of this promise, that Abraham obtained a view of the divine Saviour.

Indeed, if we remove Christ, and the promise of pardon and eternal life through faith, from this covenant, we shall array ourselves directly against the entire tenor of Scripture. Paul expressly affirms, that "the covenant was confirmed of God IN CHRIST;" and in another place, "that Jesus Christ was a minister of the circumcision for the truth of God, TO CONFIRM THE PROMISES MADE UNTO THE FATHERS; AND THAT THE GENTILES MIGHT GLORIFY GOD FOR HIS MERCY," Gal. iii, 17; Rom. xv, 8, 9.

There is, in Heb. vi, 13-19, a remarkable declaration of the apostle, with respect to the spiritual and evangelical character of the Abrahamic covenant. After having alluded to the oath which God made to Abraham, (Gen. xxii, 16,) and to the general confirmatory nature of oaths among men, he says: "On which account God, willing in the most abundant manner to manifest to the heirs of the promise [made to Abraham] the immutability of his counsel, [in condescension to human ideas and customs,] interposed with an oath: that by two immutable things, [namely, the promise and oath of God,] in [either of] which it was impossible for God to lie, we [the heirs of those promises, which have been thus abundantly attested and confirmed] might have strong consolation, who have fled for refuge to lay hold on the hope which [by the promise of this covenant] is set before us." This I conceive to be the true meaning of the passage, as the context, and the scope of the apostle's reasoning, abundantly show.

The strictly evangelical character of this covenant is further proved from the fact, that Abraham's faith, in its several promises, was accounted to him for righteousness; that is, as Paul's reasoning, in Rom. iv, 1–8, most unequivocally proves, by faith in the promises of this covenant, Abraham obtained that justification, or state of pardon before God, that we now obtain through faith in Jesus Christ. And the apostle there concludes his argument in the following manner:—"Now it was not written for his [Abraham's] sake alone, that it was imputed to him; but for us also, to whom it [faith] shall be imputed, [for righteousness,] if we believe on Him that raised up Jesus our Lord from the dead," Rom. iv, 23, 24. Now, the plain teaching of this scripture is simply this: that Abraham's faith, and consequent righteousness, were the same as every Christian's at the present day; and if this be so, it need not be said the *objects* of Abraham's faith perfectly answered to those of the Christian's faith now. Clearer testimony could not be adduced in proof of the real evangelical character of the Abrahamic covenant, and of the faith which Abraham had in the promises of that covenant. It was the "gospel preached unto Abraham," and the faith of that patriarch in those particular promises is exhibited for our instruction and imitation. Heb. xi, 8–19. "Know ye, therefore, that they which are of faith, THE SAME are the children of Abraham. . . . And if ye be Christ's, THEN are ye Abraham's seed, and heirs ACCORDING TO THE PROMISE." Gal. iii, 7, 29. Such are the views we are taught concerning the Abrahamic covenant by an inspired apostle; and to his writings, and the general light of the New Testament, we further commend the inquiring reader.

This, then, is the first link in the chain of our argument. It is the first position to be taken in defence of infant baptism. By this we ascertain the date of the church of God. It is true, before this time "men began to call on the name of the Lord," or, as it should probably read, "to call themselves by the name of the Lord;" (Gen. iv, 26;) but we have not sufficient intimation that they were organized into a church proper before the time of Abraham. After his day, allusions to the church, or "people of God," everywhere abound.

SECTION II.

1. There is a subject to which the reader's attention must necessarily be directed, and with respect to which his views should be enlightened; and we know not of a more suitable place and time than the present for its discussion. We allude to the true design of the ceremonial law, and the distinction between it and the Abrahamic covenant. We are fully aware that, unless this point be guarded, all our conclusions will be liable to be swept away by a counter current of ignorant prejudice with respect to the design of the former, and the common delu-

sion which prevails among superficial thinkers, that it was identical with the church. Nothing, however, can be more unfounded, or foreign to the truth, than such an impression. The church did not originate with Moses, and its proper identity is not to be sought for in the ceremonial law. It existed before the ceremonial was given; it still exists, though the latter has long since been abolished.

There is a proper theory which belongs to the dispensations of God, which it is of the highest importance to understand. We are not to take their parts separately and independently, or consider them as so many isolated facts, unconnected with one harmonious, comprehensive, and most wise and perfect plan. The reasons for their variety and number are not resolvable into any inscrutable, arbitrary will of Deity, but arise from the condition and relations of men; and though not always obvious to the superficial, the careless, and the skeptical, may yet be scanned, in a great measure, by the diligent and humble inquirer. "The works of the Lord are great, sought out of all them that take pleasure therein," Psa. cxi, 2.

We are not to suppose that all the laws enumerated and enjoined in the Mosaical code took their origin at the date of that code. How many of the same were known and practised by the patriarchs we cannot tell; but that many were no more than republications of more ancient, or even primitive laws, handed down by tradition, we have the fullest evidence. Thus it was with the sabbath-day, with bloody and unbloody sacrifices, with the distinctions of clean and unclean beasts, and with circumcision. Moses rather enlarged and improved the church ritual than originated it. The great church charter was first given to Abraham, but for a long time it appeared as a dead letter. The time for its taking effect had not yet arrived. Moses at length executed it so far as its first stage of immunities extended; and, "in the fulness of time," Jesus Christ developed and matured the system.

The ceremonial law is, to this day, an enigma to many. True, we understand many things respecting it; but its true philosophy, its real design, seems not to be penetrated by many. We have room only for a few outlines of thought on this subject. The strict necessity for the superaddition of the ceremonial law to the proper church charter is to be sought for in the condition of the human mind, and of society, in these early ages.

1.) Paul says, "Wherefore the law was our schoolmaster, to bring us to Christ," Gal. iii, 24. A παιδαγωγος *paidagogos*, translated here *schoolmaster*, was a person who had the care of boys, to train them at home, accompany them to the public school, &c.; so that, when the apostle says the ceremonial law was our schoolmaster, he means that, in the infancy of the human mind, God placed the church under the care and guardianship of the law, in order thereby to receive its elemental instruction and discipline, preparatory to their coming to Christ. Here, then, is the first grand reason for the introduction of the Mosaic ritual,—the human mind needed to be taught the "*elements* of the doctrines of Christ."

The ignorance of men respecting the doctrines of revealed theology, which characterized those ages, and the universal prevalence and power of a lewd, debasing idol-worship, are not generally appreciated, even by the intelligent. It is difficult, now that we are enlightened, to bring our thoughts back to those times, and form a just estimate of the state of knowledge (or rather ignorance) which then prevailed. The modern missionary alone can sympathize fully in this subject, and he feels the need of some such simple, yet imposing economy, as that of Moses, to lift the mind of the heathen from its depth of gloomy ignorance.

Many particular individuals of very ancient times, as Enoch, Noah, the patriarchs, Moses, Job, and others, partook not of the ignorance of the times. But these are only exceptions. Idol-worship annihilates all ideas of the unity, power, wisdom, goodness, and especially of the moral attributes of the Godhead. A late anonymous author of a very ingenious work, entitled the "Philosophy of Salvation," has taken the bold ground that the idea of the holiness of God, with those of other doctrines, "had to be *originated*, and thrown into the mind through the senses by a process instituted for that express purpose." This was doubtless the fact with respect to the multitude. True, the patriarchal system contained the elements of truth, but the surrounding prevalence of a base, corrupting, and licentious idolatry, together with the long servitude in Egypt, had almost effaced the last vestige of divine truth from the mind. I cannot furnish a better specimen of the ignorance of these times, than in the words of the anonymous author above mentioned :—

"At the period of the deliverance from Egypt," says he, "every nation by which they were surrounded worshipped unholy beings. Now, how were the Jews to be extricated from this difficulty, and made to understand and feel the influence of the holy character of God? The Egyptian idolatry in which they had mingled was beastly and lustful; and one of their first acts of disobedience, after their deliverance, showed that their minds were still dark, and their propensities corrupt. The golden calf which they desired should be erected for them was not designed as an act of apostacy from Jehovah, who had delivered them from Egyptian servitude. When the image was made, it was proclaimed *to be that God which brought them up out of the land of Egypt;* and when the proclamation of a feast, or idolatrous debauch,* was issued by Aaron, it was denominated a feast, not to Isis or Osiris, but a feast to Jehovah; and as such they held it. Exod. xxxii, 4, 5. But they offered to the holy Jehovah the unholy worship of the idols of Egypt. Thus they manifested their ignorance of the holiness of his nature, as well as the corruption of their own hearts."†

How could such a people be made to understand the holiness of God, and the consequent necessity of being holy themselves? They were acquainted with no words in their language to which the proper idea of *holiness*, as now set forth in the Bible, was attached. Their own

* The meaning of the last clause of Exod. xxxii, 6, "They rose up to play," is not obvious in our English. The word צָחַק *tsahak*, rendered *play*, "is of ominous import," like παιζειν, *laudere*. It means, in general, *sport*, *play*, &c., with singing, leaping, laughing, gambolling; childish sports. But when applied to heathen worship, as here, and often when otherwise applied, includes the idea of *lewdness*. The children of Israel sat down to eat and drink, and rose up to *lewd*, *debauching* sports. This word is translated "*sporting*" in Gen. xxviii, 8, and "*mock*" in Gen. xxxix, 14, 17. The reader can see in what sense it is there used. See Gesenius on this word, and also on שָׂחַק; Dr. Robinson's Lexicon, Art. παιζω; Dr. A. Clarke's comment on Exod. xxxii, 6.

† Philosophy of Salvation, p. 71.

conceptions had never reached this sublime doctrine in its maturity. All the worship with which they were acquainted, as practised among other nations, was impure; their gods were impure; and their own moral characters, by a natural and inevitable process, assimilated to that of the deities which they worshipped. How, then, could the Israelites learn to form just notions of the holiness of God, the purity of his worship, and the consequent holiness required of his true worshippers?

"The plan to originate the idea must consist of a series of comparisons.... In the outset, the animals common to Palestine were divided, by command of Jehovah, into clean and unclean; in this way a distinction was made, and the one class, in comparison with the other, was deemed to be of a purer and better kind. From the class thus distinguished, as more pure than the other, was one selected to offer as a sacrifice. It was not only to be chosen from the clean beasts, but, as an individual, it was to be without spot or blemish. Thus it was, in their eyes, purer than the other class, and purer than other individuals of its own class. This sacrifice the people were not deemed worthy, in their own persons, to offer unto Jehovah; but it was to be offered by a class of men who were distinguished from their brethren, purified, and set apart for the service of the priest's office. Thus the idea of purity originated from two sources; the purified priest, and the pure animal *purified*, were united in the offering of the sacrifices. But before the sacrifice could be offered, it was washed with clean water—and the priest had, in some cases, to wash himself, and officiate without his sandals. Thus, when one process of comparison after another had attached the idea of superlative purity to the sacrifice,—in offering it to Jehovah, in order that the contrast between the purity of God and the highest degrees of earthly purity might be seen, neither priest, people, nor sacrifice was deemed sufficiently pure to come into his presence; but it was offered in the court, without the holy of holies. In this manner, by a process of comparison, the character of God, in point of purity, was placed indefinitely above themselves and their sacrifices."*

* Philosophy of Salvation, pp. 75, 76.

Such, then, is a specimen of the processes by which God conveyed to the minds of his people those just conceptions of his character which are so peculiar to the Bible. What we have adduced under this head is offered merely as a *specimen* of the design and adaptations of the ceremonial law; our limits forbid our pursuing this theme at length. By sensible signs Jehovah conveyed to the Jews their ideas respecting their own depravity, their guilt, pardon, sanctification, the divine holiness, justice, mercy, power, wisdom, goodness; in a word, all the sublime truths revealed in the former dispensation. These external symbols and ceremonies originated and assisted their first conceptions of truth; afterward came the long line of illustrious prophets, endowed with supernatural penetration and wisdom, and expounded more fully the spiritual sense of the "law," lifting the mind of the nation through another ascending grade of divine knowledge. And when, finally, by these external means, the *principles* of theology were fully communicated; when the Jews had so associated with other nations, by commerce, travel, wars, but especially by colonizing themselves everywhere, as to incorporate their elemental ideas of religion into other languages, and in some sense to transfuse their own principles into pagan systems of philosophy and religion; when the human mind became thus, in a measure, prepared, and "the fulness of time had come, God sent forth his own Son"—the great "Teacher"—to abolish the elemental system, to mature those conceptions of truth, and to complete the illumination of the human mind.

Thus, the machinery of the Levitical dispensation subserved a most important end; but, having originated just conceptions of God and his worship, of man's character and duty, these elemental principles once mastered by the mind, they could be easily taken and applied to various subjects at will, while the external machinery which was the means of imparting them could be dispensed with. The people of God need be "no longer under a schoolmaster;" they could now "leave the first principles of the doctrine of Christ, and go on to perfection." Nor could the sublime truths of the Bible have been imparted to the human mind by any other process, unless Jehovah had altered the constitution of the mind. But this has never yet been done to meet any exigency. All our abstract ideas are derived primarily through the outward senses. Whatever *theories* of philosophy may teach about intuitive ideas, still it remains an unsophisticated fact, that our knowledge all comes, primarily, through the outward senses. Hence, all primary words in all original languages, though many of them may now stand for abstract ideas, originally represented sensible objects. Hence, children can be taught to comprehend abstract principles, at first, only by *sensible* illustrations, and by the most easy and simple processes; "so likewise we, when we were but as children in minority, though we had the promise and hope of the Messiah, were held in bondage under the discipline of the law; in which we were employed in a way suited to the imperfect circumstances of an infant state, about worldly elements, or about those inferior things which are like the letters of the alphabet when compared with that sublime sense which they may be the means of teaching."*

The reader, then, will readily perceive that the ceremonial law was not the church charter, under the former dispensation; but only that temporary discipline and system of elemental instruction under which Jehovah placed the church for a season.

2. The ceremonial law and the Abrahamic covenant are not to be confounded. This will further appear from the following considerations:—

1.) Observe the different times of their institution.

From the date of the covenant, about A. M. 2083, (we reckon from Abram's call, Gen. xii, 1, 2,) to the delivery of the law on Sinai, A. M. 2513, we reckon four hundred and thirty years. This is Paul's statement, Gal. iii, 17.

2.) In the covenant of Abraham, "all nations" were to be blessed. It contained the gospel to the Gentiles (Gal. iii, 8) as well as to the Jews.

On the contrary, the institutes of Moses were rather adapted to a high spirit of nationality, and, I may say, exclusiveness, among the Jews. One grand design of the ceremonial law was to secure the distinct preservation of the Jewish people until Christ should come.† In order to

* Doddridge's Expos. on Gal. iv, 3.

† "The danger of mixing with the rest of mankind was so great,

this, they must be kept from intermarriages with other nations, and from copying their manners, or their religion. To these ends the inexorable ritual of Moses was well adapted. By giving to the Jews a ritual of a peculiar and highly national character, burdensome, rigid, and inflexible, "a middle wall of partition" between Jews and Gentiles would be erected, and a complete separation preserved. The Jews would not be likely to copy after the idolatrous nations around them, nor the heathen after them, while the great diversity of their respective rites rendered them mutually odious to each other. Thus the Roman annalist observes: "Moses established religious ordinances altogether new, and opposite to those of all other men and countries. Whatever we [Romans] esteem holy, is with them profane. Again, they permit many things as lawful, which to us are forbidden and impure." "The Jews," says he, "are inflexible in their faith and adherence one to another; but toward the whole race besides they retain a deadly and implacable hate.... Jovial and gay were the solemnities established by Bacchus: the Jewish rituals are preposterous and rueful."* This feature of Judaism might easily and profitably be illustrated by many specific cases, but our limits, and the proper line of our argument, forbid. Well might Paul call the institutes of Moses "the *enmity*" between Jews and Gentiles, and the abolishment of these institutes the "breaking down of the middle wall of partition between them," Eph. ii, 14, 15. He elsewhere says, that the law "was ADDED" to the covenant, "because of transgression;" that is, on account of the propensity of the people to transgress, and to check that propensity. This accounts for many peculiar severities by which it was characterized. It was intended, among other uses, as a punishment for,† and a cure of, idol-worship.

that God ordered a mark to be made on the bodies of all descended from Abraham, to be *the seal of the covenant*, and the badge and cognizance of his posterity. By that distinction, and by their living in a wandering and unfixed manner, they were preserved for some time from idolatry; God intending afterward to settle them in an instituted religion."—*Bishop Burnet's Exposition of the Thirty-nine Articles*, Art. 6.

* Tacit. Hist., lib. 5, c. 4, 5.

† See Mr. Wesley's Notes on Gal. iii, 19

3.) The ceremonial law is abolished, but the covenant of Abraham is established in Christ. The former, no Christian will deny. The latter is expressly affirmed in Rom. xv, 8; Gal. iii, 16, 17; and elsewhere.

Our argument does not permit us to pursue this subject further, nor is it necessary. Enough has been said to enable the most unpractised reader to perceive that the establishment, and subsequent abrogation, of the Mosaical law, did not affect the covenant made with Abraham in any sense whatever, further than as a temporary expedient introduced for the better security of the final ends of that covenant. "The law cannot *disannul* the covenant," neither is it "*against* the promises." Gal. iii, 17, 21. The reader should keep before his mind one general fact while reading the epistles of Paul. The Jews had colonized themselves in every part of the civilized world at the time of Christ, so that wherever the apostles travelled they found Jewish synagogues and services, and Jewish influence and prejudices, to oppose. Besides, many of the Ebionite or Nazarene Christians arose in different parts in the first age of the church, and many of the Jews—the deadly enemies of Christianity—travelled into different parts, in order to subvert the infant churches planted by the apostles, and bring the converts back to Judaism. This rendered it necessary, in almost every epistle, to enter into the controversy about the alleged obligation of the ceremonial law. This the reader should keep in view while reading the epistles, and a little care and attention will supply him with correct information on the subjects connected with that controversy.

SECTION III.

The preceding section may be regarded as a parenthetical topic, being partly a digression from our proper line of argument,—a digression, however, rendered necessary by the state of opinion, or rather prejudice, and designed to remove any after objection that might arise in the reader's mind against our conclusions.

Our next proper position relates to the substantial oneness, or identity, of the Jewish and Christian churches. I say *substantial* oneness, because, although in many secondary and adventitious points they differ, still, in all the essential features of the real church of God, they are one and the same. And here it is proper to admonish the reader of the importance of this position. It is upon this ground that we rest the weight of the Bible argument for infant baptism. This position is the proper basis of evidence on which that institution rests for support, and without which, all other arguments would still be wanting in authority. It is here we stand, as upon a rock, immovable, and plead and contend for the ancient and Scriptural rite of infant dedication to God, and for their special right to the visible mark, or sign of the covenant. We are not, however, as yet, prepared for those important conclusions to which we are tending, and for which we are striving gradually to prepare the mind of the reader.

I am apprised of the fact that some men would totally discard the Old Testament, and others view it as having no necessary connection with the present dispensation of grace to men. An impression seems to have gained ground with many, that, at the appearance of Christ in the flesh, and the establishment of the Christian church, Jehovah passed a broad and final act of nullification upon all his past acts and plans, and, to use a homely phrase, "began anew." Certain it is that some such undefinable impression, that has been imbibed without investigation, and retained without authority or reason, but, in truth, against evidence, has been allowed to operate peculiarly against the conclusions and facts that have been urged in support of infant baptism. A tide of ignorant and absurd prejudice has thus been permitted to bear against the clear evidence of reason and Scripture, which could never be resisted but by such means, but which has thus proved powerless to many minds. It will be our aim to dissipate these mists—to expose the absurdity of these vague, unfounded impressions—to trace the progress and perpetuity of the church as it makes its transit from Moses to Christ—from the ceremonial law to the gospel, and substantiate the present, which, as we have observed, is the main position in our general argument. What was said under the first section of this chapter applies also, with almost equal force, to the proposition under this head. It was our aim, in that place, to prove that the true visible church *originated* in the family of Abraham, and was formed under the covenant which God made with that patriarch. It is now our business to prove that the same church has been *perpetuated* until this day—that it has been transferred to the Gentiles, or that the latter have been grafted into that original stock.

1. The reader's attention is directed to the *appellations* by which the church was anciently distinguished. We shall not dwell largely upon this point, but it is worthy of a place in the argument. The appellations given to the church anciently are the same as now. God calls them his "people;" his "sheep;" his "vine," or "vineyard;" his "children;" his "elect," or "chosen;" "his own;" his "sons and daughters;" his "church;" and also by various other endearing and peculiar titles.

In Acts vii, 38, Stephen calls the Jewish people "*the church*:"—"This (Moses) is he that was *εν τη εκκλησια en te ekklesia, in*, or *with, the church* in the wilderness." It is worthy of remark here, that although *εκκλησια ekklesia* is the word by which the Seventy generally translate קָהָל *kahal*, (*an assembly, congregation*,* &c.,) yet the same Hebrew word is also sometimes rendered, by the same authority, by *συναγωγη, a public assembly, convocation*, &c. But in the New Testament there is not the same interchange of these two Greek words. But on the contrary, *εκκλησια ekklesia* is there uniformly used, when applied to a religious assembly, to signify "*church*," meaning the Christian church; and *συναγωγη sunagoge* is as uniformly the word used to mean a Jewish assembly, or *synagogue*. When, therefore, Stephen calls the Jewish congregation in the wilderness "THE CHURCH," he uses a word in the original that, according to the *usus loquendi* in the New Testament, conveys the distinct and proper

* "The word '*congregation*,' as it stands in our version of the Old Testament, (and it is one of very frequent occurrence in the books of Moses,) is found to correspond in the Septuagint, which was familiar to the New Testament writers, to ***ecclesia;*** the word which, in our version of these last, is always rendered—not 'congregation,' but '*church*.' This, or its equivalent, '*kirk*,' is probably no other than 'circle;' that is, assembly, ecclesia."—*Archbp. Whateley on* "***the Kingdom of Christ***," p. 84, ***note***. "The disciples had been brought up in the Jewish ***church***, or (as it is called in the Old Testament) the ***congregation***, or ***ecclesia***."—***Ibid***., p. 69.

idea of the true visible Christian church. The word εκκλησια *ekklesia* comes from the verb εκκαλεω *ekkaleo*, which means *to call out*, and the people of God, or the church, was called *ekklesia*, because they were *called out*, or *separated*, from all the nations, so as to become a distinct and peculiar people. Now, such appellations could not be fitly applied to the Jews, only on the principle of their being the true visible church; and if the same distinguishing appellations which are employed in reference to the Christian church apply with equal fitness to the Jews, it strongly argues a similarity of character. Thus: Psa. xxii, 22, "I will declare thy name unto my brethren; in the midst of the CHURCH (קָהָל *kahal*, εκκλησια *ekklesia*) will I praise thee."

In this passage the triumphs of the Redeemer are celebrated. The Saviour's passion is referred to in this psalm from verse 1 to 21, and then the victories of the resurrection. The apostle quotes the passage Heb. ii, 12, and gives it precisely this application, using the same words. That the church proper, therefore, is here intended, is undeniable. Indeed, it is sufficiently obvious from a comparison of the corresponding members of the passage:—"I will declare thy name unto MY BRETHREN: in the midst of THE CHURCH will I praise thee." Also in verse 25: "My praise shall be of thee in the great *congregation*," that is, *church*. (The same Hebrew and Greek words occur in this verse.) Dr. Coke says, the word *congregation*, and *the great congregation*, (in verses 22 and 25,) "must refer to the whole body of the Christian church."*

Psalm xl, 9: "I have preached righteousness in the great *congregation*," that is, the *church*. (קָהָל εκκλησια.) See also verse 10, where the Septuagint have rendered it συναγωγης, *synagogue*. Here also I apprehend Dr. Coke has the true sense of the passage: "If," says he, "we understand it to refer to Christ, as seems most proper, then it must refer to the *righteousness of God revealed by faith*, and made known by Jesus Christ to his CHURCH." See also Bishop Horne on this psalm. These illustrations of the use of εκκλησια *ekklesia* we need not extend.

* Vide his Comment. *in loc.*

2. Matt. xxi, 43: "Therefore say I unto you, The kingdom of God shall be taken from you, and given to a nation bringing forth the fruits thereof."

The reader is requested to read the whole parable. He will there find the following doctrines taught, namely, 1. The "kingdom of God," by which we are to understand the visible church organization, with all its spiritual provisions and promises, was given to the Jews. This is illustrated by the figure of the "vineyard," which the "householder planted," and which he "let out to husbandmen." 2. God had sent his servants, the prophets, and finally his own Son, to the Jewish people, to receive the testimonials of their spiritual allegiance, and to encourage fruits of righteousness among them; but the former they ill-treated, and the latter they "slew, and hanged on a tree." 3. In consideration of their extreme wickedness, God declared their church rights and relations null and void—took from them the ordinances—and transferred the church to the Gentiles:—"Therefore say I unto you, The kingdom of God shall be taken from you, and given to a nation bringing forth the fruits thereof." Here, then, was a direct transfer of the "kingdom"—the visible church charter—from Jews to Gentiles. Whatever that was, essentially, that distinguished the Jews as a religious body, it was "taken from them," and given to another people. Language could not make the case more clear. The argument is complete and irrefragable; the Jewish and Christian churches are essentially one. The same doctrine is also taught, chap. xxii, 1–10.

3. One principal object of Paul's letter to the Romans, as also of the epistolary writings in general, was, to prove that church privileges were no longer confined to Jews, but were equally extended to Gentiles—that both Jews and Gentiles held their relations to the visible church by the same tenure—and that, therefore, there was no just ground of jealousies, and disputes, and divisions, on this subject.*

* "It is in the Epistles principally that we are clearly taught the calling of the Gentiles *to make one church with the Jews.* Our Lord, indeed, had intimated this glorious event in some general expressions, and also in some of his parables; (see Matt. viii, 1; xx, 1; Luke xv, 11, &c.;) and the numerous prophecies of the Old

The church at Rome was composed of Jewish and Gentile converts. The former considered, that, by reason of their connection with Abraham by lineal descent, and by the bond of circumcision,—their observance of the law of Moses, and their exemption from heathen abominations,—they were, therefore, entitled to higher consideration than the latter. It was hereon that they had formerly based their claims to being the true church, and also their hopes of salvation. On the contrary, the Gentiles justly considered that their own title to church privileges, and their hopes of salvation, were not impaired by the absence of these adventitious circumstances. Other topics are touched and discussed in the epistle, but I have alluded to the principal occasion of its being written.

In meeting and obviating these discussions in the Roman church, Paul first establishes the doctrine of our justification and sanctification through faith in Christ. This is a principle of universal application to both Jews and Gentiles; it excludes boasting on the part of the Jew, and removes despair from the breast of the Gentile. It places all on an equal ground. The establishment of this position occupies the attention of the apostle mainly, from chap. i. to viii. of the epistle.

The second general position taken occupies chapters ix, x, and xi, and relates to the call of the Gentiles, the rejection and future restoration of the Jews. Our present argument does not require us to pursue the analysis of this epistle any further, and we therefore call the reader's attention to the propositions already laid down. The principles laid down in these propositions, (so far as con-

Testament, which foretell the calling of the Gentiles, were sufficient to convince the Jews that, in the times of the Messiah, God would reveal the knowledge of himself and of his will to the world more fully than ever he had done before. But the extraordinary value which they had for themselves, and the privileges which they fancied were peculiar to their own nation, made them unwilling to believe that the Gentiles should ever be *fellow-heirs* with the Jews *of the same body*, or *church*, with them, and 'partakers of the same promises in Christ by the gospel,' Eph. iii, 6. This, Peter himself could hardly be persuaded to believe, till he was convinced by a particular vision vouchsafed to him for that purpose. Acts x, 28. And Paul tells us that this was a *mystery*, which was but newly *revealed to the apostles by the Spirit*, (Eph. iii, 5,) and therefore not fully discovered by Christ before."—*Horne's Int.*, part vi, ch. iii, § 2.

cerns our present purpose,) and carried out in the discussions, are clearly these :—

1.) The Jews were the true church—the chosen people of God. They were the "elect," "beloved for their fathers' sakes." "To them were committed the oracles of God;"—to them pertained "the adoption, and the glory, and the covenants, and the giving of the law, and the service of God, and the promises." Rom. ix, 4, and xi, 28. This is so plain that it needs no further notice.

2.) That God intended the ceremonial law, the rite of circumcision, and the peculiar national blessings which resulted to the Jews on the ground of their "election," and of the righteousness of their forefathers—in fine, the general exterior form of the church, as it subsisted under the old covenant—to pass away at the coming of Christ, and give place to the introduction of a new exterior model and state of things.

3.) That in consequence of the Jews stubbornly persisting in the observance of their ancient rites, contrary to the first intention of Jehovah, and, in a manner, to "frustrate the grace of God" through Christ; and also of their great and extreme wickedness and impiety, in rejecting the Messiah, and despising the gospel, God took from them their church privileges as a nation, and not only declared their national election null and void, but gave them over to "blindness" and "unbelief"—leaving them without the pale of his visible church. In this God acted judicially, as the head and chief executive of the church.

4.) That in rejecting the Jews as a nation—that is, in unchurching them—God made a distinction between the holy and the unholy. In unchurching the nation, he did not, indiscriminately, "cast away his people"—"a remnant was saved, according to the election of grace," chap. xi, 1, 5. This "remnant," called also "the election," (verse 7,) God formed after the improved model of the New Testament church. This he did not do by taking them out of one church and putting them into another—not by nullifying their old charter, and giving them a new one—not by declaring their former relations void, and forming them on a new basis; but simply by divesting them of a cumbersome ritual—now grown obsolete—which never constituted a primary element of their church compact, and which, indeed, had been superadded to their proper church constitution with a view simply to subserve a temporary, yet important end, and introducing them to new and enlarged privileges. Here, then, is the proper state of the case. The Jews, as a nation, had been unchurched—in plain language, all the disobedient ones had been excommunicated. But the Jewish church was not destroyed. The ceremonial law, and the rite of circumcision, had been abolished; but the Abrahamic covenant —the proper and original ecclesiastical charter—had not been abrogated. Most of the Jews had been rejected personally; but all the Jews, universally, had not been expelled. The branches, many of them, were broken off; but the old stock remained. The apostle argues that the church was no more destroyed by this general expulsion of the Jews, than it was in the days of Elijah, when but "seven thousand men who had not bowed the knee to Baal" could be found, while the rest were apostate. Taking away some of the branches of a tree does not impair its proper identity. And what "if some of the branches were broken off" from this "good olive-tree;" is it therefore destroyed? By no means. Here, then, is the proper nucleus of the church left—its original stock remains—its identity is unimpaired; the converted Jews who followed Christ and his apostles, however few in comparison to the body that remained in unbelief, were still the true visible church.

5.) Into this original stock—this primitive church—the Gentiles were ingrafted. Whatever this original stock was, into it, beyond all question, the Gentile converts were ingrafted, and thus was the Gentile church formed. We do not say that they were ingrafted on any limb of the ceremonial law; but we do say that they were ingrafted into the Abrahamic covenant, on which both the Old and New Testament churches stand. Thus reasons Paul:— "For if the first-fruit be holy, the lump is also holy; and if the root be holy, so are the branches. And if some of the branches be broken off, and thou, being a wild olive-tree, wert grafted in among them, and with them partakest of the root and fatness of the olive-tree; boast not against the branches. But if thou boast, thou bearest not the root, but the root thee." Chap. xi, 16–18.

Let us attend for a moment to these statements. The word ἁγιος, *holy*, in verse 16, means *devoted to God*, *set apart for God*, as by church relations, or religious rites.* The allusion to "first-fruits" and the "lump;" to the "root" and the "branches;" is for the purpose of *illustration*, intended to show that, as the whole harvest, or vintage, or mass of dough, was considered *consecrated*, when a handful of either was first taken and offered, as a first-fruit, unto the Lord; so the Jewish nation was considered consecrated by peculiar relations to God, on account of the devotion of their ancestors. "For if the first-fruit"—that is, Abraham and the heads of the Jewish church—"be holy,"—that is, were devoted to God—set apart by church rites,—"the lump is also holy"—the entire mass of the Jewish nation, their descendants, is also ecclesiastically *separated*, and devoted to the service of God; "and if the root be holy, so are the branches,"—that is, if the progenitors of the Jewish family were brought into covenant relation to God, and *consecrated* thus, so are their descendants. The immediate point to which Paul is here arguing is, that although the Jews had generally "fallen," and God had "cast them away," yet it was evident that such was not the first intention of Deity. For as the forefathers of the Jews were *holy*, so also should their descendants be reckoned *holy*, and such God evidently designed them to be; and in view of this obvious claim which they might put forth to church privileges, they ought to hope still for pardon and restoration.

But the apostle proceeds:—"And if some of the branches be broken off, and thou, being a wild olive-tree, wert grafted in among them," &c. Now, what is the doctrine here taught? We answer, evidently, that the Gentile church was not built up upon a new and separate foundation from that of the Jews—but that they both stood on the same ground. Nay, further, the figure is much

* In this sense the word is often used, merely to express a visible church relation—a *consecration*, without necessarily implying *moral purity*. Thus, Luke ii, 23, "Every male that openeth the womb shall be called *holy* unto the Lord;" that is, *devoted to his service*. The allusion is not made directly to moral character. Thus also the Jews were frequently called a holy nation, and the temple and its utensils holy.

stronger than this. It declares that the pious Jews and the converted Gentiles were both branches of the same stock, supported by the same root, and nourished by the same sap. The Jews are the natural branches, and the Gentiles were the scions cut from a foreign stock, and grafted in among them. But what was this natural stock—this "good olive-tree?" According to Paul's own phraseology it was the church organization in Abraham's family. The patriarchs, thus gathered into church relations with God, were the "*root*" that supported both the "natural branches"—their own natural descendants,—and also the ingrafted branches—the converted Gentiles, or spiritual descendants of Abraham. The figure is borrowed from Jer. xi, 16, "The Lord called thy name a green olive-tree, fair, and of goodly fruit."

Now, I am not aware that language can make the case any plainer. I do not rest the force of the argument on any peculiar construction put upon an obscure figurative expression, but upon the obvious, natural force of the apostle's argument, and the indisputable scope of his reasoning. His entire argument hinges on the complete, substantial oneness of the Old and New Testament churches, and in defence of this position we may, therefore, with propriety, cite the Epistle to the Romans.

4. The Epistle to the Galatians deserves, in the next place, our candid and critical attention.

At an early day Paul had visited Galatia, and first planted the gospel among the people in that province. Afterward, a certain Judaizing teacher came among them, inculcating the necessity of circumcision and obedience to the ceremonial law. Many of the Galatians were hereby induced to submit to circumcision, and go back to the law of Moses. It should here be remembered, also, that the church at Galatia was composed of Jewish and Gentile converts, as was the case in most places where the apostles founded churches. The Judaizing teacher above mentioned (some suppose there were many of them) aimed to invalidate the apostolic authority of Paul, and to bring him into contempt. The scope, therefore, of the Epistle to the Galatians is, to assert the apostolical authority of its author; the truth of his former doctrine; to rectify the church in regard to errors concerning justification by faith alone, the supposed obligation of the ceremonial law, and of circumcision; and to bring back and confirm the Galatians in their allegiance to the gospel of Christ.

The reader will understand that our future remarks on this epistle will be confined to its immediate bearing on the argument before us. The object of the apostle is to prove that salvation, or righteousness, comes not by the law, but by Christ. In order to this,—

1.) He establishes the doctrine of justification by faith, and the impossibility of justification by the works of the law. Chap. iii, 1–14.

2.) Paul asserts the immutability and perpetuity of the Abrahamic covenant—its distinct and separate existence from the Mosaic law—and the mere temporary character of the latter.

On the immutable character of the Abrahamic covenant the apostle holds the following language:—"Brethren, I speak after the manner of men; though it be but a man's covenant, yet if it be ratified, *οὐδεις ἀθετει ἠ ἐπιδιατασσεται, no man setteth aside or superadds;*"—not the least alteration is made to a covenant, or contract, after it is duly signed by the parties. And this rule obtains even among erring men. Let us, then, apply the illustration. "Now, to Abraham and his seed were the promises made. He saith not, and to seeds, as of many; but as of one, and to thy seed, which is Christ. And this I say, that the covenant, which was ratified before of God in Christ, the law, which was four hundred and thirty years after, cannot make *ακυροι without effect*, so as to render the promise *unproductive*, or *useless*," (*καταργησαι.*)

Language could not make it more plain, that the covenant which God made with Abraham, recorded Gen. xvii, remains without the least alteration, and without the least abatement of its original force. It was once "ratified in Christ," and no one may subtract, or superadd, or set aside. The introduction of the Mosaic law did not at all alter the covenant—did not render it without authority or without action. The law was introduced for another purpose, and was not permitted to infringe upon the covenant, so that, now that it is abrogated, the covenant remains, as it has ever stood, "ordered in all things and sure." "The law was not against the promises of God," so as to either nullify or supersede them. Chap. iii, 15–21.

3.) Their church relations, rights, and privileges as well as their hopes of pardon and salvation, were based on the covenant, and not on the ceremonial law. This is a point of so much importance to our general argument, that we bespeak for it a candid and close attention. We had intended to introduce this argument in another place, but it cannot well be passed in this connection, and we shall not attempt further to delay it. The church rights of both Jews and Gentiles, under the New Testament, were predicated of the Abrahamic covenant; and this argument is exactly to our purpose. It is proper to remark, that the extreme involution (so to speak) of the argument renders it difficult to discuss its parts separately, without seeming repetition. The reader will put on patience. The doctrine of the pending proposition is supported by the following proof:—

(*a.*) This was the core and gist of the dispute between Paul and the Judaizing teachers of Galatia. The drift of Paul's reasoning goes to show, if justification "come by the law, then Christ is dead in vain;" that the true children of Abraham are not those merely who are of his natural posterity, but those who are of faith; that it is by faith in Christ that both Jews and Gentiles become one; that the Abrahamic covenant contemplated this union, and made special provision for it; and that the removal of the ceremonial law gave place to the full development of the gracious provisions of that covenant.

In chap. iii, 18, Paul says, "For if the inheritance be of the law, it is no more of promise: but God gave it to Abraham by promise." The "*inheritance*" here spoken of is put for church rights and privileges, both spiritual and ecclesiastical. To these the Jews put forth an exclusive claim, in virtue of their natural descent from Abraham, and of their observance of the law of Moses. But Paul says that these do not belong to the "law," but to the "covenant." "God gave them to Abraham by *promise*." If, then, church rights, and spiritual blessings, are to be predicated only of the covenant, and if that covenant contemplated the conversion of Gentiles as well as Jews,—in it the gospel being preached before unto Abraham,—

then it follows that this exclusive plea of the Jews is without foundation. This hits the point of the controversy at that time going on in the Galatian churches; and this proves that church rights are, and ever have been, predicated of the covenant. In order to be "heirs according to the promise," they must, whether Jews or Gentiles, be "Abraham's seed," according to the evangelical import of that phrase; and in order to this, they must "be Christ's." Verse 29.

(*b.*) By a striking "allegory," illustrative of "the two covenants;" the one, the covenant made with Abraham, and the other the covenant of the ceremonial law, the apostle clearly asserts, "Now we, brethren, as Isaac was, are the children of *promise.*" This is a clear and unequivocal declaration of church rights on the ground of the Abrahamic covenant. Gal. iv, 21–28.

(*c.*) In chap. iv, 1–6, Paul informs the Jewish converts that God had formerly dealt with the church as a parent would with a minor;—he had placed the church under a guardian. This guardian was the ceremonial law. It was called a "schoolmaster," (παιδαγωγος, *a teacher of children, a pedagogue,*) a "*tutor*" and "*governor,*" (επιτροπος και οικονομος, *a guardian and steward.*) Chap. iii, 24, and v, 2.

It was the custom of the Greeks and Romans to place their children, in early life, under a private tutor, or overseer, whose business it was to instruct them; to direct all their gymnastic exercises; attend them in all their walks; protect them from harm; cultivate and form their manners and habits, &c.; and, in fine, to do all for them that their age, circumstances, and destination required. These pedagogues, or family teachers, are alluded to above. The apostle very properly says, "that the heir, as long as he is a *child,* differeth nothing from a δουλου *slave,* though he be lord of all; but is under tutors and governors until the time appointed of the father. EVEN SO WE, WHEN WE WERE MINORS, ὑπο τα στοιχεια του κοσμου ημεν δεδουλωμενοι *were in subjection under the rudiments of the world.*" This last sentence is full of obscurity to a common English reader. The sense is this:—"During the period of our [Jewish] minority we were subjected, by the appointment of God, to that discipline and economy (the

Mosaic law) which, by reason of its feeble light, may be called rudimental, and, by reason of its numerous external and bodily ordinances, may be termed worldly, or terrestrial." The apostle continues:—"But when the fulness of the time was come, God sent forth his Son, made of a woman, made under the law, to redeem them that were under the law, that we might receive the adoption of sons."

Now, if we analyze this figure, we shall find it to contain the following doctrines:—

[1.] The church relations of the Jews subsisted *antecedently* to the Mosaic law, and independently of it. It must be remembered that the heirship spoken of, verse 1, has strict and special reference to the title of Jews to church privileges. The Jews were brought into a family compact—they were made children—and God himself became their "Father"—long before the giving of the ceremonial law. It was in virtue of these relations that God exercised full paternal authority over them; and by an exercise of this authority he placed them under the law as their tutor. Had not these relations previously subsisted, God had not exercised this control; but as the divine purposes, in reference to the introduction of the gospel, were to be kept "hid for ages and for generations,"—as the full time for the manifestation of God in the flesh was, as yet, far distant—and as the church, till that period, were regarded as in a state of nonage,—it was deemed fit and prudential, by infinite wisdom, to place his children under a "schoolmaster, that he might bring them to Christ."

[2.] The church of God, before the law was introduced, and since it has been abolished, is one and identical. When pious Jews were admitted to New Testament privileges, it made no other change in them, in respect to church relations and rights, than to advance them from the "rudiments" of Christianity, as taught in the law of Moses, to the sublime and perfect developments of that divine science. Under the New Testament, the church is taken from under the guardianship or tutorage of Moses, and put under that of Christ; but it is the same church. It advances from minority to full age—from the state of heirship to the possession of the inheritance. But do these changes at all affect the identity of the church? By no means. The identity of the heir is not affected by his coming into the inheritance. The identity of the minor is not affected by his coming at full age. The identity of the child is not affected by his being placed under a tutor, and afterward returned again to the direct care and benedictions of the father. The proper oneness of the church is not affected by its being first placed, by parental authority, under Moses, and afterward taken again and placed under Christ. There may be stages in its improvements; changes in its ritual; variations in the external form of its worship, and of its ordinances; but its doctrines, fundamentally, remain the same in all ages of the world, and the same, also, remain the spirit and design of its institutions.

(*d.*) In Acts iii, 25, Peter, in his address to the Jews, uses the following language:—"Ye are the children . . . of the covenant which God made with our fathers, saying unto Abraham, And in thy seed shall all the kindreds of the earth be blessed."

It is sufficient to remark here, that, by virtue of the Abrahamic covenant, the Jews were placed in an attitude directly to receive all the spiritual blessings of the gospel of Christ; and thus Peter immediately adds, "Unto you first, God having raised up his Son Jesus, sent him to bless you, in turning away every one of you from his iniquities." If this be not a declaration of church rights and immunities, on the ground of the covenant of Abraham, then can we not understand the language.

5. In further proof of the substantial oneness of the Jewish and Christian churches, we call the reader's attention to the Epistle to the Ephesians. The design of this epistle is to prove, or rather to illustrate, the fact that Gentiles were entitled to equal privileges with Jews, and that both were one in Christ. Paul was called to be an "apostle of the Gentiles," to "preach among the Gentiles the unsearchable riches of Christ." In this capacity he firmly stood in defence of their spiritual rights—maintained their equality to the Jews, arguing from the genius and evident design of the Abrahamic covenant, as well as of the law of Moses—and eloquently plead and wrote against the present recognition of all such distinctions as were

involved in Jewish rites. But in this noble work he encountered great persecution. At the time of his writing the Epistle to the Ephesians he was actually a prisoner at Rome, detained there under chains, through the influence of Jewish persecutions, and for asserting the spiritual and ecclesiastical rights of Gentiles. Under these circumstances, it might well be supposed that in his address to the Ephesians he would make some pertinent allusions to Gentile rights. The church at Ephesus was composed mostly of Gentiles, and these, Paul feared, might be tempted to doubt that the strong ground he had taken in their favour was tenable, when they saw him pursued thus fiercely by the persecuting spirit of Jewish bigotry, and suffering in a dismal Roman prison. These facts, we say, prepare us to expect and to explain the many clauses and paragraphs in the epistle relating to the subject of our present discussion. We notice, first,—

Chap. ii, 11–22: "Wherefore remember, that ye being in time past Gentiles in the flesh, . . . that at that time ye were without Christ, being aliens from the commonwealth of Israel, and strangers from the covenants of promise, having no hope, and without God in the world: but now, in Christ Jesus, ye, who sometime were far off, are made nigh by the blood of Christ. For he is our peace, who hath made both one, and hath broken down the middle wall of partition between us; having abolished in his flesh the enmity, even the law of commandments contained in ordinances; for to make in himself of twain one new man, so making peace; and that he might reconcile both unto God in one body by the cross, having slain the enmity thereby; and came and preached peace to you which were afar off, and to them which were nigh. Now, therefore, ye are no more strangers and foreigners, but fellow-citizens with the saints, and of the household of God; and are built upon the foundation of the apostles and prophets, Jesus Christ himself being the chief corner-stone; in whom all the building, fitly framed together, groweth unto a holy temple in the Lord: in whom also ye are builded together for a habitation of God through the Spirit."

We cannot, perhaps, give the reader a better general view of these passages than by transcribing the paraphrase of Dr. Macknight:—

"11. Wherefore, to strengthen your sense of God's goodness in saving you, and of the obligation he hath thereby laid on you to do good works, ye, Ephesians, should *remember, that ye were formerly Gentiles by natural descent, who are called uncircumcised* and unholy, *by that* nation *which is called circumcised* with a circumcision *made with* men's *hands on the flesh,* and which esteems itself holy on that account, and entitled to the promises.

"12. *And that ye were at that time without* the knowledge of *Christ, being* by your idolatry *alienated from the Jewish nation,* which alone had the knowledge of his coming, and of the blessings he was to bestow, *and unacquainted with the covenants,* namely, that made with Abraham, and that made with the Israelites at Sinai, *which promised* and prefigured Christ's coming to bestow *these blessings:* so that *ye had no* sure *hope* of the pardon of sin, nor of a blessed immortality; *and were without* the knowledge and worship of *God,* while *in the* heathen *world.*

"13. *But now in the Christian church, ye who formerly,* after ye had attained the knowledge of the true God, *were* obliged to worship in the outward court of the temple, *far off* from the symbol of the divine presence, *are brought nigh* to God, and to the Israelites, in your acts of worship, *through the death of Christ,* whereby ye are entitled to all the privileges of the people of God.

"14. *For he is* the author of *our good agreement, who,* by dying for the Gentiles as well as for the Jews, *hath made both one* people of God, *and hath broken down* the law of Moses, by which, as by *the middle wall of separation* in the temple, the Jews were fenced in as the people of God, and all others were excluded from that honour.

"15. *And hath abolished, by his* death in the *flesh,* the cause of *the enmity* between the Jews and Gentiles, *even the commandments of the law, concerning* the *ordinances* of circumcision, sacrifices, meats, washings, and holy days; which being founded in the mere pleasure of God, might be abolished when he saw fit. These ordinances Jesus abolished, *that he might create* Jews and Gentiles *under himself,* as head, (chap. i, 23,) *into one new man,* or church, animated by new principles; thus *making peace* between them:

"16. *And* that he *might reconcile both in one body,* or

visible church, *to God, through the cross, having slain the* cause of their *enmity* to God *by it;* that is, slain the sinful passions both of the Jews and Gentiles, which were the cause of their enmity to God;* by his death on the cross.

"17. *And* to accomplish our reconciliation to God, *coming* by his apostles, *he brought good tidings of peace* with God, *to you* Gentiles *who were far off* from God, *and to us* Jews *who were nigh* to him as his people by profession.

"18. *Therefore through him*, as our high priest, *we*, Jews and Gentiles, *have introduction*, (chap. iii, 12,) *both of us, by one Spirit, to the Father* of the universe, to worship with the hope of being accepted.

"19. *Well then*, being formed into one church with the Jews, *ye* Ephesians *are not now strangers* to the covenants of promise, *nor sojourners* (see ver. 12) among the people of God; *but ye are joint citizens* in the city of God *with the Jews, and belonging to the temple of God*, as constituent parts thereof;

"20. *Being built* equally with the Jews, *upon the foundation* of the doctrine *of the apostles and prophets*, (see chap. iii, 5,) *Jesus Christ himself being the bottom corner-stone*, by which the two sides of the building are united, and on which the whole corner rests:

"21. *By which* chief corner-stone, *the whole building being fitly joined together*, as the walls of a house by the corner-stone in the foundation, *groweth*, by the accession of new converts, *into a holy temple for the Lord* Jesus to officiate in as high priest.

"22. *In which* temple, *ye* Jews *also are builded together* with the Gentiles, *to be a habitation for God*, not by any visible symbol of his presence, as anciently, but *by the* indwelling of the *Spirit*, who is bestowed on you, in the plenitude of his gifts, both ordinary and extraordinary."

The italicised words in the above denote Dr. Macknight's translation of the text.

* The "enmity" here spoken of is not merely the natural enmity of the heart against God, but particularly that hatred which subsisted between Jews and Gentiles; each regarding the other with a religious abhorrence. This mutual animosity was a great barrier to the benign purposes of the gospel, and was aggravated by the peculiarities of the Jewish rites.

In further noticing this passage, the reader's attention is solicited to the following particular views which are set forth in it:—

1.) The religious state of Jews and Gentiles, *before* the coming of Christ.

(*a.*) The Jews are represented as having had a complete ecclesiastical charter; as being brought together in one corporate, religious body. They are called "της πολιτειας *the commonwealth.*" A commonwealth is a community of persons united together under a form of government, and regulated and protected by established laws. No figure, therefore, could set forth the fact of their ecclesiastical incorporation,—or, in other words, of their true visible church constitution, by the appointment of God, more clearly than this. Their ecclesiastical charter, or church constitution, was the "covenants of promise;" namely, that made at first with Abraham, which was further illustrated, and secured in its gracious benefits in after days, by that of the law made at Sinai.

(*b.*) On the contrary, the Gentiles are represented all along as "*απηλλοτριωμενοι being alienated from* this commonwealth of Israel." At the same time, and in consequence of their being in the state of aliens from the visible church—the spiritual commonwealth—they were also strangers to the gracious promise of life eternal, which was contained in the covenant of Abraham, and adumbrated in that of the law, and were destitute of all hopes of pardon, the resurrection, and eternal life, living in a godless condition. Ver. 12. It is hence, in ver. 17, the Gentiles are denominated *τοις μακραν the foreign*, while the Jews are called *τοις ἐγγυς the nigh;* that is, citizens.

(*c.*) Previous to the coming of Christ, the Jews and Gentiles were in a state of mutual enmity. The Jews regarded the Gentiles with deep religious abhorrence; and the Gentiles as cordially hated the Jews, and abominated their institutions. It is not necessary here to enlarge upon this point. But,

2.) What was the religious state of Jews and Gentiles *after* the coming of Christ? We speak more particularly in reference to their visible church rights and privileges, and of their mutual former animosities.

(*a.*) The Jews, that is, those of them who believed in

the Messiah and embraced Christianity, remained as the true church. No essential alteration was made. They were already "THE NIGH," "THE COMMONWEALTH," "THE HOUSEHOLD OF GOD," "THE CITIZENS," &c. No alteration was necessary, when they had embraced the Saviour, save, inasmuch as the ceremonial law was abolished, to so remodel the external form of the church as to suit it to the genius of the new dispensation. The apostle, therefore, speaks of no essential change effected in the condition of Jews in this respect. They still remain upon the same foundation, and are considered as having all along made a portion of the true building.

(*b.*) Not so the Gentiles. A total and essential change is wrought in their condition, both spiritually and ecclesiastically. They, who once were "*the far off*," are now made "*the nigh;*" they who were once "strangers" and "aliens," are now made "fellow-citizens with the saints, and *of the household*, or *family*, of God." This last clause deserves a special notice. It is said the Gentiles are made *συμπολιται των ἁγιων joint citizens with the saints.* But who are the *saints?* The word *ἁγιος*, rendered *saint*, is an adjective, and signifies *holy*, *consecrated*, &c. Of course the noun *εθνος* (or *λαος*) *people* must be understood after it. It would then read, "*joint citizens with the holy people*, or *nation*." Now, how clear is this expression! It teaches us that the Jews—"the holy, or consecrated people"—were, beforehand, denizens of the city of God, that is, lawful members of the church; and that the Gentiles were "brought nigh," and made to share with the Jews in these glorious privileges. The apostle's address was to the Gentiles, whom he wished to encourage to steadfastness by the exhibition of these blessed prospects and promises; and the point to be illustrated and settled was, their perfect coequality with the Jews, on the score of church rights and spiritual prospects. This coequality was effected, not by alienating the Jews from their former privileges as the people of God, but by incorporating the Gentiles into their fraternity, and thus naturalizing these "aliens" and "foreigners." So, says Paul, they now *οἰκειοι του Θεου belong to the house*, or *family*, *of God*, and are no more strangers. Can any thing be more plain or satisfactory, or more to the point in question? Most undeniably there was a city, and to it belonged "citizens;"—a "commonwealth," a "household," a "holy," or "consecrated people," before the introduction of the gospel. And to this city the Gentiles are brought and denizenized; to this commonwealth they are introduced and naturalized; in this household they are incorporated as lawful, integral members; and are made joint participators, with this consecrated people, in the ecclesiastical and spiritual privileges of the gospel.

But if the constitution of the church, as it subsisted under the law, was dissolved—if the Jewish church was taken and planted on a new foundation—if they were thus (as they plainly must have been) disfranchised, and if the old family compact—or "household of God"—was broken up, and a new church formed at the coming of Christ—if this were so, then, we ask, where is the propriety or justness of the above phraseology? In what sense could the Jews be said to be *τοις ἐγγυς the nigh*, if they were disfranchised, unchurched, and destitute of any ecclesiastical rights? And how could the Gentiles be called *τοις μακραν the far off*, if they were no further off than the Jews, that is, if both Jews and Gentiles were alike destitute of any church character? The entire force of the apostle's reasoning turns upon this view, namely, that the Jews had a church character, which, in the case of all those who embraced Christ, was never lost, while the Gentiles, from immemorial days, were alienated from God and never possessed such a character, till, under the gospel, they were brought and incorporated into the ancient spiritual commonwealth. It should be remembered that what Paul here says of Jews, he says of them *as Jews*, and not merely as individuals. He speaks to the abstract question of Jewish prerogatives. What he says of the Gentiles, also, is in this abstract light, *as Gentiles*, and not merely as Ephesians. The importance of this suggestion need not be reiterated to an intelligent mind.

(*c*.) The complete, substantial oneness of the Old and New Testament churches, is clearly proved by the figure of a building, employed in verses 20–22. It is there stated that converted Jews and converted Gentiles "are builded together for a habitation of God by his Spirit." The church, thus contemplated under the figure of an edifice, rests upon the foundation of the doctrine inculcated by "the apostles and prophets, Jesus Christ himself being the chief corner-stone." A word of explanation is due here. The prophets were the oral and living expositors of the Old Testament dispensation to the Jews. That dispensation did not originate in the prophets. They were merely the ministers of God to expound and enforce the doctrines of the Abrahamic covenant and the Mosaic law. Through them the true light of the Old Testament dispensation displayed itself; and it is hence they are said to be the "foundation," &c. So also the apostles. The New Testament did not originate in them. They were rather sent to explain more in detail the doctrines and precepts of Christ, and to inculcate them upon the people. In them, therefore, the New Testament light was more fully displayed. But between the apostles and prophets there subsisted the most perfect congruity. The foundation of the church, therefore, was not laid in the apostles. It did not commence with them, or in their day. The church of God first rested "upon the foundation of the prophets;" that is, on the doctrines expounded and inculcated by them. This is the foundation that God himself has laid, and which he has enlarged and strengthened under the apostles. The principal corner-stone in this foundation is Jesus Christ; that is, the doctrine of the atonement, or Christ crucified. Here, again, we are brought back to the doctrine of the substantial oneness of the church, as it subsisted under the old, and afterward under the new covenant. Nor can the attentive reader fail, as he passes a candid criticism upon the phraseology and figurative language of Paul, of being convinced of the verity and soundness of this view. In vain do men say the Mosaic law is abolished: this we readily concede, but allege that this was not a dissolution of the charter of the Old Testament church. That charter was the Abrahamic covenant. In vain are we told that the Jewish nation was rejected, and disfranchised. This we concede. As a nation they were unchurched; but the "foundation" was not overthrown; a nucleus of the Jewish stock, namely, those who embraced the Messiah—"the election"—(Rom. xi, 7) still remained, and God built up these, together with converted Gentiles, on the old basis, "the foundation of the apostles and prophets," Christ being the principal stone in the foundation. Here, then, is the proper unity of Jews and Gentiles. But more on this point in another place.

6. The Epistle to the Colossians was written about the same time of that to the Ephesians; that is, about A.D. 62, while Paul was a prisoner at Rome. The design of both these epistles was the same, namely, to guard the churches against the influence of Judaizing teachers, and confirm them in their adherence to the gospel of Christ. There are, consequently, many points of resemblance between them, particularly in relation to the subject under discussion. The reader is requested to keep these facts in view as he peruses the Epistle to the Colossians, especially the third chapter. He will find the epistle to corroborate our position; but we do not design to notice it at length.

7. We call the reader's attention to the language of the third chapter of Hebrews. We insert only verses 1–6.

"Wherefore, holy brethren, partakers of the heavenly calling, consider the Apostle and High Priest of our profession, Christ Jesus; who was faithful to him that appointed him; as also Moses was faithful in all his house. For this man is counted worthy of more glory than Moses, inasmuch as he who hath builded the house hath more honour than the house. For every house is builded by some man; but he that built all things is God. And Moses was verily faithful in all his house, as a servant, for a testimony of those things which were to be spoken after; but Christ as a son over his own house; whose house are we, if we hold fast the confidence and the rejoicing of the hope firm unto the end."

1.) The first thing the reader is to notice here is, that the church of God is compared to a house. This same figure is elsewhere employed. So Peter says:—"Judgment must begin at the *house* (οἰκου) of God," 1 Pet. iv, 17. Paul also says: "That thou mayest know how thou oughtest to behave thyself in the *house* (οικῳ) of God, *which is* the *church* (ἐκκλησια) of the living God," 1 Tim. iii, 15. This figure came into use according to a very common and a very natural law of language, and is of frequent occurrence in the Old Testament Scriptures. It was very natural to call the Jews, as a religious body, the *house*, or *temple* of God, from the circumstance of their necessary connection with, and constant worship in the temple, or house of God at Jerusalem.

2.) There is but one "house" spoken of in the above passage from Hebrews; and in this house Moses acted as a "servant," and Christ as a "son," or Lord. I am aware that the present state of the English text would not be likely to convey this view, while ignorance and carelessness serve to confirm many in what I deem to be a wrong impression. In setting before the reader what I deem to be the true light of this passage, and its just bearing on the question under discussion, I observe,—

(*a.*) The proper antecedent of the pronoun *αυτου*, "*his*," in ver. 2, must first be settled. "In all his house." In all whose house? The order of the words in the text might seem to indicate that this intended Moses' house; but this is far from being the truth, as Moses is here contemplated in the light of a servant, not a proprietor or lord. This pronoun, then, evidently refers back to *ἀυτου*, *him*, that is, God, in the same verse, or else to Χριστον Ἰησουν, *Christ Jesus*, in ver. 1, considered as God. This is evident; for ver. 2 is a quotation from Num. xii, 7, where God says, "My servant Moses is faithful in all בֵּיתִי *bethi*, MY *house*." In God's house, or church, then, Moses acted as a servant.

(*b.*) To the same original noun (God) must be referred the same pronoun *αὑτου his*, and also the relative *οὑ hou*, *whose*, in ver. 6. It is to be observed that our English is not a fair transcript of the original. It does not read *οἰκον αὑτου oikon hautou*, *his own house*, as our version has it, but *οἰκον αὐτου oikon autou*, *his house*.* The difference, which will readily be seen by the critical reader, is exactly to our purpose. Indeed, the comparison between Moses and Christ, upon which the argument of Paul is founded, requires the sense we are contending for. Christ is represented as being faithful to the same person, (the Father,) as a son, to whom Moses was faithful as a servant; also Christ is represented as being *επι τον οἰκον αὐτου* OVER *his* (that is, God's) *house*, as master, or ruler; while Moses is represented as being faithful *εν ὁλω τω οικω* IN

* See Professor Stuart's Com. *in loc.*

all his (that is, God's) *house*, as a servant. But it was the same house, or church, for the apostle immediately adds, ver. 6, "*ὁυ οικος εσμεν ἡμεις* WHOSE HOUSE ARE WE." The doctrine, therefore, which we would deduce from this passage may be expressed by giving to verses 5 and 6 the following sense:—"*Now Moses truly was faithful in all God's church, as a servant,* conforming in every particular to the instructions which he received from God, relative to the formation of the tabernacle, and the Jewish ritual, &c., because these things were to stand *for a declaration of those things which were* afterward *to be spoken* by Christ and his apostles; *but Christ as a son over this same church, which church are we, provided we hold fast unto the end our confidence and joyful hope*."* But the true force and bearing of the 6th verse may not readily be perceived. I understand the apostle as affirming the church membership of his Hebrew brethren, under the gospel, on a certain condition, namely, "IF they held fast their confidence," &c. It is, therefore, with great propriety that he breaks off from the subject for a time, to warn and exhort his brethren against failing to attain to this privilege. In this caution he represents the position of the Jews of his day, in reference to the gospel, as being similar to that of their forefathers, when they stood in Kadesh Barnea. They then stood upon the borders of Canaan, and might have entered in, but their "confidence" in God failed them, and they were rejected. Paul's Hebrew brethren now stood in the very borders of the gospel dispensation,—the New Testament privileges being before them. If now they will leave Moses, and come to Christ, they shall retain their membership,—they shall be made "*partakers* of the benefit," for which they have so long hoped. "Therefore," says he, "harden not your hearts, as in the day of temptation in the wilderness;" "for," continues he, "we are made partakers of Christ," that is, we enter into the inheritance of gospel blessings, and become members of the church under its new model, of which he is the Head, or over which he is the son, "provided we hold fast to the end those first-fruits of our faith," which we gathered under the former dispensation, and also (compare verse 6) "retain the confidence and joyful hope now revealed in the gospel." So I under-

* See Stuart's Com. *in loc.*

stand την ἀρχην της ὑποστασεως, translated in our English *the beginning of our confidence.* Here ἀρχην the *beginning*, or *first*, appears to be put for ἀπαρχην *first-fruits*, as in the margin of Griesbach's Testament, and as the tenor of the apostle's argument seems to purport. He teaches his Hebrew brethren that they had gathered the *first-fruits* of gospel blessings under the old dispensation.* Now, says he, if we retain these "first-fruits,"—this "beginning of our faith,"—walking according to its true light, we shall be led to Christ, who will mature it, and give us a "confidence and bold rejoicing;" (ver. 6;) all which, if we hold fast, will justify us in the profession of being the house, or church, of God. Those Jews, therefore, who lived up to the spirit and teachings of their dispensation, were thereby brought to Christ; whom, if they embraced, they were still reckoned on as the true visible church; "whose house are we," &c.

Such, then, is a specimen of the evidence afforded to the doctrine of the substantial oneness of the Old and New Testament churches. It is not necessary further to prolong these already lengthy arguments: enough has been said to settle the question. Whoever attends to the teaching of Scripture on this subject, with any degree of candour and intelligence, must feel convinced that the New Testament dispensation is nothing else than a completion of those gracious designs which were sketched in their outlines before the eye of faith, in former ages. Christ

* It is agreeable to the original to read ver. 14, "If we preserve the *first state* of our faith steadfast to the end." It is thus αρχη *arche* is rendered Jude 6,—"And the angels which kept not την ἑαυτων ἀρχην *their own first estate.*" And this *first state* of the faith of the Hebrew brethren I take to mean Judaism, not in its ceremonial, but in its spiritual character. In Heb. vi, 1, this same word should be translated "*first principles,*" instead of "*principles;*" it being put for στοιχεια της ἀρχης *first principles* in chap. v, 12. But most clearly these "first principles of the doctrines of God" are defined to be those simpler and more elemental truths, which, as they belonged to an inferior state of knowledge, characterized an inferior dispensation. True, the Hebrew brethren were exhorted to leave them, and "go on to perfection;" but this does not mean to abandon them,—to cast them away,—as they did the ceremonies of Moses. They were only to advance beyond their limits to more mature knowledge; still holding fast to their light, and "walking by the same rule."—Vide Dr. Peck's Lectures on Christian Perfection, Lecture I.

was then, as now, the grand object of faith and worship, and the end of all their rituals. By symbols, and various external representations, they were taught the same truths by which the Christian disciple is now made wise unto salvation. "To them was the gospel preached, as well as unto us." To them "God spake at sundry times, and in divers manners, by the prophets," but now hath he "spoken unto us by his Son." What the prophets then spoke, is now fulfilled unto us. "Christ came, not to disannul the law, or the prophets," in the true import of their teaching, "but to confirm" our obligations to believe their doctrines, and obey their rules. The high adaptation of the Jewish economy to promote the faith and practice of true religion is everywhere alluded to in the New Testament, and is traceable in the exemplary piety of many of their illustrious progenitors and countrymen, of whom it is said, "They all died in faith,—of whom the world was not worthy." Words need not be multiplied further. God has never had but one visible church in the world, so far as regards identity of doctrine, and similarity of spirit and practice; although in regard to external form, and the degree of light enjoyed, there obtains a distinction.

CHAPTER II.

ORDINANCE OF INITIATION.

THE INITIATORY RITE OF THE CHURCH UNDER THE OLD TESTAMENT—ITS APPLICATION TO INFANTS.

1. THE ceremony itself, by which members were inducted into the church under the Old Testament dispensation, was circumcision. "This is [the token of] my covenant," saith God to Abraham, "which ye shall keep, between me and you, and thy seed after thee; every man-child among you shall be circumcised. And ye shall circumcise the flesh of your foreskin; and it shall be a token of the covenant betwixt me and you. And he that is eight days

old shall be circumcised among you, every man-child in your generations. . . . And the uncircumcised man-child, whose flesh of his foreskin is not circumcised, that soul shall be cut off from his people; he hath broken my covenant." Gen. xvii, 9–14.

2. As to the general import of circumcision, it was a mark or sign of inward holiness to the Jew, just as baptism is to the Christian. This does not require extended proof, as few men will deny it. We direct the reader's attention, first, to the well-known passage of Rom. iv, 11: "And he [Abraham] received the *sign* of circumcision, a *seal* of the righteousness of the faith which he had yet being uncircumcised." The sense of this clause may be more apparent to some, if we should express it thus:—"And he received the visible mark of circumcision, a token of confirmation of the righteousness by faith which he obtained while in a state of uncircumcision."* This is exactly to the point, and is of sufficient authority, being clear and unequivocal; and the plain, obvious sense not required to be altered by any other passage, to settle the question of the true spiritual import of circumcision. But we wish the reader to attend to such passages as the following:—"For he is not a Jew which is one outwardly; neither is that circumcision which is outward in the flesh: but he is a Jew which is one inwardly; and circumcision is that of the heart, in the spirit, and not in the letter; whose praise is not of men, but of God," Rom. ii, 28, 29. Even so, baptism is "not the putting away of the filth of the flesh, [merely,] but the answer of a good conscience toward God," 1 Pet. iii, 21. God says to Israel, "Circumcise therefore the foreskin of your heart, and be no more stiff-necked." "And the Lord thy God will circumcise thy heart, and the heart of thy seed, to love the Lord thy God with all thy heart, and with all thy soul, that thou mayest live." "Circumcise yourselves to the Lord, and take away the foreskins of your heart." "We are the circumcision who worship God in the spirit, and rejoice in Christ Jesus, and have no [superstitious] reliance [in the merely outward part of the ordinance, which is] on the flesh." Deut. x, 16, and xxx, 6; Jer. iv, 4; Phil.

* Vide Stuart on Romans

iii, 3. Nothing can be more satisfactory touching the religious import of circumcision.

Circumcision was not only a sign of inward purity, the Jews thereby denoting that they had "cast off the body of the sins of the flesh," (Col. ii, 11,) but it was a visible mark and sign of relationship to the church of God. We have before shown that the covenant that God made with Abraham was the first great charter of visible church rights and privileges ever granted to man. Circumcision was the rite by which men became annexed to this covenant. "This is [the token of] my covenant .... every man-child among you shall be circumcised." It was hence called the "covenant of circumcision;" (Acts vii, 8;) that is, the covenant, the token of which was circumcision. It was hence the Jews were called "the circumcised," and the Gentiles "the uncircumcised;"—this mark constituting the visible distinction between their religious states. In all these respects circumcision is shown to have answered the ends of an initiatory church ordinance, answering to Christian baptism.

3. The import of circumcision, as applied to infants, was appropriately that of a spiritual ordinance. It was given to Abraham as a token of the covenant; and when, also, applied to infants, it signified that they had a right to the blessings promised in that covenant. It was a visible mark set upon the male descendants of Abraham, and the male children of proselytes, to designate them as belonging to God by covenant ties, and as being brought into a special, visible relation to himself. This is the exact idea of Christian baptism as an inductive ordinance into the church. It was all the ceremony that was ever used, by which the male descendants of Abraham were brought into covenant, or church relations. If Jehovah had a true church on earth previously to the coming of Christ, circumcision, beyond all dispute, was the appointed ceremony of admission into that church. If the rite of circumcision did not bring the subject into proper church relations to God, then the conclusion is inevitable, that God had no church on earth. The ordinance of initiation, therefore, under the Mosaic law, retained, thus far, in its application to infants, its appropriate signification. It was to them a visible mark,—a token of confirmation of the

promises, by which they were recognised and approved as the rightful members of the covenant.

As an emblem of purity, circumcision applied to infants with equal fitness as to adults. In this, also, it fully answered the purpose of a church ordinance, and is analogous to baptism.

We wish it, moreover, to be borne in mind, that the applicability of circumcision to infants was settled by express command. This is important, as it settles the question of the design of God, with regard to the relation of infants to the church, as it subsisted under the law. The ceremony of circumcision was not only required, but it was required to be performed at *eight days old.* This specified time was an important part of the law, and clearly proves that God intended, not only that men should belong to the church, but that they should be ingrafted into it in infancy. The question of the proper subjects of the initiating ordinance, in the period of the church now referred to, is hence settled beyond dispute. God intended that, as infants were to share in the spiritual blessings of this gracious covenant, so they should bear the *sign* by which they were known and recognised as such participators. The blessings of the Abrahamic covenant were to come upon children, as well as upon adults, and circumcision was to signify their title and right to such blessings. And thus did the Jews regard it. They looked upon their children as joint and equal participators with themselves in the spiritual and temporal blessings of the covenant, and as being equally entitled to the external mark, or ordinance, which attested their mutual claim to these blessings. In these views were they educated; so that from the days of Abraham to those of Christ, every Jew was accustomed to regard his children, while yet in infancy and childhood, as lawfully connected with the visible church, and "heirs, according to the promise," of the common salvation.

CHAPTER III.

THE INITIATORY RITE OF THE CHURCH ALTERED.

THE INITIATORY RITE OF THE CHURCH ALTERED, UNDER THE NEW TESTAMENT DISPENSATION, AS TO ITS EXTERIOR FORM, AND SOME OTHER CIRCUMSTANCES, BUT NOT CHANGED AS TO ITS APPLICABILITY TO INFANTS.

SECTION I.

1. It is incumbent on us, in order to preserve the proper connection of our argument, to show in this place, first, that Christian baptism answers to, and is instituted in the place of, Jewish circumcision. We are not merely to show that a resemblance is traceable between the two ordinances, but to prove that the one succeeds to the place and office of the other. Remote analogies are not sufficient; an exact unity of purpose and import must be traced between them, and baptism must be shown to come in the place of circumcision. As this is an important link in the general argument, it is not surprising that it has been strongly contested. The reader is admonished of the importance of enlarged views of the divine economy, in treating subjects of this nature. He should bring to the investigation a disciplined and candid mind. Nothing is more pitiful, or unworthy the dignity, or irrelevant to the weakness and dependance of our understandings, than for us, on our first approach to a subject, or on a merely partial knowledge of its connections and bearings, and before we have entered into the wide and extensive designs of God, to demand or expect the same posture of things with respect to clearness and evidence, as if the present had no connection with the past, by which it might receive explanation. The great Author of all things acts upon a wise, established plan, wherein one part has relation to the other. To understand, therefore, any part of the works or ways of God, we must understand others which stand connected with it. God has not seen fit, in the world of nature, or in the dispensations of his moral government, to establish each particular fact upon a separate and inde-

pendent ground of proof, but, by establishing a just connection between all the several parts of his vast economy, one thing is thus made, by the nature of the case, to prove and illustrate the other. Thus, in directing to a certain line of duty, he does not always lay down that formal proof of facts, as if nothing had subsisted in all his former dispensations to establish faith and enjoin obedience touching this particular thing; but evidently takes into account the just amount of information that may be derived from his former acts, and adduces only what may be lacking to complete the revelation. Nothing can be more prejudicial to just views of God and his works, than to suppose his successive acts and dispensations are but so many unconnected and independent efforts, put forth, from time to time, to meet existing exigences, and not constituting a regular, progressive development of one wise, broad, comprehensive plan.

"The wisdom of God, in the arrangement of successive dispensations, seems averse to sudden and violent innovations, rarely introducing new rites without incorporating something of the old. As, by the introduction of the Mosaic, the simple ritual of the patriarchal dispensation was not so properly abolished, as amplified and extended into a prefiguration of *good things to come*, in which the worship by sacrifices, and the distinction of animals into clean and unclean, reappeared under a new form; so the era of immediate preparation [meaning the dispensation of John Baptist] was distinguished by a ceremony not entirely new, but derived from the purifications of the law, applied to a special purpose. Our Lord incorporated the same rite into his religion, newly modified and adapted to the peculiar views and objects of the Christian economy, in conjunction with another positive institution, [the Lord's supper,] the rudiments of which are perceptible in the passover. It seemed suitable to his wisdom, by such gentle gradations, to conduct his church from an infantine state to a state of maturity and perfection."*

In order to prove that baptism succeeds to circumcision, it is not necessary to adduce any formal, specific declaration of this fact in the New Testament; much less is it

* Robert Hall's Works, vol. i, p. 303.

requisite to trace any resemblance between the merely external forms of the two rites. All that the argument strictly requires is, that it be shown that baptism answers the same ends to the church, under the New Testament, that circumcision did to the same church under the Old Testament. The reader, therefore, has little else to do than recall to mind the various observations and facts which lie scattered through the foregoing pages.

1.) The church under the Old Testament, and that under the New Testament, are, substantially, one and identical.

2.) Circumcision, under the Old Testament, was the initiating rite of the church. The same is baptism under the New Testament.

3.) Circumcision was an indication of purity of heart. As the flesh, which was circumcised, was *cast away*, it indicated the "putting off" all carnal and "fleshly lusts which war against the soul;" or, as Paul says, it was "the putting off the body of the sins of the flesh," Col. ii, 11. To this sense baptism exactly answers.

4.) Circumcision attested the right of the person who bore its mark to the blessings of the covenant of Abraham, which covenant embraced the Messiah. So baptism. The New Testament is but the mature and complete developments of the Abrahamic covenant, and baptism attests our connection therewith and our right thereunto. Must not baptism, then, be considered as succeeding to the place of circumcision?

But as if to put this question finally at rest, and satisfy the most pertinacious scruples of the objector, it is decided in direct terms by the voice of inspiration. We call attention to the following passage, Col. ii, 11: "In whom also ye are circumcised with the circumcision made without hands, in putting off the body of the sins of the flesh by the circumcision of Christ; buried with him in baptism."

The reader must remember that the Colossian church was in danger of being corrupted by certain false teachers who attempted to bring them back to a corrupted species of Judaism. Paul utters the caution, "Beware lest any man spoil you . . . after the rudiments of the world, and not after Christ . . . for ye are complete in him." He then goes on to prove that they are complete in Christ, without

Jewish circumcision and the Mosaic law. As if he had said, "Does any one teach you to be circumcised? I say unto you, that 'ye are circumcised with (or *in*) Christ.'" Now here Paul expressly declares that certain Gentile converts were circumcised. But then it was *περιτομη ἀχειροποιητω* with a *circumcision made without hands*—a "circumcision of the *heart*, in the Spirit," and not outward, in the flesh. It was the substance—the thing signified by outward circumcision—that these Gentile converts had; consisting "in the putting off the body of the sins of the flesh." And this, says Paul, is *τη περιτομη του Χριστου the Christian circumcision*, which, in the very next clause, he affirms to be accomplished, emblematically, in baptism. The exact argument of Paul we conceive to be this: "The import and design of your Christian baptism, answering, in every respect, as it does, to the import and design of Jewish circumcision, renders it unnecessary that you, who have been baptized, should afterward be circumcised; ye are, in effect, already circumcised, for ye received circumcision, in the Christian sense, when ye were baptized; this ordinance signifying that ye are dead with Christ unto sin, just as circumcision denoted the 'casting off of the body of the sins of the flesh.'"

This is the exact view which the early Christian church took of this subject. Justin Martyr, who lived forty years after the apostles, says, "We, who by him have had access to God, have not received this carnal circumcision, but the spiritual circumcision, which Enoch, and those like him, observed. *And we have received it by baptism.*"* Again Justin says, "We are circumcised by baptism, with Christ's circumcision;" alluding to Col. ii, 11, 12.

St. Basil says, "And dost thou put off the circumcision made without hands in putting off the flesh, *which is performed in baptism*, when thou hearest our Lord himself say, 'Except a man be born of water,'" &c.?†

Chrysostom, in one of his Homilies, says, "There was pain and trouble in the practice of circumcision. . . . But *our* circumcision, *I mean the grace of baptism*, gives cure without pain, and procures to us a thousand benefits, and fills us with the grace of the Spirit," &c.

* Dialogue with Trypho. † Exhortation to Baptism.

Both St. Basil and Chrysostom use the exact words of Paul, and call baptism, in its mystical import, περιτομη αχειροποιετω *the circumcision made without hands.*

Now, it is to be remembered that these quotations do not merely give the private opinions of these learned men on the subject, but they express the current opinion of the times, and go to form a strong presumption that as the Christian church had derived this opinion from the very days of the apostles, so it was a doctrine which was taught to them by the apostles. The subject, then, is sufficiently clear, and needs no further argument to place it in a light more satisfactory. The early Christian church believed that baptism takes the place of circumcision.

2. The reasons for changing the initiatory ordinance of the church from circumcision to baptism, it may not become us very curiously to inquire into. Some of them, however, it may not be irrelevant to state.

1.) Circumcision was adapted only to the male sex; baptism is equally adapted to both sexes.

I am not aware that we are positively informed of the reason why God selected an initiatory rite of such partial application, nor is it at all important to our argument to show and vindicate such reason. The fact is all that concerns us. Nor is it incumbent on us to show on what principle females claimed the rights of church members. As a matter of fact, we know that they did claim such rights; and it appears most reasonable to conclude that ablutions and sacrifice answered them in lieu of circumcision, and also *that they were considered as being completely represented in the man.* However, this might possibly be one of the defects to which the church was necessarily subjected in its infantine state.

2.) The figurative, or sacramental use of water, is more obvious and simple than the ceremony of circumcision.

Although, as we have already observed, circumcision imported purity, or "the putting off of the body of the sins of the flesh," still, to a great degree, such a meaning seems forced and arbitrary. On the contrary, water is a natural and a beautiful emblem of purity; and the external application of it to the body very fitly denotes the inward "washing of regeneration." The greater *simplicity,* therefore, of the sacramental use of water, adapts it, in a higher sense, to the genius of the New Testament dispensation.

3.) The comparative severity of the two rites under consideration yields a preference in favour of baptism.

Circumcision seemed well enough adapted to the tenor of the Mosaic ritual, and to the prevalent taste and habits of the ages in which, and the people among whom, it was in vogue. It seems, too, to have been designed, by its peculiarly oppressive character, to operate as a sort of punishment, as it was certainly a severe rebuke of licentiousness—the prevalent sin of those polytheistic ages. Certain it is that it was "a yoke that neither the later Jews nor their fathers were able to bear."* Not so with baptism. Its adaptations are more universal, and its extreme mildness every way suited to the new economy.

It should be remembered that the Jewish ceremonies were unadapted to extensive proselyting. The divine intention was sufficiently indicated in the great variety and burdensomeness of these rites; and accordingly it turned out, that after having subsisted on the earth during a period of two thousand years, the Jews had made no important enlargement beyond the bounds of their own nation. Circumcision presented a peculiar obstacle to the extension of their religion among other nations; but in proportion to the hinderance it offered to such an enlargement, it evinced an adaptation to consolidate, by rendering odiously singular the Jewish people, and hence to preserve, with the most perfect entireness, the identity of their religion and of their nation. Thus the purposes of God, in regard to the birth and advent of the Messiah, and the introduction of the gospel plan, were served more perfectly. These considerations are deservedly of great weight. To a religion thus stationary, the severity of the initiatory rite could be no primary objection. But just the reverse is it with the gospel. This is eminently and emphatically a proselyting system. The original command addressed to the apostles, and through them to all Christian ministers, is, "Go ye, *disciple* all nations, baptizing them." It is obvious, then, that a system professedly adapted and designed for universal propagation, like the gospel of Christ, must adopt a proselytic ordinance as

* Vide Note A., at the end of the volume.

mild and convenient as its own genius and universal adaptation would naturally require. And such is the case with regard to baptism. It offers no practical impediment to the general extension of the gospel, but, wherever the latter may become "the power of God unto salvation" to any people, there baptism may also witness that they are "the children of the covenant."

These are probably some of the reasons for changing the initiatory rite from circumcision to baptism; but whatever may be the peculiar reasons for this change does not affect our argument; the fact is sufficiently obvious, and this is all that directly concerns us.

SECTION II.

That the law of initiation, though changed as it respects its external form, and also its adaptation to females as well as males, is not changed as to its applicability to infants, is proved from several considerations.

We have already observed that the circumstance of the applicability of the initiatory rite to infants, under the Old Testament, was a subject of express precept, and a prominent feature of that institution. The express command directed that circumcision should be performed at eight days old, and the practice of ages had so familiarized the idea of infant consecration to the mind of the Jew, that he must have associated with this point of adaptation in the law the validity of the law itself. A change in this feature of the rite must have been looked upon by the converted Jew under these circumstances with interest, as affecting the radical character of the rite; so that, if such a change has actually taken place, we may reasonably expect to find such obvious reasons for it, and, withal, such notices of the fact, if not such a positive prohibitive command, as will meet all the natural circumstances of the case, satisfy all reasonable inquiry, and settle the faith and practice of the church.

The reader will here perceive, by the posture of the subject, that we claim the entire argument from *prescription.* We place ourselves upon the ground of the ancient usage of the church, and whatever advantage of proof arises from uniform and immemorial practice belongs to us. If there be any probability that baptism applies to infants, because the initiatory rite of the church has always been thus applied, we are entitled to the benefit of that probability; and if there be any change in the meaning and application of church ordinances from their ancient meaning and application, the entire labour and responsibility of proving such a change devolves on our opponents, and not on us. Until, then, they shall prove that a change has actually taken place in regard to the applicability of the initiatory ordinance of the church to infants, it is not only our privilege to hold to the ancient usage, but we are bound so to do. And they also, if they fail to adduce clear and adequate evidence of such a change of the ordinance, are wholly unauthorized in varying the ancient practice. This, then, is the true position of the question. And here we might, in strict argumentative justice, rest the controversy, until the point in question be fully set forth by our opponents. Until that time, moreover, it is with great propriety that we exhort all to stand by "the ancient landmarks." And here it would not be enough for them to prove that the Mosaic ritual is abolished; circumcision belonged not to the law, but to the covenant: it is not enough for them to prove that circumcision is done away; the ordinance of initiation into the visible church remains. But if the applicability of baptism to infants be shown to be a chimera, it must be proved that this rite does not bear the same relation to the Abrahamic covenant under the gospel, that circumcision did to the same covenant under the law—that the applicability of circumcision to infants was an unimportant feature of that rite, not affecting its general character and design—that the state of opinion and practice among the Jews, touching this point, at the time of Christ, was such as to render it naturally and of course inexpedient and unnecessary to state that this feature of the initiatory rite was to be omitted, but that the converted Jews, who were taught that baptism was the initiatory rite under the New Testament, though they had always been taught to apply this rite to their male children, under the old covenant, yet would, without question or controversy, omit the same application of it now,—in fine, it must be shown that, expressly or impliedly, our Saviour has prohibited Christians from administering the initiatory ordinance to their children, as the Jews anciently did.

But these things can never be shown; and yet, by an unaccountable stupidity, or a want of candour, many overlook this position of the argument, and seem dead to any just appreciation of its real force.

We would admonish the reader that we are approaching an important branch of the general argument, and we request him to put on candour and patience, and closely and critically weigh the evidence now to be adduced. What we have hitherto advanced must be necessarily imperfect without that which is to follow. All that remains, to render the Bible argument complete on this subject, is to prove that the New Testament makes just such recognition of facts and principles, in relation to infant baptism, as the state of the case required, on the supposition that Christ intended infants should be baptized. Remember, we are not to show that the New Testament commands infant baptism, or even mentions it in so many words; the first was not required by the state of opinion in relation to infant consecration, and the second it is absurd to insist upon as a necessary circumstance; but we are to show that infants are spoken of just as though they were all along considered as being, as a matter of course, entitled to the initiatory rite of the New Testament church, and that this is all we could reasonably expect would be said, in view of very ancient opinion and practice. We repeat it, prescription is in our favour, and positive proof is not required, therefore, to establish the eligibility of infants to baptism; but contrariwise, positive, prohibitory law is required to be shown in order to establish their *in*eligibility to that ordinance. The position we take, then, is this; not to show that there is a new and express law of the New Testament requiring infants to be baptized, but that the ancient right of infants to the initiating ordinance has never been forfeited, and that, consequently, the application of this ordinance to them is a matter of perpetual obligation. We wait for proof that the old law has been annulled before we join with our opponents and call for a new one relating to the same point. And we argue that the ancient law which required the initiatory rite to be applied to infants is not rescinded, on the following grounds:—

1. There is no *assignable reason* for such a change. If infants had a right to the blessings of the Abrahamic covenant anciently, they have the same right now. If they were eligible to the "*token*" of that covenant—circumcision—anciently, they are eligible to the *token* of the same covenant—baptism—now. There is no reason in the nature of the case—in the change or posture of circumstances—that calls for such a change in the application of the initiatory rite. Infants are the same, as it respects their moral condition, as formerly; the covenant of Abraham is the same—it still remains that "in him and in his *seed*," which is Christ's, "all nations shall be blessed." And why should so important a principle as that which relates to the recognition of the lawful "heirs according to the promise" be causelessly altered? If the divine economy was to be so changed as to exclude infants from those privileges, and that relation to the church which they had enjoyed for nearly two thousand years by virtue of a divine charter, ought there not to have existed such a state of things as to render this change expedient and necessary? And if our opponents affirm that such a change has actually taken place in the divine economy toward infants, are we not warranted in demanding of them the proof of the requisite corresponding change of circumstances? But, we repeat it, no such change of circumstances existed. The presumption, therefore, is, that God has not changed the principles of his economy touching the admission of infants to the covenant, or, which is the same, the church.

2. That the divine economy has undergone no change that would prejudice the ancient rights of infants to the initiatory ordinance, is urged from the fact that no *publication* of such change has been made. It has never been registered upon the page of revelation. There are two ways in which a law may constitutionally pass into disuse: First, by a rescinding act of the law-making power; secondly, by the fulfilment of those specified ends for which it was first enacted. That the law in question has never been repealed is evident. No record has been made of such an act. It must be remembered that the abolishment of circumcision does not affect the point at issue. Circumcision only defined the *external form* of the ordi-

nance—this affects its *spirit*. The abolishment of circumcision was not an abolishment of the initiatory ordinance of the church, but only of the ancient *form* of that ordinance; the questions of the *import* and *applicability* of the ordinance, which were entirely distinct, remaining untouched.

The importance of this point is vital to the church. It involves not the mere question of forms and ceremonies, but of the proper and essential character of the church of God. If any importance can attach to any law, human or divine, it must lie in the intended application of such law. The great question, Upon whom, and in what circumstances, is the law intended to operate? involves all the importance that can, in the nature of things, attach to any law. And thus, in regard to any charter, the only possible question that can illustrate the theoretical or practical character of the charter itself, or the concernment that individuals may have in it, is, Upon whom, and under what conditions, are its immunities conferred? These principles are so plain as to appeal at once to the intuitive convictions and practical knowledge of mankind. And in relation to the inductive ordinance of the church of God, we repeat it, if it possessed any one feature of importance above another, that feature did not consist in its external form, but in its import, and the circumstances in which it was intended to apply to men. This question is, and must necessarily be, vital. And this, as we have already seen, was clearly settled by positive and indisputable authority, in the ancient church. If the *form* of the initiatory ordinance—circumcision—was distinctly settled by divine authority, so also were the circumstances and *subjects* of its administration clearly defined.

Now, what we wish the reader here to understand is, that if the abolishment of the external *form* of the initiatory ordinance required an express rescinding act of the Lawgiver; so, also, the question of the proper *subjects* of the same ordinance, if it is to be changed, being a still more vital point than that of the form, must also receive the same formal decision from the law-making power. The case appears very clear, but the importance of it will not justify us in dismissing this point while any obscurity remains. We maintain a wide and essential distinction between the *external form* of an ordinance, and the *essential character* of that ordinance. The former is merely accidental, the latter is the very substance of the thing itself. Take an illustration. An oath of allegiance to any government must have the same essential meaning, or import, in all nations and in all ages. Yet the *form* of such an oath may be made to differ in almost any extent conceivable, without affecting its proper and essential meaning. Indeed, the form of such an oath is wholly unimportant. It may consist of one set of words, or of another order of words, or of no words at all, but only of particular signs. And so long as the government was pleased to establish a connection between the voluntary performance of certain signs and the obligations of allegiance—so long as, by the authority of law, any particular signs were made to import the voluntary assumption of patriotic principles—just so long such signs would embody the essential character of a verbal oath of allegiance. It is the thing intended by the form of words, or the particular signs, that constitutes the substance and character of the oath. It is easy to perceive, therefore, how the form of an oath can be changed, without changing its proper character. It is so with the ordinances of the church: it is so with the initiating ordinance. The form has been changed, but its primary character remains unaltered. And we say that the change of the ancient form of this ordinance does not necessarily, and as a matter of course, draw after it, or imply, any change of its applicability to infants, or of its proper and essential character. The initiating ordinance, as we have already seen, bears the same meaning now as anciently; it is our *sacramentum*, or oath of allegiance still, although the *form* of the oath is changed. And thus must every converted Jew have considered it. When he was taught to leave Moses, and come to Christ—to leave the law, and "go on unto the perfection" of the gospel—to abstain from circumcision, and be baptized—nothing could be more natural than for him to regard his children still, as anciently, the proper subjects of the initiatory ordinance. He would naturally ask, "If we are to be initiated into the gospel church, not by circumcision, but by baptism—if the form of the initiating ceremony is to be thus changed—what is to be the change, if any, respecting the application of this ordinance to our children? How are they to be henceforward treated? Are we to regard them still, as heretofore, as the ingrafted members of the covenant?" And we hold that, as this point would be regarded with deep interest by every Jew—as very ancient law and practice would teach him to look with concern upon the covenant rights and relations of his offspring—if no prohibitory law appeared to the contrary, he would naturally, and as a matter of course, apply baptism to his children. And to have prevented such an application of this rite, an express prohibition was called for, in the nature of the case, as much as in changing the form of that ordinance.

To feel the full force of this argument one has only to place himself in similar circumstances, and ask himself if he would ever be likely to abandon, naturally, and as a matter of course, any practice that he believed to be right, and of divine injunction, and to which he was almost instinctively disposed by education, and the unvarying usage of his ancestors. Do such practices easily fall into disuse, or become obsolete in a day, like the ephemeral customs that receive their mould by the changing seasons? If any man has so imagined, he has yet to be informed that he has made an erroneous reckoning with human nature. He has constructed his theory without a just estimate of those inveterate principles of conduct which are engendered by immemorial custom—not to say, religious belief. Look, for a moment, at palpable and imposing fact. How difficult it was for the apostles of Christ to convince even those Jews that had received the gospel and submitted to baptism, that circumcision was to be omitted! How difficult to instil into their minds the doctrine that those were the truly circumcised that had become Christians—"that worshipped God in the Spirit, and rejoiced in Christ Jesus, and had no confidence in the [merely outward ceremony which was on the] flesh." But if it was one of the most difficult lessons for a Jew to learn, that he was called upon to give up and omit that outward ceremony which God had anciently instituted, and which his fathers had practised with so much religious, not to say, in many cases, superstitious, veneration; could it have been less obnoxious to his principles and prejudices to be informed that not only was he called upon to abandon this outward ceremony, to accept another, but that that feature of the ordinance which had always recognised his children to be "fellow-heirs with himself of the grace of life"—which had so largely endeared to him, as to his ancestors, the outward ceremony in question—that that feature, which touched the vitality of the ordinance, was also abolished? And if their attachments to circumcision were so inveterate as to occasion so many controversies among Christians respecting it as are recorded in the New Testament, and also to give birth to a large and powerful sect of half Jews and half Christians—which was the fact, as shown in the history of the Nazarene and Ebionite Christians—is it probable that the converted Jews, while thus, with characteristic obstinacy, contending for circumcision, would be likely to yield up the ancient covenant rights of their children—a fact so prominently recognised in the former dispensation, and imported by circumcision—and submit to the new ordinance with quiet acquiescence? Such a supposition would be characterized with too palpable and glaring improbability, and would too openly contradict all the analogies of the case, to be for a moment entertained by any intelligent mind. Every inch of encroachment on the Jewish law, by the gospel system, was disputed with all the pertinacious obstinacy of a Jewish zealot. The New Testament affords ample testimony of this statement. We sicken at the rehearsal of those puerile controversies which absorbed the intellects, and alienated the hearts of the early Jewish converts. And where analogy sheds its light so largely abroad—discovering the real state of opinion—we are warranted in the opinion, nay, we are compelled by every reasonable consideration to the belief, that had the Jews been called upon to change the relation of their children to the covenant, and in the administration of baptism to wholly pass them by, they would have submitted to this new order with less alacrity than to almost any other change.

If, then, the initiatory ordinance was to be so changed under the New Testament as to wholly omit its application to infants, such a change, being one of primary importance, would have called for an express prohibitory statute. Without such a statute, we maintain that the converted

Jew would naturally, and as a matter of course, have continued to apply baptism, as he had always applied circumcision, to his children. But the fact that no such prohibition is recorded in the New Testament is a strong presumption that it never existed. At least, with our opponents, who are so loud in their demands for positive precept, it must be admitted to possess peculiar weight. If the appeal is to be carried to positive " law and testimony," we demand positive law for changing the ancient covenant rights of children. Where, we ask, is the rescinding act to be found? When and how did children forfeit their eligibility to the initiating ordinance of the Abrahamic covenant? And on what authority do men deny them the rights which God has secured to them by positive law? These are grave questions, and we submit them to the intelligence, the candour, and the consciences, of all whom they may concern.

It becomes, then, an easy task to account for the apparent silence of the New Testament touching the question of infant baptism; and it will at once be perceived that such silence, so far from prejudicing our argument, is itself a powerful argument in our favour. It is an argument of very peculiar force. It not only proves that the initiating ordinance was applied to infants in New Testament times, but it proves much more—it proves that, such was the uniformity of that practice, not even a controversy arose in the church respecting it; and also, such was the state of opinion among converted Jews, (with whom, it is well known, the Christian church took its rise,) that it required no original command to institute and enforce infant baptism, but that the first members of the church adopted and continued the practice as a matter of course. Such, then, is the peculiar force, in our favour, of the particular circumstance of that kind of silence which the New Testament observes on this point.

3. But it may be said, " Although Christ has not prohibited the application of the initiatory rite to infants by any positive law of which we have any account, still, that ancient practice has fallen into disuse, and was designed to fall into disuse, at the 'passing away' of the Mosaic ritual." The force of this objection lies in the supposition that the doctrine of the covenant rights of infants is part

and parcel of the Mosaic economy, which was designed to cease at the coming of Christ. We know, indeed, that the sacrificial rites of Moses, and of primitive times, found their fulfilment in Christ; and that that whole economy, in a general sense, was "a shadow of good things to come," of which "the substance was Christ." This being its character, it ceased to operate, as a matter of course, and without a rescinding act, when Christ came. Still, if the reader will attend to the epistolary part of the New Testament, he will find that almost all the typical and temporary part of the ancient ritual of the church is mentioned in detail, and rescinded. Yet, in none of these specifications is the principle, touching the right of infants to the token of the covenant, infringed. Besides, the point we here insist upon is, that this belonged, not to that temporary and elemental state of policy established by Moses, but to the settled order, and essential character of the church. We have already stated that the *form* of the initiating ordinance was temporary. It was adapted to a *non-proselytic* form of religion, such as was that of the Jews, but not to the gospel plan. But the purpose of God in regard to admitting members into the church by *some* ceremony remained unaltered. The order of the church, in this respect, was perpetual. The great Lawgiver never intended to abolish the practice of admitting members to the church, or annexing them to the covenant, (which is the same thing,) by an external sign or ceremony of some sort. When circumcision was established, it fixed the form of the ordinance for the time; when it was abolished, it left the order of the church, which was in this respect settled and perpetual, unaltered;—it still remained that an external *mark* or *sign*, of some kind, must be put upon all the children of the covenant. And we say that the design of God, in reference to admitting members into his church by some external ceremony, is not temporary, but perpetual. It can no more pass away than the church itself can fail; it involves a principle, that not merely affects the external character of the church, but strikes at its very existence.

Take a perfectly parallel case. Among the Jews there was an institution, called the passover, whose chief merit consisted in its being a lively type of the sacrifice of

Christ. It seemed the design of Jehovah herein to represent and set forth the atonement to the believing Jew, in as distinct features as possible. This rite was also commemorative. Under the New Testament we are furnished with an institution, in all essential respects the same as the passover, save this, the passover celebrated the dying love and atoning merit of a Saviour yet to come, while in the Lord's supper we celebrate the same love and merit in a Saviour already come. Now it is evident that God intended, from the moment of the institution of the passover, to establish a perpetual order—a principle of unchangeable obligation in the church; namely, *that the death of Christ, as an atonement, should be celebrated through all time by the true worshippers of God.* Under the law of Moses it was celebrated in a manner suitable to the genius and character of that dispensation; and under the gospel, the outward ceremony is also adapted to the change of circumstances, and the new and enlarged measure of light. But who will say that, in changing the form of this ordinance, the *principle*, the *essential thing*, is changed? Much less will any reasonable man affirm that, at the coming of Christ and with the abolishment of the Mosaic rites, this order of the church, in regard to the celebration of the death of Christ, was also abolished, or that it of course passed away. In this we may see the distinction between what belongs to the temporary forms of church ordinances, and the immutable order of the church with respect to them.

Applying these remarks to the case in hand, we say, the principle that respected the admission of persons into the visible church, by some visible ceremony, was one of vital importance to the church, and could not have passed away with the obsolete rites of Moses as a matter of course. And after the abolishment of circumcision, it must be evident that, in whatever form the initiatory ordinance was to be continued, the essential order and settled constitution of the church, in this respect, would remain unchanged. The dress only of the ordinance was changed. And here, were it necessary, we might prove that the abolishment, or the "passing away," of the Mosaic rites, was only a disuse of forms, without any alteration of the principles or doctrine of the church. This the reader will keep in mind. The final conclusion, therefore, is, that Christ has not rescinded the law touching the application of the initiating ordinance to infants, nor has that law died any natural death, it being not of a nature to pass away in this manner, without a rescinding act.

SECTION III.

But it may be said, "The New Testament must be supposed to say something respecting this point. If Christ intended that baptism should apply to infants, surely he would somewhere have specified such an intention, and not have left so weighty a matter wholly subject to vague conjecture, or uncertain inference." We answer:—We shall presently see that the New Testament has said something on this subject. The Head of the church has not left this matter either to conjecture, or to any dubious inference; but, contrariwise, has made just such mention of it as the state of the case required;—just such mention as proves that the practice of infant baptism was universal in the primitive Christian church, and that God intended it to be so.

1. But how comes the objector to know, with such positivity, that God would have specified his intentions on this subject by any positive law in the New Testament? And how can he feel warranted in drawing a positive inference from the alleged silence of the New Testament, in *favour* of his theory, any more than *against* it? Mere silence, abstractly considered, furnishes no argument, either pro or con, on any question. It is the peculiar posture of *circumstances* in which silence occurs, that lends to it whatever meaning it may possess; and these circumstances may lend to silence a positive or a negative signification. And here we may appeal to the common sense of mankind to decide whether the apparent silence of the New Testament be positive or negative on the question at issue. It is allowed, I believe, by universal consent, where the particular posture of circumstances renders the final decision of a question highly important and necessary, in order to place such question in a clear and undoubted light, and where the interest and wish of the party which is to decide are involved in the negative decision of the question, that

silence, in such a case, is construed affirmatively. Hence, the old and trite adage, "*Malam esse causam silentio confitetur;*" or, as we say,—His silence proves the fact. The rhetoricians say that silence is sometimes more eloquent, and may produce a more powerful effect upon an audience, than any possible form of words. On other occasions silence may be set down to the score of sheer stupidity and ignorance. Mere silence, then, we repeat it, proves nothing, because it *is* nothing. Circumstances only can lend it a meaning and force; and, in the case before us, the only proper question is, What are the circumstances that must be considered as imparting a positive meaning to the alleged silence of the New Testament on infant baptism? These circumstances we have already noticed as being in our favour. It is remarkable that the objectors to infant baptism have always urged, with an air of confident triumph, the supposed silence of the New Testament as an insuperable objection to Pedobaptism. And what is the force of this objection? It is simply this:—The New Testament does not expressly mention infant baptism,—therefore infant baptism is not to be practised. And this, to many, seems unanswerable. But how came our opponents to know that they had a right to put such a construction upon the silence of the New Testament? If the mere fact of silence is to be considered, it proves as much on one side of the question as the other, and we might reason in our turn: The New Testament does not expressly mention infant baptism,—therefore it does not prohibit it,—therefore it may be practised. And thus stand the two parties. The Baptists reject infant baptism for want of a positive New Testament *precept:* we maintain it, because there is no New Testament *prohibition* of the ancient law of infant consecration, and also because the New Testament makes just such recognition of the moral and ecclesiastical state of infants as we suppose the case called for, on the supposition that they were to be baptized.

But what I wished mostly to notice, in this place, is, that our opponents have no right to demand even a positive mention, in so many words, of infant baptism, in order to establish its obligation and its practice. We readily grant, that if the practice of applying the initiatory ordinance of the church to infants had never been known or heard of before the time of Christ,—if such a practice would have been new, and the principle involved in it new to the church,—under such circumstances an express command would have been clearly necessary. But we have shown, we apprehend, that this was not the state of things at the time of the introduction of the gospel. Furthermore, we know that the apostles must have received many particular instructions from Christ, which, though they carried out in practice, they did not commit to writing. In such cases we must look to their *practice* for a knowledge of what was commanded them. Christ might have commanded them to baptize infants, and still they may not have been commanded to enter this precept upon record with the written canons of the church. The force of early practice and doctrine might have superseded this. And herein analogy is certainly against our opponents.

2. Take a case every way equally involved to the one in question. The practice of applying the initiatory rite to females as well as males, was not authorized by any ancient usage, or even possible, in the nature of the case, before the introduction of the gospel; and, being wholly unknown to the Jews, might seem to require an express direction from the lips of the divine Saviour. Such direction he undoubtedly gave; but, if so, it has never been entered upon record; thus demonstrating that, in the estimation of divine wisdom, this practice would, naturally enough, take the right direction through all successive ages, though left to mere inductions from Scriptural and rational principles; or the requisite instruction might have been given privately. Herein, then, we have an important change in the external applicability of a church ordinance, without any signified, registered intention, that it was the will of the divine Lawgiver that such a change should take place. It is true that, after the introduction of Christianity, the baptism of women was mentioned historically, and as a matter of fact, (Acts viii, 12,) proving that it was the will of God that they should be baptized. But this is proof of the very thing we have stated;—it proves it to have been an apostolic practice, *without* an express command. An historical mention of an act, is not a command to perform that act. It may presuppose a command, but the command itself must have existed prior, and is altoge-

ther another thing. Here, then, we find the apostles applied baptism to females, contrary to the ancient usage of the church, which denied them the initiatory ordinance; while their only authority for so doing was derived from the reasonableness of the case, from inference, or from private instruction that had never been entered upon the sacred record. And have we any just ground to suppose that the Saviour would particularize with greater care on other points which were less likely to be misunderstood? Have we any right to demand a positive precept, or even a mention, in so many words, of the applicability of baptism to infants?*—a doctrine clearly pointed out by ancient practice,—when the point of its applicability to females, which seemed to be forbidden by the analogy of all ancient law and practice, was not so much as alluded to in the original commission, and was never expressly commanded? Can we suppose, in the full blaze and vigour of ancient Jewish law and custom, that infant baptism

* The fact that the Jews would have gone on and practised infant baptism, as a matter of course, unless prohibited, being governed in this respect purely, or at least mainly, by the light of ancient usage, has been illustrated by a homely similitude, and yet a similitude so much in point, that I will copy it:—

"A man orders his servants to mark the sheep of his flock with a bloody sign; and is careful to add, 'See that you apply this sign to *all the lambs also.*' Afterward he sees fit to dispense with the *bloody* sign, made with a knife in the flesh; and ordains that his servants shall mark his sheep with *paint:* but he says nothing about the lambs. Now, the question is, Will those servants, because the marking is a 'positive institution,' argue that the lambs are no longer to be marked, because they are not specified, in so many words, in the second order? As they purchase more sheep, with lambs, will they mark the sheep, but say they have no order for marking the lambs?" Every man must perceive the case would be just the contrary. All the natural force of circumstances would tend to establish the conviction that no change was intended in the *mark*, further than its external character. Its applicability to the lambs, as well as to the sheep, would not be considered as being at all affected by such a change in the mark, or sign. And it is wholly unnatural to suppose that they would reason from such a fact, to the exclusion of the lambs. So in the case before us. The fact of the external form of the initiating ceremony, or mark of discipleship, being changed, is not a sufficient ground for inferring the change of the applicability of that ordinance to infants; and it is wholly unnatural and forced to suppose the apostles would have drawn such an inference.—See Hall on Baptism, pp. 156, 157.

would be any more likely to be misunderstood and neglected by the Jewish converts, in the absence of direct precept, than was female baptism? It is plain that the preponderance of probability which the clear light of analogy throws upon this question, lies against such a supposition. In this estimate we are not to consult modern prejudice and modern practice; but we are to go back to the time of Christ, place ourselves in the situation of a converted Jew, and endeavour to appreciate the influence and operation of circumstances upon his mind. And it is in this manner we have arrived at the above conclusion. How vain, then, is it for men to put forth demands for positive precept on this, or any other subject involved in similar circumstances, as an indispensable condition of their faith and practice!

3. It has been a common practice of Pedobaptist authors to introduce at this stage of the argument the subject of female communion. The use of the argument is this:—That as God has nowhere directly authorized female communion by any express precept; and as, from the reasonableness of the case, we are fully convinced it is the divine will that they should be admitted to the communion table, therefore we are warranted in believing that positive duties are sometimes left to the direction of inference and analogy, without explicit written command: and if such a subject as the right of females to the communion table has been left to inference, analogy, and the reasonableness of things, so also may the subject of infant baptism;—a subject, we repeat it, no more likely than the former to be misunderstood. And all this may serve to show how futile are the claims which some persons put forth to that highest kind of moral evidence—explicit command—as a condition of their faith. This point is so clear and evident, and so obviously parallel to the case of infant baptism, that it needs not to be amplified. But we beg the reader's attention to some further illustrations equally clear and in point.

4. The practice of the Christian church in refusing to rebaptize any person, is far from being based on positive command. No Christian minister will knowingly give baptism to any person the second time. The universal Christian church regard it as a profanation of the ordinance. But why so? Certainly there might seem to be a strong analogy, both from Scripture and reason, to favour

ana-baptism. The Jews often lustrated their bodies. Whenever they had polluted themselves by any means, they were restored by a fresh application of water to the body, in some way, or of water and blood; and why not observe the same rule among Christians? It might seem too, at first sight, to be a reasonable inference, that as apostacy makes baptism to be void, so, upon a renewal of repentance, there should be a new application of the water of baptism. But no: this is not the fact. The church does not thus reason. In the absence of all express command, the church base their practice, in this respect, on the reasonableness of the case, and on church history, but mostly upon the latter. Baptism being a dedication of the person to God, it is understood to continue in full force and vigour while the baptized person remains holy. To repeat the rite would imply a defect in its first administration, or reception, or both. It would be to declare the first administration void. But in case of apostacy and subsequent repentance, we are guided alone by church history. "Finding that the primitive church did reconcile, but not rebaptize apostates, we do imitate that their practice."* Here, then, the Baptists themselves assume authority to direct the administration of a positive institute, without a positive command. They are, with us, governed by inference, analogy, and particularly by church history, in the use of a positive institute of Christianity. Are they consistent?

5. The fact of the change of the sabbath, from the seventh to the first day of the week, rests upon the same kind of evidence as that which we claim for the support of infant baptism. It seems not to have been duly considered by our opponents, that from the earliest records of history God has delivered his commands to men through various means, and in somewhat varied kinds of evidence. If we attentively examine into the ground of evidence that we have for various beliefs, we shall find that, while for some we have the warrant of a divine positive precept or declaration, for others we have only the authority of historical testimony and inductive reasoning. And these remarks, too, apply not merely to forms and accidental usages, but to cardinal and important subjects. We make these remarks, not to intimate a suspicion that there is any want

* Bishop Burnett on the Thirty-nine Articles, Art. xxv.

of evidence in any part of Revelation, but to direct attention to the fact, that all duties are not sustained by the same kind of evidence.

"Admitting, as we must, that all positive religious rites are originally founded on a divine command, we cannot safely conclude that such a command will be repeated to all those who shall afterward be under obligation to observe such rites, or even that the original command will be preserved and communicated to them in the sacred writings. Neither of these can be considered as indispensable; because sufficient evidence of a divine institution may be afforded in some other way. It may be afforded, particularly, by an *unwritten tradition.* It is unquestionable that the knowledge of some extraordinary events of Providence, or of some divine injunctions, may be as truly and as certainly communicated in this way as in others; and we should, in many cases, consider a man who would refuse to admit the truth and authority of a tradition, to be as unreasonable as if he should refuse to admit the authority of written or printed records.

"If we should insist upon the repetition of a divine command at different times, or upon a written record of it as indispensable, we should set aside one of the methods which God has manifestly adopted in regard to the positive institutions of religion. For instance, what clear and certain proof have we that the divine command, enjoining the observance of the sabbath, or the offering of sacrifices, was repeated to the successive generations of men from Adam to Moses; or that they had evidence of either of these divine institutions from historical records? And what certain proof is there of the repetition of the divine command, or the existence of any historical records, during the period from Abraham to Moses, respecting the rite of circumcision? And, to come down to later times, what express command has God given to us, or to any Christians since the days of the apostles, requiring the first day of the week to be observed as a sabbath? And what express declaration have we in the sacred records that such a command was ever given by Christ or his apostles? In regard to this, we who observe the Christian sabbath must either say that a divine command has been given directly to us, or that a command originally given by Christ, has been preserved to us in the sacred records,—neither of which we are able to say;—or we must justify ourselves in observing the Lord's day, because some other considerations show that such is the will of God. On what ground, then, shall we proceed in regard to this subject? We must be sensible that we have no express command from God to us, and no record of any former command, to authorize us to regard the Christian sabbath as a divine institution. Shall we, then, admit that it is proper for us to fall in with the prevailing practice in regard to a religious rite, merely because we judge it becoming and useful? This we cannot admit. We must then rest the Christian sabbath on the ground of the original institution of the sabbath, as enjoined in the fourth command of the Decalogue. And we must, at the same time, admit that the original institution was particularly modified at the commencement of the Christian dispensation, although our sacred writings nowhere expressly require such a modification. It cannot but be evident, therefore, that if we should insist upon the necessity of an express divine precept, either originally addressed to us, or transmitted to us by the sacred records, in order to justify us in observing the rite of *infant baptism*, we should contradict our own practice in regard to another subject very analogous to this.* . . . My object in this place is to remove a mistake as to the kind and degree of evidence which should be deemed conclusive, and to show that demanding an express precept in favour of infant baptism,

* Is it not wholly unaccountable that the Baptists should reject infant baptism on the ground of a want of express precept, and then turn directly about, and advocate the first day of the week as the true sabbath? They are forced to defend their practice in the observance of the first day of the week as the sabbath-day, on exactly similar grounds of evidence to those from which we argue the obligation and validity of infant baptism. Why do they accept this sort of evidence in the one case, and reject it, nay, hoot at it, in the other? The Seventh-day Baptists alone are herein consistent with themselves, and must necessarily possess great advantage of their brethren who keep the first day of the week, in argument on their respective peculiarities. "They must either keep the seventh day," says a Seventh-day Baptist, "or reject the principles on which they reject infant baptism: they must give up their argument, or keep the seventh day, or else determine to act inconsistently and absurdly."—*Rev. E. Hall on Baptism*, p. 124.

that is, demanding a new and explicit command in favour of the dedication of children to God by the Christian rite of baptism, would be unreasonable and inconsistent. I wish every man to settle it in his mind perfectly and for ever, that, in a multitude of cases, other evidence ought to be received, and is received, as satisfactory.

"Consider a moment how we proceed in regard to so momentous a subject as the authority of some of the sacred writings. Take, for example, the Epistle to the Hebrews, which we receive as having been written by inspiration of God. But why do we thus receive it? What is the kind of evidence we have of its divine inspiration and divine authority? Do the other Scriptures give testimony to this epistle, and require us to receive it? No. Does the author of the epistle inform us that he wrote by divine inspiration? Does he even give us his name? He does neither. We receive this book as of divine authority, *because ecclesiastical history teaches us that it was thus received by the generality of early Christians*, whom we know to have been far better qualified than we are to form a right judgment in regard to its claims. It is primarily on the ground of such evidence as this that we admit the epistle into the sacred canon. The intrinsic excellence of the book, and its correspondence with other parts of Scripture, are, indeed, considerations of great weight in favour of its divine authority. But these considerations are of a very different nature from what we understand by *express, positive proof* from the word of God. The same as to some other parts of the Christian Scriptures. What is the kind of evidence that we have of their divine inspiration and authority? They are sanctioned by no voice from heaven; by no miracle; and by no declaration of inspired writers. But do we, therefore, reject them? No. We receive them as a part of the sacred canon on the ground of *historical* evidence. That is, the testimony of antiquity is in their favour. We rely on that testimony, because it is the testimony of men competent to judge. And why should we not proceed on the same general principles in regard to *infant baptism?* We have at least as good evidence from history in favour of this, as we have that the Apocalypse and the Epistle to the Hebrews, and some other parts of the Bible, were written by inspired men. How, then, can we consistently reject it?"*

We have ventured upon this somewhat lengthy quotation, because, after carefully weighing the whole subject, we could think of no clearer or more comprehensive view to present to the reader. After what has been said, it is needless, although it were quite easy, to multiply instances for illustration. We flatter ourselves that it is sufficiently plain that men cannot judge beforehand of the kind or degree of evidence which the Almighty may deem fit to offer in support of any particular institution; or as the foundation of our faith and obligation. It is in vain for men to say they will not believe without the most direct and positive proof. It is folly for them to assume this attitude, because it contradicts the grounds of action which they are daily impelled to adopt in reference to a thousand other matters. Thomas might have fancied himself justified in rejecting the testimony of his fellow-disciples, and demanding the palpable evidence of his senses; he might even have imagined himself more noble than the rest on this account; but the Saviour did not commend him, but, on the contrary, plainly intimated that a less skeptical and obstinate mind was not the less reasonable, and far more happy. He also taught him that the same kind of evidence that he enjoyed could not, from the nature of the case, be granted to all, nor was it necessary. He who made man, and constituted the human mind to receive and weigh evidence, he it is that best knows what kind and degree of evidence to afford on moral subjects, and how the probationary interests of man may best be served hereby. We are to take the Bible as it is—ascertain its facts and their supporting evidence—and act according to the force of those rational convictions which such evidence inspires. And if it be regarded as hazardous to adopt a line of conduct without a written testimony, in so many words, of its being duty; it is no less dangerous to the spirit of genuine piety, and offensive to the dignity of right reason, to despise such conduct in others, and spurn it from the catalogue of our acknowledged duties, because it may be sanctioned only by evidence of an inferential and

* Lectures on Infant Baptism, by Dr. Woods, pp. 17–21.

analogical character,—evidence which, in the great majority of cases, in religion, politics, commerce, and all the social walks of life, influences and governs the conduct of men.

For some further illustrations, the reader is referred to the note below.*

SECTION IV.

But the New Testament is not silent on the subject of infant baptism, but makes just such mention of it as, in view of the state of opinion at that time, proves it to have been enjoined, and universally practised. It makes just such mention of the subject as the circumstances of the case required. It is not the ordinance of baptism itself that we now speak of, but it is the application of this ordinance to infants. The institution of Christian baptism required and received an express sanction from the lips of our Saviour; and this command is registered. But the application of this rite to infants is a point that became so obvious to the mind of the Jew, and to all who were conversant with the ancient usage of the church, as to require no direct precept, or, at least, that that precept should be recorded. The light of analogy, and the force of ancient habit, precluded any such necessity. They had only need of being informed what was the initiatory rite of the new dispensation, and the fact of its applicability to infants would follow as a matter of course, unless prohibited; or, at most, would require only private direction. Under these circumstances what mention may we suppose the New Testament would naturally make of this subject? We answer: It is reasonable to suppose that it would merely *recognise* facts and principles in relation to it, in an incidental way, without any intimation of their being new, or controverted, or doubted. And this we find to be the fact in the case. The New Testament makes just such allusion to infants—recognises all those facts and principles in reference to them—as supposes them still to retain their ancient rights to the seal of the covenant, and their ancient relation to the church. Infants are spoken of in a manner wholly inexplicable on any other supposition than that of

* See Note B.

their eligibility to baptism, and in a manner to clearly indicate that there was no controversy on this point in the New Testament times. The reader will readily perceive, therefore, upon a little reflection, the proper distinctive character of our position. He will be at no loss to appreciate the distinction between a *positive command*, directing a certain line of conduct, and a *recognition* of principles and facts which imply such conduct; between an ordinance newly issued under sanction of positive authority, and an ordinance of ancient date, newly recognised in its principles, and in the fact of its existence. Proceed we then to the labour of proof:—

1. Infants are in a gracious state. By this I mean that they are included in the provisions of the gospel, and receive a title to eternal life through the atonement. It is not our present intention to enter upon the proof of this point; if any man doubt it, we must leave him to his opinion, and address our argument to those who allow the statement. We do not, furthermore, wish any controversy respecting the manner in which infants are saved through the atonement. All we insist upon is the fact that they are embraced in the economy of redemption, and, through the grace of Christ, entitled to, and prepared for, eternal life. Now, this fact, which is so fully established by our Lord's words in Matt. xix, 14, and xviii, 2–5, and by Paul in Rom. v, and elsewhere, this fact, we say, is one of primary importance; for unless infants are fit for heaven, or have a title to heaven, it is evident they are not suitable to sustain any relation to the church. All fitness for church relations must be primarily predicated of, and based upon, that moral state that constitutes a fitness for future happiness. The church militant, in its moral features, is designed to be an image and transcript of the church triumphant. In this respect, the two "kingdoms are but one." Baptism is an outward sign of an inward work of grace,—a token of confirmation that the subject belongs to the spiritual family of God, and is an heir of that grace which is promised in the covenant of Abraham. Of course, therefore, all who are the subjects of this grace, which is signified by baptism—all who belong to the spiritual family of God—are entitled to baptism. If they have the thing signified by baptism, they may, and ought

to receive baptism itself also. This principle is fully carried out and established in the Scriptures. For instance, in Acts x, 47, Peter says, concerning Cornelius and his Gentile friends, "Can any man forbid water that these should not be baptized, which have received the Holy Ghost as well as we?" The argument which he urged in favour of their being baptized, and one which he deemed sufficient and conclusive, was, that they had "received the Holy Ghost,"—they had been made the subjects of grace. At first Peter hesitated to go into the house with these Gentiles, because they were regarded as *unclean*, forbidden and rejected of God. But now, when he beholds them really the subjects of saving grace, "he commands them to be baptized." This is clear and unequivocal. "Peter went by this rule," says Mr. Wall, "one that is capable of the ends of baptism should be baptized. Mr. Tombs himself says, 'If it should be made known to us that infants are sanctified, I should not doubt but that they are to be baptized; remembering the words of St. Peter,'"* as above quoted. But one less affected with Calvinism might be more disposed to infant baptism. Now, the New Testament recognises and affirms that moral condition of infants which, in an adult, is regarded as the groundwork of a fitness for baptism and a connection with the church. Our Saviour expressly declares, "Of such is the kingdom of heaven," which, whatever else it may mean, clearly proves, in infants, a moral fitness for baptism and church relations. Whatever, then, may be urged against infants, in other respects, on the score of their alleged unfitness for baptism, their moral state can furnish no ground for such a plea. And to this our opponents themselves can find no objection, unless they are of the number of those who believe that "persons (infants included) not elected cannot be saved."†

2. Infants are capable of sustaining covenant relations to God. This circumstance also is of primary importance. If it could be proved that children are incapable of being entered into covenant with God, we cannot see but this controversy must be at an end. On the contrary, if it can be proved that children are capable of being entered into

* Wall's Dialogue on Infant Baptism.

† Confession of Faith, article "*Effectual calling.*"

covenant, and of sustaining covenant relations and inheriting covenant blessings, then, their right to the *sign* of the covenant, and to covenant relations, is easily substantiated. And here the reader will perceive, if children possess a moral fitness for church relations,—as is proved from the fact that they are fit subjects for "the kingdom of heaven,"—and if they are capable of being entered into covenant with God, then, no primary objection can be urged against their baptism; but, on the contrary, these simple considerations would, of themselves, create a powerful presumption of the truth of the doctrine which we advocate. Now, that infants are capable of being entered into covenant with God, and that the Bible so regards them, is put beyond all question.

In Deut. xxix, 10–12, Jehovah thus speaks to the children of Israel: "Ye stand this day all of you before the Lord your God; your captains of your tribes, your elders, and your officers, with all the men of Israel, YOUR LITTLE ONES, your wives, and thy stranger that is in thy camp, from the hewer of thy wood unto the drawer of thy water: THAT THOU SHOULDEST ENTER INTO COVENANT WITH THE LORD THY GOD, AND INTO HIS OATH, which the Lord thy God maketh with thee this day." In this passage the "*little ones*" are enumerated with the same formality, and are made the same account of in the "covenant," as are the "elders," the "officers," and "all the men of Israel." But if the children were not intended to be entered into covenant equally with the rest, it would have been as much in place to have mentioned their cattle, in this enumeration, as their infants.

In Deut. v, 2, 3, Moses says, "The Lord our God made a covenant with us in Horeb. The Lord made not his covenant with our fathers, *but with us, even us*, WHO ARE ALL OF US HERE ALIVE THIS DAY." Now, this covenant in Horeb had been made with these persons about thirty-eight years previously, when many of them were children and infants, and all of them in nonage.

But it is not necessary to cite particular instances; the simple fact that children were entered into covenant with God by circumcision is sufficient to put this question for ever at rest. And here, be it remembered, the question does not hinge on the spirituality of the covenant. We are not now speaking of the *moral* qualification of infants to be entered into covenant, but of the *natural fitness* of their being thus entered. The moral aspect of this question must be determined by the fitness of children for heaven; the question now before us relates to the propriety—the natural fitness—of entering them into covenant relations to God; and this, we say, is decided affirmatively by the actual appointment of God, in relation to circumcision.

And here we plead for no principle that is not recognised and sanctioned by Scripture, by all civil governments, and by the reason of mankind. The plain truth in the case is, that if infants have any interest in the benefits of the covenant, that interest ought to be *recognised* in a lawful way. If infants, equally with their pious parents, are sharers in the bounteous provisions of the atonement, (which is the great blessing secured in the Abrahamic covenant,) they obviously possess an equal right with their parents to the visible *mark*, or *token*, of participation in such blessings. Under all civil governments children have rights; it is a law of nature and a dictate of justice that these rights should be recognised and protected. The protection of the laws, the rights of citizenship, and of property, are secured to them, not on the principle of their being of a certain age, or of their being competent to judge of the value of these blessings, but on the principle of their relation to their parents. On this point we shall dwell more at large in another place. This, then, is the principle for which we contend. Children are as capable of sustaining covenant relations to God, so far as the question of natural fitness and propriety is concerned, as they are of sustaining any civil relations to government. They are as capable of possessing spiritual rights and immunities as civil rights; and are as capable of being injured in respect of the former as of the latter. Their spiritual rights are not founded on the circumstance of age or intellectual acquirements, but on the fact of their being human beings, included, equally with their parents, in the covenant of redemption. It is in view of these facts that we may well repeat the caution, "Take heed that ye despise not one of these little ones." That the New Testament recognises this view will be made to appear in the process of the argument.

3. The right of infants to the initiatory ordinance is recognised and proved in different places in the New Testament.

[1.] We call the reader's attention to Gal. iii, 29, "And if ye be Christ's, THEN are ye Abraham's seed, and heirs ACCORDING TO THE PROMISE." In this passage it is placed beyond a doubt that the believer in Christ comes exactly under the ancient charter of rights granted to Abraham, and, according to the true spirit of that ancient grant, becomes an heir of life. In other words, a true Christian comes exactly in that relation to the Abrahamic covenant that a pious Jew sustained before the time of Christ. Indeed, it is fully attested that the promise of that covenant was not to the Jews as the natural descendants of Abraham, but to all believers in Christ as the spiritual children of that patriarch. It was according to this spiritual lineage that the inheritance of grace and church privileges was to be reckoned, and not according to natural descent. To the same purport is verse 7 of the same chapter: "Know ye therefore that *they which are of faith*, THE SAME ARE THE CHILDREN OF ABRAHAM." Now, the argument is obvious. If the converted Gentile come in the same relation to the covenant as the pious Jew, we must look also, and as a matter of course, for a corresponding application of the ordinances, or institutes of that covenant. For instance, if the initiating ordinance of this covenant, under the law, applied to the Jew, and to his infant offspring, the same application of the ordinance must be made to the Christian and his children, under the gospel, if it be true that the latter comes exactly in the same relations to the covenant as the former. It makes no difference that the external form of this ordinance is changed; whatever it be as to form, it must take the same adaptations as anciently. The ancient privileges of the covenant must be maintained. The rights of the true children of Abraham are unimpaired; and if the children of ancient Jews—who were the "children of the covenant"—were entitled to certain privileges and church relations, the children of believers now—coming, as they do, in the exact relations of ancient Jews to this same covenant—are entitled to the same rights.

It must be remembered that circumcision was the seal

of the covenant, and not, as many seem to imagine, a part of the peculiar institutes of Moses. It is proper that every covenant should have its seal, which may be regarded in the light of the proper signatures of the parties, attesting the validity and binding nature of the contract. It is hence, as we have already observed, Jehovah has always annexed *seals*, or *tokens*, to his covenants. The seal, or token, of the Abrahamic covenant was to be applied to all the male children of that patriarch. This no one will deny. The question, then, is, Who are the children of Abraham? The text under consideration declares that "if we be Christ's, THEN are we Abraham's seed." Now, if baptism be the seal of the covenant under the present dispensation, as circumcision was under the former; and if Christians now come exactly in the same relations to that covenant that pious Jews sustained anciently—being as truly the "seed of Abraham" and the "children of the covenant" as they—then, does it not follow that, the covenant being the same, our relations to it the same, and the "seal" yet remaining, we are to look for an *application* of the seal corresponding to its ancient use? Would not the apostles, who were Jews, and their converted Jewish brethren, naturally understand it thus? Can any thing be more plain and undeniable than this? Here, then, is a recognition, not of infant baptism by *name*, but of principles that as naturally and necessarily involve the practice of infant baptism, as any process of moral reasoning can involve a sequence in antecedent causes. And herein is infant baptism inculcated, not directly and by name, but by analogy and inference. Antecedent principles are established, and put beyond a doubt, and the mind is left to trace, by an easy, natural, and succinct process, the proximate and obvious result; and that result is, that children of Christian parents now, possess the same covenant rights and relations as did the children of Jewish parents anciently.

[2.] The second passage we cite in proof that the right of infants to the initiatory ordinance is recognised in the New Testament, is Matt. xxviii, 19, "Go ye, therefore, and teach all nations, baptizing them in the name of the Father, and of the Son, and of the Holy Ghost."

The question to be settled in reference to this passage

is this: "Would the apostles naturally understand the words of this commission as authorizing and directing infant baptism?" We think it is perfectly plain that they would so understand their commission; and would consequently go forward in the practice of infant baptism, unless restrained and prohibited by a special interdict. This, we are aware, the reader may deem gratuitous and unfounded; but if he will follow us with patience and candour a little, we hope to be able to dispel every shadow of obscurity from this important passage. To enable the reader to judge of the argument, we shall be obliged to enter somewhat into detail, and lay before him fully all the circumstances of the case.

1.) We argue that the apostles would understand this commission as authorizing and directing infant baptism, from the fact that the children of proselytes were baptized by the Jews. They were accustomed to make proselytes of infant children, as well as of adults, by baptism. The argument will be fully comprehended by attention to the following:—

(*a.*) The passage is not happily translated. The text stands thus: "Go ye, therefore, and μαθητευσατε *matheteusate*, *make disciples*, or *proselytes*, of all nations, baptizing them," &c.*

* Baptist authors, seeing the importance of this passage, and that, if the translation we have adopted be received, infant baptism would be a very probable and natural inference, have insisted upon the common English version, which merely says, "*teach* all nations." But this is objectionable. The translation we have given is, to say the least, as consistent with the original as the one in our common English version. This the Baptists themselves will not deny. Besides, the specific duty of *teaching* is referred to in the very next verse, and is expressed in another word. Our English presents a perfect tautology, "Go *teach* all nations . . . *teaching* them." It will not be argued that this is either a smooth or forcible sense. The two words are not the same in the original, and certainly cannot be supposed, with any propriety, to bear exactly the same sense here. The first, which occurs in verse 19, enjoins upon the apostles to bring persons over to the Christian profession, which, in an adult, would imply some elementary teaching. But the second word, which occurs in verse 20, enjoins upon them to *instruct* these converts. The former word is more *general*, the latter more *specific*. Doddridge renders it, "Go forth therefore, and *proselyte* all the nations . . . *teaching* them," &c. This makes the same sense as the marginal reading, "Go make *disciples*, or *Christians*, of all nations," &c.

(*b.*) The word DISCIPLE, in the Christian vocabulary, answers exactly to the word PROSELYTE, in the Jewish. A disciple *is* a proselyte; the only difference consisting in the circumstance that the latter is employed in the Scriptures to designate a Jewish convert, while the former applies to a convert to Christianity. A Jewish proselyte was one that was brought from heathenism and incorporated into the Jewish church; a Christian proselyte, or disciple, was one that was taken either from Jews or heathen, and became a follower of Christ. But the primary idea of both words is *convert*, or *follower*. There was a class of citizens among the Jews from the earliest period of their history, denominated גֵּרִים, and בְּנֵי נֵכָר, that is, *strangers*, *sons of strangers*, *foreigners*, &c. These were, for the most part, *proselytes* to the Jewish religion who dwelt in the land,* and, though Jews in religion, were distinguished from native Hebrews by the common appellation of *strangers*. This same class of persons was afterward called *proselytes*, from προς *to*, and ελευθω *to come*, *to come to*, and signifies a person who has *left* his own country and has *come to* another—that is, *a stranger*, *foreigner;* and also, figuratively, a person who has *left* his former practices and has *come to*, or *embraced*, a new religion; or that has *left* his former teacher and has *come to* a new one,—that is, a *proselyte*, a *disciple*, a *follower*, a

Now, it is incontestable that they were commanded to *μαθητευσατε make disciples*, BEFORE they were commanded to *διδασκω teach*. If not, why are these commands enjoined in this *order?* and if both these words mean the same thing in this place, why are the *two* employed, instead of *one* word, which would have been more simple? It is therefore absurd to suppose they mean the same thing. They were to perform the first command, (to make disciples,) *before*, or rather *by*, baptism; they were to perform the second command (to *teach*, *indoctrinate*) *after* baptism.

Furthermore, the verb bears this sense elsewhere. Thus, Matt. xxvii, 57, "Joseph . . who was *εμαθητευσε made a disciple* of Jesus." Acts xiv, 21, "And when they had preached the gospel in that city, *και μαθητευσαντες ἱκανους and having made disciples of many*." That these persons of Derbe were not only *taught*, but actually *discipled*, that is, *baptized*, and brought under the denomination of *Christians*, is evident, for in verse 22 they are called *μαθητων disciples*, and in verse 23 are spoken of as church members.

* Vide Dr. A. Clarke's Com. on Exod. xii, 43. Robinson's Calmet, art. *Proselyte*.

convert, &c. The word $\mu\alpha\theta\eta\tau\eta\varsigma$ *mathetes*, disciple, primarily signifies a *scholar;* that is, one who has placed himself under the tutorage of another. A person who left his idolatry and heathen worship, and came to Moses, adopting him as his authoritative teacher and guide in religion, was called a *proselyte:* a person who "forsook all" and came to Christ, accepting him as his only religious teacher and guide, was called a *disciple.* The primary idea in both words is the same. Our Saviour used the word *disciple* instead of *proselyte*, probably for no other reason than to avoid the confusion that would result from adopting a strictly Jewish vocabulary, although that vocabulary might, otherwise, have equally served his purpose. Thus he has used *church* ($\varepsilon\kappa\kappa\lambda\eta\sigma\iota\alpha$) instead of *synagogue*, ($\sigma\upsilon\nu\alpha\gamma\omega\gamma\eta$,) although they both signify the same thing—that is, *an assembly*—merely to distinguish between a Jewish and a Christian *congregation.* Yet, if the word *synagogue* had not already been in use among the Jews, and received by them a specific meaning, it might have been used in the New Testament instead of *ekklesia* with equal propriety. We make these remarks in order to show that the original idea conveyed by the two words, *proselyte* and *disciple*, is one and the same; and also to show the probable reason why the word *disciple* was adopted in the Christian vocabulary, instead of *proselyte.* But we have still higher authority than the mere resemblance of their etymological significations, for making the two words essentially synonymous.

The *descriptions* which are given in the New Testament of a disciple are borrowed from, and answer to, the descriptions of a Jewish proselyte. For instance, "the *first* condition of proselytism among the Jews was, that he who came to embrace their religion should come voluntarily, and that neither force nor influence should be employed in this business. This, also, is the *first* condition required by Jesus Christ, and which he considers as the foundation of all the rest. '*If any man be willing* ($\varepsilon\iota\ \tau\iota\varsigma\ \theta\varepsilon\lambda\varepsilon\iota$) *to come after me*,' Matt. xvi, 24. The *second* condition required in the Jewish proselyte was, that he should perfectly renounce all his prejudices, his errors, his idolatry, and every thing that concerned his false religion, and that he should entirely separate himself from his most intimate friends and acquaintances. It was on this ground that the Jews called proselytism a new birth, and proselytes *new born*, and *new men;* and our Lord requires men to be born again, not only of water, but by the Holy Ghost. John iii, 5. All this our Lord includes in this word, *let him renounce himself*—*απαρνησασθω ἑαυτον*. Mark viii, 34. To this the following scriptures refer: Matt. x, 33; John iii, 3, 5; 2 Cor. v, 17. The *third* condition on which a person was admitted into the Jewish church as a proselyte was, that he should submit to the yoke of the Jewish law, and patiently bear the inconveniences and sufferings with which a profession of the Mosaic religion might be accompanied. Christ requires the same condition, but, instead of the yoke of the law, he brings in his own doctrine, which he calls his *yoke* (Matt. xi, 29) and his *cross*, (Matt. xvi, 24; Mark viii, 34,) the taking up of which not only implies a bold profession of Christ crucified, but also a cheerful submitting to all the sufferings and persecutions to which he might be exposed, and even to death itself. The *fourth* condition was, that they should solemnly engage to continue in the Jewish religion, faithful even unto death. This condition Christ also required, and it is comprised in this word, *let him follow me.* Matt. xvi, 24–26; Mark viii, 34–37."*

(*c.*) It is not necessary to extend remarks on so plain a case. If, then, *disciple* and *proselyte* signify the same thing—and if the apostles, in their Jewish state, had always been acquainted with a particular mode of proselyting—it is evident that they would naturally understand the command to *make disciples* of all nations as tantamount to a command to *make proselytes* of all nations, and that they would also proceed to make disciples just as they had always been taught to make proselytes, unless otherwise instructed. This is obvious. If any new method of making disciples, or proselytes, was to be adopted, that method must be pointed out. If any alteration of the old method was to be made, that alteration should and must have been clearly defined; otherwise the apostles would have gone on and understood and applied terms according to general usage, and the principles of their religious edu-

* Horne's Introd., part iii, chap. ii, sec. 3. Clarke's Com. on Mark viii, 34.

cation. Our Lord well knew what influence the former education and prejudices of the disciples would exert in the interpretation of the words of the commission,* and he therefore specifies wherein the particular mode of their making disciples was to differ from the Jewish mode of making proselytes, namely, that whereas the Jews received proselytes by circumcision, baptism, and sacrifice,† they were to make disciples of all nations only by baptizing them. Baptism,‡ then, to the exclusion of the other ceremonies, was to be the Christian method of making proselytes. So far, then, the apostles understood. But were there any further directions necessary? Was it necessary to give any direction respecting the baptism of infants? Plainly not. The circumstances of the case did not require a distinct command in order that the apostles should thus apply their commission, but just the contrary; they required a distinct *prohibition* of infant baptism if the apostolic commission was *not* to be thus construed and applied. The inquiry which now becomes necessary, in order to set this whole matter in a clear light, is, "What was the Jewish method of proselyting with reference to children?" The answer to this we have anticipated above. It is plain that whatever might have been this method, or usage, the disciples would unquestionably have copied it, and have construed their commission by this usage, unless prohibited by an express command of the Saviour.

The practice of making proselytes, with regard to children, is very well understood by all who have any knowledge of the sacred antiquities of the Jews. It was their invariable practice to proselyte, in the usual way, all the children of converted parents. The children that were born *after* their parents had become proselytes were treated, in all respects, like Jewish children: but the

* I wish the reader to bear in mind the fact, that at the time of Christ, and previously, the spirit of proselyting ran high among the Jews, and great efforts were made to bring over to their faith the Gentile nations. Thus Idumea was wholly brought over as a nation. Josephus, Ant., b. xiii, c. 9, § 1. Thus, also, in every nation the apostles found proselytes. Acts ii, 10; vi, 5; and xiii, 43. See also Josephus, Ant., b. xx, c. 3, § 4. Our Saviour alludes to the universal passion of the nation for proselyting, in Matt. xxiii, 15. Every Jew was familiar with the mode of proselyting.

† See Calmet's Dict., art. *Proselyte.* ‡ See Note C.

children that were born *before* their parents became proselytes were admitted into the church by circumcision, (if males,) baptism, and sacrifice. "Boys under twelve years of age, and girls under thirteen, could not become proselytes till they had obtained the consent of their parents, or, in case of refusal, the concurrence of the officers of justice. Baptism, in respect of girls, had the same effect as circumcision in respect of boys. Each of them, by means of this, received, as it were, a new birth."* Whenever a heathen became a proselyte to the Jewish religion, he thereby became a Jew in every sense, except by birth and early education; he thereby came under obligation to the Mosaic law, and became entitled to all the privileges of the law and of the covenant, just as though he had been born and educated a Jew, or was, as it was called, a "Hebrew of the Hebrews." Consequently it became his duty to consecrate his children to God, as the Mosaic law required of all Jews. But as those children which had been born *before* their parents became proselytes had been born in a state of heathenism, they needed, in the estimation of the Jews, the same process of purification from heathenism as their parents, and were, consequently, subjected to the same ordinances.

2.) But, furthermore, we argue that the apostles would have taken authority from their commission to baptize infants, (and would consequently have instituted the practice, unless prohibited,) from the fact, before alluded to, that infants had always been treated as the proper subjects of the initiating rite. This circumstance need not be dwelt upon here, but it must not be forgotten that its force is necessarily unequivocal and decisive.

In connection with this fact, it should be considered that baptisms were always practised by the Jews in a religious manner. Whenever a Jew had contracted any ceremonial defilement, he was temporarily suspended from the privileges and communion of the Jewish church, until, by purification, or baptism, he was again restored. These purifications were repeatedly called baptisms in the New Testament. They had all the effect of a ceremony of initiation, for they actually *restored* the lapsed Jew to his

* Robinson's Calmet, art. *Proselyte*. See Note C.

regular standing in the church. When Christ commanded to make disciples by baptism, the ceremony was by no means a new one. The baptism of John occasioned no surprise among the Jews, as it would have done had it been a novel practice, only they were a little surprised that any person less than Christ himself should administer it. John i, 25. When, therefore, in connection with this, we consider that the apostles had no idea of a church that did not contain infant members, we are forced to conclude that they would have so understood their commission as to give baptism to infants, unless expressly instructed to the contrary.

To all this it must be added, that Christ had bestowed special consideration upon children, and in a solemn manner taught his disciples also to bestow upon them a religious regard, declaring that "of such the kingdom of heaven is composed." These considerations must have exerted a powerful influence over the apostles' minds, disposing them to the baptism of infants, unless, as we have said, they had been prohibited by a special command.

And here, candid reader, I would have you pause and review the statements under this section—form a just estimate of all the circumstances of the case—and draw your conclusion. Do not mistake the nature and bearing of the argument, particularly that from Jewish proselyte baptism. This has been too often done already, and has occasioned an unreasonable prejudice against the doctrine of infant baptism. I am sorry to find, in Professor Ripley's reply to Professor Stuart on baptism—a work evincing much ability and candour—I am sorry, I say, to find in such a work so unjust a statement as the following:—"I know," says that author, "what use has been made by Pedobaptist writers of the possible, or probable, or, as they have often regarded it, certain fact that proselyte baptism was performed among the Jews before the Christian era; namely, *that it has been used as a starting point in the defence of infant baptism.*" The author then adds, "If any Christians choose thus intimately to connect their proof of what they practise as a divine ordinance with the superstitious practices of the Jews,—practices, too, the antiquity of which is so much a matter of disputation,—on themselves be the responsibility of deserting the plain, beaten path of Holy Scripture."*

We cannot disguise our astonishment and grief at finding such statements from the pen of so amiable and candid an author, calculated as they are to misguide and misinform the uninstructed reader. It takes an entirely erroneous view of the argument drawn from the "apostolic commission," and of the use made of Jewish proselyte baptism in this connection. We deduce no warrant for infant baptism from the "superstitious practices of the Jews." Nay, further, we do not deem it an essential point at all, whether the Jews ever baptized proselytes before the Christian era. All that we profess to do is that which Professor Ripley himself, and also every other expositor of the Bible, is bound to do, namely, to so estimate the history of those times, and the particular education and habits of the apostles themselves, as to be able rightly to judge of the manner in which they would naturally construe the words of their commission. And this, it is well known, involves a principle at once the most difficult and important in Biblical exegesis. How large a portion of the Bible would still remain in obscurity, but for the knowledge that has come down to us from foreign sources respecting the religious, social, and domestic habits of the ancients! Indeed, it would be trifling with time, and with the intelligence and good sense of the reader, to dilate upon this topic. Whatever goes to determine the *usus loquendi* of the sacred writings, whether it come from the errors or the orthodoxy of the ancients—their religion or their superstition—must be taken into account. "It is common," says Mr. Wall, "for a rule or law to be so worded, as that one may perceive that the Lawgiver has supposed, or taken for granted, that the people to whom it was already given did already know some things which were previous to the apprehending of his meaning; so that it was needless to express them. But though these things were ordinarily known to the people of that time and place, yet we, who live at so great a distance of time, do not know them without an inquiry made into the history of the state of that time, as to those things which the law

* Christian Baptism, p. 109. See also Robinson's History of Baptism, p. 37.

speaks of; and, consequently, without such inquiry, the rule or law that was plain to them, will, in many particulars, be obscure to us. So, for example, many of the Grecian and Roman laws, whereof we have copies yet extant, would not be well understood by us unless they were explained to us by such as have skill in the history of the state of affairs in those empires. And so many passages in the books of the New Testament of our Saviour are not rightly apprehended without having recourse to the books of the Old Testament, and other books, wherein the customs of the Jewish nation are set forth, for understanding the state of religion among the people at that time when our Saviour gave his rules."*

This, then, is the use we would make of the practice and method of proselyting among the Jews. We do not argue that infants are to be baptized now, because the Jews had a practice anciently of baptizing the children of proselytes. We do not, as Professor Ripley would intimate, and which, indeed, he has plainly stated, "intimately connect the proof of what we regard as a divine ordinance with the superstitious practices of the Jews." If any person supposes this he is wholly in an error, and if he continue to hold and teach such an opinion, he greatly abuses both himself and those who have the misfortune to believe him. But we say, that the early Jewish education of the apostles, in relation to making *proselytes*, must have had a decisive influence over their minds in determining the construction to be put upon that part of their commission which required them to "make *disciples* of all nations;" and that, as the words *proselyte* and *disciple* signified substantially the same thing, in a religious sense, the apostles would have gone forth discipling the nations in the same method by which they had always been accustomed to see proselytes made, unless they had been otherwise instructed. And all this is saying no more than that men will naturally explain language, in any given instance, according to the custom of the age, unless specially instructed to the contrary.

It is a matter of no importance to the present argument, whether the Jews fairly derived their authority for baptizing proselytes from the Bible, or only from their doctors.

* History of Infant Baptism, *Introduction.*

The truth is, they had such a practice, and they quoted the Old Testament Scriptures as their authority. Whether, therefore, the practice were rightly or wrongly founded on the sacred Scriptures, *they fully believed* it to be of divine authority, and hence, it is easy to perceive that it would have the same influence over their minds, in determining the sense of their commission, as though it had been *indisputably* of divine authority: that is, without a prohibition, they would naturally have understood it as authorizing and directing them to baptize infants. The question is not, whether the baptism of Jewish proselytes—infants as well as adults—was right? but, whether the disciples, and all the Jews, *believed* it to be right? for the influence which it would exert over their minds is not to be measured by the absolute fitness or obligation of the practice, but by *their views* of its fitness and obligation.

The argument, then, is plain. "Suppose our Saviour had ordered the apostles to require the nations to keep the Jewish feasts. If he had meant that they should not keep the 'feast of the dedication,' (which had no divine institution, but yet, being become customary, was observed by all the Jews, and even by Christ himself,) as well as the passover, and the rest which had been commanded in the law, he would doubtless in that case have excepted that. And there is the same reason in the case before us,"* [to suppose that, if the baptism of infants was to be omitted by the apostles, this exception would have been expressly made in their commission, or elsewhere; otherwise, it being a universal practice among the Jews, in regard to proselytes,—a practice which they regarded as of divine authority,—it would have been retained by the apostles, and through them by the churches.]

We are not to interpret the language of Scripture according to the opinions and usages of *our own* times, but we are to go back to the ages in which the Bible was first delivered to men—search into the opinions and practices of those ages—form a just and natural estimate of the then existing opinions and prejudices, and of the force which they would naturally exert over the interpretation and use of language, and, in view of all these modifying circumstances, we must form our opinion of the meaning

* Wall's Hist., part i, *Introduction.*

of the laws and declarations of holy writ. The principle which I am endeavouring here to define is of fundamental importance in the interpretation of the Scriptures, and I feel authorized, from this consideration, to urge it upon the reader's most candid and mature consideration. I wish him to feel its importance to the present argument, as well as the justness and propriety with which it has been here employed. Vain and fallacious, indeed, must be that method of reasoning on this subject, which makes no account of the pre-existing opinions and prejudices of the apostles themselves, and of the Jews in general. With such a reckless and blind method of constructing theories, it becomes a hopeless undertaking to search for truth.

Long as I have detained the reader upon this particular point, and great as may be the hazard of incurring the charges of prolixity and repetition, I cannot deny myself the satisfaction of closing these remarks with the following pertinent statements of Dr. Woods:—

"If, then," says that author, "it had been the uniform custom of the Jews to baptize proselytes to their religion, as we certainly have much reason to think, it is clear that the baptism of proselytes by John and by Christ was no new thing. It is, at any rate, clear that baptism, *as a religious rite*, had been familiarly known among the Jews from the time of Moses. So that the rite which John the Baptist instituted was not by any means a new rite. The question put to him [John i, 25, '*Why baptizest thou then, if thou art not the Christ?*'] plainly implies that baptism was not regarded by the Jews at that time as a new rite. It was this rite, long used for ceremonial purification, and also in the case of proselytes to the Jewish religion, which John applied to those Jews who listened to his instructions, and gave signs of repentance. Afterward Christ ordained, that this same rite, which had thus been used among the Israelites for purification, and thus applied to converted Gentiles, and to Jews who repented under the preaching of John, should, from that time, be applied to all, in every part of the world, who embraced Christianity. The work of proselyting men to the true religion had before been carried on within [comparatively] narrow limits. It was now to be carried on extensively; and baptism, in the Christian form, was now to be administered to all proselytes: 'Go ye, and proselyte all nations, baptizing them in the name of the Father, and of the Son, and of the Holy Ghost.' In judging of the true meaning and intent of this commission, the apostles would naturally consider in what manner baptism had been administered; and particularly its having been applied to *proselytes* and *their children*. This last circumstance, in addition to the other with which they were so familiar—namely, that of having children as well as parents consecrated to God by circumcision—must have had a direct and decisive influence upon the construction which the apostles put upon their commission, and must have led them to conclude that, under the Christian dispensation, *children* as well as parents were to be devoted to God by baptism, unless some contrary instruction was given to prevent such a conclusion. Knapp says, 'If Christ, in his command to baptize all, Matt. xxviii, had wished children to be excepted, he must have expressly said this. For, since the first disciples of Christ, as native Jews, knew no other way than for children to be introduced into the Israelitish church by circumcision, it was natural that they should extend this to baptism, if Christ did not expressly forbid it. Had he therefore wished that it should not be done, he would surely have said so in definite terms.'"* But no such prohibitive terms are recorded; nor have we the least evidence to believe that the apostles ever received such instructions privately; for, as we shall hereafter show, both their subsequent practice, and that of the Christian church, combine to preclude such a supposition.

[3.] The New Testament affirms that relationship of infants to the church which implies their baptism. This is tantamount to asserting their right to baptism. Indeed, it is asserting it, not directly, but by implication. Certain things were predicated of infants anciently, which, when rightly understood, implied their baptism. This is the ground we here take.

1.) The first passage I shall cite under this head is that of Matt xix, 13–15: "Then were there brought unto him little children, that he should put his hands on them, and pray: and the disciples rebuked them. But Jesus said, Suffer little children, and forbid them not, to come unto

* Lectures on Infant Baptism, pp. 50, 51.

me: for of such is the kingdom of heaven. And he laid his hands on them, and departed thence." Mark says, (x, 16,) "And he took them up in his arms, put his hands upon them, and blessed them."

In these passages are several facts stated, to which we will attend in their order.

I understand that those whom they brought to Christ were *infants*. Matthew and Mark both say, "They brought unto him *little children*." The text does not read, "They brought unto him παιδας *paidas*, *children*, or *youth*;" but the *diminutive*, παιδια *paidia*, *little children*, is used. Luke says, (xviii, 15,) "They brought unto him also βρεφος *brephos*, *infants*;" the same word is rendered *babe* in chap. i, 41, 44; ii, 12, 16; Acts vii, 19; and in a figurative sense, 1 Pet. ii, 2. I make these references that the English reader may see the meaning of the word. Indeed, the facts that they *brought* these children to Christ, (probably in their arms,) and that Christ "took them up in his arms" to bless them, sufficiently show that they were infants. I know not that this is denied.

Our Saviour affirms that infants compose the kingdom of heaven.

Two distinct and important points present themselves, in this place, for investigation. *First.* Does our Saviour intend to say that infants themselves belong to the kingdom of heaven, or only such as in moral dispositions resemble them? *Secondly.* What is intended in this place by "the kingdom of heaven?"

(*a.*) We deem it perfectly plain that Christ intended to be understood that infants themselves are the lawful members of the kingdom of heaven. We are confident that a plain, common-sense, unvitiated mind, that had no party interests to serve, nor party influence to bias his judgment, would never think of another interpretation of these very clear and comprehensible words. But such is the posture of this subject, that we should be deemed wanting in our argument did we not offer proof of this position.

1. Let the reader, then, consider that Christ was speaking to children directly. They were the exclusive *subject* of his remarks, not merely the *occasion* of them. What he affirms, therefore, he affirms of children. In Matt. xviii, 2, "Jesus called a *little child* unto him, and set him in the

midst," for the purpose of illustrating and inculcating the virtue of Christian *humility*. In that connection, therefore, as might be expected from the occasion, our Saviour, in the process of his discourse, speaks sometimes of little children *as such*, and sometimes of his true disciples as though they were little children; calling them *μικρων τουτων these little ones*, because in moral dispositions they resembled children. The whole discourse of our Saviour, in that connection, turned upon the declaration, "Except ye be converted, and become *ὡς τα παιδια hos ta paidia*, AS *little children*," &c. The primary object of that occasion was to inculcate humility upon the disciples, by pointing out the *resemblance* between little children and true Christians. And yet, it is worthy of note, that Mark, in speaking of this occasion, (chap. ix, 37,) says, "Whosoever shall receive *ἑν των τοιουτων παιδιων one of such children* in my name," &c., evidently meaning *infants* as well as those adults who resemble them in moral dispositions; and Luke expressly says, speaking of the same occasion, (chap. ix, 48,) "Whosoever shall receive *τουτον το παιδιον* THIS *little child* in my name." Language could not be more explicit. These children were to be "*received*," as well as adults who resembled them, in Christ's name. But on the occasion before us, they brought little children unto Jesus, not for the purpose, primarily, of using them to inculcate any moral lessons upon others, but that *they themselves* might receive from Christ a blessing. It is true that in the parallel places of Mark x, 13, and Luke xviii, 15, our Saviour again institutes the comparison between little children and his true disciples, but this comparison was a secondary thought—an *accident*, and not the primary *object* of the occasion; and it was made *after* he had affirmed that children composed "the kingdom of heaven."

2. But suppose (which, however, we cannot admit) our Saviour did intend to say, not that children themselves were the subjects of the kingdom, but merely that those who were *like* to them in moral dispositions belonged to this kingdom. What has the objector gained by this supposition? Has he proved that children themselves are not subjects of this kingdom? By no means. Do away the doctrine that children belong to the kingdom of heaven,

and you destroy the ground of the comparison, and the beauty of the metaphor. For instance, if children are not the proper subjects of this kingdom, they must be regarded as *aliens*. But how can an adult become a fit subject of the kingdom of God, by an exact resemblance to persons who themselves are *aliens?* How could our Lord have said, "Except ye be converted and become as *these*, (*aliens?*) ye cannot enter into the kingdom of heaven?" If children themselves are not members of the kingdom, we see not how they could fitly represent those who are. Our Saviour, we apprehend, might have hit upon a happier metaphor.* It is true that he compares his true disciples sometimes to "doves" and to "*sheep*;" but never in the strong language of the text under consideration. He never said in reference to sheep, "Of *such* is the kingdom of heaven," nor did he ever command us to receive *such* "in his name."

3. But, furthermore, it must be considered that our Saviour adduces the membership of children as a reason why they should be brought to him. This is a most decisive proof that he here intends to affirm that children themselves belong to the kingdom of heaven. If they do not belong to Christ's kingdom—if our Lord only intended to say that certain persons who *resembled* children belonged to his kingdom—then, how could he make this a reason for urging the duty of bringing *little children themselves* to him to be blessed? The sequel shows that Christ took "*little children*" into his arms and blessed them; and he commanded the disciples to "suffer them to come unto him," alleging, as a reason, that "of such is the kingdom of heaven." But what propriety can there be in assigning such a reason for bringing little children to Christ, if the pronominal adjective "*such*" refer not to children themselves, but only to those who resemble them in moral dis positions? Take the true statement of this proposition, as our opponents would understand it. It is this: "Suffer little children to come unto me, because believing adults

* "'Of such is the kingdom of heaven;' not of such only as were *like* these infants. For if *they themselves* were not fit to be subjects of that kingdom, how could *others* be so, because they were *like* them? Infants, therefore, are capable of being admitted into the church, and have a right thereto."—*Wesley's Works*, vol. vi, p. 18.

who resemble them in moral dispositions belong to the kingdom of heaven." Now, is there any sense at all in this mode of reasoning? If children themselves are not the subjects of the kingdom, our Lord might as well have applied the same phraseology to "*sheep*," and have said, "Suffer *sheep* to come unto me," because believers who resemble sheep in their innocency of temper "belong to the kingdom of heaven." In this passage, "the subject presented before the mind was, *the little children themselves*. *They* were brought to Christ for his blessing. Upon *them* the attention of all was fixed. To *them* the objection of the disciples related. And surely, what Christ said in the way of reply to that objection must have related to them."

4. To these considerations it is only necessary to add, that *τοιουτος toioutos*, rendered *such* in the text, and which is here to be taken in its literal sense, "properly denotes the *nature* or *quality* of the thing to which it is applied. 'Innuit qualitatem rei.'—*Schleusner*. '*Such*, of this *kind* or *sort*.'—*Robinson's Wahl*."

Take a few examples of the use of this adjective:—

Matt. ix, 8, "And the multitude glorified God, who had given *τοιαυτην toiauten* SUCH power unto men."

Mark iv, 33, "And with many *τοιαυταις toiautais* SUCH parables spake he the word unto them."

Mark vi, 2, "That even *τοιαυται toiautai* SUCH mighty *works* are wrought by his hands."

Luke ix, 9. Herod said, "But who is this of whom I hear *τοιαυτα toiauta* SUCH *things?*"

Luke xiii, 2, "Suppose ye that these Galileans were sinners above all the Galileans, because they suffered *τοιαυτα toiauta* SUCH *things?*"

John ix, 16, "How can a man that is a sinner do *τοιαυτα toiauta* SUCH miracles?"

In 2 Cor. xii, 2, 3, this word is used to signify *this same*. Thus Paul says, "*Such* a one caught up," &c., that is, *this same* one caught up. "I knew *τοιουτον ανθρωπον such a man*;" that is, *this same man*. The literal and usual idea of this word is, *the same* things before spoken of, *and all like them*. For instance, Paul says, Rom. i, 32, "They which commit *τοιαυτα such* things are worthy of death;" that is, those who commit *these same* things that he has been enumerating, and *kindred* crimes, are worthy of death. So also chap. ii, 2, 3, *et alibi frequenter*. In the Septuagint version we find the same use of the term. So Jer. v, 9, "Shall not my soul be avenged on εθνει τοιουτω SUCH *a nation?*" that is, *this same* nation and all *like* it.

It is unnecessary to multiply citations under this head. The use of the adjective τοιουτος *toioutos*, *such*, is sufficiently obvious. It signifies literally, *the things before specified, and all like to them.* When used *indefinitely*, it signifies *all* persons or things of the particular class mentioned, including those which are specified in the context. Our Saviour says, "*And many* τοιειτε SUCH *like things they do;*" that is, they do the things before specified, and many others of the same class. Mark vii, 8; also verse 13. So in Gal. v, 23, "Against *such* there is no law;" that is, there is no law against such particular virtues as those specified, or any acts of this class. In Matt. xviii, 5, Jesus says, "Whosoever shall receive one παιδιον τοιουτον *paidion toiouton*, *such little child* in my name, receiveth me." Now, the question is, What is the sense of *such?* It has been supposed, as our Saviour intended on this occasion to illustrate the Christian character by the similitude of a little child which he "took and set in the midst of them," that παιδιον *paidion* (*a little child*) is used figuratively, to signify a true Christian—such a one as *resembles* a *little child* in moral dispositions. This is possible; and at any rate we do not here wish to controvert it. Suppose, then, our Saviour intended to say, "Whoso receiveth one *such disciple* in my name," the question remains unchanged. Who are included in the word *such?* The answer is obvious; namely, THE disciple specified, and *any* or *all like* him. Or, suppose παιδιον (*little child*) is used *literally;* the word *such* would then include THE *little child* specified, and *any* or *all like* it. So in Matt. xix, 14; where παιδια is unquestionably used in its literal and usual sense, to signify *little children, infants;* it says, "Suffer little children, and forbid them not, to come unto me; γαρ τοιουτων εσιν ἡ βασιλεια των ουρανων *for of* SUCH (παιδιων *little children* being understood) *is the kingdom of heaven.*" Now here it is to be remembered, that it is an important rule of interpretation that no one word in any particular connection shall take a more general meaning than the *whole* of the particular subject to which it alludes. What is the subject, then, exclusively under discussion in the thirteenth and fourteenth verses of this chapter? Plainly it is this: "Whether *children*, or *infants*, might with propriety be brought to Christ for his blessing?" Infants, as being the suitable subjects of the Saviour's benediction, were the exclusive subject of remark. Here was no metaphor—no figure of speech. The subject was plain, the occasion important, and words were used in their plain and literal sense. It is obvious, then, that *παιδιον paidion* must modify and restrict the sense of *toioutos*. If the former refer to *individuals* of a particular class, the latter must refer to *all* of that particular class; including, as a matter of course, the particular individuals specified. If our Saviour intended little children *literally*, when he said, "Suffer little children to come unto me," he must have alluded to *all* little children *literally*, and *as such*, when he says immediately after, and without giving the least intimation of having changed his subject, "of *such* is the kingdom of heaven." Without, therefore, detaining the reader longer on this point, we may safely conclude that, if we can comprehend the proper use and meaning of language, our Saviour affirms, in Matt. xix, 14, that little children belong to the kingdom of heaven, as its lawful and proper subjects.

(*b.*) What, then, is intended by "the kingdom of heaven?"

1. It is of great importance, both to our pending argument and to a right understanding of many parts of Scripture, that the reader should definitely comprehend this phrase. It may appear to be used, according to the general practice of the Hebrews, with some variety of signification, but no doubt can ultimately arise as to its entire definiteness, so far as the purposes of our argument are concerned. The language of Jewish theology is, for the most part, figurative, and is borrowed from those sensible objects which seem to impose themselves with the greater boldness and frequency upon the outward senses. From the days of the ancient prophets, the Jews were taught to contemplate the Messiah in the light of a "Prince," and his doctrines, precepts, and authority, in the light of a

regularly constituted government. The Psalms are often to be thus construed. Isaiah foretold that "the government should be upon his shoulders;" and Zechariah exclaims to the "daughter of Zion," "Behold, thy *King* cometh unto thee; he is just, and having salvation." Isa. ix, 6; Zech. ix, 9. But perhaps no prophet contributed more to the formation of these views among the Jews than Daniel; who, alluding to the very age in which Christ afterward appeared, and to the very circumstance of his mission, says, "And in the days of those kings shall the God of heaven set up a kingdom, which shall never be destroyed," Dan. ii, 44. It was to this that the precursor, John, alluded, when he proclaimed, "the kingdom of heaven is at hand."

2. But this language is not a mere figure of speech; it is the faithful and literal representation of a sublime and glorious reality. The system of redemption is nothing else than a modification of the moral government of God—a special, mediatorial administration—introduced to meet the exigences, and suit the condition, of a rebellious portion of Jehovah's subjects. It was in reference to this special, remedial administration, that "all power was given unto Christ, in heaven and in earth." It is at the head of this administration that he, as Mediator, sits; and it is this authority that he is to exert, and in this kingdom that he must reign, "till he has put down all rule, and all authority and power. And then cometh the end, [of this mediatorial administration,] when he shall have delivered up the kingdom to God, even the Father," 1 Cor. xv, 24.

3. The question that directly concerns us is, What is the meaning of the phrase, "kingdom of heaven," in Matt. xix, 14? In the widest acceptation of this phrase, in the New Testament, I understand it to be synonymous with what I have above called the Mediatorial administration; that is, the provisions, promises, institutions, and laws, constituting the system of human redemption. If the reader will keep this in view, he will spare himself much perplexity on a very plain, comprehensible subject. But sometimes this "kingdom" is spoken of with reference to its Ruler, while at other times it is spoken of with reference to its subjects, or its laws, institutions, provisions, and spiritual privileges. Sometimes it is spoken of as the

system under which men receive grace on earth, and at other times as the medium by which they shall inherit glory and immortality in heaven. Sometimes it is connected with the forgiveness of sins, and at others, with the future and final judgment. Sometimes it is spoken of as being "preached," at other times as being enjoyed; and at others, as being "inherited." It is sometimes compared to a principle of spiritual life within the human heart, and at other times it is spoken of with reference to a community of holy persons, over whom is exercised, by Christ, paternal and kingly authority. These figures of speech, so common in Scripture style, by which a part is put for the whole, or the whole for a part—the subject for the predicate, or the predicate for the subject—will be readily comprehended by all those who have any acquaintance with the formation and structure of language, especially of the genius of Hebrew style.

4. In order to ascertain what is the meaning of the phrase in question, in the passage of Matt. xix, 14, let us first inquire, What is its most general and prevailing acceptation in the New Testament, and especially in the evangelical histories?

In most places in the New Testament where this phrase occurs, it takes a restricted sense; that is, it imports only a *part* of what properly belongs to, or constitutes, the kingdom of heaven. In most places, also, it is spoken of with reference to its effects upon the human heart and character; or as the system of grace and external means by which men are fitted, on earth, for the enjoyment and glory of God hereafter. In this sense it is often synonymous with our idea of *church*. Dr. Robinson says, "Our Saviour designates usually by the phrase, *kingdom of heaven*, the community of those who, united through his Spirit under him, as their Head, rejoice in the truth, and enjoy a holy and blissful life in communion with him."* The word "kingdom," where it means the "kingdom of God," or of "heaven," occurs, in the New Testament, about one hundred and seven times, without counting the parallel places in the Gospels, where it stands in the same connection. In ninety-two places it is clearly used to designate the gospel dispensation, with reference to its

* Robinson's Calmet, art. "*Kingdom of heaven.*"

operations, effects, and the circumstances of its continuance among men in this world, including, of course, the idea of the visible church. In fifteen places it appears most probably to refer to the Mediatorial government, or gospel dispensation, with reference to the future destinies of men. It is difficult to assign any general significations to this phrase more definite than the above, which shall be, at the same time, correct. In each particular place where it occurs the discriminating reader will find no difficulty in determining its specific and distinct shade of meaning, without a full enumeration in this place. It is common to generalize the different acceptations of this phrase into "the kingdom of *grace*," and "the kingdom of *glory*;" but this division does not fully meet the case. For the benefit of the more inexperienced reader, I will subjoin a few passages illustrative of the prevailing New Testament use of this phrase.

Matt. iii, 2, "Repent, for *the kingdom of heaven* is at hand." In this place it refers to the gospel, with all its primary accompaniments of means and privileges, including church organization. The same also in chapters iv, 23; ix, 35; xxiv, 14.

Matt. v, 3, "Blessed are the poor in spirit, for theirs is *the kingdom of heaven*." See also verse 10. Here, also, the idea of church is included. As if he had said, "All the privileges of my church, both spiritual and external, belong to such."

Verse 19, "Whosoever shall break one of these least commandments, and shall teach men so, he shall be called the least in *the kingdom of heaven*;" that is, the least in the community of those who compose my kingdom—or my church.

Verse 20, "Except your righteousness shall exceed, &c., ye shall in no case enter into *the kingdom of heaven*;" that is, ye shall not be reckoned, on any account, as the true subjects of this kingdom. Ye shall not belong to my church, or be entitled to my grace and protection.

In all those passages where it speaks of persons *entering into the kingdom*, or of their *not* entering into the kingdom, or of their *being* in the kingdom of heaven, where the application is evidently to this life, the distinct idea of *church* is strongly marked and clearly set forth. I do not say that the idea of church is *synonymous* with that of kingdom of heaven, but I say that the former is clearly and necessarily *included* in the latter. See Matt. xi, 11; xix, 24; xxi, 31; xxiii, 13; Mark ix, 47; x, 24; John iii, 5.

Matt. xvi, 19, "I will give to thee the keys of the *kingdom of heaven.*" This certainly refers directly to ecclesiastical power and church organization.*

Matt. xxi, 43. Christ says to the Jews, "The *kingdom of God* shall be taken from you, and given to a nation bringing forth the fruits thereof." It is obvious that our Saviour did not here intend to threaten the Jews individually with a dereliction of the spiritual blessings of his kingdom, such as pardon, sanctification, and the hopes of eternal life; but only, as a nation, with the loss of their church organization—their ancient visible church privileges and character. It is easy to perceive, therefore, that the phrase, "*kingdom of heaven,*" in this place, as in the last-quoted passage, is as nearly synonymous with "*church*" as two words can well be, and, beyond all question, the visible church is the prominent idea intended in both places.

In Heb. xii, 28, this "kingdom" is contrasted with the external character and privileges of the Mosaic dispensation, and most clearly includes the idea of *church.* But it is not necessary to extend this enumeration. What has been said is intended to aid the critical acumen of the unpractised observer. The point upon which we would fix attention is, that the phrase, *the kingdom of heaven,* wherever it applies to this life, if it be not synonymous

* "Then again, with respect to the 'keys of the kingdom of heaven,' which our Lord promised to give to Peter, the apostle could not, I conceive, doubt that he was fulfilling that promise to Peter and to the rest of them conjointly, when he 'appointed unto them a kingdom,' and when, on the day of Pentecost, he began the building of his church, and enabled them, with Peter as their leader and chief spokesman, to open a door to the entrance of about three thousand converts at once, who received daily accessions to their number. The apostles, and those commissioned by them, had the office of granting admission into the society from time to time, to such as they judged qualified. *And that this society,* or *church, was that 'kingdom of heaven' of which the keys were committed to them, and which they had before proclaimed as 'at hand,'* THEY COULD NOT DOUBT."—*Archbp. Whateley on "the Kingdom of Christ,"* pp. 78, 79.

with, evidently *includes* the idea of the *visible church.* I have taken the ground that where our Saviour affirms that infants compose the "kingdom of heaven," he affirms what is tantamount to their church membership; that is, he does, by these very words, distinctly and literally affirm their *eligibility*, or *right*, to church membership. This I regard as incontrovertible. For what is the meaning of visible church membership but a mere recognition, a public declaration, or a visible authentication of the fact, that such members possess a saving interest in the atonement, and enjoy the favour of God? And what is the grand object of the visible church but "to gather together in one [community] all things *in Christ*," whether Jews or Gentiles; and thus to erect a separate and distinct government in this sin-disordered world? Whoever, therefore, belongs to Christ, as a redeemed and justified person—whoever has received through the atonement the present forgiveness of sin, and acceptance with God—is a member of Christ's kingdom, and is, consequently, and by virtue hereof, eligible to visible church membership; for the visible church is, according to its original design, only the community of those who are the real subjects of the spiritual "kingdom of heaven," collected together, and designated by external ordinances. God intended, from the first issuing of the church charter in the covenant of Abraham, that all who were the subjects of saving grace should be thereby eligible to, and thereon admitted into, the visible church. It is true that all that are subjects of saving grace are not, as a matter of fact, "received into Christ's holy church, and made lively members of the same;" but this reflects only upon the delinquency of man, not upon the munificent provisions and designs of God.

This view, I am satisfied, is of sufficient weight of authority to decide this controversy. It is not of any *acts* of the mind, abstractly considered, that the New Testament predicates an eligibility to church membership. It is not, consequently, of repentance and faith, considered in themselves, which are acts of the mind, that the right to church membership is predicated. But it is of the *state* of the mind, or of the *moral man*, that this eligibility or right is affirmed. It is the purity of the moral man that is the groundwork of a fitness for church membership;

and this must ever be the fact, so long as the church of God on earth is an image of the family of glorified saints in heaven.

5. The reader, then, will readily comprehend our argument. The phrase, "*the kingdom of heaven*," in its most usual acceptation, applies to the nature, operations, and the circumstances of the continuance of the gospel, among men on earth. It often alludes directly to, and always, when used with the above application, *includes* the idea of, *the visible church*. To affirm, therefore, that a person belongs to the kingdom of heaven, must import one of the following things: it must mean that such a one belongs to the visible church, as a matter of fact; or that he is a subject of grace and an heir of glory, and, *as such*, is entitled to church relations and character.* Either of these acceptations will sufficiently suit all the purposes of the pending argument. But we have strong reasons for understanding the phrase in question, in Matt. xix, 14, and parallel places, as alluding directly to the visible church. Our Saviour says, " Suffer little children to come unto me, and forbid them not, *for of such is the kingdom of heaven*" [composed.] Some have rendered it, "*for to such the kingdom of heaven belongs*;" and have considered it a parallel to Matt. v, 3, 10, where *ὀτι ἀυτων ἐστιν ἡ βασιλεια των ὀυράνων* is rendered, "for *theirs* is the kingdom of heaven;" that is, "the kingdom of heaven *belongs* to them"—they have a right to all its privileges and blessings, whether external or spiritual. This makes a good sense, and is equally to our purpose, but we incline to the sense we have given above,—" of such (that is, children) is the kingdom of heaven" [composed.] Now,

* "By the 'kingdom of heaven,' in this passage, and the 'kingdom of God,' as it is expressed by Mark and Luke, we are probably to understand our Lord to mean his visible church. And by the phrases *little children*, *young children*, and *infants*, those who were literally such can alone be intended. But, if by the phrases, 'of such is the *kingdom of heaven*,' and '*of God*,' we are to understand our Lord to mean, that infants are subjects of his grace and entitled to eternal salvation, which would be using the phrase in a higher sense; then, the lower sense is also included. For it would be absurd to suppose that our Lord would say infants are the subjects of holiness and heaven, but they are unfit to be admitted into my visible church on earth."—*Sermon on Baptism, by Rev. P. P. Sandford*, p. 14.

that our Saviour alludes directly to the visible church in this phrase I think will appear, if we take all the circumstances of the case into consideration. He uses the phrase, "kingdom of heaven," somewhat suited to current Jewish ideas, and with a view to meet and oppose the particular errors of the disciples; that is, to signify a *visible organization of government on earth.* The prevailing Jewish notions of Christ's kingdom were those of a *political* monarchy. They imagined the Messiah would be a secular prince, who would redeem his people from the Roman yoke, and erect a sovereign and independent government amid the nations of the earth. Such were the views of the disciples. It was the prevalence of these views that induced their occasional disputes about precedence—that prompted the doting "mother of Zebedee's children" to solicit beforehand a favourable preferment for her sons—and that spread the gloom of despair over the disciples when the Saviour had been laid in the tomb of Joseph. It was against these views that our Saviour's rebuke was directed, when he said, (Matt. xviii, 3,) "Except ye be converted, and become as little children, ye shall in no case enter into the kingdom of heaven." It was these secular views of the kingdom of Christ that prompted the disciples to repel those that "brought unto him little children, that he should put his hands on them and pray." They probably deemed it incompatible with the character of a monarch, and with the sovereign dignity of Christ's person, to allow such familiarity on the part of the people, and such consideration to mere infants. They imagined that children had nothing to do with this kingdom. Their notions were high, and could not bend to take in the lowly maxims of the Saviour's policy. When, therefore, under these circumstances, the Saviour said that children belonged to, or composed the kingdom of heaven, he intended that visible kingdom that he was about to set up on earth, and of which the disciples entertained so unworthy and erroneous views, namely, the church. No other application of the phrase would have suited the circumstances of the case, for the disciples certainly understood *kingdom* in the sense of a *visible organization.* As if he had said, "*These little children, whom you would hinder from being brought to me for my blessing, are objects* *of my kindest regard. They, and such as they, stand in a near relation to my church. The kingdom which I am setting up is not to overlook them, but to embrace and cherish them. Peculiar favour was shown to children under the former dispensation; think not that less is to be shown them under my reign. Look not upon them, therefore, with feelings of indifference. Strive not to deprive them of my blessing. Suffer them to come unto me; for to such children the privileges of the gospel dispensation belong.*"*

(*c.*) But this passage, together with that of Matt. xviii, 5, may be seen to favour infant baptism from another view. There is a duty set forth in these places, and enjoined upon parents, guardians, and all who have the responsible, religious control of children, that cannot be fully performed but in dedicating them to God in baptism. Our Saviour commands adults to "suffer little children, and forbid them not to come to him;" that is, he commands them to *bring* little children to him. This command is broad and universal. It applies to all parents and guardians of children, in all ages of the world. This duty, moreover, is enjoined in behalf of infants *as such*, that is, *while they are yet infants*. It cannot refer, specifically, to the duty of parents to *educate* children: this may be a correlative duty, but not the primary one. But children must be brought and presented to Christ *in infancy*, or this command is not fulfilled. But how can they be brought to Christ, and be presented to him, except by an outward ordinance of consecration?—a *visible* presentation? The command evidently contemplates this. Christ says, "*Forbid* them not to come to me." Now, in whatever sense we are to understand the text as enjoining children to be brought to Christ, in that same sense, beyond all dispute, we are capable of *hindering* them. This, the word "*forbid*" clearly implies. But we are not capable of hindering children from participating in the spiritual blessings of Christ's kingdom. We cannot hinder the operations of grace upon them here, or their future salvation, if they die in infancy. We can only hinder them from *visible* covenant relations.

Furthermore: Christ has said, in Matt. xviii, 5, and he parallel places of Mark and Luke, that "whosoever receiveth one such little one επι τω ὀνοματι μου *in my name*, re-

* Woods on Infant Baptism, p. 69.

ceiveth me," &c. Now, what is it to receive a person in Christ's name, but to receive him *on account*, *in behalf*, and *upon the authority*, of Christ himself? This is its meaning in the New Testament. But a person thus received must certainly be reckoned as belonging to the Christian family. This is not the language appropriate to aliens and to sinners; it belongs to the community of God's visible church. "The ordinary meaning of the word *receive*, in the books of the New Testament, even when it stands alone, is well known to all readers of Scripture to be *to receive* or *admit to a brotherhood*, or *fellowship in Christianity;* as, (to name one place in forty,) Rom. xv, 7, Paul commands those dissenters of opinion to *receive one another*.*

" But when Christ does, moreover, add here those words, *in my name*, it more plainly still imports that they should be received to be *as his members*, his *children*, *belonging to him*." And it is easy to perceive what influence these precepts and principles, laid down by the Saviour, must have had on the minds of the disciples, in construing and applying the powers of their commission afterward. Here, then, is a recognition of the principles involved in infant baptism; and, further than this, the then existing state of opinion did not require any teaching to extend, in order to secure its general practice.

I will close this section by the following from Dr. Wall, which is itself a "picture," and may convey a good idea to some.

"I wish some good man would be at the charge of an impression of a small picture, that might be given to such as need instruction and satisfaction concerning the will and purpose of our Saviour in this matter. The proverb is true, that pictures have with vulgar men the use of books; especially if they represent some useful history of the gospel, such as this which I am going to recommend, is, being recited by three evangelists, Matt. xviii, 5; Mark ix, 37; Luke ix, 48, our Saviour holding a little child in his arms and saying to his disciples, *Whosoever shall receive this child* (in Matthew and Mark it is, *one such little child*, or, one of such children) *in my name*, *receiveth me*. If our Saviour be drawn in that posture, holding forth the child in his

* See also Acts xv, 4; Rom. xiv, 1; 2 Cor. vii, 2; Phil. ii, 29; 2 John 10; 3 John 8–10; and other places.

arms, and those words subscribed, *Whosoever shall receive such a child in my name, receiveth me;* and over against him be drawn two men standing by a font, both pretending to be ministers of Christ; and some people offering such a child to them; and one of them reaching out his arms to receive it, and the other thrusting it back: I would fain see what countenance the painter would give to that man, who, seeing our Saviour look upon him, and hearing him say those words, does dare to reject it."*

2.) The second passage which I shall cite under this head is that of 1 Cor. vii, 14: "For the unbelieving husband is sanctified by the wife; and the unbelieving wife is sanctified by the husband; else were your children unclean; but now are they holy."

This is an important passage to our present argument. The ground we take in reference to it is, that it affirms that relation of infants to the church, which necessarily implies their right of baptism. Had not the children of Christian parents at Corinth been made subjects of baptism, they never could, with any propriety of language, have been called "*holy*," in the sense in which they were so called by the apostle. Baptism is not affirmed of them, in so many words, but it is asserted by necessary implication. Infants at Corinth were declared to be in a certain *state* in regard to the church: that state necessarily implied their baptism. This is the position we take. The highly contested state of the argument, as deduced from this text, renders it necessary to go into details of proof, that would otherwise be unnecessary.

(*a*.) We first notice the *occasion* and *scope* of the passage. The Corinthians had written to the apostle, making inquiries respecting several subjects that then agitated their church. In ver. 1, of this chapter, he says, "Now, concerning the things whereof ye *wrote* unto me," &c. He then proceeds to give directions relative to those several "things." One of these questions appears to have been this; namely, whether a believing husband, or wife, may continue to live in conjugal relation with an unbelieving partner, innocently, and without forfeiting church privileges? To this question the apostle replies, from the 10th to the 16th verse.

* Defence, &c., pp. 508, 509.

The uninformed reader will not fully appreciate the true character of this question, or the importance which it assumed in the Corinthian church, unless the nature and occasion of the controversy be fully explained. It was this:—The Jews regarded even the touch of a Gentile as unclean; and as producing such a legal defilement, as to unfit them for any of the solemn ceremonies of their religion.* It was, hence, unlawful for a Jew to company with them in any way. The Pharisees, who were the most rigid in their observance of the law of any of the Jewish sects, adding many superstitions to their religion, always lustrated themselves after having returned home from the market, or any public way, or thoroughfare, lest they should have contracted uncleanness, by having touched some unclean person or thing. They also frequently purified their household furniture. It was this kind of sanctity that led them to complain of Jesus for receiving "sinners and publicans," and eating with them. It was this scrupulous state of opinion that caused Peter to hesitate, at first, to go with the messengers of Cornelius, they being Gentiles. The whole history of that transaction is a striking illustration of the power which these Jewish notions still held over the consciences of many Christian converts from Judaism.

From very ancient days God had warned his people against intermarriages with idolatrous and unbelieving nations. "Neither shalt thou make marriages with them; thy daughter shalt thou not give unto his son, nor his daughter shalt thou take unto thy son;" and the reason for this prohibition is thus given,—"For they will turn away thy son from following me, that they may serve other gods." Deut. vii, 3, 4; Exod. xxxiv, 15, 16. This was an important requisition, issued in order to secure the distinct preservation of the Hebrew people, as well as to preserve the purity of their religion. A remarkable instance is recorded in the book of Ezra, (chapters ix and x,) of an extensive breach of this command, when, after the return of the captives from Babylon, "the people of Israel, and the priests, and the Levites, did not separate themselves from the people of the land, but took of their daughters for themselves and for their sons; so that the holy seed

* Vide Dr. A. Clarke's Comment. on John xviii, 28.

mingled themselves with the people of those lands," chap. ix, 1, 2. The sequel shows that they were obliged to "put away" these heathen partners; although in some instances the dissolution of the marriage union occasioned not only a separation of husband and wife, but of parents and children. Chap. x, 44.

Such were the prevalent notions of the Jews relative to marriage, in the days of Paul. And as they had colonized themselves everywhere before the Christian era, so the apostles found them in all the cities of note, and countries where they travelled. Many of these Jews were converted to Christianity, and incorporated into the Christian church, bringing with them, frequently, their Jewish prejudices, and fomenting controversies among the Gentile converts, on many points of doctrine, which had their origin in the now obsolete forms of the Jewish ritual. Thus was it with the church at Corinth. Jewish controversies had been stirred up among the Jewish and Gentile converts,—the peace of the church had been disturbed by the introduction of these foreign, and now irrelevant, distinctions,—and an attempt had been made to bring back and apply the old law touching marriages, which Ezra had so signally enforced. The question was, Is it permitted, by the law of Christianity, for a Christian to live in marriage relations with an unconverted Gentile? They all very well knew that such a union between a Jew and Gentile was strictly prohibited by the law of Moses, and rigidly enforced by the administrators of that law. But was that law still in force? Were Christians to come under the same rule? Were these distinctions of *clean* and *unclean* to be still observed? These were important questions to the Christian church;—the controversy had spread at Corinth;—a formal appeal had been made to Paul, and the decision from his mouth was to be final.

And here I wish the reader to remark, that the question did not at all relate to the lawfulness of marriage, or the continuance of the marriage covenant, *in a civil sense*. It was a question to be settled by ecclesiastical, not by civil law. It arose purely out of the ancient ceremonial code of Moses, and not out of any condition or forms of society among the Gentiles respecting marriage. Dr. Reed has justly remarked, "If the dispute had been concerning the marriage of these persons, [in a civil sense,] or the legitimacy of their children, the Corinthians would undoubtedly have applied to the office of the town clerk, or to the public records, for a solution of the question; and not to a Christian casuist, who resided in the remote city of Ephesus."*

This, then, being the occasion of Paul's discourse, it is easy to perceive that, unless we are willing to charge the apostle with reasoning most inconclusively, the scope of all his reasoning in that particular connection is to show that it is ceremonially right and proper, on Christian principles, for a believing husband, or wife, to dwell with an unbelieving partner. If, therefore, "any brother hath a wife that believeth not, and she be pleased to dwell with him, let him not put her away. . . For the unbelieving wife is sanctified by the husband," &c.

(*b*.) The next point to be ascertained is the meaning of the words *ἡγιασται hegiastai*, *ἀκαθαρτα akatharta*, and *ἁγια hagia*, in the fourteenth verse, and rendered respectively, *sanctified*, *unclean*, and *holy*.

If the reader will attend strictly to the occasion and scope of Paul's reasoning, as above described, he will find no difficulty in fixing the sense and application of these terms. When we understand the *subject* of which an author is treating, no difficulty can occur in determining the sense in which he employs words, if he employ them according to their usual acceptation. To apply an author's words so as to make them prove a sentiment which he had not at first intended, and for which he had not himself employed them, is to do him an injustice, that no honest expositor would knowingly do. When we undertake to represent the opinions of another, we assume an obligation, from common honesty and fairness, to use his own words as he used them, and to prove nothing more or less, or different, by them, than he himself intended. Let the reader remember, then, that the subject before the apostle's mind was not one that related to civil law, or to civil relations, as such, but one which came solely under the cognizance of ecclesiastical law. It was wholly an ecclesias-

* Apology for Infant Baptism, p. 42. Dr. R. resided in New-England, where the town clerk is required, by law, to preserve a record of the marriages. We mention this merely as explaining how such an officer came to be mentioned by him in such a connection.

tical question. The words *sanctified*, *unclean*, and *holy*, therefore, are to be understood, not in a *civil*, or a *moral*, but in a *ceremonial* sense. In order to understand the import of these terms, in this connection, we must go back to Jewish usage, for the apostle uses these words here in their Levitical sense. It is true he was writing to a Christian church in Greece, and that he employed the Greek language, but the subject was one of Hebrew origin, and the terms were employed in strict conformity to Hebrew use. To this use alone, therefore, can we appeal. The question, then, is, What is the Hebrew use of these words?

As I do not consider that our English version gives the right turn to this passage, I shall first give the sense as I understand it, in a free paraphrase. "For the unbelieving husband is made ceremonially clean to the believing wife, and the unbelieving wife is made ceremonially clean to the believing husband; so that it is now admissible and proper, according to Christian distinctions, that they should live together in conjugal relation, and not, as under the Mosaic law, be obliged to separate and break up the marriage union. Were it otherwise, that is, did not Christianity regard the unbelieving partner as ceremonially clean to the believing, it would follow that the Christian church would reckon the children of such a marriage among the *unclean*, that is, among those who are not in covenant with God; but the fact that the church regards all such children, as well as all those whose parents are *both* Christians, as holy—they having been baptized, and admitted among the covenanted people*—proves that their parents are reckoned as ceremonially clean to each other." In support of this sense, I adduce the following considerations:—

First. The language of the text allows it. The words *ἡγιασται . . . εν τη γυναικαι hegiastai en te gunaikai*, which we translate, *is sanctified* TO *the wife*, are, to say no more, as susceptible of this turn of the sense, as of the one given in our English version. And so of the phrase, *ἡγιασται . . . εν τω ανδρι hegiastai en to andri*, *is sanctified* TO *the husband*. Our common version says, the unbelieving party is sanctified "BY" the believing. But this certainly makes

* This "*holiness*" is, as we shall presently see, a baptismal holiness. See also p. 294, *note*.

no sense whatever. *How*, we ask, does the believing party sanctify the unbelieving? This is a question that can never be answered. The truth is, God himself, and he alone, sanctified the whole Gentile world at the opening of the Christian dispensation; that is, he abolished those distinctions of *clean* and *unclean*, as they applied to Jews and Gentiles formerly, and as they were now being applied, at Corinth, to believers and unbelievers.

If the reader will turn to the Acts of the Apostles, (chapters x and xi,) he will perceive, in the extraordinary vision of Peter, and in his own exposition of it subsequently, in what manner God was pleased to enlighten that apostle on this subject, and to deliver him from the force of his Jewish prejudices. Peter had doubts of the propriety of "going in to men uncircumcised, and eating with them," or even preaching the gospel to them. He called them "*common*," that is, "*unclean*." He thought it would defile him, unfit him for religious privileges and duties. But God informed him that he had sanctified the Gentile world,—Jewish distinctions were abolished,—it was lawful to have intercourse with Gentiles. "What, therefore, God hath *cleansed*, or *sanctified*, (*εκαθαρισε*,) call not thou *common*," that is, "*unclean*."

But what is the nature of this *sanctification*, or *cleansing* of the Gentile world? Certainly the sanctification of which we now speak gives to the Gentile, or unbeliever, no church privileges without personal holiness. The phraseology is strictly conformable to Jewish usage, and it is here employed in the lowest sense in which the word *sanctify* was used in their religious vocabulary. Yet so clearly defined, and so strongly marked are all the circumstances of the case, that of the real meaning of the term, in the above passage cited from the Acts, and in the place before us, there can be no doubt. *It merely extended so far as to sanction the external intercourse of Christians with unbelievers.* They might now dwell together in any of the natural or civil relations; as parents and children, as husbands and wives, as fellow-citizens, as neighbours, &c., without any detriment to church relations on the part of the believer, so long as his spirit and deportment accorded with the gospel. All the innocent relations of life, whether social or commercial, might now be enjoyed between the Jew and the Gentile—the believer and unbeliever.* And thus did Peter understand his vision; for afterward, when he stood before Cornelius and his Gentile friends, he says, evidently by way of explanation of so unusual an event, "Ye know how that it is unlawful for a man that is a Jew to keep company, or come unto one of another nation; but God hath showed me that I should not call any man *common* or *unclean*." Peter considered that this sanctification of the Gentiles extended so far only as to make it lawful to have company and intercourse with them. This is exactly the sense of the word *sanctify* in 1 Cor. vii, 14, "For the unbelieving husband is *sanctified* to the wife," &c. The two parties may lawfully live together in this relation, though one be an unbeliever—the conjugal *oneness* is not now disturbed by the distinctions of *clean* and *unclean*, as they were formerly applied.

Ἡγιασται *hegiastai* is a conjugated form of the verb ἁγιαζω *hagiazo*, which means *to separate, consecrate, sanctify, make holy*, &c. It answers, in the Old Testament, to the Hebrew קָדַשׁ *kadash*, which, in the Piel conjugation, signifies to *make holy*, to *sanctify*, to *hallow*, *consecrate*.† Every person or thing among the Jews, devoted to religious use, was deemed sanctified.‡ Thus their priests, their altars, their temple, persons, sacred utensils, &c., were sanctified. But does this sense of ἁγιαζω *hagiazo* apply to the passage under consideration? Could it be said of the unbelieving husband, or wife, that he, or she, was in any sense devoted to religion? Was there any thing approaching the idea of a religious consecration?

* I hope the reader will form a just opinion of this subject. The distinctions of *clean* and *unclean* were at first purely artificial, and were established by the will of God, not in the nature of the things themselves. It is plain, therefore, that to *sanctify* these unclean things to the use of Christians, no positive change was required in the things themselves, but only that the *arbitrary prohibition* of the Lawgiver be taken off. This sanctification, then, was, after all, merely of a negative character. After the abrogation of the Levitical code, all things reverted back to their original character. It then could be said, "Nothing is unclean *of itself*;" "*All things* are pure," Levitically; "*Every creature* of God is good, and *nothing* to be rejected."

† Gesen. Heb. Lex., art. קָדַשׁ. Robinson's Gr. and Eng. Lexicon, art. Ἁγιαζω.

‡ See Note D.

A learned friend suggested to me that he considered the clause, "The unbelieving husband is sanctified to (or by) the wife," &c., to mean, "that, by reason of the connection of the believing party with the church, the unbelieving partner was thereby placed more directly before the religious sympathies of the church—made more especially the subject of prayer and religious concern by them—and that they were obligated more directly to look after his spiritual welfare, than was the case in reference to the general mass of irreligious persons; and that in this sense—the sanctity of the believing partner operating to enhance the religious privileges and prospects of the unbelieving—the latter might be said to be sanctified, or in some sense brought under religious influence by the former."* I cannot feel, however, that this is satisfactory. It appears plausible, but does not meet the point of the apostle's argument, and seems, too, rather foreign and laboured.

The exact point to which the apostle was arguing is this, namely, Whether it is lawful, according to the distinctions of *clean* and *unclean* persons, established by the law of Moses, for a Christian and pagan to dwell together in marriage relations? The apostle decided that such a union was now lawful, in a ceremonial sense. To prove this position he needed only to show that Jewish distinctions touching the case were abolished; or, in other words, God had now sanctified the Gentile world—the unbeliever to the believer. Now, it is perfectly plain that the sanctification here spoken of extends no further than to authorize the continuance of an external relation, innocent in itself, between a believer and an unbeliever. The case was this: A pagan husband becomes converted to Christianity, while his wife remains an idolater. Judaizing teachers step in and say to him, "It is not lawful for you to live with her," and they appeal to the law of Moses, where a Jew is forbidden to live in marriage relations with a Gentile. The apostle comes in and says, "If she be pleased to dwell with you, put her not away, for God has abolished these Jewish distinctions, and has thereby sanctified the Gentile world, and, in doing this, has sanctified your unbelieving

* See also Dr. Woods on Infant Baptism, p. 88.

wife to you." Now, does not every one perceive that the nature and sum of this sanctification was no more, or less, or other, than a mere *sanction* of this external marriage relation?—a rendering it ceremonially lawful for them to live together, so that the church privileges of the believing partner should not thereby be impaired?

And such is often the meaning of the word *sanctify*, whether it is expressed by ἁγιαζω *hagiazo*, or καθαριζω *katharizo*, or any word belonging to the same family. Thus:

1 Tim. iv, 5, "For it [the creature of God] ἁγιαζεται *hagiazetai*, *is sanctified* by the word of God, and prayer."

Certain men had arisen in the church, and commanded to abstain from certain meats, as being unclean. Verse 3. The apostle taught that God had made all things alike for man's good, and no creature of his was to be thus rejected, as possessing any innate or natural pollution, but all was to be received with thanksgiving. If, therefore, we received any of his creatures with thanksgiving and prayer, they were thereby sanctified to us; that is, it was made lawful for us to receive and use them. In 1 Cor. x, 23, where the apostle is speaking to the same point, instead of saying, "All things are *clean* to me," he says, "All things are εξεστιν *exestin*, *lawful* for me;" that is, I have a *right* to eat all meats. See verse 30, and chap. vi, 12. Those meats which were *unlawful* for a Jew to use were called *unclean*, the same idea being conveyed by both words. See also Titus i, 15; Rom. xiv, 14, 20. In Luke xi, 41, we are taught that by a proper use of the creatures of God all things become *pure* to us; that is, *lawful* for us to use.

This, then, we consider to be the sense of the word *sanctified* in 1 Cor. vii, 14. The unbelieving partner is made *ceremonially lawful* to the believing, so far as the conjugal relation extends.

We next inquire into the meaning of the words ακαθαρτα *akatharta*, and ἁγιος *hagios*, rendered *unclean*, and *holy*. The question here is, What is the force of these words in the sentence, "Else were your children *unclean;* but now are they *holy?*" What state or condition is described, or alluded to, by the word *unclean?* and what by the word *holy?*

We have already proved, we trust, to the satisfaction of the reader, that the word *sanctified*, in the former part of this verse, is limited by the subject to signify *rendered lawful*. This, also, we have seen, is a common use of this and similar words. We have seen that it does not refer to any church relations conferred in virtue of the faith of the believing party. But I consider the terms *unclean* and *holy* to bear a higher signification than the word *sanctified* in the same verse. I consider these words to refer directly to church distinctions, and I cannot, perhaps, render the sense of the passage more obvious to the reader than by the following: "Else were your children *pagans*; but now are they [reckoned] *holy seed*." I wish the reader to bear in mind that we offer no violence to the text, according to the general use of words, in giving it this turn. Nay, as we shall soon see, it is (we apprehend) the only sense the passage will bear. It is true that the general senses of ἁγιαζω *hagiazo* and ἁγιος *hagios* are alike, and that ακαθαρτος *akathartos* is the counter sense of the two. But this is far from proving that their significations are alike in any given connection. It is by no means an uncommon thing to find the same word occurring in different senses in different connections; but here are two words—an adjective, and a verb derived therefrom—and surely it would not be strange to find them occur in somewhat different senses in the same verse. The apostle affirms that certain unbelievers are *sanctified*, and that certain children are *holy*, and this he affirms in the same verse. But does it therefore follow that the sanctification and holiness spoken of are *one and the same*, as to character and degree? The sanctification of the unbeliever may answer one end, while the holiness of the children may refer wholly to another. And this is just the state of the case. The holiness of the children was of a higher order, a more advanced degree, than that of the unbeliever, and described a state, in reference to ecclesiastical privileges, far different from his.* This

* One of the continuators of Poole's Annotations says, with reference to the *sanctification* of the unbelieving party, "I rather think it signifies, *brought into such a state, that the believer, without offence to the law of God, may continue in a marriage state with such a yoke-fellow*." This I consider to be exactly the sense of the apostle

accords with the general *usus* of these terms in Scripture. Almost every thing pertaining to Jewish affairs was deemed holy, but the holiness of their priests was certainly of a higher order than that of their land, their chief city, and the mountains around, although the same term was employed to describe each.

Besides, the particular subject, and scope of the argument, in 1 Cor. vii, 14, make it incumbent on us to adopt such a distinction. The holiness of the children is alluded to as a well-known and accredited fact; and it is appealed to as an argument in proof of the sanctification of the unbelieving parent, and the consequent lawfulness of the continued union of the parties. But if the holiness of the children was of the same nature and degree of the sanctification of the unbelieving parent, and merely flowed from and depended wholly on the disputed fact of such sanctification, it could never, with any reasonableness, have been made an argument to *prove* that sanctification.

" The general notion of being *sanctified* is first applied to an unconverted heathen, connected in marriage with a Christian; and it is applied in reference to a particular question, that is, whether it is proper and advisible that a Christian should continue to live with an unbelieving

With reference to the holiness of the children, the same commentator says, " These are those that are called *holy*, not as inwardly renewed and sanctified, but relatively, in the same sense that all the Jewish nation were called a *holy people;* and possibly this may give us a further light to understand the term *sanctified*, in the former part of the verse. The unbelieving husband is so far sanctified by the believing wife, and the unbelieving wife so far sanctified by the believing husband, that, as they may lawfully continue in their married relation, and live together as man and wife, so the issue coming from them both shall be by God counted in covenant with him, and have a right to baptism, (which is one of the seals of that covenant,) as well as those children both whose parents are believers."—Vide *Poole's Annot.*, *in loc.*

This is exactly the difference between the words *sanctified*, as applied to the unbelieving partner, and *holy*, as applied to the children, which we intend. This we understand to be the real force of the passage. But we do not concur with the author just quoted, in representing children as being *born* in covenant with God, and, by virtue hereof, entitled to baptism. We believe they are in covenant *when* they are baptized; and their right to baptism is not derived by virtue of *natural descent*, but is predicated of their *gracious state*. On this point there appears to be some confusion with some writers.

partner. Now, when the apostle says, in relation to this question, 'The unbelieving husband is *sanctified* by [to] the wife,' it is natural to understand him of a sanctification adapted to the subject under consideration."* Such a sanctification, as we have seen, was but a negative one—the mere abolishment of Jewish distinctions—the absence of any Levitical or ceremonial prohibition to the union of the parties. But would it have been any proof of this fact to assert that their children were in the same state? All parties very well knew that if the parents were Levitically clean to each other, the children would be so of course. But the question was, Are the parents thus clean, when one is an unbeliever? The apostle affirms that they were, and, as proof, cites the well-known and established fact of the holiness of their children. Yet this would be no better than proving a thing by itself, if the holiness of the children were in no wise different from the sanctification of the unbelieving parent.

But let us more directly inquire into the meaning of the words *unclean* and *holy*. Ακαθαρτος *unclean*, according to Schleusner, signifies *that which is prohibited by the Mosaic law, or from which the people of God were required to separate themselves.* He represents it as often used to denote *a pagan, an alien from the worship of the true God*, or *one who does not belong to the people of God, or to the society of Christians.* It is this last sense we attach to the word in the passage in question; namely, *pagan, alien from the worship of God*, &c. So, also, Dr. Robinson says the word is "*spoken of persons who are not Jews, or who do not belong to the Christian community*,"† and cites this very passage, among others, in proof. Groves defines it thus: *Impure, unclean, defiled, unfit for receiving the rites of religion.*‡

In Acts x, 14, 28, *ακαθαρτος akathartos* is used to designate *a Gentile*, or "*a man of another nation*" besides the Jews. Thus is it elsewhere used. So Isa. lii, 1, "For henceforth there shall no more come to thee [Jerusalem] the uncircumcised and the *unclean* [טָמֵא *ακαθαρτος*.] Here the words *unclean* and *uncircumcised* are perfectly

* Woods on Infant Baptism, p. 93.
† Greek and English Lexicon. ‡ Ibid.

synonymous, and apply to one and the same description of persons, namely, all who were not Jews—all who were not in covenant with God. So, also, an *unclean*, or *polluted* land, is a land inhabited by pagans, or idolaters. Thus, Amos vii, 17, "And thou [Israel] shalt die in a *polluted*, or *unclean* land." [טְמֵאָה *ακαθαρτος*.] This "polluted land" was Assyria. It was in contradistinction from all such idolatrous, or pagan countries, that Canaan was called the "holy land." When Paul warned the Corinthians to have no religious intercourse and fellowship with "idolaters," "infidels," and such-like persons, who were enemies of God and aliens from the true kingdom, he says, "Touch not the *ακαθαρτου akathartou*, *unclean* person," 2 Cor. vi, 17. Our English version reads "*things;*" but this is unquestionably an error. The apostle was not speaking of *things*, but of *persons* with whom it was not lawful for a Christian to hold any religious fellowship, and he denominates them *unclean*, using the same word that is used in 1 Cor. vii, 14.

It is plain, therefore, that when the apostle says, "Else were your children *unclean*," it is in perfect accordance with the *usus loquendi* to understand him to say, "Else were your children *pagans—without the covenant*." This sense, the advance in his argument, and the nature of his subject, require us to understand.

We are confirmed in this sense, further, by the force of the next clause, "Now are they *holy*." Ἀγιος *holy* is here used in contrast with *ακαθαρτος unclean*. A *holy* person, in the language of the text, is the exact opposite of an *unclean* person, and *vice versa*. If an unclean person is the same as a *heathen*, the holy person is a *Christian*. We have seen that the word *sanctified*, as applied to an unbeliever, in the former part of the verse, is restricted in its sense by the nature of the subject, to signify merely the abolishment of Jewish ceremonial distinctions, with regard to clean and unclean persons, so as to render it now lawful for a believer and unbeliever to dwell together in marriage union, or in any other relation innocent in itself. This is perfectly plain. But the nature of the subject does not bind us to fix the same limited construction on the term *holy* in the concluding part of the passage, and we appeal to the natural force of the apostle's argument, and the general Scriptural use of the term, in support of the sense above given. I will give the reader some examples of the use of this word in Scripture :—

Matt. xxvii, 52, " And many bodies of the *ἁγιων hagion, saints* that slept, arose."

Acts ix, 13, " Ananias answered, Lord, I have heard by many of this man, (Saul,) how much evil he hath done to thy *ἁγιοις hagiois, saints* at Jerusalem." See, also, chap. xxvi, 10.

Acts ix, 32, " Peter came down slso to the *ἁγιους hagious, saints* that dwelt at Lydda."

Verse 41, " And when he had called the *ἁγιους saints* and widows, he presented her alive."

Rom. i, 7, Grace " to all that be in Rome ... called to be *ἁγιοις hagiois, saints.*"

Rom. xv, 25, " But now I go unto Jerusalem to minister unto the *ἁγιοις saints.*"

Verse 26, " For it hath pleased them of Macedonia ... to make a contribution for the poor *ἁγιων saints* at Jerusalem." See also verse 31.

Rom. xvi, 2, " That ye receive her (Phebe) in the Lord as becometh *ἁγιων saints,*" (that is, *Christians.*)

Verse 15, " Salute ... all the *ἁγιους saints,*" &c.

1 Cor. i, 2, " — to them that are ... called to be *ἁγιοις saints,*" (that is, *Christians.*)

Chap. vi, 1, " Dare any of you ... go to law before the unjust, and not before the *ἁγιων saints?*" (that is, *Christians, the members of the church.*)

Chap. xiv, 33, " God is the author of peace, as in all the churches of the *ἁγιων saints,*" (*Christians.*)

Chap. xvi, 1, " Now concerning the collection for the *ἁγιους saints,*" (that is, *Christians, church members,* who are poor.) See also ver. 15; 2 Cor. i, 1; viii, 4; ix, 1, 12.

2 Cor. xiii, 13, " All the *ἁγιοι saints* (Christians) salute you."

Besides these passages cited, the word occurs, where it is translated *saints,* about forty-one times in the New Testament; the signification in all these places being substantially the same. Here, also, I wish the reader to understand and appreciate the corroborating testimony drawn from the use of the corresponding Hebrew words. I have before mentioned that, although the apostles spoke for the most part, and wrote wholly in the foreign Greek dialect, still they were Hebrews; educated in the Jewish religion and customs, and accustomed to think and to speak according to the Hebrew idiom. Hence, they sought out and employed those Greek words that more fitly conveyed Hebrew ideas; and hence we often are obliged to resort to the use of certain Hebrew words that were used to express the same idea, in order fully to establish the sense of the New Testament language. Ἅγιος *hagios*, (*holy*,) says Dr. Robinson, "is used everywhere, in the Septuagint, for קֹדֶשׁ *kodesh* and קָדוֹשׁ *kadosh*. Hence, the ground idea is *pure, clean*."* Take a few examples.

Exod. xix, 6, "Ye shall be to me a *holy* nation;" (קָדוֹשׁ ἁγιον;) that is, *a nation of saints, a consecrated nation*.

Exod. xxii, 31, "And ye shall be *holy* men unto me;" (קֹדֶשׁ ἅγιος;) that is, Ye shall be *saints, consecrated men*. See, also, Lev. xi, 44, 45; Num. xvi, 3; *et alibi*.

The Israelites were declared a *holy people*, not because they were all morally holy; far from it; but because, by profession, they belonged to God, who had separated them from all other nations, and sanctified them unto himself by external rites; because they professed the true religion, which many among them really attained in an illustrious degree; and because "to them were committed the oracles of God," "the covenant," "and the giving of the law and the promises." They ever regarded themselves as holy. Thus they called themselves, as in Ezra ix, 2, "the *holy* seed (קֹדֶשׁ ἁγιον) have mingled themselves with the people of those lands." So, also, Daniel calls them, chap. viii, 24, and xii, 7.

I do not wish needlessly to multiply examples of the use of these words, but I knew not how to lay before the more uninformed reader a just view of the argument, without furnishing at least those above adduced. Nothing can be more plain, as appears from the examples adduced, and from the general face of Scripture usage, that ἅγιος *hagios*, and its corresponding Hebrew קֹדֶשׁ *kodesh* and קָדוֹשׁ *kadosh*, when used substantively, signify, *a worshipper of God; a*

* Greek and English Lexicon, art. Ἅγιος.

person set apart, or *devoted to religion*, either by spiritual sanctification, or by external ordinances; *a person who belongs to the community of the true worshippers of God*, as distinguished from an idolater, or an irreligious person; *a member of the church of God; a saint; a Christian.* Ἁγιος *hagios*, then, is frequently used in the New Testament in a sense exactly synonymous with *church member*, as every person knows who has examined the subject, and it is a word which is never applied to an unbaptized or uncircumcised person. It is in this sense that I conceive it to be used in 1 Cor. vii, 14. When, in that passage, children are declared to be ἁγια *hagia*, they are declared to be in that state which is exactly contrary to paganism, or Gentilism. But what is that state which is exactly opposite to Gentilism? It is *Christian church membership.* The *unclean* person was an alien from the law and the covenant,—a Gentile. The Jews were called *the holy, the clean;* and after them the Christians were also called *the holy, the clean*, or *the saints.* The members of the Christian church were the *saints*, and the *saints* were the members of the Christian church. When, therefore, Paul affirms that those children who had one parent a believer and the other an unbeliever were not "*unclean*," but ἁγια *saints*, he is unquestionably to be understood as affirming that they were not mere Gentiles,—aliens from the covenant,—"but fellow-citizens with the saints, and of the household of God." All the parts of the apostle's argument conspire to establish this meaning; and the antithesis employed and indicated in the word ακαθαρτος *akathartos* (*unclean*) demands it, for the contrast here is between a *pagan* and a *Christian*;—"Else were your children *pagans;* but now are they *Christians*"—devoted to God by a Christian rite. When it is said in Luke ii, 23, every first-born male child "shall be called ἁγιον τω Κυριω *holy*, or *consecrated to the Lord;*" the meaning of this *holiness*, or *consecration*, was, that the child was to be devoted to God in the most absolute sense, requiring redemption in order to entitle the parents to resume it, even for protection, support, and education. And although this consecration was of a peculiar kind, evidently higher than the ordinary idea of church membership, still, it illustrates the force of which the word in question is capable, even when used in a Levitical sense. When the apostle says, "the unbelieving husband is *sanctified* to the wife," he intends only that degree of sanctity that renders it ceremonially lawful for her to live with him; but when he says, "your children are *holy*, *sanctified*, or *consecrated*," he means that they belong to the Christian community, and if he does not affirm their baptism directly, he affirms their relation to the church, which implies the *fact* of their baptism;—he recognises, by necessary implication, both the principle and the fact of infant baptism. He says exactly what we might suppose him to say, on the supposition of the universal practice of infant baptism. Every Jew would have understood him as affirming the church membership of infants. He says of the children of Christian parents just what the Jews would have said of their own children, when they would express their covenant, or church relation—he says they are *holy*. It was, to their minds, an explicit declaration of church relation, in contradistinction from the Gentile, or heathenish state; and, I need hardly add, that precisely as the Corinthian disputants, in this Jewish controversy, must have understood these words, in the same manner must we now understand and apply them.

(*c.*) On the whole, upon reviewing this argument, I cannot but deem it decisive. I have endeavoured to lay before the reader all those facts which are necessary to aid him in forming his judgment of the passage; and if I have seemed to be prolix, I can only urge in my defence the highly contested state in which the text in question is found.* I crave for this argument a most patient and critical attention, convinced, as I am, that it has never been wrested from its powerful, and, I repeat it, decisive bearing in favour of Pedobaptism. But much as has already been said, I should deem the argument deprived of some of its force, did I omit to call the reader's special attention to two things:—

First. The question in the Corinthian church respected the lawfulness of the conjugal relation between a believer and an unbeliever; and one simple circumstance that speaks a volume to our purpose is this: namely, that the apostle, in deciding that the children of such parents were

* See Note E.

ἁγια *Christians*, plainly intimates that where *both* parents were believers, the children, as a matter of course, were ἁγια *Christians*. I find this argument stated with so much clearness and force by Dr. J. M. Mason, that I am persuaded the reader will be gratified with an excerpt from that author in this place. "The passage thus explained," says he, "establishes the church membership of infants in another form. For it assumes the principle, that when both parents are reputed believers, their children belong to the church of God* as a matter of course. The whole difficulty proposed by the Corinthians to Paul grows out of this principle. Had he taught, or they understood, that no children, be their parents believers or unbelievers, are to be accounted members of the church, the difficulty could not have existed. For if the faith of both parents could not confer upon the child the privilege of membership, the faith of only one of them certainly could not. The point was decided. It would have been mere impertinence to teaze the apostle with queries which carried their own answers along with them. But on the supposition that when both parents were members, their children were also members; the difficulty is very natural and serious. 'I see,' would a Christian convert exclaim, 'I see the children of my Christian neighbours owned as members of the church of God; and I see the children of others, who are unbelievers, rejected with themselves. I believe in Christ myself, but my husband, my wife, believes not. What is to become of my children? Are they to be admitted with myself? or are they to be cast off with my [unbelieving] partner?'

" 'Let not your heart be troubled,' replies the apostle, 'God reckons them to the believing, not to the unbelieving parent. It is enough that they are yours. The infidelity of your partner shall never frustrate their interest in the covenant of your God.'

"This decision put the subject at rest. And it lets us know that one of the reasons, if not the chief reason, of the doubt, whether a married person should continue, after conversion, in the conjugal society of an infidel partner, arose from a fear lest such continuance should exclude

* I shall hereafter explain the relation of infants to the church. The *fact* is all that concerns us now.

the children from the church of God. Otherwise it is hard to comprehend why the apostle should dissuade them from separating by such an argument as he has employed in the text. And it is utterly inconceivable how such a doubt could have entered their minds, had not the membership of infants, born of believing parents, been undisputed, and esteemed a high privilege,—so high a privilege, that the apprehension of losing it made conscientious parents at a stand whether they ought not rather to break the ties of wedlock, by withdrawing from an unbelieving husband or wife. Thus the origin of this difficulty on the one hand, and the solution of it on the other, concur in establishing our doctrine, that by the appointment of God himself, the infants of believing parents are born [ceremonially clean, and have a right to be admitted as] members of his church."*

Secondly. The simple circumstance that Paul cites the relation of infants to the church in proof of another subject, and one, too, of such grave importance as to involve the perpetual union of husband and wife, and the good order of families, clearly proves that the membership of infants was a point which was not only believed, but it was *universally* believed; *there was no difference of opinion, or dispute concerning it, in the Christian church.* The force of this argument I wish the reader to feel. In proving any doubtful point, the only rational method to be pursued is to advance facts, or deductions from principles which are themselves established and undisputed, and which have a relation to the point to be proved. No satisfaction could ever be realized—no approach to truth and certainty could ever be made—by advancing one disputed point to prove or establish another. In a court of justice the witnesses are called upon to state what they do *know*—what is, with them, clear and undisputed, that has a relation to the question pending. In reasoning, no argument can be deemed valid, or as entitled to any importance whatever, unless it be itself drawn from facts and principles well established, and which have a relation to the point at issue. We cannot, by the mere accumulation of doubtful or dis-

* Essays on the Church of God. *Christian Magazine*, ii, 49, 50, quoted by Dr. S. Miller; Infant Baptism, pp. 20, 21. See chap. vii. of this work.

puted arguments, add any weight of certainty to the doctrine which we would establish by them. To advance one disputed fact to establish another, is but to shift the ground of the difficulty, not to diminish it. If the testimony itself can be overthrown, it proves nothing. All the proof that arises from any given fact, in any given case, is based on the single circumstance that the fact itself is unquestioned by the parties who are to be the judges; remembering, of course, that it must have a proper relation to the point at issue.

Now, suppose infant baptism and membership had been disputed topics in the early Christian church. Suppose, when Paul declared, "your children are not unclean, but holy"—the precise phraseology which a Jew would employ to assert their membership—that, by this announcement, he had touched a disputed point among the Corinthians. And suppose he had advanced (as he certainly does) the fact that these children were thus clean, or *holy*, (by which the Jewish disciples would understand that they were the covenanted seed, the lawful members of the church,) to prove another point; I ask, Would the argument have had any weight whatever? If they had doubted that children themselves belonged to the Christian community, they certainly could not have received the assertion that they did thus belong, as proof of any other disputed point. They might very properly have said to the apostle, "True, your reasoning is very plausible and forcible to those who admit your premises. We readily grant that IF children of believing parents, or those who have one parent a believer and the other an unbeliever, do really belong to the Christian community, *then*, it must follow that the unbelieving parent was considered as ceremonially clean; but this reasoning takes for granted a disputed and unsettled point. We deny that children are members of the Christian community. And as your whole argument is built upon this mooted point—as it assumes for an axiom that which itself wants proof, at least in our estimation—it can, of course, with us, have no force whatever." But did the Corinthians make any such reply to the reasoning of the apostle? Would Paul have advanced such reasoning had he known that such a reply could have been made? Certainly not. We therefore say, that the manner of alluding to infant, ceremonial holiness, that is, infant church membership, proves, even more clearly than a direct assertion, that infants were universally regarded by the church as belonging to the Christian community. It proves that their eligibility to baptism was not only believed, but regarded as an established axiom. Had the apostle said, "Your children should all be baptized," it might have implied that some doubted, and neglected the duty. But when he advances the fact of their relation to the church, which necessarily implies their baptism, and uses this fact as the basis of an important argument, it proves that there was no doubt or disputation on the subject,—that it was a settled point of faith, an established axiom in theology.

[4.] The right of infants to baptism is recognised in those words of the apostle, recorded Acts ii, 38, 39:—"Then Peter said unto them, Repent, and be baptized, every one of you, in the name of Jesus Christ, for the remission of sins, and ye shall receive the gift of the Holy Ghost. For the promise is unto you, and to your children, and to all that are afar off, even as many as the Lord our God shall call."

In eliciting the force of the argument, from this passage, we call attention to the following particulars:—

1.) The "promise" here spoken of, refers to Gen. xvii, 7:—"And I will establish my covenant between me and thee, and thy seed after thee, in their generations, for an everlasting covenant; to be a God unto thee, and to thy seed after thee." That the reference is to this passage, appears evident, if we consider, first, the exact similarity of expression between them. The promise made to Abraham says, "*to thee, and to thy seed*:" the promise quoted by Peter says, "*to you, and to your children.*" Secondly, it better suits the analogy of the case, to refer Peter's words directly to those quoted in Genesis. Peter connects the promise with the duty and privilege of submitting to the initiating rite—baptism: the promise of Gen. xvii, 7, also stands connected with the same privilege and duty in reference to the initiatory rite of that dispensation—circumcision. In both cases the subjects of the promise were to be brought into church fellowship by virtue of its provisions and efficacy. Thirdly, the promise here spoken of includes the blessings of pardon and reconciliation. It regards man as a sinner, and brings him within the provisions of mercy, and the reach of hope. This, primarily, can refer only to the Abrahamic promise :—"I will be a God to thee, and to thy seed after thee." The promise of Joel ii, 28, 29, refers to a more mature and perfect development of the system of human redemption; not to the elemental principles of that system, as repentance, pardon, &c. But Peter exhorts to repentance, and encourages the hope of pardon, by virtue of the "promise" of God to which he alludes. It should be considered, moreover, that the promise of Joel is itself based upon the provisions of the Abrahamic covenant, and is one and identical with the promise of that covenant, with this distinction, that the Abrahamic promise included all spriritual blessings—"*I will be a God to thee and to thy seed*"—while Joel speaks distinctively of the gospel days,—the more glorious period of the covenant. After all, whether the "promise" spoken of by Peter allude to the promise of Joel ii, 28, or to that of Gen. xvii, 7, is not of essential importance to our argument; for, as we shall presently show, whatever may be the original character of this promise, it forms, most unquestionably, the ground of right and obligation to baptism, with respect to all those persons to whom it constitutionally applies.

2.) How would a Jew understand the phrase, "to *you* and to your *children*."

To know this, we must first ascertain the meaning of the word τεκνα *tekna, children.* I see no ground of dispute on this point. The *usus loquendi* sheds a perfectly clear and unequivocal light. Τεκνον *teknon* means a *child*, whether male or female. It sometimes answers to the Hebrew בֵּן *ben*, as, in the plural form, in Gen. iii, 16, "God said to the woman...in sorrow shalt thou bring forth בָּנִים *banim*, τεκνα *tekna, children.*" This is the proper meaning of τεκνα *tekna;* but it has also a wider sense, and is used Hebraistically for *descendants, posterity,* without any determinate reference to age. But the primary meaning of τεκνον is *a child;* and this is indicated by its etymology, being derived from τικτω *tikto, to bring forth.* So, also, σπερμα *sperma* literally means *seed,* as being sown, or scattered. But *tropically* it signifies *children, offspring*. It answers to the Hebrew זֶרַע *zera*. Now, the case is this:—The primary meaning of τεκνα *tekna* is *children;* and a primary figurative sense of σπερμα *sperma* is also *children*. But both words are also sometimes used in a wider sense, to signify *posterity, descendants*, and in a sense which sometimes shows that *adult* descendants are intended, as well as infants. How then can the force of either of these words be determined in any given passage? How can we determine, in any one instance where either of these words occurs, which of the two senses it is to take; that of *posterity*, in its broad application, or that of *children*, in its more restricted meaning? The answer is plain;—*the sense of the particular passage must decide.* For instance, it must be ascertained what is *affirmed* or *denied* of the τεκνα *tekna* or of the σπερμα *sperma* in the text. If any thing is affirmed of them that does necessarily belong, or may with perfect propriety be ascribed to *children*, and which cannot be properly ascribed to adults, then the word in question may be known to be there used in its literal or more restricted form, to signify *children*. But if the thing affirmed do properly belong to *adults* as well as children, then the word may be understood in its larger application, as denoting *posterity* in general. Now, in the passage before us it is said, "the promise is unto you, and to your τεκνα *children*." The question is, Does τεκνα mean children proper, or only posterity in general? To determine this, we ask, Is any thing affirmed of the τεκνα *tekna* in the text that is inapplicable to children proper? The answer is certainly in the negative. There is nothing absurd, or unsuitable, in the supposition that children should be made the subjects of a spiritual promise,—in other words, that they should be made the subjects of divine grace. Then, it follows that τεκνα *tekna* may be understood in its literal and more simple acceptation, as denoting *children* proper, although the more general idea of posterity is not excluded.

This is the more probable, because, in Gen. xvii, 7, where Jehovah promises to "be a God unto Abraham, and to his *seed*," (זַרְעֲךָ σπερματος,) the Jews understood the promise as applying to themselves and their *infant chil-*

dren; and hence, also, the *token* of this covenant—circumcision—was applied to their infant children, as indicating their right to the promise. Every Jew, therefore, would unquestionably understand the words of the apostle Peter as applying to himself and his infant offspring. "The Jews had been accustomed for many hundred years to receive infants by circumcision into the church; and this they did, as before observed, because God had promised to 'be a God to Abraham and to his seed.' They had understood this promise to mean parents, and their infant offspring; and this idea was become familiar by the practice of many centuries. What, then, must have been their views, when one of their own community [countrymen] says to them, 'The promise is unto you, and to your children?' If the practice of receiving infants [into the church] was founded on a promise exactly similar, as it certainly was, how could they possibly understand him but as meaning the same thing, since he himself used the same mode of speech? This must have been the case, unless we admit this absurdity, namely, that they understood him in a sense to which they had never been accustomed... Certainly all men, when acting freely, will understand words in that way which is most familiar to them; and nothing could be more familiar to the Jews, than to understand such a speech as Peter's to mean adults and infants. So that if the Jews, the awakened Jews, had apprehended the apostle to mean only adults when he said, 'to you and your children,' they must have had an understanding of such a peculiar construction, as to make that sense of a word, which to them was totally unnatural and forced, [and, we may add, altogether unheard of in such a peculiar connection,] to become [all at once] familiar and easy."*

But if we take τεκνα *tekna* in its broadest application to denote *posterity*, the result will be the same. For what is our idea of posterity but that of a generation, or of generations of human beings, comprising adults and infants? To say that the word posterity means adults only, is to assume a position in the argument too absurd and ridiculous to merit a serious refutation. "How idle a thing it is for a man to come with a Lexicon in his hand, to inform us

* Edwards on Baptism, pp. 67, 68.

that *τεκνα tekna, children*, means *posterity!* Certainly it [often] does, and so, consequently, means the youngest infants,"* as being necessarily included in the term.

Whatever method, therefore, we adopt for the explication of the apostle's words, we must, unless we would rush into the most palpable absurdities, understand him as meaning *adults* and *infants*, when he says, "*you*, and your *children*." Thus must the Jews have understood him, because this understanding would be according to the most natural and obvious meaning of the words. And thus must Peter have intended to be understood, unless he is to be charged with an unusual and improper use of terms, which no one will pretend. Thus did both Peter, and all the Jews, actually understand an exactly similar phraseology in the promise given to Abraham. The hortatory parts of Scripture are peculiarly simple and natural in their style. All technicalities, and words of difficult or doubtful meaning, were studiously avoided, and the words of common life only were employed. Peter, in the passage before us, uses the style and pathos of exhortation. He is a Hebrew, speaking to Hebrews. He carries them back to the Hebrew Scriptures—points them to a distinguished promise there recorded—uses words in their Hebrew sense, and constructs his argument wholly upon acknowledged principles of the Hebrew theology. To lead them to the spiritual provisions of that ancient promise (Gen. xvii, 7) was his single aim. All the circumstances, and the associations of the occasion, concur in establishing the use of *τεκνα tekna*, in its most obvious and simple sense, as we have above explained, namely, to mean *children* proper.

3.) The relation which the conjunctive particle *γαρ gar*, in verse 39, bears to the preceding part of the discourse, plainly establishes the obligation of infant baptism. The phraseology of this passage is exactly what we might expect, on the supposition that infant baptism was practised by the apostles; exactly what the Jews must have deemed sufficient to establish such a practice; and it becomes impossible fully to account for the force of the apostle's words on any other hypothesis. *Γαρ gar* is what is called,

* Edwards on Baptism.

in the language of grammarians, a "*causal conjunction*," and has the force of the English *for*, *because*; Latin, *enim*, *quippe*, *igitur*.* It always expresses the *reason* of what has been previously spoken, or implied, in the same connection. Now, the question is, to what word, or words, in the preceding part of the discourse, does γαρ *gar* refer? If we can fix its proper causal relation, we shall be at no loss to comprehend the force of Peter's argument. There are but three facts to which it can allude, and of which it can be considered as assigning a reason. Does it refer to either of these facts separately?—and if so, to which one? or does it refer generally to all the preceding part of Peter's discourse, contained in verse 38? After mature reflection, I am inclined to adopt the latter opinion. I will lay before the reader an analysis of the whole argument, so as to enable him to judge for himself. If γαρ *gar* be referred back to *μετανοησατε metanoesate*, (*repent* ye,) then the sense would be indicated by the following grammatical connection:—"*Repent ye* . . . BECAUSE *the promise is unto you*," &c. If γαρ relate to *βαπτισθητω baptistheto*, (*be baptized*,) then the grammatical connection would stand thus: "*Be baptized every one of you* . . . BECAUSE *the promise is unto you*," &c. If γαρ refer to the declaration, "*ληψεσθε την δωρεαν του ἁγιου Πνευματος ye shall receive the gift of the Holy Ghost*;" then the grammatical relation would stand thus: "*Ye shall receive the gift of the Holy Ghost*; BECAUSE *the promise is unto you*," &c. The first of the foregoing constructions would require γαρ *gar* to be understood as expressing the reason for their *repentance*; the second, the reason for their *baptism*; and the third, the reason why they should expect to *receive the Holy Ghost*. Now, either of these constructions would make a good doctrinal sense; but we consider γαρ to refer to ALL that is advanced in the thirty-eighth verse—first, because it better suits the plan of Luke, by giving very *general* statements of Peter's argument; secondly, γαρ no more fitly relates to one of the above-mentioned antecedents than another. It is as really a reason for their baptism, or their repentance, as for their receiving the Holy Spirit; and *vice versa*. Thirdly, it better suits all the

* Vide Buttmann's Greek Grammar; Robinson's Greek and Eng. Lex.; and Schrevelii Lex.

circumstances of the occasion to fix the causal relation of this conjunction to all the facts mentioned in the thirty-eighth verse. For instance, the preaching of Peter had produced a powerful effect;—"they were pricked in their heart, and said unto Peter, and to the rest... Men and brethren, what shall we do?" The first emotions of their remorse had produced a temporary despair; truly, they thought, we have forfeited not only church rights, but all hopes of mercy. Peter exhorted them to repentance—to assume church obligations in the Christian form—and encouraged them to look for the gift of the Holy Spirit. All these directions suited the urgency of the moment; and he proves their appropriateness and adaptation to his Jewish brethren by adding, "BECAUSE the [ancient covenant] promise [Gen. xvii, 7, to the fulness of which Joel has referred in chap. ii, 28] is unto you, and to your children, &c. If it were not so—if the ancient covenant promise were not to you and to your children—there would be no propriety in your repentance, (as it would be hopeless,) nor in your baptism, (as you would have no right to church privileges,) nor (much less) in your expecting to receive the fulness of the Holy Spirit." It does not appear that they were in any peculiar need of encouragement in order to enable them to embrace the promise of Joel ii, 28. On the contrary, it does seem plain that their immediate concern was to know whether they might expect pardon, and a restoration to covenant, or church blessings, (for which the Abrahamic promise directly provided;) thinking, probably, (and certainly with much reason,) that if they were not excluded from the covenant, they might yet hope for the Spirit's effusion. If, then, we suppose γαρ *gar* to refer to the several statements of the thirty-eighth verse, we understand the apostle as assigning a general reason for the exhortations and encouragements therein laid down; which certainly suits the point of the occasion much better than to refer this particle to the last clause of that verse.

But lastly, I remark, if the apostle had intended a direct quotation from, or an exclusive allusion to, Joel ii, 28, he would undoubtedly have adopted a phraseology more closely answering to the words and doctrine of that passage. In describing the persons upon whom the "Spirit" should be "poured out" in the latter (that is, gospel) days, Joel speaks only of *adults*. He speaks of "sons and daughters," of "old men and young men," of "servants and handmaids." It will not be doubted that the prophet intends only adults by these descriptions; unless the words "sons" and "daughters" should be supposed to include infants. But it is evident that he uses בָּנִים *banim* and בָּנוֹת *banoth*, as they are often used, to designate *age*, just as we would say *youth* and *maidens*, to designate an age advanced from childhood, though yet tender. And so the Seventy understood them, and rendered them by the corresponding Greek *υἱοι whioi*, and *θυγατερες thugateres*, *sons* and *daughters*. But Joel determines the question of the *age* of these *sons* and *daughters*, by immediately adding, "*they shall prophesy*." This proves that he intended only *adult* sons and daughters. Indeed, theology can sufficiently decide this question. The effusion of the Spirit, under the gospel dispensation, produces no alteration of the moral state of infants. Adults only, who are admitted to greater light and privileges, are directly affected by this event. It is plain, then, that Joel is speaking only of adults; and when he says "*all flesh*," his general terms must be limited by the other specific terms employed, and, above all, by the nature and design of the subject.

But the apostle Peter does not employ a proper phraseology to designate adults *only*, and therefore cannot be supposed to intend a direct quotation from Joel. Peter says, "the promise is *ὑμιν και τοις τεκνοις to you* (adults) *and to your* (infant) *children*." If he had intended adults only, as Joel unquestionably did, he would have employed another phraseology. *Τεκνα tekna*, though it may, and often does, mean adults, yet never means adults *only*, without being connected with qualifying and definitive circumstances. In verse 17, where Peter intends a quotation from Joel ii, 28, he uses the exact phraseology of the prophet, and says, "*οἱ υἱοι ὑμων και αἱ θυγατερες ὑμων your* SONS *and your* DAUGHTERS shall prophesy," &c. But the intelligent reader need not be informed that *τεκνα children* is not sufficiently explicit to be a quotation of *υἱοι και θυγατερες sons and daughters*, and those, too, that are old enough to "*prophesy!*" I have before shown, in this section, why the words of Peter, Acts ii, 39, may, and should, be regarded as a quotation of Gen. xvii, 7. Every circumstance, save that of a direct assertion, that can exist to determine any passage to be a quotation of another, exists in this case to determine the former to be a quotation of the latter.

It is sufficiently obvious, then, that γαρ *gar*, in Acts ii, 39, cannot refer exclusively to the promise of Joel ii, 28, or, in other words, to "the gift of the Holy Ghost," and must, consequently, be referred back, as above stated, to βαπτισθητω *baptistheto*, (*be baptized*,) or to μετανοησατε *metanoesate*, (*repent* ye,) or to all these facts in general. There is no grammatical objection to considering the conjunction in question as relating to all the statements of the thirty-eighth verse, and, for the reasons already assigned, we shall thus regard it.

4.) The argument, then, which we derive from this passage, in favour of infant baptism, is easily deduced: "*Because* the covenant promise is unto you, therefore repent and be baptized, and ye shall receive the gift of the Holy Ghost." But it may be objected, the same promise is unto their *children* also; must they repent, be baptized, and receive the gift of the Holy Ghost? If the "promise" be a valid reason for repentance, baptism, and the bestowment of the Holy Spirit's effusion, in the one case, is it not also equally so in the other? But as infants cannot repent, does not this argument wholly fail? We answer: The analogy of this argument applies as far as the nature of the case allows. That infants are incapable of repentance, is no proof that they are unsuitable subjects of baptism, or of the Spirit's influences. No possible difficulty can arise here to any candid mind, who considers that the use of words, in such a case, is always to be explained according to the nature of the subject, and the analogy of faith. The fact, which I cannot see how to avoid in view of all the circumstances of the case, is, that the "promise" in this passage stands connected, by the causal conjunction γαρ *gar*, to "baptism," and consequently to church relations. It must, then, follow that all to whom the promise constitutionally applies have a right to baptism, unless they have forfeited it by an infraction of the covenant. But the promise applies to infants; they have never for-

feited it, or any of its external provisions—therefore, they are to be baptized.

Thus was the ancient rite of circumcision connected with the covenant promise. God says to Abraham, "I will establish my covenant between me and thee, and thy seed after thee,...to be a God unto thee, and to thy seed after thee...THEREFORE thou shalt keep my covenant... This is my covenant...every man-child among you shall be circumcised." The point of analogy is this, the "promise" is the *ground* of right and obligation to church relations and ordinances. "When a positive institute is connected with a promise, all who are contained in the promise have a right to the institute. I think any one may be compelled to grant this, as it is certainly an undeniable truth; for if parents must, therefore, be circumcised because they are included in the promise, then, as infants are also included in the promise, they too must be circumcised. All this is evinced by the history of circumcision, and is, indeed, a self-evident case; because, if a promise give a right to an institute, the institute must belong to all who are interested in the promise. And, therefore, we may reason thus: If parents must be baptized because the promise belongs to them, then must their infants be baptized, because the promise belongs to them also. This mode of reasoning is the more certain, as it is confirmed, beyond all doubt, by the divine procedure; for if you ask, Who are the circumcised? the reply is, Those to whom the promise was made. If you inquire again, To whom was the promise made? we answer, To adults and infants. Again, if you ask, Who are to be baptized? the answer is, Those to whom the promise is made. But to whom is it made? The apostle says, 'To you, and to your children.' Now, what proof more direct can be made or desired for infant baptism?"*

Bishop Burnett says, "When the apostles, in their first preaching, told the Jews that the promises were made to them and to their children, the Jews must have understood it according to what they were already in possession of, namely, that they could initiate their children into their religion, bring them under the obligations of it, and

* Edwards on Baptism, pp. 74, 75.

procure to them a share in those blessings that belonged to it."*

[5.] In John iii, 5, the Saviour says, "Except a man be born of water and of the Spirit, he cannot enter into the kingdom of God."

This passage has always been regarded as having a very decisive bearing on the question of infant baptism. So it was regarded by the early fathers in the Christian church, and so it should doubtless be of right considered. That this refers to water baptism is too manifest to require proof. To say that *water* is here used only in a mystical sense, as it is in John iv, 13, 14, and not of the *material element*, is not only to contradict the voice of all antiquity, but, what is of vastly more serious import, it is to contradict reason itself, and the general analogy of Scripture usage. Of this, the intelligent reader, with a little reflection and examination, may soon become convinced. (See chap. v, sec. i, of this work.)

But is it duly considered what our Saviour has here said? Hear him: "'Εαν μη τις γεννηθη ἐξ ὑδατος και πνευματος *Except* ANY ONE *be born of water and of the Spirit*, he cannot enter into the kingdom of God." Is there any exception here? Does it not apply to all alike? to children and to adults? And let the reader turn back and compare this with Matt. xix, 14, where our Saviour affirms that "the kingdom of heaven belongs" to children. It truly belongs to them, and to such as resemble them in moral dispositions, but "none shall enter into it," according to the ordinary appointment of God, "except he be regenerate, and born anew of *water* and of the Holy Spirit;" and if the "kingdom" here means, or implies, the visible church, as it often does, then must all, without any exception, be born of water, as well as of the Holy Spirit, before they can lawfully become its acknowledged members. These awful, and very direct words of Jesus Christ, are too often lost, in their practical effect upon the heart and conduct of the believer, through the application of an allegorizing, and certainly a very dangerous, principle of interpretation. "Blessed are they that hear the word of God, and keep it," Luke xi, 28.

* Exposition of the Thirty-nine Articles, Art. xxvii.

[6.] The New Testament recognition of infant baptism is obviously set forth in the mention of "household baptisms."

There are three different places where household baptisms are recorded, namely, Acts xvi, 15, Lydia and her household; verse 33, the jailer "and all *his*;" 1 Cor. i, 16, "the household of Stephanas." The scope of this argument may be comprehended in the two following propositions: First. The *language* employed is such as may be fitly used to represent the baptism of children. Secondly. The *circumstances* concur to establish a decided probability that Pedobaptism is here intended.

1.) Whenever we would understand the meaning of any author, our first effort should be to explain his words according to the common usage, and the obvious design of the particular writer. If it be an ancient author, we must ascertain what was the use of the terms he employed at the time of his writing, and among the people to whom he wrote. The question, therefore, which we are now to decide is, Does *οικος oikos*, (translated *household*,) the word which is used in Acts xvi, 15, and 1 Cor. i, 16, properly include *infants?* The sacred history informs us that certain persons, with their *households*, were baptized; the question is, Does the phraseology properly denote that infants were, or might have been, baptized? I am fully apprized that the more informed reader will deem it wholly unnecessary and gratuitous for me to adduce formal proof of the affirmative of this question; but for the sake of those who may not readily appreciate how terms are used in the Bible, and also that the final argument may not seem to rest barely on assertion, or the mere authority of names, I cannot withhold a few statements. *Οικος oikos* primarily denotes a *house*, that is, a building or edifice, *domus*. But by a very common rule of language it also signifies all that dwell in a house, that is, *a family;* including parents, children, domestics, &c.; all those persons which we range under the general title of *family*, or *household*. The point to be ascertained is, whether infants are naturally, and as a matter of course, included in this phrase. The opponents of infant baptism take the ground that infants cannot be proved to have been included in the "households" which the apostles baptized, because they are not *specified*, and it is well known that there are households, or families, without infant children. We take the ground that, although *οικος oikos* does not specify children, yet, children are properly included within the term, as much as parents, or servants; and the presumption is that they are always thus included, unless there is a specification to the contrary. The word *family* does not necessarily specify parents,—a family may be constituted, or subsist, without the relation of parents,—but does this authorize us to infer that parents are never included in this word unless they are specified by a distinct and appropriate appellation? The same may be said of servants. The words *οικος*, *familia*, and *household*, include the idea of servants, as constituting a part of those who live together in the same house. Still, neither of these terms is the proper one to denote a servant distinctively, and there may be families where there are no servants. But are we authorized to infer, hence, that servants are never included in these words, unless they are specified distinctly by some adjunct? For instance, it is said Lydia and her household were baptized. From this we argue that, as children are properly included under the general term household, therefore, the presumption is, children were baptized. "Not so," says a Baptist; "the term household does not specify infants; there are many households that do not include one infant, therefore the baptism of households does not, in any way, prove the baptism of infants." Well said! Admirable logic! But hold: will this principle of interpretation hold good in other cases? Let us try. The term household does not specify domestics of any kind. There are many households without any servants whatever. Nor does the term specify children that are grown up. There are many households that are composed of the husband and wife, or only one of them, and the servants; therefore, the baptism of households does not prove the baptism of servants of any kind, or of children of any age, unless they are specified by a distinct and appropriate name;—therefore there were no domestics of any kind, or children of any age, baptized by Paul in the households of Lydia, the jailer, and Stephanas, because no specifications to this effect appear. Finally, as no individuals but Lydia, the jailer, and Stephanas, are specified—as the term "household" specifies no particular person, or class of persons—therefore, it cannot be proved that any particular persons but those three were baptized on those occasions. And thus endeth the first lesson on the logical use of *οικος*, according to Mr. Pengilly and the Baptists.

But we maintain that we have the same authority for supposing that children were included in these households, and were consequently baptized, as for supposing that any other individuals were included in them and were baptized. Children are as natural a branch of the household as servants, and much more so. Mr. Pengilly says, "From the word 'household,' therefore, to infer the baptism of infants, is completely *begging the question*." Just as much is it begging the question to infer that any other persons were baptized besides those specified; as, for instance, parents, adult children, servants, or any others. It is more properly begging the question to infer that children were *not* baptized in these households, because it assumes the point to be proved without any proof, and exactly against the face of a reasonable probability.

2.) We inquire, Do all the circumstances of the case so concur as to establish a decided probability that infant baptism is here intended?

The reader will understand that we are not seeking for any positive declarations in proof of our position. The nature of the case does not demand such proof, and the principles we have before laid down, by which to direct our inquiries, do not impose upon us this task. I mean by *circumstances*, all those corroborating facts that serve to shed light upon the case in point, which do not appear from a mere philological examination of the word *οικος oikos*. It will be sufficient for our argument to prove that there are no specified circumstances connected with these family baptisms that impair the force of the probability that Pedobaptism was practised, according to the natural indication of the terms employed.

(*a*.) It is a fact worthy of note, that the faith, or conversion, of Lydia only is mentioned, or even intimated; following which, as if it were a matter of course, was the baptism of her household. It is said the Lord opened HER heart, "that SHE attended unto the things that were spoken of Paul;" but it does not say that the Lord opened the hearts of her *household*, and that THEY attended unto the same things. Thus, then, stands the account: "SHE" attended unto the preaching of Paul, and "SHE" and her "HOUSEHOLD" were baptized. No more or less can be made of the words of Luke. Now we do not say positively that there were no other adults in her family, but we do say positively that no other adults are specified, and also that infant children are a very usual and natural portion of a household, which throws the force of a clear probability on the side of Pedobaptism. Another point that perhaps is worthy of mention, as indicating that Lydia only, of all the members of her house, believed, is, that when she invites the apostle and Silas to tarry for a time at her house, she says, "If ye have judged ME to be faithful, come into my house," &c. Had there been other believing adults besides herself, it might seem more modest for her to have at least hinted it, and to have said, "If ye have judged US to be faithful," &c. This might seem especially suitable, as there appeared a strong reluctance in Paul and Silas to comply with her entreaties; and if *her* faith was an argument of any strength in favour of their staying, surely the faith of the entire household (supposing them to be adults and converted) would have added weight to the argument. Lydia was a Jewish proselyte before her conversion to Christianity. It is said, verse 14, she "*σεβομενη τον Θεον worshipped God;*" that is, was *devout,*—a description that is used to distinguish proselytes from native Hebrews. The probability therefore is, that she and her household had been previously proselyted to Judaism; and as she had given up her household to God in baptism before, according to the Jewish requisition in making proselytes, so now again, according to Christ's requisition in making disciples.

"The great difficulty with the Baptists is, to make a house for Lydia, without any children at all, young or old. This, however, cannot be proved from the term itself, since the same word is that commonly used in the Scriptures to include children residing at home with their parents: as, 1 Tim. iii, 4, 'One that ruleth well his own *οικου house*, having his *τεκνα children* in subjection, with all gravity.' It is, however, conjectured first, that she had come on a trading voyage from Thyatira to Philippi, to sell purple, as if a woman [who was a native] of Thyatira might not be settled in business at Philippi, as a seller of this article. Then, as if to mark more strikingly the hopelessness of the attempt to torture this passage to favour an opinion, 'her house' is made to consist of journeymen dyers, 'employed in preparing the purple she sold;' which, however, is a notion at variance with the former; for if she was on a mere trading voyage—if she had brought her purple goods from Thyatira to Philippi to sell, she most probably brought them ready dyed, and would have no need of a dying establishment. To complete the whole, these journeymen dyers, although not a word is said of their conversion, or even of their existence, in the whole story, are raised into 'the brethren,' (a term which manifestly denotes the members of the Philippian church,) whom Paul and Silas are said to have seen and comforted in the house of Lydia before they departed!"* There is, therefore, not the least circumstance in this whole history that impairs the force of a reasonable probability that it describes an instance of infant baptism.

(*b.*) In the case of the jailer, it appears evident that there were other adults besides himself who believed and were baptized; for it is said Paul and Silas "spake the word of the Lord to all that were in the jailer's house," verse 32. But this in nowise militates against the probability that there were children also in the jailer's family, and, if so, that they were baptized. It is said of the jailer, *και εβαπτισθη αυτος και όι αυτου παντες and he was baptized, he and all who* were [ἠσαν being understood] *of him.* The relative force of *όι hoi* is not brought out in our common English version, although a kindred sense to the above is given to this passage. All I aim to make out of this sentence is, that the phraseology indicates that the jailer had children, (of what age is not specified,) and that they were baptized. But if this be so, the probability is in our favour, namely, that there were young children in his family, and, therefore, that the text is a recorded instance of infant baptism. The reader will understand that all that is claimed from this passage, in favour of infant baptism, is, that it affords a reasonable probability in its favour, and, of course, against our opponents.

* Watson's Theol. Inst., pp. 641, 642.

I am aware that it is said that, in verse 34, the historian informs us that the jailer "rejoiced, believing in God with all his house;" but it is hardly necessary to inform the critical reader that this is far from stating that all his house believed with him. Indeed, it says nothing about the faith of his house. The grammatical order of the sentence is broken by our common version, and, as I think evidently, the sense much obscured, or rather misstated. The sentence stands thus: *και ηγαλλιασατο πανοικι πεπιστευκως τω Θεου and he rejoiced in all his house, believing in God;* or, to make better English syntax, it should stand thus: *and he, believing in God, rejoiced with*, or *in, all his house.* The peculiar turn of the passage I understand to be, that *he*, (the jailer,) *believing in God, rejoiced* IN, or, as we would say, OVER *all his family.* How natural is it for a man newly converted, and whose children also are newly ingrafted into the covenant of promise, and consecrated to God, to rejoice in this conversion of his family! The jailer now looked upon his family as dedicated to God, and as fellow-heirs with himself of the grace of life. He looked upon his children (for the text certainly indicates that he had children) as subjects of grace, and as those who were honoured and blessed of the Lord. He believed in God—the adult members of his family believed, and all his family had been newly baptized by these faithful servants of God; the change was great—it was glorious. He rejoiced in the conversion of his family. He rejoiced over them just as any Christian father would rejoice in the consecration of his house to God. This I conceive to be the true force of the passage, and it is sufficient to say that no philological objection stands opposed to it. But how do we know that there were any infants in this family? We do not know;—we have not undertaken to prove this. How, then, does it favour infant baptism? We answer, The *presumption* always is that *οικος oikos*, when used in the sense of *family*, and *πανοικὶ panoiki*, (*household, all the household*, &c.,) include children. So it is said, Exod. i, 1, "The children of Israel came into Egypt, every man and his *household*." (בֵּית *πανοικὶ*.) But how do we know that *πανοικὶ panoiki*, which the Septuagint here employ, includes young children? The word itself does not positively prove that there were any infant children in these families of the sons of the patriarch. Yet, if we had no other evidence of there having been little children in these households but the mere force of the word, still the presumption would be that there were such children, because it is a proper word to designate the collective body of parents and children. But we know that *πανοικὶ panoiki* includes infants in this passage, because it is stated, Gen. xlvi, 5, that the sons of Jacob "carried their *little ones* and their wives in the wagons" to Egypt. So also may the same word be presumed to include infants in Acts xvi, 34.

I know that it is said in the English version that the jailer "rejoiced, or believed, *with* all his house;" thus indicating that all the members of his house actively united in his rejoicings, or faith. But there is no such word as "*with*" in the Greek text. It is not in the sentence, and it does not necessarily appear in the composition of *πανοικὶ panoiki*. The truth is, that *with*, or *in*, or some other particle, is left to be supplied by the sense. "He rejoiced *in* all his house;" that is, "over his entire family." From an attentive observation, therefore, of all the particular circumstances connected with the baptism of the jailer and his household, we find nothing to impair the force of the natural probability that *πανοικὶ panoiki*, and the phrase *ὁι αυτου παντες all who* were *of him*, imply and include children; and, as they were all baptized, the force of this scrap of history is evidently in favour of infant baptism.

(*c*.) "The third instance," says Mr. Watson, "is that of 'the house of Stephanas,' mentioned by St. Paul, 1 Cor. i, 16, as having been baptized by himself. This family, also, it is argued, must have been all adults, because they are said in the same epistle, chap. xvi, 15, to have 'addicted themselves to the ministry of the saints,' and further, because they were persons who took '*a lead*' in the affairs of the church, the Corinthians being exhorted to 'submit themselves unto such, and to every one that helpeth with us and laboureth.' To understand this passage rightly, however, it is necessary to observe, that Stephanas, the head of the family, had been sent by the church of Corinth to St. Paul at Ephesus, along with Fortunatus and Achaicus. In the absence of the head of the family, the apostle commends 'the house,' the family of Stephanas, to the regard of the Corinthian believers, and perhaps also the houses of the two other brethren that had come with him, for in several MSS. marked by Griesbach, and in some of the versions, the text reads, 'Ye know the house of Stephanas and Fortunatus,' and one reads also, 'and of Achaicus.' By the house or family of Stephanas, the apostle must mean his children, or, along with them, his near relations dwelling together in the same family; for, since they are commended for their hospitality to the saints, servants, who have no power to show hospitality, are of course excluded. But in the absence of the head of the family, it is very improbable that the apostle should exhort the Corinthian church to 'submit,' ecclesiastically, to the wife, sons, daughters, and near relations of Stephanas, and, if the reading of Griesbach's MSS. be followed, to the family of Fortunatus, and that of Achaicus also. In respect of government, therefore, they cannot be supposed 'to have had a *lead* in the church,' according to the Baptist notion, and especially as the heads of these families were absent.* They were, however, the oldest Christian families in Corinth, the house of Stephanas, at least, being called the 'first-fruits of Achaia,' and eminently distinguished for 'addicting themselves,' *setting themselves on system,* to the work of ministering to the saints, that is, of communicating to the poor saints; entertaining stranger Christians, which was an important branch of practical duty in the primitive church, that in every place those who professed Christ might be kept out of the society of idolaters; and receiving the ministers of Christ. On these accounts the apostle commends them to the especial regard of the Corinthian church, and exhorts '*ἱνα και ὑμεις ὑποτασσησθε τοις τοιουτοις that ye range yourselves under* and co-operate with them and with every one' also, 'who helpeth with us and laboureth;' the military metaphor contained in *εταξαν etaxan,* (*have set, devoted, arranged,* Eng. ver., *addicted,*) in the preceding verse, being here carried forward. These families were the oldest Christians in Corinth; and as they were foremost in every good word and work, they were not only to be commended, but

* Thus far the reasoning of our author is ingenious and forcible, on the supposition that Stephanas and his companions did not return to Corinth, as the bearers of the first letter of Paul to that church.

the rest were to be exhorted to serve under them as leaders in these works of charity. This appears to be the obvious sense of this otherwise obscure passage. But in this, or, indeed, in any other sense which can be given to it, it proves no more than that there were adult persons in the family of Stephanas,—his wife, sons, and daughters, who were distinguished for their charity and hospitality. Still it is to be remembered that the baptism of the oldest children took place several years before. The house of Stephanas was 'the first-fruits of Achaia,' in which St. Paul began to preach not later than A. D. 51, while this epistle could not have been written earlier at least than A. D. 57, and might be later. Six or eight years taken from the age of the sons and daughters of Stephanas might bring the oldest to the state of early youth, and as to the younger branches, would descend to the term of infancy, properly so called. Still further, all that the apostle affirms of the benevolence and hospitality of the family of Stephanas is perfectly consistent with a part of his children being still very young at the time he wrote this epistle. An equal commendation for hospitality and charity might be given at the present day, with perfect propriety, to many pious families, several members of which are still in a state of infancy. It was sufficient, to warrant the use of such expressions as those of the apostle, that there were in these Corinthian families a few adults, whose conduct gave a decided character to the whole 'house.'

"Thus the arguments used to prove that in these three instances of family baptism there were no young children, are evidently very unsatisfactory; and they leave us to the conclusion, which perhaps all would come to in reading the sacred history, were they quite free from the bias of a theory, that 'houses,' or 'families,' as in the commonly received import of the term, may be presumed to comprise children of all ages, unless some explicit note of the contrary appears, which is not the case in any of the instances in question."*

3.) The familiar, and, as we may say, matter-of-course manner of mentioning these cases of family baptisms, clearly indicates that it was in perfect harmony with the

* Watson's Institutes, vol. ii, pp. 642–644.

universal custom of the apostles. Had it been any unusual thing—had infant baptism been unknown to the apostolic church, and as abhorrent to God as it is to our Baptist brethren, it is not at all probable that these cases would have been thus registered by the direction of the Holy Spirit, without unequivocal intimations that no infant children were included in the number of the baptized. As it is, however, it leaves upon the mind of the unbiased reader the impression of a strong probability, not only that infants were included in those baptized households which are mentioned, but that hundreds, perhaps thousands, of families were baptized in the same way; which is an advance of the argument that falls little short of the highest Scriptural authority.

It cannot have escaped the observation of the attentive, intelligent reader, that the simple *fact* of the register of household, or family baptisms, as well as the *manner* in which they are registered, is in perfect keeping with the hypothesis that infants were universally baptized with their believing parents in apostolic times. There is a corroborating force to these circumstances that should not be overlooked. Such a record of baptisms certainly never would occur in the same easy, unrestricted, familiar style of history, as that adopted by the author of the Acts of the Apostles, under an anti-Pedobaptist ministration. It is true that our Baptist brethren tell us they have baptized households. Mr. Pengilly tells us, in his work on Baptism, that he "has baptized households; and, among others, a 'Lydia and her household,' and yet never baptized a child;" and concludes that "to infer the baptism of infants from the word 'household,' is completely begging the question."* His argument amounts to this: He has baptized households without ever having baptized a child, —therefore, it is begging the question to suppose that there were any children in those households whose baptism is recorded in the New Testament. But the point upon which I wish to fix attention here is, the incongruity of such registers, and such historic accounts, in the easy, familiar, and matter-of-course style of Luke, to the hypothesis that infant baptism was unknown and unpractised

* Scripture Guide, p. 43.

by the apostles. A Baptist disputant, for the sake of giving effect to his argument, may record a household baptism which he himself had performed; but would he be likely, in sending home missionary reports, for instance, to return an account of family baptisms in the same open, unqualified manner as that of Luke, in recording the baptism of Lydia's family? Or, furthermore, were a Baptist writing a history of the Baptist missions, or of the general Baptist denomination,—a history that was to be read by future generations, when its author, and all who now might have any personal knowledge of the facts recorded, would be no more—a history, one prominent object of which was to set forth the validity and true character of water baptism, as held and practised by the Baptists—were a Baptist, I say, to write such a history, would he be likely to mention family baptisms in such an indefinite, familiar, and unqualified manner as to leave the impression upon thousands of minds, that infants, being a natural part of a family, were to be baptized? Does it accord with our knowledge of the Baptists' views on this subject, to suppose that they would be likely to write so unguardedly as to leave the impression on the minds of many of their ingenuous readers that they practised infant baptism? And if the apostles, and the author of the book containing an account of their "Acts," and the primitive church, had all been opposed to infant baptism, or had been wholly ignorant of any such practice, I ask, Would they have been likely to leave such an unguarded account of their baptisms, as to give the impression to thousands that they practised infant baptism? Would an intelligent Arminian, now-a-days, write concerning the doctrine of "free grace" in terms that would be likely, from the natural force of words, to leave the impression that he was a believer in the "five points of Calvinism?" And yet, absurd as would be the affirmative of these suppositions, it would not fully illustrate the absurdity of an anti-Pedobaptist construction of the household baptisms of the New Testament. For here, according to the theory of our opponents, we not only have anti-Pedobaptist authors (for such the Baptists suppose Luke and Paul to have been) writing about baptism in terms exactly calculated to leave the impression that infant baptism was an apostolic practice, but we are bound to believe that such an absurdity was sanctioned by the authority of the Holy Spirit! for these men wrote "as they were moved by the Holy Ghost."

To illustrate this subject still further, let us suppose the following case:—"Two missionaries have for a number of years been successfully labouring for the conversion of a particular tribe of savages in the wilderness of America. We have heard of their labours, and of their success, and have rejoiced in it, but have never learned, and have never to this day inquired, whether they practised infant baptism or not. For special reasons, this now becomes a subject of inquiry; and the only means of information which we have at hand is a brief history which those missionaries have published of their labours. In that history, which is now subject to a careful examination, we find that they speak of several instances in which individuals embraced Christianity and received baptism. And they inform us that at such a time they baptized one of the chiefs, and his *family;* and that, at another time, they baptized such a man, and *all his;* and again, another man, and *his household.* This is all the information they give. They mention, without explanation, the baptism of several persons, and their *households*, and so make *family baptisms* a noticeable circumstance in the history of their mission. Would not such a circumstance lead us to think it probable that they practised infant baptism? Be sure, it might be said, that they do not expressly mention the baptism of little children, and that all who belonged to those families may have been *adults*, and adult *believers*. This, I admit, would be possible. But would it be *probable?* Would those who do not baptize children be likely to speak in this manner? Should we not think it very singular to find accounts of *family baptisms* in a history of Baptist missions?"*

The apostles wrote and spoke of them just as the Jews would in reference to household proselyting; the idea of proselyting households among the Jews was perfectly familiar, by which they understood the bringing of the parents and children over to Judaism by circumcision, baptism, and sacrifice. The practice of discipling and baptizing households among the early Christians appears equally familiar, and equally common to record. We say

* Woods on Infant Baptism, pp. 81, 82.

therefore, that family baptisms, as recorded in the New Testament, exactly coincide with, and strongly corroborate, the doctrine of infant baptism.

4.) It has been urged that the paucity of instances in which the mention of household baptism occurs is a powerful presumption against the supposition that the apostles baptized infants. In reply, we can but remark with what amusing facility some people, who are earnest partisans, overrate the comparative importance of their favourite dogma. They have a hobby, and their great wonder is, that it is not mentioned in every page of holy writ. They conceive of nothing more important than the success of their darling theory, and they wonder how the Almighty could pass it by so lightly in his revelation. Some people seem to imagine that infant baptism ought, if true, to have been mentioned with great minuteness and particularity, and with many repetitions. But is this according to the analogy of the divine proceedings? By no means. "The sabbath was instituted at the creation: and though *weeks* are mentioned in the sacred history, the *sabbath* is not again mentioned till Moses: [a period of more than two thousand four hundred years.] Yet, how important the sabbath was considered in the sight of God is well known. Again, it is not mentioned from the time of Joshua till the reign of David, [a period of about four hundred years,] and yet, as says Dr. Humphrey, 'it will be admitted that, beyond all doubt, the pious judges of Israel remembered the sabbath-day to keep it holy.' Moreover, the Bible says nothing of *circumcision* from a little after Moses till the days of Jeremiah—a period of eight hundred years; yet, doubtless, circumcision was practised all the while.

"In like manner, the Missionary Herald, each volume of which is twenty times as large as the book of Acts, is now in progress of the thirty-sixth volume. In the whole of these, containing the journals of so many missionaries, narrating every important incident with so much minuteness, and continued for so many years, there are very few instances mentioned of infant baptism. I have not the means at hand of ascertaining how many; but though I have long been familiar with them, and have long observed the fact with some curiosity, and have specially examined not a little, I am not able to find, or to call to mind, more than a very few instances previously to the last two years. But we know the missionaries of the American Board are all Pedobaptists. The paucity of these records of infant baptisms in their letters does not prove that they do not baptize infants: we know they do; and once in a while the fact is mentioned, but it is rare, though their converts amount to many thousands."* It is unreasonable, therefore, to hold that if infant baptism be true, it must necessarily be a subject of frequent allusion in the history of the apostolic churches.

CHAPTER IV.

ADDITIONAL EVIDENCE,

DERIVED FROM STRONG COINCIDENCES, AND THE GENERAL FITNESS OF THE PRACTICE.

THERE are several points which merit attention in this stage of the argument, not so much from any direct bearing they may have on the question as furnishing independent proof, as on account of the strong corroborative force of evidence resulting from their natural fitness to the doctrine of infant baptism. After a doctrine or practice is proved to be Scriptural, it is but reasonable and fair that we should expect to find that natural fitness and adaptation to all the circumstances of the case that we so uniformly find in the works and dispensations of God. If we could clearly point out an unfitness and incongruity in it to the circumstances of the case, we are ready to concede that such incongruity would necessarily weaken, if not overthrow, all the arguments that might be brought forward in its support. Revelation is consistent with itself, and with all the other works of God, as well as fitted to the condition of man. God cannot contradict himself. He suits his dispensations to the condition and circumstances of man, no less than to the perfection of his own infinite and unerring mind. All that he has commanded is befitting the

* Rev. E. Hall on Baptism, pp. 168, 169.

occasion, and is in harmony with the other parts of the system. Now, if we could point out, in infant baptism, some strong irrelevancy to other parts of the divine economy, or to other parts of the duty of Christians, it must necessarily jostle all our confidence in the professed Scriptural authority for its observance,—we should, in such a case, be forced to conclude it was not of God. This will be readily admitted on all hands.

On the contrary, if, upon a more minute examination of all the kindred circumstances, we shall find that the practice perfectly coincides with all the circumstances of the case,—if we find that there is a natural fitness in the practice to the other parts of the Christian economy, and to the acknowledged duties of Christian parents and their relation to their offspring; I say, in such a case, the presumption in favour of its divine origin would be powerful, while no objection, either from reason or Scripture, could be urged against it. Thus, then, stands the question; and we ask, Is there any thing unsuitable to all the circumstances of the case in the practice of infant baptism?

1. We have already shown that infant baptism is suitable to the *moral state* of infants. On this there can be here no controversy. Infants belong to the "kingdom of heaven," and this constitutes the groundwork of a fitness for baptism. If they *are* members of the kingdom, it is unquestionably fit that they should be *declared* such by baptism.

2. It is in perfect harmony with the avowed object for which the Christian church was erected, that infants be baptized. What was the intention of God in having a church upon the earth? Let the apostle answer: "That he might gather together in one [family] ALL THINGS IN CHRIST, both which are in heaven, and which are on earth; even *in him*," Eph. i, 10. Now, the meaning of this is, that all who enjoy a saving interest in the atonement—who are justified in Christ—are to be collected in one community, at the head of which is Christ, and this community, or church, (for they are the same,) in connection with all other holy beings, constitutes God's family. The same idea is conveyed in chap. ii, 15, where Paul says that Christ abolished the ceremonial law, "for to make *in himself* of twain [that is, of Jews and Gentiles]

one new man," &c. The object was to gather all those who were truly justified in Christ, whether Jews or Gentiles, into one fraternity—one family, or church—of which Christ was to be the head, or chief. So it is said, also, in chap. iii, 15, that "of Christ the whole family [of holy beings] in heaven and earth is named." This doctrine is largely taught in the New Testament. The only question, therefore, that can possibly arise is, Do infants belong to Christ? Are they "in Christ?" Is he their spiritual Head? their Saviour? If so, it was the intention of God "to gather them together in one" family, even his church, with all other persons who belong to Christ. Although this is a valid, and, as we regard it, a positive argument, still we have chosen to place it under the chapter of *coincidences*. We say, then, that infant baptism is altogether suitable to, and befitting, the nature of the Christian church, and God's original design in forming it.

3. Infant baptism is in harmony with the analogy of Jewish church ordinances. We have already mentioned, somewhat at large, that Jehovah, from the first organization of the church, took infants into covenant relation to himself. We need but mention the fact here. The light of analogy is clear and overwhelming, and the practice of infant baptism is just what we might expect, from a knowledge of all the past.

4. There is a particular mention of children in Eph. vi, 1, that so strikingly coincides with, and seems to corroborate infant baptism, that I deem it worthy of a mention in this place. The apostle commands "children to obey their parents in the Lord." These children were so young as not to have received their elemental instructions, as appears from verse 4. Yet they were said to be "*in the Lord.*" For "how could they obey εν κυριω *in the Lord*, if they themselves were not εν κυριω *in the Lord?*"* The phrase, "*in the Lord*," is used to signify church membership in the New Testament. Thus, the "household of Narcissus were *in the Lord*;" Onesimus was "*in the Lord*;" "Andronicus and Junia were *in Christ*." Rom. xvi, 7, 11; Philem., ver. 16. The address of the apostle, in a strain of command and promise, would have been

* Mr. Knox's remarks on Infant Baptism, inserted at the close of Dr. A. Clarke's comment on Mark's Gospel.

unsuitable to any but such as were in covenant with God. If children were not thus in covenant, we see not how they could be addressed as a distinct class, in an apostolic epistle which was professedly addressed to Christians. Mr. Jerram well says, "If children are enumerated among the various classes to whom the epistle is addressed as constituting the church of Christ, they must have been members of it; and if members, they must have been baptized in their infancy."* It is certain that when this same command, "Honour thy father and thy mother," &c., was first issued, it was addressed to children in covenant with God. The "promise," also, which was appended, was a promise included in the covenant. See Exod. xx, 12; Deut. v, 16. Comp. Gen. xvii, 8. The remarks of Mr. Knox, above alluded to, are exactly in point:—"It must not escape attention," says he, "how exactly the sequel of the apostle's address accords with the commencement; the injunction being given as to those in express covenant, 'Honour thy father and thy mother; for this is the first commandment with promise.' Had those addressed been out of the Christian pale, this language would have been inapplicable. In that case they would have been *απηλλοτριωμενοι της πολιτειας του Ισραηλ* [*aliens from the commonwealth of Israel*]—therefore not within the range of the divine commandment; and *ξενοι των διαθηκων της επαγγελιας* [*strangers from the covenants of promise*]—consequently not warranted to assume an interest in the promise. As, then, the pressing of the sacred injunction supposes the persons on whom it is urged to be *συμπολιται των ἁγιων fellow-citizens with the saints*, their acknowledged interest in the promise proves them to be *οικειοι του Θεου of the household of God.*" Eph. ii, 12, 19.

This is not only an ingenious, but, so far as I can judge, a valid argument. If the reader can clearly comprehend it, (and it is not obscure,) he will scarcely fail to be strongly influenced by its corroboration of, and its perfect and strong coincidence with, the doctrine and practice of infant baptism.

5. The consecration of little children to God, in baptism, coincides with the feelings of pious parents. The

* Conversations on Infant Baptism, p. 63.

deep and sleepless solicitude of the devout parent for the spiritual salvation of his offspring finds a natural expression in this act; and his anxiety is soothed, and his gratitude awakened, by the reflection that God has affixed to his child the token of his love, and the pledge of his protection. This, indeed, is not advanced as an independent argument for infant baptism, but merely as an important coincidence; showing such an agreement between the practice and our sanctified affections, as proves that it involves nothing impious or absurd. "What pious parent, rightly apprehending the nature and design of infant baptism, would not acknowledge it to be a benevolent appointment of God? Who would not be gratified to find such a doctrine as that of infant baptism true? Who would not deem it a privilege to perform such a duty? And who would not regard it a subject of heartfelt grief to be deprived of such a privilege? It must surely be the wish of pious parents to give up their children to God; and to do this in the temple of God, where the prayers of many will ascend with their own to the Lord of heaven and earth in behalf of their children; publicly to apply to them a sacred rite which marks them for God; which signifies that they are placed in the school of Christ, and in the nursery of the church; that they are to enjoy faithful, parental instruction, and the affections and prayers of Christians; which signifies, too, that they are to come under the influence of a divine economy, fraught with the most gracious promises, and the most precious blessings; —to apply to children a sacred rite of such import, must be inexpressibly delightful to godly parents.... Pious parents, I repeat it, who rightly apprehend the doctrine of infant baptism, cannot but wish it true. And it would seem to me that their first inquiry must be, whether they may be *permitted* to devote their dear offspring thus to God, and to apply to them the seal of his gracious covenant. If nothing is found to *forbid* their doing this; especially if they have reason, from the word and providence of God, to believe that he would approve it; I should suppose they would embrace such a privilege with the sincerest gratitude and joy, and hasten to confer such a blessing on their children."*

* Woods on Infant Baptism, pp. 110, 111.

I am sorry to find Mr. Jewett, an anti-Pedobaptist, exceeding the bounds of fairness in his statement of this point. He has overrated it, and thus has done injustice, doubtless without design, to the argument. He says, "The principle on which the reasoning proceeds is this: *Whatever observance is pleasant to the feelings of good men ought to be regarded as an institution of God.*"* This is not the ground of the argument. It is too unguardedly expressed, and it does not develop the point aimed at by the Pedobaptists. The truth is, that the natural agreement of the practice of infant baptism with the best feelings of godly parents, points out a moral fitness in the practice that is calculated to remove any prejudice that may arise against it on the supposition of its impiety or absurdity, but does not prove that therefore it "ought to be regarded as an institution of God." The proof of this fact must, and does, rest on other ground of evidence.

6. Infant baptism is compatible with the obligation of parents to educate their children for the Lord.

This obligation is of a most solemn character, and is binding upon parents at the period of the very tender age of their offspring. As early as the child is capable of forming the most simple distinctions, or of becoming attracted by external perceptions, the parent should apply a method of tuition and cultivation suited to its age and capacity, and thenceforward aim, with unintermitted and tireless diligence, to prepare the child for the duties of religion here, and the enjoyments of glory hereafter. Nor is this course of instruction urged merely in anticipation of the child's moral destiny, but because it is itself now an heir of grace, and, as such, claims, on the score of present fitness, an education suited to its moral state. Children belong to the kingdom of heaven, and therefore it is meet that they should be early dedicated to God. The philosophy of the human mind, and the Scriptures of truth, inculcate upon the parent the duty and importance of an early consecration of the child to God, and a subsequent corresponding course of instruction. If the child is a moral being—is in a state of grace—is to be, from early infancy, trained for religion—the practice of devoting it to God by baptism seems the most consonant to all these

* Mode and Subjects of Baptism, p. 73.

circumstances of any thing conceivable. It seems a most suitable auxiliary and attendant of parental obligation and duties, by yielding to them a divine sanction and encouragement. The Bible is explicit and abundant in its inculcations touching the duty of parents. Very anciently God commanded his people that the words which he delivered to them should be in their hearts: "And thou shalt teach them diligently, saith God, to thy children, and shalt talk of them when thou sittest in thine house, and when thou walkest by the way, and when thou liest down, and when thou risest up," Deut. vi, 7. David says, "God established a testimony in Jacob, and appointed a law in Israel, which he commanded our fathers, that they should make them known to their children; that the generation to come might know them, even the children which should be born, who should arise and declare them to their children; that they might set their hope in God, and not forget the works of God, but keep his commandments," Psalm lxxviii, 5–7. The obligation of parents to bring up their children according to the religion of the Bible was fully understood by the Jews. The wise man says, "Train up a child in the way he should go;" and adds, for the encouragement of parents, "and when he is old he will not depart from it." Houbigant renders it, "*Initiate, instruct, catechise; lay down the first rudiments,*" &c.

"—— Now pliantly inure
Your mind to virtue, while your heart is pure;
Now suck in wisdom; for the vessel well
With liquor seasoned long retains the smell."

So said a heathen. The Hebrew of this passage reads, "Initiate a child at the opening (the mouth) of his path." "חֲנֹךְ *hanak*, which we translate *train up*, or *initiate*, signifies also *dedicate;* and is often used to denote the *consecrating* any thing, house, or person, to the service of God. [So it is used Deut. xx, 5; 1 Kings viii, 63; 2 Chron. vii, 5.] *Dedicate*, therefore, in the first instance, your child to God; and *nurse*, *teach*, and *discipline* him as God's child, whom he has intrusted to your care. These things observed and illustrated by your own conduct, the child (you have God's word for it) will never depart from the path of life."*

* Dr. A. Clarke's Comment. *in loc.*

And thus Paul commands, Eph. vi, 4, "Bring them up in the nurture and admonition of the Lord;" or, as Mr. Wesley more properly has it, "*in the instruction and discipline of the Lord*—both in Christian knowledge and practice." Dr. Robinson says, "*παιδεια* Κυριου, that is, *such training as the Lord approves.*"*

Thus stand the oracles of truth in regard to the religious education of children. Such is the duty of parents, and such their high responsibility, with respect to the early training of their offspring, and their subsequent character and destiny. Great is the authority which God has vested in the parent, in order to secure the moral instruction and happiness of his offspring; and most sacredly and awfully is the obligation of filial submission and fidelity guarded by the word of God, with an unerring aim at the same unspeakable good. Anciently the parent had absolute power of life and death over the child; and long after this power was taken from the parent and vested in the civil magistrate, it was said, "Whoso curseth father or mother, let him die the death." How solemn are these considerations! How strict and inexorable are the injunctions of Scripture upon parent and child! And thus it must of necessity be, so long as the temporal and eternal interests of the child are so largely lodged in the power of the parent, and so deeply involved in the discipline and instructions of childhood. By the peculiar constitution of our nature, if it be not a necessary result of the structure of mind itself, early impressions constantly grow with our growth, strengthen with our strength, enlarge with the mind's development, and mature with our years. The long and faithful discipline and instruction of childhood and youth, by a wise arrangement of Providence, fits us for the duties of social life, and submission to the authorities of civil government, and prepares us, by the habit of wholesome restraint upon our passions, and salutary influences upon our hearts, "to receive," in after-life, "with meekness, the ingrafted word, which is able to save our souls." How suitable, then, to these parental duties, and to these filial obligations, is baptism! How appropriate for the parent thus to "*dedicate* his child to God, in the opening of his way!" How appropos to all the circum-

* Robinson's Lex., art. *παιδεια*.

stances of the case! How effectually must it remind the parent of his duty, and how tenderly must it affect his heart, to know that with prayer and devout supplications he has offered up his little one to the Lord in baptism! And this dedication, so concordant to the moral state and the prospective destiny of the child, shall be a divine pledge of spiritual blessings, which he has promised to the seed of the righteous. But if it were otherwise,—if there were an entire want of correspondence between infant baptism, and the duties, and obligations, and pious solicitudes of godly parents, this circumstance certainly would go far—perhaps be of itself sufficient—to invalidate all argument in favour of the ordinance. Such an incongruity, however, never occurs in any of the works or dispensations of God. "It would avail little to say, in the way of objection, that parents would be under all these obligations, and would have sufficient motives to faithfulness, without such an ordinance as baptism. The obvious design of baptism is, to cause these obligations to be felt *more deeply* and *constantly* than they would otherwise be, and to give *greater efficacy* to these motives than they would otherwise have. The influence of public rites and observances has been acknowledged in all ages, both in civil and religious concerns. In our own country, and in other countries, they are kept up, in order to perpetuate the principles of civil government. Among the Israelites they were established for the purpose of giving to one generation after another a knowledge, and a lively impression, of the principles and laws of their religion. The human mind is so constituted, that it is very doubtful whether the truths of religion could be inculcated and impressed with the necessary efficacy without the help of public rites and observances. The utility of the Lord's supper, which is generally acknowledged to be great, rests on the very same principle as that which gives importance to infant baptism. Thus it was also with the utility of the passover and circumcision. And we may as well say that the principles of religion might have been effectually taught, and impressed, and transmitted from one generation to another among the posterity of Abraham, without the passover, or circumcision, or any of their sacred rites; and that the principles of the Christian religion might be

effectually taught and impressed, and its motives rendered sufficiently powerful, without the Lord's supper, as to say that the influence of such a rite as infant baptism is unnecessary, and that parents will be as likely to feel their obligations, and attend to their duties, without it, as with it. The experience of the world is in favour of visible signs and tokens, of public rites and observances. The human mind requires them, as means of inculcating moral and religious truth. To undervalue them would be a discredit to our understanding; and to neglect them, an injury to our moral feelings,"* and, we may add, a reflection upon the wisdom of the past dispensations of God.

7. Infant baptism is suited to the import and ends of the ordinance of Christian baptism.

It is strange that on so plain a subject as the proper import of baptism there should have been so much diversity of opinion. I cannot see why men should dispute with so much pertinacity over this subject as has been exhibited by many authors. Verily the whole subject is comprised within a limited compass. The difficulty arises wholly from a misapprehension of the phraseology of Scripture; in applying terms which are used in hortatory style, and for the purpose of moral suasion, as if they were elaborated with critical precision and dull correctness, to fit a system of didactical divinity. Baptism is frequently alluded to in the New Testament for the purpose of deducing an argument, or of sanctioning an argument for the fidelity and holiness of Christians, and in such a popular strain of exhortation we must not look for that precision in the use of words, or that critical order and exactness of ideas, as we expect to find in a close argument, or a set treatise. I do not make these remarks with a view to unhinge the mind of the reader, and to create the impression that the language of Scripture is indefinite; on the contrary, I urge them only on the ground of just criticism. The Baptists insist that baptism is "everywhere regarded as *a public profession of faith* in our Lord Jesus Christ"—that by baptism we take upon ourselves a voluntary and "sacred obligation, in the presence of God, to maintain a good conscience, to be watchful against sin, and to strive after holiness." They hold also that "the New Testament

* Dr. Woods on Infant Baptism, pp. 166, 167.

represents baptism to be emblematical of the death and resurrection of Christ;" and also to be "significant of the belief of the subject of it, *in the resurrection of the body*," &c. And it is asked, "What avails all this fulness of meaning, this richness and preciousness of instruction in the gospel ordinance, if it is to be thrown away upon unconscious infancy? But if *only those who believe* are proper recipients of the ordinance, then indeed can we perceive it to be instructive, impressive, and delightful."*

These views, which are common to Baptist authors, we conceive to result from an erroneous construction of the language of Scripture. The truth is, baptism imports inward purity, and is an external token that the subject belongs to the covenant of grace. In this sense it most fitly applies to infants; and where those persons who have been baptized in infancy attain to years and understanding, and are taught the nature of baptism, nothing can be more natural for them to infer, or obvious, in fact, than that their baptism imports an obligation of voluntary and perpetual devotion to God. To the infant, as to the adult, it primarily denotes that the subject is interested in the gracious provisions of the covenant; and from this generic and primary sense it is easy, and natural, and proper, to make specific deductions to sanction duties that belong to adult age, in an exhortation, or a moral inculcation addressed to an adult. All this would not at all disparage the entire and perfect fitness of baptism to infants.

Take the case of circumcision. That it had a spiritual meaning—that it imported to the adult, "the putting off the body of the sins of the flesh"—I see not how any one can deny. Yet it was applicable to infants. It denoted entire devotion to God: "The Lord will circumcise thy heart, and the heart of thy seed, to love the Lord thy God with all thy heart." To Abraham it was a "seal of the righteousness of faith." Yet infants were circumcised. Could they "love the Lord their God with all their heart?" Could they believe? They were in a state of grace, but it could not be said with propriety that they "loved the Lord"—that they had "put off the body of sin"—or that they believed. But the fact that they were subjects of grace; that they belonged to the covenant; was enough

* Jewett on Baptism, pp. 86–89.

to constitute a fitness for circumcision; and afterward, in adult age, it was easy to perceive that circumcision bound them to a holy life. Nor were their obligations to holiness, arising from their circumcision, less sacred, or less obvious and binding, because their circumcision was performed in infancy. So is it with baptism. The analogy holds perfectly good, and forms an unanswerable refutation of all such objections as those above mentioned. (See my Treatise on the Mode, &c., of Baptism, chap. x.)

It is strange, indeed, that the Protestant Episcopal Church should have heedlessly rushed into this very error, namely, that baptism is a profession of faith; and then have trusted to the strength of their doctrine of sponsors in baptism for their escape from the absurd consequences of this admission. Bishop Hopkins, of the diocess of Vermont, says,—

"But how does this requisition of repentance and faith before baptism apply to the case of infants? We answer, that it does not apply at all; *for infants are baptized upon the repentance and faith of others*, under the solemn obligation, nevertheless, of exercising both these graces, so soon as they attain to years of sufficient discretion... We find, then, that, according to the doctrine of the [Protestant E.] Church, baptism is the ordinance appointed by the Lord for admitting sinners into his kingdom, as his regenerate, adopted children ... *that in the case of infants they are adopted through the repentance and faith of those who present them to the Redeemer; which is available before God, until they are capable of repenting and believing for themselves.*"*

Nor is the Protestant E. Church alone in this belief. Others have followed the same phantom. It were easy to quote authors, but we adduce but one, and we select him from the modern Calvinistic school. Dr. Miller says,—

"After all, the whole weight of the objection,† in this case, is founded on an entire forgetfulness of the main principle of the Pedobaptist system. It is forgotten that

* Primitive Church compared with the Protestant Episcopal Church, pp. 23, 24.

† The objection which the author is answering is, "That infants are not capable of those spiritual acts or exercises which the New Testament requires in order to baptism."

in every case of infant baptism faith is required, and, if the parents be sincere, is actually exercised. *But it is required of the parents, and not of the children.* So that, if the parent really present his child in faith, the spirit of the ordinance is entirely met and answered."* Does our author mean to say, that faith is required of the parents *in behalf* of the children?

We would seriously inquire what this vicarious repentance and faith mean? Is it assumed that infants have need of repentance and faith in order to salvation, and that, being incapable of performing these acts themselves, their performance by proxy becomes acceptable to God? What, then, becomes of those children who have no sponsors or pious parents to repent for them? Or are repentance and faith only necessary to baptism, and *not* necessary to the salvation of the infant? Besides, how is it that a being is capable of sinning, who, at the same time, has not the constitutional faculties necessary to repentance? Have infants sinned, that they need to repent? Or do they need some one to repent of Adam's sin, and then transfer such repentance to their account?

But all this theory is singularly at variance with God's word, and the principles of his moral government. "The soul that sinneth, IT shall die." There is no sinning by proxy, and there is no repenting by proxy. God requires repentance of no being in the universe but the sinner, and he will accept of no repentance, or faith, at the hand of any other being in lieu of the sinner. This idea of the transfer of moral virtues is as absurd in philosophy as it has ever been monstrous in divinity. See Ezek. xviii, 2–4. It is unaccountable that thinking men should have rushed into these delusions—that they should not have scanned the philosophy of baptism with a happier discrimination. One would suppose that their own absurdities would react upon the mind so as to produce conviction of the truth. Baptism, it is said, imports "a profession of faith," "is emblematical of a burial and resurrection," is a profession of "faith in the resurrection of the dead," and signifies the blessings of "pardon," "adoption," and "resurrection to life."† And what else? In thus attempting to prove every

* On Infant Baptism, p. 40.

† See Dick's Theol., vol. ii, pp. 387–389, and Willett on Baptism.

thing, we prove nothing. Baptism truly stands connected with many of these blessings, in the practical exhortations and admonitions of the apostles. But it is easy to perceive that all these significations are deduced from that one pervading, original, generical idea,—*the complete regeneration of the inward man.* We do not, however, believe that baptism ever imports a burial and resurrection; and as to its denoting faith in the resurrection of the dead, founded on that obscure passage, 1 Cor. xv, 29, it is enough to say that *οι βαπτιζομενοι ὑπερ των νεκρων* (translated, *who are baptized for the dead*) is too dubious, as to its real application, to be pressed into this argument.

How, then, can baptism be made to signify, primarily, any of the means, accidents, or consequences of salvation? The moment this liberty is taken, the imaginations and conceits of men are permitted to take their range, and the simplicity, beauty, and certainty of the import of the ordinance are impaired. But if baptism import regeneration—inward purity, and conformity to God—if it be an outward sign of this moral state—then, manifestly it is as applicable to infants as to adults, and cannot be any specific token or profession of "faith." It is true, faith is implied in this moral state in the case of every adult, and so also are repentance, godly sorrow for sin, and prayer. And faith is no more necessary to the justification of the adult sinner, than prayer, confession of sin, and godly sorrow. Why, then, in the nature of the case, should baptism import, distinctively and exclusively, one of these exercises any more than the other? But is there not the veriest absurdity in the supposition that baptism is a "public profession of faith?"—that applying water to a person, in any form, should be made to represent *an act of the mind?* Water is a natural and fit emblem of *purity*, and moral purity may imply, as it does in the case of adults, an act, or acts of the mind; but is water a natural and fit emblem of any mental act or exercise? It has never been regarded so, and the supposition is too preposterous and absurd to be harboured for a moment. Faith is an act of the mind. It is not in itself a virtue, nor is the profession of it in itself a virtue, but a relative virtue is ascribed to each. They do not, therefore, either of them, deserve to be the grand original, emblematical idea

of baptism. Moreover, faith does not need a separate and solemn ordinance of religion for the mere purpose of *declaring* it to the world. Such a profession is more appropriately made in another form;—" With the *mouth* confession is made unto salvation," and by the "*works*" faith can be clearly attested. But relationship to the church of God, claimed and conceded on the ground of being in a state of grace and reconciliation with God, is not so attested by the appointment of God.

If our opponents use faith as synonymous with regeneration, why, then, the controversy is at an end. It is the *thing* we contend for, *not* the name. And how explicit is the evidence of Scripture on this point! Take a perfectly parallel case. Paul says, "Abraham believed God, and it was counted unto him for righteousness.... And he received the sign of circumcision, *a* SEAL *of the* RIGHTEOUSNESS *of the faith* which he had." Rom. iv, 3, 11. But why was not circumcision a "sign" and "seal" of *faith* by which he became righteous? This would have been in exact accordance with the hypothesis we are opposing. But God ordained it to be a sign and seal of *righteousness;* which, in Abraham, was obtained through "faith," but in infants is wrought by the agency of God *without* faith. We say, then, that faith is made prominent in the New Testament, in connection with adult baptism, because with all adults it is an indispensable prerequisite to baptism—being, with such, a prominent condition of regeneration. It is its connection with regeneration that gives it all its importance as a prerequisite to baptism. If, therefore, regeneration could be obtained without faith, baptism would be equally appropriate, and faith might be altogether dispensed with as a prerequisite to the consecrating rite. It is by making faith to assume the importance and character of regeneration that it is made, *per se*, a prerequisite to baptism, whereas it is made, in fact, a prerequisite only by circumstances. It is insisted upon, not on its own account, but solely in view of its relative importance, as a condition of regeneration.

CHAPTER V.

HISTORICAL ARGUMENT.

SECTION I.

1. It becomes important to inquire into the ancient usage of the Christian church in reference to baptizing infants; not because this argument is fundamental in the nature of the case, but because of its strong collateral bearing upon the point. We go to the records of church history, not to prove the primary obligation of infant baptism,—this must be proved from the Bible,—but to prove its *antiquity*—its contiguity to the age of the apostles. And if it can be clearly and satisfactorily shown to have been the universal practice of the Christian church from the very times of the apostles,—if it were a doctrine of primitive Christianity,—the presumption is strong, and amounts to evidence almost irresistible, that the apostles themselves authorized the practice. We readily concede that mere antiquity cannot prove any doctrine to be true, or any practice to be binding on us. But if we should find a practice which a candid and close examination of Scripture would lead us to consider obligatory; which at least was not forbidden by the letter or spirit of revelation; and which had been the uniform practice of the church from the earliest times; which the church generally regarded as an apostolic commandment; which many of their most learned doctors had directly declared to be such; which was not contradicted by any heresy or schism—any individual or body of men—for one thousand years after the apostles; which does not necessarily involve an absurdity; I say, if the apostolic antiquity of a practice could be proved under such circumstances, it would be perhaps unreasonable, if it were even possible, for a person to deny its apostolic authority. This is the case with infant baptism, only the Scriptural argument is far more decisive and satisfactory than is here stated.

The force of an argument derived from tradition in support of any doctrine of religion, and the circumstances under which such an argument becomes admissible, are clearly defined by Bishop Henry U. Onderdonk, of Pennsylvania, in his charge to the clergy. The principles which he lays down are the following:—"1. If any tradition be in anywise contrary to Scripture, it is void; the greater authority cancelling the less when in opposition to it. 2. If there be an absolutely unquestioned tradition, clearly traceable to the apostolic age, the matter of which is asserted in Scripture also, the authority in the case must be accounted twofold; that of the written word, however, being from its nature the more excellent of the two. 3. If there be an absolutely unquestioned tradition, the matter of which is not found in Scripture, or believed not to be there, yet in no degree contrary to Scripture, and clearly traceable to the apostolic age, it must be regarded as having such authority without Scripture as belongs to the case.* Of this, the substitution of the Lord's day for the old sabbath will probably be deemed the best example, by those who think that they do not find Scriptural warrant for the change," &c.

If, then, a doctrine be sustained by an unquestionable tradition from the apostles, and if that doctrine be not contradicted by Scripture, but on the contrary strong intimations are given of its truth therein, although it may not be expressly declared, that doctrine is to be considered as possessing suitable and adequate authority. Yet infant baptism has far superior authority to this, as the Bible argument is more clear and satisfactory than here stated.

This, then, is the nature of the argument we propose to consider in this chapter. We adduce the testimony of the Christian fathers and early councils to prove the fact of the antiquity of infant baptism; and having fixed the date of the practice coeval with the times of the apostles, we then advance from this ascertained fact to the argument, namely, if it was handed down to us *from the very times* of the apostles, all the circumstances of the case combine to prove that it was delivered to the first churches *by apostolic authority*.

* We cannot follow the bishop in this last particular, if we understand him. We do not believe any doctrine or duty, further than relates to church government, is fully sustained by the sole authority of tradition, however "unquestionable," joined to the mere silence of Scripture. Mr. Cruden on this point is very clear. See his Concordance, Article TRADITION.

2. It will be seen that the testimony of Irenæus, in the following section, turns upon the supposition that *renascor, to be regenerated*, means, or implies, *to be baptized.* This, to an uninformed reader, who knows nothing of the use of these words in ancient times, may appear unwarrantable, and may, at first sight, tend to prejudice our argument with such. It is, therefore, proper to state, in this place, that *regeneration* was often used by the fathers to signify *baptism.* It should be recollected that the Scriptures use a language in some sense calculated to bring about such a *usus* of terms. Jesus Christ has said, "*ἐαν μη τις γεννηθη ἐξ ὑδατος και πνευματος except any person be generated*, or *born by water and the Spirit*," &c., John iii, 5. Paul calls Christian baptism, "the *washing of regeneration*," and says we are saved "*δια λουτρου παλιγγενεσιας by the washing of regeneration*, and the renewing of the Holy Spirit," Titus iii, 5. So the Jews, in conformity to the same law of language, called the water employed in ceremonial rites, the "water of purification," of "separation," &c. The Jews, at the time of Christ, were accustomed to call that proselyte who had been baptized, "born again." The proselyte was required to renounce all his former customs, and even his relations, his parents, and friends, and to assume new ones, more compatible with his new religious profession and character. He was baptized in token of having put off all these, and of having been purified from them. The change was great; it was complete and universal, and they called it "*the new birth*," or *regeneration.* So says Maimonides, "The Gentile that is made a proselyte . . . behold, he is like a child *new born.*" So the Christian fathers regarded a person *baptized* as being *newly born;* and this also is an appellation given to disciples in the New Testament. So Peter says, "*As new born babes*," &c. It is easy then to perceive how the early church came to use *regeneration* so as to include, by that term, water *baptism.*

Justin Martyr, in his first Apology, describing the manner of making Christian disciples, says, concerning their baptism,—

"We bring them to some place where there is water, *και τροπον αναγεννησεως ὁν και ἡμεις αυτοι ανεγεννηθημεν, αναγεννωνται and they are regenerated by the same way of regeneration by which we were regenerated;* for they are washed with water [that is, baptized] in the name of God the Father and Lord of all things, and of our Saviour Jesus Christ, and of the Holy Spirit. For Christ says, 'Except ye be regenerated, you cannot enter into the kingdom of heaven.'.... And that we shall obtain forgiveness of the sins in which we have lived, *by* or *in water,* [εν τω ὑδατι,] there is invoked over him that has a mind to be *regenerated* [αναγενηθηναι] the name of God, the Father and Lord of all things.... and this washing [or baptism] is called the enlightening," &c.

Irenæus says, "When Christ gave to his apostles the commission of *regenerating* unto God, (regenerationis in Deum,) he said unto them, 'Go and teach all nations, *baptizing* them in the name of the Father, and of the Son, and of the Holy Spirit.'"

Gregory Nazianzen says to the baptized person, to deter him from falling back into sin, "*ουκ ουσης δευτερας αναγεννησεως* there is not another *regeneration* afterward to be had, though it be sought with never so much crying and tears;" and yet grants, in the very next words, that repentance may be exercised after baptism; but he means that *baptism* is not to be repeated.

St. Austin being asked, whether a parent carrying his child, which had been baptized, to the heathen sacrifices, does thereby obliterate the benefit of his baptism, says, "An infant does never lose the grace of Christ, which he has once received, but by his own sinful deeds, if when he grows up he proves so wicked: for then he will begin to have sins of his own, quæ non regeneratione auferantur, sed alid curatione sanentur, which are not removed by *regeneration,* [*baptism,*] but will be healed by some other method."

St. Hierom, discoursing in praise of virginity, "Christ was born of a virgin, and *regenerated* [that is, *baptized*] by a virgin;" alluding to John Baptist, who was unmarried.

St. Austin calls the persons by whose means infants are *baptized,* those by whom they are *regenerated; cos per quos renascuntur.**

Mr. Whiston, a learned Baptist, says, "That regenera-

* Wall's History of Infant Baptism, part i, cap. ii, sec. 4, 5, and cap. iii, iv.

tion is here, [in John iii, 5,] and elsewhere, (generally, if not constantly,) used with relation to baptismal regeneration, is undeniable;" and adds, "not as supposing the bare outward ceremony to deserve that name."*

"The ancient doctors of the church," says Dr. Waterland, "in explaining regeneration, were wont to consider the *spirit* and the *water* under the lively emblem of a *conjugal* union, as the two *parents;* and the new-born Christian as the offspring of both. . . . Whatever aptness or justness there may or may not be in the *similitude*, yet one thing is certain, that the ancients took *baptism* into their notion of *regeneration*."†

In accordance with this sense the reader is to understand the quotation from Irenæus, to be hereafter given.

Dr. Gale, in his Reflections upon Mr. Wall's History of Infant Baptism, has attempted to evade the force of this, by showing that regeneration does not always mean baptism, and also that it is not used in the above particular instances as a perfect synonym of baptism.‡ But it is easy to perceive that he mistook the real question, and Mr. Wall has not failed to discover his vulnerable positions.§ The question is not, whether regeneration *is* baptism, according to the sense of the fathers? but, whether regeneration necessarily *includes* or *implies* baptism? Dr. Gale, in assuming the former, has missed the mark, and Mr. Wall himself is not always sufficiently careful to keep clear distinctions. Dr. Waterland's statement above is as definite and satisfactory as any thing I have ever met with. The fathers *included* baptism in their idea of *regeneration*, but the two terms are not synonymous.

SECTION II.

We now proceed to lay before the reader a just view of the argument for infant baptism, as derived from the testimony of the Christian fathers, during the first four hundred years of the Christian era.‖

* Primitive Infant Baptism, p. 7. † On Regeneration, p. 9.

‡ Reflections, &c., pp. 481–483, 514, &c.

§ Defence, &c., p. 363, &c.

‖ As the following summary of the argument from church history is chiefly derived from Mr. Wall's well-known and valuable History

1. Justin Martyr, who was a learned Samaritan, was converted to Christianity about A. D. 133, and wrote about forty years after the death of St. John, who was the last of the apostles. Justin says, "We also, who by him have had access to God, have not received this carnal circumcision, but the spiritual circumcision, which Enoch, and those like him, observed. And we have received it by baptism, by the mercy of God, because we were sinners: and it is enjoined upon all persons to receive it in the same way." Again: "We are circumcised by baptism, with Christ's circumcision."* Again: "Many persons among us, of sixty and seventy years old, of both sexes, who were *discipled* (εμαθητευθεσαν) to Christ in their childhood, (εκ παιδων,) do continue uncorrupted."†

The testimony of this most ancient father may be thus summed up:—

1.) He maintains that baptism answers to circumcision. This admission, especially in a dialogue with a Jew, such as Trypho was, and with a professed intention of justifying the Christians in their neglect of Jewish circumcision, can be regarded in no other light than that of an acknowledgment of infant baptism. If baptism succeed to circumcision; if it be fitly called *τη περιτομη του Χριστου the Christian circumcision*, or, as Justin here calls it, *πνευματικην*

of Infant Baptism, I deem it proper, for the sake of those who may not be acquainted with this celebrated work, to give the following notice of it. Dr. Wall is regarded as a very correct and judicious historian. He has written with great ability, candour, and impartiality.

"On Feb. 9, 1705, the clergy of England, assembled in general convention, 'ordered, that the thanks of this house be given to Mr. Wall, vicar of Shoreham, in Kent, for the learned and excellent book he hath lately written concerning infant baptism, and that a committee be appointed to acquaint him with the same.' Dr. Atterbury, a leading member in said convention, says, 'that the History of Infant Baptism was a book, for which the author deserved the thanks, not of the English clergy alone, but of all churches.' Mr. Whiston, also, a very learned man, well acquainted with the writings of the fathers of the four first centuries, and a professed Baptist, in his address to the people of that denomination, declares to them, 'that Dr. Wall's History of Infant Baptism, as to facts, appeared to him most accurately done, and might be depended on by the Baptists themselves.'"—*Memoirs of his Life*, part ii, p. 461; quoted by Dr. Ridgeley, Body of Divinity, vol. iv, p. 209, *note*. See also Advertisement to Mr. Cotton's edition of Dr. Wall's History, &c., 4 vols., 8vo. Oxford.

* Dialogue with Trypho. † Apologia Prima.

περιτομην *spiritual circumcision,* it is plain that its application to infants must be similar now to what it anciently was.

But it must be distinctly kept in mind that Justin is not speaking here either of *external* circumcision, or of *external* baptism, exclusively, but of the *spiritual import* of these ordinances. He speaks of them in their emblematical sense, but of course the external ordinance is implied. If this be remembered, the reader will find a ready solution of all the learned and laboured objections of Dr. Gale.* On this point Mr. Wall's expressions appear sufficiently guarded, who says, that in this place, from Justin, and also in Col. ii, 11, 12, circumcision "refers both to the *inward* and *outward* part of baptism;" whereof the *inward* part is done *without hands:* and accordingly the ancients were wont to call baptism, περιτομην αχειροποιητον "*the circumcision made without hands.*"†

2.) Justin predicates the *necessity* of baptism, of the common corruption of our natures.... This is more clearly shown in other parts of his writings. This is not only a primitive, but it is a Scriptural doctrine; and it argues equally strong in favour of infant, as for adult baptism.

Here, however, the reader must remember, that the point is not whether Justin conceived a right opinion of the necessity of infant baptism, but the fact that he had such an opinion, argues equally in favour of infant, as of adult baptism; and it is the *fact* of infant baptism, and not its *reasonableness,* that we are now proving.

3.) He expressly declares that many persons in his day, of sixty and seventy years old, were made disciples in childhood. The word rendered *made disciples,* is the same as in Matt. xxviii, 19, where our Saviour commands the apostles to go "*make disciples* of all nations, baptizing them," &c. This shows that children were discipled, (and, if so, baptized of course,) as well as adults; and these persons of whom Justin speaks, being now sixty and seventy years old, might have been baptized by the apostles themselves, as they certainly were baptized long before John died. We merely add, in reference to this

* Reflections on Mr. Wall's History of Infant Baptism, pp. 395, 396, 466–477.

† History of Infant Baptism, part i, cap. ii, sec. 2.

father, in the words of Mr. Waddington, "As Justin flourished only one century after the preaching of Christ, we are not extending the value of tradition beyond its just limits, when we consider his opinions as receiving some additional weight from their contiguity to the apostolical times."*

2. Irenæus was bishop of Lyons (in France) about A. D. 178, and consequently flourished about seventy years after the death of the apostle John. Some suppose he was born four years previous to the death of John, but it was not far from the time of that event, either way, that we are to reckon the date of his birth. Irenæus, though afterward bishop of a western church, was educated in Asia, where St. John had lived and died. In early life he was accustomed to hear Polycarp converse of the apostle John. Polycarp was John's companion, and was appointed by that apostle to be bishop of the church at Smyrna; (see Rev. ii, 8.) In his old age Irenæus speaking of Polycarp, says, "I remember the things that were done then better than I do those of later times, so that I could describe the place where he sat, and his going out, and coming in; his manner of life, his features, his discourse to the people concerning the conversation he had had with John, [the apostle,] and others that had seen our Lord; how he rehearsed their discourses, and what he had heard them that were eye-witnesses of the Word of life, say of our Lord, and of his miracles and doctrine: all agreeable to the Scriptures."† Such was the proximity of this father to the apostles and to Christ. The passage we quote from him is the following:—

"For he [Christ] came to save all persons by himself: all, I say, *qui per eum* RENASCUNTUR *in Deum; infantes, et parvulos, et pueros, et juvenes, et seniores; who by him are* REGENERATED [that is, *baptized*] *to God; infants, and little ones, and children, and youth, and elder persons*."‡

To appreciate the force of this passage the reader must remember,—

1.) The Christian fathers often used the word *regeneration* as synonymous with, or as including, *baptism*. This

* History of the Church, p. 81.

† Wall's History of Infant Baptism, p. 21. See Euseb. Hist., lib. v, cap. xix.

‡ Second Book against Heresies.

no one will doubt who is acquainted with their writings, or who candidly looks at the evidence already adduced in its support, in a previous section of this chapter. It was a common mode of speaking of baptism, and we are authorized, therefore, to take the testimony of Irenæus in the case, as positive.

2.) Consider his proximity to the apostles, and how little probability there is that he has, in this matter, deviated from their rule.

3.) What he says, we are to receive, not as his private opinion merely, but as the doctrine of the church in his time. His private opinion might be more easily questioned, as to its truth or propriety, as he was but a fallible man, though a firm Christian. But his testimony concerning what the church in his age believed, is above impeachment, and cannot be questioned. And it is to this point that we especially direct the attention of the reader.*

3. Tertullian flourished about one hundred years after the apostles. He was made presbyter of the church at Carthage about A. D. 192. He was a man of very irregular and contradictory principles and habits, possessing a sour, monastic spirit. "Tertullian is described by Jerome as 'a man of eager and violent temper;' and he appears to have possessed the usual vice of such a temperament—inconstancy. The same is the character of his writings; they contain some irregular eloquence; much confidence of assertion, and a mixture of good with very bad reasoning. He wrote many tracts against heretics, and then

* The reader will be astonished to learn, that on this single quotation, from Irenæus, Dr. Gale has expended forty-one octavo pages in "Reflections," with a view to wrest it from the hands of Pedobaptists; and Mr. Wall has devoted no less than eighty-four pages, octavo, in his "Defence," in order to restore the passage to the Pedobaptist cause. It will not be expected of me to give even a syllabus of the arguments *pro* and *con* in this small treatise. Mr. Gale, apprized that this passage from Irenæus is important, attempts to invalidate its force, 1. By denying its *genuineness;* 2. By asserting that *regeneration* does not *always* mean, or imply, *baptism.* 3. That *infants*, according to the *usus* of the term by Irenæus, are persons under ten years of age. The arguments on either side are too lengthy to be cited, even in a condensed form, with any satisfaction to the reader. Those who wish to see the subject exhausted, and more than exhausted, and, withal, the entire force of the passage in favour of Pedobaptism fully vindicated, can consult Mr. Wall's Defence, &c., pp. 321–405; Hist., p. 77, &c.

adopted the opinions of the least rational of all heretics, the Montanists, [so called from one Montanus, who gave himself out to be the Paraclete, or Comforter, promised by our Saviour.] But in spite of many imperfections, his genius, his zeal, and his industry, place him at the head of the Latin fathers of that period. His moral writings must have been eminently serviceable to converts who had been educated with no fixed principles of morality; and his 'Apology' is among the most valuable monuments of early Christianity."* I have said thus much for the reader's better understanding of Tertullian's character, and for his better appreciation of his testimony which is to follow. I must add, moreover, that Tertullian imbibed an error, which now began more than ever to prevail in the church, and which gave a peculiar turn to his notions on infant baptism. The error which I refer to was, that baptism removed all previous guilt, and hence, as the newly baptized person was deemed pure, and fitted to enter paradise, so the practice of deferring baptism until just before death grew to be prevalent. Tertullian was a strenuous advocate of this practice, as will appear in the quotation we shall make from his writings, and yet, with characteristic inconsistency, he elsewhere as vehemently urges baptism without delay. He says,—

"But they whose duty it is to administer baptism are to know that it must not be given rashly. 'Give to every one that asketh thee,' has its proper subject, and relates to alms-giving: but that command rather is to be here considered, 'Give not that which is holy unto dogs, neither cast your pearls before swine.' And that [command also,] 'Lay hands suddenly on no man, neither be partaker of other men's faults.' Therefore, according to every one's condition and disposition, and also their age, the delaying of baptism is more profitable, especially in the case of little children. For what need is there that the godfathers should be brought into danger? because they may either fail of their promise by death, or they may be mistaken by a child's proving of wicked disposition. Our Lord says, indeed, 'Do not forbid them to come to me.' Therefore let them come when they are grown up: let them come when they understand: when they are instructed whither

* Waddington's Church History, p. 52.

it is that they come; let them be made Christians when they can know Christ. What need their guiltless age make such haste to the forgiveness of sins? Men will proceed very warily in worldly things: and he that should not have earthly goods committed to him, yet may he have heavenly. Let them know how to desire this salvation, that you may appear to have given to one that asketh."*

In regard to this testimony of Tertullian, the reader will notice,—

1.) The simple fact that he speaks of infant baptism as a well-known and general practice in his day—proves it to have been instituted long before his day. If Tertullian opposed infant baptism, then it is incontestible that infant baptism existed. This is the best kind of proof we could possibly have. But if the practice of infant baptism existed before the days of Tertullian, that is, within less than one hundred years after the death of the apostle John, when, we ask, did it commence? and with whom did it originate? Can our opponents tell us? Could such a practice, which affects (in the estimation of our opponents at least) the essential character of the ordinance as well as that of the church,—could such a practice, I say, originate in merely human authority, and become general over Europe, Western Asia, and Northern and Eastern Africa, within less than a single century after the apostles, and yet its novelty not be objected to by one who opposed the practice? Tertullian was, as we have seen, opposing, under certain circumstances, infant baptism. Now, whatever would make for his argument, we know he would have had no scruples in using. Many pitiful and puerile things we know he did say, for want of better material to work with. Could he have found more powerful and plausible weapons at hand, unquestionably he would have used them. Suppose, then, infant baptism had been an invention of some doctor, or doctors, in the church, since the days of St. John; such a circumstance, had it been true, could not have escaped the knowledge of such a man as Tertullian, and had he been knowing to such a fact, he certainly would not have failed to urge it. Why, then, did he not come out at once, and say, "First of all, this doctrine of infant baptism is a novel thing, and without

* Tertull. de Baptismo.

any authority whatever from Christ and his apostles; therefore it ought to be abandoned, and baptism deferred to adult age?" Why, I say, did he not urge its *novelty*, and its utter want of Scriptural authority, against its being practised? Why did he not point out the innovator who first introduced the custom, and brand him as a heretic? All this would have been directly to his purpose, and would have weighed a thousand times more in argument than the contemptible puerilities over which he makes a pitiful display of reasoning. Why, then, did he not use these important facts? Why? To this there can be but one answer: Because no such facts existed in truth—because infant baptism bore a date and an authority coeval and coequal to the date and authority of adult Christian baptism.

2.) It is a matter of still further moment to attend to the *principle* on which Tertullian opposed infant baptism. Indeed, strictly speaking, he did not oppose it. Infant baptism, *as such*, he did not oppose. His opposition to it rested, primarily, on the ground that it was better to defer baptism, in all cases, till just before death, or till the individual was beyond the reach of peculiar temptation; and this notion arose out of the prevailing belief that baptism washed away all previous guilt, and not from any objection to infant baptism *per se*. This made sin after baptism appear to them the more terrible, inasmuch as the ordinance could not be repeated. On the same principle Tertullian advises all single persons, widows, &c., to defer baptism until they are either married, or confirmed in continence, lest they, being exposed to temptation, should fall into sin. "They that understand the weight of baptism," says he, "will rather dread the *receiving* it than the *delaying* it." In this connection he is not speaking of infant baptism exclusively, nor of the delay of infant baptism only, but of the delay of baptism in all cases where there is no immediate expectation of death, and where there is any peculiar danger from temptation. Hear him: "Therefore, ACCORDING TO EVERY ONE'S CONDITION AND DISPOSITION, AND ALSO THEIR AGE, THE DELAYING OF BAPTISM IS MORE PROFITABLE." But where there is an approach of death, or a case of necessity, he strongly advocates even lay baptism, and says, if a person "neglects at such

a time to do what he lawfully may, (that is, to baptize, or to discharge the office of a bishop toward the person in necessity,) he will be guilty of the person's perdition." From this view, then, of Tertullian's peculiar notions respecting the ordinance of baptism, the *character* of his far-famed opposition to infant baptism assumes quite another aspect. It is true that he advances arguments (such as they are) against the baptism of infants; but at the foundation of all his objections to this practice lay this primary error, namely, that baptism, in all cases, should be delayed, unless a case of clear necessity urged its prompt administration, and then, even lay baptism was to be tolerated, if a bishop or presbyter could not be procured. It was not infant baptism, in itself considered, that he really opposed, but only an improper *haste* in receiving the ordinance, which infant baptism seemed to him to indicate, but to indicate no more, according to his own showing, than baptism in many cases in adult age, for he says, after laying down his reasons for deferring infant baptism,—"FOR NO LESS REASON unmarried persons ought to be deferred, who are likely to come into temptation," &c. And in confirmation of this view, we may add that the older editions of Tertullian's writings, instead of the clause above quoted, "For what need is there that godfathers should be brought into danger?" &c., it reads, "What occasion is there, *except in case of necessity*, that godfathers should be brought into danger?" &c.* This, and many other corroborating circumstances, are adduced by Mr. Wall. But enough has been said on this point.

3.) The reader must here also recollect, that it is not the individual opinion of Tertullian that gives an importance to his testimony on this point, but it is his testimony as to what were the opinions and practices of his age that attaches a value to his statements. Even his errors and absurdities are equally to our purpose, for we are not now proving the reasonableness of infant baptism, but its antiquity. This we have now proved. That is, Tertullian's testimony alone proves that it was much older than his day, and if so, it is impossible to date it later than the apostles and Christ. For when, and where, we again ask,

* See a note by Mr Cotton, in his edition of Wall's History, vol. iv, pp. 412, 413.

did it arise? Where is the account of the controversy in the church, upon the occasion of its first introduction? Could it have been introduced without producing the slightest shock to the previous faith of the Christian church? Nay, without even exciting sufficient attention to secure from some of the historians and writers of that age a bare mention of its origin? Let those who can believe without evidence, or, rather, against evidence, credit this fiction.

4. Origen was born A. D. 185. He descended from a long line of Christian ancestry, and his father suffered martyrdom A. D. 202, when Origen was but seventeen years old. He was a native of Egypt, and was learned in all the knowledge and philosophy of the times. He was early called into the service of the church, and his learning, and the success of his labours, not only revived greatly the suffering church, but procured for himself a first rank in the list of the early fathers. Origen had his errors, as was the case also with all the fathers of the Christian church, but he is not accused of any error on the subject of baptism by the men of his times. He held, on this subject, what was, in his day, the orthodox doctrine. He says,—

"Besides all this [evidence of original sin,] let it be considered what is the reason that whereas the baptism of the church is given for forgiveness of sins, *secundum ecclesiæ observantiam etiam parvulis baptismum dari, infants* also, *according to the usage of the church, are baptized:* when, if there were nothing in infants that wanted forgiveness and mercy, the grace of baptism would be superfluous to them."* Again:—

"Infants are baptized for the remission of sins. Of what sins? or when have they sinned? Or how can any reason of the laver in their case hold good, but according to that sense we mentioned even now, [namely,] 'None is free from pollution though his life be but of the length of a single day upon the earth.' And because by the sacrament of baptism our native pollution is taken away, therefore infants may be baptized. Parvuli baptizantur in remissionem peccatorum.... Et quia per baptisma sacra-

* Eighth Homily on Leviticus.

mentum nativitatis sordes deponuntur, propterea baptizantur parvuli."*

In another place, speaking of original sin, and of its affecting infants, he says, "Pro hoc ecclesia ab apostolis traditionem suscepit etiam parvulis baptismum dare: *For this* [cause] *the church received from the apostles a tradition* [that is, *an order*] *even to give baptism to infants.* For they to whom the divine mysteries were committed knew that there is in all persons the natural pollution of sin, which must be done away by *water* and the *Spirit*."†

There are other parts of Origen's writings which would also serve our purpose, but we have quoted sufficiently to answer our present demand, and to satisfy the reader of the decided bearing of the testimony of this father. In summing up the evidence of the foregoing quotations, the reader will remember,—

1.) Origen was born only about eighty-five years after the death of St. John. At this distance of time many of the events that transpired in the times of Christ and his apostles must have been still measurably fresh. It was a remove of only two generations from the days of the founders of Christianity. It is more than probable that Origen's grandfather saw and conversed with some of the apostles, or, at least, it is certain he lived in their day. Here, then, is a contiguity that affords this Christian father large opportunity to know from unwritten and uncorrupted tradition, as well as from the written Scriptures, and other documents, many things that the apostles did and taught.

2.) The reader must recollect that Origen was one of the most learned men of his day, and had access to all the writings of his age.

3.) His orthodoxy, with respect to baptism, was never questioned, so that we are to take his statements as a candid expression of the current and prevailing doctrine of the church in his times, and previous. It is not the private opinion of this father that we are searching out, but it is his testimony, as an author, as to the opinions of the church in his day. And to give a clear and intelligent testimony he was amply prepared. He was born and educated at Alexandria, and "had lived in Greece and at

* Homily on Luke. † Comment on Epistle to Romans.

Rome, and in Cappadocia and Arabia, and spent the main part of his life in Syria and Palestine."

4.) I merely add, Origen was of Christian parentage. Eusebius, in his Ecclesiastical History, enters into this point particularly. He says, "*the Christian doctrine was conveyed to him from his forefathers;*" or, as Rufinus translates it, "from his grandfathers, and his great-grandfathers."* The Christian ancestry, then, of this father gave him a more important proximity to the apostles, in reference to a true knowledge of apostolical doctrine and practice, than that of any of the preceding fathers. When he says that "the church had received from the apostles a custom or tradition to baptize infants," his testimony is clear, important, and above impeachment, for his Christian ancestry gave him uncommon advantages for knowing, and, as he had no controversy with any one on the subject of infant baptism—as he had no possible interest in making a false statement—as his statement was spontaneous and unbribed—so it should be taken without abatement or gainsaying.

5.) We see, then, a great and learned man, and devoted Christian, whose ancestors were Christians from the days of the apostles, within two hundred years from the death of Christ, and a little over one hundred from that of the apostles, bearing repeated testimony to the fact that infant baptism was the prevalent custom of the church in his age, and that this custom had been received direct from the apostles themselves. Now, upon the supposition that infant baptism had been a recent invention of the church—that it was not handed down from the apostles themselves, we again ask, When and where did it originate? This unwelcome question has never been answered.†

* Wall's History, p. 43.

† Dr. Gale has very hotly contested the admission of Origen's testimony, on the ground that it is not authentic, the most of that father's writings having come down to us only through Latin translations of his original works, some of which are deemed faulty by the learned, in many respects, and Dr. Gale has attempted to invalidate his whole testimony in favour of infant baptism, on the ground of these faults in the translations. I cannot here rehearse the arguments pro and contra; the reader can, if he choose, refer to the works of Drs. Wall and Gale. Dr. Wall has fully shown the unfairness of Dr. Gale's attempt, What is of the most importance for the reader to know is, that the translations of Rufinus, which are those complained of, are generally

5. Cyprian was converted from heathenism to Christianity late in life, and was soon after raised to the see of Carthage, in A. D. 250, by the general approbation. This honour, however, he did not long enjoy, as he fell a martyr to Christianity in A. D. 258. Cyprian was a man of learning, and of amiable and irreproachable character; though less remarkable for his learning than for his piety and humility. In A. D. 253, three years after he was raised to the bishopric of Carthage, a council, composed of sixty-six bishops, was held in that city. This council was convened, according to the usual custom, to consult and determine upon any important concerns that might affect the purity and well-being of the church. Fidus, a country bishop, sent a letter to the council, inquiring, among other matters, whether, in case of necessity, an infant might be baptized before it was eight days old? To this they returned the following answer:—

"Cyprian, and the rest of the bishops who are present at the council, in number sixty-six, to Fidus, our brother, greeting.

"We read your letter, most esteemed brother, in which you write of one Victor, a priest, &c.... But to the case of infants: Whereas you judge 'that they must not be baptized within two or three days after they are born, and that the rule of circumcision is to be observed, so that none should be baptized and sanctified before the eighth day after he is born:' WE WERE ALL, IN OUR ASSEMBLY,

allowed to give Origen's sense in the main. They contain the *substance* of that father's writings. Also, there existed no reason why Rufinus should give a false representation of Origen's views of infant baptism, except, as he denied (though for the most part secretly during his life) the doctrine of original sin, it would have been much to his interest to have denied infant baptism, if he had dared. But this renders his testimony to infant baptism more clear from suspicion. If Origen had not held to it, Rufinus would not have inserted it in the translation, because it was his interest to deny it.

Besides, the Homily on St. Luke was translated by St. Hierome, whose translation is allowed to be a faithful one. He himself says, that in that translation he had "changed nothing; but expressed every thing as it was in the original." (See Wall's History, p. 107, &c., and Defence, pp. 426, 427, &c.) So that the reader may turn back and review the quotation from this part of Origen's writings, and satisfy himself of the reality of that father's views on infant baptism. These remarks will enable him to perceive what hard toiling our opponents have to breast the torrent of historical evidence which is against them.

OF A CONTRARY OPINION. For as for what you thought fitting to be done, there was not one that was of your mind, but all of us, on the contrary, judged that the grace and mercy of God is to be denied to no person that is born. For whereas our Lord, in his Gospel, says, 'The Son of man came not to destroy men's souls, [or lives,] but to save them;' as far as lies in us, no soul, if possible, is to be lost.... So that we judge that no person is to be hindered from obtaining the grace by the law that is now appointed: and that the spiritual circumcision [that is, *the grace of baptism*] ought not to be impeded by the circumcision that was according to the flesh, [that is, Jewish circumcision,] but that all are to be admitted to the grace of Christ; since Peter, speaking in the Acts of the Apostles, says, 'The Lord has shown me that no person is to be called common or unclean.'

"If any thing could be an obstacle to persons against their obtaining the grace, the adult, and grown, and aged, would be rather hindered by their more grievous sins. If, then, the greatest offenders, and those that have grievously sinned against God before, have, when they afterward come to believe, forgiveness of their sins, and no person is prohibited from baptism and grace; how much less reason is there to refuse an infant, who, being newly born, has no sin, save that being descended from Adam according to the flesh, he has from his very birth contracted the contagion of the death anciently threatened? who comes for this reason more easily to receive forgiveness of sins, because they are not his own, but others' sins that are forgiven him.

"This, therefore, most esteemed brother, was our opinion in the assembly, that it is not for us to hinder any person from baptism and the grace of God, who is merciful and kind, and affectionate to all. Which rule, as it is to govern universally, so we think it more especially to be observed in reference to infants and persons newly born. To whom our help and the divine mercy is rather to be granted, because by their weeping and wailing at their first entrance into the world, they do intimate nothing so much as that they implore compassion.

"Dearest brother, we wish you always good health."*

* Cyprian's Epistle to Fidus.

Other quotations might be given from this father, but the above is all-sufficient, and our limits do not allow of very extended citations. In order fully to estimate the evidence of this quotation from Cyprian, the reader will please observe,—

1.) The exact point to be established by it is, not what were the opinions of these bishops merely, but, what was the universal usage of the church in those times. It is not a question of *opinion* that we are to settle, but a question of *fact*. It is not, whether infant baptism be right or wrong; but, whether, as a matter of fact, the churches generally believed it to be right, and therefore practised it. The doctrinal opinions of these bishops, though deserving much respect, could not be decisive in the case, but their testimony to the state of opinion and practice in their times is to be received without abatement, and is decisive. These bishops were assembled from different and distant parts. Each one would certainly know what was practised in his own diocess, and he also would know whether such practice accorded with the general usage of the church in Europe and Asia. As they were all approved and devoted men, and especially Cyprian, who was revered and beloved by all for his orthodoxy and piety, and as their decision in this case was never revoked or censured by the church, it is absurd to suppose they spoke any thing but the general faith.

Besides, the question was not, whether infants are to be baptized at all. This nobody disputed. But the question was, *May they, in cases of necessity, be baptized before they are eight days old?*

2.) Consider the means of knowing the truth in the case that this council possessed. They not only were competent to tell what was the practice of their own times in reference to infant baptism, but it is clear that they were amply competent to decide whether that practice was according to the apostles' doctrine and usage. This council was convened only one hundred and eighty-eight years after the death of Paul and Peter, and only about one hundred and fifty years after the death of the apostle John. Now, two, or, at the most, three persons, could have sufficed to hand the true practice of the apostles, touching this subject, to the members who composed this council.

Doubtless many of these bishops were aged men, and if seventy or eighty years of age, might have conversed with men that had seen the apostles, or, at least, that had lived in the apostles' day, and were acquainted with their practice in a matter so important as that of infant baptism. Tradition must have been still fresh, and the fathers, or, at least, the grandfathers, of these bishops must have had personal knowledge of apostolic times. Certainly, in the sixty-six dioceses over which they presided, there must have been many old men whose information on these points was ample, and whose recollection was clear. Take sixty-six intelligent and aged ministers, holding high and responsible offices in the church, and whose very offices, as well as ministerial profession, oblige them to study and understand the history, the doctrines, and the usages of the church—take sixty-six men of this class, I say, in this day, and assemble them together in council, and then propose to them a question, whether it it be lawful, according to the doctrine and usage of the church, to do a particular thing or not? I say, would not these men be fully competent to expound the doctrine of the church, so as to decide such a question? I allude now only to questions of *fact*. I need not say that they would be fully competent to such a task. And with all the advantages resulting from the extensive personal knowledge of these African bishops—their access to the records of the church, and to the writings of the earlier fathers—and the fresh gushings of the fountain of traditionary information—I say, with all these advantages, this African council could have been at no loss to understand what was the usage of the church then, and what it had been since the days of the apostles. And let it be remembered,—

3.) That the council were *unanimous* in their decision. "*Not one was of Fidus's mind*, that infant baptism must be delayed until the eighth day, in conformity to the law of Jewish circumcision. Much less was there any of opinion that it was not to be used at all."

4.) The only question, then, that can possibly arise to occasion the shadow of a doubt as to the apostolical character of this decision, is that which respects the moral honesty, or the true Christian integrity, of these bishops. Have they given us the true doctrine of the apostles, or have they, with all their advantages of correct information, given us only a figment of superstition, which owes its origin to the apostacy and corruption of the church? I know not that I can better shape a reply to this question than in the language of Dr. Milner. Speaking of this council, he says,—

"Here is an assembly of sixty-six pastors, men of approved fidelity and gravity, who have stood the fiery trial of some of the severest persecutions ever known, and who have testified their love to the Lord Jesus Christ in a more striking manner than any anti-Pedobaptists have had an opportunity of doing in our days; and if we may judge of their religious views by those of Cyprian,—and they are all in perfect harmony with him,—they are not wanting in any fundamental of godliness. No man, in any age, more reverenced the Scriptures, and made more copious use of them on all occasions, than he did; and, it must be confessed, in the very best manner. For he uses them continually for PRACTICE, not for OSTENTATION; for USE, not for the sake of VICTORY in argument. Before this holy assembly a question is brought,—not whether infants should be baptized at all—none contradicted this,—but whether it is right to baptize them immediately, or on the eighth day? Without a single negative, they all determined to baptize them immediately. This transaction passed in the year two hundred and fifty-three. Let the reader consider: If infant baptism had been an innovation, it must have been now of a considerable standing. The disputes concerning Easter, and other very uninteresting points, show that SUCH an innovation must have formed a remarkable era in the church. The number of heresies and divisions had been very great. Among them all, such a deviation from apostolical practice as this MUST have been remarked. To me it appears impossible to account for this state of things, but on the footing that it had EVER been allowed; and, therefore, that it was the custom of the first churches."*

6. Optatus, bishop of Melevi, in Numidia, was a person of some note, a man of orthodox faith and genuine piety. He wrote against the Donatists—a schismatical, rather than heretical party in the African church—about A. D. 370

* History of the Church, cent. iii, chap. xiii.

Mr. Wall places him two hundred and sixty years after the apostles. Among other things he refers to baptism. The question, however, was not, whether infants are to be baptized; but, whether a person, coming over from the Catholic Church to their party, should be considered as baptized, or, (as Mr. Wall sarcastically expresses it,) whether they "must be baptized afresh by some such pure men as the Donatists were." This question, therefore, does not prejudice the cause of infant baptism.

The only quotation from this writer which it concerns us to make is the following. Optatus had been comparing a Christian's putting on Christ at baptism to the putting on of a garment; and had compared Christ, so put on, to a garment, &c. He then adds:—

"But lest any one should say, I speak irreverently, in calling Christ a garment, let him read what the apostle says, 'As many of you as have been baptized in the name of Christ, have put on Christ.' O what a garment is this, that is always one, and never renewed; that decently fits all ages and all forms: it is neither plaited for infants, nor stretched for men, and without alteration is suitable to women."*

All I wish to notice, in connection with this citation, is the familiar manner in which infant baptism is referred to. Nothing can more clearly point out the settled unanimity of faith in the church, touching this subject, than that easy, familiar, and matter-of-course way of alluding to it, that seems to take for granted that all parties, whether Catholics or schismatics, orthodox or heretics, believed and practised alike.

7. Gregory, commonly called Gregory Nazianzen, was born at Arianzum, an obscure village in the province of Cappadocia, about A. D. 320. He was a man of great learning, and, though inclined to the ascetic life, was raised in succession to the sees of Sasimi, Nazianzus, and Constantinople. He was an intimate friend of St. Basil. He died in A. D. 389. The testimony of Gregory, in favour of infant baptism, is clear and abundant. In his eulogy upon St. Basil, his intimate friend, (who, though the younger, died before Gregory,) he relates the baptism

* Fifth book concerning the Schism of the Donatists.

of that father in his infancy, as one of the commendable things in his history. With this account we shall not detain the reader. Before citing from this author, it is important to observe, that the practice of deferring baptism from year to year had become alarmingly prevalent. Persons would remain in the state of catechumens until just before death, and then receive baptism, and be admitted into the church. This practice, which had now received the example of the emperor Constantine, had, as we have before mentioned, grown out of a superstitious notion of the saving efficacy of baptism. They considered that it removed all previous guilt; and, as the ordinance could not be repeated, and as they feared they might stain the purity of their baptism afterward, if baptized in early life, they were easily betrayed into the habit of deferring it. This exact view it is important to remember, and against it Gregory levels the artillery of his argument and the polished shafts of his eloquence. He reminds them of the danger of losing baptism by sudden death—that such procrastination is often a mere pretext for living longer in carnal pleasures—that it is a wily stratagem of the devil to cheat souls, which he calls upon them to resist; and then says,—

"Art thou a youth? fight against pleasures and passions with this auxiliary strength: list thyself in God's army. Art thou old? let thy gray hairs hasten thee. Strengthen thy age with baptism.... Hast thou an infant child? Let not wickedness have the advantage of time. Let him be sanctified from his infancy. Let him be dedicated from his cradle in the Spirit. Thou, as a faint-hearted mother, and of little faith, art afraid of giving him the seal, [that is, baptism,] because of the weakness of nature. Hannah, before Samuel was born, devoted him to God, and as soon as he was born, consecrated him, and brought him up from the first in a priestly garment, not fearing on account of human infirmities, but trusting in God. Thou hast no need of amulets, or charms.... Give to him the Trinity, that great and excellent preservative. *Δος αυτω την τριαδα, το μεγα και καλον φυλακτηριον*." Again:—

"Some of them [those who neglect baptism] live like beasts, and regard not baptism. Some have a value for baptism, but delay the receiving it, either out of negligence, or a greediness longer to enjoy their lusts. But some others have it not in their own power to receive it, either because of their *infancy* perhaps, (*η δια νηπιοτητα τυχον*,) or by reason of some accident utterly involuntary... And I think of the first sort, [that is, those who despise baptism,] that they shall be punished, as for their other wickedness, so for their slighting of baptism. And that the second shall be punished, but in a less degree, because they are guilty of their own missing it, but rather through folly than malice. But that the last sort, [those who omit baptism involuntarily, as infants,] will neither be glorified nor punished by the just Judge; as being without the *seal*, [that is, baptism,] but not through their own wickedness; and as having *suffered* the loss rather than occasioned it." "——We must, therefore, make it our utmost care that we do not miss of the common grace," &c. "Some may say, Suppose this to hold in the case of those who can desire baptism: what say you of those that are as yet infants, and are not in capacity to be sensible, either of the grace or the want of it? Shall we baptize them too? Yes, by all means, if any danger make it requisite. For it is better that they be sanctified without their own sense of it, than that they should be *unsealed* and uninitiated. *Και τουτου λογος ἡμιν ἡ οκταημερος περιτομη and our reason for this is circumcision, which was performed on the eighth day*, and was a typical *seal*, and was practised on those who had no use of reason. As for others, I give my opinion that they should stay three years, or thereabouts, when they are able to hear and answer some of the holy words; and though they do not perfectly understand them, yet they form them: *οὑτως αγιαζειν και ψυχας και σωματα τῳ μεγαλω μυστεριω της τελειωσεως and that you then sanctify them in soul and body with the great sacrament of consecration.* For though they are not liable to give account of their life before their reason be come to maturity, yet, by reason of those sudden and unexpected assaults of dangers that are by no efforts to be prevented, it is by all means advisable that they be secured by the laver [of baptism.]"*

A few remarks it may be proper to subjoin to this lengthened citation.

* Discourse on Baptism.

1.) The peculiar notions of Gregory, or of his age, concerning the efficacy of baptism, &c., we do not quote with approbation of their moral or theological tendency. These errors do not affect the testimony of this father, in reference to the points upon which we intend his testimony to bear.

2.) The principle upon which persons deferred baptism, in his day, was of such a nature as not to argue in the slightest degree against infant baptism, *as such*. The validity of infant baptism was not called in question, any more than adult baptism. The delay of baptism till just before death was urged by many, purely on the ground of its supposed efficacy in removing past sin, and the danger of losing the grace of the ordinance by subsequent transgression; and on this ground Gregory took up the objection.

3.) Gregory and Tertullian are the only two that speak of delaying infant baptism at all; the latter till the age of reason, the former till three years. Both one and the other, however, are to be understood, where there is no danger of death in the meanwhile: which is plainly expressed in the above extract from Gregory, and in Tertullian is collected from his other speeches.*

4.) According to the testimony of Gregory, then, infant baptism was fully believed to be Scriptural in A. D. 370, and was commonly practised in the Christian church, except where such superstitious notions of the ordinance as those above noted occasioned its delay, which exception is no detriment to our argument.

8. The statements of St. Basil, in his discourse to the catechumens, possess not sufficient importance to merit a full recital here. He does not profess to speak directly to the subject of infant baptism. Mr. Wall says, the most material evidence that can be derived from this father in support of infant baptism is taken from his practice. He then proves it to have been the practice of St. Basil to baptize infants, by citing, from Theodoret, the instance where he (Basil) recommended to the emperor Valens to have his child baptized by a person of the catholic faith. (The word *catholic* distinguishes only from the Arian faction, in this place.) The child, however, was baptized

* Wall's History of Infant Baptism, part i, c. xi, sec. 10.

by an Arian. This child was *an infant son* of Valens, according to Socrates.*

9. Ambrose was born in Gaul about A. D. 338. He was educated in Italy, and his talents and conduct early brought him into notice, and raised him to high civil honours. He was elected bishop of Milan, in A. D. 374, by the unanimous voice of the people. With some weaknesses and equivocal traits of character, he was still a great and useful man. He died in A. D. 397, after enjoying a life of universal celebrity.

After having mentioned the miracle of Elijah, in dividing the waters of Jordan, he adds:—

"But perhaps this may seem to be fulfilled in our time, and in the apostles' time. For that returning of the river waters backward toward the spring head, which was caused by Elias when the river was divided, (as the Scripture says, *Jordan was driven back*,) signified the sacrament of the laver of salvation, which was afterward to be instituted; per quæ in primordia naturæ suæ qui baptizati fuerint, parvuli a malitia reformantur, *by which those infants who have been baptized are reformed from* [their] *perverseness, to the primitive state of their nature*."† Again; he cites those words of our Saviour, "Except any person be born again of water, and of the Spirit, he cannot enter into the kingdom of God;" and then adds, by way of comment,—

"Utique nullum excipit: non infantem, non aliqua preventum necessitate, *Certainly none is excepted: not an infant, not one that is prevented from necessity.* But," he adds, "suppose that such have that freedom from punishment, which is not clear, yet, I question whether they shall have the honour of the kingdom."‡

A few remarks are necessary here.

1.) Ambrose expressly refers infant baptism to the apostles' times. He says: "Sed fortasse hoc supra nos et supra apostolos videatur expletum, *But perhaps we see the fulfilment of this in our own and the apostles' times;*" that is, as he immediately adds, it appears to be fulfilled in infant baptism. The contingency expressed in the sentence does not apply to the *fact* of infant baptism being

* Wall's History, part i, c. xi. † Comment on Luke i, 17.
‡ Ambrose concerning the patriarch Abraham.

practised in the apostles' day, but to the circumstance of the *application* of the figure as made in the passage.

2.) The puerility of the figure here employed, to set forth infant baptism and its efficacy, does not militate against the testimony of Ambrose to the fact that he believed in the doctrine, and that he also believed in its apostolic origin, as also that it was the current doctrine of his day. We know that the Christian fathers employed many silly comparisons and weak arguments to defend Christianity, but that they employed weak and even silly arguments does by no means prove their cause to have been weak. This would be a strange mode of reasoning. We all know that they were given, unhappily, to an allegorical interpretation of Scripture, especially after the days of Origen, which often betrayed them into the most vague and idle conceits, but this does not affect their testimony to the great doctrines of revelation as believed and practised in their day: this does not affect the credibility of their testimony to an unbroken tradition, handed down, through them, from the apostles. The same may be said of their erroneous notion of the saving efficacy of baptism, as we have before stated.

3.) It is proper to state also, for the information of the more uninformed reader, that the last quotation from Ambrose evidently teaches the doctrine of a *middle state*—a place, after death, that partakes not fully of the qualities either of happiness or misery—to which place unbaptized infants, and others, were supposed to go. It is not our business to dwell upon these errors, either to explain or refute them. We simply wish the reader to understand that such errors do not discredit the testimonies of these men to the fact of infant baptism in their day, or the fact of its traditionary transmission from the apostles.

10. Chrysostom, bishop of Constantinople, was born at Antioch about A. D. 354. He died A. D. 407. He was renowned for his eloquence, and the people used to say that they would rather the sun would not shine than that John should not preach. He was a man of great powers of mind, having many imprudences of conduct, and not a well-balanced and tempered zeal. In contrasting the two rites of circumcision and baptism, he says,—

"But our circumcision—I mean the grace of baptism—

gives cure without pain, and procures to us a thousand benefits, and fills us with the grace of the Spirit: and it has no determinate time as that had, *ἀλλ ἔξεσι και εν αωρω ἡλικια, και εν μεσῃ, και εν αυτω τω γηρα γενομενος τινα ταυτην δεξασθαι την αχειροποιητον περιτομην, but one in immature age, or in middle life, or that is in old age, may receive this circumcision made without hands;* in which there is no trouble to be undergone, but to throw off the load of sins, and receive pardon for all previous offences."*

From a homily of St. Chrysostom's on Baptism, which is not now extant, the following passage is quoted by St. Austin:—

"*Δια τουτο και τα παιδια βαπτιζομεν καιτοι αμαρτηματα μη εχοντα, for this reason we baptize infants also, although they have no* [actual] *sins.*"

In another place he is censuring the women for "a custom that they had of rubbing the forehead of the child with a sort of dirt, prepared with some magical tricks, which was to preserve it from being bewitched. He tells them that such a practice, instead of guarding and purifying the infant, makes it abominable." His words are:—

"He that anoints an infant so with that dirt, how can he think but that he makes it abominable? How can he bring it to the hands of the priest? Tell me, how can you think it fitting for the minister to make the sign on its forehead, where you have besmeared it with the dirt?"†

In these quotations from Chrysostom, then, it is expressly declared that baptism is appropriate *εν αωρος ἡλικια in immature*, or *newly begun, age*,—that is, in *infancy;*—that the church actually did baptize infants; and he inveighs against the superstitious practice of putting dirt on children's foreheads, as unseemly and improper, because it has no relevance to the consecrating ordinance of baptism which their children received from the priest.

BEFORE THE PELAGIAN CONTROVERSY.

I shall follow the order of Mr. Wall, and give quotations from the fathers who lived during the Pelagian controversy, distinguishing those quotations which date prior to that controversy from those which date subsequently to its

* Homily xl, on Genesis. † Homily xii, on 1 Corinthians.

origin. The reason of this is, that the Pelagian controversy had a direct effect, more than any other event since the days of the apostles until that time, to call forth definite opinions and positions in relation to infant baptism.

11. St. Hierome, in a letter to a lady, about A. D. 380, urges the duty of the right education of her child, from the fact that God will require the sins of children at the hands of their parents. He says,—

"But he that is a child, and thinks as a child, his good deeds, as well as his evil deeds, are imputed to his parents. Unless you suppose that the children of Christians are themselves only under the guilt of the sin, except they receive baptism; and that the wickedness is not imputed to those also who would not give it them, especially at that time when they that were to receive it could make no opposition to the reception of it."*

The meaning, or doctrine, of this passage is simply this:—Infants are not chargeable with any sin in the omission of their baptism. Such a delinquency could be imputed only to their parents, or those who withheld baptism from them.

12. Austin, or Augustin, lived three hundred years after the apostles. He was a man of great eloquence; he wrote much, and exerted a powerful influence over all parties in the church during a long life. Our limits do not permit us to go at length into quotations; we shall give all that are necessary to the complete purposes of our present argument. In one of his books against the Donatists, who were a schismatical party of the Christian church in Africa, this father is showing that if a person be baptized in insincerity, like Simon Magus, or, like him, be baptized with erroneous and crude notions of the Trinity, still, having attained better views, and having repented, he is not to be rebaptized—his former baptism is yet to be held valid. He says,—

"So that many persons increasing in knowledge after their baptism, *and especially those who have been baptized either when they were infants, or when they were youths*; as their understanding is cleared and enlightened, and their 'inward man renewed day by day,' do themselves deride, and with abhorrence and confession abjure the former

* Letter to Leta.

opinions which they had of God, when they were imposed on by their own imaginations. And yet they are not therefore accounted either not to have received baptism, or to have a baptism of the same nature of their error. But in their case, both the validity of the sacrament is acknowledged, and the vanity of their own understanding rectified." Again:—

"And as the thief, who by necessity went without baptism, was saved; because by his piety he had it spiritually: so where baptism is had, though the party by neces sity go without that [faith] which the thief had, yet he is saved: quod traditem tenet universitas ecclesiæ cum parvuli infantes baptizantur, *which, being handed down to them, the universal church holds, with respect to infants who are baptized;* who certainly cannot yet believe with the heart to righteousness, or confess with the mouth to salvation, as the thief could; nay, by their crying and noise, while the sacrament is being administered, they disturb the holy mysteries; and yet no Christian will say they are baptized to no purpose.

"Et si quisquam in hac re auctoritatem divinam quærat: quanquam quod universa tenet ecclesia, nec conciliis institutum sed semper retentum est, non nisi auctoritate apostolica traditum rectissime creditur, *and if any one do ask for divine authority in this matter, though that which the universal church practices, which has not been instituted by councils, but has always been observed, is most justly believed to be nothing else than a thing delivered* [or *handed down*] *by the authority of the apostles:* yet we may, besides, take a true estimate, how much the sacrament of baptism does avail infants, by the circumcision which God's former people received.

"——Therefore as in Abraham the righteousness of faith went before, and circumcision, the seal of the righteousness of faith, came after; so in Cornelius, [the centurion,] the spiritual sanctification by the gift of the Holy Spirit went before, and the sacrament of regeneration by the laver of baptism came after. And as in Isaac, who was circumcised the eighth day, the seal of the righteousness of faith went before, and (as he was a follower of his father's faith) the righteousness itself, the seal whereof had gone before in his infancy, came after: so in infants baptized the sacrament of regeneration goes before, and (if they put in practice the Christian religion) conversion of the heart, the mystery whereof went before in their body, comes after.

"And as in that thief's case, (alluding to the thief upon the cross with our Saviour,) what was wanting of the sacrament of baptism the mercy of the Almighty made up; because it was not out of pride or contempt, but of necessity, that it was wanting: so in infants that die after they are baptized, it is to be believed that the same grace of the Almighty does make up that defect, that by reason, not of a wicked will, but of want of age, they can neither believe with the heart to righteousness, nor confess with the mouth unto salvation. So that when others answer for them, that they may have this sacrament given them, it is valid for their consecration, because they cannot answer for themselves. But if for one that is able to answer for himself, another should answer, it would not be valid.

"—— By all which, it appears that the sacrament of baptism is one thing, and conversion of the heart another; but that the salvation of a person is completed by both of them. And if one of these be wanting, we are not to think that it follows that the other is wanting; since one may be without the other in an infant, and the other was without that in the thief: God Almighty making up, both in one and the other case, that which was not wilfully wanting. But when either of these is wilfully wanting, it involves the individual in guilt."*

The reader is particularly requested to notice,—

1.) St. Austin gives the general opinion of the church. All believed in the utility and necessity of infant baptism. He says, Nullus Christianorum, *No Christians* will call infant baptism useless. All who believed in any water baptism at all (and there were a few who denied all baptism) held to infant baptism.

2.) This father directly affirms that no council of the church had instituted the rite—that it was the universal practice—that it had been practised from the first—and that, with the strictest propriety, it was regarded as

* Fourth Book against the Donatists, concerning Baptism.

* I think so too

A. H. Wilson

having been delivered to the church by the authority of the apostles.

3.) He holds, as is common with all the fathers, a strict analogy between circumcision and baptism.

(Besides these references, there are others that belong to about this date, A. D. 408, which we might make equally to our purpose. For instance, a bishop by the name of Boniface writes to St. Austin, propounding questions in relation to infant baptism. Austin answers him at length. In both epistles the utility and divine authority of the practice are taken for granted, and the fact that the church did generally practise infant baptism at that time fully attested. So also, in Austin's book on our Lord's sermon on the mount, and his books on free will, which our limits do not allow us to notice.)

This father further says,—

"Consuetudo tamen matris ecclesiæ in baptizandis parvulis nequaquam spernenda est, neque ullo modo superflua deputanda nec omnino credenda nisi apostolica esse traditio, *Yet the custom of our mother, the church, in baptizing infants, is by no means to be disregarded, nor be accounted needless, nor believed to be other than a tradition of the apostles;*"* [that is, an institution handed down from the apostles. *Tradition* is something *handed down*, as from father to son; and when infant baptism is said to be esteemed as a tradition of the apostles, the meaning is, that it is a doctrine and practice handed down from the apostles, and of course by their authority.]

In a letter to St. Hierome, St. Austin says,—

"I ask where the soul contracted that guilt, by which it is brought to condemnation, (even the soul of an infant who is surprised with death,) if the grace of Christ do not relieve it by the sacrament whereby infants are baptized."

Speaking of the question, whether the soul of man is a new creation of God, or generated in the same way as the body; and of the different modes of settling this question; he says,—

"Before I know which of them is to be chosen, this I know, that the one which is true does not oppose that most firm and established faith by which the church of

* St. Austin's tenth book on Genesis.

Christ believes that even the new-born little ones of mankind cannot be freed from condemnation, but by the grace of the name of Christ, which he has commended to us in his sacraments."

In his letter to eighteen Pelagian bishops afterward, being an answer to one they had published, he says,—

"But this I say, that original sin is so plain by the Scriptures, and that it is forgiven to infants in the laver of regeneration, is so confirmed by the ANTIQUITY and AUTHORITY of the Catholic faith, so NOTORIOUS BY THE PRACTICE of the CHURCH, that whatsoever is disputed, inquired, or affirmed of the origin of the soul, if it be contrary to this, cannot be true."

13. In the forty-eighth canon of the third council of Carthage, held about A. D. 397, we find the following:—

"In reference to the Donatists, it is resolved that we do ask the advice of our brethren and fellow-bishops, Siricius and Simplicianus, concerning those only who are in infancy baptized among them; whether in that which they have not done with their own judgment, the error of their parents shall hinder them, that when they, by a wholesome purpose, shall be converted to the church of God, they may not be promoted to be ministers of the holy altar."

It appears that the consent of these bishops was obtained; for four years afterward, in another council held at Carthage, Aurelius, bishop of that city, addresses the council thus:—

"You remember that in a former council it was resolved that they who were, in their infancy, before they were able to understand the mischief of that error, baptized among the Donatists, and when they came to age of understanding, acknowledging the truth, &c., they were received by us. All will grant that such may undoubtedly be promoted to church offices, especially in times of so great need.

"Some that have been teachers in that sect would come over with their congregations, if they might have the same places among us. But this I leave to a further consideration of our brethren. Only that they will consent to our determination, that such as were baptized by them in infancy may be admitted to orders."

In the sixth canon of the fifth council of Carthage, held about A. D. 400, we have the following:—

"It is resolved concerning infants of whose having been baptized there are no positive witnesses that can give certain evidence, and they themselves are not capable of giving any account of that sacrament having been administered to them, by reason of their age; that such be, without any scruple, baptized," &c. This was the received doctrine of the church in regard to all doubtful cases.

There are many testimonies that might be introduced here, but as they are of a nature to require introductory and explanatory remarks in order to give a full view of their force to the reader, and as our limits do not permit this, and as, also, there are many others directly to the point that are not so involved in circumstances that require lengthy explanation, we therefore omit them. It is enough that we assure the reader that there is no want of evidence, or any *contrary* current of testimony, that induces any omission.

AFTER THE COMMENCEMENT OF THE PELAGIAN CONTROVERSY.

We have now arrived at the period of the origin of the Pelagian controversy. Pelagius was a native of Britain, a monk, and a man of the first order of intellect and genius. He associated with him Celestius, a native of Ireland, and a man of talent. The Pelagian heresy began to make its appearance about A. D. 405. In A. D. 410, when the Goths took and plundered Rome, these heresiarchs, who were then residing in that city, fled, Celestius to Carthage, and Pelagius to Palestine, after which they attained more note than ever. Never before had the doctrine of infant baptism been subjected to such a test as by this controversy. Its antiquity, its utility, and its Scriptural authority, were points upon which the event of the controversy largely depended. The hinging point was, original sin, and the necessity of divine grace in order to salvation. In a council of fourteen bishops, held at Diospolis,* in Palestine, in A. D. 415, the following errors were charged

* This place is called in Scripture, *Lydda.*

upon Pelagius, which he was compelled at the time to abjure, though he did not afterward forsake them:—

1. That Adam, whether he had sinned or not, would have died.

2. That his sin hurt himself only, and not mankind.

3. That infants newly born are in the same state that Adam was before his fall.

4. That neither by the death, or fall, of Adam does all mankind die, nor by the resurrection of Christ does all mankind arise.

These are, in substance, what were charged upon Celestius four years previous, in a council held at Carthage. I have inserted these points from the creed of Pelagius, in order that the reader may the more perfectly comprehend the force of the testimonies soon to be adduced. As Pelagius and Celestius denied original sin, it would seem that they would of course deny the necessity of infant baptism, for all the Christian world believed that baptism was "for the remission of sins." Infants, indeed, were not supposed to have any actual sin, but yet there was that liability to punishment, that unfitness for heaven, that, without the atonement of Christ, is an inseparable property of our nature, and this the ancient Christian church held was removed by, or at, baptism. A denial of the doctrine of this innate depravity, therefore, appeared to carry with it, necessarily, a denial of the fitness and obligation of infant baptism. And so it did. Accordingly the great spirits in the church who opposed Pelagius ceased not to press him with this argument, "If infants are without fault in their nature, as you affirm, why then are they baptized?" Now, any person can at once perceive how it became the interest of Pelagius to invalidate the practice and obligation of infant baptism, if he could. He never met with a more difficult and troublesome argument, in all the circle of this famous and furious controversy, which shook and menaced the church in Asia, Africa, and Europe, than this simple one with which he was constantly beset. In vain did he attempt to shelter himself from the charge of denying the utility and obligation of infant baptism, by holding that infants needed baptism, not for the remission of any guilt, which he denied their having, but in order to fit them for the kingdom of heaven. In vain,

I say, did he urge this distinction. He was met with the argument, "If infants need baptism in order to fit them for heaven, then, previous to their baptism they were *un*fit for heaven, which would argue their sinfulness." "As for infants that die without baptism," says Pelagius, "I know whither they do not go; but whither they do go I know not, that is, I know that they do not go to the kingdom of heaven; but what becomes of them I know not." But why all this difficulty—this hard labour with the argument? Why not cut the knot at once by denying infant baptism? by pointing out its want of Scriptural authority; and by demonstrating the fact that it had crept into the church in an evil hour, under the auspices of ambitious and corrupt men? Let those who deny infant baptism reply to these questions. Meantime we call the reader's attention to the evidence elicited by the history of this controversy.

(12.) St. Austin, in one of his books concerning the guilt and forgiveness of sins, and baptism of infants, says,—

"The whole church has of old constantly held that baptized infants do obtain remission of original sin by the baptism of Christ." "For my part," continues he, "I do not remember that I ever heard any other thing from any Christians that received the Old and New Testaments, non solum in Catholica ecclesia, verum etiam in qualibet hæresi vel schismate constitutis, *neither from such as were in the Catholic church, nor yet from such as belonged to any sect or schism.* I do not remember that I ever read otherwise, in any writer that I could ever find treating of these matters, that followed the canonical Scriptures, or did mean, or did pretend so to do."

In connection with this declaration of St. Austin, we wish the reader to recollect that this father was well versed in the history of the church, and a few years afterward wrote a "history of all sects and opinions" that were or had been in Christendom.

(11.) St. Hierome, in one of his books against Pelagius, after having crowded him hardly with the argument derived from the practice and obligation of infant baptism, as being irreconcilable with the notion that they were without sin, says,—

"This one thing I will say, that this discourse may at last have an end: Either you must set forth a new creed, and after the Father, the Son, and the Holy Ghost, baptize infants into the kingdom of heaven: or else, if you acknowledge one baptism for infants and for grown persons, you must own that infants are to be baptized for the forgiveness of sins."

14. In a letter of Pelagius to Innocent, bishop of Rome, he complains of his opponents, and says,—

"Men do slander me as if I denied the sacrament of baptism to infants," &c. He further declares,—

"Nunquam se vel impium aliquem hæreticum audisse, qui hoc quod proposuit de parvulis, diceret: *that he never heard even an impious heretic who would affirm this concerning infants;* [namely, that they were *not* to be baptized.]

He still continues:—

"Quis enim ita evangelicæ lectionis ignarus est, qui hoc non modo affirmare conetur, sed qui vel leviter dicere aut etiam sentire possit? Denique quis tam impius, qui parvulos exortes regni cœlorum esse velit, dum eos baptizari et in Christo renasci vetat? *For who is so ignorant of the reading of the evangelists, as to attempt (not to say to establish this* [doctrine,] *but) to speak of it heedlessly, or even have such a thought? In fine, who can be so impious as to hinder infants from being baptized, and born again in Christ, and thus cause them to miss of the kingdom of heaven;* since our Saviour has said, that none can enter into the kingdom of heaven that is not born again of water and the Holy Spirit? Who is there so impious as to refuse to an infant, of what age soever, the common redemption of mankind, and to hinder him that is born to an uncertain life from being born again to an everlasting and certain one?"

Before we pass to another citation, we beg the reader to pause and consider that this man, (Pelagius,) who affirms his belief of infant baptism, and complains of being slandered when it is reported that he denies it—that declares he never heard of any person so impious or so ignorant of the gospel, not even among heretics, that presumed to deny the doctrine, or even call it in question—this very man, we say, would, as has been mentioned, have found it greatly to his interest to have been able to cast discredit upon the practice. Could he have proved that infant baptism was of human invention, or any thing short of apostolic authority, it would have made more in favour of his cause than almost any other argument he could have advanced. As it was, he was obliged to maintain the obligation of the practice in connection with his notion of the innate purity of infants, which was an absurdity too gross to be concealed by all the arts of his sophistry. And this letter to Pope Innocent was written in A. D. 417, only three hundred and seventeen years after the apostles. Could not Pelagius have traced out and exposed the spurious origin of infant baptism, if such an origin it really had? To doubt it requires more faith than we can command at the mere challenge of a cavilling objector.

15. Celestius wrote a creed, or book of faith, which, though it differed somewhat from Pelagius's views, sufficiently sets forth his own. The work is not extant, but St. Austin quotes from it, and we take from him. Celestius says,—

"Infantes autem debere baptizari in remissionem peccatorum, secundum regulam universalis ecclesiæ, et secundum evangelii sententiam, confitemur; quia Dominus statuit regnum cœlorum non nisi baptizatis posse conferri; quod quia vires naturæ non habent, conferri necesse est per gratiæ libertatem: *But we acknowledge infants ought to be baptized for the remission of sins*, ACCORDING TO THE RULE OF THE UNIVERSAL CHURCH, *and* ACCORDING TO THE SENTENCE OF THE GOSPEL, *because our Lord has ordained that the kingdom of heaven shall be bestowed upon no person except he be baptized;* which, as men do not receive it by nature, it is necessary to confer by the power [or liberty] of grace."

Here Celestius plainly admits infant baptism for the remission of sin, which was according to the opinion of the church; but this can hardly be regarded as any thing else than an insincere profession, designed to allay the violence of opposition. And so St. Austin regarded it. Pelagius himself, when pressed hard by friends to renounce his objectionable tenets, at last confessed to them: "Infantes in remissionem peccatorum percipere baptismum,

Infants are to receive baptism for the remission of sins." Yet, they denied that infants had any sin. Their most common and plausible argument was, that infants are baptized for admission into the kingdom of heaven, because our Saviour says, "Except a person be born of *water* and of the Spirit, he cannot see the kingdom of God:" but that they were not baptized for the remission of sins, because they had no sin. The Constantinopolitan creed declared, "*We acknowledge one baptism for the remission of sins.*" So said the whole Christian world. But Pelagius's doctrine of the purity of our nature rendered infant baptism, in this view of it, an absurdity. Why, then, did he not deny the obligation and Scriptural authority of the practice? He never was able to give a rational account of the utility and necessity of infant baptism—he tried every possible way to evade the argument derived from its obligation and import—he was restless under its weight, while it chafed him on every side—but still he did not deny it, and thus take the shorter, and certainly the more consistent way, in the estimation of his opponents, to rid himself of its annoyance. Still, both he and Celestius confess that they never heard of any sect or person who denied infant baptism. Mr. Wall has justly said,—

"If there had been any such church of anti-Pedobaptists in the world, these men could not have missed an opportunity of hearing of them, being so great travellers as they were. For they were born and bred, the one in Britain, the other in Ireland. They lived the prime of their age (a very long time, as St. Austin testifies) at Rome—a place to which all the people of the world had then a resort. They were both for some time at Carthage, in Africa. Then the one [Pelagius] settled at Jerusalem, and the other [Celestius] travelled through all the noted Greek and Eastern churches, in Europe and Asia. It is impossible there should have been any church that had any singular practice in this matter but they must have heard of them. So that one may fairly conclude that there was not at this time, nor in the memory of the men of this time, any Christian society that denied baptism to infants. This cuts off at once all the pretences which some anti-Pedobaptists would raise from certain probabilities, that the Novatians, or Donatists, or the British church of those times, or any other whom Pelagius must needs have known, did deny it."*

16. A council, composed of two hundred and fourteen bishops, was held in Carthage, A. D. 418, at which they considered the Pelagian error concerning infant baptism, and also the question, whether infants may be baptized before they are eight days old; which, it seems, some doubted. The violence of the Pelagian controversy was well calculated to elicit definite statements; accordingly we have them. The council thus decree :—

"Also we determine that whosoever does deny that infants may be baptized when they come recently from their mother's womb; or does say that they are indeed baptized for forgiveness of sins; and yet that they derive no original sin from Adam, (from whence it would follow that the form of baptism for forgiveness of sins is in them not true, but false,) let him be anathema."

17. That infant baptism was the universal practice of the church, from the days of the apostles, is strongly forced upon our belief from the fact that there was no sect, or schism, in the church that did not hold it. The reader will recollect that we have mainly attended to the practice of the general, or catholic church, in the foregoing pages. But from the body of the church there separated various and numerous disaffected, or heretical parties. These were all distinguished from the church by some peculiar doctrine, or principle. But among all these, during the period through which we have thus far travelled, none are found who denied infant baptism. Let us attend for a few moments to this point :—

1. Irenæus wrote a history of all the sects and heresies that had arisen up in the church before his time, from the history of Simon Magus, mentioned in the Acts of the Apostles. He wrote his treatise about seventy-seven years after the death of the apostle John. We have before noticed that Irenæus was acquainted intimately with Polycarp, who was the companion and friend of St. John. After having resided in Smyrna during the earlier part of his life, Irenæus was appointed bishop of Lyons, in France. Thus he became conversant with the churches both in Asia and Europe, by actual residence and intercourse

* Wall's History of Infant Baptism, part i, c. xix, sec. 36.

among them, as well as by his general learning, and his office. Irenæus mentions all the different sects that had sprung up with particularity, but he mentions none that held any doctrine contrary to the general church touching infant baptism—that is, he mentions none that denied infant baptism. Had there been such a sect, or had there been any variety of practice on this subject among the Christians anterior to his day, he must have known it;—if he had known of such a case, he certainly would have mentioned it. "Inasmuch, therefore, as Irenæus, among all these observations, says nothing, *pro* or *contra*, about baptizing infants among the heretics, it may, as I said, be concluded that they had nothing singular in that point, but practised as the catholics [or general church] did;"* that is, baptized their children.

2. Epiphanius, about A. D. 374, wrote an account of all the sects that had appeared until his time. He enumerates, in all, eighty heresies, which, he says, "were all that he had heard of in the world." "He says nothing of their baptizing or their not baptizing infants," but, after he has spoken of all the heretical sects, he speaks of the doctrines of the general church, and mentions baptism, stating that it is to us "instead of the old circumcision," &c. Had there ever been a denial of infant baptism, he would undoubtedly have known it, and, if so, of course recorded it.

3. Philastrius wrote an account of all the heresies up to about A. D. 380. He is very minute, "making a difference of opinion about any trifling matter a heresy," of which he numbers above one hundred. "He mentions no dispute about infant baptism."

4. St. Austin wrote his history of all the sects about A. D. 420. He reckons eighty-eight heresies in all, of which that of Pelagius was the last. He expressly declares that he never knew of any sect, or heresy, that denied infant baptism. The Pelagians held to infant baptism on a different ground from that which was held by the church, but the thing itself they did not deny.

5. Theodoret, bishop of Cyrus, in Syria, wrote about the same time. He classifies all the heretics under four divisions. He mentions some, who were of the most

* Wall's History, part i, c. xxi, sec. 3.

impious character, who denied all baptism; but of those who admitted any baptism, he mentions none who denied it to infants. Thus, says Mr. Wall, "they none of them mention infant baptism either as practised, or as not practised, by the sectaries,—a plain proof that they held nothing in that point different from the ordinary practice of the church."*

Thus have we followed the church through the first three hundred and thirty years after the death of the apostles. We might have added many other testimonies, but we have now brought forward the strength of the argument from church history, and we do not wish to embarrass or weaken its force by cumbersome and needless citations. If the foregoing testimonies be not sufficient to settle the question as to the real doctrine which church history teaches, then, verily, it will be trifling to add others. After the time of St. Austin, no one doubts that infant baptism was the general practice of the church. This the Baptists admit, and hence there is no reason why we should pursue the argument down to a later date. Cassander, who wrote in the twelfth century against the novel heresy that had sprung up, and had been propagated by Peter Bruis, who denied infant baptism, aggravates the charge of novelty by stating, that if infant baptism were only a mock baptism, as Bruis alleged, then, "as all France, Spain, Germany, and Italy, and all Europe, has had never a person baptized now for three hundred, or almost five hundred years, otherwise than in infancy, it has had never a Christian in it."† I produce this quotation to show the general and prevailing practice of infant baptism in the middle ages. Dr. Gale gives up the argument from church history, after the time of Cyprian of Carthage. The first body of men, says Mr. Wall, that ever denied baptism to infants were the Petrobrusians, (so called from one Peter Bruis, the founder of the sect,) A. D. 1128, of whom some account is given in the Appendix to this work.‡ "To those who say that the custom of baptizing children was not derived from the apostolic ages, the traditional argument may fairly run, in language nearly Scriptural, 'If any man seem to be contentious, we

* History, part i, c. xxi, sec. 4.
† Wall's Hist., part ii, c. ii, sec. 2.
‡ See Note F.

have no such custom, neither the churches of God:'—we never had any such custom as that of confining baptism to adults."*

If infant baptism was received from the hands of the apostles, then all is clear, and universal history and tradition speak an intelligible language. But if it was introduced at some subsequent period, then, what period was that? Why have we no account of the first person, or persons, who introduced the practice? Why have we not an account of some sect who still held to the old apostolic doctrine of adult baptism during the first four centuries of the Christian era? How came the church to glide into this practice so imperceptibly as not to know the time when it originated; and at the same time so universally as not to occasion the slightest controversy? Can our opponents tell? No: they cannot tell. They have never told. These questions admit of no solution on the principles of their hypothesis. Infant baptism came from the apostles, and if, in after-ages, it became associated with errors, as was the fact,† still, this cannot invalidate the truth and obligation of the ordinance, much less the simple fact (which is all we have aimed to prove in this chapter) that it has been received down from the apostles.

SECTION III.

1. But some ask, Why, then, was it not mentioned more fully and more explicitly in apostolic times, and by Justin Martyr and Irenæus, who followed so soon after the apostles? Also, several very ancient authors do not mention infant baptism at all. This has been urged by the Baptists as being incompatible with the supposition that it was universally practised.

At first blush this objection may appear to have weight. But let it be remembered, infant baptism was not a debated subject in apostolic and primitive times. It is not to be wondered at that a subject which elicited no question or controversy, should be wholly omitted by some writers, and but occasionally alluded to by others. Besides, the church was engrossed in other and more important concerns. The doctrines of the unity of the Godhead, the atonement

* Milner's Church History, cent. iii, ch. xiii. † See Note G.

by Christ, the fall of man, salvation by faith, the resurrection of the body, and future retribution,—these, with the "great fight of afflictions" that the church was early called to endure, absorbed its attention, and engrossed its powers. The numerous enemies from without gave them little leisure to attend to the minor points of doctrine.

"The same remark, I think, ought to be made upon that objection which the anti-Pedobaptists do so much insist on, namely, that St. Luke, in reciting the lives and 'Acts of the Apostles,' does not mention any infants baptized by them. Whoever observes the tenor of that history, and considers the state of those times, will perceive that St. Luke's aim is to give a summary account of the principal passages of their lives; and of those passages especially in which they found the greatest opposition. And in such a history, (which is but short in all,) who can look for an account of what children they baptized? Suppose the life of some renowned and laborious modern bishop, or doctor, were to be written, (say of Bishop Usher or Stillingfleet,) and that in a volume ten times as long as the book of the Acts of the Apostles, who will expect to find an account there of what children he christened? And yet there is no doubt but he did christen hundreds. [The fact, that no mention is made of his having christened infants, would not prove that he had not christened any; much less would it prove that he was opposed to the practice. So in the case before us.] The main business of an apostle was to preach, [plant churches,] attest the truth of Christ's resurrection, [doctrines,] and miracles, *and not to baptize*, as Paul says, 1 Cor. i, 17. The baptizing of such as the apostles had convinced, and especially of their children, would of course be left to deputies. Yet of the six baptisms, (which are all that St. Paul is mentioned to have been concerned in,) three were the baptisms of whole households: such a one, *and all his*. And this is as much as can reasonably be expected of so minute a circumstance."*

2. It has been objected to the argument for infant baptism derived from church history, that infants were introduced to the communion table, and made to partake of the

* Wall's History, part ii, chap. x, sec. 3. See also closing remarks of chap. ii. of this work.

consecrated elements; and that if history prove infant baptism to have been practised, it also proves infant communion, with other absurdities; and so by proving too much, it proves nothing.

1.) It is easy for an ignorant, cavilling mind, "to darken counsel by words without knowledge;" alias, in modern phrase, "to raise a dust" on any subject. Powerless and unfair as is this pretended objection, we shall give it a brief notice for the sake of those who may not have the information beforehand to detect its fallacy. Let it be reiterated, then, for the last time, that it is not the truth and obligation of infant baptism that we attempt to prove (save in a secondary manner) from church history, but simply *the fact of its apostolic antiquity.* This is a question of *fact*, to be decided by *testimony*, and the testimony we have adduced is not to be invalidated by any doctrinal errors of the witnesses on other, or even kindred topics. Their *testimony* to the existence of certain opinions is unimpeachable, while those opinions themselves may even be absurd.

2.) But the main facts in the case are these:—It appears most probable, says Mr. Wall,* that in Cyprian's time, A. D. 250, the people of the church of Carthage did sometimes bring their children, younger than ordinary, to the communion; and that in St. Austin's and Pope Innocent's time, A. D. 400, in the western church, the communion was given to infants from a belief of its necessity in order to salvation, inferred from the words of Christ, "Except ye eat the flesh, and drink the blood, of the Son of man, ye have no life in you,"—"The bread which I give is my flesh, which I give for the life of the world," &c. That the practice continued about six hundred years after this time, namely, till about A. D. 1000, when the doctrine of transubstantiation coming into credit, occasioned the omission of the elements to infants, and the council of Trent, A. D. 1560, finally prohibited the sacrament of the supper to infants formally. The Greek church, being always inferior to the Latin, borrowed the practice from them, and, as they did not receive the doctrine of transubstantiation, and consequently had not the same ground for dropping the practice, they continued it on, and practise it to this day.

* History of Infant Baptism, part ii, chap. ix, sec. 15–17.

Now, what force this absurd practice may have to invalidate the antiquity of infant baptism, and the presumption that, if it came from the very times of the apostles without controversy, and as the universal practice of the church, it came by their sanction and authority, I leave the reader to judge.

Dr. Miller has justly remarked, that "infant communion derives not the smallest countenance from the word of God; whereas, with regard to infant baptism, we find in Scripture its most solid and decisive support. It would rest on a firm foundation, if every testimony out of the Bible were destroyed.

"The historical testimony in favour of infant communion is greatly *inferior* to that which we possess of infant baptism. We have no hint of the former having been in use in any church until the time of Cyprian, about the middle of the third century; whereas testimony more or less clear in favour of the latter has come down to us from the apostolic age.

"Once more: Infant communion by no means stands on a level with infant baptism as to its *universal*, or even *general*, reception."* We have seen what was the prevalence of the latter; the former was manifestly an *innovation*. We can trace out its origin; its spread through the churches; its discontinuance in the Latin church, and the reason for it; but we cannot point to the time when infant baptism originated, nor to the sect who denied it. The two cases, then, have no resemblance to each other.

3. Another attempt to evade the force of the historical argument has been made in the pitiful effort to prove that infants proper are not intended in the earlier mention of infant baptism. Mr. Robinson says,—

"The fact is, infants appear three times, at three different and distinct periods, and the baptism of them is each time claimed for a new and different reason. The first time, *it is an infant in law*, able to ask to be baptized, and accompanied by his sponsor or guardian. This happens in the time of Tertullian. The second is an infant of eight days old. This happened about forty years after the former, [in the time of Cyprian.] The last is a new-born babe," &c.†

* On Infant Baptism, p. 46. † Hist. of Baptism, pp. 165, 166

1.) The reader must understand that all the Baptist writers assert that infant baptism was first mentioned by Tertullian, and that he opposed it. This, they say, was the date of the first attempt to introduce the practice. To this, however, it is enough to reply, that Tertullian speaks of infant baptism, of sponsors, &c., as *facts*. He recognises them as *already* known, and not as then *about to be introduced*. Besides, he does not mention the circumstance of *novelty* as an objection to the practice. Perceiving this, and not willing to fully confide in the hypothesis that this was the proper *origin* of infant baptism, our opponents have fitted up a life-boat of the assertion that *infantes*, *parvulos*, &c., do not mean *infants* "in the modern popular English sense of that word." Mr. Robinson undertakes to make out that Tertullian and Irenæus speak only of "*minors*"—"*infants in law*," &c.; and he finally concludes that these infants mentioned by Tertullian might have been *seven* years old.* He says, "they were *boys*, and not *babes*." Dr. Gale had previously taken the same position in regard to the meaning of *infantes*, &c.; and had ventured upon the opinion that those spoken of by Irenæus were children of any age under *ten* years.† Later writers have been pleased to catch at the same straw. So Mr. Hinton, after occupying a section, embracing five pages of his work, to prove that the Greek and Latin words employed to designate *children*, *youth*, *infants*, &c., do not always express a definite sense with regard to age, concludes that we must have something more than the force of these terms to make out a case of infant baptism, or to prove that, where they relate to baptism, a *babe* was baptized.‡

2.) To this it is sufficient here to reply, that Tertullian describes the kind of little children, or infants, which he intends: they are "such as cannot ask;" such as cannot, of themselves, "come to Christ;" such as are of "guiltless age;" "such as know not whither it is that they are brought," when they are brought to baptism; in fine, they are exactly the same description of infants as those which they "brought to Christ" in the days of his flesh, for Tertullian says, respecting them, "Our Lord says, indeed,

* History of Baptism, pp. 159, 167, &c.
† Reflections, &c., pp. 524–527. ‡ Hist. of Bapt., p. 226, &c.

* Rather lame point
A. N. Wilson

'do not forbid them to come unto me,' therefore, continues he, let them come *when they are grown up*, *when they understand*, *when they are instructed whither it is that they come*, let them be made Christians [baptized] *when they can know Christ*." Are not these infants proper?

The infants of which Origen (who lived at the same time with Tertullian) speaks are those who have never committed any actual sins—who have no need of any forgiveness, except of original sin. The reader can turn back and read the descriptions which these two fathers give of the *parvulorum* of whom they speak. Irenæus lived at the same time with Tertullian and Origen, only he was the oldest of the three, and used words, of course, as they used them. In the same place he enumerates the various stages of life with respect to age, and mentions *infantes*, *et parvulos*, *et pueros*, *et juvenes*, *et seniores*, *infants*, *and little ones*, *and children*, *and youth*, *and elder persons*. Yet we are gravely told that *infants* here do not denote *babes* proper, but children under *ten*, (according to Dr. Gale's conjecture,) or of about *seven* years, (according to Mr. Robinson's.) And then, these children of *ten* years, and under, are alleged capable of repentance and confession of faith, and hence capable of believer's baptism. Thus infant baptism, after all, is said not to be proved by the earlier fathers. Will our opponents tell us what word Irenæus should have used to denote an infant proper?

4. 1.) Baptist writers have resorted to another plan to bring the historical argument for infant baptism into discredit,—a plan well calculated to take with the ignorant. It is a favourite method with them to preface all their chapters on this subject with a long, dolorous, piteous complaint concerning the corruptions of the church in the first five, and even the first three, centuries. All the sayings of all the authors that have ever written on the early church, which go to cast a shade upon its reputation, are studiously sought out, and industriously scraped together, to make one appalling picture of corruption and depravity. The ultimate design of all this is, to make people think that the Christian fathers are not worth believing, let them say what they may respecting the primitive and apostolic antiquity of infant baptism. When they affirm that the universal church believed infant baptism to be of Scrip-

tural authority, and practised from the earliest times, lo! they are met with the reply, that the age in which they lived was a very corrupt age, and therefore their testimony is not to be received!

2.) It is stoutly affirmed that infant baptism first made its appearance in Africa—a place, it is said, noted for its fertility in error;—and the country of its alleged nativity, and the times of its alleged origin, are declared sufficient to account for such a corruption of the Christian ordinance. All this is said, merely because it was in Africa that the first *disputes* concerning infant baptism arose. Do not our opponents know that Tertullian and Cyprian, as well as all others who mention infant baptism, speak of it *as an* EXISTING custom? How can it be said to have *arisen* in Africa, when the earliest mention we have of the practice speaks of it as ALREADY ESTABLISHED, and as *already being* the UNIVERSAL and UNDISPUTED faith of the church? The earliest disputes (if such they may be called) concerning infant baptism all recognise the practice to have been ESTABLISHED. This is the fact which, all along, we have endeavoured to press upon the attention of the reader. Yet our opponents take these very notices of the practice, which do not relate to its validity, or its Scriptural authority, and which unanimously concur in speaking of it as an *established* custom—they take these notices, I say, as so many proofs of the simultaneous *date* of the practice. And, furthermore, because it happened to be in Africa that these notices were first taken, *therefore* it was in that place that the practice of infant baptism originated.

The most curious part of these truly wonderful arguments is their *logical* conclusiveness:—Infant baptism is first noticed in *Africa*, (instead of Europe or Asia,) therefore it is a corruption of Christianity. Again: Infant baptism was first disputed about in corrupt ages of the church, therefore it is itself corrupt. The major propositions to these syllogisms the reader will readily supply.

3.) But we are far from wishing to slander the early ages of the church. They had their blemishes, their errors, their childish and ridiculous opinions on many topics; yet, the corrupt ages of the church, properly so called—the apostate age—dates after the conversion of Constantine, in the former part of the fourth century. But how can existing corruptions in the first three centuries affect the credibility of the testimony of the writers of that period concerning a matter of fact? Such corruptions might shake our confidence in the correctness of their *opinions*, but do they invalidate their testimony to an existing *fact?* It is amusing to witness the management of our opponents. No people have ever made a more ostentatious display of the musty records of Christian antiquity to corroborate any doctrine than the Baptists, to set forth their theory of exclusive immersion. Whole books have been written on the "history of baptism," with no other ultimate aim than to set forth the authority of history (as far as possible) in favour of this doctrine among others; and in these compilations no corruptions of the church—no darkness of the age—no heterogeneous, affiliating errors—deter them from taking down whatever of testimony they can find, and wherever they can find it. And yet, if a Pedobaptist cite witnesses from the first three centuries, (the purest ages of the church before the time of Luther,) forthwith a *hue and cry* of CORRUPTION is raised, and a vulgar prejudice is excited against the testimonies thus brought forward.

5. The world, too, have been warned to withdraw their confidence from all traditionary evidence in support of Scriptural doctrine. Long sections have been written in illustration of the Popish character of all reliance upon tradition in matters of Christian faith and practice. Baptist authors have laboured hard to fix the impression upon their readers that Pedobaptists, in this case, exalt tradition to an equal authority with the Scripture canon.* They have openly charged us with *Romanism*—with "preaching another gospel"—with "making void the law of God" by tradition—while for all this they have had no better grounds than the fact that we have insisted upon the real force of the historical argument—not as the basis of authority for, but as strong corroborating evidence of, the apostolic origin of infant baptism. If individual Pedobaptist authors have at any time expressed an undue reliance upon tradition in respect of this or any other subject, still, our opponents should know that this is not a sufficient warrant for the broad allegations they have laid at our door. But the fact

* Dr. Gale's Reflections, &c., p. 243, &c. Hinton's History p. 209, &c.

is, Baptist writers begin by denying that the Scriptures contain *any* proof of infant baptism, and then, by making the *entire* proof rest upon tradition, they easily fabricate and deal out their uncharitable censures. All their trumpet alarms about Romanism and semi-papacy in the Protestant church, respecting this subject, are but as "sounding brass," the moment it is admitted that the sacred Scriptures do authorize infant baptism. All their charges are predicated solely on the assumption that they are right, and that we are wrong, touching the Bible argument. Modest men! Can they ask for more? Mr. Hinton magnanimously says,—

"In our closing chapter it will be demonstrated that one of the great evils of the unhappy perversion of the ordinance of baptism is, that it tends materially to weaken the attachment of those DELUDED by it to the great Protestant principle, or rather principle of the true church, that 'the Bible, and the Bible ALONE, is sufficient for ALL matters both of faith and practice.' Indeed it is manifest that whenever Pedobaptists engage in a contest with the advocates of Popery, they find their position on the subject of baptism one of great embarrassment, to say the least, and giving great advantage to their opponents."*

How happy it is for the church, and the world, that some pure Protestants yet remain!—Protestants who have not defiled their garments with the corrupting doctrine of infant baptism, or adulterated their faith by the muddy streams of tradition! And how unassuming is it, in our Baptist brethren, to advertise themselves to the world as being this same class of Protestants!

In closing this chapter, I have only to assure the reader that I have not designedly omitted any argument or objection that has any important bearing upon the subject. I have endeavoured so to exhibit the whole evidence in the case as to enable him to judge for himself; and though it were easy to swell this single chapter into a volume, yet I feel confident that he has the just dimensions and real merits of the historical argument before him. Dr. Gale, as we have before stated, gives up the controversy at Cyprian, and acknowledges that afterward infant baptism was practised. Mr. Robinson represents Austin as making

* History of Baptism, p. 214.

"efforts to bring in the baptism of babes." I have, therefore, carried the subject down to that father's time. I have seen much to pain me in the process of the investigations necessary to complete this chapter, so that, I confess, I reluctantly throw aside my pen even now, and yet the reader may think, perhaps, that an apology is due for having detained him so long.

CHAPTER VI.

OBJECTIONS ANSWERED.

Objection I. It is urged against infant baptism that the Bible requires "*faith*" in order to baptism; but as infants are incapable of exercising faith, therefore they are not to be baptized.

This is one of the most prominent and specious objections that has ever been urged against the practice for which we contend. It appears, at the first blush, to be fair and unanswerable; and being easy of comprehension, and summary in its logic, it has proved a very successful weapon in the hands of the opponents of Pedobaptism. And here it must be conceded, that if the doctrine of this objection be true,—if the Scriptures do require faith in Christ, in all cases, to precede baptism, then the controversy is at an end; infants are not the fit subjects of the consecrating ordinance. But it is proper to admonish the reader, that after all the evidence which has been adduced in support of infant baptism, no objection can be presumed to be valid against it, before a most careful and rigid investigation of its character. The objector himself is bound to make out a fair and valid objection, of clear and indisputable authority, before it can be admitted to have any weight against arguments of so just and conclusive a nature as the Scriptures furnish in support of the affirmative. Indeed, as we have once before remarked, if a doctrine be fairly proved, no valid objection can possibly lie against it. Truth cannot contradict itself. Either the argument, therefore, or the objection, must fall to the ground. Proceed we then to canvass the merits of the present objection. And

1. It is based upon a wrong application of the language of Scripture.

The Scriptural authority for making faith an indispensable and an invariable prerequisite for baptism is professed to be derived from the words of the apostolic commission, and from the history of the early Christian baptisms, as recorded in the Acts of the Apostles, where preaching the gospel to the individuals, and repentance and faith on their part, are mentioned as having taken place before baptism was administered. But

1.) Does the apostolic commission teach any doctrine irreconcilable with infant baptism? The words, as recorded by Mark, chap. xvi, 15, 16, run thus: "Go ye into all the world, and preach the gospel to every creature. He that believeth, and is baptized, shall be saved; but he that believeth not shall be damned." This, say our opponents, clearly places "faith" *before* "baptism," and hence excludes infants. But is this a lawful inference? Are we authorized to conclude against infant baptism from any thing that appears in this passage? I must confess I cannot so view it. It is true, that if no other circumstance existed, that would naturally lead the apostles to practise infant baptism, unless expressly prohibited,—if no evidence existed, aside from this text, to render this practice lawful and binding; in such a case we could not infer, or take authority for it from the words of this passage. But even in such a case the text itself could not, so far as I can appreciate, be urged as any *impediment* to the doctrine. For, first, the very general terms of the commission, and its exceeding brevity, forbid us to expect any details, or specifications, that do not strictly belong to a commission to "preach the gospel." Those points on which the apostles might have received instruction previously, or even subsequently, by other means, were here altogether omitted. The grand object of the Saviour seems to have been, simply to authorize them, from his own lips, to promulgate his gospel to all nations. The details of church ordinances, of church government and institutions, were left to be supplied from other sources, or at a future time. The occasion and manifest design, therefore, of this commission do not authorize us to expect great particularity in the settlement of church ordinances. What information we have in this commission, on the subject of church institutions, further than the most general allusion to baptism, seems rather incidental to the main design. The holy supper is not alluded to at all.

Secondly. It being a commission to "preach the gospel" and to administer baptism, comprised in the most succinct and comprehensive form of words, it is, as a matter of course, and as all documents of so public and general a character naturally should be, addressed to adults. The duty of preaching, specifically, has reference to adults, or to persons whose reason is so far developed as to sustain a moral responsibility. To preach, is to *publish*, *proclaim*, *announce;* and presupposes persons capable of attending to what is published, proclaimed, or announced. This is a primary and distinctive duty of all the ministers of Christ. Now it is evident that publishing the gospel has relation only to adults; and it is evident also that this specific duty of the ministers of Christ has no exclusive bearing upon the privileges or the condition of children. A command to publish the gospel to those who are old enough to act under a moral responsibility in receiving or rejecting it, is not a command, either expressly or constructively, to exclude children from baptism. Nor is a command to baptize those who believe the published truth any command, either directly or impliedly, to exclude children from that ordinance. But on the contrary, as it is evident that our Lord intended to authorize the apostles, not only to publish the gospel and to baptize, but also to plant churches, administer discipline, and do all other things necessary to the final and most universal success of their ministry; and as these varied powers of their office are not specified, but, so far as respects this passage, are wholly *constructive;* and as infant baptism may be, and is, sustained on other ground of evidence; it follows that this commission may, and must, be so construed as to authorize the practice for which we contend.

It is evident that a command addressed to adults, containing duties appropriate only to adult, or responsible age, cannot conclude either for or against the privileges and condition of infants. So far, therefore, as this commission is *specific* in the duties it enjoins, or in the powers which it confers, it must be regarded as leaving the question of infant baptism wholly untouched; and in this light, we should not feel authorized, from the text, either to affirm or deny the doctrine. But it is evident that the commission itself confers large constructive powers upon the apostles, while it leaves out, and seems to pass over, the greater amount of church institutions and ministerial functions. It appears to be a general commission to the apostles, and to all ministers of Jesus Christ, to do all things requisite to the existence and purity of the church, and the universal success of the gospel; that is, all those things that are directly, or by necessary construction, taught in the word of God.

I cannot pass from this point without noticing an unfair statement of it, which, as it occurs in a work of somewhat recent date, evinces that the Baptists do not, even now, always appreciate the ground taken by their opponents. The author says: "But it is said, 'The directions of Christ here refer only to those who are capable of believing, and the language does not *forbid* the baptism of infants.' True, these directions command none but believers to be bapized.... But the terms of the commission, while they enjoin the baptism of believers, *do, most certainly, exclude the baptism of any but believers.* If I commission my agent to purchase for me a lot of Webster's *large* dictionaries, does he not violate his instructions, if he also buy on my account a lot of the *abridgments?* But, he says, 'You did not *forbid* the purchase of the abridgments.' Did not *forbid* the purchase! I answer, It was not necessary for me to insert in your commission a prohibition against purchasing other books. Your instructions were definite; and when I directed you to buy the *large* books, you must have known that you had no authority to buy *small* books; you have done it at your own risk."* All this shows just how far some authors look into a subject before they pronounce upon it. The analogy, however an unpractised reader may be influenced by it, is an unfair and perfectly puerile statement of the case. For in the first place, Pedobaptists do not take their *authority* for baptizing infants from the mere *absence of a prohibition* of such a

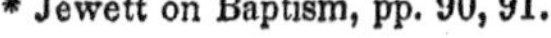

* Jewett on Baptism, pp. 90, 91.

practice, as the pretended analogy teaches. We know not, indeed, how a Christian author could make such a representation of the opinions of his brethren. All we affirm touching this point is, that the total *absence* of a prohibition, in this particular commission, does not *prove* an universal prohibition; it proves nothing at all, either *pro* or *con*. And yet our author attempts to prove that the absence of an express prohibition, in this specific case, *does* directly prove a general prohibition. Furthermore, the analogy is without any just force whatever, because, although a command to buy *large* books, is no authority for the purchase of *small* books; and a command to baptize *believers* is no authority for baptizing *infants;* yet, as such commands contain no prohibition, there may exist circumstances, or there may, in another way, be instructions communicated, to authorize the purchase of the small books, alias the baptism of infants; and this may be such a perfect matter of understanding between the master and the "agent," as to render it wholly unnecessary to specify it. And this, we maintain, is the exact state of the case in relation to infant baptism.

But if we turn to Matt. xxviii, 19, 20, we shall find the directions contained in the apostolic commission so arranged as to exactly suit the practice of infant baptism. The command there reads, "Go ye therefore and *make disciples*, or *Christians*, of all nations, *baptizing* them, &c. . . . *teaching* them to observe all things whatsoever I command you." This text we have already noticed.

One incontestable proof that our Lord speaks exclusively of adults, in Mark xvi, 15, 16, and that, therefore, his words cannot be urged as any objection to infant baptism, is, that whatever force this text may be supposed to exert against the doctrine of infant baptism, it exerts in an equal degree, and by perfect parity of reasoning, against the salvation of infants. It is contended that want of faith incapacitates infants for baptism; but it is said also, "he that believeth not shall be *damned*." Does want of faith incapacitate, and unfit them for salvation? If these words are to be so construed as to bear against infant baptism, on the score of their want of faith, we urge the principle still further, and say, for the same reason they must be "*damned*." Now, by proving too much from these words our opponents have proved just nothing at all, and we are brought back to the point from which we started, namely, that the phraseology of the text does not conclude either *for* or *against* infant baptism, the language being intended for, and appropriate to, adults only.

But we have pursued this argument thus far, on the supposition that the text decides the order of baptism, in relation to faith. This, however, is not the case. It does not say, "He that believeth, and *afterward* is baptized;" but, "He that believeth, and IS baptized." Two things are here required—*faith* and *baptism*. The requisition is put forth to adults. The questions are, first, Do they believe? Secondly, Have they been baptized? If both precepts have been fulfilled, the claims of the apostolic commission have been fully met. And infant baptism may meet the requisition as fully as baptism in adult age. Nor is this a mere quibble. It is a plain and literal statement of the fact. The verb βαπτισθεις *baptistheis* is in the Aorist passive participial form; and the sentence literally reads, "He that believeth, *having been baptized*, shall be saved," &c. This turn of the passage exactly suits the hypothesis of infant baptism.

Baptist authors have felt the force of the fact, that if children are not to be baptized for want of faith, so neither could they be saved, and for the same reason; and Mr. Carson, one of their most celebrated writers, has boldly attempted to escape from the dilemma by the following extraordinary declaration:—"With reference to Mark xvi, 16, 'He that believeth, and is baptized, shall be saved; and he that believeth not, shall be damned'—it is said, '*If we infer* that a person must actually believe, else he cannot be baptized, we must also infer that he must actually believe, else he cannot be saved; hence, *infants* cannot be saved.' Certainly, if there were no way of saving infants but by the gospel, this conclusion is inevitable. The gospel saves none but by faith. But the gospel has nothing to do with infants, nor have gospel ordinances any respect to them. The gospel has to do with those who hear it. It is good news; but to infants it is no news at all. They know nothing of it. The salvation of the gospel is as much confined to believers as the baptism of the gospel is. None shall ever be saved by the gospel who do not believe it. Consequently, by the gospel no infant can be saved Infants are saved by the death of Christ, but not by the gospel, not by faith. They are to be regenerated, but not by the gospel; they must be sanctified for heaven, but not through the truth revealed to man. The position is therefore good; none can be saved by the gospel but such as believe the gospel; none can be baptized with the baptism of the gospel but such as believe the gospel. There is no exception in either case."*

All this only serves to show how hardly the author was pressed with the difficulties of his position, and into what labyrinths of absurdity men will sometimes plunge, in their vain attempts to escape from the consequences of their untenable and indefensible dogmas. If infants are not saved by the gospel, then, unless the merest quibble is intended on the word *gospel*, have they not been affected by the fall.

2.) And thus also must the history of adult baptism be understood in the Acts of the Apostles. The requisition of faith before baptism, in the case of the eunuch, and others, proves indeed that the apostles did not baptize unbelieving adults—that faith is an indispensable qualification for baptism with reference to all such as can believe; but further than this it does not prove. It does not amount to an exclusion of infants.

2. The objection is founded upon a wrong view of the nature and importance of evangelical faith.

This, I am apprised, may seem bold. What we mean is, that faith is made to assume the place of regeneration, or that work of grace wrought upon the heart by the Holy Spirit, whereby man is created anew in the image of God. Now faith, in an adult, is only the instrument, or medium, of this great work, of which baptism is an outward sign and seal. Why, then, should it be said that baptism primarily, and in its most original sense, is to be "regarded *as a public profession of faith* in the Lord Jesus Christ?"† True, faith is a prominent idea embraced in the import of adult baptism, but it is not the *original* idea. As the *instrument* of our salvation it is the most proximate of all the means, but it is not the salvation itself. "Receiving the END of your *faith*," says the apostle, "EVEN THE SALVA-

* See Jewett on Baptism, p. 93. † Ibid., pp. 86–89.

TION OF YOUR SOULS," 1 Peter i, 9. Why, then, should the *means* be so publicly celebrated by a distinct and separate ordinance of Christianity, when the great "END" of this means is not mentioned? Now the idea which we are striving to bring to light here, we apprehend, is quite simple, and is all-important to a right understanding of the ordinance under consideration. When, for instance, the traveller visits Breed's Hill, near Charlestown, Mass., he beholds a towering obelisk. He asks its meaning; and is very properly told that it is designed to commemorate the great battle which was fought there in 1775. The idea is simple, and he readily calls to mind all the circumstances of that great and awful event. The idea of the battle is simple, that is, comprehended by one effort of the mind, though *generic.* It is embraced in one word —in one thought. Yet it comprehends under it a great variety of circumstances—of means and accidents—of causes and effects. But who would be silly enough to suppose that the grand, original intent of the monument pointed to any isolated circumstances? One man might say, The battle never could have been fought without arms and ammunition,—therefore the obelisk commemorates these *means*, without which no stand could have been made against British valour and discipline. Another man might say the battle would not have been fought but for the indomitable prowess of freemen,—therefore the obelisk commemorates the unexampled valour of simple yeomen. And this might seem a plausible account. But no. It is a mistake. The grand, original idea is the *battle;* other circumstances are necessarily included, but they are all subordinate to this. This illustration, though crude, may serve the more unskilful reader a good purpose. Baptism is not, indeed, a *commemorative* ordinance, like the holy supper, but it stands as an outward sign of something unseen, because spiritual. As a *sign* it must, of course, *signify* something, and that which it signifies, or points to, must, according to all analogy, be simple. It may be generic, but the original idea must be *one* and *singular.* That idea is *regeneration*, taken in its broadest sense. Baptism, as we have before mentioned, is not an emblem, or a representative of faith, or of repentance, or of godly sorrow, or of prayer, or of any of the *means* of salvation,

but of THE SALVATION ITSELF—the regeneration of the entire man. If, therefore, children be the subjects of regenerating grace, they may be, and are, in virtue of this state, entitled to baptism. And if faith be, as it is in the case of adults, required before baptism, it is solely because it is necessary to place the adult in a justified and regenerated state before God, in which state he is on a perfect parity of standing with the child, in respect of a moral fitness for baptism. Faith, then, is mentioned, not on its own account, but simply as being an immediate and indispensable condition of justification, which alone is the groundwork of fitness for baptism, both in adults and infants.

OBJECTION II.—It is objected to infant baptism that it is opposed to the spiritual nature of Christ's kingdom.

Mr. Jewett has thus stated the objection, which he quotes from the Christian Review:—"The ecclesiastical constitution which commenced in the family of Abraham, and was fully organized by the ministry of Moses, was not only religious, but political. Church and state were then one, for the civil government was then a theocracy. It embraced all who were natives of Judea. To be a member of the Jewish church and a subject of the civil government was the same thing; for to the church God held a political relation. But to the Christian church God holds no political relation. Though the Son is king in Zion, and wields a mighty sceptre, yet he rules by a spiritual, not a civil sway. If, then, the kingdom of Christ is strictly spiritual; if the subjects of it 'are born, not of blood, nor of the will of the flesh, nor of the will of man, but of God;' if they are not to say within themselves, We have Abraham for our father, because God is able, of the very stones, to raise up children unto Abraham,—then how incongruous is it with the nature of that kingdom, to give one of its sealing rites to those who can furnish no evidence of a spiritual regeneration, and who are connected with the subjects of it only by ties of natural or civil relationship! What a confounding is this of the relations of nature and of grace, of the claims of the flesh and of the Spirit, of the immunities of the church and of the world!"*

* Jewett on Baptism, pp. 85, 86.

Such loose, and yet somewhat plausible, reasoning has had its effect upon many minds. But it is sophistry, and adapted only to mislead. What if Moses gave to the Jews a political code? Does this corrupt, or in the least degree modify, their proper church character? It is true that the civil and the ecclesiastical laws of the Hebrews emanated from the same divine authority, but does this prove that they were one and identical? or that the plan of the Jewish church was half spiritual and half political? The church was in its state of minority, or nonage, (Gal. iv,) but it was the church of God—it was the Christian church in *fact*, but not in *maturity*. It is easy to perceive that the above objection calculates on making capital out of the very obnoxious word "*political*." In this respect it is a mere *argumentum ad ignorantiam*, and will weigh only with the ignorant. We have already fully vindicated the proper church character of the Jews. If children were ingrafted into a spiritual covenant by an ordinance of spiritual import anciently, surely they may be ingrafted into the same covenant by an ordinance of exactly similar import now. If the spirituality of the covenant was no impediment to their membership then, so neither is it at the present time. If children are in a state of favour with God, they are spiritually fit for baptism; and if so, the spirituality of the church presents no obstacle to their being baptized.

But there are statements in the above extract that are strange indeed. With what propriety or evidence it is asserted that the Jewish "church and state were one," is not easy to perceive. Their magistracy and their priesthood were totally separate; the ruler, the judge, the king, had no sort of control over the ecclesiastical affairs, except sometimes, as in the case of the Sanhedrim, to settle questions judicially. The king was not regarded as the spiritual head of the nation, nor was the high priest, or prophet, endowed with political sovereignty. The priest was not appointed or deposed by government,* nor were the functionaries of government elected or removed by the priests. Circumcision did not make a man a member of the nation of the Hebrews, or a subject of the Jewish

* It is true, this was the fact in the corrupt and degenerate ages of the nation, but we speak only of what the Mosaic law enjoined.

government, as is ignorantly asserted in the above objection. It gave him no title to an inheritance in the Holy Land. Hundreds, and probably thousands, were circumcised among the Gentiles who never saw the Promised Land, and who never submitted to the political code of Moses. Yet they were Jews in their religion, and of the spiritual seed of Abraham. How, then, could the Jewish religion be so mixed up with politics as to destroy the proper spirituality of the Old Testament church? The truth is, our opponents aim to make out that the Jewish church was a sort of ecclesiastico-political constitution—not a church—a something, they know not exactly what; but any thing to make it dissimilar to the New Testament church, so as to make all reasoning from the former to the latter without foundation, and without force. In this they will never succeed. They might as well attempt to convince the world that the Church of England is not a branch of the true church of God, because it is a national establishment, as to convince men that the political code of Moses annihilated their proper church character, or destroyed its spirituality. Indeed, it appears that the church to which Abraham, Moses, David, Isaiah, and Daniel belonged, is not spiritual enough for our opponents! The genius of those doctrines and church institutions which fostered such exalted piety in them, and in innumerable others, does not meet the high requisitions of their more enlightened views. All these things are of no avail. It is of no avail that God himself has declared that "he is not a Jew which is one *outwardly*; . . . but he is a Jew which is one *inwardly*;" that circumcision is not that which is *outward on the flesh*, but circumcision "*is of the heart, in the spirit*;" it is in vain that God has declared, all along, to his ancient people, that "the sacrifices of God are a broken and a contrite heart"—that God requires truth "*in the inward parts*"—that it was of no avail that they, at any time, "drew nigh unto him with their *mouths*, and honoured him with their *lips*, while their *hearts* were far from him;"—in vain, I say, hath all this, and a thousand times more testimony, been borne to the spirituality required and expected, and in many instances illustriously attained, in God's ancient church; all, all is in vain. It was *not* a spiritual church! It was an "ecclesiastico-

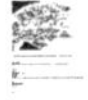

political" one! *Such a church as might admit infant members!* I would not be sarcastic, but really, what reply could be made to such assuming ignorance?

The hinging point of the present objection, however, is this: Are infants in a state of grace? If so, which we affirm, the spirituality of the church is no objection to their baptism; unless the church is too pure to admit all of God's redeemed ones.

OBJECTION III.—Infant baptism implies no exercise of reason, or of choice, and therefore forms no presumption of the truth or excellence of Christianity.

I find this objection stated in the following language by Mr. Robinson; and as it bears so general an endorsement by the Baptists, it is worthy of an insertion here:—"When the subject [of writing a history of baptism] first darted into my mind," says that author, "I own I was not thinking of baptism, but of the evidences of Christianity. I was entering on that argument, which is taken from its rapid progress, and the multitude of its professors; and I was the more struck with it by observing that the first ecclesiastical historian, Luke, in the book of Acts, makes frequent use of it; but I could not help at the same time observing, that the same argument is not valid now, because a profession of Christianity doth not now imply an exercise of reason and assent, but is put upon infants by extrinsic force. The conduct of a multitude of wise, free, and virtuous men forms a presumption in favour of the reasonableness of their actions; but a multitude of beings of no character cannot form even the shadow of a presumption. The first are the thousands of whom Luke wrote; the last are the modern professors of the Christian religion."*

We do not deem this objection as meriting a formal notice; but as its high endorsement invests it with a borrowed importance, we think it should not be wholly omitted. It may appear plausible to some, but, after all, what is its real force? All the force it can possibly possess is derived from the assumption that baptism is, primarily, a profession of faith in the Christian religion. Destroy this notion, and the objection falls to the ground. Now

* History of Baptism, *Preface.*

we readily grant that, in the case of an adult, baptism implies both the fact and the obligation of faith in the Christian religion. But is this its primary and leading signification? By no means. Nor does this admission at all militate against the fitness of applying the ordinance to infants. The principle is the same as that involved in circumcision. But as we have so fully explained this principle already, we forbear any further remarks in this place. The whole difficulty originates in a very common blunder with respect to the import of baptism. If this point were set right, the others would correct themselves. Baptism, like circumcision, is, primarily, a seal of *righteousness*, not an emblem, or a profession of *faith*. If faith, and a declaration of doctrine, be necessary to salvation, they are then and there necessary to baptism. But if not necessary to salvation, they are not necessary to baptism. The true philosophy of this subject is astonishingly misapprehended by many.

Objection IV.—Infant baptism is incompatible with those natural rights of man by which he is entitled to choose for himself the religion he professes.

Mr. Robinson says,—"Nor doth infant baptism appear less incongruous with the natural rights of mankind, than it is with the wisdom and equity of Christianity. Of personal liberty, one of the dearest branches is liberty of conscience, the liberty of choosing a religion for one's self, of which none is capable during infancy. It is the parent, or the magistrate, who chooses what religion the infant shall profess, and this is depriving him of a natural birthright."*

Mr. Woolsey, a Baptist, in his Treatise on Baptism, has a section (p. 322) under the following caption:—"INFANT BAPTISM DEPRIVES THE SUBJECT OF THE RIGHTS OF PRIVATE JUDGMENT, AND THEREFORE IS CONTRARY TO THE WORD OF GOD."

"Who but admires," says he, "those noble and evangelical sentiments of the framers of the Declaration of American Independence, 'That all men are created equal; that they are endowed by their Creator with certain inalienable rights; that among these are life, *liberty*, and the

* History of Baptism, *Preface*.

pursuit of happiness!'"—"Our parents," continues he, "have not the right to *take advantage of our infancy*, and then and there impose upon us what shall fetter our conscience when come to years of accountability."*

I have known some sincere Christians to take this ground. "Children," say they, "should grow up, and choose for themselves; then they will be satisfied. But if we cause them to be baptized without their choice, and they grow up and become dissatisfied with their baptism, and at the same time do not wish to become Baptists, they will be subjected to many unpleasant, and even painful circumstances. They will either be obliged to join the Baptist church, which may not be the church of their choice, in order to receive 'believer's baptism,' or else remain in a Pedobaptist church, with the painful conviction of having never received what they believe to be Christian baptism, for no Pedobaptist minister would rebaptize them. Thus their liberty of conscience is restricted, and we therefore prefer that our children should grow up and choose the form and kind of baptism that their own consciences approve. Then they will be satisfied, and will not have to reproach us." This is the substance of the objection we wish here to meet. In reply we observe,—

1. This is not the principle upon which the question of our duty in the premises is to turn. If it be a Christian institution, enjoined by divine authority, we are to practise it, without reference to any such future contingencies as are contemplated in the objection; but if the Bible has not sanctioned or enjoined it, then we are to omit it, not because it may have a supposed repugnance to the rights of conscience, but because the Bible does not require or sanction it. This is the principle by which our conduct is to be governed. Yet, if infant baptism, or any other practice or institution, plainly and really trenched upon the natural rights of conscience, or the moral liberty and right of choice which God has given to every man as an inalienable property, and constituent part of his moral nature, I could not doubt but such a practice, or institution, must be plainly and essentially antiscriptural.

2. But the same objection is equally conclusive against

* Vide Rev. E. Hall on Baptist Errors, p. 101.

all religious training, and especially that education in a particular system of doctrine which it is the pious concern of every conscientious and devout parent to impart to his child.

The moment the parent engages to instruct the child in the Christian religion—or to pre-engage its faith and affections in favour of any particular system of doctrine—that moment he undertakes to commit the child, by the strongest principles that govern human conduct—namely, those of early associations and religious habit—in favour of one particular faith, to the exclusion of all others. The parent uses his own superior reason and experience, to control the pliant sensibilities and docile intellect of the child, and to mould them according to a model that, in after-life, it may disdain and utterly renounce. The child is not consulted—it has no option—it is wholly submissive and obedient to the authority of the parent, whose instructions it is taught to receive without gainsaying, and to regard as infallible. The child, in such a case, cannot be said to have chosen its own religion. It may, in after-life, approve it, and be willing to lay down his life for it, but it is a religion which the parent first chose for the child, and in which, availing himself of all the advantages which nature and Providence had put in his hands, he had taken unwearied pains to establish the child, before it should arrive at that period wherein it could be said to be capable of choosing for itself. Now, what is all this but choosing a religion for another? What is it but abridging the rights of conscience, according to the notion of the objection aforesaid? If infant baptism be repugnant to the natural freedom and rights of conscience, so also, on the same principles, is the religious education of children.

It may be supposed, however, that the two cases are not parallel. But wherein do they differ? Are the obligations of Christian *institutions* in any wise different from those of Christian *doctrine?* Have the former a binding force upon the conscience different in kind or degree from the latter? Is it any more the duty of parents to pre-engage their children in the belief of the one, than in the practice of the other? Or is it any easier to break away from the restraints of one than of the other, in after-life? The principle is involved in this simple question, whether a child, before the period of personal choice, may be committed in favour of any one religious doctrine or institution, to the exclusion of its opposite, without impairing its natural liberty of choice. Infant baptism, if true, is no more binding than any doctrine of revelation; and if false, is as easily thrown off, in after-life, as the force of any particular doctrinal education. The natural liberty of conscience is affected no more in the former case than in the latter. Is it not plain, therefore, that

3. This objection is based on a licentious interpretation of the natural rights of conscience? Nothing is more clear, as a dictate both of revelation and nature, than that the responsibility of giving a right direction to the mind and conscience of the child devolves wholly on the parent. But could there exist such a responsibility, in the absence of a power and a right, both to choose for the child and to enforce instructions? The thought is absurd. Where, then, is the right of the infant to choose for itself? Or, which is the same, where is their right to claim to be left alone and neglected, as to their religion, until they can choose for themselves? If the infant is endowed with such rights, then, plainly, the parent can claim no antagonistic right. Nature cannot contradict herself. If the infant has a right to remain without a religious education, or a religious bias, previous to the period of personal choice, then it is clear that the parent can have no right to impart and enforce such instructions during all the term of immature reason. But is this a doctrine of the Bible? Is it a dictate of nature? Is it in accordance with reason? Is it not rather a latitudinarian construction put upon the doctrine of our natural rights?

A cognate principle to the above, and one which is often assumed by our opponents, in this controversy, is, that infant baptism confers no obligation upon the child, because the latter does not become a subject of the ordinance, or a party to the covenant, by personal, voluntary choice. Such objections appear the more plausible to some, because they seem to coincide with the full and unrestrained moral freedom of the actor. But how fallacious are all such reasonings! Are moral beings under no obligation to obey their Creator previously to their voluntarily engaging to obey him? Does the voluntary choice of duty make it any more sacred, or truly obligatory? Baptism originates no obligation. It is, at most, merely the sign, or recognition, of a pre-existing obligation. It is the pledge and memorial of our devotion to God; but can it make the obligation of that devotion more sacred than it was before? Was the duty of the "son," to "go and work in his father's vineyard," any more sacred after he had said, "I go, sir," than at the moment that he uttered the undutiful words, "I go not?" Did his own personal choice in the matter alter the nature of his obligation, or modify or enhance it in the slightest degree? Who does not see that it did not? So neither can the want of personal choice in infants affect the binding nature of their baptism. They are obligated, if they grow up, to lead holy lives, according to the import of their baptism, no less than as if they had chosen their own baptism in adult age.

"Consent is not necessary; for infants receive inheritances. This is by force of municipal laws. But are not the laws of God of equal force? 'Baptism [it is said] implies obligations, which can be founded only on consent.' Then it will follow that infants are not bound by human laws, for they have not assented to the social compact. They are [moreover] under no obligations to obey parents, guardians, or masters, because they either did not choose them, or were incompetent to make such choice. [Nay, further,] they are not bound by the laws of God himself, because they have not consented to his authority; and if they never consent, they will be always free equally from all obligations and all sin. Such are the consequences of the above objection."*

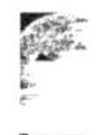

It is folly to pursue this point further. Reason and piety revolt at such doctrines. Why, then, have our opponents descended to such things, and consented to employ such sophisticated weapons against the doctrine of infant baptism? In this their zeal has betrayed them into consequences which they no more believe than we ourselves. If Christian parents believe it to be their duty to consecrate their children to God in baptism, they ought to do it, and no fancied rights of conscience on the part of the infant should deter them. The mature reason and con-

* Ridgeley's Divinity, vol. iv, p. 187.

science of the parent must act for the child, while its own remain undeveloped; and whatsoever the parent judges to be right, according to the best means of information in his power, it is his duty and his prerogative to do. If, after all this, he errs, it is the child's misfortune—the parent's infirmity—and to God alone is he held amenable. The whole subject, then, resolves itself back into the question, Is infant baptism a divine institution?

4. It is obvious, therefore, that the objection assumes, as an established principle, the very point to be proved. It assumes that infant baptism is an antiscriptural institution. If it be a divinely authorized institution, there can be no doubt but it ought to be practised; if not, it ought not, on any ground, to be allowed in the churches.

5. As to the fact that some persons, who have been baptized in infancy, having grown up, become dissatisfied with their baptism, this can never be made a valid objection to the practice. The dissatisfaction that an adult may feel with regard to his baptism in infancy can form no conceivable objection to the truth and validity of the ordinance. How many persons become dissatisfied, in after-life, with their early religious education! Men are constantly shifting their position, in regard both to doctrine and to church government. And if this circumstance might be urged as a proof of the truth of their new faith, the world would be confused more than ever with the heterogeneous testimony of conflicting partisans. That a man abjures his former faith is no evidence of its being an error; and that he becomes a willing martyr to his new doctrines is no evidence of their truth. The circumstances of the case may fully attest his *sincerity*, but can furnish no proof whatever of his *infallibility*. And what if some persons renounce their baptism, because it was received in infancy. Is this an argument to prove that infant baptism is an error, and not to be administered? We have known persons to become dissatisfied with their baptism, though received, by their own choice, in adult age; but does this prove the ordinance void, and that it ought not to be administered? Must we wait until a man has shifted his opinions for the last time, before we may venture to administer to him the ordinances, and then administer them in a way to suit the final state of his opinions? We

cannot forestall what changes the faith of an individual may undergo, nor are the ordinances at all affected by these things. The only fact that it concerns the administrator to know, as the guardian of the purity of the ordinance, is, that it fitly applies to the candidate, according to its true spirit and intent, *at the present time.* His duty is then obvious—the administration is then fully authorized, and completely guarded.

But the point we are now considering is of small importance. The broadest dimensions of this objection are too insignificant to beget any alarm among Pedobaptists, or to justify any flattering expectation of triumph on the part of their opponents. The probability that children will become dissatisfied with their baptism, in after-days, on the supposition of their having been properly educated in religion, and instructed in this particular topic, is so small, as to be wholly unworthy of a special consideration. If parents do not seriously intend to train up their children "in the nurture and admonition of the Lord"—if they do not intend to instruct them in the nature of baptism, and in the obligations of which it is a recognition, as well as the fact that they themselves have been early dedicated to God by this solemn rite; if, I say, they do not teach their children these things, it would doubtless be better that they should wholly omit their baptism. It would be trifling with sacred things, and with the awful mysteries of religion, to consecrate a child to God by a divine ordinance, and then neglect to educate and bring it up in a manner suited to such a solemn dedication. But if proper pains were taken with children, to inform them as to the fact and nature of their baptism, and their obligation to answer its holy and mystical import, there is no reasonable probability that they would ever become dissatisfied in after-life. Few, very few, even now, indulge any doubt of the entire sufficiency of their early consecration, notwithstanding the too prevalent irregularities perceptible in the plan of religious education generally adopted in reference to children.

Objection V.—It is objected to infant baptism, that it can do no good. It is often asked, "What good can it do to baptize an unconscious babe? Does it confer any spiritual benefit? Will it make its salvation more sure, if it should die in infancy, or its manhood more exemplary and pious, if it attains to years? Is the infant conscious of any advantage received, or capable of appreciating or receiving any personal good through this means? And, if not, where is the benefit of infant baptism?"

There is, to this objection, such an air of impertinence, that I have hesitated long on the question of noticing it. But when it is considered that it has its influence over many sincere minds, who are not much accustomed to argumentation, and who, therefore, do not always appreciate what belongs to a valid objection, the prominence we here give it will be the more readily excused. Our object is to attain to truth, and to disabuse the minds of sincere inquirers after truth of all erroneous impressions, as far as it may be discreet and obligatory upon us to pursue the evasive forms of error. In attempting to seize, and detain before the mind of the reader, the Protean shapes of this objection, we remark,—

1. It assumes to judge of divine institutions by the test of utility. The moment a man brings the institutes of religion to this test, he is in the greatest danger. True, the institutes of religion are all useful; and if any one could be pointed out and clearly demonstrated not to be subservient to a useful end, one could not reasonably doubt that it emanated from some human source. But the question is, Is it our prerogative to subject the truth and authority of the Christian institutes to such a test? Are we at liberty to receive or reject them, according to our notions of their utility, or their inutility? That all divine institutions are useful, we doubt not; but is our opinion of their usefulness to be the *ground* on which we are to receive them? I think no Christian is prepared to assume this position. If evidence is afforded sufficient to produce a rational conviction that a certain act, or course of conduct, is required of God, it doubtless becomes our duty to obey, without calling in question the utility of the requirement. Human wisdom is ever rife with suggestions for the improvement of the divine economy. Adam might have questioned the wisdom and fitness of the prohibition laid on the tree of knowledge. Abraham might have plead eloquently for the privilege of remaining in his parent

country; and human wisdom would have suggested an emigration of the patriarch at that time eastward, instead of westward, although after-history has demonstrated that such a movement would have defeated the great objects of his "call." How numberless are the dangers that beset such a course of reasoning! The mind would soon be led into the wilderness of skepticism, and left to "stumble upon the dark mountains" of unbelief. If we are satisfied God has required of us any particular act, we should cheerfully obey, not doubting its ultimate utility, or questioning its propriety, or, above all, cavilling where we ought to acquiesce.

2. We have not the slightest objection to meeting our opponents on this ground, and, as far as it is permitted to man to judge of the divine commands by his perceptions of their utility, to rest the fate of this subject on the issue of this argument. But our opponents must remember that they cannot hold us to any principle, or rule of judging, in this case, that does not hold equally good, and that they themselves will not cheerfully abide, when applied to doctrines *ex confesso* of divine origination.

The Romish doctrine, as expressed by the council of Trent, declares the sacraments to confer grace *ex opere operato*, that is, by the external administration of them. This the Protestant principle contradicts. We do not hold that an inherent efficacy resides in the external ordinances themselves, that by the mere act of administration is made over to the recipient. In this sense, according to Protestant principles, baptism could be of no service either to adults or infants. How, then, can infants be benefited by baptism? We answer, Their gracious interest in the covenant is thereby attested; the pledge of the divine blessing is thereby given; their own gracious state is recognised; and they are thus, by divine direction, made members of the Christian family, according to the rules of which they are required to be brought up, and to live. This subject will be fully noticed in another chapter.

But the important feature of this objection, to which we invite particular attention, is, that it assumes that an infant is incapable of being benefited by a religious ordinance, because it cannot now reflect, and reason, and comprehend the nature of things, like persons of maturer years.

The phrase, "*unconscious* babe," is a favourite expression with our opponents, to which they often give a peculiar emphasis. But what is the force of this objection? What force ought to be conceded to it, when it openly contradicts established facts, and empties its contempt upon usages which Jehovah himself has sanctioned! What good did it do to the "unconscious babes" that were brought to Jesus, that "he took them up in his arms, put his hands on them, and blessed them?" Were they *conscious* of the deed performed by our Saviour? Could they reason upon it? Could they at all comprehend it? We hope our Baptist brethren will answer these questions. But whether it availed any thing or not, the Saviour said, "Suffer little children, and forbid them not, to come unto me;" and this command is as binding on us now as on the disciples anciently.

But stranger still. God commands Abraham, and his natural descendants, to circumcise their male infants. Can any person inform us what good this ever did them? I know our opponents would escape by saying that circumcision was a mere mark of Jewish descent, and served only a political purpose; although it unfortunately happens that God himself has declared that that is *not* circumcision which is merely outward, on the flesh, "but circumcision is that of the heart, in the spirit, whose praise is not of men, but of God;" and also that Abraham's circumcision was "a seal of the righteousness of faith," Rom. ii, 29, and iv, 11. These are all-important facts for our opponents to account for, on the principle that an "*unconscious babe*" can derive no benefit from a religious ordinance, before they approach us with this same principle, and claim the privilege of applying it to the disproof of infant baptism. If they urge the application of the principle in the latter case, we shall certainly urge it in the two former; and if they hold it to be an objection to infant baptism, we shall hold it to be an objection to the wisdom and fitness of circumcision, and a reason why our Lord ought not to have taken up little children in his arms and blessed them. Strange that the Saviour did not know that "unconscious babes" *could not be* blessed! Will not our Baptist brethren count the cost of their own arguments before they adopt them? But let them beware The Saviour may rebuke them, as he did the disciples, with the significant words, "FORBID THEM NOT."

OBJECTION VI.—An objection to infant baptism is founded on the omission of a word in Acts viii, 12. It is there stated that the Samaritans, "when they believed Philip, preaching the things concerning the kingdom of God, were baptized, both men and women." Here, it is said, if but a single word had been added, this whole controversy about infant baptism might be brought to a close, or, rather, would never have occurred. If it had read, "men and women, and *children*," the text would have furnished a clear precedent for infant baptism, and all doubt of its Scriptural authority would be removed.

Great use is made of this trifling circumstance by Baptist writers; and their appeals, *ad ignorantiam*, (for they are no better,) are not without their effect. The circumstance of so trifling an omission, where so much depended upon explicitness; and also the total omission of the mention of children, where the historian professes to be very explicit, and where, according to the Pedobaptist theory, it is supposed infants must have been baptized; these circumstances are dilated upon with great seriousness, as possessing vast weight in the present controversy. But let us examine this matter:—

1. We call in question any man's right to assume what the Scriptures ought to say on any given subject, and then construct an argument, *pro* or *con*, on the mere authority of that naked assumption. With such a license a man could decide any controversy whatever. It is well known that in former days a great controversy raged in the church as to whether the earth moved round the sun, or the sun round the earth; whether the earth was round, or flat; whether it had a *foundation*, or was pendulous, &c.; and many carried their appeals directly to the Bible. These controversies gave rise to severe persecutions, and lasting disgrace to religion. A few words, direct to the point, had they been inserted in the Bible, had prevented all this scandal.

The geological age of the earth has been asserted to contradict the chronology of Moses; and the enemies of revelation have, for many years past, exulted in the supposed discovery, at last, of arguments drawn from the solid framework and superficial strata of our globe itself, sufficient to destroy the credibility of our sacred writings. Many Christians have felt their confidence shaken for a time, and long and painful has been the suspense of many minds respecting the issue. Science has never made so formidable an attack upon revelation as by the skeptical geology of modern days. The event, with many minds, is not yet decided. Yet, if Moses had added *two words* to the second verse of Genesis,—if he had written, " And *ages afterward* the earth was waste and desolate," (or " without form, and void,") no apparent ground of difference between the Mosaical and geological antiquity of the earth could ever have existed. How much, apparently, would have been spared to the cause of truth! But are we at liberty to reject revelation on the ground of such an omission?*

So is it with the doctrines of the Trinity, of the divinity of Christ, of vicarious atonement, and indeed of every other doctrine which has ever been a subject of dispute among men. If certain express words had been *added* to the present text, touching them severally, painful controversies had been spared the world. Every man who doubts any doctrine of Scripture imagines he has found a radical defect in the present Scriptural proof of that doctrine, and that if the Holy Spirit had ever intended to teach it at all, he would have taught it in a particular form of words, which he has now, at length, discovered to be the only suitable method of conveying the doctrine. Thus, every man proposes to the Author of revelation his own condition of faith. It would be endless to enumerate all the demands, of a perfectly kindred character to the one in question, which have been made upon revelation for additions here, and additions there. So it is. After all the miracles of Christ's spotless life, yet some cannot believe on him; an important item of evidence is omitted; " *If he be Christ,* the chosen of God, *let him now come down from the cross.*" How easy it is to make converts!

* I would not seem to betray any doubt, in my own mind, of the sufficient clearness of the Mosaic account, and of its entire harmony with the real facts of geological science. I merely allude to the controversy as an existing fact, and an evil that might have been prevented by a few express words, had they been inserted in the Mosaic narrative.

2. The phraseology of the text in question does not, as the objection assumes, preclude infants. We are not to suppose that infants are excluded, merely because they are not specified; this would involve us in difficulty when we came to apply the same principle to the explanation of other texts. If our opponents assume that children were not included in the number of baptized Samaritans, *merely because they were not expressly mentioned*, then we understand them, and they must not complain if we hold them to the same principle of interpretation in all similar cases. Now, let us try the principle.

It is said that Joshua and the Israelites destroyed the city of Ai, and that "Joshua drew not his hand back... *until he had utterly destroyed* ALL *the inhabitants of Ai.*" Now, the question is, *Were there any infants destroyed in this city?* The sacred historian says, "And so it was, that ALL that fell that day, BOTH OF MEN AND WOMEN, were twelve thousand, EVEN ALL THE MEN (*population*) OF AI," Josh. viii, 25, 26. Here, then, it is stated that ALL the population of the city was destroyed, and *men* and *women* are enumerated, just as they are in Acts viii, 12. But no mention whatever is made of *infants*. Were there, then, any infants in this city? And remember, the question is not, whether, judging from other causes, the city probably contained infants; but, whether the mere *omission* of infants, in the enumeration of "men and women," &c., *proves* that there were no infants. And I believe, if any man should assert that, because "men and women" are expressly mentioned, and infants are wholly omitted, in this enumeration, therefore we are to infer that this city of twelve thousand inhabitants contained no infants; I believe, I say, that such a man would be commiserated by every Baptist in the land, as one that had lost his senses. Why, then, will they continue to urge upon us such a sheer puerility in the shape of an argument? Is it because they are in want of valid arguments?

The reader may also turn to Judges ix, 49, 51. He will there find, in verse 49, an account of the destruction of "about a thousand *men and women*" in the tower of Schechem. Infants are not enumerated. Is this proof that there were none? In verse 51 he will find an account of the flight of "all the *men* and *women*" of the city of Thebez to the tower within the city. Children are not mentioned. Had this city *no* children? According to the principle of interpretation which our opponents have applied to Acts viii, 12, we are to infer that Thebez, the tower of Schechem, and the city of Ai, contained *no children*, because, after an express enumeration of "men and women," as composing their population, no infants, or children, are *mentioned*. If the principle hold good in one case, it holds equally good in all the rest.

We see, therefore, that nothing can be gained by our opponents from the circumstance of the omission of infants in the enumeration of Acts viii, 12; and the most we can make of that enumeration is, that it is a mode of expression merely tantamount to "*male* and *female*"—"they were baptized, both *male and female*."

3. But finally, if the text in question had read, "They were baptized, *men*, *women*, and *children*," still, we have no reason to believe our opponents would have been satisfied. Doubtless they would have gone to work to prove that it meant an "*infant in law*"—a "*minor*"—and not an infant proper. This they have done already in a case where far less depended on the argument than would be the case in the passage before us, if the word *children* were added. Tertullian, in the second century, speaks of the baptism of children, and not only calls them *little children*, (*parvulos*,) but *describes* them as such. (See page 227, &c., of this work.) Yet page after page has been written by Baptist authors, to prove that the Greek and Latin words for *children*, *infants*, &c., meant, often, only *minors*—*infants in law*. So we apprehend it would be if the word *children* had been inserted in Acts viii, 12. It is in vain that men call for Lazarus to convince them, when they reject Moses. They would not receive him.

Objection VII.—An objection to infant baptism is founded on 1 Peter iii, 21, "Baptism doth also now save us, (not the putting away of the filth of the flesh, but the answer of a good conscience toward God.")

The stress of the objection lies on the supposition that infants are incapable of the ends of baptism. Baptism imports the "answer of a good conscience toward God;" infants are incapable of this; therefore they are improper subjects of baptism.

1. The word *επερωτημα eperotema*, translated *answer*, is supposed to refer to the answer to questions propounded to the candidate at baptism, or to those questions themselves—as the word sometimes means *demand*, as well as *answer*—or to the whole *examination*, including both question and answer. Dr. Robinson says, "The word is spoken in the New Testament of *a question* put to a convert at baptism, or rather of the whole process of question and answer, that is, by implication, *examination*, *profession*," &c.* The word occurs in no other place in the New Testament, and but once in the Septuagint, in Dan. iv, 17, (Sept. iv, 14,) where it is rendered in the English, *demand*. The verb *επερωταω eperotao*, from which it is derived, signifies to *ask*, *inquire*, *demand*, &c. So, also, its corresponding Hebrew שָׁאַל *shaal*. See Gen. xxiv, 47; Judg. iv, 20; *et alibi*.

Now, it is plain that the apostle here intends the spiritual import—the essence itself—of baptism; namely, that it is not merely an outward washing, but a washing of the mind, or purity of conscience. He speaks of baptism here, just as it is natural to speak of it—as it applies to adult age, and as obligating to a holy life. As if he had said, "Baptism doth now save us; however, the ends of baptism are not answered when the person has answered certain questions of doctrine, but when the conscience gives a right response to God." I say, the address of the apostle is made to adults, and to such his words are particularly applicable. But this does by no means exclude the idea of infant baptism. Infants are placed under the same obligations by baptism, to profess sound doctrine and lead holy lives, as age and reason shall render them capable.

But the particular point I would notice here is, that subjects are often spoken of as if they had an application only to adults, when, at the same time, they have an equal application to infants; or as having an application only to males, when they equally apply to females. The point to

* Greek and English Lexicon.

which we allude is what is called speaking of a subject *in the abstract.* Baptism is often thus spoken of in the New Testament; and a grievous error with many persons in ordinary, who reason on this and other topics, is, that they take the language which was used only as applicable to an abstract question, and apply it to a specific case. For instance, to illustrate the principle, in Gen. vi, 5, it is said, "And God saw the wickedness of *man* that it was great," &c. Here the masculine gender only is employed. But will any one argue that the female sex were excepted in the divine mind from participating in this general wickedness, merely because this wickedness is affirmed of *man?* Every one sees that it is the *fact, in the abstract*—the fact of general depravity of morals—that is asserted, without any attempt to distinguish between the comparative corruption of the sexes. And when Jehovah threatens that his "Spirit shall not always strive with *man*," and that he will "destroy *man* from the face of the earth," does not the dereliction in the one case, and the visitation in the other, apply to *human beings*, of whatever sex? And so of a thousand other cases we might mention, where a distinction is to be made between a general question and a given case; and where the language is to be explained accordingly.

Saving grace is often mentioned as coming "through faith." "By grace are ye saved through faith." "He that *believeth*, shall be saved; and he that *believeth* not, shall be damned." "Whosoever *believeth* on him shall not perish, but have everlasting life." Here grace is limited to the exercise of faith. Infants are not excepted. No intimation is given here of any special adaptation of the atonement to infants. And this, too, is in harmony with the tenor of Scripture phraseology. Yet, does the Saviour exclude infants from heaven for want of faith? What I wish the reader to notice is, that language is often addressed to adults which seems appropriate only to them, and yet that same language does not imply an exclusion of infants from sharing an equal interest in the things thus set forth. The reader can easily apply these remarks to circumcision, which was often spoken of as applicable only to adults: thus, "Circumcise the foreskin of your heart, and be no more stiff-necked." "Circumcision is not that which is outward on the flesh...but circumcision is that of the heart, in the spirit, and not in the letter; whose praise is not of men, but of God." Deut. x, 16; Rom. ii, 28, 29. This high spiritual and practical import of circumcision was as impracticable to infants then, as "the answer of a good conscience toward God" is to the same class of persons now. Yet, the Jewish child, as he grew up, was taught his duty to assume these obligations, (which, indeed, God had already devolved upon him, and which did not, and, in the nature of things, could not, *originate* in baptism,) and to carry out the purport and meaning of his circumcision. So with the baptized child now. But

2. The scope of this passage from Peter is most decidedly in favour of infant baptism. Here we have presented to view a *family* saved by the operations of the faith of its head. "By faith NOAH, being moved with fear, prepared an ark TO THE SAVING OF HIS HOUSE," Heb. xi, 7. "In like manner baptism doth also now save us." As *Noah and his family* were anciently saved by water, so now also may *believers and their families* be saved by baptism. Let every believing parent, then, receive the ancient admonition and command of Jehovah, which was addressed to Noah, "Come thou, AND ALL THY HOUSE, into the ark." For a further illustration of this passage, I beg to refer the reader to my treatise on the Mode, &c., of Baptism, chap. vii, sec. 2.

CHAPTER VII.

BENEFITS OF INFANT BAPTISM.

Some observations which might properly fall under this head we have already forestalled, and shall endeavour not to repeat them here. The subject of the present chapter has this indication of truth and merit, that it has drawn down upon itself the sneer and ridicule of such as could oppose to it no better weapons. The reader will understand that we have no compliment to pay to such illiberal and grovelling attempts, and, passing them by, shall address our remarks to his candour and his understanding.

The errors that have been held in connection with infant baptism by its friends, as well as the prejudices that have been enlisted against it by its enemies, make it incumbent on us, before we commence our enumeration of its benefits, to state what it does not accomplish for the subject.

SECTION I.

1. Baptism does not, in any peculiar sense, accomplish the *regeneration* of the infant; nor do we consider that the child is regenerated AT baptism any more than *before*, or *after*. We do not consider that baptism accomplishes any more for a *child* than for an *adult*.

It is well known to the student in church history, that the Christian fathers associated a saving efficacy with this ordinance. Their ideas, however, do not appear to be always clear, or satisfactory to themselves. A general tendency existed to overrate the virtues of baptism, although their expressions are often such as an ultra Protestant himself could not hesitate to adopt. We are far, however, from adopting, without exception, either their style, or their sentiments, touching this point. But whatever excess, and tendency to superstition, might have marked the progress of opinion on this subject during the first three centuries after the apostles, it is evident that the extravagant dogmas of Romanism, in after-ages, were far in advance of the theology of the fathers.

The Church of Rome not only associate a saving virtue with the administration of baptism, but derive that virtue directly from the administration of the external ordinance itself. (See Objection V, of the chapter on "Objections," &c., in this work.) It is not easy to define this idea. "This barbarous phrase, *opus operatum*, which is utterly unintelligible without an explanation, signifies the external celebration of the sacraments. It has been defined by Popish writers to be the performance of the external work, without any internal motion; and sacraments have been said to confer grace *ex opere operato*, because, besides the exhibition and application of the sign, no good motion is necessary in the receiver. All that is required is, that no *obstacle* shall be opposed to the reception of grace, and the only obstacle [which they admit] is mortal sin. But as sins of this class are reduced by Roman casuists to a very small number—all others being accounted venial—the exceptions to the efficacy of the sacraments which are made by this negative qualification are quite inconsiderable.... It is in vain to ask any proof of this doctrine from Scripture, for none is to be found."*

Another dogma of the Church of Rome respecting the efficacy of sacraments is, that the priest who administers the sacrament "must *intend* to do what the church does." The meaning of this is, that the intention of the priest is essential to the efficacy of the rite. If he intend the sacrament to be efficacious, it is efficacious; but if he intend it otherwise, it is then a mere external symbol, without any accompanying grace. This absurd and impious doctrine invests the priest with absolute power to lock up or unlock, at will, the mysteries of the kingdom of heaven. But it is not our intention to pursue this error. It bears its own refutation upon its forehead.

Baptismal regeneration is a doctrine that has been charged upon the Protestant Episcopal Church, and other branches of the Protestant family.

It is difficult to affirm that the Church of England believes this or that respecting this doctrine; and it is difficult because, while one party in the Church affirm, and the other deny it, and while both alike hold to the Liturgy, and while both these parties are large and re-

* Dick's Theology, vol. ii, p. 360.

spectable, it is not an easy matter to say which is the Church. The Church of England certainly could not be supposed to hold to both sides of this question. Doubtless one of these parties holds the doctrine of *the Church*, while the other holds a *dissenting* opinion. The present state of opinion on this and other topics, in the English Church, is thus alluded to by Dr. Pusey, in a letter to "Richard, lord bishop of Oxford:"—"I own, my lord, I have myself shrunk from stating fully the degree of evidence which there is, that baptismal regeneration is the doctrine of the Church of England, lest in these days, when men hold so laxly by their Church, and are ready to quit her upon any ground of difference,—ready to suspect her, and very slow to suspect themselves,—the result of proving that baptismal regeneration is the doctrine of our Church, would be that men would rather forsake their Church than embrace her doctrine....

"Not as if I entertained any doubt, my lord, that *we speak with our Church* on this point, and that every syllable of her teaching in her services for baptism, confirmation, and the catechism, goes the same way; and that her Articles imply the same thing; but that it seems useless and ungracious for us to press upon them, that their Church holds the doctrine, until their prejudices against it shall first be, as those of many are being, somewhat softened."*

But what is meant by baptismal regeneration? The doctrine of the Church of England (we speak of what is called the "high-Church party") is, that the child is, ordinarily, regenerated AT baptism, and BY baptism, *as a means*. This is according to the ordinary appointment of God. Regeneration, they hold, is the result of two concurrent causes,—the outward washing of baptism, and the Holy Spirit. The outward ordinance is the *instrument—the means of conveyance*—the Holy Spirit is the *agent*. They do not believe that regeneration is always *necessarily* confined to baptism, but that it is ordinarily so; that by the appointment of God men are thus to be regenerated, although salvation is not necessarily dependant on baptism. On this subject, however, we are constrained to say, their language is often strong.

Dr. Waterland says,—"Every one must be born *of water*

* Letter, pp. 79, 80.

and of the Spirit: not *once* born of water, and *once* of the Spirit, so as to make *two* new births, or to be regenerated *again* and *again*, but to be once new born of *both*, once born of the Spirit, in or by water; while the Spirit primarily and effectively, and the water secondarily and instrumentally, *concur to one and the same birth*, ordinarily the result of *both*, in virtue of the divine appointment."... "Regeneration is the work of the *Spirit*, in the use of *water;* that is, of the Spirit *singly*, since water really *does* nothing, is no *agent* at all."...

"If we look either into the New Testament, or into the ancient fathers, we shall there find that the sacrament of baptism, considered as a *federal rite*, or transaction between God and man, is either declared or supposed the ordinary, necessary, *outward instrument* in God's hands of man's *justification:* I say, an instrument in *God's* hands, because it is certain, in that sacred rite, God himself bears a part, as man also bears his," &c.*

Immediately afterward the same author proceeds to show from Scripture, (according to his understanding of Scripture,) that "baptism is, ordinarily, the necessary *outward mean*, or *instrument*, of *justification*, the *immediate* and *proximate form* and *rite of conveyance*" of that blessing.

Dr. Hook says,—"So, again, with respect to the sacraments. On this subject all must admit that the language of the Church of England is peculiarly strong.... She declares the sacraments to be generally necessary to salvation, and she defines a sacrament thus necessary to salvation 'as an outward and visible sign of an inward and spiritual grace given unto us, ordained by Christ himself, as a means whereby we receive the same, and a pledge to assure us thereof,'—*a means to convey grace*, a pledge to assure the worthy recipient of its illation. Of

* On Regeneration, pp. 9, 15, 48. "Few names," says Bishop Van Mildert, "recorded in the annals of the Church of England, stand so high in the estimation of its sound and intelligent members as that of Dr. Waterland. His writings continue to be referred to by divines of the highest character, and carry with them a weight of authority never attached but to names of acknowledged pre-eminence in the learned world." It is proper here to state that I quote from an American edition of Dr. Waterland's work, entitled "Regeneration stated and explained according to Scripture and Antiquity: with a summary View of the Doctrine of Justification. Philadelphia, 1829."

baptism she states the inward grace of which it is the means, to be 'a death unto sin, and a new birth unto righteousness.' She quotes the third chapter of St. John, in which the necessity of a new birth is asserted, as a chapter implying, on *that account*, 'the great necessity of baptism where it can be had;' in the baptismal offices she expressly connects the regeneration of infants always, and of adults duly qualified, with baptism; in the office for confirmation she does the same; in the Homilies, the font is designated as the 'fountain of our regeneration,' while it insinuates that by baptism we are justified; and she teaches our children in the catechism that they were, at baptism, made members of Christ, children of God, and inheritors of the kingdom of heaven."*

Bishop Latimer says, "In all ages the devil hath stirred up some light heads to esteem the sacraments but lightly, as to be empty and bare *signs*."

Nonconformist's Memorial, Introduction, p. 9:—"So evidently does the Church connect baptism with regeneration, that the Puritans in Queen Elizabeth's time, and the Nonconformists in the reign of Charles II., justified their secession on the ground that '*the Church clearly teaches the doctrine of real baptismal regeneration.*'"

Archbishop Cranmer, Works, vol. ii, p. 302, says,—"Christ hath ordained one spiritual sacrament *of spiritual regeneration in water.*" And in Works, vol. iii, p. 65,—"And when you say that in baptism we receive the spirit of Christ, and in the sacrament of his body and blood we receive his very flesh and blood, this your saying is no small derogation to baptism, wherein we receive not only the spirit of Christ, but also Christ himself, whole body and soul, manhood and Godhead, unto everlasting life, as well as in the holy communion. For St. Paul saith, 'As many as be baptized in Christ put Christ upon them.' Nevertheless, this is done in divers respects; *for in baptism it is done in respect of regeneration*, and in the holy communion it is done in respect of augmentation."

And in his sermon on Baptism, pp. 1, 7:—"And the second birth is by the water of baptism, which Paul calleth 'the bath of regeneration,' *because our sins be forgiven us in baptism, and the Holy Ghost is poured into us as into*

* A Call to Union, &c., pp. 20, 21.

God's beloved children, so that by the power and working of the Holy Ghost we be born again spiritually, and made new creatures. And so by baptism we enter into the kingdom of God, and are saved for ever, if we continue to our live's end in the faith of Christ.... When we are born again by baptism, then our sins are forgiven us, and the Holy Ghost is given us, which doth make us also holy," &c.

Bradford says, "*As, therefore, in baptism is given to us the Holy Ghost, and pardon of our sins,* which yet lie not lurking in the water; so in the Lord's supper is given unto us the communion of Christ's body and blood, without transubstantiation, or including the same in the head. By baptism the old man is put off, the new man is put on, yea, Christ is put on without transubstantiating the water. And even so it is in the Lord's supper."—Sermon on the Lord's supper, quoted in Wordsworth's Life of Latimer, vol. iii, p. 236.

Mr. Simeon, Works, vol. ii, p. 259, says,—"In the baptismal service, we thank God for having regenerated the baptized infant by his Holy Spirit. Now, from hence it appears, that, in the opinion of our reformers, *regeneration and remission of sins did accompany baptism.*"*

"By this doctrine," [of baptismal regeneration,] say the Oxford tractarians, "is meant, first, that the sacrament of baptism is not a mere *sign* or *promise*, but actually *a means of grace—an instrument—by which, when rightly received, the soul is admitted to the benefits of Christ's atonement, such as the forgiveness of sin, original and actual, reconciliation to God, a new creature, adoption, citizenship in Christ's kingdom, and the inheritance of heaven,*—in a word, REGENERATION."

"But the two sacraments of the gospel, as they may be emphatically styled, *are the instruments of inward life*, according to our Lord's declaration, *that baptism is a new birth*, and that in the eucharist we eat the *living* bread."†

With respect to the initiation of Christians, says Bishop Pearson, "It is the most general and irrefragable assertion of all, to whom we have reason to give credit, *that all sins*

* See Appendix to "Call to Union," &c., a sermon by Dr. Hook, vicar of Leeds, and chaplain in ordinary to the queen, from which several of the foregoing extracts have been taken.

† Tracts for the Times, Nos. 76 and 90.

whatsoever any person is guilty of, are remitted in the baptism of the same person." Again: "It is, therefore, sufficiently certain that baptism, as it was instituted by Christ after the preadministration of John, wheresoever it was received with all qualifications necessary in the person accepting, and conferred with all things necessary to be performed by the person administering, *was most infallibly efficacious*, as to this particular, that is, *to the remission of all sins committed before the administration of this sacrament.*" Again: "And therefore the church of God, in which remission of sin is preached, doth not only promise it at first *by the laver of regeneration*, but afterward, also, upon the virtue of repentance; and to deny the church this power of absolution, is the heresy of Novatian." Again: "St. Peter made this exhortation of his first sermon, 'Repent, and be baptized, every one of you, in the name of Jesus Christ, for the remission of sins,' Acts ii, 38. In vain doth doubting and fluctuating Socinus endeavour to evacuate the evidence of this scripture; attributing the remission either to repentance without consideration of baptism, or else to the public profession of faith made in baptism; or, if any thing must be attributed to baptism itself, it must be nothing but a declaration of such remission. For how will these shifts agree with that which Ananias said unto Saul, without any mention either of repentance or confession, 'Arise, and be baptized, and wash away thy sins?' and that which St. Paul hath taught us concerning the church, that Christ doth 'sanctify and cleanse it with the washing of water?'"*

The Church of England, in her baptismal service, instructs her ministers to say, concerning an infant after its baptism, "Seeing now, dearly beloved brethren, *that this child is regenerate*, and grafted into the body of Christ's church, let us give thanks," &c. And in the collect which is immediately to follow, the minister says, "We yield thee hearty thanks, most merciful Father, that it hath pleased thee *to regenerate this infant* WITH THY HOLY SPIRIT," &c.

In the catechism to be used before confirmation, the bishop asks the name of the candidate, and then asks, "Who gave you this name?" Ans. "My sponsors in bap-

* Exposition of the Creed, Art. x, pp. 549–551.

tism, WHEREIN *I was made a member of Christ, the child of God, and an inheritor of the kingdom* of heaven."

If the reader thinks I have been tedious in these extracts, I must urge the great importance of the subject as my apology. The question of baptismal regeneration is agitating the churches. It is destined to "trouble Israel" in its progress and results, and it is folly for us to be blinded or ignorant respecting its true nature and bearings. Baptist writers have taken great advantage of this point in the controversy on infant baptism, and I am sorry to add, they have not always dealt in fairness.

Respecting the efficacy of the sacraments, the Calvinistic and Arminian schools, with the general family of Nonconformists, do not hold with the Church of England. We, who are styled of the more ultra Protestant school, take entirely a different view. There may be a tendency among us to undervalue external ordinances, and our jealousy for a spiritual religion, and abhorrence of the Romish rituals, may have betrayed us, in some cases, into this ultra tendency. I say, this may be, to some extent, a truth which candour would oblige us to admit. Still we are not sensible of such a tendency. It is true we have among us those who reject water baptism, and discard all outward ordinances. We have Quakers, and mystics of different classes. But the soundness of the general Protestant view, with regard to the efficacy of the sacraments, we do not consider affected by these exceptions.

The tendency of all formalism is, to exalt the virtues of outward rites. But it may still be questioned, that Romanism, in attempting to exalt the character of the sacraments, has not lowered their true dignity. Indeed, the real degradation of the sacraments is traced in nothing more clearly than in an attempt to associate with them, in so high a sense, a saving efficacy. We are hereby led to contemplate them no longer in the simple light of their being beautiful and instructive emblems, but as being possessed of charms, and to be rendered efficacious by a sort of incantation.

That the Church of England has stopped short of the true meaning of the sacraments, in her secession from the Papal thraldom, is the candid belief of a large portion of the Protestant family. I say, a large portion, for not all

Protestants who are not of the Church of England are agreed as to the real nature of the sacraments. Luther and his followers, says Dr. Wall, do indeed speak more doubtfully of this; [that is, whether baptism is strictly necessary to salvation;] and do lay so much stress on actual baptism, as that they allow a layman to do the office in times of necessity, rather than that the infant should die without it.*

"A late Lutheran," says Dr. Pusey, "admits that 'as to the sacrament of baptism, there is no controversy of much moment between the two churches,' Lutheran and Roman."† This is an astonishing admission, and taken in connection with the doctrine of consubstantiation, places the Lutheran Church, in respect to these two sacraments, in fearful proximity to Rome. It is painful to make these reflections, and happy should we be to believe the English Church pure in this matter. But how far short of Romanism do they fall? How far do they come from the doctrine that sacraments confer grace *ex opere operato?* Not that they hold to this doctrine, but that the doctrine which they do hold is liable to objections scarcely less serious.

The exact doctrine of the Church of England touching the efficacy of baptism, and the certainty of its saving results, is this: that the person is always regenerated at, or in baptism, *unless some obstacle intervene to prevent.* In the case of infants no impediment can be opposed to the grace of baptism; therefore such are always regenerated in that ordinance. Hear them:—

"In the case of infants, their innocence and incapacity are to them instead of repentance, which they do not need, and of actual faith, which they cannot have. They are capable of being savingly born of water and of the Spirit, and of being adopted into sonship with what depends thereupon; because, though they bring no *virtues* with them, no *positive* righteousness, yet they bring no OBSTACLE, NO IMPEDIMENT."‡

"The principle of St. Augustine, on the contrary, that children *being able to put no bar of an opposite will, God's goodness flows unrestrained toward them,* is, in our own

* History of Infant Baptism, part ii, chap. vi, sec. 8.

† Letter to the Bishop of Oxford, p. 73.

‡ Dr. Waterland on Regeneration, p. 19.

Church, thus beautifully expressed by Hooker:—'He which, with imposition of hands and prayer, did so great works of mercy for restoration of bodily health, was worthily judged as able *to effect the infusion of heavenly grace* into them, whose age was not yet depraved with that malice *which might be supposed* A BAR *to the goodness of God toward them.* They brought him, therefore, young children, to put his hands on them and pray.'

"In the same way again Archbishop Bramhall: 'Secondly, we distinguish between the visible sign, and the invisible grace; between the external sacramental ablution, and the grace of the sacrament, that is, interior regeneration. We believe that whosoever hath the former, hath the latter also, *so that he do not put a* BAR *against the efficacy of the sacrament by his infidelity or hypocrisy, of which a child is not capable.*'*

"And, next, baptism is considered to be rightly received, *when there is no positive obstacle*, or *hinderance* to the reception, in the recipient, such as impenitence or unbelief would be in the case of adults; so that infants are necessarily right recipients of it, as not being yet capable of actual sin."†

Thousands in the Protestant E. Church, both in England and America, justly complain of this language as too strong. The words of the baptismal service, catechism, and Homilies, are so softened by them as to leave the rite of baptism where our Saviour and his apostles undoubtedly intended to leave it. Yet, that the above is really the doctrine of the Church of England, however some of her more evangelical children may dissent, cannot be denied. Nor is it irrelevant to press this subject upon the American churches. The Episcopal Church of this country is following close in the steps of the Anglican mother.

A treatise on baptism by a late clergyman of that denomination, which bears the warm commendations of Bishop Chase, of Illinois, and others, contains the following:—

"Christ rebuked those who forbade little children to be brought unto him. What shall he say to those fathers or mothers who neglect or refuse to bring unto him their own children? They have need of redemption through

* Vide Dr. Pusey's Letter, &c., pp. 75, 76.
† Tracts for the Times, No. 76.

him as well as yourselves, and will you deny them the privilege of coming unto Christ in the way he hath appointed? I by no means insinuate, that if an infant die without baptism, its future state is thereby rendered worse. It was no fault of its own. But it is neither unreasonable, nor against the Scriptures, *to believe that some distinguishing marks of goodness shall be conferred on those infants in another world who have entered into the door which the Church hath opened.* And to a parent that regards Christianity, *I cannot but think it is a just cause of uneasiness, when his young child dies without baptism*, through his neglect."*

All this is in itself too strong language—doctrine to which we cannot subscribe:—besides, it seems to intimate a latent suspicion in the author himself, that infant baptism may possibly be necessary to infant salvation after all. Why, else, should the delinquent parent feel "*uneasy?*" Sorrow he may feel for not having dedicated his child to God in baptism, and thereby signified his acquiescence in a divine direction; but *uneasiness* at the thought of this delinquency, *as affecting the future destiny* of the child, is extending the efficacy of baptism far beyond what we consider to have been the intention of its Institutor.

Yet, Archbishop Laud says, "That baptism is necessary to the salvation of infants, (in the ordinary way of the Church, without binding God to the use and means of that sacrament to which he hath bound us,) is express in St. John iii, 5, 'Except a man be born of water,'" &c.

"Concerning the everlasting state of an infant," says Dr. Wall, "that by misfortune dies unbaptized, *the Church of England has determined nothing*, (it were fit that all churches would leave such things to God,) save that they forbid the ordinary office for burial to be used for such a one; for that were to determine the point, and acknowledge him for a Christian brother. And though the most noted men in the said Church from time to time, since the reformation of it to this time, have expressed their hopes that God will accept the *purpose* of it for the *deed; yet they have done it modestly*, and much as Wickliffe did, rather not determining the negative, than absolutely determining

* Rev. Alexander Hay on Baptism, pp. 129, 130.

the positive, that such a child shall enter into the kingdom of heaven. Archbishop Laud's words, we see, are, 'We are not to bind God, though he hath bound us.' And Archbishop Whitgift, disputing with Cartwright, says, 'I do mislike, as much as you, the opinion of those that think infants to be condemned which are not baptized.' But there are, indeed, some, who make a pish at any one who is not confident, or does speak with any reserve about that matter."*

Before passing to notice the doctrine of our own (the Methodist Episcopal) Church, we wish to offer a few thoughts on the foregoing views.

1. We have already stated that, in our own opinion, the stress laid upon baptism by the Church of England is too great. Its efficacy is overrated; and the primary cause of this error is, the too literal interpretation of a few passages of Scripture. Language which has been employed evidently in a figurative sense, has been pressed too closely to the *letter*, and the metaphor has been thus made to assume an importance which belonged only to the thing itself, which was represented by it.

These texts are such as John iii, 5; Acts ii, 38, and xxii, 16; Rom. vi, 4; Gal. iii, 26, 27; Eph. v, 25, 26; Titus iii, 5–7; 1 Pet. iii, 21. Admitting that some Protestants may have attached too lax and unworthy views to these strong expressions of Scripture, still it is but figurative language, and baptism is made to be only an outward rite, having no efficacy beyond the force of a *sign* and a *visible pledge*.

2. It is contrary to the analogy of Scripture doctrine, as well as to the nature of the case, that an outward rite, applied to the flesh, should be made an "*instrument*," (in the proximate sense of that term,) or "*means of conveyance*" of spiritual regeneration.

It is contrary to the analogy of Scripture doctrine, because nowhere is an outward ceremony appointed as the proximate instrument of regeneration. Circumcision, to which baptism now answers, was given to Abraham, not as a *means of conveyance* of regeneration, but, as "*a seal of the righteousness* WHICH HE HAD YET BEING UNCIRCUMCISED," Rom. iv, 11. Paul, when speaking of the efficacy

* Wall's History, part ii, chap. vi, sec. 8.

of all outward ablutions under the law, admits merely that they "sanctified to the *purifying of the* FLESH," and in direct antithesis to this he asserts that "the blood of Christ" only is the proximate *means* by which God will "purge our consciences from dead works." But the blood of Christ is here spoken of figuratively, as being sprinkled, or used as a material instrument. Analogy, therefore, is against this doctrine.

But reason no less repudiates it. How can a physical rite *convey* grace to the soul? It may represent that grace, but can it *convey* it? Can the chasm between mind and matter be so closed as to bring the two into proximity? Nay, more, can a *moral* change be effected *through* a physical medium? God alone, who is a "spirit," can carry his grace to the heart and conscience of man. Water can go no further than the *flesh;* there it must stop. Beyond that it cannot be used as any "*means of conveyance*," because, beyond that it does not *go*. But beyond this God's Spirit enters, and regenerates the heart. As baptism is not, therefore, the *means*, in propriety of language, of regeneration, so regeneration is not confined to baptism, either from the nature of the case, or the ordinary appointment of God.

I wish the reader to appreciate that it is not a mere phantom, or a mere form of words, that is here opposed. Dr. Waterland says, "From these several passages of the New Testament laid together, it sufficiently appears, not only that baptism is the *ordinary instrument* in God's hands for *conferring* justification; but also, that ordinarily there is no justification conferred either *before* or *without* it. Such grace as *precedes* baptism, amounts not ordinarily to justification, strictly so called: such as *follows* it, owes its force, in a great measure, to the *standing virtue of baptism* once given.*

So then, whether a person have *faith* or not, before baptism, it is all one, "ordinarily," so far as respects complete justification, or "justification *strictly so called!*" This is utterly out of the question. Again: "In baptism is the *first solemn and certain reception of justification*."† Such quotations might be easily multiplied. If nothing more were meant, by all these strong expressions, than

* On Justification, p. 54. † Ibid., p. 48.

that baptism is *a means* of grace, a peculiar means, if you please, so that the word *means* were used in its ordinary acceptation, as denoting that which helps the soul to embrace Christ, or answers some spiritual end, we would here drop this controversy. And let it be remembered, the question is not whether a person *may be* regenerated at baptism? but whether baptism is the appointed instrument of conveying that blessing? Whether by the special appointment of God, regeneration, or justification, takes place, in all ordinary cases, at that time, and by that means? and, consequently, whether it is reasonable and Scriptural to expect either without baptism, where baptism can be had? Whether the importance of baptism be such as to leave a doubt respecting the future happiness of those infants which die unbaptized? so that it is modest for the Church, in reference to such, to express no opinion as to their future happiness or misery? Whether a child will receive "some distinguishing marks of goodness in another world," for having been baptized in this? And whether a parent has "a just cause of *uneasiness*, when his young child dies without baptism, through his neglect?" These are grave considerations, and they are this day agitating the church of Christ, in many parts, with a deep and terrible convulsion.

I know that it is said the Church of England holds to regeneration by the Holy Spirit *only*, and that baptism is not abstractly *necessary* to salvation, but only necessary in the ordinary appointment of God. All this we understand. But we deny that regeneration by the Holy Spirit takes place AT baptism, any more than BEFORE that ceremony. We hold to the fitness of baptism, BECAUSE the subject is regenerated. And we hold, also, that baptism is no more essential to salvation than any other appointed outward means of grace.

3. It is astonishing to reflect how completely these views, which we oppose, mistake the *genius* of gospel ordinances. It seems to be entirely overlooked that the ordinances have reference strictly to the church *in its militant state.* All their suitableness arises from the circumstances of the church in its *earthly* relations. We need no external ceremonies to fit us for, or induct us into, "the church of the first-born, which are enrolled in heaven."

Baptism has no prospective relation to another life. All its significancy, all its intentions, are fully met and answered in this life. It is designed to give *visibility* to the church, not to confer on it a *spiritual* character. This is conferred only by the Holy Spirit, in his direct communications to the heart. We do not, therefore, conceive any fitness in baptizing a dying person, merely because he is dying. It is proper to bear testimony to the truth, and to show our spirit of obedience, by embracing the sacraments at any suitable time. But the importance of baptism to the individual recipient is not enhanced by the mere circumstance of the near approach of death. The church triumphant recognises no such outward rites, and the terms of membership there relate to the essential purity of the moral man, not to any accidents.

Indeed, this is the very essence of superstition, to place the eternal happiness of the soul upon some outward and accidental circumstance of the person here. God has never placed the spiritual destinies of men upon such precarious footing. It is not in the power of one man thus to withhold salvation from another, or to confer it upon him, in the strong sense which this doctrine of baptismal regeneration supposes. Such a notion is no less revolting to all our natural sense of justice, than it is repugnant to Scripture and right reason. Men have always had a contest with the Almighty as to which should hold the greater sway over their consciences and moral destinies, themselves or their Maker. Man loves to do the work of God better than his own; and if he dare not always assume the prerogative of plenary remission of sin, he will make his consequence to be felt by linking himself somewhere in the train of causes that are to result in such remission. If he dare not assume to regenerate the heart, he will fain think that the Almighty has been pleased to subject himself, as to the *time* of regenerating, and the *means* of justifying, "ordinarily," to the moment of his own convenience, and the ministry of his own hands. These may be deemed uncharitable expressions, but we utter them not in such a spirit. We do not wish to impute any such sentiments as the above to any living men. As a matter of fact, we are aware many, very many, of the Church of England, as well as Episcopalians in this country, repu-

diate all such pretensions. But this, we say, is the tendency of the language of the Liturgy and standard writings of their Church; and if they sincerely regard the general interests of truth, and at the same time revolt at the general construction put upon their statements, why do they not condescend to a more popular, and hence a more comprehensible phraseology? This has long been a subject of just complaint by many of the evangelical sons of their own communion. But have they at all heeded these complaints? A reconciliation with the evangelical party within her pale the Church of England earnestly wishes, but, unhappily, wishes it on the ground stated by Dr. Pusey,* in the following words: "And to this reconciliation it may perhaps the rather tend, if I add, that we do not wish to enforce any technical view of baptismal regeneration: for myself, I should be fully content with any view, which acknowledged in its simple sense the words which our Church teaches every child to say of itself, 'wherein I was made a child of God, a member of Christ, and an inheritor of the kingdom of heaven;' meaning, of course, really what is here said, *a real child of God*, and *a real member of Christ*, not *simply* an outward member of an outward body of people called Christians:"—that is, the Rev. doctor would be satisfied with any view of the words in the baptismal service, catechism, and homilies, peradventure such view accorded with *his own*, and that of the high-Church party! and all this he would do for the sake of reconciliation!

The Methodist connection, it has been covertly insinuated, holds to the doctrine of baptismal regeneration. Mr. Hinton asks, "Is Methodism clear of baptismal regeneration?" and then says: "It will be perceived that although the prayers in this service [meaning the baptismal service prescribed in the Methodist Discipline] closely resemble those of the Episcopal Church of England, yet, by avoiding the *thanksgiving* at the close, the Methodist is allowed to escape the assertion that the baptized child *is* 'sanctified with the Holy Ghost,' and 'is received into the ark of Christ's church,' and has received 'the fulness of grace;' though in the prayer, 'ever *remain* in the number

* Letter to the Bishop of Oxford, p. 81.

of thy faithful and elect children,'* it is clearly intimated that the child was about to become one."†

This, to be sure, is a very curious statement. First, Mr. Hinton gravely tells his readers that the Methodist Church, by avoiding the *thanksgiving* which the Church of England employ after the baptism of an infant, is "allowed to escape the assertion that the baptized child *is* sanctified," &c.; that is, by omitting to *affirm* the doctrine of the Church of England, the Methodist Church is allowed to *escape* the assertion of that doctrine! This is extraordinary! Secondly. In the prayer, "ever *remain* in the number of thy faithful and elect children," &c., it is *not* "intimated that the child is *about to become* one" by baptism, but that it is *already* a subject of grace and an heir of heaven, and *therefore* is entitled to the seal of the covenant.

Mr. Hinton has ventured upon the following statements: "It is not necessary," says he, "to enter more minutely into the investigation of this ordinance as found in the Methodist Church, *since the authorized statements respecting it are exceedingly loose and indefinite*," &c. And in a footnote remarks, "I am aware, however, that in some instances the authority of great names in the Methodist Church may be found sanctioning some of the wildest fancies of the fathers respecting infant baptism; but wherever fidelity will permit, it is pleasing to exercise *forbearance*."‡

I think it cannot be denied by the intelligent and candid of the Methodist Church, that some of our standard writers have adopted too far the phraseology of the Church of England. Some of them were educated for the ministry in that Church before they became Methodists, and others were drawn into particular modes of speech from a long intimacy with her justly admired standard writers, as well as from the force of educational connection with her ritual. Mr. Wesley was, in the earlier period of his life, a *high-Churchman*. Afterward his views of doctrine and church government, it is well known, became greatly changed. He always retained, however, those forms of expression concerning baptism which are employed in the Liturgy,

* See collect before baptism.

† History of Baptism, p. 348. ‡ Ibid., p. 349.

attaching to them, invariably, that modified sense of which they are capable, and which, in his guarded method of using them, could not be greatly objectionable even to a Baptist, and certainly could not be misunderstood. Mr. Wesley's real views of the efficacy of baptism were Scriptural, according to the most settled principles of the Protestant school, and his predilection for the forms of speech used in the Liturgy of the Church of England, of which he was a member, is not to be ascribed to any obsequious copying after the Christian fathers. He understood John iii, 5, and Titus iii, 5, to refer to Christian baptism, and considered his language no stronger than that employed in Scripture. But whatever objection may be had to his language, none can be urged against his *meaning*, which is repeatedly and explicitly set forth in his sermons.*

We could have wished, also, that Mr. Watson had, in one or two single expressions, employed words less liable to be misunderstood; as when he says, "Baptism *conveys* also the present blessing of Christ"—"It *secures*, too, the gift of the Holy Spirit, in those secret influences by which the actual regeneration of those children who die in infancy is effected, and which are a *seed of life* in those who are spared." We say, a more guarded phraseology might have been adopted, in strict accordance with Mr. Watson's views, and hence, we could have wished it had been, for the sake of the more fastidious. Mr. Watson's views are fully and most unexceptionably expressed thus: "In a word, it is, both as to infants and to adults, the *sign* and *pledge of that inward grace* which, although modified in its operations by the difference of their circumstances, has respect to, and flows from, a covenant relation to each of the three *persons*, in whose *one name* they are baptized."† Yet it is possible Mr. Hinton imagined he saw in these expressions "some of the wildest fancies of the fathers respecting infant baptism"—expressions "exceedingly loose and indefinite;" although common sense, combined with common honesty, would have taught him to understand their words as they had explained them, in which case no objection, doctrinally, can lie against them.

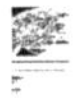

The doctrine of the Methodist E. Church respecting

* See Note H. † Institutes, part iv, ch. iii, sec. 2

the sacraments is expressed in her 16th article of faith: "Sacraments ordained of Christ are not only badges, or tokens, of Christian men's profession; but rather they are certain signs of grace, and God's will toward us, by the which he doth work invisibly in us, and doth not only quicken, but also strengthen and confirm our faith in him." Of baptism she says, in her 17th article of faith: "Baptism is not only a sign of profession, and mark of difference, whereby Christians are distinguished from others that are not baptized: but it is also a sign of regeneration, or the new birth." What apology a man can have, after all these statements, (to which we might add others, to an indefinite length,) for representing the Methodist Church as holding loosely and indefinitely to the doctrine of infant baptism, I shall not trouble the reader to divine.

Before dismissing this subject, I beg leave to state that I apprehend some confusion of ideas has resulted from the use of the word *sacrament*. A sacrament is defined to be an outward sign of an inward grace; consisting, consequently, of two parts, the one *visible*, and the other *invisible;* and in baptism one part of the sacrament is *water*, the other *regenerating grace*. It is evident, therefore, that, according to this definition, baptism, or the outward washing, is not of itself a sacrament, but only the *visible*, or *outward part* of a sacrament—the lesser half. How improper, then, to use the words *baptism* and *sacrament* as synonymous! By this means an obscurity has sometimes rested upon language. No one ever believed that baptism, or the outward washing, regenerates; but only that a person is regenerated *at* baptism, and that regeneration is a necessary part of the sacrament, of which baptism is the other part. We could mention many cases where an unguarded use of terms has led to false issues on this point. The question is, Has God appointed that regeneration should ordinarily accompany baptism? We all admit that regeneration is the work of the Holy Spirit—that baptism adumbrates it; but while the Church of England holds that it ordinarily accompanies baptism, and that baptism is a *means of conveyance*, or *instrument*, of this grace, we hold that regeneration takes place ordinarily *before* baptism, and that baptism is appropriate *because* the person is regenerated, and is, also, a sign and seal of such regeneration.

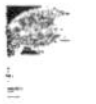

SECTION II.

1. The relation of baptized infants to the church, it is important to our general subject that we should understand. The following distinctions should be observed:—"A person may be a member of the catholic, or universal, church of Christ, while he is not a member of any particular church. Baptism introduces a person into the catholic church of Christ. Baptism alone does not constitute him a member of any particular church. To become a member of a Presbyterian church, or a Methodist church, &c., something more is required besides being baptized. Therefore, when an infant is baptized, though he is introduced by baptism into the church of Christ, he is not thereby constituted a member of any particular branch of Christ's church; and if the baptism be performed by a Presbyterian or a Methodist minister, he does not baptize him by virtue of his being a Presbyterian or a Methodist, but by virtue of his office as a minister of Christ. He does not, therefore, by virtue of his office, introduce him by baptism immediately into the Presbyterian or Methodist Church. But he does introduce him, by baptism, immediately into the church of Christ."* ✕

It is a favourite objection with our opponents, and one which they often urge against the baptism of infants, that, in virtue of their baptism, infants have a right to communion at the Lord's table; but as this is allowed on all hands to be absurd, and as it is alleged that baptism invariably confers upon the recipient this privilege, hence, it is inferred that infant baptism itself is absurd. In reply to this popular objection, and in order to place the true relation of infants to the church in the true light, we observe,—

1.) It is a great mistake to suppose that baptism alone confers upon the patient all the privileges of the visible church. This principle is constantly assumed by our opponents, but it is not admitted by us to be valid. Cases exist where baptized adults are properly excluded from the communion. Something more than mere baptism is requisite. No Christian thinks of claiming a seat at the Lord's table simply on the ground of his baptism. This fact, which needs no proof, (as none will deny it,) is suffi-

* Rev. P. P. Sandford on Baptism, p. 18.

✕ N.B. The child then is formally a member of the General church of Christ.

cient to overthrow the principle upon which the above objection is founded, and hence, to overthrow the objection itself. If mere baptism do not entitle an *adult* to communion, certainly it cannot be supposed to give *infants* such a title, and therefore it is not absurd, *per se*, to baptize infants and then deny them the Lord's table. If something else besides baptism is necessary to this privilege, then manifestly it cannot be predicated of baptism alone. If mere baptism gives permission to sit at the Lord's table, then, why do our Baptist brethren ever suspend from communion some of their own members? but if not, why do they reproach us for not making mere baptism a sufficient qualification for the same privilege? Will they answer?

The truth is, the two ordinances differ in this respect: He that "eateth" at the communion table must "*discern the Lord's body*," in order to partake "worthily." But the design of baptism, as a *sign* and *seal* of covenant grace, does not thus exclude infants from participation, on the score of incapacity; unless it be proved that they are not in a state of grace.

Besides, how do our opponents know that baptism warrants the privilege of communion, any more than it does other church privileges? For this they have no sort of proof; it is mere assumption. Now, it is incontrovertible that baptism does not confer full church privileges in all cases. All females are prohibited for ever all eligibility to ministerial or church offices:—"I suffer not a woman to *teach*, or to usurp *authority*"—"Let them keep silence in the churches, for it is not permitted unto them to speak," 1 Cor. xiv, 34, 35; 1 Tim. ii, 11, 12. Here, then, are half the lawful members of Christ's church ecclesiastically disfranchised and laid under perpetual ecclesiastical disabilities;—church members, denied the *rights* of church members! Now, we mention this merely to show that baptism alone does not always introduce to all the rights of church membership, and, so far as the abstract principle is concerned, it is no more paradoxical and absurd to deny the communion to baptized infants, than to deny other church rights to baptized females. I am aware, however, that for an *ad hominem* argument this is an unfortunate one, for our opponents admit females to sit in judgment on the opposite sex in their church assemblies. But whether

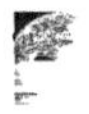

in this feature of their congregationalism they claim to follow the letter of Scripture as closely as in baptism, we cannot say.

2.) The principle involved in this question is clearly recognised in the common sense and universal practices of mankind. We know, indeed, that this is not an adequate sanction for any religious practice, *as such;* but it may suffice for illustration, and, withal, it clears us from the charge of acting absurdly. Children are entitled to some of the immunities of law from their earliest infancy. From their birth they are recognised as citizens. Yet are they disabled, during all the period of minority, from holding any share in certain rights which belong to citizens. They belong to the nation—are citizens—are capable of enjoying some of the immunities of law—and yet are physically and legally incapacitated to share in the full privilege of citizenship.

So it is with a child who is heir to an estate. Who will dispute his title on the ground of his age? Yet his title does not give him possession of the inheritance during nonage. So that it may truly be said, "Now an heir differeth nothing from a servant, though he be lord of all; but is under tutors and governors until the time appointed." Here is a title without possession. Here is admission to some rights, and exclusion from others, while at the same time the individual holds an equal *title* to ALL. Nonage cannot invalidate the *title*, but it does legally, as it of right should, in the eye of reason, suspend the *possession*, and, consequently, the plenary *enjoyment*. So do we regard the case of infants with respect to communion. They are subjects of grace—they may bear the seal of the covenant—they are entitled to the blessings of the church—"the kingdom of heaven *belongs* to such"—but the period of actual inheritance, when they come into the exercise and enjoyment of all the privileges of their gracious birthright, is postponed to the age of maturer reason. Our opponents, then, will remember, that Scripture, reason, and the common sense of mankind, do sanction the principle involved in the practice of denying the communion to baptized infants. If they wish to ridicule it, therefore, it must be at their own expense. We are vindicated.

3.) But we have higher authority still for this practice.

We are able to settle, not the abstract principle only, but the thing itself, by a case so nearly analogous, as justly to be regarded as a precedent, and as to remove all reasonable ground of doubt respecting its propriety. It is matter of fact that circumcision did initiate into the visible church under the law of Moses. This our opponents will not deny, unless they deny the existence of *any* visible church at that time. It is a fact, also, that male infants, among the Jews, were circumcised, and that ALL infants, of both sexes, were considered as belonging to the church, and as having an equal interest with their parents in the covenant. Yet we know that it was physically impossible for them to partake of the *passover* as early as they were required to be circumcised. We know, also, that they could not have shared in the other feasts, nor in the sacrifices, offerings, and ablutions required by the law. Here age was wanting. Age alone could give capacity.

If we attend to the tenor of the law respecting the observance of the passover, as recorded in Exod. xxiii, 15–17, we shall find that it would have been impracticable for young children to attend that feast. The reader will there find that "three times in a year all the males were to appear before the Lord," in the place which he should choose, and they were not to appear empty. The passover formed one of these occasions. But it does not appear at all probable that their male infants were required to be present at the passover with an offering. Indeed, this would not have been practicable. On the contrary, it is plainly intimated in Exod. xii, 25, and elsewhere, that children were not brought to these annual feasts until they were old enough to inquire of their parents, "What mean you by this service?"

And hence it was that the Jewish "custom," or law, prohibited children from these privileges of the church. We learn from Luke ii, 41, 42, that Jewish children were admitted to the passover at "twelve years old." This was the age at which our Saviour first went up to Jerusalem to this feast. Calvin remarks, that "the passover, which has now been succeeded by the sacred supper, did not admit guests of all descriptions promiscuously; but was rightly eaten by those only who were of sufficient age to be able to inquire into its signification."

The same distinct statement is also made by the Rev. Dr. Gill, an eminent commentator of the Baptist denomination:—"According to the maxims of the Jews," says he, "persons were not obliged to the duties of the law, or subject to the penalties of it in case of non-performance, until they were, a female, at the age of twelve years and one day, and a male, at the age of thirteen years and one day.* But then they were accustomed to train up their children and inure them to religious exercises at an earlier age. They were not properly under the law until they had arrived at the age above mentioned; nor were they reckoned *adult* church members until then; nor then neither, unless worthy persons; for so it is said, 'He that is worthy, at thirteen years of age, is called a son of the congregation of Israel.'"†

This, then, is sufficient to settle this point. No objection can lie against the practice of excluding baptized children from the Lord's supper, that does not equally lie against the exclusion of circumcised children from the passover. But the latter is settled by divine authority and

* The German author, Frederick Strauss, represents the custom of the Jews as allowing children to go up to the passover at an earlier age than twelve or thirteen years, if they discovered a capacity for enjoying that sacred feast. In his "Pilgrimage of Helon," which was designed to furnish a "picture of Judaism, in the century which preceded the advent of our Saviour," he describes a procession of Jews going up to Jerusalem to attend the passover. As the vast multitude passed on, with every demonstration of holy joy, "before a house in Bethshur stood a fine boy of *ten years old.* Tears streamed from his large, dark eyes, and the open features of his noble countenance had an expression of profound grief. His mother was endeavouring to comfort him and to lead him back into the court, *assuring him that his father would take him the next time.* But the boy listened neither to her consolations nor her promises, and continued to exclaim, 'O father, father, let me go to the temple! I know all the psalms by heart.' He stretched out his arms to the passers-by in earnest entreaty; and happening to see among them a man of the neighbourhood whom he knew, he flew to him, and clinging to his girdle and his upper garment, besought him with tears to take him with him, till the man, moved with his earnestness, asked his mother to allow him to go, promising to take care of him till he should find out his father.

"'And this,' said Helon, 'is the object of children's longing in Israel; so early does the desire of keeping the festival display itself.' Brought up in Palestine, he felt it would have been with him exactly as with the child."—*Helon's Pilgrimage*, &c., pp. 96, 97.

† Comment on Luke ii, 42. See Miller on Baptism, p. 52.

the nature of the case; the former, therefore, cannot be absurd or irrelevant. The great difficulty lies in assuming the principle that children cannot be members of the church *in any sense,* without being so *in the fullest sense,* and, consequently, if entitled to *any,* entitled to *all,* the privileges of the church. This principle we have seen to be absurd. Our opponents will not abide its consequences when applied to other subjects, or to the case of circumcision, which is perfectly analogous to the one in point. Why, then, will they continue to urge it? Baptized children, therefore, are members of the church just as far as all children are members of the nation, or subjects of the government to which they belong; just as far as all circumcised children were members of the Jewish church; *they are members of the church so far as to entitle them to all the spiritual benefits that belong to their age and capacity.*

2. Infant baptism, as well as that of adults, is an affecting memorial of the sinfulness of our nature, and of our consequent need of inward sanctification by the Holy Spirit.

One primary intention of all outward ceremonial ablutions is, to impress man with the truth of his own pollution by sin. "Behold," says David, "I was shapen in iniquity, and in sin did my mother conceive me," Psa. li, 5; and Job justly inquires, in reference to the depravity of Adam's descendants, "Who can bring a *clean* thing out of an *unclean?*" Job xiv, 4. "We are *by nature* children of wrath," Eph. ii, 3. No method could have been adopted which could have more fitly aroused the human mind to a just sense of the corruption of our nature, and of our utter need of inward sanctification, in order to the enjoyment of God, than the Jewish ritual respecting outward washings. The same emblematical sense is preserved in the Christian ordinance of baptism, and in this sense is fitly applied to infants.

"Infant baptism," says Dr. Wardlaw, "contains a constant memorial of *original sin;*—of the corruption of our nature being not merely *contracted,* but *inherent.* And this doctrine of original corruption, of which infant baptism is a standing, practical recognition, is one of fundamental importance; one, I am satisfied, to inadequate conceptions and impressions of which may be traced all the principal perversions of the gospel. In proportion to its relative importance in the system of divine truth is it of consequence that it should not be allowed to slip out of mind; the baptism of every child brings it to view, and impresses it [upon the mind.] If in any case it should be otherwise, the fault is not in the ordinance, but in the power of custom, and in the stupidity and carelessness of spectators, of parents, of ministers. It teaches very simply, but very significantly, that, even from the womb, children are the subjects of pollution; that they stand in need... of purification from the inherent depravity of their nature, in order to their entering heaven."*

3. The moral influence of infant baptism upon parents and children merits attention.

Never was a maxim uttered with more propriety and truth than was that of the apostle: "With the pure, all things are pure; but to them that are defiled is nothing pure." That principle of human nature developed by this maxim ceases not to affect the opinions and conduct of men in all departments of society, and in every variety of interest. Men will contemplate things through the medium of prejudices and opinions previously formed, and truths, presenting themselves to the mind through these media, will borrow their hues, and appear more or less to blend with their character. As the colour and appearance of external objects are, to our vision, affected by the medium through which we view them, so are doctrines and facts affected by the disposition and prejudices of the mind before which they are presented. Cameleon-like, even truth cannot come before the mind without seeming to take the hues of surrounding notions with which it becomes thus associated.

Such reflections have forced themselves upon our minds, as we have followed the general strain with which Baptist authors have treated this subject. They have represented the moral influence of infant baptism, upon both the subject and the parent, as most hostile to the best interests of Christianity and good morals; and, if the reader can maintain his gravity, and credit our statement, as dangerous to the liberties of these United States!† Religious declen-

* Dissertation on Infant Baptism, p. 179.

† "Now, I ask, what is the moral influence all this infant baptizing

sion in all the Protestant churches is traced back to this practice, as the "spring head" and fountain of all impurity; and indeed, the reader would be likely to infer, from the reading of most Baptist authors on this subject, that but one thing was necessary to remove the great obstacles to the conversion of the world, namely, the abolishment of infant baptism. Dr. Gill called it "a part and pillar of Popery," and he has been echoed and re-echoed by later writers till this day. So the Papist sees nothing but transubstantiation in the words, "this is my body"—the Episcopalian nothing but "the apostolic rite of confirmation" in the words, "the doctrine of baptisms and the laying on of hands"—and the predestinarian his peculiar tenet in Rom. ix, 18. Men will be likely to judge of evidence, and of the moral influence of doctrines, by the force of preconceived opinions in their own minds. These constitute the glass through which they look, but which often, unhappily, discolours all objects before the mind. Let us endeavour to break away from this thraldom of prejudice, and contemplate the moral influence of infant baptism according to the true philosophy of things.

It must always be remembered that the moral influence of all external ceremonies of religion is to be judged of simply by their adaptedness to excite and encourage moral dispositions in the recipient, and in those who may be witnesses of the administration. And this moral influence is not conferred upon the patient by the mere external act of administration. No inherent virtue resides in the ordinances themselves; and none, therefore, can be evoked

is *adapted* to produce in the minds of those involuntary members, either of the Greek, Episcopal, Presbyterian, or Methodist Churches? The grace of God may, in many instances, prevent it,—*but the natural tendency of this system is to produce disgust and alienation*, where all would be most desirous to secure respect and kindly feeling."... "*To my own knowledge, spiritual embarrassment and confusion of the most stupifying, or else distressing kind, is the result of this system*... I do not design to encourage the insinuation that Pedobaptists, either Catholic, Episcopal, Presbyterian, or Methodist, have any *present design* TO ERECT A NATIONAL ESTABLISHMENT ON THE RUINS OF OUR FREE INSTITUTIONS!!.. BUT IT MUST BE EVIDENT TO EVERY REFLECTING MIND, THAT IF ANY ONE PEDOBAPTIST DENOMINATION WERE TO ABSORB ALL OTHERS, AND THERE WERE NO 'IGNORANT AND CONTENTIOUS' BAPTISTS REMAINING, THAT A NATIONAL ESTABLISHMENT WOULD THEN BE INEVITABLE!!"—*Hinton's History of Baptism*, pp. 363, 369, &c.

from them by any sort of incantation. Their moral influence depends on the moral dispositions of those concerned in them, and the uses to which they are applied.

Take an example. It will not be doubted that the Jewish ritual was highly adapted to excite and encourage pious and devout feelings among the Jews. Their numerous ablutions were well calculated to impress them with a sense of their own impurities, and of the necessity of holiness; their sacrifices taught them their guilt, and their dependance upon the great Atonement for pardon; their feasts called back to mind those great events of their history, so illustrative of the principles of the moral government—of the character of God—and of their own duty; their offerings were a thankful recognition of an overruling and bounteous Providence; and thus it was that, by external ceremonies, the great principles of the natural and moral governments of God were kept before the mind. This was the natural tendency of these ceremonies, when observed with an enlightened sentiment and a devout heart. Yet, they possessed no conceivable power, in themselves, to change the heart, or to avert the severity of divine justice. At a time when the nation was most exact and most constant in the observance of the law, as to all its outward ceremonies, it was most abhorred in the sight of God. Thus it was in the days of Isaiah, (see chapters i. and lviii,) and in the days of Christ.

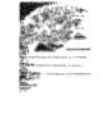

But would it become us to cavil, and to ask, "Of what use, then, were all these ordinances?" We know, indeed, that the Christian ordinances are often unproductive of any visible good, even in adults; but does this prove that they are, by any philosophical necessity, unprofitable? We know that they cannot save the soul in any case, and that they never can supersede, in the least degree, the necessity of the atonement, of the divine agency of the Holy Spirit upon the heart, of repentance and faith on the part of the adult, in order to salvation; but shall we, hence, discard them? Shall we say they are but useless forms? Shall we call that common, which God has called clean; or that idle, which he himself has appointed? All objections which are urged against infant baptism, on the score of *inefficacy*, may be urged equally against all outward rites, Jewish or Christian; and especially against the rite of circumcision, which, in this respect, is a perfectly parallel case.

It must be remembered that the tendency of an ordinance to produce a good moral effect is not to be judged of by the actual effect which it may have produced in any given cases. Infant baptism, we are sorry to say, has often been unproductive of good. The same, also, may be said of adult baptism. But for this failure the ordinance itself cannot be held accountable. Errors have been associated with the rite that have, in some instances, contributed to bring about this result; and in others, a general want of piety, and sense of religious obligation, have neutralized its happier tendencies. Yet, what can be more directly adapted to encourage and stimulate the pious exertions of the parent, in training its little one for God, than the recollection that he has already consecrated that little one to God in baptism? The parent beholds, with humble gratitude and holy joy, that God has been pleased to affix the seal of the covenant to his tender offspring—to enter into covenant "with him and his seed"—to recognise his child as an heir of salvation, and place upon it the visible mark, or pledge, of his protection and grace—all these considerations, presenting themselves to the parent's mind, could not fail to produce, if rightly improved, a deep and abiding impression. This, I say, would be their tendency.

And the child, when come to years of reason, if properly instructed in the nature and obligations of its baptism, would, if inclined to religion at all, acquiesce in the order of God—recognise the validity and propriety of its early consecration—assume, *in propria persona*, all the obligations consequent upon that act, and feel grateful to his parents for their early and prompt attention to his spiritual welfare, and to God for having blessed him with such parents. This, I say, would be the natural tendency of infant baptism, when rightly used.

But I need not say to the reader, that all these salutary influences depend wholly upon the moral state and education of the parties concerned. The faith of the parent in the divine authority for this practice is an indispensable condition of its salutary effect. If the parent believe that God has directed it, and do it, therefore, from a principle of obedience to a divine order, attending to all the several duties belonging to the same rite, from the same principle, under such circumstances, the rite itself is highly adapted to the happiest effects upon the parent, securing the happiest results to the child. But if the parent do not believe it to be of divine obligation, or neglect the other duties belonging thereto, we readily conceive how, to him, the practice would be likely to be attended with mischief, rather than good.

So with the child. Should it be permitted to grow up, after baptism, in ignorance of its duty to God, and of the nature and obligations of its baptism; and, withal, should it be taught to believe, either by its parents or others, that infant baptism is a mere human invention, a corruption of the Christian ordinance, "a part and pillar of Popery," and the highest imposition that could be practised upon "helpless infancy;" I say, under these circumstances it is not possible, in the nature of things, that an unhappy and mischievous effect should be prevented. Still, the moral effect would be rather negative than positive—they would only fail to derive any good from the ordinance, without being made positively worse on that account. Infant baptism, as it cannot confer grace *ex opere operato*, so neither can it confer any possible evil, in the same way, by those who afterward treat it unworthily. I mean there is nothing *peculiar* in infant baptism, in this respect. It is always an occasion of evil, in a greater or less degree, to misapprehend and misapply the truth and ordinances of God. But all orthodox Christians hold that outward ceremonies are not to be reckoned among the essentials of religion.

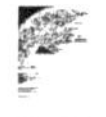

It is easy, then, to perceive how the Baptists have arrived at their notion of the mischievous moral tendencies of infant baptism. They form their estimates wholly on the supposition that neither the parent, at the time he devotes his child to God in baptism, nor the child, in after-days, fully credits the Scriptural obligation of the ordinance. They first introduce skepticism in the minds of all the parties concerned, and then calculate the tendency of infant baptism in the light, and by the operation, of that skepticism. Now, the question is not, "What would be the tendency of infant baptism, if all believed it to be a mere human invention?" but, "What would be its tendency, if all believed it to be of *divine* origin?" What is its *natural* tendency, when faithfully practised, and carried out in all its parts?

Will any man, in his senses, believe that it is calculated "to produce disgust and alienation" in the mind of the child, to inform it that it has been dedicated from early infancy to God? Disgust it may produce in the mind of a vicious youth, who is now informed for the first time that he was dedicated to God in infancy. Such a mind will turn with equal repugnance from all the institutes and precepts of Christianity. But would this be a proper test of the natural tendency of infant baptism, any more than of Christianity in general? If this same youth had felt predisposed, from the influence of early teaching, and from early divine influence, (which is rendered effectual, ordinarily, by such teaching,) to revere the institutes of religion and submit to its precepts,—if he felt disposed to give his heart to God—would he now feel "disgust" to know that he had been, in early life, dedicated to God by a solemn ordinance of religion? Exactly contrary to this would be the effect. It is perfectly obvious, therefore, that our opponents calculate the moral tendencies of infant baptism in the light of skepticism, and not in the light of faith;—they calculate what its moral effects would be likely to be upon an *impure*, not upon a *pure* mind;—a method of procedure this, as unfair as it is absurd.

But it is worthy of our constant attention that God has settled this question by his word, and by the very constitution of our nature. The question is simply this:—"Is the fact of having dedicated a child to God in baptism calculated to exert a bad moral influence over the mind of that child in after-life?" And on this question there is about as much room for controversy as on this: "Whether it would be calculated to alienate the child from God, in after-life, to bring it up from early childhood in the principles of the Christian religion?" We cannot trifle with the reader's understanding, and, above all, with the word of God, to dwell upon such themes. We wished, however, to say, that the divine obligation of infant circumcision settles for ever the question of the moral tendency of infant baptism, for the two cases are exactly parallel.

As to the question, whether the general practice of infant baptism would lead to national establishments, or the union of church and state, we deem the matter too childish to merit attention. Our opponents can harp upon it, if they can find any one to listen to them. We are not anxious. But the charge of a general tendency to "formalism" and spiritual lethargy is one of very serious consequence, and which, if it fitly apply to infant baptism, must refute all its claims to Scriptural authority.* The philosophy of some men amounts to a literary curiosity. Their method of tracing out cause and effect, and the logical principles by which they deduce and apply evidence in particular cases, ought to be written for the general admonition, or, perhaps, diversion, of mankind. Baptist authors have attributed the formalism and spiritual lethargy of the national establishments of Europe principally to the practice of infant baptism.† They might as well have attributed it to monarchy, or to the wars of Charlemagne.

But to cut this matter short, we must address a sort of *argumentum ad verecundiam* to our opponents, and dismiss the point. It is painful to be obliged to assert one's own good character, or to be under a necessity of comparing and off-setting moral characters with an opponent, in order, by a sort of final appeal to respectability, to terminate a tiresome controversy. This is an issue which, to say the least, is unpleasant. Modesty recoils, while duty and necessity urge forward. We are somewhat comforted, however, when we reflect that Paul, the great apostle, once condescended to the same thing. When driven to this necessity, he did, finally, assert that his character was as good as that of his opposers. He finally consented to take this issue with his adversaries,—"Seeing that many glory ... I will glory also," 2 Cor. xi, 18. So say we; and we appeal to the truth-telling page of history in support of the assertion, that Pedobaptist churches (Protestant) do exhibit as truly and as extensively the genuine signs of orthodoxy

* "Here begins to appear the most lamentable moral influence of infant baptism; *it has the very contrary effect to that for which baptism was designed by its Founder.* Instead of SEPARATING the church and the world, IT ACTUALLY UNITES THEM," &c. See Hinton's History of Baptism, p. 366, &c.

† Hinton, p. 367.

and vital godliness, as do the Baptist churches in this or any other country. "I am become a fool in glorying; *ye have compelled me.*" We consent, then, that the moral tendencies of the respective doctrines of exclusive *adult* and *infant* baptism should be judged of by the spiritual state of the churches respectively who hold these tenets; though still we say, "It is not expedient for us, doubtless, to glory."

That additional matter which otherwise would fall under this head, the reader will find contained mostly in the third and fifth chapters of this work.

CHAPTER VIII.

THE GROUND OF AN INFANT'S ELIGIBILITY TO BAPTISM.

1. All infants are, by nature, in the same state, as it respects moral condition; all are under condemnation. "We are, by nature, children of wrath." But at the moment when the period of personal existence commences—at the moment when the identity of the human being is established, so that it is capable of moral happiness or misery—at that moment we consider the soul to come within the gracious provisions of the atonement, which secures unconditional salvation to all such as die in infancy. All children, we consider, are alike in this respect. All are on a perfect parity of standing; and, in so far, all are equally eligible to baptism, the seal of that covenant of grace by which they are saved. And this we regard as the proper, primary ground of eligibility to this ordinance. We know of no principle, either of reason or revelation, which authorizes us to make any distinctions between different children as it respects moral condition.

2. Yet does it not necessarily follow that all children, without distinction, should be brought to baptism. Other circumstances, of a secondary nature, must be taken into account. Infant baptism contemplates, from its very nature, early religious education. Its obligations are prospective. If they are not met and fulfilled, both by the

parent and the child, its grand intention is unanswered, and its efficacy lost. Just so with the adult; if, *after* baptism, he fail to keep the law, his baptism is void. In the language of a Jew in a parallel case, "his circumcision is counted for uncircumcision." If parents do not educate their children for God, it is no better than solemn mockery to offer them up in baptism.

Now, it is reasonable that some *pledge* of the suitable education of the child should be required of the parent before the child is admitted to baptism. Without this, the ordinance would not be sufficiently guarded, and would inevitably fall under public scandal. But ungodly parents cannot give this pledge, from the nature of the case; therefore it is unsuitable to admit the children of ungodly parents to baptism.

3. It will be perceived by this, that we do not hold to the right of children to be baptized, on the ground of natural relation to the parent, (if we understand that phrase.) It is not by virtue of natural descent, as some authors have loosely expressed it, that children derive any claim to the sealing ordinance. The ties of nature, and those of grace, are not to be thus confounded. The one can confer no title to the privileges of the other.

Children of believing parents are not "*born* members of the church," as Dr. Mason has strangely asserted.* This is a doctrine fraught with monstrous consequences. Yet it is probably a mere unguarded phrase, as no individual, or body of Christians, ever believed that a person, adult or infant, could be made a member of the church otherwise than by baptism; that is, if they held to water baptism at all."†

* Christian's Magazine, vol. ii, pp. 49, 50.

† Such a thing as birthright membership in the church of God was never yet known. Among the Jews none were thus reckoned. Circumcision, not natural descent, was the initiating ceremony. Nor were they born ceremonially *clean*. Both the mother and the child were reckoned *unclean;* the child till eight days, and the mother from forty to eighty days, according to circumstances. Lev. xii. The mother and child were restored to a state of purity by the sprinkling of blood, and sacrifice. See Luke ii, 22–24. All this certainly does not look like being born either *clean*, or *members of the church*.

Tertullian thinks the apostle intended to be understood, in 1 Cor. vii, 14, that the children were "holy," only by baptism; they were *designed for holiness*, says he, (*sanctitati designati*.) "Every soul,"

On this point, unhappily, many loose, unguarded expressions have been made. The idea of the "federal holiness" of the children of Christian parents is not well defined, and ought to be omitted. In paraphrasing 1 Cor. vii, 14, Dr. Mason, as above quoted, says, speaking to the "believing" partner concerning his or her children, "They are holy, *because* you are so." This certainly does not necessarily follow from the words of the apostle, and the doctrine is too liable to objection to be received on such ground. It is carrying Jewish distinctions further than is warranted in the gospel.

4. Nor is it relevant to admit of "sponsors," in lieu of parents, while the latter are yet living. Parents are the natural guardians of children,* and their control over their children precludes that exercise of authority and discipline on the part of sponsors, which are requisite to the fulfil-

continues he, "is reckoned as in Adam, till it be anew enrolled in Christ, and so long unclean, till it be so enrolled."—*De Anima*, c. 39, 40.

Bishop Burnett says, "Their children were not *unclean*—that is, not shut out *from being dedicated* to God."—*Expos. of the Thirty-nine Articles.*

This is the true idea. All children are born *without* the covenant; that is, they do not come within the covenant by virtue of natural generation, but by grace, and baptism is the *visible token* of that covenant.

As a matter of fact, the children of pious parents in Paul's day were, by their parents, designed for *holiness*—that is, *church relations;* and so were baptized. But their right to baptism was not founded on the piety of their parents, but on the fact that, though by natural birth they were "children of wrath," yet by grace they were included in, and made partakers of, the promise of life; and it became fit and proper to baptize them, because the piety of their parents became a *pledge* and *guarantee* that the ordinance should not be abused, but should be made to answer its appropriate ends. We say again, it would be absurd for ungodly parents to dedicate their children to God. This could not be done in sincerity.

* "The law of nature and of nations puts children in the power of their parents; they are naturally their guardians; and, if they are entitled to any thing, their parents have a right to transact about it, because of the weakness of the child; and what contracts soever they make, by which the child does not lose, but is a gainer, these do certainly bind the child. It is then suitable, both to the constitution of mankind, and to the dispensation of the Mosaical covenant, that parents may dedicate their children to God, and bring them under the obligations of the gospel."—*Bishop Burnett on the Thirty-nine Articles*, Art. xxvii.

ment of their obligations to the baptized child. If the parent, by reason of his impiety, incapacitates himself to become the spiritual sponsor of the child, and thus deprives it of baptism, still the case, we consider, is without remedy. No other person has any right to step in and assume the control of the child, in such a degree as to justify the obligations of a sponsor. In order to this, the child should be formally surrendered to, and adopted by, the sponsor. At least the latter should be invested with an entire discretion, to bring up the child *as if* he were its parent.

This we consider the true philosophy of the case. If a child have Christian parents, or, according to the apostolic rule, (1 Cor. vii, 14,) if it have only one Christian parent, and the parents both concur in this, it is proper to baptize the child. The pledge of the believing parent is sufficient. If it have unbelieving parents, it is irrelevant to baptize the child; not because its moral state is not upon a perfect par with that one which has Christian parents, but because there is no adequate *pledge* that the ends of baptism, so far as relates to early education, will be answered in the child. Yet, if the child were wholly surrendered to, and adopted by, some person, or persons, who would proffer and redeem the requisite pledge, it might with propriety be baptized. And thus, if a child were found, whose parents could not be ascertained, and were adopted by Christian parents, it would be proper to baptize it at their request. But no person can act as a godfather or a godmother (very awkward words, by the by) to the child of another, while at the same time the person thus acting as sponsor has no further control over the child than to see that it is instructed in certain doctrines of religion, and certain catechetical forms. The practice is absurd, and leads to very mischievous consequences. The parent, either by nature or by formal adoption—the person who has the responsible supervision of the entire conduct of the child—can alone become responsible for the religious training of the child; and he alone, therefore, could, with any propriety, present the child in baptism.

This, then, is the true doctrine of sponsors in baptism; not, indeed, as it is held and practised by the Church of

England,* but as it may be justified by the nature of the case, and the principles of religion.

5. However, there is a modified form of this practice which may, under particular circumstances, be harmlessly retained. Parents alone can stand directly pledged for the child; but persons of approved gravity, piety, age, and experience, may pledge themselves to *assist* the pious efforts of parents, taking a sort of collateral responsibility. And this, under certain circumstances, may be not only harmless, but highly expedient.† Especially might this be expedient in case of the death of the parents, and in times of great persecution in the church.

"I have nothing to except," says Dr. Ridgeley, "against the first rise of this practice, (of having sponsors in baptism,) which was in the second century, when the church was under persecution, and the design thereof was laudable and good, namely, that if the parents should die before the child came of age, whereby it would be in danger of being seized on by the heathen, and trained up in their superstitious and idolatrous mode of worship, the sureties promised that, in this case, they would deal with it as though it were their own child, and bring it up in the Christian religion; which kind and pious concern for its welfare might [however] have been better expressed at some other time than in baptism, lest this should [come at length to] be thought an appendix to the ordinance. However, through the goodness of God, the children of believing parents are not now reduced to those hazardous circumstances; and, therefore, the obligation to do this is the less needful. But to vow, and not perform, is not only useless to the child, but renders that only a matter of form, which they promise to do in this sacred ordinance."‡

* See the exhortation to godfathers and godmothers after baptism, prescribed by the Church of England.

† Vide Wesley's Works, vol. vi, pp. 235, 236.

‡ Body of Divinity, vol. iv, pp. 228, 229.

APPENDIX.

Note A.—Referred to page 66.

Some information respecting circumcision cannot fail to be acceptable to the reader, particularly as such information is commonly rare, and the physical nature of the transaction but little understood by people in general.

1. Circumcision was known and practised by other nations besides the Jews; the Egyptians, Samaritans, Arabians, Saracens, Ishmaelites, Colchians, and Ethiopians. The Colchians were originally a colony from Egypt, and probably derived this practice from the parent country. The Egyptians most probably received it from the Arabians, who, together with the Saracens and Ethiopians, derived it from Ishmael. Gen. xvii, 11, 25, 27. The statement of Herodotus, that the Jews derived it from the Egyptians, is not worthy of credit. "Those who assert that the Phœnicians were circumcised, mean, probably, the Samaritans; for we know, from other authority, that the Phœnicians did not observe this ceremony." (See Calmet.) No account is given by these nations as a reason of their practising this rite, and it never was insisted on among the Egyptians as an indispensable condition of their enjoying national privileges, as among the Jews.

2. "Circumcision," says Mr. Stackhouse, "is the cutting off the foreskin of the member which in every male is the instrument of generation; and whoever considers the nature of this operation, painful if not indecent in those of maturity, and to such as live in hot countries highly inconvenient, if not dangerous;—an operation wherein we can perceive no footsteps of human invention, as having no foundation either in reason, or nature, or necessity, or the interest of any particular set of men, we must needs conclude that mankind could never have put such a severity upon themselves, unless they had

been enjoined and directed to it by a divine command. Nay, this single instance of Abraham, who, at the advanced age of ninety-nine, underwent this hazardous operation, and the very indecency of it in a man of his years and dignity; these two considerations are in the place of ten thousand proofs that it was forced upon him; but nothing but the irresistible authority of God could be a force sufficient in those circumstances. So that the strangeness and singularity of this ordinance is so far from being an argument against it, that it is an evident proof of its divine institution; and what was originally instituted by God, cannot, in strictness, be accounted immodest, though we, perhaps, may have some such conception of it; since 'unto the pure all things are pure,'" &c.—*Hist. of the Bible*, book iii, sec. 1.

3. "The manner of this ceremony's being performed," says Calmet, "whether in the public synagogue or in private houses, is this:—The person who is appointed to be the godfather sits down upon a seat, with a silk cushion provided for that purpose, and settles the child in a proper posture on his knees, when he who is to circumcise him (which, by the by, is accounted a great honour among the Jews) opens the blankets. Some make use of silver tweezers, to take up so much of the prepuce as they design to cut off; but others take it up with their fingers. Then he who circumcises the child, holding the razor in his hand, says, 'Blessed be thou, O Lord, who hast commanded us to be circumcised;' and while he is saying this, cuts off the thick skin of the prepuce, and then, with his thumb nails, tears off a finer skin still remaining. After this he sucks the blood, which flows plentifully on this occasion, and spits it out into a cup full of wine. Then he puts some dragon's blood upon the wound, some coral powder, and other things to stop the bleeding, and so covers up the part affected. When this is done, he takes up the cup wherein he had spit the blood, moistens his lips therewith, and then, blessing both that and the child, gives him the name which his father had appointed, and at the same time pronounces these words of Ezekiel, 'I said unto thee, when thou wast in thy blood, Live; (chap. xvi, 6;) after which the whole congregation repeats the one hundred and twenty-eighth Psalm, 'Blessed is

every one that feareth the Lord,' &c.; and so the ceremony concludes. Only we must observe, that, besides the seat appointed for the godfather, there is always one left empty, and is designed, some say, for the prophet Elias, who, as they imagine, is invisibly present at all circumcisions."—*Calmet's Dict.*, Art. *Circumcision.*

Note B.—Referred to p. 88.

On the subject of the kind and degree of evidence which any particular subject requires, and which we may reasonably demand as a condition of our assent, much may be said. The subject itself deserves our most mature and candid consideration. Most persons who, in a moment of hasty dispute, and when urged and chafed by the argument of an opponent, put forth a demand for a certain kind or degree of evidence to support the contested doctrine, without duly counting the cost. They are generally apt to be short-sighted, blinded by the precipitancy of their zeal, and deceived as to the relative importance of their mooted doctrine. We wish our opponents and the world to know that we adopt such principles of reasoning and interpretation in the present case, and such *only* as we are prepared to adopt and carry out in all our investigations of the word of God. And we wish them and the world to know, also, that we shall hold them steadily and inflexibly to their own principles. If they have adopted, in the case of infant baptism, a theory of interpretation and evidence by which they consent to abide; and if they hold us to certain conclusions, according to the principles of their own theory; our only resort is to test the soundness of that theory. And we, in our turn, have a right to hold them answerable for the consequences which result from the application of their own principles. It would be an easy thing to adopt a principle, or rule of evidence, in one particular instance, to help us out of a present, galling dilemma, if we had no other concernment or responsibility in the matter than the mere application of such particular rule to the case in hand; but it is quite another thing to conduct an argument skilfully and successfully, according to principles of reason and evidence which are of acknow-

ledged and universal authority. We are athirst, but let us not, therefore, rashly accept the poisoned draught, lest, while we escape from a partial evil, we do thereby plunge ourselves into general destruction.

In addition to the illustrations offered on this point in the body of this work, I beg leave to adduce the following from the pen of the shrewd and eloquent George Stanley Faber, B. D. Although his remarks applied to another subject, they are designed to illustrate the same principle as that under consideration:—

"If, indeed, we be required to produce, in so many words, a specific declaration that, *at the commencement of patriarchism, God himself instituted the rite of expiatory sacrifice*, a task is certainly imposed upon us, which can never be performed: but a truth, I apprehend, may be clearly and distinctly conveyed in other modes than that of a regular scholastic enunciation.

"1. A modern Socinian writer has challenged us to bring forward a single text in which *the twofold nature of Christ* is unequivocally asserted: and he boasts that, although such a challenge has often been given, it has never yet been accepted.

"Doubtless he may make the boast with perfect safety: for, after the most careful examination of the whole Bible, from the beginning of Genesis to the end of the Apocalypse, we must fairly confess that the precise words, *Christ has two natures*, nowhere occur. Yet, we do not, on that account, the less hold the doctrine.

"Why, then, it will be asked, do we deem ourselves fully authorized to maintain it? Simply, because, in some passages, we find Christ expressly declared to be *God*, while, in other passages, we find him no less expressly declared to be *man*. These two declarations, each alike resting upon inspired verity, we combine in a single proposition: and the clear RESULT is *the doctrine of Christ's double nature.*

"2. The same remark, and the same mode of reasoning, may be extended to the all-important doctrine of the Holy Trinity.

"That doctrine forms the very nucleus of sound religion: but still, I fear, we must confess, that nowhere, in the regular scholastic form of an article or a symbol, are we taught that *God is one essence, and three in personality.* Yet, notwithstanding this omission of a direct enunciation in some one specific text, every sound Catholic holds the doctrine to be of vital necessity: nor will he allow the silence of Scripture to be any proof of its *neutrality.*

"How, then, does he proceed, for the purpose of establishing his position, and of vindicating his belief?

"With Athanasius of old, he examines the Bible: and, since he there finds the essential unity of the Godhead expressly maintained, while the identical things predicated of the Father are also predicated of the Son and of the Spirit, he perceives that in no way can Scripture be reconciled with Scripture, save by the reception of *the doctrine of a trinity in unity.*

"The demonstration is, I think, clear and invincible: but, after all, we must acknowledge that it rests upon *induction;* after all, we must confess that God has not revealed, in so many precise and formal words, that *the Deity is three in regard to personality, and one in regard to essence.....*

"3. I have yet to learn in what part of the Mosaic narrative, or even in what part of the entire volume of Scripture, *the primitive divine institution of a perpetually recurring sabbath, to be observed by man as matter of ordained religious obligation, is* PRECISELY AND SCHOLASTICALLY ENUNCIATED. I vainly look for an absolute COMMAND, that the subjects of the patriarchal dispensation should observe a perpetually recurring sabbath.

"The record is brief, and simply historical:—

"'On the seventh day, God ended his work which he had made; and he rested on the seventh day from all his work which he had made. And God blessed the seventh day, and sanctified it: because that in it he had rested from all his work, which God created and made.' Gen. ii, 2, 3.

"The FACT that God, having rested on the seventh day from the work of creation, sanctified the precise seventh day on which he rested from all his work, is indeed distinctly specified: but, in regard to *the positive* INSTITUTION *of a perpetually recurring sabbath,* we are neither indefinitely told that EVERY *successive seventh day was sanctified,* nor are we definitely taught that EVERY *successive seventh day should always be set apart* BY MAN *for the duties and purposes of religion.*

"4. By those who advocate the theory of Bishop Warburton and Mr. Davison, we are assured that *the primitive divine institution of expiatory sacrifice is nowhere mentioned in the Mosaic history.*

"With respect to this allegation, I freely confess that, IN THE FORM OF A REGULAR PROPOSITION, *the primitive divine institution of expiatory sacrifice, immediately after the fall*, is nowhere mentioned.

"I myself hold the primitive divine institution *both* of the sabbath and of piacular sacrifice: and, in *each* case, I hold it much upon the same principle. Yet were I to set up any difference between the two, I should not hesitate to assert, that the evidence for *the primitive divine institution of piacular sacrifice* is stronger and more direct than the evidence for *the primitive divine institution of the sabbath.* For almost at the very commencement of the patriarchal dispensation, we can produce a specific instance where the devotement of a sin-offering is COMMANDED: [which manifestly intimates that such was the DUTY of Cain, to whom the command was addressed, in consequence of a well-known, already existing divine institution.] But throughout the whole book of Genesis (which, from the creation, brings us down well nigh to Moses) we are unable to produce a single instance where either the observance of the sabbath is *enjoined*, or where it is mentioned as a *positive institution*, or even where it is barely noticed *as a mere occurrence.*"*

I have ventured upon this extract merely to illustrate further to the reader the method by which we often arrive at truth. I wish him fully to appreciate what would be the condition of theology should the principles of reasoning and evidence adopted by our opponents, in the case of infant baptism, be universally adopted in reference to all other subjects. The great doctrines of Christianity *need* no other evidence than that which they *have;* but it cannot be denied that many of them utterly fail of that kind of evidence which results purely from clear and express statement. Yet this is the evidence which our opponents demand for infant baptism.

* Faber on Primitive Sacrifice, pp. 188–199.

NOTE C.—Referred to p. 99.

The fact that the Jews baptized their proselytes at the time of Christ, is now generally admitted without controversy among the learned. It is a remarkable fact that the Jews felt no surprise at the fact that John baptized his disciples, which they certainly would have manifested had baptism been a novel thing. Nay, they even go to John and ask, "Who art thou?" He assured them he was not the Christ. They reply, "*Why baptizest thou then,* IF *thou be not that Christ,* nor Elias, neither that prophet?" John i, 25. Here is no surprise manifested at the simple fact of baptism—this they seemed to have expected when Christ should come—but they merely wished to be informed how it came to pass that a person of less authority than Messiah could baptize. This indicates most clearly a familiarity, on their part, with baptism as a religious ceremony, in which light John employed it.

When our Saviour talked with Nicodemus, and announced the startling doctrine that, "except any person (so it reads in the Greek) be born of water and of the Spirit, he cannot see the kingdom of God," the Pharisee was surprised, and his surprise arose from a want of clear comprehension of the nature of the new birth, and also from the fact that our Saviour made no exceptions in favour of the Jews, but affirmed the necessity of the regeneration of them as well as of Gentiles. Our Lord, in turn, expressed his astonishment that he, being a "master in Israel," should not understand this doctrine. As if he had said, "Dost thou, as a spiritual master in Israel, command proselytes to be baptized with water, as an emblem of a *new birth;* and art thou unacquainted with the *cause, necessity, nature,* and *effects* of that new birth?" (See Dr. A. Clarke on the place.)

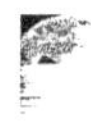

Nicodemus did not seem to be surprised at the *phraseology* of Christ, but only at the *sense* he attached to this phraseology, and its application to Jews as well as Gentiles; and Christ expressed his wonder that this language, which was so generally employed by the Jews, as applying to proselyted Gentiles, should not be comprehended in its true import by one whose office it was to be an instructor of the ignorant, and a guide to the blind. He did not comprehend the meaning of that very language which was familiar to every Jew from the practice of proselytic baptism.

The Jews derived authority for baptizing proselytes from the fact that, before they themselves were entered into covenant with God at Mount Sinai, they were commanded to sanctify themselves, washing their clothes, &c., which was called a baptism. At this time, therefore, they considered that their whole nation was baptized, and thus, in connection with the use of circumcision and sacrifice, they were entered into covenant. Then, it was written in their law, Num. xv, 15, 16, "One ordinance shall be for you, and also for the stranger (that is, proselyte) that sojourneth with you... As ye are, so shall the stranger be before the Lord. One law and one manner shall be for you, and for the stranger that sojourneth with you." As they themselves, therefore, considered that they had acquired, and still retained, their standing as Jews by circumcision, baptism, and oblation; and as one law must serve equally for them, and the stranger, or proselyte, that sojourned with them, it is obvious from whence their authority for baptizing proselytes proceeded. As to themselves, however, they considered that as their nation was once dedicated to God solemnly by baptism, (Exod. xix, 10, &c.,) there was no necessity that their children should afterward be baptized, being born of parents already legally clean, or holy.

But these notions, whether well-founded or not, have no weakening force upon our argument. All that we are concerned to prove is, the *fact* that the Jews uniformly baptized proselytes at the time of Christ. Indeed, they knew of no way of making disciples, or proselytes, but by baptism. So Maimonides says,—

"*And so* IN ALL AGES, when a Gentile is willing to enter into covenant, and gather himself under the wings of the majesty of God, and take upon him the yoke of the law, *he must be circumcised, and baptized, and bring a sacrifice.* As it is written, 'As you are, so shall the stranger be.' How are you? By circumcision, and baptism, and bringing of a sacrifice. So also the stranger, [or proselyte,] THROUGH ALL GENERATIONS; by circumcision, and baptism, and bringing a sacrifice.....

"At this time, when there is no sacrificing, they must be circumcised and baptized. And when the temple shall be built, they are to bring the sacrifice. A stranger that is circumcised, and not baptized; or baptized, and not circumcised; he is not a proselyte till he be both circumcised and baptized."

The Talmud of Babylon says, "When a proselyte is received, he must be circumcised: and when he is cured [of the wound of circumcision,] they baptize him in the presence of two wise men, saying, 'Behold, he is an Israelite in all things.'"

The Talmud of Jerusalem testifies to the same point, only specifying "sacrifice" in addition to circumcision and baptism.

The Gemara of Babylon, a Jewish commentary on the Mishna, says, "The proselytes entered not into covenant but by circumcision, baptism, and sprinkling of blood."

So they believe Jethro, Moses' father-in-law, was proselyted, and all others who came into the Jewish church after his day. Hence, Arrianus, who wrote about A. D. 147, calls the Jewish proselytes, in derision, "*the baptized.*"

As baptism was well understood and practised by the Jews in our Saviour's time, so also was infant baptism. Maimonides says, "If an Israelite take a Gentile CHILD, or find a Gentile INFANT, and baptize him in the name of a proselyte, behold he is a proselyte." Rabbi Joseph says, that persons who are made proselytes in *infancy* may retract when they are grown up, &c.

Rabbi Hezekiah has this rule, in regard to proselyting a person in the name of a free man, or a servant: "Behold, one finds an infant cast out, and baptizes him in the name of a servant: do thou also circumcise him in the name of a servant. But if he baptize him in the name of a free man: do thou also circumcise him in the name of a free man."*

"In regard to this subject," says Dr. Woods, "let the following things be well considered:—

* See Dr. Lightfoot's Horæ Hebraicæ Talmudicæ; also his Harmony of the New Testament. Dr. Hammond's Annotations; also his Six Queries on Infant Baptism. Quoted by Wall, History, part i, *Introduction;* and Dr. A. Clarke, at the close of his comment on Mark's Gospel.

"1. The rabbins unanimously assert that the baptism of proselytes had been practised by the Jews in all ages, from Moses down to the time when they wrote. Now these writers must have been sensible that their contemporaries, both Jews and Christians, knew whether such a practice had been prevalent, or not. And had it been known that no such practice had existed, would not some Jews have been found bold enough to contradict such a groundless assertion of the rabbins? At least, would there not have been some Christians, fired with the love of truth, jealous for the honour of a sacred rite, first instituted by Christ, who would have exposed to shame those who falsely asserted that a similar rite had existed for more than a thousand years? But neither of these things was done.

"2. Had not the Jews been accustomed to baptize proselytes previously to the Christian era, it is extremely improbable that they would have adopted the practice afterward. For their contempt and hatred of Christianity exceeded all bounds, and must have kept them at the greatest possible distance from copying a rite peculiar to Christians.

"3. It seems to have been perfectly consistent and proper for the Jews to baptize proselytes. For their divine ritual enjoined various purifications by washing, or baptism. And as they considered all Gentiles to be *unclean*, how could they do otherwise than understand the divine law to require, that when any of them were proselyted to the Jewish religion, they should receive the same sign of purification as was, in so many cases, applied to themselves?"*

NOTE D.—Referred to p. 128.

Cruden enumerates four senses in which the word sanctify is employed in Scripture:—

"1. It signifies, to confess and celebrate that to be holy which in itself was so before. Matt. vi, 9. And thus it is to be understood, wheresoever God is said to be sanctified.

"2. To make persons holy, [in a moral sense,] who

* Lectures on Infant Baptism, pp. 48, 49.

were impure and defiled before. 1 Cor. vi, 11. And this is the sense of the word in those passages of Scripture where the elect are said to be sanctified.

"3. To separate and set apart some things, or persons, from a common unto a holy use, as the tabernacle, temple, priests, &c. [This is proper ceremonial sanctification.]

"4. To employ a thing in holy and religious exercises, in the worship of God in public and private, and the celebration of his works; in this and the former sense, the seventh day is sanctified. Exod. xx, 8."

Not to mention that the last two of these significations seem necessarily to involve each other, and hence, to be one and the same thing substantially, the great fault of this enumeration is, that it overlooks the very sense in which ἁγιαζω occurs in 1 Cor. vii, 14, and, indeed, in many other places. Things were deemed *sanctified* that were not devoted to any particular *religious* use, but which were merely lawful for a Jew or a Christian to use, as has been noticed in the body of this work.

Note E.—Referred to p. 138.

It is proper that the reader should be informed of the various opinions that have been held with regard to this passage, in order that he may the more clearly settle his own opinion respecting the true meaning. I have given, in the body of this work, what I conceive to be the true sense of the terms employed, and the real force of the apostle's argument. I shall here endeavour briefly to notice others that have elicited the most considerable share of attention from writers on both sides of the question.

First. There is an opinion which Pedobaptists have held respecting this passage, which is set forth in the following paraphrase: "For it has ordinarily come to pass, that an unbelieving husband has been brought to the faith, and so to baptism, by his wife; and likewise an unbelieving wife by her husband. If it were not so, and if the wickedness or infidelity of the unbelieving party did usually prevail, the children of such would be generally kept unbaptized, and so be unclean. But now we see, by the grace of God, a contrary effect, for they are generally baptized, and so become holy, or sanctified."*

This view requires us to understand the words *sanctified* and *holy* as applying to moral character, and as implying *baptism*. The reasons urged in favour of this construction are the following:—

1. The grammatical form of the sentence is said to indicate it. It stands thus: ἡγιασται γαρ ὁ ἀνηρ ὁ ἀπιστος ἐν τη γυναικι *for the unbelieving husband* HATH BEEN SANCTIFIED *by the wife*, &c. The verb ἡγιασται *sanctify* is in the *perfect passive*, and not in the *present active* form, as our translators have rendered it.

2. This is the view entertained by many of the fathers of the Christian church.

3. It is supposed to accord better with the scope of Paul's reasoning, for he expressly says in verse 16, "For what knowest thou, O man, whether thou shalt save thy wife?" &c.; as if the scope of his argument all along is, to show that the salvation (and hence baptism) of the unbelieving partner might be, and often had been, effected through the instrumentality of the believing partner, and this should induce them to live together, as it would sanction their continued union.

Mr. Wesley seems to have been of this opinion. He says, "For the unbelieving husband hath, in many instances, been sanctified by the wife, &c., else would your children have been brought up heathens, whereas now they are Christians." (See his Notes on the place.)

So also Bishop Burnett: "The apostle does appoint the Christian to live with the infidel, and says that the Christian is so far from being defiled by the infidel, *that there is a communication of a blessing that passes from the Christian to the infidel*, the one being the better for the prayers of the other, and sharing in the blessings bestowed on the other: the better part was accepted of God, in whom mercy rejoices over judgment."—*Expos. of the Articles*, Art. xxvii.

In reply, it is sufficient to say, 1. As to the grammatical form of the sentence, it equally accords with the version and particular turn of sense we have given to the passage. We might read, "For the unbelieving husband *has been*

* See Wall's History of Infant Baptism, part i, c. xi, sec. 11.

sanctified to the wife," &c., and it would equally make to our purpose. 2. It appears strange that writers should have found so much trouble with the little particle εν *en.* Our English text has it *by*, and this is, I believe, the translation more commonly given. It is this translation of this small word that has occasioned so much misunderstanding of the passage, and which, indeed, is the basis of the above view. If this particle were rendered *to*, instead of *by*, the whole argument of Paul would assume another aspect. Indeed, the opinion above stated does not give a true view of the force and character of the argument. The question in the Corinthian church was this, whether it was ceremonially lawful for a believer to dwell with an unbeliever? But it is no proof that such a union would not render the believing party *now* unclean, to say that *sometimes* the unbeliever has been sanctified by the instrumentality of the believer, and that the latter might, in this case, *hereafter* be the means of accomplishing the same good.

Secondly. It has been maintained by Baptist authors, at whose head, in this respect, stands Dr. Gill, that the word "*unclean*," ver. 14, is to be understood in the sense of *illegitimate*, and the word "holy" in the sense of *legitimate*, or *lawfully begotten.*

Dr. Gill has thus expressed this view:—"'The unbelieving husband is sanctified by the wife, and the unbelieving wife is sanctified by her husband; else were your children unclean; but now are they holy.' The parties spoken of are duly, rightly, and legally espoused to each other;—otherwise, that is, if they were not truly married to each other, the children must be *spurious*, and not *legitimate.* 'Else were your children unclean, but now are they holy;' that is, if the marriage contracted between them was not valid, and if, since the conversion of one of them, it can never be thought to be good; then the children begotten and born, either when both were infidels, or since one of them was converted, must be unlawfully begotten, base-born, and not genuine, legitimate offspring; but as the parents are lawfully married, the children born of them are, in a civil and legal sense, holy, that is, legitimate."

This view of the text is endorsed by the American

Baptist Publication and Tract Society, as it is the view of Mr. Pengilly, whose tract on baptism that society have published: although, to be sure, they have published another view of the text in the same tract, which we shall notice hereafter.

The most plausible argument in favour of this construction is, that it appears to coincide with the scope of Paul's reasoning. He certainly is arguing to the question, whether a man and woman may innocently live together, under given circumstances, in marriage relations; and it appears, at first blush, to be a natural and a satisfactory reply to this inquiry, to show that the parties were lawfully married at first. The great objections lying against this theory, however, are,—

1. If it had been a question of civil law, or relating to the lawfulness of marriage in a civil sense, it is not probable, as we have before observed, that the Corinthian church would have applied to Paul, now residing at Ephesus. Why did they not appeal to civil law at once?

2. To understand *ακαθαρτος akathartos* and *ἁγια hagia* in the sense of *illegitimate* and *legitimate*, is contrary to the *usus loquendi*. "It puts a sense upon these words which is widely different from the prevailing sense; yea, different from the sense which they have in any other passage of Scripture. And Dr. Gill himself does not pretend that either of the words is used in the sense he contends for, in any other text. He does, indeed, attempt to support his rendering by referring to the use of the Hebrew קִדֵּשׁ in the Talmudic books, where it has the sense of *espousing* merely. But Schleusner objects to the argument, and says, 'that the notion of espousing, which certain interpreters have attributed to the word *το ἁγιαζειν*, from the use of the word קִדֵּשׁ in the Talmudic books, is, as any one must see, manifestly foreign to this place. There is not one of the senses of קָדַשׁ, given by Gesenius, and not one of the many senses of *ἁγιαζω*, given by Schleusner and Wahl, which favours the rendering of Dr. Gill. The same is true of the adjective *ἁγια*. Schleusner and Wahl give a great variety of senses, but none of them relate to the *legitimacy of children*. Nor is *ακαθαρτος*, nor the corresponding Hebrew טָמֵא, ever used to

designate a *spurious*, or illegitimate offspring. Good use, then, is entirely against the rendering of Dr. Gill."* We have already, in the body of this work, illustrated the Scripture use of these words.

3. Such a meaning as this of Dr. Gill, and his disciples, does not meet the *design* of the apostle. We have before noticed the true occasion and design of Paul's reasoning; and we here refer the reader's attention to those remarks. The question before the apostle arose purely from Jewish *ceremonial* distinctions, and not from any state or condition of the civil law respecting marriage;—it respected, therefore, only their *ceremonial purity*, and not the *legality* of their marriage, or the *legitimacy* of their offspring.

4. It has been urged against this view that it represents the apostle in the puerile effort of trying to prove a thing by itself. It represents him as proving the lawfulness of the marriage of the parties by the legitimacy of their offspring—"You are lawfully married, because your children are not bastards." A shorter method of arguing, on the same principles, would have been to say, "You are lawfully married, *because* you are lawfully married."

This opinion concerning the sense of 1 Cor. vii, 14, the Baptists have long held, and many of them still hold it. But by many also it is totally discarded, so that it does not seem necessary to extend our notice of it further.

Thirdly. The next opinion which deserves notice in this place is, so far as I am informed, original with the Rev. John L. Dagg, formerly pastor of the Fifth Baptist church, Philadelphia. His views are published by the directors of the Baptist General Tract Society, in an appendix to Mr. Pengilly's Scripture Guide to Baptism. Mr. Dagg takes the words "unclean" and "*holy*" in their usual sense, and brings forth the following paraphrastic exposition of the passage:—

"The apostle," says he, "decides, in verses 12 and 13, that they [the believing and unbelieving partners] may lawfully dwell together; and in ver. 14, for the convincing and silencing of any members of the church who might object to the decision, he in substance says, '*The unbelieving husband is not unclean, so that his wife may not*

* Dr. Woods on Infant Baptism, p. 85.

lawfully dwell with him; the unbelieving wife is not unclean, so that her husband may not lawfully dwell with her. If they are unclean, then are your children unclean, and not one parent in the whole church must dwell with or touch his children, until God shall convert them; and thus *Christians will be made* to *sever the ties that bind parents to their children, and to throw out the offspring of Christian parents into the ungodly world, from their very birth, without any provision for their protection, support, or religious education.*"

Mr. Hinton, in his History of Baptism, (p. 150,) adopts this view at large, as the most probable one he had met with. Mr. Jewett also (Baptism, p. 79) adopts the same opinion. Mr. Woolsey seems to prefer the opinion advocated by Dr. Gill. Which of the two constructions is nearer the truth, in the estimation of the Baptist General Tract Society, they have not informed us. They have offered both to the public on equal authority, and, with much liberality, have left the matter to our election. We prefer neither. However, they both serve to show how troublesome is this text to their peculiar theory.

The reader will perceive that the pronoun *your*, our author understands to refer, not exclusively to those parents of whom one was a believer, and the other an unbeliever, but to the *whole church.* He thinks that if the apostle had intended to speak of those children only who had one parent a believer, and the other an unbeliever, he would have said, *τεκνα αυτων tekna auton, their children,* instead of *τεκνα ὑμων tekna humon, your children;* the use of the latter pronoun being more customary in addressing the *whole* church, while the third person is more generally employed to designate *individuals* of the body. He thinks also that the present tense of the verb, "your children *ἐστι are* unclean," is a mode of speaking more suited to a parallel than a dependant case.

The objections to this view are the following:—1. It is based upon a supposition that is wholly improbable and absurd, and which contradicts all analogy. It supposes that if it be not ceremonially lawful for a believing husband or wife to live in conjugal relation with an unbelieving partner, so neither would it be lawful, on the same principles of reasoning, for Christian parents to live with their children. Now, the cases are by no means parallel, and the latter cannot be inferred from the former. It does not follow, by parity of reasoning, if a Christian and a heathen cannot live together as husband and wife without the ceremonial defilement of the Christian, that, therefore, Christian parents cannot live with their children, whether born before or after the conversion of the parents, without contracting ceremonial pollution in an equal degree. Analogy is altogether against such a supposition. The history of ceremonial distinctions clearly informs us that where *both* parents were clean, the *children*, who should be afterward born, would be clean also. And if among Jews or Christians a believer has been reckoned defiled by living with an unbeliever, or children have been reckoned unclean when but one of their parents was converted, (both which held true among the Jews,) certain it is that children have never been reckoned unclean where *both* their parents were converted before their birth, any more than two Jews or two Christians have been reckoned unclean merely by living with each other. We know not, indeed, where our author derived his authority for advancing such a supposition, or by what authority the "directors of the General Tract Society" endorsed it; but this we do know, that it is unauthorized by any precedent or parallel in the entire range of analogy.

"If," says Dr. Woods, "we admit the above-mentioned interpretation, what sense would there be in the apostle's argument? Speaking of a believing wife who is connected with an unbelieving husband, he says, Such a husband is sanctified to his wife, so that she is under no necessity to leave him;—and the same as to a believing husband and an unbelieving wife;—and then he adds, *addressing himself unquestionably to the same persons*, 'otherwise,' that is, were it not for this innocency of relation, which the believing partner has to the unbelieving, 'your children would be unclean;—but now,' in consequence of this favourable relation, 'they are holy;' are to be regarded and treated as a *holy, consecrated seed.* The whole relates to the particular case described. What sense can the passage have if we understand it as addressed to the Christian husbands and wives generally, both parties being believers? 'Else were your children unclean!' How? Why?

The apostle says that it would be so, were it not that the unbelieving partner is sanctified to the believing. But here, according to the supposition, there is no unbelieving partner. And then, what sort of relation has the conclusion to the premises? The reasoning supposed consists of two parts. First. If the unbelieving partner were not sanctified to the believing partner, *the children of all other Christians would be unclean.* Secondly. But now as the unbelieving partner *is* sanctified to the believing, *the children of all other Christians are holy.* The first could not be true. If the unbelieving partner were not sanctified to the believing, it would indeed follow that *their* children would be unclean, but it would not follow that *other* children would be unclean, where both parents were believers. The conclusion in the second part is true,—but it does not follow at all from the premises. The children of the church generally, where both parents are believers, are indeed *holy*, in the sense of the apostle; but not because an unbelieving partner is sanctified to a believing."*

2. If the above supposition were true;—if we concede to our opponents all the claims of the above argument, still, we frankly confess, we cannot feel that it possesses force. What is the argument? Why, simply, "that if it be not ceremonially lawful for a believing husband or wife to live with an unbelieving partner, so neither is it lawful, by parity of reasoning, for Christian parents to live with their children." But wherein lies the force of this argument? Simply in the supposition that it is more unnatural and shocking to humanity for parents to refuse to live with their children, than for husbands to refuse to live with their wives, or wives with their husbands. Destroy this supposition, and the argument has no conceivable force.

Why should the fact, that parents may not refuse to live with their children, be urged as an argument to prove that husbands should not refuse to live with their wives, or wives with their husbands, except on the supposition that the former is self-evidently unnatural and shocking, while the latter is not? If there be any thing

* Infant Baptism, p. 98.—I have slightly altered the phraseology of this extract, merely to suit the turn I have given to the text in the translation I have adopted, but not so as to alter the bearing of the argument as intended by the author.

in the philosophy of Mr. Dagg's argument, this is it. But if we appeal directly to nature, or to the common sense of mankind, we shall find that it is no more repugnant to the social feelings, the good order and happiness of society, nor more appalling to humanity, for parents to refuse to live with their children, than for husbands and wives to refuse to live together. The former is not more strongly prohibited by nature itself, by revelation, or by the disastrous consequences that would ensue, than the latter. It is plain, therefore, that the unnatural wickedness of the one cannot be a forcible argument against the performance of the other, where the wickedness of both would be equal. Our author, then, undertakes to prove a doctrine, first, by stating a parallel, which indeed is found to be no parallel; certainly not such an obvious one as to entitle it to become the basis of a new theory! and, secondly, by deducing from this supposed parallel appalling consequences, which, indeed, are no more appalling or impious than those of the original error which they are intended to refute.

The consequences, moreover, are unfairly drawn. The fertility of the author's genius in deducing corollaries has betrayed him into a most amusing excess. It appears as if he had attempted to storm the imagination, and take the judgment prisoner by a sort of *coup de main*, but it proves a failure. If we should suppose that Christian parents could not live with their children without ceremonial defilement, and to avoid profaneness, were consequently obliged to separate from them until they had grown up and become converted, still it would be far from following, (and that man must be crazy indeed who could suppose that it *must* follow,) as a necessary alternative, that they must "*sever the ties that bind them to their children, and throw out their offspring into the ungodly world from their very birth,* WITHOUT ANY PROVISION FOR THEIR PROTECTION, SUPPORT, OR RELIGIOUS EDUCATION!!" *Facinus horrendum!* On the contrary, even if Christian parents could not be allowed to live with their children, still they could love them, and make any other provision for them in their power, for "their protection, support, and religious education."

3. After all, this mode of reasoning seems nothing bet-

ter than proving a thing by itself; a method of procedure absurd and senseless, and expressly rejected by Mr. Dagg himself. If it be an absurd mode of reasoning to say, "You are lawfully married, because your children are lawfully begotten," (and Mr. D. says it *is* absurd,) then, also, is it equally absurd, and by perfect parity of reasoning, to say, (as Mr. D. *has* said,) "You are clean, because your children, which are born of you, are clean." If the *cleanness* or *holiness* in both cases is the same, answering the same ends, then has Mr. D. adopted a mode of reasoning which he himself had repudiated in Dr. Gill. And this is not merely an *argumentum ad hominem*, for in both cases the reasoning is to be rejected.

NOTE F.—Referred to p. 222.

In connection with the historical argument in support of infant baptism, it becomes necessary to furnish the reader with some account of the Waldenses, Albigenses, &c., and particularly of the sect called Petrobrusians. The reader should be apprized that the Baptists have made great searchings into the ecclesiastical records of Christian antiquity, to find some sect, or broken fragment of the church, or independent society, through which to reckon the descent of anti-Pedobaptism from the apostles. They have found a society, answering their purpose in part, in the character and history of some obscure people, who began to attract attention in the middle ages, but whose antiquity and true history are shrouded, in a great degree, to this day, in impenetrable night. The people to which I allude are now more commonly designated by the general name of Waldenses and Albigenses. Before entering upon the brief account of this people which we intend to give, it is proper to premise, that after the Christian church began largely to corrupt itself by the usurpation of temporal dominion, the use of images in worship, and a hundred other departures from the simplicity of the gospel, which it is not necessary to mention, there arose, from time to time, small parties who opposed these existing abominations. These, always being in the despised

minority, and mostly of obscure birth and fortunes, were overawed in the populous cities, where church power was dominant, and quickly expelled. Hence they confined themselves mostly to the obscurer parts of the kingdoms in which they arose. The Waldenses seem to have arisen up, and more generally to have remained, in the mountainous regions of Italy and France. Here, in the retirement and solitude of a rural life, hedged in with lofty mountains, God gave them, for a long time, that liberty of conscience and freedom to worship him, without Papal interdiction, which their seclusion from the world, their distance from Rome, their paucity of numbers, and their unostentatious pursuits, seemed so naturally to guaranty. In the principality of Piedmont, in Italy, and in the late province of Dauphiny, in France, (now comprising the departments of Drome, Isere, and Upper Alps,) as well as in many parts bordering on the Pyrenees, are beautiful and fertile valleys, where, under a genial sun, are cultivated all the fruits and luxuries which belong to any of the districts of France or Italy.

In these regions, on account of the greater security which the situation offered, arose numerous sects, at different times, widely differing from each other, and all enemies of the Catholic Church. The word Waldenses simply signifies *valleys*, *inhabitants of valleys*, &c., and applied to all the sects generally who inhabited these valleys. Of the sects that arose in these regions, some were Manichees,* and, with many impious and absurd tenets, denied all water baptism, retaining only a "baptism by fire," as they called it, which they administered only to adults. Mr. Wall says, "Though the authors do not well distinguish the names, yet, most generally, this sort that denied all baptism, and held the other vile opinions, are denoted by these names, *Cathari*, *Apostolici*, *Luciferians*, *Runcarians*, *Popelicans*, alias *Publicans*."†

After minutely searching out the histories of all the different sects that inhabited these *valleys*, and which are modernly denominated Waldenses, he fixes upon *one sect only* of those who held to water baptism at all, who yet

* For an account of the Manichean heresy, vide Dr. Mosheim's Ecclesiastical History, century iii, chapter v.

† History, part ii, chap. vii, sec. 7.

denied infant baptism. This sect was the Petrobrusians. Ecclesiastical historians complain much of the obscurity that rests upon the history of these times. The history of these sects we derive from their enemies and persecutors, the bigoted monks, and others who took part against them. Hence they are sometimes charged with denying particular doctrines, and, among the rest, infant baptism, evidently to slander them. The whole evidence of there being any sect, or society of men, among those generally called Waldenses, that denied infant baptism, who, at the same time, held to any water baptism at all, is but *probable*. So says Mr. Wall, and so many others regard it.

"The modern Waldenses in Piedmont and Provence, who are the descendants of those ancient ones, practise infant baptism. And they were also found in the practice of it when the Protestants of Luther's Reformation sent to know their state and doctrine, and to confer with them. And they themselves say that their fathers never practised otherwise; and they give proof of it from an old book of theirs, called the Spiritual Almanac, where infant baptism is owned. Perin, their historian, gives the reason of the report that had been to the contrary. He says, 'Their ancestors being constrained for some hundred years to suffer their children to be baptized by the priests of the Church of Rome, they deferred the doing thereof as long as they could, because they had in detestation those human inventions that were added to the sacrament, which they held to be the pollution thereof. And forasmuch as their own pastors were many times abroad, employed in the service of their churches, they could not have baptism administered to their infants by their own ministers. For this cause they kept them long from baptism; which the priests perceiving, and taking notice of, charged them with this slander.' There are many other confessions of theirs of like import, produced by Perin, Baxter, Wills, &c. This is the account the Waldenses give of themselves in those confessions, some of which seem to have been published about two hundred years ago, (that is, about 1505.) One, of the Bohemian Waldenses, is dated 1508."*

* Wall's History, part ii, chap. vii, sec. 3.

These various sects that arose in the tenth, eleventh, and twelfth centuries, were known by different names in different places. In France they were mostly known as Albigenses, so called from Albi, a city in Languedoc, where they became very numerous; or, perhaps more accurately, from Albigesium, the general denomination of Narbonnese Gaul in that century. So some of them also were called Lyonists, or the poor men of Lyons.

The antiquity of these various sects cannot well be computed. The exact date of their origin is not a matter of history. Peter Waldus, a native of Lyons, an opulent merchant and a layman, became so affected with the existing corruptions of the church, that he began to inveigh against them. He began his ministry about A. D. 1160. In the course of his exertions he became acquainted with a people in the valleys of Piedmont, of spirits congenial to his own. These were what were afterward called the Waldenses, or "men of the valleys." By the influence and labours of Peter, his disciples from Lyons became intimately associated with those in the valleys of Piedmont. But the latter had long subsisted there previously to this date. Some believe that they had existed from the days of the apostles. Others ascribe to them an indefinite antiquity. St. Bernard says they must have derived their origin from the devil, since there is no other extraction which we can assign to them. Waddington says we must admit that the direct historical evidence is not sufficient to prove their apostolical descent. He supposes the general sect of the Waldenses may have gradually crept into existence, and extended from the eighth to the eleventh century. It still appears, says he, that the name is not mentioned in any writing before the twelfth century; and there is no direct, specific evidence of the previous existence of the sect. Nevertheless, as its origin was confessedly immemorial in the thirteenth century, and as there has not, perhaps, existed, in the history of heresy, any other sect to which some origin has not been expressly ascribed, we have just reason to infer the very high antiquity of the Vaudois, or Waldenses.*

But the antiquity of this sect, or, we should say, perhaps, of these sects, is of very little importance to the

* History of the Church, p. 290.

argument of our opponents, so long as it is by no means clear that they denied infant baptism. Indeed it is clear that they did not deny it, if we except a single party of a later origin. Mr. Gilly, an English clergyman, who made excursions among the modern Waldenses of Piedmont in 1823, has shown that they now practise infant baptism; and Mr. Jones, in his History of the Waldenses, has attempted to evade the force of this by showing that the present inhabitants of the valleys of Piedmont are not the true descendants of the ancient Waldenses, and that they do not hold the same faith of the latter. His proofs, however, do not appear fully satisfactory touching the point of infant baptism, to say no more. For where he quotes the ancient Waldenses as saying that antichrist "teaches to baptize children into the faith, and attributes to this the work of regeneration," &c., it does not necessarily follow that they intended to condemn infant baptism itself, but only the making it to be equal to regeneration, and indeed what immediately follows proves this to have been the point of their meaning. So when they speak of professing faith before baptism, it may only refer to adults, which is a very common mode of speaking.*

But allowing the ancient Waldenses to have denied infant baptism, still this can hold true only of one of the many sects that went under that name, namely, the followers of Peter Bruis, hence called Petrobrusians. Peter began to preach about A. D. 1126, in the province of Dauphiny, in France. His sect spread over much of the southern part of France, both in country and city, particularly in Toulouse. He was arrested and burnt as a heretic in A. D. 1144. He was succeeded by one Henry, who took the lead of the party for some time. Henry was arrested, and it is probable that he was executed, about A. D. 1147 or 1148. St. Bernard had been sent out by Pope Eugenius to suppress this sect, and, after the death of Henry, "it is said that those who had erred were reduced, the wavering were satisfied, and the seducers so confuted that they durst nowhere appear. And a little after this, Bernard sends a letter to the people of Toulouse, congratulating their recovery from the confusions that had

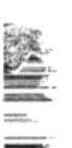

* See Jones's History of the Waldenses, vol. ii, pp. 335–338; and Preface to fifth edition, *Philadelphia.*

been among them on account of those opinions."* Here then, was the suppression of the only sect, of which we have any authentic and positive knowledge, for the first eleven hundred years after the apostles, who denied infant baptism. Their distinct existence as a sect seems not to have continued more than about thirty years. After this, there is no direct account of any sect who denied infant baptism until the rise of the Anabaptists in Germany early in the sixteenth century, (A. D. 1522.) This sect might have arisen, like the phenix, from the scattered ashes of the former.

I have now laid before the reader, very briefly, the prominent facts in the case, in relation to the Waldenses, so far as they stand connected with our subject. The question, then, arises, What does all this make for the argument of our opponents? In other words, What is the force of the argument for anti-Pedobaptism, derived from the fact that the Waldenses, or some who passed under that general name, denied infant baptism? Really we cannot see that it has any force whatever. All the force that the argument can possibly have, in the nature of the case, is derived from the supposition that there existed, in the northern part of Italy and in the southern part of France, a sect who, from the days of the apostles, denied infant baptism, and held to believers' baptism only. If anti-Pedobaptism cannot be traced through these men up to the apostles, the argument is good for nothing. The argument from church history is brought in merely to prove the antiquity of the practice; and if it can be traced up to the apostles themselves, as the uniform and uncontested practice of the church, it furnishes a powerful presumption, nay, almost a demonstration, that it was instituted by the apostles. This, in regard to infant baptism, we have shown to have been the fact. But is this the state of the case in reference to anti-Pedobaptism? Far from it. What if all the Waldensian sects denied infant baptism? What if they had united to ascribe their origin to apostolic times, and their practice to apostolic teaching? All this could have proved nothing, any more than the antiquity of the Chinese can be proved from their mere pretensions. In the absence of authentic records, or of powerful circumstantial testimony, we can

* Wall's History, part ii, c. vii, sec. 7.

place no reliance whatever upon mere rumour, or upon mere sectarian pretension. The Waldenses did not come fully into notice till the twelfth century, and the denial of infant baptism dates no further back than the year 1128. Beyond this is, with reference to this subject, the fabulous age—the age of fiction and conjecture. All the Christian world regarded the doctrine as *new* when it then appeared, first in the Alpine regions of Dauphiny.

But it should be remembered (which we have not before stated) that the *principle* on which infant baptism was denied by the Petrobrusians is such as to indicate sufficiently its new and heretical character. "Christ sending his disciples to preach," say they, "says in the gospel, 'Go ye into all the world, and preach the gospel to every creature. He that believeth, and is baptized, shall be saved; but he that believeth not shall be damned.' From these words of our Saviour it is plain that none can be saved unless he believe and be baptized: that is, have *both* Christian faith and baptism. For not one of these, but both together, doth save. So that infants, though they be by you baptized, yet, since by reason of their age they cannot believe, *are not saved*. It is therefore an idle and vain thing for you to wash persons with water, at such a time when you may indeed cleanse their skin from dirt in a carnal manner, but not purge their souls from sin. But we do stay till the proper time of faith: and when a person is capable to know his God and believe in him, then we do (not, as you charge us, rebaptize him, but) baptize him. For he is to be accounted as not yet baptized who is not washed with that baptism by which sins are done away."* The principle, then, upon which this sect denied infant baptism was plainly this, that infants, *baptized or not baptized, are lost*, so that it is unfit that they should be subjects of any religious ordinance, not being subjects of grace. A practice founded on a principle so erroneous (not to say shocking) cannot commend itself to us with authority, or yield any important aid to the cause of modern anti-Pedobaptism.

* Vide Wall's History, part ii, c. vii, sec. 5.

NOTE G.—Referred to p. 223.

The Church of Rome hold that the administration of baptism belongs chiefly to bishops, priests, and deacons; but, in case of necessity, men or women, Jews, infidels, or heretics, may do it, *if they intend to do what the Church doeth.*

The ceremonies that are used in baptism are the following:—

1. Chrism, or oil mixed with water. This is a token of salvation.

2. Exorcism, composed of certain words, prayers, and actions, for expelling the devil out of the person, and also out of the salt to be used. The priest is to blow in the face of the child after the form of a cross, saying, "Go out of him, Satan!"

3. The forehead, eyes, breast, &c., are to be crossed, to show that by the mystery of baptism the senses are opened to receive God, and to understand his commands.

4. Then some exorcised salt is to be put into the mouth, to signify a deliverance from the putrefaction of sin, and the savour of good works. And the priest, in putting it into the mouth, saith, "N., take the salt of wisdom, and let it be a propitiation for thee to eternal life. Amen."

5. Then the nose and ears are to be anointed with spittle, and then the child is to be brought to the water, as the blind man to Siloam, to signify it brings light to the mind.

After baptism, 1. The priest anoints the top of the head with chrism; and adds, "Let him anoint thee with the chrism of salvation."

2. He puts a white garment on the baptized, saying, "Take this white garment, which thou mayest bring before the judgment-seat of Christ, that thou mayest have life eternal."

3. A lighted candle is put into the hand, to show a faith inflamed with charity, and nourished with good works. Vide Wesley's Works, vol. v, pp. 785, 786, from which this is taken.

Now, can all these senseless and ridiculous ceremonies, which are evidently only the inventions of men, prove that infant baptism itself was also nothing but an invention of man? If such an argument holds good against infant baptism, it certainly holds equally good against all baptism whatsoever, for adult baptism was involved in the same superstitious corruptions. On the same principles of reasoning also the divine institution of the eucharist is invalidated, and proved to be a human invention, because it was corrupted with not only silly superstitions, but monstrous absurdities.

How pitiful, then, is all this attempt to get up an ignorant prejudice against the apostolic institution of infant baptism, merely on the ground of its having been abused by the superadditions of a foolish superstition, to meet the vitiated taste of an apostate church! It is amusing, and at the same time pitiful, to trace the laboured efforts of Mr. Robinson, and of his copyist and admirer, Mr. Benedict, in their Histories of Baptism and the Baptists, through tiresome pages, wrapping themselves in an endless verbosity, and saying many silly things, and all to show that infant baptism had its origin in the middle ages! and arose from the general despotism of the laws, the ignorance of the people, the licentiousness of the clergy, &c., &c.! We say, considered in the light of either sober argument or authentic history, all this is pitiful—is contemptible. It is a mere play upon the presumed ignorance and credulity of their readers. See Robinson's History of Baptism, pp. 269–282; and Benedict's Hist. of the Baptists, vol. i, pp. 60, 61, &c.

Note H.—Referred to p. 278.

In his sermon on "Marks of the New Birth," Mr. Wesley says,—

"Say not, then, in your heart, 'I *was once* baptized, therefore I *am now* a child of God.' Alas! that consequence will by no means hold. How many are the baptized gluttons and drunkards, the baptized liars and common swearers, the baptized railers and evil speakers, the baptized whoremongers, thieves, extortioners! What think you? Are these now the children of God? Verily I say unto you, whosoever you are, unto whom any one of the preceding characters belong, 'Ye are of your father the devil, and the works of your father ye do.' Unto you I call, in the name of Him whom you crucify afresh, and in his words to your circumcised predecessors, 'Ye serpents, ye generation of vipers, how can ye escape the damnation of hell?'

"How indeed, except ye be born again! for ye are now dead in trespasses and in sins. To say, then, that ye cannot be born again, *that there is no new birth but in baptism*, is to seal you all under damnation, to consign you to hell, without help, and without hope....

"'Verily, verily, I say unto you, Ye,' also, 'must be born again.' 'Except ye' also 'be born again, ye cannot see the kingdom of God.' Lean no more on that staff of a broken reed, that ye *were* born again in baptism. Who denies that ye were then made children of God, and heirs of the kingdom of heaven? But, notwithstanding this, ye are now children of the devil. And let not Satan put it into your heart to cavil at a word, when the thing is clear. Ye have heard what are the marks of the children of God: all ye who have them not on your souls, baptized or unbaptized, must needs receive them, or, without doubt, ye will perish everlastingly. And if ye have been baptized, your only hope is this, that those who were made the children of God by baptism, but are now the children of the devil, may yet again receive 'power to become the sons of God;' that they may receive again what they have lost, even the 'spirit of adoption, crying in their hearts, Abba, Father!'"—*Works*, vol. i, pp. 160, 161.

In his sermon on "the New Birth," he says,—

"I proposed, in the last place, to subjoin a few inferences which naturally follow from the preceding observations.

"1. And first, it follows that baptism is not the new birth: *they are not one and the same thing*. Many, indeed, seem to imagine that they are just the same; at least, they speak as if they thought so; but I do not know that this opinion is avowed by any denomination of Christians whatever. Certainly it is not by any within these kingdoms, whether of the established Church, or dissenting from it. The judgment of the latter is clearly declared in their large catechism: 'Q. What are the parts of a sacrament? Ans. The parts of a sacrament are two: the one, an outward and sensible sign; the other, an inward and spiritual grace, thereby signified. Q. What is baptism? Ans. Baptism is a sacrament, wherein Christ hath ordained the washing with water, to be a sign and seal of regeneration by his Spirit.' Here it is manifest, baptism, the sign, is spoken of as distinct from regeneration, the thing signified.

"In the Church Catechism, likewise, the judgment of our Church is declared with the utmost clearness: 'Q. What meanest thou by this word sacrament? Ans. I mean an outward and visible sign of an inward and spiritual grace. Q. What is the outward part or form in baptism? Ans. Water, wherein the person is baptized, in the name of the Father, Son, and Holy Ghost. Q. What is the inward part, or thing signified? Ans. A death unto sin, and a new birth unto righteousness.' Nothing, therefore, is plainer than that, according to the Church of England, baptism is not the new birth.

"But, indeed, the reason of the thing is so clear and evident as not to need any other authority. For what can be more plain than that the one is an external, the other an internal work; that the one is a visible, the other an invisible thing, and therefore wholly different from each other?—the one being an act of man, purifying the body; the other a change wrought by God in the soul: so that the former is just as distinguishable from the latter, as the soul from the body, or water from the Holy Ghost.

"2. From the preceding reflections we may, secondly, observe, that as the new birth is not the same thing with baptism, *so it does not always accompany baptism: they do not constantly go together.* A man may possibly be 'born of water,' and yet not 'born of the Spirit.' There may sometimes be the outward sign, where there is not the inward grace. I do not now speak with regard to infants: it is certain our Church supposes, that all who are baptized in their infancy are at the same time born again; and it is allowed that the whole office for the baptism of infants proceeds upon this supposition. Nor is it an objection of any weight against this, that we cannot comprehend how this work can be wrought in infants. For neither can we comprehend how it is wrought in a person of riper years.

But whatever be the case with infants, it is sure, all of riper years who are baptized are not, at the same time, born again. 'The tree is known by its fruits:' and hereby it appears too plain to be denied that divers of those, who were children of the devil before they were baptized, continue the same after baptism; 'for the works of their father they do:' they continue servants of sin, without any pretence either to inward or outward holiness."—*Ibid.*, pp. 404, 405.

From these extracts it appears most obvious that Mr. Wesley's view of baptismal regeneration is of the most modified form, differing far less with the general class of dissenters than with the high-Church party. His catechetical and liturgical forms of expression differ, sometimes, from those which we prefer to adopt, but his explanations, and practical uses of the doctrines of baptism and regeneration, are evangelical and sound. His Christian character and doctrines were too highly evangelical to admit of an error here. No man, since the days of Paul, ever exhibited the necessity of inward holiness with a greater clearness of expression, or enforced it upon his hearers with a bolder energy of diction. He levelled his fearless rebukes against the formalism of his day—against all that tendency to exalt the outward means to the disparagement of real godliness which was bringing the Church, with a fearful proclivity, in a retrograde movement toward the enormities of the tenth century—against these deteriorating tendencies, I say, Wesley opposed the most pungent rebukes of the oracles of God, and hurled the polished shafts of the quiver of truth. He is the last man upon whom suspicion of formalism can fix her venomous fang.

THE END.

CHRISTIAN BAPTISM.

PART II.—MODE, OBLIGATION, IMPORT, AND RELATIVE ORDER.

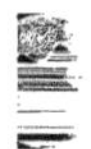

NOW I PRAISE YOU, BRETHREN, THAT YE . . . KEEP THE ORDINANCES AS I DELIVERED THEM UNTO YOU.—PAUL.

PREFACE.

THE reader will probably first expect my apology for presuming to fan the embers of a tiresome controversy, which has promised, or rather threatened, a continuance coextensive with human frailty. My apology is, that I judged the argument could be placed in a better light than that in which it is generally found in treatises on the mode of baptism; besides, several important points have not been duly noticed in any work that has come under my observation. The controversy is often encumbered by matter totally foreign to the subject, and hence we often find people arguing in a manner that leaves them further apart in the end than they had supposed, or, in fact, were at the beginning. The argument is a Bible argument—purely, and most absolutely, a Bible argument To this limit I have kept it. While there is difference of opinion among Christians on any subject, it is natural, it is right, to render a judgment of the case. I have given mine, not without hope that it may contribute its mite of influence to establish the opinions of the candid who ask for light.

If ever this controversy on the mode of baptism be settled, it will be effected, in my sober judgment, by giving that position to the philological argument that I have given to it in this work. I mean, this will be the main engine that will tend to the accomplishment of this desirable end. And here I wish to record my sense of obligation to the writings of that shrewd polemic and accomplished scholar, the Rev. Edward Beecher, president of Illinois College. Some years since I had partly taken the same ground in writing on the same subject. But it was President Beecher's lucid "Criticisms on Βαπτιζω *baptizo*," published (and now being published) in the American Biblical Repository, that settled my views, and induced me to take the position I have in this work, in relation to the import of βαπτιζω. I have, therefore, freely borrowed, as the reader will see, from that author's published numbers; although it is but just to myself to say, that many of the coincidences that occur between that author's views and my own are not chargeable to any plagiarism in me.

The reader should remember that the argument is cumulative. No single argument can decide the controversy to entire satisfaction; but various arguments, brought together from different sources, uniting in their evidence to support the same general position. In such a case, the force of the evidence is greater than that of all the arguments separately, and than the *sum* of all the arguments; above all these, there is the force of the *coincidence* of the different parts. Hence the reader should be patient in his investigations, and never abandon the subject till he has followed it out in all its ramifications.

I have said nothing in this treatise concerning the proper *subjects* of baptism. This omission has not resulted from any light estimation of the subject of infant baptism; on the contrary, it is one that lies very near my heart But I have an insuperable objection to such a mutilation of the argument on this important doctrine, as must result from an attempt to compress it into one or two brief chapters. It is itself worthy of a separate treatise, as it certainly forms a distinct and independent subject. The reader will find little or no allusion, therefore, to infant baptism. Indeed, no side is herein taken on that subject; but neither the silence that prevails throughout the following pages respecting it, nor any particular phraseology that may occur, must be construed into a want of belief in, or appreciation of, infant baptism, on the part of the author; nothing could do greater injustice to my established convictions.

The subject has been kept from a controversial aspect as far as practicable. It is true an "opponent" has been kept in view, and an eye has been had to the main force of the opposite sentiments; but this has been discovered only so far as it was judged important to the better understanding of the proper merits of the subject. The object has not been to defeat an antagonist, but to elicit truth. All extraneous matter has been studiously avoided, and many minor, collateral arguments have been neglected, from a wish not to embarrass and weaken those arguments that are clear and direct.

The reader is particularly commended to the philological argument on those chapters on βαπτω *bapto*, βαπτιζω *baptizo*, and the Greek particles. These, in the order of argument, should properly have come first; and they must necessarily exert a determining influence on the question, *pro* or *con*.

The present work is the result of a careful and anxious

investigation, carried on at intervals for several years past. I felt it more difficult to abridge than to swell its limits; but can confidently say, that the just dimensions of the argument, as I conceive it, are contained in these few unpretending pages. If they prove successful in settling the opinions of any of my Christian brethren, and leading them to juster views of the subjects of which they treat, I shall not regret my labour of writing.

F. G. H.

GENEVA, *April*, 1843.

CHRISTIAN BAPTISM.

MODE OF BAPTISM.

CHAPTER I.

JOHN'S BAPTISM.

SEC. I.—JOHN'S BAPTISMAL STATIONS.

VARIOUS views are entertained in relation to the baptism of John. Some regard it as identical with Christian baptism, while others will deem an apology due for introducing it at all in the present discussion. The character of John's baptism will be noticed hereafter; at present we shall turn our thoughts to an investigation of the *mode* of his baptism. It is not greatly to be wondered at that the advocates of exclusive immersion should so readily have imbibed the belief that John performed his baptism by immersion; but it is truly unaccountable that persons of the opposite sentiment should, in any instance, have conceded to them this ground on so slight investigation. Still, whatever may be the final determination in regard to the mode of John's baptism, it can have no direct tendency to fix the evangelical mode of Christian baptism, any further than to throw light upon the use and application of the word *baptize*.

Before stating the arguments in support of our own views, we shall notice some of those which have been brought forward in defence of the hypothesis that John immersed. The argument of our opponents derived from the word *baptize* we shall consider in a future number. We notice at present only those circumstances which stand connected with the notices of John's baptism, and which are supposed to favour the idea of immersion.

It is urged in favour of the immersion of John's disciples, that he "baptized *in* Jordan." The force of the Greek particle (εν) will be discussed in its appropriate place; but we introduce it here, merely to give a logical cast to the argument. What, then, is the argument, when logically stated? It is this, viz.:—John baptized *in Jordan*, therefore he baptized by *immersion*.

But it is further urged, in support of immersion, that "John baptized in Enon, near to Salim, because there was much water there," John iii, 23. The circumstance of John's choosing a place where there was much water is supposed to favour the doctrine of immersion. Hence the question is asked, with an air of argumentative triumph, Why did John choose a place of "*much water*," if he merely *sprinkled* the people? And so, as if the argument were complete, it is inferred that John chose such a place for the purpose of immersion only. Now we are not bound to show the real cause of John's choosing such a place. If any man assert that it was for the purpose of immersion only, why, the *onus probandi* lies with himself; let him prove it. We have not, like our Baptist brethren, taken upon ourselves any such responsibility. But mark the singular logic of the argument above alluded to. It amounts to this, viz.:—John baptized at Enon because there was *much water* there; therefore John *immersed*. Doubtless this mode of reasoning proves satisfactory to some, but we cannot participate in a faith which rests upon such evidence. Where, then, is the proof that John immersed? We know of none. But observe,

1. Considering the vast multitudes that followed John, "much water" was requisite for the convenience of baptism in any form. But, as this will not obviate the point of difficulty with our opponents, we remark,

2. That, as the history does not inform us whether the *much water* was needed for baptism or for some other purpose, we are left to conjecture the necessity of its demand by the light of circumstances. Now we know that baptism may be performed in a small body of water. But there were other circumstances, besides simple baptism, for which John was to make provision. In that country the mercury ranges, in winter, from forty to fifty degrees, and in summer from eighty to one hundred, and in the plains

of Jordan, where John was baptizing, often much higher. Water, therefore, was in constant demand, not merely for baptism, but more especially for the uses of the people and for their beasts. And this necessity of the people John must see and provide for, whenever he would fix his position for baptizing, unless he would endanger the lives of the people. In connection with this observe,

3. The Greek (πολλα ὑδατα) is in the plural number, and may be rendered here, as it is in other places, "*many waters.*" This suggests the fact that John selected a place for baptism which abounded in living springs and running brooks, water which the people might drink.* This translation is supported by historical facts. 1. John had been previously baptizing in the Jordan near Bethabara. But the water of the Jordan is unfit to drink until it has stood several hours in vessels, and settled. The river itself is bold and rapid, and its waters always turbid and dark. Hence the Jordan was sometimes called, by the Greeks, μελας, which signifies *black.* The multitudes, therefore, that thronged to John's baptism at Bethabara were probably inadequately supplied with wholesome water, which determined the course of John northward, to Enon, where this inconvenience might be obviated. 2. Another circumstance, and one which seems to be altogether overlooked by the Baptists, is, that John had left Bethabara, where there was *more water*, for Enon, where there was *much water.* Why should it be said that, because there was much water at Enon, John chose that place for baptism, when he had all along baptized at Bethabara, where the Jordan is much broader, and, consequently, where there was a much larger quantity of water? If the mere *quantity* of water is to be understood, we can assign no reason why John preferred Enon to Bethabara. Upon this supposition the passage in question is perfectly enigmatical. But, if Enon was supplied with many springs of water suited to the necessities of so vast a multitude as followed John, then we perceive a reason why John should select such a place, and we perceive also a propriety in the translation we have adopted. Strange therefore as it may seem, we are nevertheless bound to the conclusion, by all the evidence in the case, that it was the *quality*, and not

* See note A, at the end of the volume.

the *quantity* of water that determined the baptismal station of John northward at Enon; and that the Greek phrase translated *much water* should read *many waters*, applying to many living springs and running rivulets.

This passage, therefore, which has been quoted with such peculiar confidence by the Baptists as favouring their views, is found to have no possible connection with the point in dispute. It leaves the question of the mode of John's baptism where it found it; and we again demand of our opponents proof that John immersed.

SEC. II.—MODE OF JOHN'S BAPTISM.

We shall now inquire more particularly into the facts recorded in connection with John's baptism, with a view to ascertain the practicability of immersion. In doing this our observations will necessarily become more extended. In constructing our argument we shall direct our inquiries to three several particulars,—the population of Palestine, what proportion of the entire population John baptized, and what length of time John was employed in his public ministry.

I. *The population of Palestine.*—The reader must not be startled to find a population in Palestine, in the commencement of the Christian era, vastly superior, in proportion to its extent of territory, to that of our own country; or to most, if not any, of the modern nations. Many circumstances contributed to the formation of a dense mass of inhabitants; among which may be reckoned, the universal passion among the Jews for a numerous offspring;* their religious predilection for their native soil; and their aversion to the manners and customs of all other nations. Besides, their religion and their customs were so highly national, and so peculiarly their own, as to render all intercourse with other nations, either social or commercial, extremely difficult. These powerful causes checked emigration, and penned the Jews within the narrow confines of their own territory. It was not until the disastrous consequences of the Assyrian and Babylonian invasions had torn them away from the land and the graves of their

* See note B.

sires, that they first thought of planting themselves on heathen ground. Afterward, though they emigrated to different parts of the civilized world, still, the universal prejudice of the nation, (and particularly of the Aramean party,) in favour of their own land, was expressed in the current maxim, "Israel is Israel only in the Holy Land." Hence, we are not surprised to find, in the days of King David, one million three hundred thousand "valiant men that drew the sword," exclusive of the tribes of Levi and Benjamin. And in this census was not reckoned any person from twenty years old and under. Now, if we reckon five persons to every warrior, which, considering the multitude under twenty years, with the aged and those otherwise disabled from bearing arms, together with all the female population, is not an extravagant estimate; and if we reckon the tribes of Levi and Benjamin to number one hundred thousand each, (which is not their proportion,) we shall make the entire population of Palestine to amount to six millions seven hundred thousand. We might corroborate this statement by references to the population of other ancient countries, but our limits forbid such a digression.* We make these statements merely to show the probable correctness of the following account given by Josephus of the population of Palestine, A. D. 66.

That author says, (*Wars*, b. ii, chap. xiv, sec. 3,) "While Cestius Gallus was president of the province of Syria, no body durst so much as send an embassage to him against Florus; but when he was come to Jerusalem, upon the approach of the feast of unleavened bread, the people came about him not fewer than three millions; these besought him to commiserate the calamities of their nation, and cried out upon Florus as the bane of their nation," &c. Now this Florus was governor of Judea; and when the Jews said he was the "bane of their nation," they intended that part of their nation over which he ruled, viz., Judea; and hence it is probable that these three million Jews who complained to Cestius about their governor were mostly citizens of the single province of Judea.

At another time, when Cestius would take the census of the Jewish population, in order to report the same to

* See note C.

Nero, he applied to the priests for aid, who, in order to facilitate the end, counted the number of the paschal sacrifices slain at the passover, which were found to amount, in all, to two hundred and fifty-six thousand five hundred. (Jos., *Wars*, b. vi, chap. ix, sec. 3.) Now, it was not lawful for the Jews to eat the passover alone, and it often happened, according to the original command, (Exod. xii, 3, 4,) that two or three small families united in the purchase and consumption of the lamb. Josephus says there were often twenty persons to one lamb. But suppose the average number of persons to each paschal lamb to be twelve, it would follow that there were in attendance, at the feast of the passover, three millions and seventy-eight thousand persons. But observe, in both of the above instances is given the number of those persons only who were *holy* or *legally clean*, and in actual attendance at Jerusalem on the feasts. Consider, then, the number and variety of legal impurities which, by the law of Moses, disqualified the subject from attending the feasts. So numerous were those legal impediments, and so large a proportion of the people being necessarily disqualified thereby from attending at Jerusalem on the first passover, that it was enacted in the law of Moses, (Num. ix, 9, 11,) and thereafter became a custom among the Jews, to hold a "*second* passover" on the fourteenth day of the second month of their ecclesiastical year, (which month answers to the moon of our April,) for the accommodation of those who were thus, by accident, ceremonially defiled, or otherwise prevented from attending on the regular day. (An example of this is found in 2 Chron. xxx, 1, 3.) Consider, also, the number who, through poverty or business, were detained at home, and we cannot reasonably reckon upon more than half the adult population as being in attendance on these occasions. Indeed, it is hardly supposable that such a proportion of the people would venture from home at any one time. But, by this estimate, the whole Jewish population of Palestine would amount, according to the latter census mentioned, to six millions one hundred and fifty-six thousand. But there were other Jews at Jerusalem on these occasions, from remote countries. Bating, therefore, the one hundred and fifty-six thousand as an offset against the number of foreign Jews, we have six millions left as the probably true population of Palestine. And whoever takes into account the number of Jews in the days of David,—their deeply rooted aversion to other nations—their own love of country, which confined them mostly to Palestine—and also the immense population of other ancient nations,—will not deem this an exaggerated statement. Josephus says, one million one hundred thousand perished in the siege of Jerusalem, A. D. 70.

II. *We next inquire what proportion of the population of Palestine attended John's ministry and were baptized of him.*—The reader will not look for great arithmetical exactness in our calculations, when he considers that a few general facts constitute our only data; nor will he, on the other hand, regard our conclusions as "air built and baseless," when he reflects that those general facts are the express declarations of Scripture.

Previously to all direct investigation of the subject, it is important that we have enlightened views of the object of John's mission. John was sent to "prepare the way of the Lord." He was sent to no private sect or party, but to the Jewish nation—to the great Jewish family, resident in Palestine. He was received by the Jews as a nation. There was no such division of public sentiment in regard to John as prevailed in reference to Jesus Christ. The Pharisees and Sadducees in general submitted to his baptism,* ambitious of the distinction thus conferred, and all parties coalesced in the popular sentiment that John was a divine prophet. Indeed, nothing short of this general reception would have fully answered the intent of John's mission. "He was a burning and a shining light, and the Jews were willing, for a season, to rejoice in his light." These considerations furnish a strong presumption that the major part of the people were baptized of John.†

In exact accordance with this presumption are the express declarations of Scripture. Matthew says, (chap. iii, 5, 6,) "Then went out to him JERUSALEM, and ALL JUDEA, and ALL THE REGION ROUND ABOUT JORDAN, and *were baptized of him in Jordan*, confessing their sins." Mark informs us, (i, 5,) "that there went out unto him ALL THE

* See note D. † See note E.

LAND OF JUDEA, and THEY OF JERUSALEM, and were ALL baptized of him." Luke says, (iii, 21,) "And when ALL THE PEOPLE were baptized, it came to pass that Jesus himself, being baptized," &c.

Josephus, the great Jewish historian, informs us that there were so many who followed John, that Herod the tetrarch, fearing that John might secretly harbour treasonous designs, and, in the event, head an insurrection, apprehended, and caused him to be executed. Let us attend for a moment to these testimonies. That of Matthew goes to prove by specific statements that the population of the city of Jerusalem, the province of Judea, and the great valley of the Jordan, went out and were baptized of John.

The province of Judea comprehended nearly *one half* of the entire territory of Palestine west of the Jordan. The "region round about Jordan," by which we are to understand the great valley of the Jordan, lies between the mountains of Israel on the west and those of Hermon, Gilead, and Abarim on the east, reckoning from the northern extremity of the sea of Tiberias (according to Burkhardt) to the embouchure of the Jordan. This "region" embraces most of the territories of Samaria and Perea, besides a large portion of Galilee. The description of Matthew, therefore, is found to embrace the heart of the Jewish population. Mark and Luke agree, in substance, with Matthew; the former saying that ALL *the land of Judea, and they of Jerusalem*, went out, and were ALL baptized, and the latter simply stating that ALL THE PEOPLE were baptized. Besides, many foreign Jews, who were at Jerusalem at the passover, which was celebrated toward the close of John's ministry, probably received his baptism. Twelve of the foreign Jews, disciples of John and afterward Christians, were found by Paul at Ephesus. Acts xix, 1-7. How many others from abroad received his baptism history does not inform us, but the number was, probably, not inconsiderable.

The only difficulty that can arise in fixing the sense of the evangelists lies in the use and limitation of the general terms employed. The word "*all*," in the several connections cited, must necessarily mean something. It cannot be argued, with good reason, that it here amounts to a mere Hebraism for a great multitude.* There exists no reason why the word, in the above connections, should be understood in a proverbial, and not in a narrative, sense. No impossibility or absurdity is necessarily involved in taking the word literally, or to signify a great majority which is a very common acceptation. Or, if any absurdity be involved in such an acceptation, it can be so only on the principles of our opponents, and must therefore lie against their theory, which supposes that John immersed his disciples one by one. It must be remembered that the evangelists are historians who narrate the events of which they, for the most part, were eye-witnesses. Independently of the question of their inspiration, they are above suspicion as faithful narrators. They were not biased by party zeal or heated by passion, so that they would be likely to colour their descriptions. Unless therefore we are willing to discredit and prepared to disprove the historical accuracy of the New Testament, we cannot reasonably suppose the word "ALL" to signify less than the *major part*. But, to make the most liberal allowance in favour of our opponents, we will suppose John baptized *one half* the entire population of Palestine; it would then follow that he baptized, in all, three millions of persons. No doubt many, who may not have given to the subject a previous attention, will be startled at the first view of this aggregate result. John may not have baptized, in fact, so many. Still, we think the words of the sacred history oblige us to understand something like the result to which we have attained; which certainly is far from being absurd, or impossible, considered as a matter of fact. John was sent to preach "repentance" to all the Jews, and to baptize all that submitted to his doctrine. The query arises, "Was it the duty of all to repent and be baptized?" If so, which all admit, then, evidently, must there have been allowed *time* for the process. It could never have been the duty of the Jews to submit to John's baptism when a natural impossibility precluded such an act of submission. The physical strength of John—the time allotted to the continuance of his ministry—the manner and circumstances essentially connected with the valid administration of his baptism—

* See note F.

must all be taken into the account, and in view of all these considerations it must have been clearly possible for John to baptize all whose duty it was to repent and submit to the claims of his doctrine; otherwise there was clearly an absurdity—a discrepancy indicative of a want of forethought—in the adaptations and different parts of John's dispensation.

III. *We now inquire into the duration of John's public ministry.*—According to Luke, (chap. iii, 1, &c.,) John opened his ministry in the fifteenth year of the reign of Tiberius Cesar, (reckoning the three years of his reign conjointly with Augustus,) which, according to our most approved chronology, answers to the thirtieth year of John's life. It is generally agreed by chronologers that our Saviour was born December the twenty-fifth, A. M. 4000. John the Baptist was six months older than Christ, (*vide* Luke i, 30, 31, 36, compared with ver. 13,) and, consequently, was born the twenty-fourth of June previous. Allowing, then, John to have opened his ministry at the age of thirty, in the latter part of June, year of the vulgar era 26; and supposing, as Luke says, (chap. iii, 21, 23,) Jesus was baptized when he was thirty years of age, i. e., about December the twenty-fifth of the same year;* it would then follow that John had been engaged six months in his public ministry at the time of Christ's baptism. The Greek Church hold that Christ was baptized on the Epiphany, which is the sixth of January, new style. But the difference of a few days, either way, cannot materially affect the weight of our argument. How long John continued baptizing subsequently to this period we are not definitely informed. But, from a careful collation of facts, we can safely limit the period of his after labours to four months.

The last account we have of John, previously to his imprisonment, states that he was "baptizing at Enon near to Salim," John iii, 23. This was immediately after our Lord had attended his first passover, which was celebrated on the fourteenth day of the month Nisan, which, as the

* I suppose it will be understood that the birth of Christ is reckoned to have actually taken place FOUR YEARS (strictly, three years and eight days) before the commencement of the vulgar era, or Anno Domini, so that A. D. 26 answers, in reality, to the thirtieth year of our Saviour's life.

Jews reckoned their years by lunar months, answers to the moon of our March. As a necessary consequence of their reckoning time by the phases of the moon, the celebration of their passover sometimes fell on the latter half of the month of March, and sometimes on the fore part of April. We cannot therefore be exact to a day; but, by closely following the circumstances in the evangelical history, we shall arrive at a reasonable certainty that John did not continue his ministry beyond the period above assigned him. The whole chain of facts runs thus:—After Jesus was baptized he went into Galilee, where, on the third day after his arrival, he attended the marriage at Cana. John ii, 1. After this he went to Capernaum where he stayed "not many days," ver. 12. Leaving Capernaum he returned into Judea to attend the passover at Jerusalem. Ver. 13. Here he purged the temple, (ver. 14,) and held conversation with Nicodemus. John iii, 1–21. Leaving the city of Jerusalem, he went out into the province of Judea, and baptized. Ver. 22. At this time, "John also was baptizing at Enon near to Salim," (ver. 23,) about twenty miles distant. Their mutual proximity, and the increasing popularity of Jesus, led to disputes among the Jews, (verses 25, 26,) and excited the jealousy and malice of the Pharisees. John iv, 1–3. "When, therefore, the Lord knew how the Pharisees had heard that Jesus made and baptized more disciples than John, he left Judea, and departed into Galilee." Here, then, it is stated that Jesus "departed into Galilee," while John was in the vicinity of Enon baptizing, immediately after the first passover which our Lord attended—i. e., the latter part of March, A. D. 27, nine months after John had commenced his public ministry. But, by comparing Matt. iv, 12, and Mark i, 14, we find that Jesus did not depart into Galilee at this time, until after "he had heard that John was cast into prison." The conclusion, therefore, is, that John was arrested during his stay at Enon; and Jesus, in view of the commotion excited in Judea by that event, and also of the controversies going on there, concerning himself and John, prudently withdrew, for a season, into the remoter parts of Galilee.

Various circumstances corroborate this conclusion. It is evident, both from Josephus and the New Testament, that John was arrested by Herod Antipas, governor of Galilee and Perea. (Jos., *Antiq.*, b. xvii, chap. viii, sec. 1.) But Enon lay at the southern extremity of Herod's dominions on the west of the Jordan; therefore, if John had been south of Enon, he would have been beyond the jurisdiction of Herod. And, as we never read of John's going north of that place, we conclude he was arrested at Enon.

Again, our Lord did not fully open his mission until after John was cast into prison. Matt. iv, 12–17, and Mark i, 14, 15. The popularity of John presented an impediment to the ministry of the Saviour. Indeed, it is natural to suppose that two such great characters, labouring in the vicinity of each other, would inevitably produce a great division of public sentiment. Jesus, therefore, prudently withheld himself until John had "fulfilled his course." But, from the nature of the case, he cannot be supposed to have thus withheld long, the object of his mission being of such paramount importance to that of John's.

Thus have we followed John, in his public ministry, during the space of nine months. He had introduced Christ to the Jews, and having thus fulfilled the object of his mission, (John i, 31,) he retired, by a singular providence, from the field of his labour, some time in the month of April, A. D. 27. That he continued his ministry longer than about nine months cannot be proved from the Bible, and we shall, therefore, fix the entire period of his public labours at ten months, as being the utmost limit to which it can be extended with any shadow of evidence.

But here are several facts to be considered.

1. John could not have commenced baptizing immediately upon the opening of his mission. Some time must necessarily have elapsed before the people would become so acquainted with him as to apprehend his character and the purport of his mission, and be induced to receive his baptism. We will suppose, then, he preached two weeks before he began to baptize.

2. John's term of public labour included one wintry season, wherein, though the climate in that country is much milder than in our own, stil., there would be an unavoid-

able loss of time, occasioned by foul weather. This, with those who are acquainted with the calendar of Palestine, will not be deemed an insignificant item. During the winter, the inhabitants of Palestine often experience storms, especially during the rainy seasons, at which time there is little travelling abroad. This, together with the time occupied in moving from place to place, would require another deduction from John's time for baptizing, of not less than twenty days.

3. Forty-three sabbaths are to be deducted, wherein, according to the Jewish observance of those days, it was unlawful for John to baptize. Thus we have left, in all, two hundred and twenty-seven days, in which we may suppose John exercised the function of his ministry.

We next inquire how many hours per day John was employed in the very act of baptizing. If he immersed his disciples, according to the modern mode, he could not have thus laboured more than six hours per day, pursuing his labours in the same ratio for two hundred and twenty-seven days. John was unsustained by any miracle, and we must calculate his labours as we would those of any other man, according to a medium ratio of physical strength. And no man could rationally suppose John to have stood in three feet depth of water more than six hours in a day, and for the number of days above mentioned, labouring at the top of his strength, without an iron-bound constitution, or a miracle of aid. But, according to this estimate, the whole number of hours in which John was employed in the very act of baptizing amounted to one thousand three hundred and sixty-two.

We are now ready for the argument.

1. John baptized, in all, three million persons.

2. The whole time in which John may be supposed to have been engaged in the very act of baptizing did not exceed one thousand three hundred and sixty-two hours.

Therefore John must have baptized, in one hour, two thousand two hundred and two; in one minute, thirty-six, or a little over *one* in every two seconds. And he must have pursued these labours in the same rapid ratio during six hours per day, for the space of two hundred and twenty-seven days.

Here, then, is an expose of the real facts in the case.

Let not the advocates of the hypothesis that John immersed deem the subject unencumbered with difficulty. We are not at liberty to construct our theories irrespective of facts. That age of fanciful philosophy wherein *theory* subsisted antecedent to investigation has passed. *Investigation* is now the great talisman of the inquirer after truth. We are, however, far from being tenacious, to a unit, of the exact arithmetical aspect of the above calculation. The perfect triumph of our argument does not require it. It would not become us in view of the very *general* character of those facts which have constituted our principal data. All that we fix upon *tenaciously* is, the UTTER IMPRACTICABILITY of immersing the multitudes which John is said to have baptized.

It may be supposed, by some, that our argument is as conclusive against sprinkling as immersion: that it was impracticable for John to have baptized such numbers in any form. And so it certainly was on the supposition of his taking them one by one, according to the practice observed in Christian baptism. But there is no just ground for supposing this to have been the fact. The nature of his baptism did not require it, and the force of the language employed to describe his baptism does not prove it. I take the following facts to be established:—

First. The water of baptism was administered to the people by John's own hand. This is evident from the force of the words, "And were baptized ὑπ' αυτου BY *him*," &c., Matt. iii, 6; the preposition *by* here denoting, according to its usual acceptation, the efficient cause.

Secondly. There is no necessity of supposing him to have baptized them one by one. This would not only have been totally impracticable, but the Jewish law did not require it. It must be remembered that John made no innovation upon the Mosaic rites, but employed the existing ceremonies of purification to the purposes of his own ministry. This is evident from several circumstances: 1st. If the reader will refer to John iii, 25, 26, he will find that both John's baptism and that of Christ, before the resurrection, had reference only to Jewish ceremonies of purification, taken and applied to the higher purposes of John's ministry. 2d. No controversies were ever started about the validity of John's baptism.

This is, alone, sufficient to satisfy any candid, intelligent person, that John did not depart from the usage of Moses. It is unaccountable that the Pharisees and lawyers who did not submit to be baptized of John should have held their peace, and failed to have used so plausible and powerful a pretext for their opposition to John as that which would have been furnished them by the fact of an innovation. They questioned every assumption of power made by the Saviour; and complained of every fancied breach of Moses' law, or even of the tradition of their elders. And had John introduced any new external right, they would, beyond all doubt, have disputed his authority. But we have no account of such a dispute. 3d. Furthermore, John was not sent to abolish the Jewish rites, but to resuscitate the languishing state of the Mosaic religion. The spirituality of that dispensation had suffered an almost total eclipse from the incorporation of numerous traditions, and the supplementary glosses of their expositors. Practical piety was in a low state. John was sent to revive the spirit of ancient institutions, and excite an immediate expectation of Messiah.

If, therefore, John's manner of baptism was taken from the Jewish law, it is not difficult to conceive of the practicability of his baptizing such multitudes. The Jews had a mode of purifying the people by dipping a bunch of hyssop into water and sprinkling it upon them. So it is said of Moses, "When he had spoken every precept to all the people according to the law, he took the blood of calves and of goats, with water and scarlet wool, and hyssop, and sprinkled both the book and all the people," Heb. ix, 19. Now it is worthy of remark that the people numbered, at this time, six hundred thousand warriors; which, reckoning five of the common people to one warrior, leaves a round number of three million persons. These Moses sprinkled. The occasion was one of the most grand and awful import of any similar one recorded in the Old Testament. It was "the dedication of the first testament;" and not only were "ALL THE PEOPLE" then solemnly dedicated to God, but also the tabernacle and all its utensils. Heb. ix, 18–21; Exod. xxiv, 6; Lev. xiv, 16. But if Moses dedicated the people to God by sprinkling, and if such forms of consecration were familiar

2

with the Jews, and if John adopted a Jewish rite for the purposes of his ministry, then, evidently, we may suppose he sprinkled the people by means of a hyssop branch, dipped in the water. If this were the actual manner of John's baptism, (or purification, see chap. iv,) he might have performed the labour with comparative ease, administering to many at the same instant of time, as they might pass before him in ranks. I am aware that this ground will be contested, standing, as it does, so directly opposite to the commonly received opinion. But let the objector candidly weigh the difficulties that lie against the Baptist theory; let him consider that the common hypothesis, that John baptized the people separately, is wholly assumed, and is without any supporting evidence; let him consider that the hypothesis we have advanced is sufficiently in harmony with Jewish usage; and, withal, let him remember that we have not theorized beyond the obvious bearing, and, what appeared to us, the necessary requirement of facts. And if, finally, he should not be satisfied with our conclusions, let him exercise himself a little in arithmetic, and ascertain, to his abundant satisfaction, what probable number John could have immersed (taking them one by one) within the space of *ten* months. When he has found that six thousand persons is an almost incredible estimate, then let him compare the result of his calculations with the inspired declarations on the subject, and with the incidental notices of John's popularity and success; and if, after all this, he be not satisfied of the improbability and impossibility of the Baptist theory, we must, perhaps, leave him in the undisturbed and everlasting repose of his chosen, yet baseless faith.

SECTION III.

One view of John's baptism remains to be taken, viz. *the difference between it and Christian baptism.* Many suppose the baptism of John to be identical with Christian baptism, and hence they argue from the former to the latter without reserve or qualification.

The arguments, proving their total distinctiveness, may be thus epitomized. The baptism of John is proved to be different from Christian baptism,

1. *From the time of its institution.*—John began to preach and baptize six months before our Lord entered upon his public ministry, previously to which he performed no official act. Those, therefore, who maintain that John administered the ordinance of Christian baptism, involve themselves in the following absurdity, viz., that Christian baptism was administered six months prior to any official act being performed by the founder of Christianity; i. e., that the initiating ordinance of the Christian system existed six months previous to Christianity itself! According to this, then, it would follow most unquestionably that Jesus Christ did not institute Christian baptism, unless it can be proved that he instituted it before he entered upon this public ministry—which no one, in his senses, will affirm.

Moreover, the law of Moses was still in force, and the Christian ordinances which superseded the Mosaic institutes could not, consequently, have been in vogue. The law of Moses did not end in John, but in Christ.

2. *Its distinctive name.*—It is called "*John's baptism.*" But if it be identical with Christian baptism, why does the Holy Ghost employ this distinctive appellation? Why was it ever called any thing, in the Bible, but Christian baptism? The Bible calls things by their proper names. But if John administered the Christian baptism, then it would be as egregious a misnomer to call it *John's baptism*, as it would be to call it *Peter's baptism*, because the same ordinance was administered by that apostle. And thus, on the same principle, we should have a Paul's baptism—a Philip's baptism—a Timothy's baptism—and so on *ad infinitum.*

3. *Its distinctive nature.*—John baptized his disciples on a creditable profession of their repentance. The adult Christian candidate receives baptism on profession of regeneration. *Vide* Acts xix, 4; ii, 38; Gal. iii, 27.

4. *The faith of John's disciples, required, in order to baptism, does not answer to the faith of the lawful adult candidate for Christian baptism.*—1. *John did not require faith in the Holy Trinity.* Whether John was well informed on this fundamental doctrine of Christianity, we cannot say. It was not a distinctive feature of Judaism, although obscurely taught in the Old Testament scriptures. But certain it is

that John did not require of his disciples any formal profession of belief in this doctrine at the time of baptism; nor was there at such times any formal recognition made of it, as is the case in valid Christian baptism. These circumstances form a primary distinction between John's baptism and the Christian ordinance. (*Vide* Acts xix, 2, 3; comp. Matt. xxviii, 19.) 2. *John required of his disciples, in order to their baptism, faith in a Messiah to come.* Hence, John always referred his disciples forward to him who came "after him," i. e., Christ. Paul says, (Acts xix, 4,) "John verily baptized with the baptism of repentance, saying unto the people, that they should *believe on him that should come after him*, that is, on Christ Jesus." The words we have italicised seem to have comprised the substance of John's formula of baptism. But the same apostle affirms that Christian baptism imports faith in, and conformity to, the *death* of Christ. Thus, "Know ye not that so many of us as were baptized into Jesus Christ were baptized into his *death?*" Rom. vi, 3. This clearly proves that, whatever else Christian baptism imports, it plainly implies, on the part of the candidate, faith in the reality of the *death* of the Messiah. But in this it is diametrically opposed to John's baptism. If a person, in these days, should adopt the exact faith of a disciple of John in this respect, he would be accounted a Jew or an antichristian, and would be rejected from the communion of all our Christian churches. No Christian minister would baptize a person on profession of such a faith, but under pain of church censure. 3. *John did not so much as baptize in the name of Jesus.* For, if he did, he must not only have used his *name* in baptism, but also have taught his *character* and *doctrines;* so far, at least, as to make his disciples rudimental Christians. To baptize in the name of Jesus, of whose character the adult candidate is left in ignorance, is a sheer mockery of sacred things. But the general ignorance of the people concerning Christ, even after he came, proves that John had not baptized in his name. During John's life, it is said, (Luke iii, 15,) "All men mused in their hearts, of John, whether *he* were the Christ or not." Toward the close of our Saviour's ministry he propounds the following question to his disciples: "Who do men say that I, the Son of man, am?" The disciples, who certainly had a good opportunity of knowing the state of public opinion concerning Christ, reply, "Some say that thou art John the Baptist; some, Elias; and others, Jeremias, or one of the prophets," Matt. xvi, 13, 14. Here, to be sure, was a great diversity of opinion, and not one of them right, which is unaccountable on the hypothesis that John baptized the people in the name of Jesus. It seems, further, that John's personal knowledge of the Saviour was very imperfect, as, previous to the baptism of Christ, John expressly says, "I knew him not," John i, 32, 34. But whence has arisen this opinion, so prevalent with many, that John's baptism was identical with the Christian ordinance of washing? Can any enlightened Christian entertain, for a moment, the supposition that John inculcated upon his disciples the doctrines which belong, distinctively, to the Christian system? It is said that "he that is least in the kingdom of heaven (meaning the Christian dispensation) is greater than John the Baptist." But if all John's disciples were indoctrinated into the Christian faith, (and nothing short of this would have justified a Christian baptism,) and baptized with a Christian baptism, it is difficult to conceive on what grounds of propriety or truth our Lord could have made such a statement. But,

5. *The apostles paid no regard to John's baptism, but rebaptized his disciples.*—This they certainly would not have done, had they believed the dogma we are opposing. The proof of our position is found in the history of the Acts, chap. xix, 1–5. There has been, however, a mode of construction invented for this passage which makes it speak a directly contrary doctrine from what we have supposed. The two different constructions placed upon this passage take their origin from diverse opinions in regard to the real author of the fifth verse. The common opinion is, that that verse is the language of Luke, where he again takes up the thread of the history of the disciples of Ephesus after the short interruption of Paul's speech in the fourth verse. The opposite construction assumes that the fifth verse is a simple continuation of Paul's discourse, commencing with verse 4, and that, consequently, the pronoun *they*, in the fifth verse, refers to the collective noun *people* in the fourth verse, and not to *disciples*, in verse 1.

The vast contrariety between these constructions is seen at a glance, by applying them respectively in the reading of the whole history. It is not our design to take up the controversy on this passage at length. A primary objection, however, to the latter, which we regard as a spurious construction, is found in fixing the proper antecedent of the pronoun *them* in the sixth verse. For if the pronoun *they*, in verse 5, be the true representative of the collective noun *people*, in verse 4, then, according to every principle of grammatical criticism, the noun last mentioned is also the true *original* of the pronoun *them*, in the sixth verse. The legitimate consequence of this construction, then, is, that where it says, in verse 6, that "Paul laid his hands on *them*," &c., it does not mean that he laid his hands on the twelve "*disciples*" of Ephesus, but, on the "*people*" whom John baptized, mentioned verse 4.

"Either this must be supposed, or the words which, in their original structure, are most intimately combined, must be conceived to consist of two parts,—the first relating to John's converts in general, the second to the twelve disciples at Ephesus; and the relative pronoun, expressive of the latter description of persons, instead of being conjoined to the preceding clause, must be referred to an antecedent removed at the distance of three verses. In the whole compass of theological controversy, it would be difficult to assign a stronger instance of the force of prejudice in obscuring a plain matter of fact."*

6. If John administered the ordinance of *Christian baptism*, then, most unquestionably, his disciples were christianized. If so, then the greater part of the Jewish nation were Christians at the very point of time in which Christ opened his public ministry, but immediately afterward they apostatized and became the most embittered and malignant foes of the Christian name. Now, it would have been wonderful, indeed, to behold a whole nation so generally turning to God, and submitting to the initiating ordinance of Christianity, all within the space of a few months; but it surpasses our conceptions to account for their total apostacy, within a period of time much shorter; and it is still infinitely more mysterious that the New

* Rev. R. Hall's Works.

Testament history should pass over such mighty revolutions of opinion (supposing them to be true)—revolutions which form the most interesting subjects of sacred history —in profound silence, while it records incidents of inferior note with such studied care. Our Lord never reproaches the Jews for their apostacy from Christianity; but, for their defection from the spirit of the Mosaic institutes, and for their actual sins, he publicly and repeatedly condemns them.

"There is attached to apostacy a character of perfidy and baseness peculiar to itself—a species of guilt which the inspired writers frequently paint in the darkest colours; yet, strange to tell! though they had no motives to conceal or palliate the conduct of their countrymen in their treatment of the Messiah, but many motives to the contrary, not a syllable escapes them of the charge of apostacy. What terrible energy would that accusation have lent to Peter's address! What unspeakable advantage for alarming their consciences would he have derived from reminding them of their baptismal vows, and of their unspeakable impiety in crucifying the divine person to whom they had previously dedicated themselves in solemn rites of religion. When Paul, in writing to the Thessalonians, gives loose to one of his finest bursts of indignant feeling and rapid eloquence, in a brief portraiture of the character of his countrymen, the circumstance which would have given incredible force to the picture is suppressed, and he seems to entertain no suspicion of their having been baptized in the name of Jesus."*

* Rev. R. Hall's Works.

CHAPTER II.

CHRIST'S BAPTISM.

HAVING concluded our remarks on John's baptism, something should be said of the baptism of our Saviour; and we shall not find a more appropriate place for this subject than in the present stage of the general argument. We have, therefore, assigned to it a special chapter. If any suppose that we are wandering from the direct point at issue, we readily concede the justness of their views; but we urge, as a sufficient apology, the real state of the controversy. The baptism of our Saviour has been drawn into the controversy on Christian baptism, and is appealed to, by the advocates of immersion, as possessing decisive authority, both in regard to the duty and mode of baptism.

I. As to the *mode* of Christ's baptism the Scriptures furnish no information, save what may be gathered from the import of the Greek word *baptize*, and from the force of two or three vague *particles*. These we shall not at present notice, but shall consider them in another place.

II. The *character* of Christ's baptism is a question fraught with more importance, and deserves a more extended notice. But our opponents must be reminded that we are under no obligation, from the posture of the controversy, to prove what was the real character of his baptism. We do not profess to know positively, on this subject, what the Bible has not positively expressed, or what may not, by fair implication, be attributed to it. Should our views of the subject prove unsatisfactory to any, let us not therefore be faulted. We shall render what we deem to be the Bible and rational account of the matter, making no account of the baseless assumptions or ignorant prejudices which have been entertained by many. Our proper position, in relation to this question, is on the negative side. Our Baptist brethren have assumed that Christ received a *Christian* baptism. The labour that lawfully devolves upon us will be fully accomplished when we shall have disproved the correctness of this assumption,

In order to place this subject fully before the understanding, we remark:—

1. *The baptism of our Saviour did not partake of the character of John's baptism.* For, (*a*) John baptized his converts "unto repentance;" i. e., after they had repented, and in testimony of the fact. Therefore, if our Lord's baptism partook of the nature of John's baptism, inasmuch as the latter witnessed to the repentance of the candidate, he must have previously repented of sin—which is blasphemous to assert.

(*b*) John required of the candidate faith in the Messiah about to come. "John verily baptized with the baptism of repentance, saying unto the people that they should believe on him which should come after him, that is, on Christ Jesus," Acts xix, 4. If, therefore, Christ was baptized with John's baptism, he must have believed in a Messiah *to come*, and to this faith John must have exhorted him. But the absurdity and heresy of such a doctrine need not be mentioned.

(*c*) The ultimate design of John's baptism was to "prepare the way of the Lord;" i. e., to prepare the hearts of the people for the reception of the Messiah, in all his gracious offices. This was the great aim of all his labours. But was our Saviour baptized with this intent? Could the proper import of John's baptism apply to the Saviour in any form? But it is idle to push these arguments. If a man will labour to support the hypothesis we are opposing, it is, perhaps, trifling with time and with reason to oppose him.

2. *Christ's baptism did not partake of the nature of Christian baptism.* For,

(*a*) Christian baptism was not instituted until after the resurrection of our Saviour. Matt. xxviii, 18, 19, and parallel places. We have already sufficiently exploded the notion that John's baptism was identical with Christian baptism, and we certainly have no account of the administration of the latter until the day of pentecost. If, therefore, Christ received Christian baptism, the event must have taken place about three years previous to the actual institution of that ordinance, which is absurd to suppose.

(*b*) Christian baptism is performed in the name of the

Father, Son, and Holy Ghost; thereby importing the faith of the candidate in the existence, and his dedication to the glory, of the three persons in one God. But if Christ had been baptized in this profession, it would have been, to say the least, irrelevant and trifling. There is a manifest propriety, a sublime significance, in *our* being baptized in the name of Christ the Son, in token of our devotion to his service; but there is an inconceivable absurdity in the idea of Christ's being baptized in his *own name*, in profession of his devotedness to *his own cause and person*. Yet we must suppose all this, if we suppose that Christ was baptized with a Christian baptism.

(*c*) The *import* of Christian baptism is totally inapplicable to the person and character of Christ. For, baptism is both a *sign* and *seal*. As a *sign*, it witnesseth to our inward washing and regeneration by the Holy Ghost, which, from the nature of the case, presupposes defilement by sin. Remove the idea of antecedent pollution by sin, and you annihilate the grand intent of baptism as a sign. As a *seal*, baptism becomes the *pledge*—

(*a*) Of our fidelity to God:

(*b*) Of the divine faithfulness in bestowing upon us the blessings of the new covenant; as repentance, pardon, regeneration, sanctification, &c. Such then being the true import of baptism, can any person, in his sober senses, presume it to be applicable to the Saviour of the world? We could hardly persuade ourselves that any Christian would assume so preposterous ground, if the fact did not exist to demonstrate the monstrous absurdity. And yet our Baptist brethren will maintain that Christ received a Christian baptism. They cannot, surely, intend by this that baptism, in the case of the Saviour, imported the same that it does in believers,—that it was emblematical of the inward washing of the Holy Ghost, and implied previous defilement,—that it was with him, as with us, the *seal* and *sign* of the covenant of grace. We cannot in charity suppose this to be any part of their meaning when they advance the strange doctrine in question. What then do they mean? We cannot take upon ourselves positively to decide this question. But if they have embraced a theory, in the ardour of their zeal, without investigation, we can

excuse them, and forbear to urge upon them its deductions, which they no more believe than we ourselves.

It is possible that some may imagine that the outward form of baptism was used in the case of our Saviour, while the *import* of the ordinance was, in reference to him, set aside. I am not aware that this opinion is entertained, but I state it as a possible case. This indeed would shield them from the impiety of the above conclusions, but would involve them in the absurdity of supposing that, in the case of Christ, a hypocritical, a mock baptism was used; a baptism destitute of all meaning and personal application to the candidate, or which was endued with a significance altogether extraordinary, concerning which the Bible has given us no account.

3. What then was the real design of Christ's baptism, and wherein lay the necessity of his being baptized at all? Before attempting any direct answer to this question, we shall inquire into the *supposed* design of it. It has been alleged by the Baptists that our Saviour was baptized in order to furnish his followers an example. Hence they exhort young converts to go forward in baptism, following the example of Christ. Hence young Christian disciples themselves, who are, in this respect, of the Baptist faith, are often heard to express their anxiety to imitate the example of the Saviour; i. e., to be immersed. Hence the phrase "going down the banks of the Jordan" is understood, in the technology of the Baptist faith, to mean being immersed, in imitation of the example of our Saviour. An effort is made to associate the baptism of Christ with our duty of baptism, and particularly with the alleged duty of immersion, so as to sanction the latter by the former.

The effect which this mode of reasoning has upon many minds is truly powerful. The pious sensibilities of the young disciple are deeply moved by every appeal to the example of Christ. Always anxious, while prompted only by the ardour of his first love, to tread in the very print of his steps, who is set forth in the gospel as our great exemplar of moral conduct, he is the more willing to imbibe, without investigation, the dogma in question. In the whole circle of this controversy I am not aware that the Baptists have wielded a more successful argument *ad captandum vulgus* (pardon the expression) than this appeal to the example of Christ. But we pause to demand proof of this assumed faith. Where is it written in Scripture that our Saviour was baptized for the purpose of setting his followers an example? There is no such declaration in the Bible. Nor is the doctrine deducible, by any correct rules of criticism, from the sacred text. Where then is the proof required? Candid reader, there is *no* proof.

But that our Saviour was not baptized with a view to furnish his followers an example may be argued, in addition to what has been already adduced, from the following considerations.

(*a*) The example would be essentially defective in one of its most prominent features. Christ was thirty years of age when he was baptized. Does the putting off of baptism until that age comport with the early piety of Jesus? Would it be walking in all the commandments and ordinances of God blameless, for pious youth to defer baptism (after the example of the Saviour) until thirty years of age? Our opponents would rather make the blessed Saviour to furnish an example of *procrastination* than otherwise. Besides, Luke says, "Now when all the people were baptized, it came to pass that Jesus also, being baptized," &c., Luke iii, 21. The other evangelists also relate the *baptism of the people* as taking place previously to that of Christ. Does this appear like an example? A strange example this for the age then present, when ALL THE PEOPLE had been beforehand in the same matter! Why was not our Saviour baptized in youth, to have furnished an example for the young? Why did he wait until thousands had gone before him in the discharge of their duty? Will our Baptist brethren inform us?

(*b*) The example, if such it be, is unreasonably partial, and hence analogy is against it. If Christ submitted to Christian baptism in order to furnish his followers an example, it is both natural and rational to inquire what was his conduct in reference to the other ordinance of Christianity, viz., *The Lord's supper.*

If there was a call for his example in one instance, so also there was in the other. But we know that our Saviour did not partake of the sacramental elements. When he handed to the disciples the sacramental cup, he says,

"*Drink* YE *all of it*," &c., "but I say unto you, I WILL NOT DRINK *henceforth*," &c. Besides, such was the nature of the ordinance itself, as to preclude all participation of the elements on the part of the Saviour.

If, then, our Lord has left us no example of the celebration of the eucharist, there is, at least, a strong presumption against the hypothesis of his having given us one in his personal submission to baptism.

4. We have hitherto taken only a negative view of the question. In changing, therefore, the tenor of our remarks, we inquire—Has the Bible furnished us with any statement of the reason which rendered the baptism of Christ necessary? We answer, Jesus Christ has certainly furnished the true reason for his baptism, in his reply to John's scruples, in the following words,—"for thus it becometh us to fulfil all righteousness." This answer, whatever may be its real import, perfectly satisfied John of the propriety of baptizing the Saviour. For previously to this, "*John earnestly hindered*" (διεκωλυεν) his baptism; but, after the above reply of Christ, it is immediately added,—"then he suffered him." There can be no doubt that all the reason that ever subsisted, rendering the baptism of Christ necessary, is couched in the above words of the Saviour. The only possible difficulty, therefore, which can, in the nature of the case, be realized in settling this tiresome controversy on the import of Christ's baptism must lie in our mode of understanding the particular phrase rendered "*to fulfil all righteousness*." It is an established rule of criticism, that, in the explication of terms, where the literal and ordinary import can be retained without violence to the particular scope of the passage, or to the analogy of faith, it then and there becomes the only true and lawful sense of such particular terms. "The received signification of a word," says Horne, "is to be retained, unless weighty and necessary reasons require that it should be abandoned or neglected."* In the case before us our Lord may be supposed to use a slight metonymy, putting *righteousness* for *ordinance* or *institute;* or he may be supposed to use *righteousness* in the sense, not of *ordinance*, but of the *fulfilment of*

* Introd., part ii, b. i, sec. 2.

law. In either case the result would be the same, and the whole clause may therefore be better understood by reading it,—"*For thus it becometh us to fulfil every ordinance.*" In support of this sense of the clause, we urge—

(*a*) A kindred word is frequently thus rendered; as "Then verily the first covenant had also *δικαιωματα ordinances*," Heb. ix, 1; *vide* also Rom. i, 32; Rev. xv, 4; Luke i, 6, *et al.*

(*b*) This is the obvious import of the same, or a similar mode of expression, throughout the New Testament. Thus, when Paul says, (Rom. viii, 4,) *ἱνα δικαιωμα του νομου πληρωθῇ εν ἡμιν*, he means,—"*that the* PRECEPTIVE CLAIMS *of the law might be answered* or *obeyed in us.*"

Every mind must perceive that this is the same form of expression used by our Lord, when he says,—"*For thus it becometh us πληρωσαι πασαν δικαιοσυνην to obey* or *fulfil every* PRECEPT; i. e., *of the law.* To "*fulfil all righteousness,*" to "*fulfil the righteousness of the law,*" and to "*fulfil the law,*" are phrases in the New Testament, of exactly similar import. For instance, our Saviour says to the Jews,—"Think not that I am come to destroy the law or the prophets: I am not come to destroy, but to *fulfil.*" This form of speech answers exactly to the above reply to John, and we consider them both to refer to the fulfilment of the Mosaic law. Matt. iii, 15, and v, 17. The verb *πληροω pleroö, to fulfil,* is used variously in the New Testament. It stands in connection with different prophecies about twenty-two times, and signifies their *accomplishment.* It is used in connection with righteousness, or *law,* either ceremonial or moral, about ten times, where it always intends its *fulfilment,* or the *right observance* of its precepts. The verb in this connection points us *retrospectively* to an *existing statute.* To talk, therefore, of "*fulfilling* all righteousness" by acts which are uncalled for by any statutory claim, is a mode of speech altogether unknown in the New Testament.

(*c*) An inquiry into the proper *antithesis* of the phrase, "*fulfil all righteousness,*" will tend to elucidate and establish the above construction. If we can ascertain the true antithetical reading of this clause, we shall the more readily arrive at the genuine *thesis* of our Lord's reply.

The phrase in question must necessarily admit of a *counter sense.*

The inquiry therefore is—What is that *reading* which is directly opposed to the phrase, "*fulfil all righteousness?*" In order to supply the antithesis, and give the entire sense of our Lord's reply, paraphrastically, we would read it, "For thus it becometh us to *fulfil every institution* of the law of Moses, so as finally to answer its typical intention, and not, arbitrarily, *to dissolve all obligation to its observance,* before it has thus received its accomplishment in me." This sense is fully corroborated by our Lord's statement, Matt. v, 17. In that passage, our Lord uses καταλυσαι τον νομον, *to abrogate the law,* in direct contrast with πληρωσαι τον νομον, *to fulfil the law.* And so also we consider καταλυσαι τας δικαιοσυνας, (or, δικαιωματα, for they are sometimes interchanged; *vide* Rom. v, 18; Rev. xix, 8,) *to abrogate the ordinances,* to be the true antithetical reading of πληρωσαι πασαν δικαιοσυνην, *to fulfil all righteousness,* or *every ordinance.* And this antithesis our Lord here omitted by ellipsis, but supplied it, as we have seen, in chap. v, 17.

I know not how any person of candor and information can elude the force of this argument. The term "*righteousness,*" in the text in question, cannot be supposed to stand in contrast with *personal unrighteousness.* He who is Lord of the institution of the sabbath, who was "IMMANUEL, *God with us,*" could not have been dependant for his *personal justification,* or rectitude of character, upon the act of submission to baptism! We cannot suppose our Lord sustained any personal obligation to obey the law, without fatally detracting from the merit of his obedience. Had he refused baptism, he would still have been "as holy, and as harmless, and as undefiled," as the immortal divinity within him could have rendered his immaculate nature. Wherein, then, lay his obligation to baptism? We answer,—It grew out of his assumed relations to the law, as our vicar, it being a function of his priestly character to accomplish the intent of the Mosaic ritual. The question, therefore, was, whether an ordinance of the law should then receive its ultimate fulfilment in the person of Christ, and then *pass away,* as an obsolete form of worship that had constitutionally passed the specified term of its duration, or whether it should be immaturely abrogated by the same authority that framed it at the first.

(*d*) The word itself rendered *righteousness* in the English text, is elsewhere used in the sense of *institution*, *ordinance*, *appointment*, *method*, or *rule*. Thus Paul, (Rom i, 17,) " For I am not ashamed of the gospel of Christ, for therein is the δικαιοσυνη *righteousness* of God revealed," &c. By the " righteousness of God" is here meant, the *method* of God for saving sinners. This, says Professor Hodge, is consistent with the meaning of the word in the original. Again, in chap. x, 3, " For they being ignorant of God's *righteousness*, and going about to establish their own *righteousness*, have not submitted themselves unto the *righteousness* of God." We may understand the word rendered *righteousness* in the sense of *justification*; " *justification* of God" being taken as equivalent to " *God's method* of *justification*." They being ignorant of God's *method* of justification, and going about to establish their own *method*, have not submitted themselves to the *method* which he has proposed.* In the same sense the word is probably used John xvi, 8.

But the same result is realized if we take δικαιοσυνη in its usual acceptation, to signify *righteousness* instead of *ordinance*. For righteousness is *that which fulfils the preceptive claims of law*. This is its literal import. We might as reasonably talk of extension without space, or of an accident that has no subject, as to talk of a righteousness that does not imply the existence and fulfilment of law. If, then, " Christ fulfilled all righteousness," he did it by answering the claims of existing laws.

The next step of our inquiry will be to ascertain what law, then in vogue, required the Saviour to be baptized. There were various ordinances of ablution among the Jews, but these, in general, could not be supposed to apply to Christ. We cannot suppose our Lord to have previously contracted any ceremonial defilement which was the reason of his baptism. But observe the particular juncture. Our Lord was about to enter upon his public ministry. He had attained his thirtieth year—the age at

* Professor Hodge's Comment on Romans.

which, by the appointment of God,* the priests under the law were to undertake the duties of their office,—and he was a "high priest." This was the character in which he was to display the infinite love of God to man, and illustrate that justice in whose even scales the sinner had been found wanting. If we examine the whole code of Moses, we shall find no law that required Christ to be baptized, at this particular juncture, but the law enjoining and regulating priestly consecration, recorded in Exod. xxix, and Lev. viii. That our Saviour's baptism was a priestly consecration, is corroborated by all the accompanying circumstances recorded in the evangelical history. And in addition to all we have advanced under this head, we will simply say, Christ did exercise the office of a priest when he purged the temple; and when the chief priests and elders demanded of him, on that occasion, by what authority he did these things, Christ appealed to the baptism of John. Matt. xxi, 12, 23–27. This is worthy of particular notice, as he evidently appealed to John's baptism for a vindication of the authority he had exercised. And had the Jews then acknowledged the baptism of John to have been from heaven, our Saviour would undoubtedly have replied, "John bore witness of me, and foretold you of my authority, and actually consecrated me to the priestly office according to your law." To this the captious Jew could have made no reply; against it he could have uttered no complaint. What was done, among the Jews, by an accredited prophet of Jehovah, was as irreversible as the mandate of a Roman dictator.

We cannot finally close our remarks under this head without again reminding the reader that, though we have taken up the positive side of the question, we were under no obligation so to do. Enough has been said to rescue the baptism of the Saviour from the erroneous construction of our opponents; but what was its real character we are not responsible for showing. If our remarks under this head suit the reader, he has them gratis; if not, we shall not complain—they do not affect our proper field of argument.

* Some of the Levites were entered as probationers at twenty-five years, to do some kinds of service, and in the days of David at twenty years. Num. viii, 24, 25; 1 Chron. xxiii, 24.

CHAPTER III.

CRITICISM ON ΒΑΠΤΩ *BAPTO.*

The theme, or root, of βαπτιζω *baptizo* is βαπτω *bapto* whose etymological syllable, according to Professor Stuart, is the triliteral βαπ *bap*, "whose leading and original signification seems to have been *dipping*, *plunging*," &c.

The former word only is used in the New Testament to describe the rite of Christian baptism; but as some knowledge of the use of βαπτω *bapto* will facilitate a correct appreciation of the meaning of its derivative, and shed a collateral light upon its New Testament use, serving to show, at the same time, upon what untenable ground our opponents have constructed their main argument, we shall bestow upon it a suitable degree of attention.

"I would say thus much," says Mr. P. Edwards, "of the term βαπτω, *bapto*, that it is a term of such latitude of meaning, that he that shall attempt to prove, from its use in various authors, [the exclusive sense of] an absolute and total immersion, will find that he has undertaken that which he cannot finally perform."*

"I do not intend," says Dr. John Dick, "to deny that βαπτω *bapto* ever means *to dip*, but that this is its only sense; and hence we may fairly conclude, that although its derivative βαπτιζω *baptizo* means *to immerse*, it does not follow that this is its only signification."†

This is a plain statement of the case. That the word under consideration, and its derivative, signify *to dip*, *immerse*, &c., we do not deny. This, indeed, need hardly be stated; and this, being allowed on all hands, we shall not undertake to prove. But that these are the only senses which apply to the above terms, as our Baptist brethren affirm, we deny. In prosecuting the present inquiry, therefore, we shall mainly endeavour to establish the following propositions:—1. That exclusive immersion cannot be proved from the import of the Greek word *baptize*; and, 2. It cannot be proved to have been practised in the

* Candid Reasons, &c., p. 136.

† Theology, vol. i, p. 375.

first century by any *circumstances* connected with the history of baptism in the New Testament.

The senses are various in which βαπτω *bapto* occurs in the wide range of classic and Hebrew Greek; we shall only enumerate some cases, supporting our views by citations from Scriptural Greek. The word, as has been observed, primarily signified *to dip*, *immerse*, &c. It afterward, according to a very natural law in the general analogy of language, came to signify *to dye*, or *colour*, because articles were generally dyed by *dipping* them into the colouring liquid. At length it came to signify *to stain*, without any allusion to the manner, and where the circumstances were such as to preclude immersion, or dipping. In the range of its use it is employed, also, to signify to *partially dip*, to *smear*, to *moisten*, or *bedew*. We notice, then, the following senses:—

I. To *smear over*, to *moisten*. Lev. xiv, 16: "And the priest shall *smear* (βαψει *bapsei*, Eng. ver. *dip*, Heb. טָבַל *tabal*) his right finger απο του ελαιου *with the oil* that is in his left hand."

In this passage βαπτω cannot mean to *dip* or *immerse*, for how could the priest immerse his right finger in the oil that was in the hollow of his left hand? The utmost that could be effected was to *moisten* the end of his finger in the oil. The verb here will not, therefore, bear the sense of *immerse*. It simply means to *smear*, or *wet*. This sense, also, suits the other part of the sentence. The preposition απο *apo*, does not compare with the idea of dipping, properly. The priest did not plunge his finger *of* or *with* the oil, but he *wet* it *with the oil*, or *smeared* it *with the oil*.

So also verse 6: "As for the living bird, he shall take it, and the cedar wood, and the scarlet, and the hyssop, and shall *smear*, or *moisten* (βαψει *bapsei*, Heb. טָבַל *tabal*, Eng. *dip*) them and the living bird (εις το αἱμα, בְּדַם *be dam*) *in the blood* of the bird that was killed over the running water."

We have adopted the above translation because we consider it agrees best with all the circumstances of the case. That the Greek *bapto*, and the Hebrew *tabal*, will not, in this passage, bear the sense of *immerse*, seems evident from the following circumstances.

1. It was not necessary to immerse the hyssop and living bird. The purposes of this ceremony did not require it. The object, or intention, was, "to sprinkle upon him that was to be cleansed from the leprosy, seven times." This did not require an immersion of the hyssop and bird, or any thing more than that they be *wet*, or *moistened*, in the blood and water. The same ceremony was performed by putting the end of the right finger in some oil contained in the left hand. Ver. 16.

2. The quantity of the liquid used seems wholly to preclude an immersion. They were required to take some running water in a clean earthen vessel, in quantity about a quarter of a log, "or an egg shell and a half full," according to the rabbins,* and with this clean spring water they were to mingle the blood of the bird killed, and in this mixture they were to *smear* (*immerse?*) the living bird and hyssop. These circumstances seem to dictate the rendering we have given above.

Lev. iv, 17: "And the priest *shall smear*, or *moisten*, (βαψει *bapsei*, Heb. טָבַל *tabal*, Eng. version, *dip*,) his finger απο του αἱματος, מִן־הַדָּם *min ha dam, with the blood.*"

It is only necessary here to observe, 1. That the rendering we have given is a lawful one. The Hebrew preposition *min*, and the Greek *apo*, will bear the sense of *with*, *by*, *by means of*, &c. This rendering also suits the circumstances, and comports with *bapto* better than a rigid adherence to the primitive sense of the verb and prepositions, which would require us to read, "And the priest shall *plunge* his finger *from* the blood," &c.

2. The sense of βαπτω *bapto* is, here, that of *smearing* only, and not that of *dipping*, or *plunging*. The priest might, as a matter of fact, have plunged his finger in the blood; but the meaning and intent of the command did not necessarily require it, and it would have been equally complied with if he had *poured* a little blood on his finger, because this would have *smeared* or *moistened* it in the blood sufficiently for all the legal purposes of the ceremony.

Exod. xii, 22: "And ye shall take a bunch of hyssop, and βαψαντες απο του αἱματος *having smeared*, or *moistened*

* *Vide* Dr. A. Clarke, *in loc.*

[it] *with the blood,*" (Heb. וּטְבַלְתֶּם *vootebhaltam, ye shall* SMEAR, &c. Eng. version, DIP.)

Here it is to be observed, the quantity of blood was, probably, insufficient for an immersion of the hyssop;—a *partial dipping*, a *smearing*, or *moistening*, was all that was required by the circumstances of the case; and here, also, the occurrence of *απο apo* with the genitive after the verb, constitutes a form of speech unadapted to convey the idea of dipping.* The original (to follow out the

* It is proper here to remark, that the original form of the sentence sometimes admits of another turn in the sense. Hence, Professor Ripley has attempted to evade the force of the above passages by availing himself of this other method of translating them. To give the English reader an idea of the posture of the argument, we adduce the following observations.

1. It is contended by Professor Ripley that the Heb. מִן *min*, which is translated in the Greek by *απο apo*, has the sense of OF, and is used, in Lev. xiv, 16, *et al.*, as a *partitive*. This would require the passage to be read thus: "And the priest shall *dip* his right finger [in some] *of* the oil that is in his left hand." This retains for *βαπτω* the sense of *dip*.

2. We have given *βαπτω bapto* the sense of *smear*, and to מִן *min*, and *απο apo*, the sense of *with*: thus, "And the priest shall *smear* his right finger *with* the oil," &c.

In support of our translation we have said that it was a sense in which the above prepositions sometimes did occur. Thus the phrases, "*red* (*dark*) WITH *wine*"—"*white* WITH *milk*"—"BY (*by means of, through, with,* denoting the efficient cause) *the odour of water it sprouts up.*" "WITH *dreams thou dost terrify me*"—"*No more shall all flesh be cut off* BY, or *by means of*, (or *with*, denoting the instrumental cause,) *the waters of the deluge.*" Gen. xlix, 12; ix, 11; Job xiv, 9; vii, 14. *Vide* Gesenius. So also, in Dan. iv, 33, Nebuchadnezzar's body is said to have been wet *απο της δροσου του ουρανου* WITH, or BY MEANS OF, *the dew of heaven.*

The sense of the connection in Lev. xiv, 16, clearly determines that the Hebrew preposition is not there used partitively. It would be absurd to say, "he shall *dip* his finger *in some of* the oil in his left hand," when *all* of it was insufficient for a dipping, that is, if we understand *dip* in the sense of *immerse*. The context generally intimates with sufficient clearness when מִן *min* is to be used as a partitive, and when it is not. For instance, in Lev. iv, 18, it reads: "And the priest shall put *of* the blood upon the horns of the altar." Here the sense is, evidently, that he shall put a *part* of the blood, or *some* of the blood, &c.; and our English translators have very properly added the word *some*—"*some* of the blood," &c. And we know that the sense of the preposition is that of a partitive, denoting that only a *part* of the blood is to translation of our opponents) exhibits a form of speech like the following English: "And ye shall take a bunch of hyssop, and *having plunged* it *from*, or *of* the blood," &c.—a translation wholly without meaning.

I am disposed to conclude that the passage in Matt. xxvi, 23, "He that *dippeth* (εμβαψας) his hand with me in the dish," &c., may be classed also under this head. Certain it is that βαπτω *bapto*, in this passage, does not signify *immerse*, and *smear* makes a good sense.

Here is a plain reference to a mode of eating similar to that which is now practised by the Turks, Arabs, and others in the East; viz., by taking the food out of a common dish, or platter, using the fingers instead of forks or spoons. It is a point of etiquette among the Turks, and others in that country, (Western Asia,) while eating, to present any delicate morsel, *in the fingers*, to the mouth of a distinguished or favourite guest. This is a mark of special consideration. Thus, Dr. Jowett, speaking of their manners, says, "But the practice which was most revolting to me was this: when the master of the house found in the dish any dainty morsel, he took it out with his fingers and applied it to my mouth. This was true Syrian courtesy and hospitality; and had I been sufficiently well-bred, my mouth would have opened to receive it."* This is precisely the conduct of our Lord related John xiii, 26; where, instead of "*sop*," it should read *morsel;* "And when he had dipped the *morsel*, (ψωμιον,) he gave it to Judas Iscariot, the son of Simon."

To dip the hand in the dish, or platter, was not to submerge it up to the wrist in the liquid contained therein, but simply to take food therefrom with the fingers, in true Asiatic style, instead of using a fork, or spoon, after the manner of the Europeans. The idea, therefore, intended by the word βαπτω *bapto*, in Matt. xxvi, 23, is not that of *immerse*, but rather that of *smear*. The hand was said to

be put upon the horns of the altar, because it is immediately added, "he shall pour out ALL [THE REST OF] the blood at the bottom of the altar." But there is no such reason why we should understand the Hebrew *min*, in the above connections, partitively, and there are good reasons against it.

* Christian Researches in Syria, &c. *Vide* Rob. Calmet; Article, Eating.

be baptized when the ends of the fingers only were *smeared* in the liquid contained in the dish. Or, *βαπτω bapto* may be used here to signify merely the downward and reflective motion of the hand in taking the food.

But in John xiii, 26 the sense of *smear* is plainly carried out. The Saviour says, "He it is to whom *βαψας το ψωμιον επιδωσω I shall give the morsel when I have* SMEARED it," i. e., in the oil, or liquid. "And *εμβαψας το ψωμιον when he had* SMEARED it (i. e., in the liquid or sop) he gave it to Judas." This, we apprehend, is the sense of the passage, and exhibits the true force of *βαπτω bapto* in that connection.

II. It means to *stain*, or *colour*, where the circumstances of the case show that the colouring was not performed by dipping, but by *bespattering*, *sprinkling*, &c.

Psa. lxviii, 23: "That thy foot may be *stained βαφῇ* with the blood of thine enemies." English version, "*dipped in* the blood," &c.

Bishop Horne has hit the exact imagery of the text. He says, "Thus Jehovah had promised to repeat in Israel, by David, his glorious acts; to work as signal victories and deliverances for his people as he had formerly done in the field of Bashan, and at the Red Sea; when they saw their enemies *dead at their feet*."* It was in the battle-field that their feet were to be *baptized*, or *stained*, by the blood of their enemies slain. The idea does not come up to the sense of *plunging*. It comports equally well, and indeed much better, with the notion of *pouring*, or sprinkling. The blood of their enemies *gushed out* upon them as they trod them down in the day of battle.

Rev. xix, 13: "And he was clothed with *ἱματιον βεβαμμενον αἱματι a vesture* STAINED *with blood*." Our English version has it "*dipped* in blood;" but the idea, most unquestionably, is not that of a *dipping*, but of a *staining*, and the circumstances show that this staining was performed by *bespattering*, or *sprinkling* the blood upon the garment.

The imagery of the whole passage is twofold. First, that of a conqueror, leading his triumph, followed by his victorious army, having his "garment *stained*" by the blood

* Comment. *in loc.*

of his enemies. This *staining* is called *baptizing* his garment in blood, which, from the nature of the case, could not have been effected by *dipping*, but by *aspersion*, as this alone is the mode in which a general's garment is stained by the blood of his enemies in battle. Secondly, the allusion is made to the vintager, whose garment is supposed to be *stained* by the juice of the grape, while he is engaged in treading the wine-press. The question therefore arises, "How would the garment of the vintager become stained (i. e., *baptized*) by the juice of the grape?" Surely not by *dipping*, unless the person himself who wore it was also *dipped* into the wine-vat! but by the occasional *gushing out* of the juice of the grape upon it. Neither was the garment *wholly stained*, as if it had been dipped. The allusion, in either of the above cases, is at the furthest remove from the idea of a dipping. A general's garment may be stained in various places by the blood of his foes, but it is never *wholly dyed* in their blood; and so of the garment of the vintager. The garment of our Saviour, to which allusion is made in the text, could not be supposed to have been *dipped* nor yet to have been *wholly dyed*, as if it had been dipped into his own blood. But his blood may be supposed to have *gushed out upon it and to have stained it in places.*

To place the whole subject at once before the eye of the reader, we shall subjoin the following synopsis of the passage in question and its parallel reading in Isaiah:

Who is this that cometh from Edom, with *dyed garments* from Bozrah?

Wherefore art thou red in thine apparel, *and thy garments like him that treadeth the wine-press?*

I have trodden the wine-press alone; and of the people there was none with me: for I will tread them in mine anger, and trample them in my fury, *and their blood shall be* SPRINKLED *upon my gar-*

And I saw in heaven, and behold a white horse; and he that sat on him was called Faithful and True, and in righteousness he doth judge and *make war.*

And he was clothed with a vesture *stained* (βεβαμμενον *bebammenon*, Eng. ver. *dipped*) with blood: and his name is called the Word of God.

And out of his mouth goeth a sharp sword, that with it he should smite the na-

ments, and I will STAIN *all my raiment.* Isa. lxiii, 1–3.

tions: and he shall rule them with a rod of iron: *and he treadeth the wine-press of the fierceness of the wrath of Almighty God.* Rev. xix, 11–15.

Here then is an instance wherein a garment is said to have been *baptized*, (or stained,) where, from the nature of the case, the baptism, or staining, could be effected only by *sprinkling*, or *aspersion;* and where a parallel passage directly affirms this to have been the mode.

III. It signifies to *moisten, bedew, wet.*

Dan. iv, 30, (Eng. ver. iv, 33:) "His body *απο της δροσου του ουρανου εβαφη was wet*, or *moistened, with the dew of heaven.*" (Chal. צְבַע *to wet, moisten, imbue.*)

Here the reader will remark: 1. The thing set forth by the expression. The object was not to describe what a vast quantity of dew fell upon the king; but simply to make it clear that the king, in his severe punishment, lodged in the open field, and not in a palace. Hence in ver. 12 (Eng. ver. 15) it simply says, "*Και εν τη δροσω του ουρανου κοιτασθησεται, And he shall go to rest*, or *lodge, in the dew of heaven;*" that is, exposed to falling dew. The grand idea of the passage is conveyed in the following words: "And let his portion be with the beasts, in the grass of the earth." He was to live like a beast, and not like a man. This, then, being the force of the expression, the sense of *βαπτω bapto* does not turn upon the *amount* or *quantity* of dew that fell upon the king, but upon the simple fact that it did fall; the idea of *quantity* being foreign to the thoughts of the speaker.

That the word *bapto*, in this connection, is adequately explained by the verb *moisten*, or, as our English has it, *wet*, I can see no just reason to doubt.

To urge that the dews in that country are copious, and that, therefore, the body of Nebuchadnezzar was *drenched*, does not remove the difficulty. Besides, it is far from being manifest that his body was as thoroughly wet by the dews of heaven as though he had been dipped in the Euphrates. No competent critic would advance this position. But, as this is a difficult passage for our opponents, they have cast about with uncommon diligence to find some mode of explication suited to their restrictive theory. Professor Ripley says, "I consider the word βαπτω *bapto* as hyperbolically used in the book of Daniel."* But wherein lies the necessity of considering the term an hyperbole? The dews in Babylonia were phenomena in their domestic meteorology with which both the prophet and the king were acquainted. All the effect of exposure to falling dew was perfectly understood by both. What then could the prophet have gained by heightening his picture by such an hyperbole as the professor supposes, but to have exposed himself to the ridicule and contempt of the king and court? Under such circumstances it could have added no force to his descriptions, but wolud rather have weakened them by an ostentatious display and pomp of language. Besides, it should be remembered, the word occurs in plain, narrative style, where we are not to look for poetical figures and exaggerated suppositions. The fidelity of the author, in this case, required of him a plain, unequivocal diction.

2. The Chaldee word, as we have already shown, which answers to *bapto* in the Septuagint, is not the word that is used to import an immersion, but means *moisten, wet, tinge, imbue*, &c.†

3. To carry out the translation of our opponents we must read, "And his body was *plunged*, or *immersed, from* the dew of heaven." The verb *bapto* in the Greek takes after it απο *apo* with the genitive, which constitutes a mode of speech, as shown above, wholly irreconcilable to the hypothesis of dipping. It will not be contended that απο is here used Hebraistically in a partitive sense, and that the passage is, therefore, to be rendered, "His body was dipped [in some] of the dew of heaven." No hypothesis will shift the force of this passage from its fatal bearing against the construction of dipping.

But if to become wet by exposure to falling dew be tantamount to a baptism, how are we to appreciate the authority by which we are told that βαπτω *bapto*, and its derivative βαπτιζω *baptizo*, always correspond in sense to the Latin immergo, and to the English immerge, or im-

* Examination of Stuart, p. 37. † *Vide* Gesenius and Parkhurst.

merse? To what credit are the critical opinions of men entitled when they are at war with the facts of an authentic history? Let no one be awed, or deceived by the display of learning which has been arrayed in defence of this pseudo philology. No rules of verbal criticism can alter the stubborn nature of authenticated facts When, therefore, it shall be proved, that to be wet with the dew of heaven is tantamount to an immersion, then also will it be proved that sprinkling *is* immersion.

Leaving the reader to sum up the evidence adduced in this chapter, and to give it a candid and rational bearing upon his own belief, we shall close our remarks under this head, by stating that the Rev. John Groves, the Greek lexicographer, was certainly a man possessed of an honest and independent mind, when, with Parkhurst, and other great names before him, he said,—βαπτω *bapto* signifies, "*to dip, plunge, immerse; to wash; to wet, moisten, sprinkle; to steep, imbue; to dye, stain, colour.*"

CHAPTER IV.

CRITICISM ON ΒΑΠΤΙΖΩ *BAPTIZO.*

In the foregoing chapter we cited instances, wherein βαπτω *bapto* is used to signify something less than *immerse.* We have already observed, that this word is not employed to designate the rite of Christian baptism, although it is well known that, by the laws of etymology, it has a philological bearing, collaterally, in fixing the sense of *baptizo.* As derivative words branch off from their roots, they lose some of their primitive force, and assume new shades of meaning. Hence, whenever we would attain an accurate knowledge of the meaning of derivative words, we trace their pedigree, and, as we follow them back to the parent word, we find their sense more restricted and definite. It becomes lawful, therefore, to presume, antecedently to all direct investigation, that in the case before us, βαπτιζω *baptizo* may lose some of the force and restrictedness of meaning that belongs to its primitive βαπτω *bapto.*

As we have now arrived at an important part of this controversy, and are about to investigate the point upon which the whole must hinge, we beg the reader's patient attention to a few preliminary remarks. Every thing depends upon correct and intelligent views of the subject of this chapter; and I need hardly forewarn the reader, that, if he start with wrong notions, or from wrong premises, he never may hope to arrive at a right conclusion. The exact subject of inquiry should be clearly ascertained, and its just dimensions lucidly defined. Many, from mistaken notions of the proper point of inquiry here, and of the proper field of argumentation, have undertaken to show what is the primary meaning of βαπτιζω, and have gone to the classic Greek for arguments and illustrations in support of their views. From these sources they have argued to the New Testament meaning of the word, and to its use in a religious sense. They might as well have gone to Homer, Aristotle, and Xenophon, to prove the doctrines of St. Paul.

The only question here to be settled, is, "*What is the meaning of βαπτιζω baptizo, in the New Testament, when used in a religious, or ritual sense?*" A right decision of this question must for ever hush the unsettled elements of this wordy and tiresome controversy. The reader must understand, furthermore, that we are not at liberty to travel out of the bounds of Hebraistic Greek in search of arguments. Nay, further, even Josephus and Philo could render us no decisive aid; and we are to confine our researches to the Septuagint and New Testament Greek—particularly the latter. The Bible has certainly given us a clew to the meaning of this word, and Scripture usage must be the criterion of judging of Scripture terms.

The reader should be apprised of the difference between classic Greek, or the writings of those Greek authors who were educated in the philosophy and doctrines of heathenism; and Hebraistic Greek, or those books which were written in Greek by Jews, who had been educated in the doctrines of the Bible; and who, though they spoke in the Greek language, yet they thought as Jews, or Christians. Aristotle would naturally express only the ideas of a heathen in Greek words; but St. John, when called upon to write in that language, would as naturally express, in Greek, the ideas peculiar to a Jew converted to Christianity. Hebraistic Greek is, therefore, nothing else than Hebrew ideas expressed in Greek words. And where converted Hebrews are called to write the history and doctrines of Christ, in the Greek language, it is evident that their words may not, at all times, be used in strict accordance with the *usus loquendi* of either the Septuagint or classic Greek, but may take still another idiom, and one conformed to the peculiar doctrines of the Christian system. Many Greek words have become entirely changed in their meaning, by being thus transferred from a native Greek to a Hebrew, and then to a Christian. The doctrines of Christianity could never have been expressed in Greek, as they have been, without altering the meaning of many words. The reason is obvious. The Greeks never had any conception of many of the doctrines of Christianity, and consequently, had no words in their language primarily adapted to express them. Wherever, therefore, the New Testament differs from the notions of the heathen; wherever Christianity becomes peculiar to itself—*sui generis*—if some circumlocution of the pliant Greek be not employed; we may look for a change in the meaning of words, corresponding to these new opinions, and we must there appeal to the usage of the New Testament, and not to that of the classics.*

I am aware that it has been urged that the sense of βαπτιζω *baptizo* has not been changed by its Hebrew use; but we shall see, in the course of this discussion, whether the objection has been advanced on good and tenable ground.

Another fact, of indispensable moment to a right appreciation of the point now at issue, is, that a word may have different meanings, in different connections; meanings which may not bear a very obvious relation to their primary sense. It is not always easy to trace those operations of the mind which lead on to a change in the use of words; yet we may certainly know that certain words

* See note FF.

are changed from their former meaning. It is not easy to assign a reason for a change in the meaning of the word *prevent*, within the last two centuries; still, we know such to be the fact. To argue from the primitive meaning of a word, to prove its sense in a given connection, is a procedure condemned by all just rules of philology.* It is equally inadmissible to argue that a word bears a particular sense in a certain connection, because it bears the same sense in a different connection. These principles will not be denied by any man, unless his ignorance and party spirit overbear all appreciation of truth and justice. It will not be denied that, although βαπτω *bapto* primarily means to *dip*, still, like the Latin *tingo*, it is sometimes used to signify *tinge*, *dye*, *colour*, &c., and when it is used to signify *tinge*, or *colour*, it drops its primary meaning altogether, and no longer signifies *to dip*. Suppose it should be proved that βαπτιζω *baptizo* means *immerse*, in every place in the Bible, except where it applies to a religious rite—would that prove that the same word bears the same sense also in the latter class of texts? As well might we argue that, because αιωνιον primarily, and almost always in the Bible, means *everlasting*, that therefore it has that meaning in each and every place where it may occur. But we know that it sometimes applies to things that have an end.

It seems, also, not to have been sufficiently considered that when a word is used purely in a religious sense, or to denote a religious rite, that it is likely to assume a meaning different from that which it bears in common use. Who can believe that our Lord meant to attach no higher sense to βαπτιζω, when he said to the disciples, "Teach all nations, baptizing them," &c., than Josephus did, when he spoke of his shipwreck, and of the vessel in which he sailed being *baptized*, or *sinking*, (βαπτισθεντος,) in the Adriatic Sea? It would be easy to enlarge in illustrations upon these remarks, but we apprehend it is not necessary.

Furthermore, we wish to premise, that, whatever the meaning of βαπτιζω may be, when used in a ritual sense in the New Testament, in any one place, it must be

* See note FFF.

uniform in its meaning throughout, in all similar connections. If it describe an external act, or the manner of performing an external rite in one place, then also must it have the same restricted sense in all other places. But if it have a *generic* sense; if it signify the *effect* of some outward mode of using water, as, for instance, *purify* or *cleanse*, then also must it be uniform in this sense, in all similar places. If it mean to *sprinkle*, it cannot mean to *immerse*, and vice versâ. And if it mean either sprinkle or immerse, it cannot mean *purify*, and vice versâ.

"Whichever way we decide, as it regards the import of the word, we ought to be uniform in its use as applied to baptism. For though the same word may have diverse meanings when applied to different things and in various circumstances, yet it certainly cannot, when applied to the same thing and under the same circumstances.

"Hence, if we adopt the generic meaning *purify*, or *cleanse*, we must adhere to it at all times when speaking of the rite. On the other hand, if we adopt a specific meaning, as *immerse*, or *sprinkle*, we must adhere to it in the same way, and not pass from the generic to the specific, and from the specific to the generic, according to exigences, on the ground that the word βαπτιζω may, in the whole circuit of its use, mean sometimes one thing and sometimes another. Nor must we adopt both, for, however numerous the possible meanings of a word may be in its various usages, it has in each particular case but one meaning, and in all similar cases its meaning is the same. Hence, the word βαπτιζω, as applied to a given rite, has not two, or many meanings, but one, and to that one we should in all cases adhere.

"If we adopt a generic meaning, denoting an effect, we are not limited by the command to any specific mode of fulfilling it, and are at liberty to vary the mode according to circumstances. But if we adopt a specific meaning, denoting an external act, we are limited, by the very import of the command, to the range of that meaning.

"Hence, if the command is purify, or cleanse, we are not limited by the command to any one mode, but may choose that which seems to us most appropriate, whether it be sprinkling, pouring, or immersion.

"But if the command is specific, as *immerse*, then we are limited by the range of that word, and cannot fulfil the command by sprinkling or pouring, for these are not modes of immersion, any more than riding is a mode of walking, or writing is a mode of painting.

"It is true that sprinkling and pouring may be modes of purifying; and so is riding a mode of going. But if the command is not *purify*, but *immerse*, then all debate as to the mode is at an end, for you can immerse, not by sprinkling, but only by immersion."*

I know not that the case can be stated with greater perspicuity. It is plain that if I command that an article be *cleansed*, I do not command that it be sprinkled, or dipped,—I enjoin nothing with respect to the *mode* of cleansing; I only enjoin that a certain *effect* be produced by the application of water, leaving the manner of applying the water wholly at the disposal of other circumstances, or at the option of the person to whom the command is addressed. My command would be fulfilled when the effect was produced, whether the manner of producing it were by sprinkling or pouring water upon the article, or by dipping the article into water. But if I should command that the article be dipped in water, the command would be specific, and could not be fulfilled by sprinkling or pouring water upon it, because sprinkling is not a mode of dipping. It is so with the word baptize. Where our Saviour commands the apostles to "baptize all nations," if the word "baptize," in that connection, means *immerse*, then plainly the command can never be fulfilled by sprinkling; but if it mean to cleanse or *purify*, or *consecrate*, then the command is generic, and only enjoins, not the manner of performing an external act, but the production of a certain effect, without any allusion whatever to the manner of producing it. It must be remembered, also, that if the original command to baptize be generic, merely enjoining purification by water, without respect to the mode, the word must retain the same sense in all those places where it occurs in the New Testament in a ritual sense.

If the reader has attended to the foregoing remarks, he

* President Beecher's crit. on Βαπτιζω, Bib. Repository, 1840-1.

may be now ready for the direct investigation of the point at issue. We are, then, to show, not what is the primary meaning of βαπτιζω, not what are its meanings in the wide range of classic and Hebrew Greek, not what is its general use in Scripture, but, *what is its meaning when used in a ritual sense in the New Testament;* and we take the ground that it means, in all such connections, to *purify*, or *cleanse*, and is exactly synonymous with καθαριζω *katharizo*, which is a word in the Jewish ritual signifying to *purify* or *cleanse*, without any allusion whatever to the *mode* of cleansing.

I. Nothing less than this would have been sufficiently definite and significant. All will agree that a word which is used as the descriptive title of a rite should signify the most considerable trait, or circumstance, of that rite. It was so in the word passover; it was so in the title sabbath—that institution denoting, primarily, rest. The title should give some clew or index to the nature, or history, or design, of the rite or institution. Indeed, this is no more than saying that things ought to be called by their proper names. Suppose, now, the Saviour had said to the apostles, "Disciple all nations, washing them," &c.; thus using λουω in the sense of *wash* instead of βαπτιζω *baptizo;* every one must perceive that this would have been a vague manner of expressing the utility or design of this external rite. For although *wash* may be used to signify *purify*, yet it does not necessarily take that meaning; but, on the contrary, if the liquid used in washing be impure, the sense of the word wash would be that of *pollute*, or *soil.* Thus we speak of the wash of the street—of a kitchen—"red wash," "yellow wash," &c.

Besides, the word wash sometimes drops the idea of purify, and merely denotes "a copious, superficial application of water. So we speak of the sea as washing the shores or rocks." In this instance the idea of cleansing is wholly set aside, and we have simply the idea of the copious application of water, without denoting any design, or any effect whatever. The mere idea of wash, therefore, is too vague to attach to the cognomen of the Christian rite of baptism.

But suppose we understand βαπτιζω in the sense of *immerse*, and take the ground that the Saviour used it thus, and that, therefore, the command to baptize is a command to immerse. This is the point insisted on by our opponents. But is this satisfactory? Is it definite? Is it at all intelligible? Our opponents must be philologists enough to know that whatever βαπτιζω *baptizo* may mean, in the Saviour's command, its meaning must be simple, not complex. It cannot mean *to dip, in order to cleanse*, any more than ἱππευω *hippeuo* means *to ride, in order to health. Hippeuo* means *to ride*, without any allusion to the object or design of riding, which may be health, or business, or pleasure. Just so *baptizo*, if, in Matt. xxviii, 19, it signify immerse, this is all its meaning in that place, and in all other places in the New Testament where it denotes the performance of a Christian rite; and the design of immersing could be gathered only from circumstances, not from the word. Things are dipped, sometimes, to cleanse them, if it be in pure water; otherwise, if dipped in impure water, it may be to tinge, or to befoul them. So Job ix, 30, 31: "Though I wash myself in snow water—yet shalt thou *plunge* (i. e., *defile*, εβαψας *baptize*) me in the ditch, and mine own clothes shall abhor me." A person may be plunged into water for his health, for physical cleansing, for merriment, or with a malicious intent to drown him.

Now suppose the Saviour had commanded the disciples simply to immerse, that is, to put the converts under water. Would the command have had any meaning whatever? As immersion is performed for various purposes, it might with great propriety be asked, For what purpose should they immerse the converts? The word immerse would never give a clew to the solution of this question. Philology could never settle it. History might determine it. But the word baptize, as the cognomen of a rite, would be wholly uninstructive and meaningless. If it have the sense of immerse, it cannot have the sense of purify, for immerse and purify are not synonymous, nor are they correlative, or necessarily connected at all. And on the other hand, if it mean purify, it is gratuitous and absurd to say it means immerse, or that it necessarily implies immersion.

But suppose we understand βαπτιζω in the sense of *purify*, and that our Saviour said to the disciples, "Go disciple all nations, *purifying* them," &c. This would make the sense complete, and βαπτιζω would then denote the grand *intention* of the ceremonial use of water. And now, does not every one know that it is according to the analogy of all language that words which were primarily used to denote an external act, afterward, by a very natural transition of the thought, have been used to signify the *object* or *intention* of that act? Thus βαπτω *bapto* primarily meant *to dip*, but, as people frequently dipped articles in order to colour them, it afterward came to signify *to dye*—that is, it came to signify, not *to dip*, but the *object* or *end* of dipping; and finally, it was used to signify *to dye*, when the facts of the case proved it was by sprinkling. So also βαπτιζω *baptizo* may primarily mean to *immerse;* but, as people often immersed for the purpose of *purifying*, so the word might, according to the laws of analogy, be used to mean *purify*, and thus drop all reference to the mode of purifying. This is, indeed, so plain a case that we cannot think it will be misunderstood by any, or doubted by any who understand it.

The sense of *purify*, therefore, without any allusion to the mode of purifying, is the meaning we are to attach to βαπτιζω in the New Testament, when used in a ritual sense. There is no philological objection against such a construction; it is in perfect keeping with the general use of words, and consistency and the nature of the case seem to require it.

II. The Jews expected the Messiah would baptize when he came, but they did not expect him to immerse. There is no way of accounting for this expectation of the Jews, but by understanding βαπτιζω *baptizo* in the sense of καθαριζω *to purify*. It was a subject of ancient prediction that Messiah should purify; John Baptist reiterated this prediction, and revived the expectation and faith of the Jews on the subject, but he uses the word βαπτιζω *baptizo*, instead of καθαριζω *katharizo*. That such an expectation existed among the Jews is proved from John i, 25: "Why baptizest thou then, if thou art not that Christ?" That the Messiah should immerse is nowhere foretold; but that he should *purify* is often and fully predicted. But especially is this foretold in that last and prominent prophecy of Malachi, (iii, 1–3,) which was designed to fill the eye of the mind of the nation until he came.

"He is here presented to the mind in all his majesty and power; but, amid all other ideas, that of purifying is most prominent. He was, above all things, to purify and purge, and that with power so great, that few could endure the fiery day. 'Who may abide the day of his coming, and who shall stand when he appeareth? for he shall be as a refiner's fire!'

"Suppose the word *βαπτιζω* to mean as I affirm—the whole nation are expecting the predicted purifier; all at once the news goes forth that a great purifier has appeared, and that all men flock to him and are purified in the Jordan. How natural the inference! the great purifier, so long foretold, has at length appeared; and how natural the embassy of the priests and Levites to inquire, Who art thou? And when he denied that he was the Messiah, or either of his expected attendants, how natural the inquiry, 'Why purifiest (baptizest) thou then? It is his work—of him it is foretold; why dost thou intrude into his place, and do his work?'

"In view of these facts I do not hesitate to believe most fully, that the idea which came up before the mind of the Jews when the words Ιωαννης Βαπτιστης [*John the Baptist*] were used, was not John the immerser, or John the dipper, but John the purifier—a name peculiarly appropriate to him as a reformer, as puritan was to our ancestors, and for the same reason.

"This view has to my own mind the self-evidencing power of truth, for there is not the slightest presumption against it; all probable evidence is in its favour; and it explains and harmonizes the facts of the case as no other view does."*

The bearing of this argument cannot but be felt by every attentive, candid mind that contemplates it; and we request the reader to take his Bible and examine the passages referred to, and kindred ones, and then ask himself if Malachi, and other prophets, with John the Baptist, did not conspire to raise an expectation among the Jews that Jesus would purify, and if this expectation was ever expressed by them, save in the question about baptism.

III. "The contrast made by John between his own

* President Beecher on *βαπτιζω*.

baptism and that of Christ illustrates and confirms the same view. This contrast exists in three particulars,—the subject, the agent, and the means.

"In the case of John, the subject was the body; in the case of Christ, the mind. In the case of John, the agent was material, that is, a man; in the case of Christ, the agent was the Holy Spirit. In the case of John, the means was water; in the case of Christ, they were truth, and the emotions of God.

"Now, the idea to purify is perfectly adapted to illustrate and carry out such a contrast, but to immerse is not. The sense to purify can be with ease applied to the body or the mind, to human agents or to the Holy Spirit, to water or to truth and divine influences.

"How simple and how natural the statement! 'I indeed purify you with water, but he shall purify you with the Holy Spirit. I perform an external and symbolical rite, by which the body is cleansed with water, but he shall perform a higher cleansing, or that in which the mind itself is purified by the Spirit of God.' And how harsh, how forced, how unnatural to say, I immerse you in the Holy Spirit, and in fire! Such a use of language, to denote such a thing, is entirely foreign to all the laws of the human mind. Indeed, so much is the force of this felt, that in this part of the antithesis, many resort to a new modification of the idea, and maintain that it means, to imbue largely; to overwhelm with divine influences. But this destroys the whole symmetry of the antithesis. John does not mean to say, I immerse you largely with water, but either, I immerse you in water, or I *cleanse* you *with* it; and whichever sense we adopt in one part of the antithesis, we ought to retain [the corresponding one] in the other."* If, then, John intended to say, "I purify you with water," we must retain the corresponding sense in the other part of the antithesis, and say, "but he shall purify you with the Holy Spirit:" but if we suppose John to say merely, "I immerse you in water," we must also say, to carry out the sense in the corresponding part of the contrast, "but he shall immerse you in the Holy Spirit and in fire."

* President Beecher on βαπτιζω.

Now we appeal directly to the reader's understanding, and ask which of these two senses (for one of them we *must* adopt) is the most natural and obvious; the most suited to all the circumstances of the case, and most in accordance with the easy, and natural, and correct interpretation of language? Is there not a violent improbability against the construction, "He shall immerse you in the Holy Ghost and in fire?" Is there a principle of philology, of exegesis, or of divinity, that requires such a construction? On the contrary, does not the construction, "He shall purify you with the Holy Spirit and with fire," better suit the symmetry of the antithesis, better accord with the prophetic descriptions, and better harmonize with the obvious, and easy, and correct use of words? If so, we are bound to attach to βαπτιζω the sense of *purify*, in the connections above cited, and in kindred places. This view is still further confirmed by comparing the language of John with the passage from Malachi already quoted. It seems to be at all times his great desire to lead them to apply those words to Christ, and not to himself. As if he had said, "Do not think that I am that great purifier spoken of in those words.—After me cometh one mightier than I, the latchet of whose shoes I am unworthy to loose. He shall purify you with the Holy Spirit and with fire; whose fan is in his hand, and he will thoroughly purge (διακαθαριει, *purge through*) his floor," &c. But all the force, correspondence, and natural illumination of those passages depends on giving the word βαπτιζω the sense of purify. It should be remembered that the Holy Spirit is the efficient agent of spiritual baptism. The apostle says, "For by one Spirit we are all baptized into one body, and have been all made to drink into one Spirit," 1 Cor. xii, 13. It is by the Spirit's influences that we are baptized. Now, to say that the Spirit immerses us into himself, is as monstrous a figure in rhetoric as it is absurd and gross in theology. But to say that the Spirit purifies us by his influences through the truth, is at once beautiful and proper. We are again brought back, therefore, to the conclusion, that βαπτιζω, used in a religious sense, signifies to *purify*, without respect to the mode of purification.

IV. An appeal to the *usus loquendi* of βαπτιζω *baptizo* in Scripture, where it occurs in a religious sense, will show that it bears the sense of *purify*, *cleanse*, &c., in such connnections.

Our object is not to examine all the passages of Scripture wherein the word occurs, but only, or at least chiefly, those wherein it is used in a religious sense. It is the religious use and meaning of *baptizo* that we wish to ascertain. We have already brought forward some passages, and offered some remarks that might fitly apply under this head to some extent. But they were judged, on the whole, to belong to another class of argument. Without repeating what has been said, we shall turn our attention to the general religious use of *baptizo*, with a view to elaborate, in the course of our remarks, the philological argument.

Although the controversy must be finally decided by an appeal to the canonical Scriptures, especially the New Testament, still, as shedding a few rays of collateral light upon the meaning of βαπτιζω *baptizo*, we shall first adduce two passages from the apocryphal writings. I need hardly say to the reader that the Greek of the Apocrypha is the same, considered in a literary point of view, as that of the Septuagint version.

SECTION I.

The first passage is that of Judith xii, 7: "And Judith *washed herself* (εβαπτιζετω *ebaptizeto*) at a fountain by the camp." We do not suppose this was a ceremonial, or religious washing, or baptism; yet we think it is entitled to a consideration in this place. It is evident that the sense of the Greek verb baptize, in this passage, is that of *cleanse*, *purify;* although the cleansing or washing was a common, and not a ceremonial one. The idea of *immerse* does not meet the force and meaning of the verb. Judith was in the camp of Holofernes, with whom she was striving to form such acquaintance as might further her deep-laid scheme. It was all-important, according to the fastidious notions of the orientals respecting female delicacy, that she should bestow uncommon attention to the purity of her person, in order to render her daily appearance before the haughty Assyrian desirable and engaging. This, in that hot climate, and in the dust and filth of a camp, became no easy task. Frequent *washing* was therefore indispensable. Simple immersion, or bathing, could not have sufficed: she must *cleanse* or *purify* her person. That she bathed or *immersed* herself in the process of cleansing, might, as a matter of fact, have been. But this is not the obvious meaning of the Greek verb *baptize*. It does not suit the exigence of the case: it does not answer the manifest purpose for which she went to the fountain; she might have immersed herself and still returned without the necessary cleansing. We say, therefore, that βαπτιζω, in this connection, has the sense of *cleanse, purify;* and not that of *immerse;* and the English translators have therefore very properly rendered it "*washed herself.*"

Besides, the structure of the whole sentence in the original is peculiarly unadapted to convey the idea of immersing. It stands thus: εβαπτιζετω εν τη παρεμβολη επι της πηγης του 'υδατος, [Judith] *baptized herself within the camp* AT *the fountain of water.* It does not say she baptized εις την πηγην IN, or INTO *the fountain;* but επι της πηγηνς AT, or BY *the fountain.* The English here is as exact a transcript of the aspect of the Greek as can be given. Now, no man will be willing to adopt the translation, "she *plunged*, or *immersed* herself AT the fountain." She might have *washed* or *purified* herself AT the fountain, but if she immersed at all, she immersed herself *into*, or *in* the fountain. This the Greek text does not affirm; but it does affirm just the contrary. Prof. Ripley, feeling the force of this, attempts to evade it by the usual resort—the invention of *baths.* "There surely may have been conveniences for bathing the whole person 'AT the fountain,' in the immediate vicinity of it, and conveniences which were supplied with water from the fountain.....Is it unlikely that a Jewish city [as Bethulia] thus furnished with natural supplies of water, would also be furnished at the fountain or fountains with artificial accommodations for bathing?"* Now, what has all this to do with the philological argument? Verily, nothing. But, furthermore, the text says that she baptized herself εν *in*, or *within* the camp. This would not be a suitable place to bathe, attended as

* Examination of Stuart, pp. 27, 28.

she was by only a female servant. Still, to this circumstance we attach no great weight. All things considered, whether Judith baptized herself for a religious purpose, (as seems to be intimated, chap. xi, 7; xii, 9,) or for a physical cleansing, the word βαπτιζω *baptizo* evidently takes the sense of *purify*, *cleanse*, &c., or, as our English has it, *wash*.

SECTION II.

The second citation from the Apocrypha is from Eccl. xxxiv, 30, (Eng. version xxxiv, 25,) "He that *cleanseth himself* (βαπτιζομενος *baptizomenos*, Eng. ver. *washeth himself*) *from* a dead body, and toucheth it again, what availeth his *washing?*" (λουτρο *loutro*, *washing.*)

In rendering the above, "He that cleanseth *from* a dead body," &c., we have exactly followed the original. Our English is a kind of periphrasis, introduced, it would seem, to make a smoother sentence.

The reader should here be informed that an allusion is made in this verse to the statutes of Moses relating to the purification of those persons who had touched a dead body. These statutes are recorded in Lev. xi, 25, 28, 31, 39, 40; Num. xix, 11–19. In order, therefore, to determine the sense of βαπτιζω in this passage from Ecclesiasticus, we must compare it with the words used in the Mosaic prescriptions. We consider the reference made especially to the cleansing from a human corpse, and shall, therefore, only refer to the foregoing passage in Numbers. It is there recorded: "He that toucheth the dead body of any man shall be unclean (ακαθαρτος *akathartos*) seven days. He shall *purify himself* (ἁγνισθησεται *hagnisthesetai*) on the third day, and on the seventh day, and he shall be *clean* (καθαρος *katharos.*) ... And for an unclean person they shall take of the ashes of the burnt heifer of purification for sin, and running water shall be put thereto in a vessel; and a clean person shall take hyssop and dip it in the water and SPRINKLE it upon him that touched a bone, or one slain, or one dead, or a grave: and the clean person shall SPRINKLE upon the unclean on the third day, and on the seventh day; and on the seventh day he shall purify himself, [that is, he shall finish purifying himself,] and shall WASH (πλυνει *plunei*, *wash*) his clothes, and shall WASH

HIMSELF (λουσεται *lousetai, wash,* Heb. רָחַץ *rahats, wash*) in water, and shall be clean at even."

In this somewhat lengthy quotation the reader is required to notice:—1. The unclean person is required to purify himself. The words used in the Seventy, to set forth this command, are αγνιζω *agnizo, to purify, separate, sanctify,* &c., and καθαριζω *katharizo, purify, cleanse,* &c. This command is not a command to immerse, to bathe, to sprinkle, or wash; but a command to purify. 2. Specific directions are given as to the external manner of applying the water to the body of the unclean person. The requisite purification was to be attained by sprinkling, and by washing with water. 3. In all this process immersion is not once enjoined. The Greek *louo,* and the Hebrew *rahats,* answer to the English word *wash,* and do not imply bathing, or immersing, any more than they do pouring or sprinkling. They denote a general use of water, but do not specify the mode of using it. The English translation *bathe,* therefore, in verse 19, is not strictly correct, because bathing denotes a specific mode of cleansing, whereas *rahats* and *louo* are not specific. Hence the Greek word περιλουω *perilouo* signifies, not to *bathe all around,* but, to *wash all around,* as if by casting water upon the body. Our English, therefore, should read *wash.*

Now, the argument is obvious. 1. The mode of cleansing an unclean person from the pollution of a dead body being complex; that is, including different methods of using water, such as sprinkling and washing, βαπτιζω *baptizo,* in Eccl. xxxiv, 30, cannot refer to this outward mode, because *baptizo* is not a complex term—it does not signify, in the same place, both to *sprinkle* and *wash.*

2. If it should be still urged that *baptizo,* in this connection, refers to the outward mode of using the water of purification, then we ask, to which of the words, in the original command of Num. xix, 11–19, does it answer in signification? Does it answer to περιρραινω *perirhraino, to sprinkle around upon,* or to λουω *louo,* answering to the Hebrew רָחַץ *rahats, wash?* These are all the words that are used in the original command to describe the outward act, or mode of using water. Indeed *louo* is not specific. It denotes a general use of water upon the body, in dis-

tinction from νιπτω *nipto, to wash* hands, and πλυνω *pluno, to wash* clothes, but it does not specify the *mode* of using the water. We ask, then, to which of these original words does βαπτιζω *baptizo* refer? Which of the two positions will our opponents adopt? Are they not fairly grounded? And will not their theory *overwhelm* them in difficulties if they do not speedily abandon it?

3. But the sense of *purify*, or *cleanse*, may be attached to *baptizo* in Eccl. xxxiv, 30, and the sense is complete. It would then answer to καθαριζω *katharizo*, or αγνιζω *agnizo*, in the passage in Numbers, both of which signify *to purify, cleanse*, &c.*

* I do not wish to exhaust this passage by multiplying remarks upon it, but the posture of the controversy seems to require that some notice be taken, from time to time, of what has been advanced by our opponents. It is contended, by Rev. Willard Judd, in his review of Stuart on Baptism, (p. 35,) that the passage from Ecclesiasticus should read, "He that is *immersed* from a dead body," &c. In support of this he argues, that where the law requires the Jews to *wash*, (Heb. *rahats*, Greek *louo*,) they understood it to mean *immerse*. To sanction this construction he cites the Talmuds and Maimonides; and he might as well have appealed to Zoroaster and the Zendavesta. Why did he not appeal to the Old Testament use of *rahats* and *louo?* This would have settled the question at once. The question is not, "How did the Talmudical writers understand רָחַץ *rahats?*" but, "How did the Holy Spirit employ the word in the Old Testament scriptures?" We do not inquire whether the Jews did, as a matter of fact, *bathe* themselves, but whether the original word, *rahats*, *required* them to immerse.

Mr. Judd also appeals to 2 Kings v, 10, 14, where Elisha commands Naaman to *wash* (λουσαι) in the Jordan, and the latter complied by *dipping himself* (εβαπτισατο.) But here the argument holds just as strong in favour of giving βαπτιζω the force merely of λουω, as vice versâ.

The nearest approach that Mr. Judd makes to an argument in support of his version, is when he says, the phrase "'*immersed from the dead*' may be compared with '*washed from sins*,' Rev. i, 5; and '*sprinkled from an evil conscience*,' Heb. x, 22. Cleansing is, (continues he,) in each case, implied as a consequence, but not expressed in either." The error of the author results from his rigid adherence to the physical sense of *baptizo*, supposing it to have undergone no change of meaning in its ritual use. But is his position sustained by his appeal to what he supposes to be parallel phrases? We cannot think it will be so regarded. The sentence "*washed* from sins" does not mean "*bathed* from sins," nor "*dipped* from sins," nor "*sprinkled* from sins," but it means "*purified* from sins;" λουω *louo* here, dropping its literal and taking its metaphorical sense, signifies, not the external act or mode of washing, but the *effect* of washing, viz., *purity*. So, also, the

SECTION III.

But we come now to inquire into the New Testament meaning of *βαπτιζω baptizo*, when used in a religious sense.

Mark vii, 4: "And when they come from the market, they eat not except they *purify themselves*, *βαπτιζωνται baptizontai*," Eng. ver. "*wash*."

Luke xi, 38: "And when the Pharisee saw it, he marvelled that he had not first *been purified* (*εβαπτισθη ebaptisthe*, Eng. ver. '*washed*') before dinner."

These passages, having a common allusion to the same subject, or ceremony, we have placed together. The reasons we assign for the translation we have given are the following:

1. It gives a good sense; it meets all the circumstances of the case; it gives an easy, natural, expressive turn to the passages; it is not unphilological, but perfectly in accordance with the general usage of language, to suppose such a change in the use of *baptizo*, and there is no other word that so well meets all the circumstances of the case. The sense of *purify*, therefore, should be the received sense of *baptizo* in these connections.

2. In the passage from Luke it seems pretty evident that *purify* is the sense of *baptizo*, from the ready recurrence of the Saviour's mind to that subject.

"The Pharisee marvelled that he had not *εβαπτισθη baptized* before dinner; and the Lord said unto him, Now do ye Pharisees *καθαριζετε purify* the outside . . . but rather give alms, and behold, all things are *καθαρα pure* unto you." Now the subject of the Pharisee's wonder was in relation to the Saviour's not *baptizing* before dinner; and the Saviour, in shaping his reply to meet the point of the Pharisee's objection, and to obviate his perplexity, addressed him on the practice of *purifying* the outward person, and of being over-exact in mere legal (or rather

phrase "*sprinkled* from an evil conscience" means "*purified* from an evil conscience;" *ραντιζω rantizo* being there used to signify, not the external act of *sprinkling*, but its *effect*, viz., *purity*. And so the sentence "*baptized* from a dead body" does not mean "*immersed* from a dead body," or "*plunged* from a dead body!" but simply, "*purified* from a dead body."

superstitious) distinctions between *clean* and *unclean* things. As if he had said, "Do you wonder that I have not *baptized* (*purified*) myself before dinner? I say unto you Pharisees, that ye do indeed labour to *purify* the outer man, and ye abound in nice distinctions of *clean* and *unclean* things; but rather consecrate your substance to God by distributing to the needy, and behold, all things are pure unto you." We ask, then, does not the obvious, natural force of this whole passage go to show that βαπτιζω is here used in the sense of καθαριζω *katharizo*, *purify?* We are not to strain the words and circumstances, so as to make them fit to a particular dogma. We are not to try if, by some stretch of the imagination, *baptizo* may not be made to mean *immerse*. We are to take the natural, easy, obvious sense, and that alone will be the true sense. And in this view, we think, all must feel that our position is the right one. Indeed, we must suppose that, either the Pharisee used *baptizo* in the sense of *purify*, or that our Saviour did not speak at all to the point. The latter none will admit; the former, we believe, all must concede.

3. The sense of *purify* better suits the advance in the thought which is perceptible in reading the third and fourth verses of Mark vii. There is an advance in the sense from *species* to *genera*, from a given case to a common custom, from νιπτω *nipto*, *to wash* hands, to βαπτιζω *baptizo*, *to purify*, whether the purification be that of persons or things, and whether it be effected by *sprinkling* or *immersion*. The passage stands thus: "For the Pharisees and all the Jews, except they νιψωνται τασιχειρας *wash their hands*, eat not; . . . and returning from the market, except they βαπτισωνται *baptisontai*, *purify themselves*, they eat not." In the first case they are said to have washed their hands; in the second case they are said to have had a custom of purifying their persons as the nature of the case required, whether in whole or in part.

That βαπτιζω *baptizo* does not bear the sense of *immerse* in Mark vii, 4, and Luke xi, 38, is evident from the following considerations.

1. The *character* and *frequency* of these purifications render it improbable that they were effected by immersing the whole body in water. (*a*) Their character being religious, or ceremonial, and sprinkling being efficacious in

all ordinary cases for the purification of the unclean person, it is highly probable that sprinkling, or aspersion, was the common method employed. This, of course, is only presumptive evidence. (*b*) The frequency of these purifications would render their accomplishment by immersion inconvenient, to an extent that throws the reasonable probability against that hypothesis. It must be remembered hat these baptisms were performed always before eating, and after returning from market. This the reader will perceive by comparing the passages above, from Mark and Luke. The Jews ate three times a day. How often they returned from market we know not. The market, among the Greeks and Romans, and also among the Jews, after they had copied the manners of those nations to some extent, was a place of resort for those who wished to trade—for philosophers to teach wisdom—for magistrates to administer justice—for poets, dramatists, and actors to amuse the people—and for the unemployed to seek for that society and conversation suited to their tastes. Hence we find Paul disputing with philosophers in the market, and Paul and Silas accused before the magistrate in the market-place. Acts xvii, 17, and xvi, 19. Hence the Pharisees "loved salutations in the market-places," Mark xii, 38. Their visits to the market would not be casual, but frequent and necessary. Many were called thither by the nature of their avocations, many from motives of pleasure, and many others from sectarian pride. But did they always immerse on returning from market? We know that the *argumentum ab inconvenienti* in this case will not pass very current with our opponents; but still we say, it throws the reasonable probability against the theory of immersion.

2. Besides, it being clear that they baptized themselves for a religious, and not for a common purpose, it becomes still more improbable that they immersed on these occasions, from the fact that their *clothes* would need to be submerged in water equally with their bodies. According to Jewish laws, and notions of legal defilement, whatever operated to defile the person tended equally to defile all the clothes which he had on at the time; and the clothes, under such circumstances, needed to be purified equally with the man himself. If the Pharisees, then, on account

of their high notions of legal sanctity, immersed their bodies in water on returning from market, and before eating, they must also have submerged their clothes in water, or the touch of their own garments would have rendered them still unclean. But who can believe that they were in any such habit of drenching their clothes three or more times a day?

3. A corroborating circumstance is found in John ii, 6. We there read, "There were set six water-pots of stone, after the manner of the purifying of the Jews, containing two or three firkins apiece." The word μετρητας, rendered "firkin," denotes a measure with which we are not well acquainted. According to Bishop Cumberland, as quoted by Dr. A. Clarke, it contains about *seven pints and one eighth of a pint*. Others suppose the capacity of the vessel here referred to, to be much larger, sufficient to hold *ten gallons*. In 2 Chron. iv, 5, it answers to the Hebrew בַּת *bath*, of about seven and a half gallons. The following may throw some light upon the subject of the capacity of these stone pots. "While Mr. W. Rae Wilson (who visited Palestine in 1819) was at Cana, 'six women having their faces veiled came down to the well, each carrying on her head a pot for the purpose of being filled with water. The vessels were formed of stone, and something in the shape of the bottles used in our country for containing vitriol, having great bodies and small necks, with this exception, that they were not so large. Many had handles attached to the sides; and it was a wonderful coincidence with Scripture, that the vessels appeared to contain much the same quantity as those which the evangelist informs us had been employed on occasion of the nuptial celebration,' viz., '*three firkins*,' that is, about twelve gallons each."* Such, then, being the capacity of the vessels which were appropriated to the common purifications of the Jews, the idea of their frequent immersions becomes manifestly improbable, if not absurd and impossible.

4. It appears quite probable that the washing of hands was alluded to as the principal omission on the part of our Saviour and his disciples. This, indeed, we know was

* Wilson's Travels in Egypt and the Holy Land, p. 339, first edition, quoted by Horne, Introd., part iii, chap. v, sec. 3.

the ground of the repeated complaints of the Pharisees, as the reader will perceive by referring to Matt. xv, 2 ; Mark vii, 2. It was the omission of that kind of washing, or purification, which was peculiarly appropriate before eating. So also in Luke xi, 38 : "And when the Pharisee saw it, he marvelled that Christ had not *first washed before dinner*." Also, "When they come from market, they *eat not*, except they *wash*," Mark vii, 4. The foolish superstitions of the Jews taught them that to eat with unwashed hands was a great sin ; and that the food of such persons was subject to an evil spirit they called *shibta*. (*Vide* Dr. A. Clarke on Matt. xv, 2.) This washing of hands, also, was a religious ceremony. Hence our Lord says, in reply to these superstitious notions, "Not that which goeth into a man defileth a man," &c. Hence he says also, to the Pharisee, The true way to make "all things *pure*" is, not merely to purify your hands before eating, but to "give alms of such things as ye have," thus rendering your substance to God.

These considerations strongly force themselves upon our minds as convincing evidence that the Pharisee, in Luke xi, 38, was offended because the Saviour omitted the ceremony of washing his hands before dinner. "It is no more likely that a want of *immersion* offended the Pharisee, in the case of Christ, than it is that this was the ground of offence in the case of the disciples, Mark vii. It does not appear that Christ had been to the market. Nor is it likely at all that an immersion was expected, as a matter of course, before every meal, even on coming from a crowd. The offence in the case of the disciples was, that they had not washed their hands. An immersion was not expected of them, though they had been in crowds. Why should it be of Christ?

"Kuinoel, on this passage, well remarks, that the existence of any such custom of regular immersion, before all meals, cannot be proved. And the opinions and statements of Jewish writers in after ages are of very little weight."*

Other considerations might be urged, to show that the washing of hands was the principal thing alluded to in

* President Beecher on βαπτιζω.

Luke xi, 38, and Mark vii, 4; but the reasonable probability already appears in favour of that position, and this is sufficient to justify an argument from the mode of washing hands.* It becomes, then, a proper subject of inquiry, "What was the mode of washing hands among the Jews?"†

Customs never change in the East. What was practised in the days of David was still in vogue in the days of Christ, and has been handed down, with little alteration, to the present time. That the Jews washed their hands by pouring water upon them is evident from 2 Kings iii, 11, "Here is Elisha Ben-shaphat, who poured water on the hands of Elijah." The same practice prevails, to this day, in the East. So Pitts, speaking of the Mohammedans, says, "The table being removed, before they rise from the ground on which they sit, a slave, or servant, who stands attending on them with a cup of water to give them drink, steps into the middle with a basin or copper pot of water, something like a coffee-pot, and a little soap, *and lets the water run upon their hands*, one after another, in order as they sit. Such service, it appears, Elisha performed for Elijah." On the same subject D'Ohsson says, "The Mussulman is generally seated on the edge of a sofa, with a pewter or copper vessel, lined with tin, placed before him upon a round piece of red cloth, to prevent the carpet or mat from being wet: a servant, kneeling on the ground, *pours out water for his master;* another holds a cloth destined for the purifications. The person who purifies himself begins by baring the arms as far as the elbow. As he washes his hands, mouth, nostrils, face, arms, &c., he repeats the proper prayers. It is probable that Mohammed followed, on this subject, the book of Leviticus."‡

The same custom, substantially, prevailed in the time of Christ, as appears from John xiii, 45, where Jesus performed the office of servant, as above described.

The argument, then, is plain. Βαπτιζω *baptizo* is used, in Luke xi, 38, and Mark vii, 4, *generically* to mean *purify*. It does not there mean *immerse*, or *sprinkle*, or *pour*, or *bathe*, but only *purify*. The Jews had a custom of purifying them-

* See note G. † See note GG.

‡ *Vide* Robinson's Calmet, art. Baptism.

selves, and all their furniture, often. Sometimes they purified their whole persons; sometimes they purified their hands only. Sometimes they purified by bathing, sometimes by sprinkling, and sometimes by pouring water on the hands. The purifications which were performed before eating were emphatically of the latter kind. The stone pots which were set for purification were, unquestionably, for the purpose of sprinkling; and in this the custom of the Pharisees bears a strong resemblance to modern Roman Catholic ceremonies. These purifications were called *baptisms*, not because they were immersions, or sprinklings, or pourings, but because they were *purifications*, *baptizo* being used for *katharizo*.

5. But that the βαπτισμους *baptisms* of Mark vii, 4, were not *immersions*, is put for ever beyond the region of doubt from the circumstances of the case. It is said that the Jews not only *baptized* their persons, their "cups, and pots, and brazen vessels," but also their κλινων *beds*, or *couches*. Our English word "*tables*" is not correct. In order to place the subject fully before the reader, we remark:

1. The word *bed*, in Scripture, is used to denote a kind of hammock, or mattress, and pillow, such as the Orientals use to this day to recline upon. They are composed of a thick quilt of cotton, or some similar substance. Such was the bed spoken of Matt. ix, 2. Such beds they could conveniently carry; hence the command, "Arise, take up thy bed and walk." Now, with this definition of the term *bed*, we admit the abstract possibility of their being immersed. But then, does even this seem a rational probability? Would it have been practicable to have dipped these beds into water as often as the superstitious nicety of the Pharisees required a lustration, and still to have kept them in a state fitted for use? The rich might have sustained this expense, but the poorer classes could not have furnished themselves with the requisite supply of beds.

2. The word *bed* is used to denote that on which the hammock or pallet was laid; in other words, a bedstead, couch, or sofa. (*Vide* Prov. vii, 16, 17; Amos vi, 4.)

"It should be observed that the use of chairs is unknown in the East. The Orientals sit, or recline, on a duan, divan, or sofa; that is, a part of the room raised above the floor, and spread with a carpet in winter, and in summer with fine mats, and having cushions, or bolsters, placed along the back to lean against. These divans frequently serve the purpose of a bed, with the addition of two thick cotton quilts, one of which, folded double, serves as a mattress, the other as a covering."*

These beds were not made to suit the size of the person, but rather that of the room. Thus the bed on which Og, king of Bashan, reclined, was about *fifteen feet and a half* long, and *six feet ten inches* broad. The size of the bed was somewhat proportionate to the dignity of the person, and to his voluptuous manner of living.† Whenever an unclean person sat or reclined upon these divans, or couches, they were thereby rendered unclean, and, by the law of Moses, whosoever afterward sat upon, or touched them, previous to their purification, was, in like manner, defiled. The Pharisees carried their notions of legal purity to a superstitious exactness. In order to guard against any possible impurity, they lustrated their beds, and other furniture, much more frequently than the law of Moses required. And as they used their beds to recline upon while taking their meals, it seems perfectly consonant with their other practices to suppose they lustrated them always before eating. But that they immersed them, no man in his senses, and with the facts already adduced before him, will assert.

"Mr. Carson seems to feel this point keenly, and yet manfully maintains his ground. He says he will maintain an immersion until its *impossibility* is proved, and suggests that the couches might be so made as to be taken to pieces for this end! He has proved, he says, the meaning of the word,—the Holy Ghost affirms that the couches were immersed,—and to call this absurd, is to charge the Holy Ghost with uttering an absurdity; and he is filled with horror at the thought, and warns his opponents to beware of so fearful a crime, and he has a long dissertation on the infidel and Unitarian tendencies of allowing difficulties to shake our faith in the assertions of God. But what is all this to the point? The question is not, 'Will we be-

* Robinson's Calmet, art. BED. † See note GGG.

lieve that the couches were immersed *if the Holy Ghost says so?*' but this, *Has he said so?* And what has Mr. Carson proved? Why, truly, that, in other instances, βαπτιζω means immerse. But does this prove that it means so here? Not at all. The probability, as we have shown, is all the other way. Hence, the demand to prove an impossibility of immersion is altogether unreasonable. And it is against his own practice in other cases. Does he not admit that βαπτω *bapto* means to dye, or colour, when it is applied to the beard and hair? And is it impossible to dip these? Improbable it surely is, but not half so much so as the immersion of couches.

"The fact is, that the whole reasoning against the sense claimed for βαπτιζω *baptizo*, in these passages, rests on false principles. It assumes a violent improbability of the meaning in question, and resorts to all manner of shifts to prove the possibility of immersion, as though that were all that the case required, while the truth is that no such improbability exists, but one directly the reverse, and the whole scope of the passage demands the meaning claimed, that is, to *purify*."*

"There is no reason to think," says Dr. Dick, "that this baptism consisted in immersion. 'Cups, and pots, and brazen vessels,' may have been baptized by being plunged into water; but, as the operation could have been performed equally well by pouring water into them and upon them, we can draw no certain conclusion respecting the mode, and the words βαπτιζειν and βαπτισμος convey nothing more than the general idea of *washing*. The last word in the passage, κλινων *klinon*, is improperly rendered *tables* in our version, and the proper translation is *beds*, or *couches*. These were the couches on which they reclined at their meals. They were so large as to hold several persons at the same time; and, from their size, it seems reasonable to suppose that they were *baptized*, not by being *immersed* in water, but by being *washed with the hand*, or *sprinkled*, to remove any real or fancied impurity."†

The following is the opinion of one of the first Oriental critics of the present age:—"As the word βαπτισμους *baptisms* is applied to all these; and as it is contended

* Pres. Beecher on Βαπτιζω. † Theology, vol. ii, p. 375

that this word, and the verb (*baptizo*) whence it is derived, signify *dipping*, or immersion *alone*, its use in the above cases refutes that opinion; and shows that it was used, not only to express *dipping*, or *immersion*, but also *sprinkling* and *washing*. . . . *Baptisontai* may mean either to *wash*, or *dip*. But instead of the word in the text, the famous *Codex Vaticanus*, *eight* others, [MSS., quoted by Griesbach and others, of very respectable authority,] and *Euthymius*, have ῥαντισωνται *rantisontai*, *sprinkle*."* According to these authorities, then, the Jews *sprinkled* themselves before eating, and on returning from market or, they may have used ῥαντιζω *rantizo*, as we construe βαπτιζω *baptizo* to mean *purity*.

SECTION IV.

John iii, 25, 26: "Then there arose a question between some of John's disciples and the Jews about καθαρισμου *katharismou*, *purifying*. And they came to John and said unto him, Rabbi, he that was with thee beyond Jordan, to whom thou bearest witness, the same βαπτιζει *baptizeth*, and all men come to him."

Here is an incontestible proof of our position, viz.. that βαπτιζω and καθαριζω are synonymous, in their religious use, both meaning *to purify*. The subject of dispute was purification, to settle which, an appeal was made to John on the subject of baptism. The argument, then, is obvious. If the decision of a question on baptism could settle a controversy on the subject of purification, and vice versâ, it needs no great powers of logical or of philological discrimination to perceive that the two terms are perfectly synonymous. The argument then is complete; nothing more need be added. No room is left for further controversy.

This text also clearly fixes the *character* of John's baptism. It was a Jewish purification, taken and applied to the higher purposes of John's ministry.

SECTION V.

The history of spiritual baptism completely corroborates and establishes our view.

* Dr. A. Clarke on Mark vii, 4, 6.

In Joel ii, 28, 29, we find this remarkable prophecy and promise: "And it shall come to pass afterward that I will εκχεω *ekcheo, pour out* my Spirit upon all flesh;.... and also upon the servants and upon the handmaids in those days will I εκχεω *ekcheo, pour out* my Spirit." This was a promise of the effusion of the Holy Spirit which was to be accomplished in gospel days. John the Baptist revived the expectation of the Jews on this subject, and excited them to look for an immediate fulfilment of the ancient promise. But when John comes to speak of it, he calls it a *baptism*. Referring to Christ, through whom this promise was to be fulfilled, he says, "he shall *baptize* (βαπτισει) you with the Holy Spirit, and with fire."

When our Saviour was about to take leave of his disciples, to return "to their God and to his God," although he had sanctioned their apostolic commission by the highest authority in heaven and in earth, yet he commanded them to delay the exercise of their new and important functions, until they were endued with the plenary inspiration of the Holy Spirit. He then renews the promise at first made by Joel, and reaffirmed by John, in the following words: "For John truly *baptized*, or *purified* (εβαπτισεν) with water, but *ye shall be baptized*, or *purified* (βαπτισθησεσθε) with the Holy Ghost, not many days hence," Acts i, 5.

Ten days after the ascension of Christ, this "promise of the Father" was fulfilled. The event is thus described by Luke, Acts ii, 3, 4: "And there appeared unto them cloven tongues, like as of fire, and it *sat upon* ('εκαθισε) each of them, and they were all filled with the Holy Ghost." Peter, afterward explaining to the Jews this extraordinary dispensation, says: "This is that which was spoken by the prophet Joel, And it shall come to pass in the last days, saith God, I will *pour out* (εκχεω) my Spirit upon all flesh," &c. Some time after this, Peter was preaching to Cornelius and his Gentile friends, when, it is said, "the Holy Ghost *descended upon* ('επεπεσε) all them that heard the word.... and as many as came with Peter were astonished, because that on the Gentiles also was *poured out* (εκκεχυται) the gift of the Holy Ghost," Acts x, 44, 45.

Although this last instance mentioned, of the effusion of the Holy Ghost, took place subsequently to the spiritual baptism of the apostles, it nevertheless stands directly connected with that event, and is embraced, specifically, in the fulfilment of the promise of Christ recorded Acts i, 5. This is evident from the import of the particle "*also*," in the 45th verse; "because that on the Gentiles ALSO was poured out," &c.; and also from the words of Peter in his vindication, chap. xi, 15, 16: "As I began to speak," says he, "the Holy Ghost fell on them, AS ON US AT THE BEGINNING. THEN remembered I the word of the Lord, how that he said, John indeed baptized you with water, BUT YE SHALL BE BAPTIZED WITH THE HOLY GHOST."

This clearly demonstrates that Peter regarded this affusion of the Spirit as an instance of the fulfilment of the divine promise of a spiritual baptism, to which his mind so readily and so naturally reverted.

After this collation of passages, let us pause to give place to the sober bearing of the argument. We have seen that the promise of a spiritual baptism made by John and by Christ was fulfilled on the day of pentecost, and in subsequent effusions of the Holy Spirit. Now, βαπτιζω *baptizo*, as used by John, (Matt. iii, 11,) and by Christ, (Acts i, 5,) must denote, either the external act of *baptism*, or it must signify the *effect* of baptism; that is, it must mean *purify*. If it be used in the sense of purify, this is what we contend for; and thus the controversy is at an end. But if it denotes the outward act, or form of baptism, then, most undeniably, it is employed in a sense exactly synonymous with εκχεω *ekcheo, to pour forth*, επιπιπτω *epipipto, to fall upon*, καθιζω *kathizo, to sit down upon*. So far as the effect of the argument is concerned, we are not anxious to know which of these two senses our opponents will contend for. In any case, their theory is totally prostrated. But truth, and the just principles of criticism, require us to understand *baptizo* here, in the sense of *purify*. Our Lord, in Acts i, 5, promises that the apostles "shall be *purified* with the Holy Ghost not many days hence." This was not a promise of immersion, or of sprinkling, but of purification. The word βαπτιζω having the sense of purify, does not, of itself, indicate the mode. But the circumstances, and the use of other terms, most triumphantly and unequivocally show that the mode

of spiritual baptism was not by immersion. The *baptism* or *purification* by the Holy Ghost was effected by a *pouring out*, a *descending upon*, a *sitting upon*, &c. The Holy Spirit appeared in the form of a luminous body directly over the apostles' heads, and then divided off in the shape of fiery spires, or tongues, each spire resting, or, in the language of Luke, *sitting upon*, one of the disciples. The appearance seems to have been that of a beam of light, taking the hues of fire, as if it had been *poured out* from above upon the heads of the apostles: a mode of *baptism*, or purification this, as far removed from the idea of immersion, as the force of language and of literal descriptions can place it.

SECTION VI.

A remarkable passage occurs, 1 Cor. x, 2: "All our fathers were under the cloud, and all passed through the sea; and were all *consecrated* (εβαπτισαντο *ebaptisanto*, Eng. *baptized*) unto Moses in the cloud and in the sea."

1. It should be remembered that our English Bible, in this place, gives no translation whatever of βαπτιζω *baptizo*. It merely gives an English termination to the Greek verb, using it as a technic, without attaching to it any definite sense whatever. To say "they were all *baptized* unto Moses," &c., is to say nothing. The word *baptizo* conveys no idea. But if we should say, "they were all *immersed* unto Moses," or, "they were all *sprinkled* unto Moses," or, "they were all *consecrated* unto Moses," we should then attach a definite meaning to *baptizo*.

2. The translation we have given makes a good sense, and is, evidently, the real meaning of the word in this place. Moses was the "mediator of the old covenant." To be "baptized unto Moses," was to be devoted, by a solemn act, to the doctrines and duties of that dispensation of which he was the mediator; just as the New Testament phrase imports. To be "baptized unto Jesus Christ," is to be *consecrated* or *devoted* by a solemn rite to Christ, as the Mediator of the new covenant. This, then, we conceive to be the true sense. The words *consecrate* and *purify* are not exactly synonymous, but they are exactly *correlative*. To be *purified*, implies a separation from a common, and devotion to a sacred purpose; and to be

consecrated, or *devoted*, in a religious sense, presupposes the exact idea of purification. We consider, then, that *baptizo*, in 1 Cor. x, 2, retains its *generic* use, purification being the leading idea.

3. The word βαπτιζω will not bear the sense of *immerse* in this connection. If its generic sense, for which we have contended, be still rejected; if it be still maintained that it refers to a specific, outward act, then must our opponents reconcile the sense of *immerse* with the historical allusions of the text, or they must admit that *baptizo* imports *sprinkling*. But this is, and ever has been, a difficult passage for our opponents, and it justly merits a more extended notice.

Various have been the hypotheses resorted to, by Baptist authors, in order to evade the direct and manifest bearing of this text, and to retain for *baptizo* the sense of *immerse*. But the favourite one is to regard the baptism of the Israelites as merely figurative; and thus, having thrown the whole subject into the regions of ideality, they can theorize and speculate at will. "The language," says Professor Ripley, "is evidently figurative, and is intended to represent the Israelites, not as being *literally baptized*, (*immersed*, I suppose the professor means,) but as submitting themselves to the special authority and guidance of Moses," &c.*

That the learned professor has distinctly stated the *import* of their baptism, we unhesitatingly concede; but, that their baptism, and their act of submission to the doctrines and authority of Moses, were *one*, and *identical;* that is, that their baptism implied nothing more than their voluntary devotion to Moses, without the use of water; that it was wholly "*allusive;*" that it was merely typical and shadowy, we can never admit, except with a deliberate consent to a use of βαπτιζω *baptizo*, for which we know of no warrant in its *usus loquendi* in the Holy Scriptures. It is remarkable, too, that our opponents should here resort to an unexampled use of *baptizo*, without any other necessity for so doing but to save their own theory. In vain do we call upon them for a vindication of this new and extraordinary sense of the word. As

* Christian Baptism, p. 100.

a last and forlorn shift, they have here left the beaten path of criticism, and fled to their own imaginations.

Professor Ripley gravely inquires, " What though they were not touched with the water?"* assuming that they were not. How it is that people can be baptized in an aqueous element, and yet not be touched with water, we leave the reader to judge. The voice of inspiration declares they were " all baptized *in the sea* and *in the cloud*." Others have supposed that the cloud stood over their heads during the passage of the Red Sea, which, with the walls of the waters on both sides, *surrounded* the Israelites, so as in a manner to *immerse* them. Beautiful imagery! Our imaginations are indeed regaled, but our understandings are still unfruitful. But it is unfortunate for this hypothesis that the " cloud," during the passage of the Red Sea, stood, not over their heads, but *behind* the Israelites. Ex. xiv, 19, 20.

We cannot attain a just view of the meaning of βαπτιζω *baptizo*, in 1 Cor. x, 2, without removing some rubbish from the historical allusions of the passage which erroneous hypotheses have accumulated, and exhibiting all the circumstances in a plain and unencumbered light.

It seems to have been generally taken for granted that the baptism " in the *cloud* and in the *sea*" took place at one and the same time; whereas, it is by no means clear that this was the case. The grammatical structure of the passage in Corinthians fairly conveys the idea of *two* distinct times of baptism: one " in the cloud," and the other " in the sea." With this hypothesis also agree the Old Testament accounts. Want of attention to this has occasioned much confusion. Professor Stuart says, speaking of the passage of the Red Sea, " The cloud on this occasion was not a cloud of rain."† Admit it. But what is gained or lost by this supposition? Verily, nothing. But though the cloud which stood behind the Israelites, during the passage of the Red Sea, was not a cloud of rain, still, there was a cloud of rain that attended them on their journey. It should be remembered that the cloud (or clouds) which followed them served a fourfold purpose;—it was their guide in

* Christian Baptism, p. 101.

† Essay in Biblical Repository for April, 1833, p. 336.

the desert; it gave them light by night; it overshadowed them by day; and it supplied them with water. Thus the psalmist, (cv, 39,) "*He spread a* CLOUD *for their* COVERING." Allusion is also made to the uses of the cloud, Isa. iv. 5. It should be remembered that the people required some shelter from the heat of the sun, and vast and constant supplies of water for themselves, and for their numerous herds and flocks. Whence did they derive this water? During thirty-eight years they were supplied miraculously. There is no method of supplying them mentioned, (save in one or two special instances,) but by the cloud.

The apostle says that "all our fathers were *ὑπο την νεφελην* UNDER *the cloud*," and were "all baptized *εν τη νεφελη* IN, or WITH *the cloud*." This shows that the cloud *in*, or *with* which they were baptized stood over their heads at the time; and this agrees with the statement Psa. cv, 39. But their baptism in the cloud does not apply to the time of their passing the Red Sea, but to a subsequent period, and the cloud in which they were baptized was not the same as gave them light by night. We cannot better illustrate our views on this subject than by furnishing a synopsis of Old and New Testament representations of the affair. Thus:

O God, when thou wentest forth before thy people, when thou didst march through the wilderness, . . . thou, O God, *didst send a plentiful rain*, WHEREBY THOU DIDST CONFIRM thine inheritance when it was weary. Psa. lxviii, 7, 9. Lord, when thou wentest out of Seir, when thou marchedst out of the field of Edom, the earth trembled, the heavens *dropped*, *the clouds also dropped water*. Judg. v, 4.	Moreover, brethren, I would not have you ignorant, how that all our fathers were under the cloud, . . . *and were all* BAPTIZED *into Moses* IN THE CLOUD. 1 Cor. x, 1, 2.

The Septuagint render Judg. v, 4, thus: Ὁ *ουρανος εσταξε δροσους, και ἁι νεφελαι εσταξαν ὑδωρ*, *The heavens distilled moist-*

ure, and the clouds dropped water. The Hebrew simply says, "*The heavens* DISTILLED, *also the clouds dropped waters.*" But this is an elliptical mode of speaking, with which the Hebrew abounds. The meaning is, "The heavens *distilled* or *dropped* moisture." The Hebrew נָטַף *natap* answers to the Greek *σταζω stazo*, Lat. *stillo*, Eng. *distil, to drop*, or *trickle down.* In Psalm lxviii, 8, the same language is employed. If we follow the Septuagint, who, we believe, have given the right turn to the sentence here, we shall read, "The land shook, and also *οἱ ουρανοι εσταξαν απο προσωπου του θεου του Σινα*, [אַף־שָׁמַיִם נָטְפוּ מִפְּנֵי אֱלֹהִים זֶה סִינַי] *απο προσωπου του θεου Ισραηλ the heavens* DISTILLED [water] *from the face of this God of Sinai*, [even] *from the face of the God of Israel.*" Then the ninth verse immediately gives an intensive repetition of the thought: "Thou, O God, didst send גֶּשֶׁם נְדָבוֹת *gasham nedboth, abundant* or *liberal rain.* (*Pluvia larga*, says Gesenius.) Sept. *βροχην εκουσιον spontaneous* or *plenteous rain.*"

It is not a little surprising that some commentators should have construed these passages so as to wholly set aside the idea of rain. They seem to think of nothing else but showers of manna and quails around the Israelitish camp. Why should we not understand the psalmist to speak of rain literally? The Israelites were in need of water no less than of manna. They tarried in the desert of Sinai about *eleven months and twenty days*, and the rains they there received are associated, by the psalmist, with the other miraculous and wonderful phenomena which they witnessed while at that station. The cloud of rain attended them also on their journeyings, and was a circumstance of such large importance to the preservation and well-being of the nation that it deserved to be commemorated in song in after ages.

How beautiful is the sentiment of the psalmist! When that immense multitude were moving over a tract of desert, described by Burckhardt as "the most barren and horrid tract of country he had ever seen;" which M. Rüppell denominates "a frightful desert," and which Moses calls a "great and terrible wilderness;"—when, I say, the Israelites were traversing this monotonous waste of "chalky hills, alternating with rolling plains,"—exposed to the burning rays of an Arabian sun, and prompted, by a parching thirst and numerous privations, to tempt God, and to doubt the divine legation of Moses,—then it was that "God did *send a plentiful* RAIN, whereby he CONFIRMED his inheritance," in their allegiance to him and to Moses their leader. And this, we apprehend, is what the apostle calls being BAPTIZED *in the cloud.* For, as Christian baptism is an outward seal and confirmation of our obedience to Christ, so did these *rains* CONFIRM God's people in their devotedness to him. And it is with strict philosophical propriety that the apostle says they were baptized *in* or *with* the cloud, when that cloud was being distilled upon them in drops of rain.

That the Israelites, then, were baptized by means of water, we can see no just ground to deny. Besides, if *βαπτιζω baptizo*, in 1 Cor. x, 2, is not intended to denote or suggest a *real* use of water, why should it be said they were *baptized* "in the cloud and in the sea," any more than *in the passover* and *in the manna*, or *in the waters of Meribah* and *in the Jordan*, or, *in the plagues of Egypt?* Were not the great miracles they witnessed all contributory to their confirmation, and to their submission to Moses? Yet how absurd to say "they were baptized into Moses in the passover and in the manna!" But why not in these, as well as in the cloud and in the sea, if *baptizo* does not purport the use of water? It would be no greater perversion of the sense of *βαπτιζω* in one case than in the other.

As to their baptism in the sea, we know it was not by immersion. The Egyptians were, indeed, immersed, for it is said, "The depths have *covered* them, *they sank into the bottom as a stone*," Ex. xv, 5. But "the children of Israel *walked upon dry land* in the midst of the sea," Ex. xiv, 29. It is true the Bible gives us no account of the positive mode of their baptism. But as, from the nature of the case, immersion is precluded, we must necessarily suppose some other mode. It seems most probable that, as the climate was oppressively warm, and as the people, being closely pursued by the Egyptians, were greatly fatigued, God refreshed them (and thus *baptized* or *consecrated* them to Moses as their earthly mediator) by sprays of the sea being blown over them. We know, indeed, that this must have been a necessary consequence, as "a strong wind prevailed all that night," Ex. xiv, 21. And as this was so opportune to the necessities of the people, and also so analogous to their baptism in the cloud, it is the more probable. The reader can adopt our hypothesis or not; we are not solicitous. But the argument drawn from the text in question, against the theory of our opponents, is, and must for ever be, complete. We only add, that the translation of the Campbellite Testament, as well as the Baptist construction, which requires us to read, "And were all *immersed* into Moses, in the cloud and in the sea," is an outrage upon common sense, no less than upon the right use of language, and contradicts the attested facts in the history.

SECTION VII.

We come now to a very extraordinary passage, furnishing a most incontestible and triumphant argument in favour of our position. In Heb. ix, 10, speaking of a particular class of the Levitical institutes, the apostle says, they "stood only in meats, and drinks, and διαφοροις βαπτισμοις *diaphorois baptismois*, *different purifications*," &c. Eng. version, *divers washings*.

We request the reader's patient attention to the following considerations:—

1. The apostle was here speaking only of those external ceremonies which the worshipper, under the old covenant, was obligated to perform on account of their *personal* effect, but which could not deliver his conscience from a sense of guilt. Hence, when he comes to speak of the Jewish purifications, which he calls *different baptisms*, he does not allude to those particular rites for the purification of cups, skins, clothes, vessels, &c., but only those ceremonies which had an application *to the body of the worshipper*. This will be obvious to the reader if he attends to three things:—

(*a*) The apostle all along (see the context) contemplates the effect that these ordinances of purification, or baptisms, were supposed to have upon *the conscience of the worshipper*. Now, the purification of inanimate things, as vessels, clothes, furniture, &c., we all know, had no possible effect upon the *conscience* of the worshipper, and they were never designed, even typically, to remove his guilt. All the effect that was produced by such ceremonies was upon the things themselves, and no effect whatever was realized upon the conscience of him that performed the service. It was only when water, or blood, or the ashes of the heifer, *was sprinkled upon the body of the unclean person himself*, that it had any personal effect.

(*b*) Besides, the apostle expressly calls all that class of ordinances, of which he is speaking, δικαιωμασι σαρκος *dikaiomasi sarkos*, *ordinances of the flesh*, (ver. 10,) or, as it might read with equal propriety, *ordinances of the person*, in distinction from those ordinances which related to the purification of inanimate things. Our English has *carnal ordinances;* but the word *carnal* does not convey the proper idea. The whole connection is thus exhibited by Professor Stuart:—"Oblations and sacrifices are offered which cannot fully accomplish what is needed for the conscience of him who performeth the services, being imposed (together with meats and drinks, and *divers washings—ordinances pertaining to the flesh*) only until the time of the reformation."*

(*c*) The antithesis of the apostle's argument proves that the *washings* here referred to were lustrations of the body of the worshipper only, and not those of vessels, and of inanimate things. The apostle's main intention is to draw a contrast between the supposed virtue of these outward lustrations required by the law of Moses, and the real virtue of that purification effected by the blood of Christ. Jewish lustrations, he says, were applied to the body—they were *fleshly ordinances;* but the blood of Christ is applied to the mind. The blood of bulls, and of goats, and the ashes of a heifer, sprinkling the unclean, *sanctified to the purifying of the* FLESH, but the blood of Christ shall *purge your* CONSCIENCE *from dead works,* to serve the living God.

Now, without multiplying remarks, it is most obvious that in all the context the apostle speaks only of those ordinances of purification which related to the *person*, or *flesh* (σαρκος) of the worshipper.

2. This, then, being clearly understood, it is evident

* Commentary on Hebrews.

that the mode of administering those Jewish ordinances of purification becomes a fit and important subject of inquiry. For if the noun βαπτισμοις *baptisms* refer to a particular class of Jewish lustrations, it becomes necessary, in order to settle the true sense of the word, to understand how these lustrations were enjoined; that is, the manner in which they were required to be performed. If these Jewish lustrations were to be performed by *immersion* of the body, then βαπτισμοις, undoubtedly, in Heb. ix, 10, mean *immersions;* but if not, then, undeniably, the Greek noun does not import immersions, and our opponents are, consequently, obliged to recede from the ground they have taken in regard to the meaning of the word.

And here, let it be understood, we are not to show whether the Jews did, or did not, as a mere matter of fact, immerse themselves on different occasions, in performing their ceremonies of ablution; but only to show what was actually *required* of them, in order to effect the purification of the unclean. We do not now ask, What was the *practice* of the Jews? but, What was the *language* of the law? What *words* are employed by the Holy Spirit to enjoin bodily lustrations? And is *immersion* ever enjoined, under any circumstances, as necessary to effect a purification? These questions are now in point; and we are happy to be able to answer them in the following language of President Beecher:—

"No immersions of persons are enjoined under the Mosaic ritual. As this fact does not appear to have been noticed as it ought, and as many assume the contrary, it is necessary to furnish the proof of this assertion.

"It lies in this fact, that no washings of persons are enjoined by the word טָבַל *tabal,* to *immerse,* even in a single instance, nor by any word that denotes immersion; but, as I think, without exception, by the word רָחַץ *rahats,* which denotes to *wash,* or *purify,* without any reference to the mode.

"Those who read the English version might suppose that where the direction to *bathe* occurs, immersion is enjoined; but in every such case the original word denotes only to *wash.*

"If any doubt whether this is the true view of the import of רָחַץ *rahats*, let him take a Hebrew concordance and trace it through the whole of the Old Testament, and he will have abundant proof. He will find it used to denote the washing of any thing in any way,—of the feet, the hands, the face, the body, or the mind. Its translation in the Septuagint denotes how wide its range of meaning is; for it is at one time [translated by] λουω *louo*, [which denotes a general washing of the body by whatever means,] at another by νιπτω *nipto*, [which denotes a more partial *washing*, as that of the hands, and hence, I believe, always takes χειρες *cheires*, *hands*, after it,] and at another time πλυνω *pluno*, [which is used to denote the washing of clothes,] just as the circumstances may seem to require. If ever it is applied in cases where bathing was probably performed, the idea depends not at all on the word, but on the circumstances of the case. So a Baptist writer thinks that, in the case of Pharaoh's daughter, (Exod. ii, 5,) the word denotes *bathing;* but all our evidence lies in the fact that she went down to the Nile, and not at all in the word רָחַץ *rahats*, and therefore our translators have very properly rendered it *wash*.

"I would quote passages to illustrate all these assertions, did not the proof lie so plainly on the surface of the whole usage of the word that I do not suppose any one who has investigated the subject will think of denying it.*

"It is perfectly plain, therefore, that whatever was the practice of the Jews, no immersions of persons were enjoined, and the whole Mosaic ritual, as to personal ablution, could be fulfilled to the letter without a single immersion. I do not doubt that immersions were common, but nothing but washings of the body was enjoined; and immersions fulfilled the law, not because they were immersions, but solely because they were washings.

"The only immersions enjoined in the Mosaic law were immersions of *things*, as vessels, sacks, skins, &c., to which no reference is had in Heb. ix, 10."†

These facts are important to be remembered. No immersions of *persons* were enjoined under the law, but only *inanimate things* were sometimes (but not often) required to be immersed. But Paul, in Heb. ix, 10, is not speak-

* *Vide* note GGGG. † President Beecher on βαπτιζω.

ing of all the purifications required by the law of Moses, but only those *personal purifications*—or that class of lustrations which, as he says, ἁγιαζει προς την της σαρκος καθαροτητα *sanctify to the purification of the* FLESH ; (ver. 13;) and which, of course, applied to the body of the worshipper.

This fact, we apprehend, is, therefore, unequivocally clear. But if the above statements be correct, the argument is conclusive and irresistible against the theory of our opponents. Βαπτισμος *baptismos* is here found to be not only synonymous with καθαρισμος *katharismos*, *purification*, but, to refer to a distinct class of purifications—a class wherein immersion, or bathing, was rarely admissible, and where it was NEVER enjoined.

A circumstance that adds great weight to this argument is, that in the class of legal ablutions we are now speaking of, and which the apostle calls *baptisms*, sprinkling was by far the most common, and the most important ceremony. Hence it is said, in Num. xix, 20, "But that soul that shall be unclean, and shall not purify himself, that soul shall be cut off from among the congregation . . . the water of separation hath not been SPRINKLED upon him; he is unclean." And so Paul, in Heb. ix. After having referred to the *personal purifications* under the law, and called them *baptisms* in verse 10, when he afterward, in verse 13, has occasion to allude to these baptisms, for the purpose of summing up his argument, he only mentions one mode, "*sprinkling*," this being by far the most prominent and efficacious, and hence a fit representative of the efficaciousness of the entire system of bodily ablutions, or baptisms, in the Levitical code.

In Heb. vi, 2, Paul refers to the same subject, and uses the same language. The βαπτισμων διδαχῆς *instruction concerning purifications* (Eng. ver. *doctrine of baptisms*) refers to the Levitical law enjoining and regulating bodily ablutions. This the Jews had been taught as altogether indispensable, in order to retain their covenant relations to God. But now Paul exhorts them to leave της αρχης του Χριστου λογου *the beginning*, or *former state*, *of the doctrine of Christ*, (that is, Judaism,) and go on to perfection—to the maturer developments of the gospel. Among the instructions they were wont to receive, was the "doctrine of baptisms," or *purifications*.

SECTION VIII.

Under this section we adduce various passages in a connected view, merely to show that the sense of βαπτιζω *baptizo*, in the New Testament, bears the sense of *consecrate, devote, purify*, &c. We again remind the reader that the word *baptize*, in the English Bible, is not a translation of the Greek word, and to an English reader it conveys no sense whatever, being used merely as a sort of technic. The word *baptize*, from its frequent and long use, may seem to have a smooth sound to many English ears, and many may have necessarily associated with it a meaning of some sort, from a long habit of using the word, and not from any philological examination of its use. It is hence even possible that, from mere habit, and long usage of the term, the Anglicised form *baptize* may sound smoother to some, than any translation of the word we could put in its place. We should not have made these remarks, had we not been aware of the force of such habits and prejudices, especially over those who are little accustomed to philological investigations.

We remark also that it is the *generic* use of the word *baptizo* for which we are contending. Hence, when we render it *consecrate*, although it is not exactly synonymous with *purify*, yet the generic use is retained; the leading idea is *purify;* and the rendering is also in harmony with the usage of language.

(*a*) Rom. vi, 3, 4: "Know ye not that so many of us as were *consecrated* unto Jesus Christ, were *consecrated* into [a communion with] his death? Therefore we are buried with him, by [means of this] *consecration* into [communion with his] death."

The reader will perceive that we have given εις *eis* a force and peculiarity of meaning which, to a superficial observer, may seem improper. It would be easy here, however, to justify this construction by citations from commentators and divines, but it is not our desire to encumber and embarrass a plain subject. In 1 Cor. xii, 13, we find the following language: "ἡμεις παντης εις ἑν σωμα εβαπτισθημεν *we all are baptized* (*consecrated, initiated*) INTO *one body;*" that is, INTO *communion* or *fellowship with one body.* "Here," says Professor Stuart, "εις *eis* plainly designates *participation*, and the meaning of the phrase is, that by baptism we come to belong to *one* body, to participate in one body, to be members of one body. . . . The idea is, for substance, that 'by baptism we become consecrated to any person or thing, appropriated (as it were) to any person or thing, so as to belong to him, or to it, in a manner peculiar, and involving a special relation, and consequent special duties and obligations.' This sense is such a one as fits the passage of Rom. vi, 3. Thus interpreted it would mean, 'As many of us as have become *devoted* to Christ by baptism,' &c."*

(*b*) 1 Cor. i, 13: ". . . were ye *consecrated* (εβαπτισθητε *ebaptisthete*, Eng. *baptized*) in the name of Paul?"

To be "baptized *into the name* of a person," and to be "baptized *into* a person," are phrases of exactly similar import. The word ὀνομα *name* is, in such places, *expletive*.

Verses 14–17: "I thank God that I *consecrated* none of you but Crispus and Gaius; lest any should say that I had *consecrated* in mine own name. And I *consecrated* also the household of Stephanas: besides, I know not that I *consecrated* any other: for Christ sent me not to *consecrate*, but to preach the gospel."

I have presented these passages mostly to show the reader that *consecrate* gives an easy, smooth, natural, and expressive sense to βαπτιζω *baptizo*. Besides, although our opponents may retain the sense of *immerse* in these passages, still, they are forced to lug in some *ad*-signification to make out the sense of *consecrate*.

(*c*) Gal. iii, 27: "For as many of you as have been *consecrated* unto Jesus Christ, have put on Christ."

Before taking our leave of the phrase "baptized *into* Christ," we may remark that it has given commentators and divines abundance of trouble. Professor Ripley prefers to retain the more common acceptation of the phrase, understanding it to mean, "baptized INTO *an acknowledgment of* Christ." So also, "to be baptized into Christ's death," is to be "baptized INTO *an acknowledgment of* his death;" and the phrase, he thinks, may compare with Matt. iii, 11, "*I baptize you* INTO (εις) *repentance*," that is "*into an acknowledgment of repentance*."

* Commentary on Romans.

In respect to the last quotation from Matt. iii, 11, we wish only to say that εις *eis* has the meaning of *unto*, *with respect to*, *on account of*, &c.: "I baptize you *in respect to*, or *in consideration of*, repentance." This seems to be the force of the particle in Gal. iii, 27, "baptized *into* Christ," that is, "*consecrated* TO *Christ*."

(*d*) 1 Pet. iii, 21. In order to present the true, unencumbered sense of this passage, we subjoin the following free paraphrase :—"Eight souls were saved in Noah's ark by water; and *in like* manner *the antitype*, which is the ordinance of *consecration*, (βαπτισμα *baptisma*,) *doth also now save us* (*not*, indeed, that mere outward purification, *the putting away of the filth of the flesh; but*, that inward and real consecration of the soul, *the answer of a good conscience toward God*) by the resurrection of Jesus Christ." Here the Greek noun *baptism* is evidently used in the generic sense, signifying the *effect* of using water ceremonially upon the body; that is, it signifies *purify*, or *consecrate*. And the apostle was so exact in this use of the word that, to prevent misconception, he introduces his parenthetical exposition, expressly declaring this to be the true sense.

(*e*) Acts viii, 16: "For as yet he [the Holy Spirit] was fallen upon none of them; only they were *consecrated* TO the Lord Jesus;" the words εις το ὀνομα *in the name* being *expletive*.

See also chap. xix, 3, 4, 5.

It is not necessary to adduce any more passages under this head. The argument which we wish to draw out and commend to the reader's judgment is this: βαπτιζω *baptizo*, in every passage in the New Testament where it occurs in a religious sense, may be rendered by the English verb *purify*, or *consecrate*, and in all such connections it has a *generic* sense, leaving the outward *form* or *mode* of applying the water of baptism wholly out of the sense. On the other hand, to render βαπτιζω *baptizo* by *immerse* is to involve many passages in utter obscurity and in irretrievable confusion. Besides, the word *immerse* never meets the full exigences of the case so well as *purify*, or *consecrate*, even where the former may seem to give a lawful sense. How uncouth and how ridiculous would it be to read, "For as many of us as have been *dipped* into Jesus Christ have been *dipped* into his death; therefore we are buried with him by *dipping* into death!" We apprehend the turn we have given to this passage will convince the reader, after this comparison, that we have hit its true force and meaning. Compare also our version with the following: "I indeed *dip* you in water, but he that cometh after me shall *dip* you in the Holy Ghost and *in fire!*" "As many of you as have been *immersed* into Jesus Christ have put on Christ." "And were all *immersed* into Moses, in the cloud and in the sea."

Can any person in his senses be made to believe that, in these passages, to instance no more, a faithful translation of βαπτιζω has been given? Never yet was a man *immersed* in the Holy Spirit and in fire. Never were the Israelites *dipped* into the cloud, or in the Red Sea. Baptism is figuratively called "the washing of regeneration." But if *baptize* means *dip*, why not, when the allusion is made to baptism, use the word *dip*, and read, "the *dipping* of regeneration?" Beautiful simile! Rhetoric extraordinary!

SECTION IX.

It has been stoutly maintained by our opponents that as *immerse* is the primitive and literal sense of βαπτιζω *baptizo*, therefore the word must bear this sense in all those places in the New Testament where it is used to describe a religious rite.

Let us, for a moment, suppose this method of reasoning from the primitive sense of a word to its sense in a particular connection to be valid. We will propose to the reader a parallel case:—The word δειπνον *deipnon*, in the New Testament, signifies a *supper*, which, with the Hebrews, was the principal meal of the day. It also signifies *feast*, *banquet*. Luke xiv, 12, *et alibi*. Now, it is well known that Paul uses this same word to signify the institution of bread and wine, called the "Lord's supper," Κυριακον δειπνον. 1 Cor. xi, 20. Hence, if we adhere strictly to the primitive meaning, and general usage of the word, we shall arrive at this conclusion, viz., that the Lord's supper is a *sumptuous repast*, a *full meal*, a *feast*, a *banquet*, which is exactly contrary to the true meaning of the word in that connection, and to the proper manner of celebrating that institution. But there is no reason, so far as the mere philology of the question is concerned, why we should use βαπιζω in its primitive sense *immerse*, and not as uniformly use δειπνον in its primitive sense of a *feast*, or *banquet*. And if we can obey the command to "eat the Lord's supper" by eating a *morsel* of bread and taking a single *sip* of wine, analogy would teach us that we might obey the command to be "*baptized*" by having a small quantity of water applied to us.

And here we may rest the philological argument from the import of the word βαπτιζω *baptizo*. More might be said by way of shedding collateral light, but the strength and just dimensions of the argument are before the reader. We have striven to simplify the whole so as to bring it within the comprehension of any attentive observer, and we must here be excused from a recapitulation. If the reader has attended to the various parts of the argument, he, we apprehend, will believe with us, that βαπτιζω *baptizo*, when used in a religious sense in the New Testament, may be translated by *purify*, *consecrate*, or (sometimes) *wash;* that it is a *generic* term, in all such places, signifying the *effect* of the ceremonial use of water, without any allusion to, or stress put upon, the particular mode.

CHAPTER V.

GREEK PARTICLES.

"Hitherto we have found nothing to justify the confidence with which it has been asserted that βαπτιζω necessarily signifies *to immerse*. But to supply what may be wanting in the evidence arising from the word itself, it is alleged that such phrases are joined with it, as clearly show that it was by dipping or plunging that baptism was originally administered."* An examination of this hypothesis will lead us to notice the Greek prepositions employed in connection with the history of baptism in the New Testament. These are four in number, viz., εν, εις, απο, and εκ, or εξ.

* Dick's Theology, vol. ii, p. 375.

The frequent interchange of these particles—the different senses in which they are used, together with the rareness of their occurrence in connection with water baptism,—all concur to render their testimony to the cause of our opponents so dubious, that we should deem it altogether unworthy of any formal notice, had it not assumed an importance in the estimation of some who, for want of investigation, seem not to have appreciated its real merits.

"Prepositions which mark a *removal, derivation*, or *motion from a place*, viz., απο and εκ, as well as those which signify *motion to a place*, as εις, are often interchanged with those which mark *rest in a place*, as εν, and vice versa."* It is not, however, our purpose to treat of the prepositions at large, but only to adduce those instances wherein they occur in connection with baptism, and wherein they are supposed to favour the idea of immersion. In order, therefore, to the greater perspicuity, we shall treat them separately.

1. Εν. Its primary meaning is *in*, and it denotes *rest in* a place. The first sense we shall notice as belonging to this preposition, where it stands connected with baptism, makes it synonymous with our English preposition, AT. Thus—the people were baptized by John εν τω Ιορδανη "AT *the Jordan*," Matt. iii, 6. Our common English version reads "*in* Jordan." It is well known that the Baptists claim this passage in their favour, supposing that, if John stood *in* the waters of the Jordan when he baptized, it must have been for the purpose of immersion only. But in this it is easy to perceive that they have assumed the very point to be proved. Nay, they have assumed it *against* proof. If John stood *in* the water, still it is altogether gratuitous to assert that, therefore, he immersed. As well might we maintain that εν Ασια certainly imports *under the soil of Asia*, and εν Βεθλεεμ *under Bethlehem*, as that εν Ιορδανη necessarily imports, in the above connection, an immersion. In translating εν by *at*, as above, we do not intend to deny that John ever stood *in* Jordan, when he baptized. We suppose he may sometimes have stood *in* the water and sometimes *out* of the water when he

* Valpy's Greek Grammar, edited by C. Anthon.

performed the ceremony. But the object is to show that the force of the preposition has nothing to do with the *mode* of baptism, but only serves, in the passage adduced, to denote *rest in a* place, i.e., it merely fixes John's general *position* to be in the vicinity of the Jordan. This will appear plain from the following parallel places. Mark says, John baptized εν τη ερημω "*in the desert.*" Luke says, he came "preaching the baptism of repentance (i.e., preaching repentance and baptizing) in all the περιχωρον *country* ABOUT Jordan;" while John declared he baptized περαν του Ιορδανου "BEYOND *Jordan* εν *in* Bethabara," and also, at another time, εν "*in* Enon."* What, then, becomes of the force of the particle εν? What connection does it hold with the doctrine of immersion? If the phrase "baptized *in* Jordan" denotes immersion, what is denoted by the phrases, "baptizing *beyond* Jordan"—"baptizing *in* Bethabara"—"baptizing *in* the wilderness?" Our opponents must surely abate the tenor of their criticism, or difficulties will accumulate upon their hands. But if we suppose the evangelists merely intended to relate that John stood AT, or *in the vicinity of* Jordan, Bethabara, Enon, &c., when he baptized, the statements are all reconciled. We might add to this, that εν is elsewhere rendered *at.* Thus, "the tower εν *at* Siloam"—"εν *at* the right hand of God," Luke xiii, 4; Rom. viii, 34. But it is needless to prolong these remarks.

The second sense of εν, when used in connection with baptism, is properly expressed by our English WITH, denoting the *instrumental cause*, or *means* by which a thing is performed. Thus—"I indeed baptize you εν ὑδατι WITH *water*," not "*in* water," Matt. iii, 11; Luke iii, 16. In this sense the same preposition is elsewhere frequently employed. Thus, (Matt. xxiii, 37,) "Thou shalt love the Lord . . . εν *with* all thy heart, and εν *with* all thy soul, and εν *with* all thy mind."

Luke xiv, 34: "If the salt have lost his savour, εν τινι WITH *what* shall it be seasoned?"

Matt. vi, 29: "Solomon εν *with*, i. e., *by means of*, all his glory was not arrayed like one of these."

The translation of εν, therefore, by *with*, in the connec-

* Matt. iii, 6; Mark i, 4; Luke iii, 3; John i, 28; ii, 23.

tion of Matt. iii, 11, and parallel places, is justified by the *usus loquendi* of that particle, and it is here used to import that it was by the application of water that baptism was effected, without the most distant allusion to the quantity of water used, or to the mode of using it.

A third use of the particle εν, which our subject requires us to notice, is to denote the *efficient cause*, or *agency*, by which a thing is effected. Thus, (Acts i, 5,) "But ye shall be baptized εν BY the Holy Ghost." See also chap. xi, 16. The same sense is attached to this particle, Luke i, 4: "Jesus . . . was led εν BY the spirit into the wilderness." Matthew (ch. i, 4) explains it by ὑπο, BY.* That the Holy Ghost is the efficient agent of spiritual baptism, we are abundantly taught in the Holy Scriptures. And that this was the doctrine specifically taught, in the above passages from the Acts, as well as in Matt. iii, 11 and Luke iii, 16, admits of no reasonable doubt. Still we are presented with the following version of Acts i, 5 "For truly John *immersed in* water; but ye shall be *immersed in* the Holy Ghost," &c. And this, we are gravely informed, is the philological rendering. Doubtless it accords well enough with the philology of those who, in constructing their exegesis, consult the rules of etymology more than the principles of sound theology, or the undeniable facts of history. The doctrine taught by our Saviour, in the passage last mentioned, is plainly this, that, as water was the *instrument* of their outward baptism, which they received at the hands of John Baptist, so the Holy Ghost should be the immediate *agent* of that spiritual and more important baptism to which they were referred by the outward washing. And the particle εν *by* is here used to denote that *agency* which the Holy Ghost should exert upon them, without any allusion to the *mode* of spiritual baptism. The version of our opponents, therefore, as above noticed, not only fails to convey the true sense of the passage, but it gives a palpably false rendering—leading the mind to overlook the grand idea of the text. It represents the Holy Ghost as a passive, inert element, in which the believer is plunged, as a man is plunged in water—than which nothing can be more ab-

* *Vide* Dr. Gerard's Biblical Criticisms, p. 335.

surd in the light of reason, to forbear all comment upon the theological bearing of such a doctrine.

But our opponents pay as little deference to facts as to theology, in their zeal for a literal translation. In describing the mode of the Spirit's baptism, Luke says, (Acts ii, 3,) the Holy Ghost "SAT UPON" the apostles; although our opponents would have it that the apostles were *immersed in* the Holy Ghost.

I will not here, as I at first intended, introduce the question respecting the use of the dative instead of the accusative case, after the active verb βαπτιζω *baptizo*. The argument is too indeterminate to beget any degree of satisfaction in ordinary cases, and I cannot believe that the question at issue hinges on such refinements. Whether the evangelical writers borrowed their use of εν from the Hebrew preposition בְּ *be*, which has the force of the Greek εν, εις, ὑπο, &c., and of the English *in*, *into*, *by*, *with*, &c.; or whether they borrowed their use of that particle from Greek classic usage, is certainly a matter of no importance to the present controversy. An appeal to New Testament usage must finally settle all such disputes. We have shown the use of the particle εν when employed in the New Testament in connection with water baptism, and that it has no bearing whatever upon the question of the *mode* of baptism.

2. Εις *into*, εκ *out of*, απο *from*.—I have placed these prepositions together, and in connection with their primary significations, because it will not be convenient to treat of them separately. It must not be forgotten that they frequently bear other senses different from what are annexed to them above, so that it is not always a conclusive or satisfactory mode of arguing to depend upon their primitive force in a particular connection. It is recorded in Mark i, 9, "Jesus was baptized by John εις *into* the Jordan." This passage presents a solitary example, in the New Testament, of the use of εις with the accusative case after the active verb βαπτιζω *baptizo*, and, philologically, furnishes as good proof of immersion as any passage in the New Testament. Still we are by no means satisfied that it presents a clear case of immersion, and we shall state the ground of our doubts in the following considerations:—

(*a*) This is, as we have already mentioned, a solitary use of εις with the accusative, after the verb *baptize*, where such a construction would affect the question at issue. The dative, with or without εν *in*, is more generally employed, (*vide* Matt. iii, 6 ; Mark i, 5, *et al.*,) not with reference to the *manner*, but to the *means* of baptism. (See the preceding section.)

(*b*) This is plainly an instance of the frequent interchange of Greek particles where εις *into*, is put for εν *in*, or *at*.

(*c*) The passage in question is made to prove immersion only by supposing the Greek word *baptize* to signify immerse *only;* otherwise the particle εις has no force at all in fixing the mode of baptism. This throws the whole controversy back on the significance of the verb *baptize*, which is a manifest abandonment of the whole argument derived from the Greek particle. Indeed, it is quite obvious that the meaning of the verb, and not that of the particle, is, after all, the proper ground of controversy in this passage, for it is the sense of the verb that fixes that of the particle, and not *vice versa*.

(*d*) The sequel intimates that Jesus had not been *into*, but only *to*, the water. Thus it says: "And forthwith ascending απο *from* the water," &c. Ver. 10. Precisely the same language is employed by Matthew, (iii, 16,) although in both cases our English version reads "*out of* the water," which certainly is not the true rendering.

The second and last place where εις *into* occurs in connection with baptism, in a manner to affect the present question, is found in Acts viii, 38: "And they went down both εις *into* the water, both Philip and the eunuch," &c. The circumstance of going *into* the water is urged as proof of immersion. It is true that the more considerate advocates of immersion do not urge this as proof positive of their distinctive theory, but then it is no less true that it is claimed by all as a proof text of immersion, and is usually quoted with great approbation and an air of triumph, on occasions of baptism. But wherein lies the stress of the argument for immersion? Surely not in the circumstance of their going "*into* the water," for that is affirmed of "*both*" of them. Whatever, therefore, is proved from this circumstance in relation to one, must hold equally conclusive with regard to the other. Besides, the act of baptism is said to have taken place *after* they had "both gone down *into* the water," and is described by another word. So far, indeed, is this text from proving the immersion of the eunuch, that it does not necessarily prove that he went further than the margin of the water, i. e., *to* the water. For though it is said "they went down both εις το ὑδωρ," still there can be no philological objection to our reading it thus: "They went down both TO the water," &c. Numerous examples might be here adduced to show that such a rendering would be in entire accordance with Greek usage. A few, however, must suffice. Acts xxvi, 14: "And when we" (Saul and his company) "were all fallen εις *to* the earth;" not *into* the earth. John xi, 38: "Jesus therefore cometh εις *to* (not *into*) the tomb" of Lazarus. John xx, 3–8: "Peter therefore went forth, and that other disciple, and came εις *to* the sepulchre. So they both ran together; and that other disciple did outrun Peter and came first εις *to* the sepulchre, ... yet went he not εις *in*. Then cometh Simon Peter, following him, and went εις *into* the sepulchre .... Then went εις *in* also that other disciple that came first εις *to* the sepulchre." These examples are to the point. Others might be given, but it is not important. Any person who is at all conversant with his Greek Testament may readily satisfy himself as to the use of the prepositions by the New Testament writers. If, therefore, εις το μνημειον means TO *the sepulchre*, and εις την γην means TO *the earth:* the preposition merely denoting the *point to which* the motion is made: so also may εις το ὑδωρ signify TO *the water*, and in the connection of Acts viii, 38, may mean no more than that Philip and the eunuch both went *to the margin of the water*.

We are aware that it will be said, "they both came up εκ *out of* the water," thus implying that they had previously been *into* the water. But it is probable that εκ, *out of*, in this passage, has only the force of απο, *from*. At least such a construction would be in harmony with its *usus loquendi* in the New Testament.

(*a*) It cannot have escaped the observation of the intelligent reader who has perused his Greek Testament with any reference to this point, that εις *into* often stands in contrast with *απο from*, instead of *εκ out of*. Instance passages like the following: "*απο from* city *εις to* city:" "*απο from* Jerusalem *εις to* Jericho:" "The way that goeth down *απο from* Jerusalem *εις to* Gaza," &c. This circumstance we conceive to have great force in settling the controversy about the terms employed to describe the eunuch's baptism: for if *εις eis* is indifferently put in contrast with *απο apo* and *εκ ek*, nothing can be clearer than that it may signify either *to* or *into*, according to the circumstances of the case. So that the far-famed and favourite argument for immersion, drawn from the connection of *εις* and *εκ* with an active verb in Acts viii, 38, falls to the ground. The importance of this argument justifies a few further remarks. It has been argued that the phrase "*from* city *to* city," means "*out of* one city *into* another;" just as the phrase "going *to* Boston" includes the idea of entering *into* that city. Popular usage may, and doubtless often does, include the idea of entering *into* the city or place, when only a motion toward, or an approach *to*, such place is expressed. But the question is not whether, for instance, in the passage, "Jesus went down *εις to* Capernaum," (John ii, 12,) the Saviour did, as a matter of fact, go *into* the city; but whether the force of the preposition necessarily requires us to suppose that he actually entered into the city. Now, we have no doubt that Jesus did enter into the city. But this is not the question. The only question is, "Does the force of the particle *εις* necessarily import such a fact?" Every person must see that it does not; and that if any man would prove that Jesus actually entered into Capernaum at that time, he would find himself obliged to search for other evidence than that afforded by the particle in question. If Jesus had only gone to the gate of Capernaum, it might be said, in Greek phrase, that *κατεβη εις Καπερναουμ he went down* INTO *Capernaum.* If the reader be still in doubt of the truth of our assertion, let him turn to Luke viii, 23. It is there stated that "a storm of wind came down *into* the lake," (*κατεβη . . . εις την λιμνην.*) Yet we know, from facts resulting from natural causes, that the "storm" did not enter *into* the lake, but came only *on* or *to* the lake. In Rev. xiii, 13, the following somewhat remarkable passage occurs: "And he (the beast) doeth great wonders, so that *πυρ ποιη κατα-*

βαινειν εκ του ουρανου εις την γην *he maketh fire come down* FROM *heaven* ON (or TO) *the earth.*" Here the prepositions εις and εκ are put in contrast, and both stand connected with an active verb, exactly similar, so far as the present criticism would require, to the passage of Acts viii, 38, 39; and yet in this text cited from the Apocalypse, they have only the force of the English prepositions *from* and *to*. Now, apply this last example to the case in hand. If it be good New Testament Greek to say, "he maketh fire come down εκ του ουρανου εις την γην FROM *heaven* TO *the earth*, or ON *the earth*," then, beyond all controversy, it is also in accordance with good usage to say of Philip and the eunuch, "they both κατεβησαν εις το ὑδωρ *went down* TO *the water*," and, after baptism, ανεβησαν εκ του ὑδατος, *they ascended* FROM *the water*.

We have already observed, that both Matthew and Mark use απο *from*, instead of εκ *out of*, when they describe the act of our Saviour, in leaving the water after baptism. They simply say, he came *from* the water. The passage therefore, in question, is a solitary case in the history of baptism, where εκ is put in contrast with εις, denoting motion *to*, and *from*, *or into*, and *out of*, the water of baptism. This circumstance, to say the least, renders their testimony to the doctrine of immersion extremely unsatisfactory. But, furthermore, it is well known that εκ is often used to denote simply the *point from which* a motion is made. Thus: "Howbeit there came other boats εκ *from* Tiberias." "Get thee εκ *from* thy kindred." "Who shall deliver me εκ *from* the body of this death," &c. John vi, 23; Acts vii, 3; Rom. vii, 24. It would, therefore, be every way consistent with the general use of the prepositions in question, to adopt our translation, and read, "And they went down both *to* the water .... and when they were come up *from* the water," &c. Besides, it should be remembered, that the act of coming out of the water, as well as going into the water, is affirmed of both Philip and the eunuch, and has no more to do with the act of baptism than with their riding in the chariot. The Greek prepositions, employed in this narration have the same latitude of meaning as our English *into* and *from*, or *out of*. And, in popular language, a person goes *into* the water when he enters to the depth of six inches; and, when he recedes from that point, he comes *out of* the water. Professor Ripley here proposes a question that is, indeed, singular enough. It is, whether the preposition εις indicates, that they went far enough into the water for immersion. How such a question is to be determined satisfactorily, I am unable to judge. Certain it is, that philology can never settle it. But, while the subject of the eunuch's baptism is before the reader, I will adduce a few considerations, which may tend to corroborate the foregoing statements, and show that an immersion was not probably practised on this occasion.

(*a*) The *place* where the eunuch was baptized was "*desert.*" Vide ver. 26. The word *desert*, in Scripture, sometimes means a barren waste, and sometimes merely a country place, in contradistinction of a city. The former is probably the true sense, in this connection. For when the angel said to Philip, "Arise, and go toward the south, unto the way that goeth down from Jerusalem to Gaza, *which is desert*," if he intended merely a country place, the description would have been trifling. It was already understood, as a matter of course, by Philip, that the place was rural; but that it was a desert proper, might not have been so obvious. But to find a body of water in a desert proper, sufficient for immersion, would be strange indeed!

(*b*) *The body of water itself*, in which the eunuch was baptized. The account says, "They came επι τι υδωρ *to* SOME *water*." No more or less can be made of Luke's statement. But what is *some* water? How much? The pronoun τι (*some*, *any*) has sometimes a diminutive sense, and so here. "They came to *a little* water," &c. Our English reads "a *certain* water;" as if our translators had in view a particular watering-place for travellers or caravans. And so the eunuch, when he saw it, exclaimed with evident emotion, Ιδου 'υδωρ, *Behold water.* He does not say how much water, but seemed a little surprised and pleased to find any water in such a place. Indeed, it was in this vicinity—in the valley of Gerar—the valley in which, according to our most accurate maps, the city of Gaza stands—that Abraham and Isaac were obliged to dig wells, to procure water for their flocks. It was here that "the herdmen of Gerar did strive with Isaac's herdmen, saying, The water is ours." It could not have been far from this place where Philip baptized the eunuch. We sometimes, in Scripture, read of "springs in the desert," boiling out of the ground, (Gen. xxvi, 19,) and it was probably such a body of water in which the eunuch was baptized. Whence, then, has arisen all this fancied abundance of water sufficient for an immersion, where herdmen would contend for a "*well*" to water their flocks? The reasonable presumption is against it. We want more proof.

(*c*) Whether or not it may be considered as having much force in the present connection, I cannot forbear recalling the reader's attention to the phrase, "they went down *into* the water." It would seem that this phrase is supposed to be a natural indication of immersion. So also, when our Saviour went "to the Jordan" to be baptized, the circumstance of his going to a river to be baptized, as also that of John's choosing a river to baptize in, is supposed to indicate the practice of immersion. But, certainly, it is altogether a fanciful argument—an argument that has no force but in the imagination of its author. We wish only to refer the reader, in this place, to a passage recorded in Tobit vi, 2. The passage runs thus: "And when the young man κατεβη περικλυσασθαι *went down to wash himself all round*," &c. That is, he went down to the river Tigris to wash himself all round, by *casting water over his body*, as the word imports; and that he went *into* the water is evident from the sequel, for he was attacked by a "fish," which he "drew to land," ver. 3. We do not suppose the story itself to be true, but it is, nevertheless, equally in point for our purpose. Here then is a case where a young man went down into a river of water for the purpose of purifying himself, and although the case itself allowed immersion, and the heat of the climate might seem to determine in favour of such a mode of cleansing, still, he *went down into the river* to purify himself *by casting water all over his body*. So also Philip might have gone *down into the water*, not to immerse, but *sprinkle* the eunuch. At least, it may edify our Baptist brethren to know that it is said a man once *went down into a river*, in a hot climate, to purify himself by *casting water all round his body*.

In concluding our remarks under this head, we wish to apprise the reader that a cursory and hasty perusal of this chapter will not be likely to beget a very high state of satisfaction in his mind, as to the real merits of the argument drawn from the Greek prepositions, unless he is already somewhat accustomed to philological investigations. The argument itself, indeed, is not deep. It lies on the surface. A habit of close and correct observation of the meaning of words will render the above citations and remarks fully comprehensible without a knowledge of the Greek. For, while we have endeavoured to exhibit every important phase of the subject, and to enter into such detail as to be able to draw out and explain the several points which we judged to have any important bearing; still, we have striven so to simplify the whole, and to retrench unnecessary and unimportant views, as to disencumber the whole, as far as possible, from that embarrassment which would be likely to accrue to the mere English reader. But if, after the argument shall have been mastered, he find that it has no great force, *pro* or *con*, in the question at issue, he will have exactly attained to our settled opinion on the subject; always remembering that, while the force of the prepositions determines neither the one side nor the other of this controversy, the bearing of their aggregate and almost uniform evidence is manifestly against the hypothesis of exclusive immersion. If it be said we have bestowed too much attention upon a branch of the argument which, after all, is indeterminate, we must beg to assure the reader that the posture of the controversy required all this at our hands. Besides, it should not be forgotten that the evidence which the subject admits is not demonstrative, but cumulative. No single argument is sufficient to decide the whole question and to establish general and satisfactory convictions; but we must patiently build our conclusions upon various data, brought together from different sources and compared, deriving from each one its tribute of support to the establishment of the general result.

CHAPTER VI.

CHRISTIAN EXAMPLES.

1. At this stage of the argument it is proper to inquire into the practice of the early Christians, with a view to determine the specific bearing of their example on the question at issue. On this subject I feel constrained to depart from that popular opinion which is ever prone to pay a blind veneration to the practices of early Christians. I feel incapable of appreciating the views of those who congratulate themselves in a fancied pre-eminence of virtue, or of orthodoxy, merely because they find a precedent to their conduct, or a sanction to their belief, in the history of the opinions and practices of the primitive church. It must be acceded that those who enjoyed the personal instructions of our Saviour and his apostles possessed, from opportunities of private conversation, advantages from which we, at this distance of time, are necessarily excluded; advantages which would seem to invest their example with a degree of authority over the faith of all succeeding generations of the church. Still, it will not have escaped observation, that these advantages on their part are more than counterbalanced by our superior state of moral and intellectual improvement, as the facts in our comparative histories abundantly demonstrate. The early churches were formed from Jewish or Gentile converts, who had alike been bred in the vilest superstitions. The potency of their early education was felt long after their espousals to Christianity. Even under the pruning hand and vigilant eye of Paul, there sprang up, in the bosom of the church, the rank weeds of a barbarous religion. The solemn ordinance of the holy supper was turned into a bacchanalian revel! Endless disputes, on points of no importance, were warmly prosecuted—disputes which are generated only by superstitious and ignorant minds. So prone were they to abuse the institutions of Christianity, that Paul, in his letter to the Corinthians, (chap. i, 14, 15,) gives utterance to this strange declaration: "I thank God that I baptized none of you but Crispus and Gaius; *lest*

any should say that I baptized in mine own name." But if we pass into the second and third centuries, we shall find a state of things far more deplorable. Here the true genius of the Oriental philosophy, mingling with a variety of vulgar superstitions, began to display itself. Who can forget the ridiculous ceremonies at baptism, of exorcism, unction, giving salt and milk to the candidate, attiring him in a snow-white robe, and crowning him with an evergreen? Who, I say, can forget all this, and persuade himself that these very Christians, so prolific of superstitious refinings and innovations upon the rite of baptism in every thing else, did yet, in regard to the *mode* of baptism, remain infallible?

But the appeal is carried up to apostolic practice; and here, doubtless, the weight of the argument from church history mainly hinges. Let us not, therefore, be misunderstood. We do not suppose that either primitive or apostolic practice could, *from the nature of the case*, decide this controversy. We have already observed that the verb *baptize* is a *generic* term, like our verb *purify*, or *wash*, and therefore comprehends under it a variety of particular modes of ablution. Whatever, therefore, may have been the precise mode of baptism practised in the early church, it can never constitute any obligatory rule of faith or practice for us, so long as the command to be baptized is not *specific* as to the mode. The climate of Palestine, and also of many of the other countries where the gospel was preached by the apostles, is warm. This rendered bathings frequent; and this latter circumstance, of itself, might naturally be supposed to have begotten in them a predilection for immersion, even though it were not required, but only allowed, by the original command. But in a more rigorous climate, where bathings are unfrequent, and attended with greater inconvenience and exposure, a diverse propensity would naturally exist. The practice of the church, therefore, in any age, setting aside denominational prejudices, would be likely to shape itself, in general, according to the climate and the corresponding habits of the people. There is more weight, I am persuaded, in these remarks, than a prejudiced mind would be willing, readily, to concede. The aquatic habits of a Greenlander and an Otaheitan,—I mean their habits in relation to bathing, swimming, diving, &c., although respectively engendered by climate,—are totally different. And when we say that a Greenlander, when left to the direction of his own choice in relation to the mode of baptism, would feel a natural bias to the practice of aspersion instead of dipping, and that an inhabitant of the Society Isles would be naturally inclined to an opposite choice to that of his shivering brother, we pay no more than a reasonable tribute of respect to the prejudices of climate. And when we consider that these prejudices are not only innocent and unavoidable, but highly salutary to the health and comfort of the body, we cannot but admire the wisdom and characteristic goodness of the Author of our religion, in so graduating his command, touching the duty of baptism, as to harmonize with the various conditions of his great family. If, therefore, it should be found, upon examination, that the apostolic churches did practise immersion, still, if the foregoing remarks be correct, that circumstance can be sufficiently accounted for on other ground than that of a specific command of Christ.*

2. But, from an examination of all the instances of baptism recorded in the New Testament, we are far from being satisfied that immersion was uniformly practised; so far, indeed, that in many cases the circumstances seem to preclude all idea of immersion. Instance, the baptism of Saul. Acts ix, 18, and xxii, 16. The account simply states that he was required to "*stand up*" (ανιστημι) and be baptized. Lydia was indeed baptized by "a river;" still, nothing can be inferred from this circumstance in favour of an immersion, inasmuch as the apostles went to the river, not to baptize, but to pray. Acts xvi, 13, 15. Peter, when he would baptize Cornelius and his friends, made no proposition to leave the spot; no preparations are made for an immersion; but he modestly inquires, Can any man forbid water that these should not be baptized which have received the Holy Ghost as well as we? (Acts x, 47,) i. e., in plain English etiquette,—"Will some one present be kind enough to fetch some water, that these may be baptized?" The language of

* See note H.

Peter deserves a little further notice. The verb κωλυω *forbid*, implies, in this connection, as in other places, the power (sometimes including the right) of imposing a prohibition on the thing or act specified. Thus: Num. xi, 28, "Joshua said, My lord Moses, *forbid* them," (i. e., Eldad and Medad, from prophesying.)

Mark ix, 39: "But Jesus said, *Forbid* him not."

Mark x, 14: "Suffer little children, and *forbid* them not, to come unto me."

Luke vi, 29: "He that taketh thy cloak, *forbid* not to take thy coat also."

Nothing is more obvious than that the prohibitive phrase in these passages fully recognises the power of granting or withholding at option; and this power is also clearly recognised in the persons to whom Peter's address was made. Had they possessed no such power as the one in question, the appeal of Peter on this occasion would have been trifling and senseless. For instance, if it had been the intention of Peter to repair to some public pool, a pond, or a river, in order to immerse the candidates, it is manifest that the persons present would have had no power of interference to prohibit such an act. And in such a case it would have been senseless to inquire, "Can any man present prohibit the use of a *public* water that these should not be baptized?" &c. But if the apostle intended to baptize the Gentile converts on the spot, and by aspersion, and consequently needed only a vessel of water to be brought in; a service which it was certainly in the power of any one present to *grant* or *withhold*—it was with the greatest propriety of language—which at the same moment evinced true delicacy of sentiment, combined with the most disciplined courtesy—that he couched his request for a vessel of water in that interrogatory appeal, "Can any man forbid water that these should not be baptized which have received the Holy Ghost as well as we?" These words of Peter, therefore, when rightly understood, present a singular difficulty to the theory of exclusive immersion; and, so far as we now can judge, are irreconcilable with it.*

The baptism of the Philippian jailer was performed in

* See note I.

his own house, in the jail. The jailer could not have quitted the jail, during the night, in company with the apostles, as some suppose, without a breach of fidelity, and a forfeiture of his life to the laws of his country. The guilt or innocence of the apostles could not have affected his duty as jailer, which was, not to award to them the sentence of the law, but to immure them safely within the walls of the prison, until that sentence should either be finally executed, or revoked. But Paul himself virtually affirms they had not been out, in his refusal to be "thrust out privily." This refusal would have been urged with a poor grace, and with no very scrupulous regard for consistency if they had already been "out privily" during the night preceding, in quest of a pond or a river of water wherein to have immersed the jailer. But, as if to remove all difficulties and silence all controversy, resort is had to the old and convenient hypothesis; an hypothesis which has peculiarly befriended our opponents on other occasions of need, viz., that there was, in all probability, a private *bath* in the jail which served them on this occasion for a place to immerse. It is unfortunate, however, for this hypothesis, that Philippi lay under latitude 41° north, in a climate where baths are little used; and that the person supposed to have furnished the bath on this occasion was a *jailer* and *not* a gentleman.

The account of Luke (Acts ii) goes to prove that three thousand persons were baptized and added to the church on the day of Pentecost; but does not specify the mode. If, however, we attend critically to all the circumstances of the occasion, we shall find the weight of evidence to lie against the idea of their being immersed. Proceed we then to notice—

1. *Their time for baptism.* Peter began to preach "about the third hour of the day;" i. e., nine o'clock, A. M. Ver. 15. Judging from the nature of the occasion and from the drift of his discourse, as given by Luke, he continued at least an hour. Luke says, "With many other words Peter testified and exhorted," &c. Ver. 40. Peter's sermon being ended, the converts must be selected from the multitude, and questioned as to their faith and experience. This was not the work of a moment. If they were immersed, they must have been provided with a change

of raiment. This must have occasioned great delay. For when the multitude came together, at first, it was with some confusion and no expectation of Christian baptism or conversion. Then, apartments for men and women must be procured adjacent to the place of baptism. Before all these preliminaries could be disposed of with decency, it must have been afternoon; say one o'clock. The Jewish day closed at six P. M., and Luke says they were baptized and added to the church "the same day." Consequently they had but five hours left, in which to perform their labour. But if the twelve apostles baptized three thousand persons in five hours, they must have averaged for each apostle, two hundred and fifty; which would be, for each, fifty persons per hour, or five persons in every six minutes. This, I need not say, would have been impossible. But if the apostles baptized by aspersion, they thereby saved much time, and might have performed the task with comparative ease. I know it has been said that the seventy disciples aided on this occasion. But where is the proof that they were commissioned to baptize? It is not found in Luke x, where we are furnished with an account of their call and commission. The authority to baptize was one of those important functions originally invested in the apostles only. It was, at first, distinctively, an apostolic prerogative: subsequently, they transmitted this power to others, whom they judged men of established reputation for integrity, piety, and understanding, who felt moved by the Holy Ghost to take the office of the ministry. "Lay hands hastily on no man," was an apostolic maxim in reference to priestly ordination. 1 Tim. v, 22. But we have no account of the apostles having ordained any person to the work of the ministry during the ten days that intervened between their commission and the day of Pentecost. We do know, however, that our Saviour himself commanded them to suspend the exercise of all their apostolic functions until the descent of the Holy Ghost, which took place on Pentecost. Luke xxiv, 49; Acts i, 7, 8.

Besides, Luke seems very explicit in giving us to understand, that, if the seventy were present at all, they were present only as private individuals, and took no part in the transactions of the day. In ver. 14, he says, "But Peter, standing up with the eleven," &c. But why not mention the seventy, if they also took a part? Certain it is, if they took so considerable a part on the occasion as to assist in baptizing, this partiality of Luke is rather unaccountable, especially as he professes to be explicit.

2. *They had no place for the immersion of such a multitude.* The brook Kidron, (Cedron,) which ran along the east side of the city, was, at its maximum, but a turbid stream,—always dry in the hot season, and it was now about June; so that its waters must have been failing fast. Besides, soon after it issued from its source, it received, from a common sewer, all the blood and ordure of the sacrifices, and the common filth, both of the temple and the northern section of the city. This alone would have rendered it unfit for baptism. As to public pools, we have account of only two, Bethesda and Siloam. The latter was three-fourths of a mile from the spot where the apostles had preached. We have no account of their marching off three thousand persons, with all the multitude of spectators that would naturally follow, this distance. Besides, their time would have failed them. Bethesda lay within the precincts of the temple, and was used in the temple service for the washing of sacrifices, &c. It was, therefore, in the hands of the priests, the avowed and mortal enemies of Christ and his apostles; and I believe it will not be pretended that the dignitaries of the Jewish church, after their recent hard-earned and diabolical triumph over Christ and his followers; their concerted and undisguised hostility to the Christian name; their settled and incurable malice, now newly festered by the alarming success of the apostles,—it will not, I say, be pretended that, under these circumstances, they would have peaceably surrendered their claims to the use of Bethesda, in order to have accommodated the apostles of Christ with a place for Christian baptism; particularly, as the time for the evening sacrifice came on between three and four o'clock, P. M., when the use of the pool was always needed; and it being now Pentecost, and the sacrifices numerous and important, its use would have been wholly indispensable. In addition to all this, (if any additional remark be necessary,) both Siloam and Bethesda were probably of inadequate dimensions to admit twelve men,

(much less the seventy disciples,) for the purpose of im mersing. In the porches of Bethesda, the sick constantly reclined, waiting to receive the benefit of its healing waters. Where, then, did the apostles immerse the three thousand converts? Are there not difficulties attending that hypothesis?

CHAPTER VII.

FIGURATIVE LANGUAGE.

SEC. I.—GENERAL ARGUMENT FROM ANALOGY.

We come now to treat of an important branch of the general argument. The inquirer after truth will scarcely fail to be convinced of the general correctness of our position, in proportion to the intelligence and candour with which he investigates the following argument. This we predicate, not so much of the presumption that we shall present the subject in its happiest light, as of the intrinsic force of the argument, when once it is fully and clearly received in the understanding.

There is no controversy among Christians, as to whether baptism be emblematical; nor is there any dispute in regard to the fact, that outward baptism is an emblem of inward purity. All agree that baptism with water derives its entire efficacy from its emblematical character, while none deny that it also signifies *purity of heart.* But while the Baptists maintain that baptism is designed to adumbrate inward purity, as procured through the death, burial, and resurrection of our Saviour; we hold, in common with all Pædo-baptist churches, that it is a simple and beautiful emblem of the Spirit's agency upon our hearts, operating as the efficient cause of inward holiness. They regard baptism as a recognition of the death, burial, and resurrection of Jesus Christ, as the procuring cause of moral purity; but we regard the ordinance as a recognition of a divine agency upon our hearts, "working salvation." This distinction I have been the more careful to state, as it forms the basis of important conclusions. The Baptists, regarding baptism as a recognition of a burial and resurrection, with strict propriety, insist upon exclusive immersion. Professor Ripley says, "It is most readily granted, that if purification be the *only* thing represented by baptism, then there is by no means so much need of opposing a departure from immersion. But something else is also intended to be represented, which renders immersion necessary; and, as the purification represented in baptism is purification obtained through the death and resurrection of Christ, it is surely not surprising that the apostle should teach that in baptism there is a recognition of this death and resurrection, and of our obligation to die unto sin as Christ died for sin; and to rise to a new and holy life as Christ arose to a new and glorious life. Conceding then that sprinkling, or pouring, or washing may have a significancy, it does not follow that it has all the significancy that the baptismal rite was intended to possess."*

I have made this quotation to show, on good authority, what use is made in this controversy of the construction which the Baptists have fixed on the mystical import of baptism. It is plain from this, that they could abate the strictness of their theory, if it could be made to appear that their views of the emblematical sense of baptism were erroneous. If they err here, "then" (we quote their own words) "there is BY NO MEANS *so much need of opposing a departure from immersion.*" It is conceded, too, that "sprinkling, pouring, and washing may have a significancy." All this, to be sure, looks like an approximation to a friendly coalition of sentiment. The field of controversy appears much narrower than before, which encourages the hope of a final reconciliation on some common Scriptural ground of faith.

But here it is of the last importance to the issue of this controversy, that the reader settle it in his own mind, once for all, that the two opinions above stated, in regard to the mystical signification of baptism, cannot both be correct. If baptism represent a burial and resurrection, it cannot, in the nature of things, at the same time be a lively emblem of the *agency* of the Holy Ghost upon our hearts. Two transactions, so totally diverse in their forms, could not be

* Examination of Stuart, p. 123.

adumbrated by one and the same act. These two prototypes, therefore, would necessarily require diverse forms of administration of the consecrating element, in order to create that similitude on which the very notion of an *emblem* is founded. On this subject Dr. John Dick has justly observed, "It is by no means probable that God would speak of his own operations in one way, and symbolically represent them in a different way; that he should promise to sprinkle or pour out his Spirit upon us, and, to confirm this promise, would command us to be plunged into water. There would be no analogy in this case between the promise and the seal; and the discrepance would give rise to a confusion of ideas."* It is evident, therefore, that whichever of the two views already mentioned be substantiated, the opposite must, of necessity, fall to the ground. We hold, in common with all Christian churches, that regeneration and sanctification are changes wrought in the moral man by the power of the Holy Ghost. And that, in the great scheme of redemption, if the death of Christ were necessary, as a government act, to vindicate before the universe the moral rectitude of the divine Lawgiver in the public overtures of pardon to the guilty; the agency of the Holy Ghost is no less necessary in order to render that atonement available or efficacious in the personal salvation of the sinner. The ground we take, then, in this discussion is, that baptism is the symbol of the regenerating and sanctifying agency of the Holy Ghost, and that, therefore, the *form* of baptism should be adapted to represent the *manner* in which the Holy Spirit bestows his influences upon the heart.

If we scan the figurative language of Scripture, we shall find that two distinct ideas are comprehended under the general ceremonial use of water, namely, *regeneration* and *purification* of heart. The one is founded on the *resuscitating*, and the other on the *purifying* qualities of water. This distinction will be observable in the process of the argument. In order to give somewhat of a classification, or rather, a division of our thoughts, we shall,

1. Inquire into the ancient Jewish import of the ceremonial use of water. It seems almost superfluous to en-

* Theology, vol ii, p. 377.

large upon this part of the argument, so plain is it to every reader of the Old Testament. The whole history of bodily ablutions among the Jews speaks but one language, and yields a united testimony to one point. We shall content ourselves with a few passages, and the reader may extend the line of citations *ad libitum.*

David says, Psa. xxvi, 6, "I will wash my hands in [token of] INNOCENCY." Psa. li, 2, 7: "*Wash* me thoroughly *from mine iniquity*, and *cleanse* me from my sin." . . . "*Purge* me with hyssop, and I shall be CLEAN: *wash* me, and I shall be *whiter than snow.*"

Isa. i, 16: "*Wash* you, make you CLEAN; put away the *evil* of your doings." Isa. iv, 14: "O Jerusalem! *wash* thy heart from WICKEDNESS."

Evidently, in these instances, the outward washing represented *inward purity.* These passages also accord with the universal tenor of the Old Testament. But the ancient oracles are more explicit. They describe the *manner* in which the purifying and refreshing graces of the Spirit are bestowed, by the pouring or sprinkling of water, either ceremonially or otherwise.

Isa. xliv, 3: "I will POUR WATER upon him that is thirsty, and floods upon the dry ground; I will POUR MY SPIRIT upon thy seed, and my blessing upon thine offspring." What a lively—what a beautiful emblem! "I WILL POUR WATER . . . I WILL POUR MY SPIRIT."

Ezek. xxxvi, 25, 27: "Then will I SPRINKLE CLEAN WATER upon you, and ye shall be CLEAN; from all your filthiness and from all your idols will I cleanse you. . . . And I will PUT MY SPIRIT WITHIN YOU," &c. Here also the Spirit's influences are associated with the sprinkling of water.

Hos. x, 12: "Seek the Lord till he come and RAIN *righteousness* upon you." Hos. xiv, 5: "I will be as the DEW unto Israel."

In these last citations from Hosea the prophet beautifully represents the *refreshing* influences of the Spirit by a metaphor taken from the falling of *dew* and *rain.*

Psa. lxxii, 6: "He [Messiah] shall *come down* like RAIN upon the mown grass." "And what image," says Bishop Horne, "can convey a better idea of those most beneficial and blessed effects, which followed the descent of the Son of God upon the earth, and that of the Spirit at the day of Pentecost."*

Joel ii, 28, 29: "And it shall come to pass afterward, that I will POUR OUT my Spirit upon all flesh." . . . "And upon the servants, and upon the handmaids, in those days will I POUR OUT my Spirit." Comp. Acts ii, 16–20.

These passages will suffice to show the opinion of the ancient Jews in regard to the import of the emblematical use of water; and also in regard to the most significant *mode* of using the water of ablution. They also clearly designate the manner of the Spirit's operations. It is hardly necessary to add, that the idea is at the furthest remove imaginable from that of a burial and resurrection.

2. This ancient sense attached to the ceremonial use of water is fully corroborated and sustained by the typical import of John's baptism. The baptism of John was a visible token of reformation on the part of the recipient. But, in addition to this, it was also manifestly typical of the dispensation of the Holy Ghost which was ushered in with so much power and grace on the day of Pentecost. Hence, when John baptized with water, he exhorted the people to look forward through the shadowy medium of that outward ordinance to the more important baptism of the Holy Ghost. The prospective and typical relation of John's baptism to that of the Holy Spirit is fully established by the following passages:—

Matt. iii, 11: "I indeed baptize you with water; . . . but he [Christ] shall baptize you with the Holy Ghost." *Vide* also Mark i, 8; Luke iii, 16.

Acts i, 5: "John truly baptized with water; but ye shall be baptized with the Holy Ghost not many days hence." These are the words of our Saviour to his apostles just previous to the ascension. The object was to revive and continue, in the minds of the apostles and disciples, that expectation of the effusion of the Spirit that John the Baptist had at first inspired by the exhortations above alluded to. In order to this, he reverts to their attention to John's baptism, to which they had already submitted, and to its typical character, and then renews the promise of its fulfilment in the dispensation of the Holy

* Commentary on Psalms.

Ghost. So Peter also, when he saw the Holy Ghost descend upon the household of Cornelius, felt his mind to be instantly drawn, retrospectively, to the promise of the Saviour. Speaking of that event, he says, "Then remembered I the word of the Lord, how that he said, John indeed baptized with water; but ye shall be baptized with the Holy Ghost," Acts xi, 16; comp. chap. x, 44. But why associate thus John's baptism with that of the Holy Ghost, unless there be a mystical connection between the two? The above passages clearly establish such connection. Here, again, we pause, to give the argument its just weight and bearing. John's baptism represented the purifying and renovating agency of the Holy Ghost. It was not merely a *symbol*—it was a *type* or *image* of the latter. And as it is always required that there be a fit application of the type to the antitype, so also in this instance. Do we ask, then, What was the mode of John's baptism? The answer is at hand; and it is involved in the inquiry, What was the mode of the Spirit's baptism? For if the baptism of John typified the baptism of the Holy Ghost, there must be a *resemblance* between the two, so that a knowledge of the *form* of one would lead to a knowledge of the *form* of the other. This view of the subject will not be objected to by any person who is acquainted with the nature of a *type;* nor can it be overthrown but by subverting the established relation which subsists between a type and its antitype. But, in relation to the mode of the Spirit's baptism, we have already (in a former chapter) had occasion to remark that it was a "*pouring forth,*" a "*descending upon,*" a "*sitting upon,*" &c. We ask, therefore, Could such an act of the Holy Ghost be adumbrated by plunging a man in water? Would not the *pouring out* or *sprinkling* of water upon him be a more expressive emblem? It is needless to dwell upon an argument so plain. Nor will the force of it be shuffled off by such miserable attempts as appear in the new-fangled version of our Testament, where we find Acts i, 5, and cognate passages, distorted so as to read, "John *immersed in water;* but ye shall be *immersed in the Holy Ghost.*" But this also has been noticed in a former chapter. Thus have we shown, we trust to the satisfaction of the candid reader, that the ancient church of God, up to the time of Christ, had always regarded bodily ablutions, and emblematical uses of water, as expressive of that inward purity, and regeneration, produced by the agency of the Holy Ghost, and were total strangers to the modern doctrine, that ceremonial washing imports a burial and resurrection. I am aware, however, that our Baptist brethren take the ground, that the doctrine that ceremonial washing signifies a burial, &c., is a doctrine which belongs peculiarly to the Christian dispensation. But, of this there is no proof. And certainly analogy is against it. The idea, moreover, is wholly unnatural and arbitrary. But,

3. We inquire into the New Testament views of baptism. The object of this inquiry is to ascertain whether our Saviour and his apostles taught that ceremonial washing, or, in other words, baptism, is a symbol of the purifying and regenerating influences of the Holy Ghost; that is, whether the Old and New Testament doctrines, in regard to the emblematical sense of ceremonial ablution, accord. The following passages will serve to elucidate the New Testament argument on this subject:—

John iii, 5: "Except a man be born of water and of the Spirit, he cannot enter into the kingdom of God." Whether our Lord alludes in this place, distinctively, to Christian baptism, has been matter of dispute, and is not important to our argument. We may suppose our Lord here to allude to Christian baptism, or we may suppose him to allude to all outward ceremonial washings, as such —Jewish or Christian. As if he had said, "Except a man be born [not only] of water, [which, as the mere emblem, is the less important, but also] of the Spirit, he cannot enter into the kingdom of God."

Acts ii, 38: "Be baptized every one of you . . . and ye shall receive the gift of the Holy Ghost." Here, Christian baptism stands associated with "the gift of the Holy Ghost," in a manner clearly to indicate its mystical relation to the latter.

Acts x, 47: "Can any man forbid water that these should not be baptized, which have received the Holy Ghost as well as we?" It should be observed that Peter urged the propriety of their baptism on the ground that they had already "received the Holy Ghost."

Acts xix, 2, 3: Paul said to the Ephesian disciples, "Have ye received the Holy Ghost since ye believed? And they said unto him, We have not so much as heard whether there be any Holy Ghost. And he said unto them, Unto what, then, were ye baptized?" The words *εις τι into what*, in the last clause, refer to the *faith* or *doctrine* which they professed at baptism. As if Paul had said, "Into what (or in respect of what) profession of faith were ye baptized?" Paul was evidently astonished at the ignorance of these disciples, and perplexed to know the cause. It is worthy of special remark, however, that, finding them ignorant of the effusion of the Holy Ghost, he instantly, and, indeed, very justly, questions the validity of their baptism. As if he had said, "What! are ye so ignorant of Christianity as not to have ever heard of the effusion of the Holy Ghost? Unto what profession of faith, then, were ye baptized? How could you have received Christian baptism, understandingly, and still have remained in ignorance of this all-important doctrine, which is shadowed forth and signified thereby?" All, however, was explained when Paul was informed that these disciples had only received "John's baptism." They were, probably, still looking forward in prospect of the gift of the Holy Ghost, as John exhorted them, (Matt. iii, 11,) or, possibly they were still ignorant of the real nature of the doctrine. From this scrap of history, we are plainly taught, that when outward baptism (I mean Christian baptism) does not teach the doctrine, and inculcate upon the disciple the necessity and duty of receiving this inward washing and gift of the Holy Ghost, it is, by the word of God, meaningless and void.

Acts xxii, 16: Ananias saith to Saul, "Arise and be baptized, and *wash away thy sins*, calling on the name of the Lord." 1 Cor. vi, 11: "But ye are washed... by the Spirit of our God." Eph. v, 26: Christ gave himself for the church, "that he might sanctify and cleanse it by the washing of water by the word." Heb. x, 22: "Having our hearts sprinkled from an evil conscience, and our bodies washed with pure water." In all these passages it is plain that water, ceremonially applied to the body, represents the cleansing operations of the Holy Ghost upon the heart.

Titus iii, 5: "He saved us, by the *washing of regeneration*, and *renewing of the Holy Ghost*."

I have placed this last quotation by itself, and lastly, because it merits particular attention; and I deem it of sufficient authority to settle our opinion on this subject. Baptism is here denominated, "the *washing* of regeneration." That is, the washing that stands as the outward sign and seal of regeneration. This is, obviously, the purport of the phrase. The "washing" stands conjoined with the "renewing of the Holy Ghost" in a manner to evince its true emblematical character.

With respect to the *manner* of the Spirit's operations upon the heart, in addition to what has already been said, it may be proper to notice another class of texts. When our Lord would bestow the graces of the Spirit upon the apostles, "He BREATHED ON THEM, and said unto them, Receive ye the Holy Ghost," John xx, 22. He did not *immerse* them into the Holy Ghost. So when the apostles afterward communicated the full power and privilege of the gospel kingdom to believers: "THEY LAID THEIR HANDS ON THEM, [in token of the manner of the Spirit's communication,] and they received the Holy Ghost," Acts viii, 17. The same form was observed when any peculiar power, or privilege of a spiritual or ecclesiastical nature, was to be conferred on any individual. Acts xiii, 3; 1 Tim. iv, 14; Heb. vi, 2, *et al.*

Without attempting any further adduction of evidence in support of our position, we might here pause, and, waiving for the present the allusions of Rom. vi, 4, and Col. ii, 12, require proof of the opposite hypothesis. Where is the emblematical use of water conjoined with the death, burial, and resurrection of Christ, so as to authorize the doctrine of exclusive immersion on the ground of the mystical import of baptism? The passages from Romans and Colossians admit of an interpretation opposite to that insisted on by the Baptists; and under these circumstances, they will never convince those who are acquainted with the rules of Biblical interpretation, that those mooted texts are of sufficient authority to counterbalance and nullify the whole argument drawn from analogy. Indeed, it is difficult to comprehend upon what ground of consistency their professors in theology can advance their position, with respect to these texts, and shelter themselves under an appeal to the laws of Biblical interpretation. It cannot be denied, or evaded, that if baptism be an emblem of a burial and resurrection, it cannot, at the same time, represent the effusion of the Holy Ghost. We have, then, arrived at this new and important (and alarming) discovery in the science of sacred hermeneutics, viz., that the authority of two texts, wherein one and the same allusion occurs, in figurative style, and which may admit of a different interpretation, is yet sufficient to establish a new and extraordinary doctrine—a doctrine of which we hear nothing in other parts of the Bible, and against which the usage of all antiquity bears a uniform testimony.

But we shall abide the decisions to which we are conducted by antique usage, which has never been either contradicted or impaired. We cannot allow an innovation upon the ancient and established meaning of the emblematical use of water, for which there is not only no necessary demand, but which alters in so important and vital respects the aspect of New Testament doctrines and allusions.

If, therefore, according to the general analogy of Scripture, water be used ceremonially, as an emblem of the purifying and regenerating operations of the Holy Spirit; and if God has uniformly spoken of the latter as being *poured out* upon men—as *falling upon*—as *sitting upon* them, &c.; and has also signified it, symbolically, by the *falling of dew*—by the *descent of rain*—by the *pouring out of water*—by the *sprinkling of water*—by Christ's *breathing upon the disciples*—by the "*laying on of hands;*" and, if to this general, emblematical sense of ceremonial ablutions, accord the particular teachings of the New Testament in regard to Christian baptism;—it follows, that, by the sanction of all Jewish usage—by the analogy of water and spiritual baptism—and by the common law of interpretation of all symbolical rites—the water of baptism should be applied by SPRINKLING OR POURING. And here, candid reader, pause and review the argument. Let ridicule and low wit be left to the disingenuous and to the ignorant. Start not—falter not at the sound of words. Have courage to think—to deliberate—to determine. Have candour to confess. You will not appreciate the entire bearing of the foregoing remarks by a single perusal, unless you have given the subject an investigation at some previous time.

Thousands of intelligent and conscientious Christians repose their faith on this rational and Scriptural ground. Etymology is a science which often becomes so abstruse as to render its deductions altogether unsatisfactory, and in this controversy we cannot concede to it the authority claimed in its behalf by our Baptist brethren. Philology, properly so called, fails, in repeated instances, to effect conviction upon the great mass of mind, owing to an inevitable, or an accidental ignorance. Besides, although it is a primary, still it is not the only source of argument. But the argument deduced from the analogy of *ceremonial* and *spiritual* purifications, while it emanates from a source every way calculated to inspire confidence and satisfaction, is also open to the inspection and comprehension of all capacities; and is, so far as we can judge, unanswerable.

SEC. II.—BIBLE ALLUSIONS.

There are various allusions to baptism in the New Testament, illustrative of its import; but we recollect of no passage where an allusion is made for the professed purpose of setting forth the mode in which it should be administered. Had not certain passages of an allusive character been pressed into the service of our opponents, contrary to what we deem to be just and fair rules of argumentation, we should not feel that the cause of truth would demand of us the matter of this section. Several allusions to baptism have been briefly noticed in the former section of this chapter. Two only remain, which, from the manner of their having been interpreted and used by our opponents, seem to deserve a particular notice.

1. The first we shall notice occurs in 1 Pet. iii, 21. After having stated that "eight souls were saved by water" in Noah's ark, the apostle says: "The like figure whereunto baptism doth also now save us." It is well known that Dr. Macknight has given to this clause the following rendering: "*To which* WATER the antitype baptism doth now save us also, by the resurrec-

tion of Jesus Christ." He observes that the relative ᾧ *which*, being in the neuter gender, its antecedent cannot be κιβωτος *the ark*, which is feminine, but ὑδωρ *water*, which is neuter. After this exegesis, the doctor goes on to a still further elucidation of what he no doubt thought to be the doctrine of the text, aided alone by fancy, and deducing three grand particulars, wherein he attempts to show that the flood was a type or emblem of baptism. The bearing of the whole is to press the text into the service of the theory of immersion. The subject does not deserve a lengthened notice, although Dr. Macknight has been copied, I believe generally, by succeeding commentators. The principal thought that engaged the mind of Peter at this time, was the point of analogy between the circumstance of Noah and his family's being saved by the water of the deluge, and our being saved [emblematically] by the water of baptism. No reference whatever can be supposed to be made to the manner of Christian baptism, without the aid of a somewhat lively fancy. Every person must feel that Dr. Macknight's translation is very unsatisfactory. It gives an unnatural awkwardness to the phraseology of Peter; besides, it makes *baptism*, which is an ordinance, to stand as the antitype of *water*, which is a liquid element. Now the proper antecedent of ὡ *which*, is, we apprehend, neither κιβωτος *ark*, or υδωρ *water*. The whole difficulty is removed, and the whole sentence restored to an easy and natural construction, if we understand the noun τροπος *manner* after the relative ὡ *which*. It would then read, "*In* or *after which* MANNER the antitype baptism doth also now save us," &c. An objection may arise against this construction, from the fact that ᾧ *hō* is in the neuter form of that pronoun, while τροπος *tropos* is in the masculine. This objection is removed, however, if we suppose ᾧ *hō* in the dative neuter to be put for ὁ *ho*, a contract of ὁυ *hou* in the genitive masculine, as in the margin of Griesbach's Testament. This makes the relative and noun agree in gender, and justifies our translation.

The force of the text, then, is, that as Noah and his family were saved by water, so we are now saved by baptism. The two cases are put in juxtaposition by the apostle, merely because they possess in common that remote point of resemblance, viz., salvation by means of water. Yet the apostle, in his parenthetical qualification, guards us against running too close an analogy. What then has this text to do with the mode of baptism? Verily, nothing. Peter alludes to Noah's deliverance by water, and then says, "after which manner we are now saved by the antitype baptism."

If, however, the copyists of Dr. Macknight, like the editor of the Comprehensive Commentary, should insist upon the circumstances of Noah's being enclosed in the ark, like one laid in a tomb, and his emerging therefrom, like one rising from the dead, &c., as being typical of a burial in water, and a resurrection therefrom at baptism; we have only to remind them that they have left the beaten path of exposition, and have turned aside after their own fancy. Noah was not immersed in the water. He was borne up above the waters, and sprinkled with the rain. David's hiding in a cave, and then coming forth, was just as much a type of immersion as was this case of Noah.

2. But the allusion most worthy of our notice at this time is contained in Rom. vi, 4. It occurs also in Col. ii, 12, and is supposed to embody an irrefragable argument for exclusive immersion. The stress of the argument rests wholly upon the supposition that baptism imports a burial and resurrection. We institute our analysis of the subject by inquiring into

(*a*) *The scope of the passage.* In the preceding chapter, the apostle had dwelt somewhat at large upon the statement, that "where sin abounded, grace had superabounded." In the commencement of the sixth chapter, he anticipates an abuse of that doctrine which might possibly arise, and which he states in the following words: "What shall we say then? Shall we continue in sin, that grace may [continue to] abound?" Against this preposterous conclusion—the monstrous offspring of an ignorant and perverse mind—the apostle argues, from the second to the eleventh verse consecutively. His first argument is drawn from the *nature* of the Christian religion, showing its opposition to sin. "How shall we who are dead to sin, live any longer therein?" Ver. 2. As if he had said, "If the sinner's justification by faith, not only implies his renunciation of sin, but also exemption from its power and dominion, how can he, consistently with the nature of that justification, continue to live in the commission of sin?" Paul's second argument against the doctrine of the continuance of believers in sin, is a confirmation of the first, and is deduced from the *import* of Christian baptism. "Know ye not that so many of us as were baptized into Jesus Christ were baptized into his death?" That is, "Do ye not know that so many of you as have received Christian baptism, have been thereby taught your obligation to conform to the death of Christ—to die *unto* sin as he died *for* sin?" "Therefore, we are buried with him by baptism into death: that, like as Christ was raised up from the dead, by the glory of the Father, even so we also should walk in newness of life." Upon this (fourth) verse we offer, at present, no paraphrase. The question now is, "What did the apostle aim to set forth and prove in this passage?" We answer, He intended simply to set forth the reality of our death to sin, proved by the significance of baptism.

The scope of the passage, therefore, does not require us to suppose that the apostle alludes at all to the outward form of baptism: that subject was not embraced in the author's intention. But, by a strong figure he endeavours to place in undoubted certainty the doctrine that salvation by grace implies a moral death to sin. We consider, then, that Paul here uses an *intensive* form of speech; as if he should say, "Know ye not that so many of us as were baptized into Jesus Christ, were baptized into his death? Wherefore, in respect of the death of Christ, we do as truly hold fellowship with him therein, according to the true import of our baptism, as though we were already entombed with him." The allusion to a burial is not made (as we suppose) for the purpose of lugging into the argument any proof of the external form of baptism; but it is added in order to give an intensity or vigour to the idea. A burial is the last and most indisputable proof of natural death; so is baptism, in the true force of its mystical signification, an undeniable evidence of our death unto sin. Our remarks, thus far, are intended simply to show, that the faithful interpretation of the text in question does not require us, necessarily, to suppose that any allusion is made to the external form of baptism; and that, therefore, the construction fixed upon it by our opponents, is not, of necessity, the correct one, but is rather foreign to, and possibly at variance with, the scope of the author.

(*b*) But the "*burial*" spoken of, ver. 4, is not a *physical* burial in water, as our opponents affirm, but a *moral* "burial unto death." We have already remarked that the whole stress of the argument for immersion rests upon the hypothesis that baptism is an emblem of a burial and resurrection. Captivated by the mere sound of words without due attention to their connection and meaning, hundreds have rushed to the conclusion that the *burial* of Rom. vi, 4, is an outward one; and, in the ardour of their zeal, have overlooked the legitimate consequences of their theory. Others, who have, with a happier penetration, forestalled the consequences, have in no wise suffered themselves to be intimidated thereby, but have, like the fabled fox, boldly leaped into the deep well, trusting to their learning, or their ingenuity, or the fancied strength of their cause, for their safe deliverance. If, however, the burial be a physical one in water, as Baptist authors affirm, then also must the resurrection, which is its proper antithesis, in order to compare with the nature of the burial, be a physical resurrection,—a resurrection of the body from under the water. But, on the other hand, if the burial be taken purely in a *moral* sense, then also must the resurrection, which is to supply the antithesis of the thought, be a moral one,—a resurrection of the moral man from the death of sin to a life of holiness. It is thus, therefore, that, by ascertaining the nature of the resurrection which the apostle opposes to the burial, we are furnished with the undoubted signification of the latter, by means of an argument as satisfactory as it is logical.

The construction for which our opponents contend would require us to read the passage thus: "Therefore we are buried with him by baptism into the water: that like as Christ was raised up from the dead by the glory of the Father, even so we also, having been raised out of the water, should walk in newness of life." So great a falling off from the force of the apostle's reasoning must inevitably occasion surprise in every mind. But a little attention to facts will show, that, however unwelcome such a construction may appear, it is the only sense that can, in fairness, be attached to the doctrine, or be deduced from the statements, of our opponents. A physical, baptismal burial, such as our opponents contend for, we have already observed, could be made only "*in water*," not "*into death*." A resurrection corresponding to such a burial must be a resurrection, or an emerging *from the water*. But is this the sense of the apostle? Is there any thing expressed in relation to their being raised out of the water? "I take it for granted," says Professor Stuart, "that after ἡμεις [*we*] in ver. 4, εγερθεντες [*having been raised up*] is implied, since the nature of the comparison, the preceding ὡς ἐγερθη Χριστος, [*as Christ was raised up*,] and also ver. 5, make this entirely plain."* The passage would then read:—"that like as Christ was raised up from the dead by the glory of the Father, even so we also, having been raised up, should walk in newness of life." Walking "in newness of life," necessarily presupposes a resurrection. But the question is, Is that resurrection physical or spiritual? This question hardly admits of debate. It was in virtue of the resurrection that they were enabled to walk "in newness of life;" they must, therefore, have experienced a resurrection unto moral, or spiritual life. In other words, they experienced a moral resurrection; and it is this, and this only, that could be placed in contraposition to a "burial into death."

In the fifth verse the apostle speaks of a spiritual resurrection—"We shall be also in the likeness of his resurrection." In ver. 8 he says, "Now if we be dead with Christ, we believe that we shall also LIVE *with him*." Also ver. 11: "Reckon ye also yourselves to be dead indeed unto sin, but ALIVE *unto God*." To *live with Christ*, to be *alive unto God*, are phrases which imply a spiritual resurrection to this spiritual life. And the reader will plainly perceive that the apostle, all along, preserves the

* Commentary on Romans.

moral death and the moral resurrection in exact juxtaposition.

If we turn to Col. ii, 12, we shall find the same doctrine, clothed in a similar form of speech to this passage in Romans, with this advantage, that the former fully carries out the antithesis of the figure in the expression. The following paraphrase may assist the reader in apprehending our views of this passage: "For ye are as truly dead to sin as though ye were already buried with Christ, as ye have witnessed at your baptism; in which ordinance also ye are risen with him through that faith which is inspired in your hearts by the energy of God, who hath, by the same power, raised up Christ from the dead."

It will readily be perceived that I have supposed the relative ὡ *ho* to refer to the noun βαπτισματι *baptismati*, and not to the pronoun αυτω *auto*. This gives to the passage exactly the sense of our English version, which seems, most of any other construction, to favour our opponents and for which Professor Ripley contends. Now, the argument of our opponents is this, that as the burial is said to be performed *in* or *by* baptism, and as baptism is a physical rite, therefore the burial itself must be physical. Carrying out the antithesis, therefore, of such a burial, so as to make a correspondence of sense throughout, we affirm that the resurrection should be a physical resurrection. But does this accord with the statement of the apostle? Assuredly not; for he declares that the resurrection is attained "*through the faith of the operation of God.*" But if it be attained through *faith*, it certainly cannot relate to raising the body out of the water *by muscular strength*. Faith, then, being the instrumental cause of the resurrection, determines its character to be spiritual; but a spiritual resurrection can stand opposed only to a spiritual burial; and if both be spiritual, they cannot refer to the outward form of baptism, and consequently the passages in question can yield no aid to the cause of our opponents.

Professor Ripley seems to feel the force of this argument, and finding no other way to escape from its conclusive bearing on the question, he undertakes to show that the apostle runs a double comparison, the one spiritual and the other physical,—that "on the one hand there is a moral death and an emblematical burial; on the other, an emblematical resurrection and a holy life."*

All this is but a web of fancy. We cannot see that the words of the whole connection sustain or allow any such hypothesis, and we see powerful reasons against it.

If we take the relative ὡ *ho* in Col. ii, 12 as referring to αυτω *auto, him*, or rather to the original noun Χριστου *Christ*, in ver. 8, the passage will then read, "Buried with him in baptism, *with whom* also ye are risen through the faith of the operation of God, who hath raised him from the dead." The relative is thus rendered in the eleventh verse,—"*In whom* (εν ὡ) also ye are circumcised," &c.; and also in ver. 3,—"*In whom* (εν ὡ) are hid all the treasures of wisdom and knowledge." Language could not make it plainer that a spiritual resurrection alone is intended. The text declares that believers are raised up by the power of God, through faith, and by the same divine power, too, that raised up Christ from the dead.

It should be remembered, also, that the same phrase,—"*raised up with* Christ," or "*risen with him*,"—elsewhere has the same moral sense. See Col. iii, 1; Eph. ii, 6.

If it should be urged that, admitting the resurrection to be moral, and thus to compare fitly with the death, which also is moral, still the allusion to a burial seems unaccounted for, and that the ground taken in this argument is insufficient to meet all the circumstances of the case; we remark, 1. The phrases in Scripture, *dead to sin; dead with Christ; buried with him by baptism into death; buried with him in baptism; baptized into his death*,—are terms which we understand as synonymous, with this exception, the allusion to a burial gives energy to the expression. This we have already alluded to. It seems not to have been sufficiently noticed that a *death* and *burial* may be spoken of in the nervous, figurative style of a hortatory address, and where the object is moral suasion, when nothing further than the idea of a *death* is intended, and where, in narrative style, this word only would be used. 2. The words *death* and *burial* constitute no more than a proper antithesis of the word *resurrection*, especially in the style just alluded to, which is that of Paul in Rom. vi. So

* Examination of Stuart, p. 89.

Professor Stuart: "The reason why *συνεταφημεν we are buried with* is used in Rom. vi, 4, and in Col. ii, 12, seems to be, that the language employed may be a full antithesis of the word *resurrection*, which is used in a corresponding part of the comparison. 'You who are buried with Christ' gives energy to the expression. A dead body would indicate that life had departed; but a body *dead* and *buried* would indicate more thoroughly the entire removal of it. Such is the strong language, evidently to be taken in a figurative sense, which the apostle has here employed."*

(*c*) If we admit the burial to be a physical one in water, how shall we dispose of the last clause of the sentence, *εις τον θανατον into death*, which stands so intimately connected with the verb *συνεταφημεν, we are buried with?* The words *into death* are unquestionably to be understood in a figurative sense, and they evidently modify the sense of the verb *συνθαπτω, to bury with*, (used in the passive voice.) How, then, can the burial be physical? The text affirms, in so many words, "We are buried with him . . . . *into death*," and its syntactical structure, in the original, bears an exact resemblance to Mark i, 9, "Jesus was baptized . . . *into the Jordan*." In the latter case we have no doubt of an outward baptism, and the words *εις τον Ιορδανην into the Jordan*, beyond all contradiction, affix to the verb *baptize* its literal signification. But, instead of the present form of that text, suppose it had read, "Jesus was baptized . . . *εις τον θανατον into death*;" would not the last words of the sentence, *into death*, standing as they do in such relation to the verb baptize, suggest to the expositor of Scripture the necessity of attaching to *baptize* a *figurative* sense somewhat like that which it bears in Matt. xx, 22, 23?

Apply this reasoning to the case in hand. If the passage in Rom. vi, 4 had read, "Therefore we are buried with him . . . *εις την γην into the earth*;" or if it had read, "Therefore we are buried with him . . . *εν τω μνημειω in the sepulchre*;" who does not perceive that the words *earth* and *sepulchre*, in these sentences, would determine the *physical* character of the burial? And what commentator would ever think of maintaining that the verb *θαπτω, to bury*, must be understood in a figurative sense, when it stood in

* Commentary on Romans.

such connection with γη *earth*, or μνημειον *sepulchre?* Furthermore, if this much-litigated passage of Romans had read, "Therefore we are buried with him, by baptism, εις το ὑδωρ *into the water:* that like as Christ was raised up from the dead by the glory of the Father, even so we also, being raised εκ του ὑδατος *out of the water*, should walk in newness of life;" I say, if the passage had thus read, no doubt could have remained upon any mind of the physical character of the burial. But, as the text reads, the case is far different. It is, indeed, altogether another statement. The apostle does not say we are buried into the *earth*, nor in the *tomb*, nor yet into the *water*, but, *into death.* No one would think of understanding the phrase, *buried in the ground*, in a *figurative* sense, and yet they would have the same reasons, philologically, for such a construction, that we now have for understanding the phrase, *buried into death*, in a *physical* sense. We apprehend, therefore, that to others, as to us, the words *into death*, in Rom. vi, 4, will appear to have a decisive bearing in determining the spiritual character of the burial.

(*d*) In the eighth verse, the apostle recapitulates the main proposition of his argument thus: "Now, if we be dead with Christ." Hence the attentive reader will readily perceive that, in all the preceding argument, the apostle has attempted to establish nothing more than the reality of the Christian's *death unto sin*, to which idea, in the fourth verse, he gave an intensive energy by the additional allusion to a burial. Hence, also, the words συνεταφημεν αυτω εις τον θανατον *we are buried with him into death*, (ver. 4,) seem evidently to be synonymous with the words απεθανομεν συν Χριστω *we are dead with Christ*, (ver. 8,) with this exception, that the former expresses the sense with more energy than the latter. And the apostle, in finally summing up the whole argument, in verse 11, and in deducing his final corollary, says, "Likewise reckon ye yourselves to be νεκρους μεν τη ἁμαρτια *dead indeed to sin*," &c.

Nothing can be plainer, then, than that the doctrine of the believer's death to sin was the true and only idea that the apostle placed in juxtaposition with the "life of holiness," and which occupied the unbroken tenor of his thoughts. And to force upon the fourth verse a construction differing (save in the degree of the *energy* of the thought) from that of the eighth and eleventh verses, is plainly acting without authority from the context, inasmuch as the substance of all the former statements is contained in each successive breviary of the argument, as here shown.

(*e*) That the apostle does not allude to the outward form of baptism, appears evident from the fact that he uses a *mixture of figures* designed to set forth the same doctrine. For instance, in verse 4, he speaks of our being "buried with Christ by baptism into death;" in verse 5, of our being "*grafted** together in the likeness of his death;" in verse 6, of our being "crucified with Christ, that the body of sin might be destroyed." In every instance it is our death with Christ unto sin that is the thing set forth. Paul, first, illustrates it by an allusion to the import of baptism; secondly, by a metaphor taken from grafting; and thirdly, by a crucifixion. Now, are we warranted by the context in taking one part of the apostle's argument literally, and the rest symbolically? If so, which part is to be understood in the literal sense? Is it the baptism, or the grafting, or the crucifixion? Does he allude to the external form of baptism, any more than to an external grafting, or to an external crucifixion?

Besides, if we turn to the passage in Colossians, we shall find still another figure employed, and the whole subject placed in a clear light. The apostle there declares we are not only buried with Christ in baptism, but we are "circumcised with Christ." Professor Ripley has fallen into a singular inadvertence here. He says, "Mr. Scott, (the commentator,) I apprehend, has fallen into an error as to the last expression, 'circumcised with him,' that is, Christ. I have searched in vain for this expression in the Scriptures."† We will satisfy the professor's doubts. Here is the expression:—"ἐν ῳ και περιετμηθητε *with whom* (i. e., *Christ*) *also ye were circumcised*," Col. ii,

* The word συμφυτοι *sumphutoi*, translated *planted together*, is derived from συν *with*, and φυω *to grow*, and signifies *to grow together with*. "Dr. Taylor reckons it a beautiful metaphor taken from *grafting*, or making the scion *grow together* with the new *stock*."—*Dr. A. Clarke's Commentary*.

† Examination of Stuart, p. 88.

11. But does the apostle intend a literal and outward circumcision? Certainly not; for he strictly guards against such a construction by immediately adding that the circumcision was "made without hands." And as if to make the subject still more plain, and to assure them that he alluded, not to the outward circumcision, but to its spiritual *import*, he further adds, that the circumcision to which he alludes consisted "in the renunciation of the body of the sins of the flesh,"—that they had not received a mere Jewish, but a Christian circumcision, and had been circumcised "*εν τη περιτομη του Χριστου with the circumcision of Christ.*" Then, after having deduced an argument from the import of the Jewish ordinance of consecration, to show that they were truly dead to sin, Paul argues to the same point from the import of the Christian ordinance of consecration. They were not only "circumcised with Christ," but they were "buried with him in baptism." All which goes to prove the reality of their death to sin, and nothing else. But if Paul alludes to circumcision when he only intends the *import*, and not the *external form* of that rite, is it lawful to infer that when, in the same connection, and for the same purpose, he refers to baptism, he intends any thing *more* than the import?

(*f*) It is an objection of no inconsiderable weight against the hypothesis of our opponents, that baptism is nowhere in Scripture declared to import a burial. Bodily ablutions, among the Jews, signified *purity of heart.* This is its emblematical sense in the New Testament, as we have shown in another place. But in those familiar and constant allusions to the emblematical sense of external washings—allusions which are dispersed over the entire range of Scripture history—there is not found, in one solitary instance, the most distant approach to the idea of a burial and resurrection. I ask, then, Is it safe—is it in accordance with the established laws of Scriptural interpretation, to add a new emblematical sense to baptism—a sense altogether extraordinary, and comparatively modern in the history of bodily ablutions—which contradicts and sets aside all Jewish analogy—and this on the authority of a single disputed allusion of holy writ?

(*g*) Furthermore, the hypothesis we are opposing, by

assuming a similar ground, goes far to supersede the holy supper. In the sacrament of bread and wine we have, emblematically, set forth the death of our Saviour: "We do thereby show forth the Lord's death," 1 Cor. xi, 26. Where, then, is the propriety of having another ordinance to signify the same thing? If baptism be emblematical of the death of Christ, we can see no reason why it should not displace the other ordinance. Professor Ripley observes: "Baptism is to be regarded as reminding us of the *manner in which purity is attained*, viz., through the *death* and *resurrection* of Christ..... Thus it is a token of our recognising Christ's *death*, *burial*, and *resurrection*, on account of sin."* But I ask, So far as baptism is "a token of Christ's *death* on account of sin," is it not manifestly superfluous; coming, as it does, upon the identical ground occupied by the ordinance of the supper? Is not the one necessarily supplanted by the other? But the error of the quotation just cited consists in its overlooking the grand *agency* employed in our conversion. The sacrificial death of Christ constitutes the *meritorious ground* of our salvation; this is signified by the ordinance of the supper. But inward purity, including regeneration and sanctification, is wrought in us by the *agency* of the Holy Ghost, through the truth; and this *agency*, or *efficient cause* of our salvation, is adumbrated by the water of baptism. It does not belong to this discussion to enter at large upon the distinction between the two ordinances of Christianity, and the distinctive grounds they occupy, but suffice it to say, that this distinction, besides being supported by Scripture, has this merit also, it preserves the ordinances of Christianity from an unmeaning sameness.

Other remarks might be offered under this head, and such, too, as have been considered to possess an influence on the argument; but we think of nothing of sufficient importance to justify a greater length to this section. The strength of our argument is already brought forward. We have laboured to adjust the scales of candid and impartial criticism, and to ascertain the bearing which this far-famed passage has upon the question of the external form of baptism. In conclusion we can but remark, that,

* Examination of Stuart, p. 94.

so far as we can now judge, the construction of our opponents, though it seems to be generally sustained by the popular voice, cannot abide the severity of criticism. We cannot see but it is subject to powerful and, indeed, insurmountable objections. Verily, the text admits of another construction, and one, too, we judge, less liable to serious difficulty. When we consider this, and reflect upon the strength of evidence adduced in support of the *generic* use of βαπτιζω *baptizo* in the New Testament, we cannot suppress or disguise our astonishment, that this passage from Romans should have been urged by our opponents, as a proof text of their theory, and with a tone of unmeasured confidence.

Finally, whatever support this passage may be supposed to yield to the theory of exclusive immersion, its support is but circumstantial and unimportant. Suppose our opponents are correct in their construction, what have they proved? "Why," says one, "they have proved the universal obligation of exclusive immersion,—they have finally and triumphantly established their theory; inasmuch as Paul says, 'AS MANY OF YOU as have been baptized,' &c., plainly showing that all had been baptized in one and the same way; and 'οσοι *hosoi* also means *whoever*, that is, *all without exception*."

So thinks Mr. Judd: "What he (Paul) affirms, he affirms of baptism as baptism, and not of an occasional or particular mode of administration."* From all this we feel constrained, from a common regard of right rules of interpreting language, to dissent. That Paul spoke to the abstract question, touching the *import* of Christian baptism, we readily enough concede; but that he thus spoke in relation to the *form* of baptism, or that the text obliges us to suppose he alluded to the form of baptism at all, we cannot admit. Baptism imports *death to sin;* so did circumcision. Immersion is not necessary to make the emblematical sense complete; and a burial is alluded to, to give intensity to the idea of a *death.*

It is possible the Roman Christians were, as a matter of fact, immersed. But whatever might have been their practice, or that of the early Christians, with respect to

* Review of Stuart, p. 74.

the *mode* of baptism, it does not bind us. This has been noticed elsewhere. If the apostle alluded to the outward form of baptism, his argument must have been, to the Roman and Colossian Churches, of the *ad hominem* character. But still, we say, we are unable to comprehend the necessity of such a construction; and the allusion, if such there be, must be obscurely couched somewhere, like Milton's adversary, at the ear of Eve, " squat like a toad," which needs the spear of Ithuriel to rouse it up.

CHAPTER VIII.

OBJECTIONS ANSWERED AND PROPOSED.

SEC. I.—OBJECTIONS ANSWERED.

Some notice should be taken of certain objections, which, though trivial in their character, are yet common, and not without their influence over many sincere, though, generally, uninformed minds.

1. It is objected to sprinkling and pouring, that they are insufficient modes of baptism. It is not easy to state the objection in specific terms; but its force lies imbodied in the following interrogatory, which is advanced with an air of supercilious exultation: " How can a filthy garment be cleansed by merely sprinkling or pouring a little water upon it?" And hence, as if the argument were complete, it is inferred that baptism also, if performed by aspersion, would be a mere mock cleansing. At the outset, we inform the reader, we are not disciples of the earl of Shaftesbury, and do not endorse his strange maxim, that "ridicule is one of those principal lights or natural mediums by which things are to be viewed, in order to a thorough recognition." We do not aspire to compass our ends by such low artifice, which is often resorted to by disputants, ostensibly for the detection of error, but, in truth and reality, to cast grave subjects into the most ludicrous light, and which certainly leaves the mind in an unfavourable state for the sober investigation of truth. Vain,

indeed, is that contempt with which some affect to view the practice of sprinkling. Vain are those weapons of sophistry,—those insidious comparisons,—by which it is assailed. The intelligence, the piety, the candour of the age will resist them.

In reply to the above objection we remark,

(*a*) It proceeds upon a false assumption in regard to the original design of baptism. The analogy which is here drawn between the washing of a filthy garment, in order to purge it from an offensive matter, and the ceremonial washing of the body in baptism, gives a total misrepresentation of the meaning of the ordinance. Will it be contended by our opponents that baptism was originally designed to remove that common filth which, from personal neglect, accumulates upon the surface of the body? And yet, strange as it may appear in their own eyes, this is the identical construction which they themselves have fixed upon the ordinance, by pressing too closely the analogy between common and ceremonial washings. If ceremonial ablutions were intended originally to effect a kindred purpose with that of household washings, we readily concede that, under such circumstances, the quantity of water and the mode of applying it would materially affect the efficiency of their administration. But the case is far otherwise. Domestic washings are used only to effect a *physical* cleanliness, while ceremonial washings borrow all their importance from their *mystical* signification, not from their *visible* effects; and hence the mere *quantum* of water is not a circumstance of primary moment. We, indeed, marvel that such an objection should ever have found its way into this world of error; and it is a wonder, surpassed only by the ignorance in which it originated and through which it is uttered by a thousand mouths at the present day.

But do not our Baptist brethren perceive that their weapon, in this instance, with which they thought to do mischief to the cause of their opponents, has, like the elephants of King Pyrrhus, turned back upon their own ranks? By their own showing, they are defeated on their own principles, no less than we. If the analogy above alluded to is to be thus hardly pressed,—if sprinkling is to be denounced on the score of inefficacy, according to the doctrine advanced in the objection,—certainly the difficulty is not removed by a resort to immersion. If sprinkling a garment will not cleanse it, I know of no one so silly as to imagine that simple immersion would cleanse it. And thus the doctrine of the objection is as fatal to immersion, the Baptists themselves being judges, as it is to sprinkling.

(*b*) The common sense of mankind, too, in settling a principle of this nature, merits a decent respect, especially where it lies imbodied in religious ceremonies of great antiquity, and which, though now abolished, were originally founded upon divine authority. For instance, "It was a custom among the Hebrews, Greeks, and Latins, to wash their hands in token of their innocence, and to show that they were pure from any imputed guilt."* So also, according to the Mussulman's creed, ablution consists in washing the hands, feet, face, and part of the head. The devotee is then pronounced *wholly clean.* Thus, by different nations, in different ages of the world, has the principle been clearly recognised, that *perfect* or *entire purity* may be significantly represented by applying water to a *part* of the body only. But what renders this circumstance of weight in the present controversy is, that the Bible itself has given sanction to the principle, in the form of religious duty. Anciently, among the Hebrews, when the body of a murdered man was found, and the guilty perpetrator had eluded discovery, the elders of the city nearest the spot where the body was found were required to *wash their hands* over a slain heifer, as a public protestation of their innocence of the murder whose author was unknown. Deut. xxi, 1–9. But why were they not required to immerse themselves, if the principles of our opponents be correct, and if, consequently, a *partial* washing may not represent *entire* purity? David says, "I will wash my hands in innocency," Psa. xxvi, 6. Here, undeniably, the washing of the *hands* betokened the entire purity, or innocence, of the *whole man.* So, also, Pilate "took water and washed his hands, saying, I am innocent of the blood of this just person," Matt. xxvii, 24. But why did he not immerse himself in token of his alleged innocence? See Psa. lxxiii, 13.

* Dr. A. Clarke's comment on Matt. xxvii, 24.

(*c*) But, doubtless, our opponents will call for other testimony in support of our position; and certainly the subject admits of other proof, which shall be adduced, in compliance with so reasonable a demand. We subjoin a few passages only.

Psa. li, 7: "SPRINKLE (ῥαντιεῖς) me with hyssop, and I *shall be clean.*"

Ezek. xxxvi, 25: "Then will I SPRINKLE clean water upon you, and you *shall be clean.*"

Heb. x, 22: "Having your hearts SPRINKLED from an evil conscience."

Heb. ix, 13: "The blood of bulls and of goats, and the ashes of a heifer, SPRINKLING the unclean, sanctifieth to the purifying of the flesh."

Again do we admonish the reader of the error and disingenuity of a misapprehension of our position. We do not adduce these passages and statements as direct proof that Christian baptism should be performed by sprinkling, but simply to show that Jehovah has long since settled the principle in his church, that a partial washing, or sprinkling the body with water, may suffice to represent an entire cleansing of the moral man. And we wish our opponents to bear it distinctly in mind, that when they ridicule the practice of baptism by sprinkling, on the score of its inefficacy, they ridicule a *principle* that God himself has, from the remotest antiquity of the church, settled by his own authority. We know it is quite convenient for men, when arguing on this subject, to blind the eyes of the more uninformed, and create a tide of ignorant prejudice by the *hue and cry* of JUDAISM, whenever we would make an allusion to Old Testament practices or principles. We are not pleading for the restoration of the obsolete rites of Judaism; nor are we in doubt that, with the intelligent and candid, the position we have taken will be estimated according to its legitimate bearing upon the point at issue. But we have something more to do with the principle under consideration. The subject assumes too serious an aspect to be scouted away by the frivolity of superficial thinkers. When the Bible speaks of the application of the blood of Christ to the heart, in order to effect (not a ceremonial, but) a *real* cleansing, it employs the following allusion: "Elect . . . through sanctification of the Spirit . . . and SPRINKLING *of the blood* of Jesus Christ," 1 Pet. i, 2. The same reference is also made, Heb. ix, 13, 14, and x, 22. So also Heb. xii, 24: "Ye are come . . . to Jesus and to the *blood of* SPRINKLING."

But why is not the allusion made to immersion instead of sprinkling? Will our opponents ridicule the idea of cleansing the heart from moral defilement by having the blood of Christ *sprinkled* upon it? Why, then, should they speak lightly of having water sprinkled upon the body, when the object is merely to represent this moral cleansing? "There are three," says John, "that bear witness in earth, the Spirit, the water, and the blood," 1 John v, 8. We are acquainted with the operations of the Spirit, and the application of the blood of atonement, only by their AFFUSION upon the heart. This is the mode in which they uniformly yield their testimony to the divinity and Messiahship of Christ. Analogy, therefore, would teach us that the water of baptism, in order the more forcibly to "agree in one" testimony with the "Spirit and the blood," should agree with them also in the *mode* of its application, i. e., should be sprinkled or poured upon the body. There is a remarkable instance recorded in Isa. vi, 7, of the entire purgation of the prophet, by simply applying a coal of fire to his lips. "Lo," says the seraph, "this hath touched thy lips, and thy iniquity is taken away, and thy sin is purged." So far as the principle under consideration is involved, we might ask, Is there any thing more absurd, in supposing that an application of water to *one part* of the body may represent the entire purgation of the whole man from moral defilement, than in supposing such a purgation to be actually effected by applying a coal of fire to the lips only?

2. It has been objected to the practice of sprinkling, that "there is no *cross* in it;" while the cross of being immersed is a circumstance urged in proof of the superior and exclusive merits of that mode. Of course the cross of Christ is intended. Simple as this objection may appear, it is not without its influence over many sincere Christians. The process of reasoning by which it comes to possess that influence is also simple and summary. It is something like the following:—All Christians must bear the cross of Christ. That is a cross to which we

feel a strong repugnance. And hence, it is loosely inferred, to overcome our repugnance to a particular act, is to bear the cross of Christ. This is evidently somewhat the process of thought by which many attain their peculiar views of this subject. They seem to measure the cross of Christ, in any particular duty, according to their re.uctance to perform it. This, I am well assured, is the popular view taken of this subject. And if people would examine the subject with candour and impartiality, they would find that what generally passes under the specious appellation of the cross of Christ in immersion, is nothing else than the irrepressible risings of a constitutional repugnance of such treatment of the body. To persons living in frigid climates there is a strong resistance to being plunged into the water. This resistance arises, not from the force of theological opinions, but from the natural effects of climate on the physiological constitution. On the other hand, in the torrid regions, to be dipped into the water is a luxury ardently craved by every impulse of the languishing system. Yet the cross of Christ no more strongly marks the immersion of an Icelander than that of a Cingalese. The Author of our being has implanted in our natures, for our own welfare, an instinctive propensity to resist any sudden or unexpected hazard of our safety. The operations of this instinct are involuntary, and without the co-operation either of the will or of the rational faculty. Thus, if a man stumble in his walk, he makes an involuntary effort to recover his upright position. This effort is made before he has time to reflect upon his danger, and consequently without any concurrence of his reason or his will; it is the operation of an instinct of self-preservation. It cannot be denied, that to plunge a man backward under the water gives a most unnatural and helpless posture to the body—a posture that inevitably renders the safety of tne body a little precarious, and which cannot be maintained for any length of time without actual strangulation. Indeed, the candidate often comes out of the water, not in the serene dignity of a newly consecrated disciple, but *in spasms for breath!* Great precaution and self-possession are requisite to avoid drawing the water into the nostrils, and thus obstructing the channels of respiration. This is a matter of so much importance, in order to preserve the order and solemnity of the scene, as often to become the subject of special instruction from the minister previous to baptism. But all this, together with a little apprehension of danger, arising from the constant liabilities of the minister himself to accident or blunder, involves so much mental calculation and concern on the part of the candidate, as often to produce a powerful diversion of mind from the solemnity of the ordinance. We know, to be sure, that immersion might be practised in such a place, and under such circumstances as to preclude any risk of personal safety. It is also true that in many cases, as immersion is now practised, by dint of the rational faculty, the jealousies of the instinctive principle of self-preservation are quieted. But in many other instances, it is equally true, it gains the entire ascendency, prompting the candidate to involuntary efforts to regain his feet before he has been submerged; which requires the minister to make two successive efforts to effect a complete immersion, and presents him in the attitude of an adversary to the candidate—the latter struggling for freedom and the former for control. It is my settled conviction, founded upon somewhat extensive observation, that many, very many, who deeply imbibe the doctrine of exclusive immersion beforehand, still, at the moment of baptism, experience so much agitation and alarm as utterly to preclude that sense of religious obligation and devotional awe that should wholly pervade and possess the mind. Witness the hurried, convulsive respiration—the stifled sigh—the violent palpitation—the alarm depicted upon the pale visage—the spasmodic grasp of the candidate on the arm of the minister—these are the common symptoms which give evidence of a resistance in the human frame and temperament to such treatment of the body; and proclaim also, that the mind of the candidate is occupied with anxious thoughts of safety, and not with the devotional solemnities of religion. Yet all this agitation of body and mind, which is the result of natural causes, passes for the cross of Christ. I am fully apprised that these statements will give umbrage to some; but how unreasonable—how groundless—is that offence! I do not state these things because they give me pleasure, nor because I wish to have them so. Herein I speak, not as a polemic writer, but as a narrator of facts—

facts over which I am unable to exert the slightest power, either to reverse or modify. Whatever censure, therefore, may fall upon the above remarks, let it be understood that we are exculpated. He who gave man his present constitution—he alone is the opponent of the Baptists in this case.

Still we are taunted,—(nay, reader, do not deem us unguarded, or uncharitable, in our choice of terms. "We speak," not without pain, "that we do know,")—yes, I repeat it, we are taunted with the opprobrium of avoiding the "*cross*,"—of inclining to a mere fleshly, selfish ease,—to the subversion of a pure administration of Christian baptism,—and this, because we deny the theory of exclusive immersion. We have not courted this controversy; but we shall not shrink from meeting any form of attack our opponents may please to adopt. We are not swayed by a vain elation of our orthodoxy, or of our fidelity to the primitive institutes of Christianity; nor would we disparage others by an invidious comparison. The Baptist Church have signalized themselves in the field of Christian philanthropy, and it is just that their praise should be, as it is, pronounced in the churches. But is it quite modest for them to compare themselves with other churches? Nay, is it just for them to impugn thus the motives of other Christians? Are the Baptists themselves well aware that they do not rest an undue stress upon this one rite? Are they as rigid—as jealous of encroachment—in the practice of all other duties as in this fanciedly primitive practice? On the other hand, have not the Pedobaptist churches advanced to the front ranks in the great strife, and shown themselves valiant for the truth? Have they slunk into concealment in the hour of persecution and the times which have tried men's souls? Have they ever betrayed the common cause, or given any just ground for a latent suspicion (much less a public proclamation) on the part of the Baptists, that, like the apostate Galatians, they wished to "avoid the cross of Christ?" Where, then, is the justice—where the truth of these insidious whisperings of defection? We repudiate the ungenerous reflection thus cast forth upon the fair reputation of the great body of the church; while we assure the reader, that if, in his estimation, we have descended to an odious personality in our *argumentum ad hominem*, it has not resulted from our choice, but from the delicacy of our position in this ill-fated controversy.

SEC. II.—MISCELLANEOUS OBJECTIONS AGAINST EXCLUSIVE IMMERSION.

Several considerations combine to stamp the hypothesis with a decided cast of certainty, that immersion, however appropriate under some circumstances, was, nevertheless, never designed for universal application. It is the glory of the Christian institutions, that, like the moral precepts of the Bible, they are adapted to the universal condition and capacities of mankind. Their observance was designed to be commensurate to the spread and authority of evangelical truth. Hence, they were graduated according to a just and merciful precognition of the diverse and changing circumstances of human life; and are now brought to bear upon us with a mildness which marks the legitimacy of their origin. The great error of the Baptists, we conceive, to lie in their substituting a *specific* for a *generic* term. We have already noticed, that the Greek word *baptize* is a *generic* term. We have deduced from the original word and its derivatives, as used in the Bible, by rules of interpretation which we are more than willing should be submitted again to the scrutiny of unsparing (if intelligent and just) criticism, the following senses, viz.: *to besmear, to bedew, to pour, to sprinkle, to purify, to wash.* Now, what is the fair and candid conclusion, but that it was the intention of the Holy Ghost, in selecting a term of such large application to designate the ordinance of baptism, to leave the *particular mode* of baptism to be determined by circumstances? But, contrariwise, the Baptists have affixed to the Greek verb in question a *specific* sense. They have affirmed, that it signifies *to immerse* only. They have left nothing to circumstances; and have thus caused the requisition of Scripture, touching baptism, to lay very unequal claims upon different members of the human family,—claims which, as we shall hereafter see, in numerous instances, can never be met but by an imminent and criminal hazard of health and of life. Turn we, then, to an investigation of the condition and ability, not of any particular class of men, or of any local section of the human race, but of the universal family of man, in reference to the observance of such a specific and restrictive command.

1. We call the reader's attention to the objection lying against the Baptist theory, arising from climate.

When the missionary penetrates northward into those regions traversed by the sixtieth parallel of latitude, he finds himself already in a temperature where wells are frozen at a great depth, and where, for the most part of the year, water can be obtained only by melting snow or ice. In the region of the Esquimaux, the lakes and standing waters, unless deep, are generally in winter frozen to the bottom. They continue frozen from seven to nine months of the year. "In Greenland, Lapland, and the coldest countries of this region, brandy and mercury freeze during the winter." "During the winter, the inhabitants of the coldest parts remain crowded together in small huts. The whole inside of a hut, or ship, is usually lined with ice, formed from the vapour of breath, which must be cut away every morning. The inhabitants of Siberia stop the openings of their houses with ice, and use it instead of glass. If the cold air suddenly enter the house, the vapours fall in a shower of snow. Every part of the body must be covered in going out, or it is instantly frozen. The air when breathed seems to pierce, and even rend the lungs. The cup often freezes to the lips, if it be touched in drinking. The provisions must be cut with hatchets and saws. Trees and the beams of houses are split by the frost, and rocks are rent with a noise like that of fire-arms."*

In a country thus bound in "thick-ribbed ice," for most of the inhospitable year, can it be supposed that immersion is practicable? For how, we demand, could they obtain their supply of water during the severe season? Could they obtain it by melting snow or ice? Could they furnish baths? Could they endure the process? No sensible man would maintain that they could. And yet in these regions of terrible frost dwell *millions* of the human species. How difficult it is to practise immersion

* Woodbridge's Universal Geography, p. 145. *Seventh edit.*

in our own climate during the severer parts of the year! But we are not in the habit of having our deep wells frozen, or the mercury congealed in the bulb of our thermometers. But allowing the abstract possibility (and this is the utmost that candour can demand, or truth concede) of practising immersion generally, during the wintry season, in Labrador, Lapland, Siberia, Iceland, Greenland, and other countries lying within the polar and frozen regions, where the mean annual temperature is often below, and seldom much above freezing point, still there will be found none presumptuous enough to pretend that such a requisition, which for the inhabitants of those countries would be enormously expensive and burdensome, would bear any analogy to the mild and merciful character of gospel institutions. Let not the reader dismiss this argument with a leering suspicion of its candour or its justice. Can it be doubted that the condition of this portion of our race, now under consideration, forms a fair and necessary exception to the universal practicability of immersion? As Humboldt and others have traced the isothermal lines, not less than eight millions of human beings inhabit the polar and frozen regions. To these the gospel must be promulgated. Churches must arise in the very bosom of their heartless winters. To these must the gospel ordinances be administered as well as to us. But to the administration of immersion nature has interposed a barrier for two-thirds of the year,—a barrier which, to them, would render immersion more galling than the bloody rite of circumcision. Does it argue well for either the wisdom or goodness of the Author of Christianity, that he has established an ordinance of perpetual obligation, which, though it may be tolerably adapted to the condition and convenience of some of the human family, must in the nature of things bear oppressively upon others?

But the above remarks are designed to apply only to those who inhabit regions of almost perpetual frost; whereas, with some modification, they may be made to apply to a much larger portion of the world's population. About *one-eighth* of the entire population of our earth inhabit regions north of our own latitudes, in climates more ungenial than ours. Their winters extend through six to ten months of the year, while they experience an average temperature through the year (taking their climates collectively) of only about thirty-eight degrees. In many populous places, as at Stockholm and Petersburg, the mercury ranges below freezing point during six months of the year. We, who live in the northern section of what is called the *temperate region*, enjoy a mean annual temperature of about fifty degrees, while our winters continue only from three to four and sometimes five months. But even with us, there may be reckoned six months of the year wherein immersion cannot be performed without great inconvenience, and producing those unpleasant and even painful sensations of body, which possess no imaginable power to improve the heart, and are altogether at variance with the analogy of New Testament institutions. If, indeed, we are to attach a merit to such physical sensations according to a papist's idea of penance, or a Brahmin's notion of self-mortification, we readily acknowledge, that so far from regarding snow, and ice, and arctic winds, and a temperature of two degrees of Fahrenheit, as impediments to immersion, we should exult in them, as being joyful circumstances, which would enhance the merit of our obedience, and ensure its acceptance. But we have not learned divinity in such schools; and we repeat it, that the theory of exclusive immersion lays very unequal, and, in many instances, oppressive claims upon the human family.

From all that we have adduced, thus far, under this head, the reader will clearly perceive our opponents to be fairly and irretrievably lodged in one of the following conclusions, viz.: that, either God has established a Christian ordinance of universal and perpetual obligation, which, during most of the time from year to year, by the unalterable course of nature, is rendered, either totally impracticable, or, at least, oppressively burdensome, to a large portion of the human family; or, that exclusive immersion is not of divine appointment.

We cannot dismiss this topic without adverting to a very singular passage which we find in Professor Ripley's treatise on baptism. That author says, "The difficulties supposed to be connected with the ancient rite [immersion] are only imaginary; and are of little power except in the hands of an adversary, to excite dread and disesteem against the ordinance. Among those who always practise immersion the mention of such difficulties only provokes a smile, and it serves to show how empty is mere theory when contrasted with facts."* So exulted the invincible Alexander when he had pursued his conquests down the Indus to the shores of the Indian Ocean, and vainly imagined he had reached the boundaries of the universe! But, like the Grecian monarch, our author is doomed to disappointment. He has, as yet, conquered but half the world. His "imaginary difficulties" are still overcome only in *imagination*. The universal practicability of immersion has never yet been proved; and the Baptists, in their confident exultation and boasting on the subject, are altogether premature. Happy for their theory, that they have always kept themselves within prudent latitudes. In this they have done wisely. While other Protestant sects of Europe have extended their lines far north into Norway, Lapland, and Greenland, the Baptists have prudently kept themselves mostly confined within Germany, the southern part of Poland, and some of the northern states of Austria. The Baptists have sent out their missionaries to India, Africa, and among the aborigines of North America; but we have never seen the experiment of a Baptist church rising up in Labrador, Siberia, Greenland, or central Russia. Doubtless they would not "smile" at the "difficulties of immersion," nor deem them altogether "imaginary," in these regions.

The Greek Church, which includes, with other countries, most of Russia, baptize by trine immersion. Of course they have to contend with the frosts of a Russian winter, although in the eastern and northern parts the people are scarcely reached by any religion whatever. But in the Greek Church, previous to the administration of baptism, "the baptismal water is consecrated, and *in winter* WARMED, and perfumed with sweet herbs."† Of course the reader will understand that they generally use fonts, or baptisteries. This practice of warming the baptismal water is the legitimate offspring of necessity; but it is a practice which cannot be carried into the coldest regions, for want of fuel, fonts, and suitable houses.

* Examination of Stuart, p. 128.

† Robinson's History of Baptism, p. 455.

"In the twelfth century a Swedish Catholic bishop, named Otho, travelled into Pomerania and taught a great number of the natives, whom he caused his assistants to baptize in bathing-tubs let into the ground and surrounded with curtains; and, as the weather was excessive cold, he ordered large fires to be made, it should seem, *for the purpose of dissolving ice to supply the tubs with water.* In such a rigorous season it was a case of necessity."* The same author observes, that the missionaries who introduced Christianity (rather popery) into Iceland, in the tenth century, found some difficulty with the inhabitants in persuading them to be baptized. When it was proposed to them to be baptized, "they refused to comply, except on condition that they should be baptized *in hot baths,* for they unanimously declared 'they would not be baptized *i kalt vatn,* IN COLD WATER.' "† They were consequently baptized in some of the natural hot baths with which the country abounds by reason of its volcanic heat. This, our author says, "was mere caprice" in these Icelandic converts. But we think they acted wisely. At least, the above facts will serve to show how hard it is for the missionary to grapple with the rigours of northern climates, in order to support the theory of exclusive immersion. These climates engender a settled aversion to being immersed in cold water; and it is only superstition in the Catholics of that region that prompts the infatuated devotee to overcome this aversion, and exult in those bodily pains which result from such a practice, and which bear a stronger resemblance to heathen than to Christian rites.

If we turn from these inclement skies and ice-bound shores, to contrast the scenes of a tropical climate, we shall find a very natural and satisfactory solution of the allegation, which to many has been perplexing, and to the Baptists an occasion of triumph, that those people who enjoyed the first teachings of Christ and his apostles, generally, in the first century, practised immersion. We have already suggested, in a former chapter, that *climate* is sufficient to account for this circumstance. We introduce the subject here, in juxtaposition with the foregoing remarks, that the reader may the better judge of the can-

* Robinson's History of Baptism, p. 456. † Ibid.

dour and correctness of our position. Upon a very superficial view, many have supposed that the reason of the first churches practising immersion was, that they better understood the import of Christ's command; that is, that they better understood the meaning of the word *baptize*, than we. This is certainly more than any man can prove. To illustrate our views we subjoin the following extract from Woodbridge, which he takes from Humboldt:—"Snow is here [in the tropical regions] almost unknown. The streams are never frozen, and vegetables grow through the winter. The *thermometer* sometimes rises above one hundred, and continues at this height during the night. Travellers have been obliged to wet their clothes, and even wrap their head and face in wet cloths, at night, to protect themselves from the scorching air."* Within this climate lies the land of Palestine. It was such a climate that originated the demand for baths, and pools, and fountains, throughout the East, and made the practice of bathing to be common. And, we repeat it, it was this universal custom of bathing,—a custom so indispensable to pleasure, to decency, and to health, among the Orientals,—which, more than any thing else, gave a bias in their minds to immersion instead of affusion. And as, during the first ages of the church, the Christian religion did not spread very far northward; and as the foreign churches always maintained a deference to the practices of the church in Judea, so, in this also they probably became obsequious, and thus transmitted a practice, which was only suited to warm regions, to climates for which it has no adaptation. But had our Saviour opened his mission in the heart of Siberia, or in central Russia, it is undeniable that the people, left to their own option as to the mode of baptism, (which we maintain to be the true state in which our Lord left the ordinance,) would have chosen affusion. Christianity, though first planted in Palestine, is a native of every clime, and adapted to every people under heaven. While it flourishes in one region, it is not doomed to protract the sickly existence of an exotic in another. Its ordinances and its precepts possess a universal adaptation to man as he is. But this cannot be said of exclusive immersion. But,

* Universal Geography, p. 137.

2. Not only does the practice of immersion require a moderate temperature, but it also makes a demand for a certain degree of *health*, which the candidate does not always possess. Can it be credited, that the compassionate Author of Christianity has instituted an external ordinance of religion, of universal obligation, so irrespective of the frailties of his creatures, as that thousands, by the irreversible necessity of circumstances, are for ever debarred all participation therein? And this, too, while he has ever bestowed the most distinguished compassion, in every other respect, upon this very class (the sick) of our race. How large a proportion of our race are actually labouring under chronic diseases which, for months and even years together, deprive them of the power of being immersed! Those who repent and obtain pardon upon their death-beds, not having been previously baptized, though they may afterward linger for weeks, or even months, with the most devout solicitude to receive this ordinance, are for ever denied the privilege of putting on Christ by baptism. Moreover, a want of Christian baptism, according to the settled usage of the churches, incapacitates them for receiving the elements of bread and wine in memory of the Saviour's death; and thus, however Christians may indulge a hope for their salvation after death, they are still cut off from all hopes of obtaining any *visible* relation to Christ's body, and consequently from all church communion with his saints on earth. Thus it is clear, according to the theory of our opponents, that the ability to fulfil the command touching baptism is not commensurate to the ability of men to repent, which evinces a discrepancy not to be charged upon true Christianity. And hence, about the middle of the third century, during a tiresome and virulent controversy in the church on another question respecting baptism, Cyprian, bishop of Carthage, decided, "and certainly," says Dr. Milner, "with much propriety, that those whose weak state of health did not permit them to be washed in water, were yet sufficiently baptized by being sprinkled:—Cyprian observes that the virtue of baptism ought not to be estimated in a carnal manner, by the quantity of external apparatus."*

* Milner's Church History, cent. 3, c. 13.

Mr. Robinson, the Baptist historian, notices this fact, and acknowledges that sprinkling was introduced and practised, before the Reformation, from *necessity*, and that in such cases it was held valid. This, one would suppose, would be sufficient, of itself, to suggest to such a mind as Mr. Robinson's, that exclusive immersion is too unadapted to the universal conditions of men, and too severe in its exactions upon the sick and enfeebled, to justify the high and unqualified pretensions to divine authority claimed for it by its advocates.*

I now distinctly recollect the case of Mrs. ——. She was a member of my charge, and we all thought her to be a sincere Christian. Two whole years rolled away, and she lived in the neglect of baptism. She had strongly imbibed the notion, that, for her, nothing would be baptism but immersion. But she was in ill health, and deferred. I was never able to engage her to receive baptism; nor could I ever seem to impress upon her mind the incongruity of her faith to a reasonable requirement. The last that I knew of her she was unchanged in her belief, with the gloomy prospect of carrying the same enfeebled body to the grave. To be baptized was her constant and ardent wish; but she felt that, if she would be immersed, she must abandon every prudent consideration, and rush into the jaws of death. Do you affect pity for her imbecility, and say, that, if she had "*faith*," she would come out of the water unhurt? I know that faith is the *sine qua non* with many, and is supposed to possess the power of preventing disease. But whether this notion agree better with Christian or heathen theology, we leave the reader to judge. Where, we demand, is the Scriptural ground of such faith? Whence did our opponents derive their peculiar views on this subject? Does it become them to exhort a frail being to an act which a little knowledge of physiology would condemn as rash and hazardous, and then appeal to Scripture to sanction their temerity? I know not how others may view this subject, but it strongly forces itself upon my mind, that this liberty which is taken with the evangelical doctrine of trust in God, bears a kindred likeness to that recorded Matt. iv,

* *Vide* Robinson's History of Baptism, p. 116.

6. It is saying to a frail, dependant mortal, "Cast thyself down, for he shall give his angels charge concerning thee, and in their hands they shall hold thee up." So reasoned the young, and sprightly, but sincere —— ——. When all the shivering group stood upon the frost-bound shore, muffled in their *double enveloppe*, her slender form, exposed to the keen arctic winds, was let down through the ice into the cold liquid element below. She afterward stood upon the shore, clad in her icy garments, until several more were immersed; and then, with a body benumbed with cold, and quaking under the effects of such unnatural treatment, she was conveyed to her chamber, whence, after a few weeks of rapid decline, she was removed in a hearse to the lonely domicil of the dead. Thus died the youthful —— ——; however sincere, yet the victim of her own imprudent zeal. Her friends regarded her death as the consequence of her exposure at baptism. Do you say she died a martyr? Do you deem her death enviable? Nay, my friend; think not that God has ever established an ordinance in his church, which, in so many instances, is at war with the very health and existence of his creatures. Think not that God has ordained that rigid system which denounces all modes but immersion as antichristian—papistical innovations upon the rite of baptism,—that requires of the candidate at all times, and under all circumstances,—whether he dwell under the wintry skies of Lapland, or inhabit the sunny shores of India; whether he exult in the vigour and the bloom of health, or gasp his stinted breath in the infected atmosphere of a sick chamber,—to come under the same yoke—a yoke which, many very many, are not able to bear. Still, the prejudices of the reader against us are pre-engaged by being told that the difficulties of immersion "are of little power, except in the hands of an adversary, to excite dread and disesteem against the ordinance." Professor Ripley further says,—"Shall I be told that men have actually, by their practice of immersion, contracted disorders, and met with accidents, which have terminated in death? May I not also ask, Did never a minister die in the pulpit? Did never a man come to his dissolution while on an errand of mercy?"* But the learned profes

* Examination of Stuart, p. 128.

sor should know that this is not an adequate apology for the unwholesome and deleterious bearing of immersion. In the one case, a servant of God comes to his end by unjust and violent proceedings; a Stephen is stoned, or a Paul beheaded; and this takes place in a course of providential government: but, on the other hand, Jehovah is supposed to have ordained a ceremony of religion, of perpetual and universal obligation, which, in numerous instances, is condemned as rash and hazardous, on physiological principles. And, furthermore, the question is not whether, on the supposition that immersion is the only true mode of baptism, its obligation would remain unchanged in the case of sick persons. The professor, in arguing to this question, has missed the mark. There is no room for controversy on such a question, among men who have their senses. But the question is this: whether Jehovah has established an ordinance of universal and perpetual obligation, which his own infinite knowledge must have foreseen, (and which facts now abundantly demonstrate,) to be unadapted to the condition, and at war with the health and happiness, of a large portion of the human family?

CHAPTER IX.

OBLIGATION OF BAPTISM.

"The *obligation* of baptism," says Richard Watson, "rests upon the example of our Lord, who, by his disciples, baptized many that by his discourses and miracles were brought to profess faith in him as the Messias;—upon his solemn command to his apostles after his resurrection, 'Go and teach all nations, baptizing them in the name of the Father, and of the Son, and of the Holy Ghost;'—and upon the practice of the apostles themselves, who thus showed that they did not understand baptism, like our Quakers, in a mystical sense."*

That the example of our Lord, as above quoted, fur-

* Institutes, part iv, chap. iii.

nishes any valid ground of obligation to receive Christian baptism, we are not prepared to concede. We would rather regard it as a supplement to John's dispensation, and as *preparatory* to the Christian system, which, at that time, was still future.

Christian baptism was not instituted till after the resurrection of Christ, and the obligation of the ordinance properly rests upon the Saviour's original command. We have no account of the ordinance being administered to any person prior to the day of Pentecost, after which the history of water baptism makes a prominent feature of the early history of the church.

Plain, however, as is the evidence that water baptism was instituted by Christ, and practised by his apostles, the practice has been boldly assailed, and repudiated with abhorrence, as the relic of a spurious religion, by a large body of men, calling themselves Christians, and professing veneration for the sacred oracles. It is well known that the Society of Friends not only deny the obligation and validity of water baptism, but hold it (together with the Lord's supper) in deep religious abhorrence, as a carnal rite, adverse to the spirituality of the Christian religion. The views of this society are so well known, that little is incumbent on us at present to perform by way of exhibiting them; and they have been so often and so ably refuted, that, were it not that some notice of the subject became a necessary part of a treatise on baptism, we might be excused from the task altogether. The views of the Society of Friends could not, perhaps, so far as opposition to baptism is concerned, be more readily expressed than by an extract from a joint letter from Messrs. J. Forster, S. Gurney, and G. Stacey, of London, to Elisha Bates; and also an extract from the minutes of the morning meeting of the ministers and elders of the Society of Friends, "held 10th of tenth month, 1836." Mr. Bates was an accredited minister of the society, belonging to the Ohio yearly meeting. He went to England in the spring of 1836 on business, and, during a short residence in the vicinity of London, obtained several interviews with the celebrated Dr. J. Pye Smith, by whom he was at length baptized. In relation to this event Mr. B. was addressed by the above named Friends in a joint epistle. Part of their letter runs thus:—"We heard with much concern, after thou left London, that thou hadst thought it right to undergo the rite of water baptism, and cannot but deeply lament so painful a symptom of alienation from those spiritual views of the gospel dispensation which our society has ever thought it right to uphold. . . . . Much do we desire that the importance of the spiritual character of the gospel of our holy Redeemer, as set forth in the Scriptures of truth, may be upheld among us, intimately connected as we consider it to be with the disuse of water baptism, which is, in our apprehension, a practice to which the language of our yearly meeting's epistle of 1835 applies—'that no shadows, in the worship of God, were instituted by our Lord, or have any place in the Christian dispensation.'"

The extract from the minutes of the morning meeting, above alluded to, runs thus:—

"This meeting thinks it right, in much Christian love for Elisha Bates, to record its deep concern on the occasion, [of his baptism,] and its continued sense that the practice thus adverted to (against which our society has uniformly believed itself called upon to bear a public testimony, as no part of the Christian dispensation) was not instituted by our Lord and Saviour, whom we have always acknowledged as the only and supreme head of his church."

When we read such statements, made, not only by professing Christians, but by those who profess a *purer* Christianity than is cherished by other sects, we are utterly at a loss to appreciate those principles of evidence by which their faith has been formed, or those rules of exegesis which they would apply to the sacred text. "The spiritual character of the gospel intimately connected with the disuse of water baptism!"—"No part of the Christian dispensation!"—And this society feels itself "called upon to bear a public testimony against it!"

We are aware that this is a trite subject; but while hundreds, and thousands, are affected by the above error, we cannot pass it by without directing the eye of the reader to the antidote.

It might suffice, it would seem, to modify the confident tone of Quakerism on this point, to state that the Bible has nowhere, either expressly or constructively, prohibited water baptism. We know, indeed, that they have attempted to make out the argument from constructive evidence; but their peculiar rules of interpretation are wholly inadmissible. We call for proof of the prohibitive law.

Certain it is, if the language of the New Testament means any thing, that Jesus commissioned and commanded his disciples to baptize. But it is said this was a *spiritual*, not a *water* baptism.* And here we join issue with that mystic divinity whose leading result has ever been to dissipate and nullify the palpable and effectual truth of God. We hold that the command of the Saviour, Matt. xxviii, 19, "Go, teach all nations, baptizing them in the name of the Father, and of the Son, and of the Holy Ghost," is a command to baptize with *water*. Quakerism teaches us that it is a commission and a command to baptize *with the Holy Spirit*. In meeting this absurdity, we remark:

1. The apostles were never commissioned to baptize with the Holy Ghost.

John said, speaking to the Jews of Christ, "HE shall baptize you with the Holy Spirit and with fire." He further says, "He that sent me to baptize with water, the same said unto me, Upon whom thou shalt see the Spirit descending and remaining on him, THE SAME IS HE WHICH BAPTIZETH WITH THE HOLY GHOST," John i, 33. God says: "In the last days" (i. e., gospel days) "*I* will pour out my Spirit upon all flesh," &c. Acts ii, 17.

Indeed, we recollect of but one individual in apostolic times that imbibed the dangerous error that any being but God could baptize with the Holy Spirit. This person was Simon Magus. Acts viii, 18. What is a spiritual baptism? Is it not the emotions, or agency of the invisible God upon the human soul? How, then, can such a prerogative be delegated to mortal man? The absurdity of this theory is its own ample refutation. Were the apostles ever sent to forgive sins? to regenerate the heart of man? to bestow the emotions of God upon the soul? We know that in these extraordinary senses the pope of Rome

* *Vide* Barclay's Apology, pp. 432, 433, &c.

claims extensive power, as God's vicegerent upon earth. But who would have suspected an unpretending Quaker of holding such an absurdity?

John Baptist was very particular and exact in his teachings, to convey the impression distinctly and clearly that *he* did *not* baptize with the Holy Spirit: "I, *truly*, baptize with *water*." At the same time he was equally explicit in teaching that Christ alone would baptize with the Holy Spirit. Peter says, that Christ, "being by the right hand of God exalted, and having received of the Father the promise of the Holy Ghost, HE *hath shed forth this*." Christ had promised "to send the Comforter." The apostle informs us, that while they (the apostles) preached, God *co-witnessed to* (συνεπιμαρτυρουντος) the truth "with gifts of the Holy Ghost κατα την αυτω θελησιν *according to* HIS *pleasure*;" or, (says Professor Stuart,) *as it seemed good in his sight.*

Now, here it is expressly taught, first, that God only bestowed the Holy Spirit which accompanied the apostles' preaching; secondly, that the Holy Spirit was given according to the divine will, or discretion, and not according to any apostolic discretion. In the effusion and gifts of the Holy Spirit, God attested the truth and authority of apostolic preaching. But this *seal*, affixed to their apostleship, was the privy seal of the kingdom of heaven, committed to no created being. Christ alone possesses the keys—"he alone shuts and no man opens—he alone has the residue of the Spirit." It is hence Paul says, "for unto the angels hath he not (much less to *men*) put in subjection the world to come, whereof we speak." The phrase, την οικουμενην την μελλουσαν, translated *the world to come*, is equivalent to τω αιωνι μελλοντι, *the age*, or *world to come*, (Matt. xii, 32,) and signifies, in Jewish phraseology, *the gospel dispensation*, or, *the world as under the gospel kingdom.* This, God has never committed to men, or angels, but to Christ only. (See context of Heb. ii, 4.) But if Christ had intrusted the apostles with the power of baptizing with the Holy Spirit, they must have received, in this important commission, the very keys of the spiritual kingdom. But this error does not deserve to be further pursued under this head.

2. The commission of the apostles to baptize would

naturally have been understood by them of water baptism, unless special instruction had been given them to the contrary.

This is so plain, that I know not how it should have failed to prove a greater obstruction than it seems to have done to the faith of the disciples of George Fox.

The original command, or commission, specified "*teaching*" and "*baptizing*." This was the mode of operation to be observed by the apostles in evangelizing the world. Now, this had been the manner in which the Jews had long been accustomed to make proselytes. The disciples, were Jews, and as such, must have well understood this method of making Jewish proselytes; viz., by teaching, circumcision, and baptism. They also had been inducted into John's dispensation in the same way, circumcision only excepted. Teaching and water baptism were the accredited and common means of making converts hitherto, and thus the apostles, as Jews or as Christians, must have understood the words of their own commission. Christ himself had already practically taught them how to take these words, for, under his direction, they had already made converts by water baptism. See John iv, 1, 2. But,

3. The apostles did understand their commission as referring to water baptism, as is most clearly shown by their subsequent practice.

The first exercise of the apostolic functions put forth after the ascension, was in teaching and baptizing. Thus Peter, on the day of Pentecost, said to the inquiring multitude, "Repent, and be baptized every one of you, in the name of Jesus Christ, for the remission of sins; and ye shall receive the gift of the Holy Ghost." Here observe the order of duty—repentance, water baptism, and *then* they were promised the gift of spiritual baptism.

So, also, the baptism of the eunuch by Philip was a water baptism: "See, here is water; what doth hinder me to be baptized? . . . And they both went down into (or to) the water; and Philip baptized him," Acts viii, 36, 38.

In the case of Cornelius and his household, Peter says, *after* the Holy Spirit had descended upon them, "Can any man forbid water, that these should not be baptized, which have received the Holy Ghost as well as we?" Acts x, 47.

Here, as in other places, the baptism of water, and that of the Spirit, are plainly distinguished; and it should be remembered that water baptism was administered, either in direct anticipation of receiving the Holy Spirit, or in view of his influences already bestowed. It should be further remembered, that many of the instances of water baptism recorded in the New Testament, occurred under the direct and special suggestions of the Holy Spirit. Peter was sent on a special embassy to teach and baptize the house of Cornelius; and so of Philip and the eunuch. The reader may also consult Acts xix, 1–6, and other passages.

Now, water baptism we find to be most plainly an apostolic practice. We also find persons, professing Christianity, holding the practice in great repugnance, as a carnal rite, and "*as no part* of the gospel" of Jesus, and also holding that "the spiritual character of the gospel is intimately connected with its disuse." Here, then, we are brought to a direct issue, and one of the following conclusions is irresistibly forced upon us; viz., that either the apostles erred, and acted, not only *without* divine authority, but *against* that authority in a matter so vital as that which involved the spirituality and uncorruptness of the religion of Jesus; or, water baptism is a divinely instituted rite of the Christian religion. But if it be a divine institution, the duty of submission thereto needs no further argument. The proof is complete. "What man is he that feareth the Lord? Him shall he teach in the way that he shall choose."

CHAPTER X.

IMPORT OF BAPTISM.

We do not inquire in this place, what is the philological sense of βαπτιζω *baptizo?* but, what is the theological import of the rite of Christian baptism? Much that categorically belongs to this chapter has been brought forward in the course of the general argument on the mode of baptism. This became necessary to the complete developement of that subject, and we shall not repeat the same in this place.

Valid baptism assuredly comprehends a wider meaning than simple washing, or plunging in water. All washings do not equally constitute a baptism in the Christian sense. Some signification, *sui generis*, there doubtless is, which distinguishes baptism from all other washings. We have maintained the ground that *baptizo* means *purify*. This we believe to be its sense when used to express a religious rite in the New Testament. But the rite has a further meaning; it has an ad-signification, which a philological investigation of the word would not fully discover; and it also implies certain other circumstances, necessary to a valid administration. In setting forth our views under this head, we remark,—

1. In a general sense, Christian baptism confers the mark of *religious distinction*. Those who are baptized are thereby separated and distinguished from the common mass of irreligious men. A mark of discrimination is hereby applied to the Christian, and he is known as being devoted to Christ, just as a Jew, by circumcision, was distinguished from a Gentile, and known to be devoted to the law of Moses. It is the external and visible badge of Christianity. Some writers have indulged in a degree of fancy on this subject. Mr. Robinson says: "Baptize is a dyer's word, and signifies to dip so as to colour.... the word, then, conveys two ideas, the one literal, *dipping*, the other figurative, *colouring;* a figure, however, expressive of a real fact; meaning, that John, by bathing persons in

the river Jordan, conferred a character, a moral hue, as dyers, by dipping into a dying vat, set a tinct or colour."*

The author's theory would be well enough, if it were founded in evidence. He has deduced a secondary sense of βαπτω *bapto*, and applied it to βαπτιζω *baptizo*. The latter does not mean, to *dye*, or *colour*, anywhere; and how the author fell into the mistake is not easy to say. We do not, moreover, believe that baptism *confers* a *moral* tinct. This would be too much like regarding it as a regenerating rite. But it does confer an outward and visible relationship to Christ; and it constitutes the most considerable line of distinction, externally, between those who are the disciples of Christ, and those who are not.

2. Baptism is a *sacrament*. The word sacrament is not found in the New Testament, but comes from the Latin *sacramentum*, and has been borrowed from the writers of the Latin Church, and applied to baptism, and also to the institution of the holy supper. It is not for the word that we contend, but for the sense, the meaning, the idea. Sacramentum, among the ancient Romans, signified a gage, or pledge in money, deposited in court by the adverse parties that went to law, which, "being forfeited by the party that was cast, was devoted to *sacred* uses, and hence was called *sacramentum*."†

The word signified, also, an oath, because of its sacredness, but was especially applied to the military oath which the Roman law required of every soldier when he entered into military service, and which bound him to be true to his country and his general. Hence, the word was used by the Latin fathers to denote those ordinances of religion by which men came under an obligation of fidelity to the gospel. These, on account of their sacredness, and of their being a token of voluntary submission, were deemed binding as an oath. This sense was evidently in the minds of those who first adopted the term into the vocabulary of Christian theology, "as there are occasional allusions in the writings of the ancients to the military oath, when speaking of the sacraments.‡

By a very natural transition of thought, sanctioned by the universal consent and use of language, that which origi-

* History of Baptism, pp. 17, 18. † Dick's Theol., vol. ii, p. 353.
‡ Ibid., p. 354.

nally signified an oath, on account of its peculiar sacredness, at length became applicable to that which partook of the nature of, and was deemed equally sacred to, an oath.

Baptism, then, as a sacrament, confers upon its subjects the obligation of fidelity to God, arising in the scale of religious sanctity to the awful considerations of a formal oath. If common oaths among the Romans were sacred, their military oath was peculiarly so. The public service was important, and could not be intrusted to individuals, except under the most jealous and restrictive policy. Hence, not all citizens were admitted to the honour and rank of soldiers. Persons possessing no property were not supposed to be animated with sufficient patriotism, and were not included in the general rule of requisition as to military service. And none were admitted without the *sacramentum*, or military oath; as if the public safety required the most ample indemnity against the abuse of that power which was lodged in the military department. Delinquency, mutiny, desertion, were prohibited by the sanction of oaths, and the menace and terror of punishment.

With these views we may illustrate our baptismal obligations of fidelity to the cause of truth. This world is the theatre of one mighty struggle, not between belligerent states or empires, for political sovereignty, but, between truth and error, holiness and sin. Jesus Christ has appeared as the great captain of our salvation, leading forth the votaries of truth. The alien armies have leagued for the suppression and subversion of Bible truth and purity The parties have already taken the field; the battle-ground is squared, and the armies are now engaged. The rebel arms have triumphed over many lands that now dwell in the region and in the shadow of death. The enemy lies intrenched in surrounding error, superstition, and crime. Dark and strong are his holds; deep and almost impenetrable are his fastnesses. His spies and emissaries are abroad; they have gone up into the high places of the earth; they have entered into the very courts of God. Literature, laws, and religion, are menaced. Meantime, "wisdom hath uttered her voice in the streets; she hath cried in the chief place of concourse: unto you, O men, doth she call." She counsels, she warns, she expostulates with all, to turn to the defence of truth and righteousness; to "put on the whole armour of God." God has determined to leave the cause of truth in the earth, intrusted to human fidelity. Instrumentally, we are to achieve its final triumphs. Baptism is our sacramentum, or oath of fidelity; we take it, and arrange ourselves on the side of Christ. Every thing lodges here, subordinately, with human means, and human responsibility. Fidelity shall be crowned with life,—eternal life; "but if any man draw back, my soul shall have no pleasure in him."

We might seem to be wanting here, should we omit to notice the manner of explaining the sacraments adopted by divines in general, and sanctioned by the common usage of church formularies. It has been disputed what was the real occasion of the adoption of the term *sacrament* into Christian theology, and its application to the rites of baptism and the Lord's supper.* The correctness of the view we have taken above is not denied, but it has been supposed that the word sacrament was adopted mainly for another reason. Dr. Dick says, "I have long been disposed to doubt whether this is the true account of the ecclesiastical application of the term. In the writings of the early Christians it received a new meaning, of which I believe there is no example in the classics. It signifies a *mystery*, as every person knows who is conversant with the ancient records of the church, and as any [person] may learn by looking into the Vulgate translation. To give a few examples: 'Great is the *mystery* of godliness' is there rendered, 'Great is the *sacrament* of godliness,' '*magnum est pietatis sacramentum.*' For the words of Paul subjoined to the institution of marriage, 'This is a great *mystery*, but I speak concerning Christ and the church,' we have, 'This is a great *sacrament*,' &c., '*sacramentum hoc magnum est;*' and in the Revelation, 'The *mystery* of the seven stars, which thou sawest in thy right hand,' is, 'The *sacrament* of the seven stars,' &c., '*sacramentum septem stellarum.*' This is the translation of

* The Church of Rome hold to seven sacraments. In addition to baptism and the eucharist, confirmation, penance or penitence, orders, marriage, and extreme unction. We shall not, however, here consider their claims to this character.

the word μυστηριον *musterion*, [*mystery*,] which was used by the Greeks to denote, not only the profound and incomprehensible doctrines of the Trinity and the incarnation, but also baptism and the Lord's supper, and especially the latter, which was called ἁγιον μυστεριον, [*the holy* or *sacred mystery*,] partly, no doubt, because under external symbols spiritual blessings were veiled, but partly also on account of the secret manner in which it was celebrated. As the heathens had their mysteries, to which none but the initiated were admitted, so the church came at an early period to allow none to be present, when the Lord's supper was administered, but the baptized; and heathens, Jews, excommunicated persons, and catechumens, were excluded. Now, I think it probable that the word *mystery* having been used by the Greeks to express baptism and the Lord's supper, and the word *sacrament* having been used by the Latins as synonymous with mystery, it is in this way that we are to account for its application to those symbolical institutions. The sacraments are the mysteries of our religion. I do not deny, at the same time, that the other sense of the word may have had some influence, as there are occasional allusions, in the writings of the ancients, to the military oath, in speaking of the sacraments."*

This view is evidently sustained by the authorized instruction of orthodox churches. In the Confession of Faith of the Presbyterian Church, chap. xxvii, it is said, "Sacraments are holy signs and seals of the covenant of grace, immediately instituted by God to represent Christ and his benefits." "There is, in every sacrament, a special relation, or sacramental union, between the sign and the thing signified." In the larger catechism it is asked, "What are the parts of a sacrament? Ans. The parts of a sacrament are two: the one an outward and sensible sign, used according to Christ's own appointment; the other an inward and spiritual grace, thereby signified." Here, it is evident, the ground is taken that the adoption of the word sacrament is mainly in view of the *sacred*, or *mysterious*, spirtual relation that subsists between the outward ceremony or rite, and the inward grace. Thus, also,

* Lectures on Theology, vol. ii, pp. 353, 354.

the Church of England defines sacraments to be "not only badges and tokens of Christian men's profession; but rather they be certain sure witnesses and effectual signs of grace, and God's good will toward us, *by the which he doth work invisibly in us*, and doth not only quicken, but also strengthen and confirm our faith in him."* The same doctrine and phraseology are adopted by the Methodist Episcopal Church, in her sixteenth article of religion.

What weight is to be attached to the hypothesis that *sacrament* in Latin and *mystery* in Greek, as applied to the Christian ordinances, are borrowed from the usage of the heathens in regard to their mysteries, denoting the exclusion from these institutes of all but the initiated, we shall not undertake to decide. The above facts will aid the reader in forming an opinion of the import of baptism, so far as the nature of a sacrament is concerned: it denotes our obligation of fidelity to Christ, and it mystically adumbrates spiritual blessings.

3. But in contemplating baptism as the *sign* of spiritual blessings, we are conducted to a distinct view of the subject. Without repeating what has been said in another part of this work, on the import of baptism as a ceremonial washing, we may remark that it stands, generically, for the whole work of grace wrought in the soul; but by a common figure of speech, whereby a part is put for the whole,—a figure often used in Scripture,—it is sometimes spoken of as representing a particular portion only of this work. We are not to suppose, however, that baptism stands, distinctively, for the blessings of pardon, regeneration, the resurrection, &c., as some have fancifully maintained; but for the entire work of salvation *as a whole.* To this work there are, indeed, different stages, and a diversity of spiritual influences is manifest throughout, but it is the grand *total* of these operations,—the new creation,—that is set forth by baptism. This is the view set forth in John iii, 5; Titus iii, 4–6; 1 Pet. iii, 21; and in other places. For further remarks on this point the reader is referred to chap. vii of this work, on figurative language of Scripture, sec. 1.

4. Baptism is the *seal* of the new covenant. It is God's

* Twenty-fifth article of faith.

mark or *signature*, affixed to the all-important document, containing rules for human conduct, promises of eternal life to the faithful, and declarations concerning the future destiny of men.

In regard to the use of *seals* in general, it may be proper to premise, that it is a custom of immemorial usage, resorted to as a convenient mode of attesting the genuineness or authenticity of the instrument sealed. Anciently, when the art of writing was little known, and in all cases attended with great expense and trouble, the practice of sealing contracts was extensively adopted. Every man had his seal, which he affixed to an instrument instead of signing his own proper name. As the seal stood for the signature of the person who possessed it, whatever contract or document bore the seal of an individual, it thereby bound that individual to all the conditions, duties, &c., therein contained. The practice originated in necessity, at a time when few could write; but having once obtained, as a general custom, it continued long after the necessity which gave it birth had ceased to exist. The Bible contains various interesting allusions to this custom of sealing, which the proper line of our argument does not permit us here to notice.

God has always affixed his *seal*, or *mark*, or *sign*, or *signature*,—whatever we may please to call it,—to his dispensations; and, in doing this, he has accommodated the simplicity of the sign to the state and circumstances of man. Of this nature, it is reasonable to suppose, was the tree of life in the garden of Eden. It seems most probable, that Adam partook of its fruit sacramentally; that is, it was to him a token or pledge of the life which was promised him in case of obedience, while his act of partaking was a voluntary recognition of his obligation to obey, and a renewal of his fidelity.

When Jehovah covenanted with Noah, after the diluvial catastrophe, promising "not to smite any more every living thing," he "set his bow in the cloud;" and "God said, *This is the* TOKEN *of the covenant* which I make between me and you and every living creature. . . And it shall come to pass, that when I bring a cloud over the earth, that the bow shall be seen in the cloud: AND I WILL REMEMBER MY COVENANT which is between me and you and every living creature of all flesh; and the bow shall be in the cloud; AND I WILL LOOK UPON IT, THAT I MAY REMEMBER THE EVERLASTING COVENANT between God and every living creature..... And God said unto Noah, *This is the* TOKEN *of the covenant* which I have established between me and all flesh that is upon the earth," Gen. ix, 11-17.

It is here observable, that the *token*, or *sign*, (σημειον,) exhibited thus, was to be as a remembrancer of the obligation, and a perpetual pledge of the fidelity of Jehovah in the performance of the promises of the covenant.

This simple form of binding parties in a transaction was suited to the genius of those times, and may be familiarly illustrated by the affair of Laban and Jacob, recorded Gen. xxxi, 44-49. They formed a mutual covenant, and Jacob and his brethren gathered stones, of which they made a heap. This heap they called "*the heap* of witness." Its use and meaning was to remind either party of the covenant there formed, and equally bind both to the observance of the stipulations. In the case of default of either party, this heap of stones would witness against the delinquent; that is, it would attest the validity and genuineness of the contract.

I need not inform the intelligent reader, that these transactions belong to a rude and simple state of society, in which written contracts are little if at all known. In civilized society, altogether a different method obtains. A written instrument is drawn up, bearing the proper signatures of the contracting parties, and they are thus holden to the agreement.

Circumcision was the seal of the Abrahamic covenant, under the Mosaic law. At the time of its institution Abraham was informed, that it should "be *a* TOKEN *of the covenant*" between God and him. Gen. xvii, 11. Thus also Paul: "And he [Abraham] received the SIGN of circumcision, a SEAL of the righteousness of the faith which he had," &c., Rom. iv, 11. Circumcision, therefore, among the lineal descendants of Abraham, was the *visible mark* which Jehovah annexed to this covenant,—it became the impress of Jehovah's *seal*, whereby he attested the validity and binding nature of the covenant, and offered assurance to the Jews of his own faithfulness; just as a man would bind himself in a contract, by affixing his *seal*, *signature* or *mark* to the instrument. I need hardly say, that, in receiving circumcision, the Jews voluntarily became a party in the covenant, and assumed the obligations that it devolved upon them.

Of this nature is baptism, under the New Testament dispensation. It is a seal of the covenant which God has graciously entered into with man. It should here be remembered, that the gospel is nothing more than the complete development of the Abrahamic covenant. This covenant stretches through all time, and comprehends all nations within its liberal provisions. It was a covenant of grace and mercy, of pardon and eternal life, conditionally, to universal man; not merely of secular good to a partial few. Hence, says Paul, "*If ye be Christ's*, THEN *are ye Abraham's seed, and heirs* ACCORDING TO THE PROMISE." He declares the gospel was preached to Abraham when the promise was made: "In thee shall all nations be blessed." "For the promise, that he should be the heir of the world, was not to Abraham, or his seed through the law, but through the righteousness of faith." See Gal. iii, 7, 9, 16, 29; Rom. iv, 13, &c.; comp. Gen. xii, 2, 3, and xxii, 18. The blessings of this covenant were partially revealed and bestowed under the law of Moses. At that time it bore the seal or mark of circumcision. But in these gospel days God has appointed baptism as the sign or seal. "For as many of you as have been baptized into Christ, have put on Christ. There is [therefore, now,] neither Jew nor Greek, there is neither bond nor free, there is neither male nor female: for ye are all one in Christ Jesus." Other remarks might here be offered; but as, in our estimation, the proper idea of baptism, as a seal, is now before the reader, the just limits of our subject do not allow us to go into collateral views for general improvement. Baptism authenticates the divine word and promise to the proper subject, while the latter, by submitting thereto, becomes a willing party to the covenant, and underwrites his name to the doctrines and duties of the cross.

5. Baptism is a badge, or profession, of Christian discipleship. It confers an obligation, or rather is a recognition and avowal of an obligation, to be like Christ. In Rom. vi, 3, 4, it imports our obligation of death unto sin

and life with respect to holiness. This has been elsewhere noticed. (*Vide* chap. vii.) Paul says to the Galatians, (chap. iii, 27,) "For as many of you as have been baptized into Christ have put on Christ." The verb ἐνεδυσασθε, translated *ye have put on*, is a reflexive form of the verb ενδυνω, *to clothe, to invest, to array*. As if the apostle had said, "For as many of you as have been baptized into Christ *have clothed yourselves* with Christ." To *put on* a person, or *to be clothed* with a person, was a figurative mode of expression among the Greeks, signifying the most *exact imitation* of that person. To "put on Christ" is a phrase of frequent occurrence in the New Testament, and means, says Professor Robinson, "to be filled, imbued with Christ's spirit, to be like him."* When we clothe ourselves with or put on Christ, we assume his character and act as he acted. "The mode of speech is taken from the custom of stage-players; they assumed the *name* and *garments* of the person whose *character* they were to act, and endeavoured as closely as possible to imitate him in their spirit, words, and actions."†

By baptism, then, we publicly invest ourselves with Christianity. We assume the *name*, and *habits*, and *profession* of Christ. We publicly engage to act as he acted,—to carry out his spirit and doctrines in our lives,—to *imitate* his example,—in a word, to be *Christians*. It is only in cases where baptism is wrongly applied, where the candidate is insincere and hypocritical, or unfaithful to his baptismal engagements, that the ordinance loses its original power and signification, and becomes an empty and an idle ceremony.

* Greek and English Lex. † Dr. A. Clarke on Rom. xiii, 14.

CHAPTER XI.

RELATIVE ORDER OF BAPTISM.

THE question on the mode of baptism borrows all its importance from the question, "Is Christian baptism itself essentially prerequisite to a Scriptural participation of the Lord's supper?" This latter topic has been treated adjunctively with the question of the mode, and lends to it an unspeakable interest. Divines have not entered the polemic arena to show their skill and tact at debate. The long and painful controversy on the subject of the mode of Christian baptism has not been merely a display of intellectual parts. The Corinthians are justly censurable for wasting time and intellectual power, and brotherly charity, in a controversy concerning "meats and drinks, and new moons, and holy days;" the schoolmen have exhibited themselves to the ridicule of all succeeding generations, for their fruitless and eternal disputations on such points as, whether there is any possible distinction between essence and existence—whether an angel, or pure spirit, can pass from one absolute point to another without passing over the intermediate space; and nearly allied to such topics must be the question of the mode of baptism, if it have no further importance than the mere convenience or fitness of an outward ceremony. But the case is far otherwise. The bearing which the *mode* of baptism is alleged to have on the *validity* of the ordinance; and the connection which it bears to the lawful approach to the Lord's table, and to the rights and immunities of church fellowship; these invest it with a character of paramount importance. The question no longer respects merely a ceremony of religion, but has assumed the bold and alarming aspect of CHURCH OR NO CHURCH! Every ordinance, every institution, every rite and privilege of visible Christianity, is drawn along and merged into the bosom of this doubtful controversy. Within its ample folds are embraced the questions of true Protestantism and pure Christianity; while its capacious vortex has set in motion the very pillars of the visible church, threatening to whelm it in its troubled waters. The issues of this controversy are to decide whether the Pedobaptist churches are the true churches of Christ; whether their ministers hold their commission to administer the ordinances by a lawful tenure; whether their members have any right to approach to the table of the Lord, and whether the privileges of the church may be conceded to them without desecration. Verily, the question of the mode of baptism is a far-reaching subject. Without controversy it is a grave theme.

Before entering upon the argument before us, it is but just to remark that in one principle the Baptist and Pedobaptist churches agree. They both agree in rejecting from communion at the table of the Lord, and in denying the rights of church fellowship to, all who have not been baptized. Valid baptism they consider as essential to constitute visible church membership. This also we hold. The only question, then, that here divides us, is, "What is essential to valid baptism?" The Baptists, in passing the sweeping sentence of disfranchisement upon all other Christian churches, have only acted upon a principle held in common with all other Christian churches; viz., that baptism is essential to church membership. They have denied our baptism, and, as unbaptized persons, we have been excluded from their table. That they err greatly in their views of Christian baptism, we, of course, believe. But, according to their views of baptism, they certainly are consistent in restricting thus their communion. We would not be understood as passing a judgment of approval upon their course; but we say, their views of baptism force them upon the ground of strict communion, and herein they act upon the same principles as other churches, i. e., they admit only those whom they deem baptized persons to the communion table. Of course, they must be their own judges as to what baptism is. It is evident that, according to our views of baptism, we can admit them to our communion; but with their views of baptism, it is equally evident, they can never reciprocate the courtesy. And the charge of *close communion* is no more applicable to the Baptists than to us, inasmuch as the question of church fellowship with them is determined by as liberal principles as it is with any other Protestant churches, so far, I mean, as the present subject is concerned; i. e., it is determined by valid baptism.

Now, this being the case, does it not become a measure of responsible moment to decide upon the question of the mode of baptism? Indeed, so awful are the aspects of this subject, that thousands have feared to assume a decided position in reference to it. They have held to exclusive immersion, and at the same time have held to catholic communion, or communion with persons who have not been immersed,—an anomaly and absurdity that presents a singular contrast to the characteristic symmetry of Christian theology. Robert Hall thinks it may be doubted that the belief of close communion is the sentiment of the majority of the Baptist denomination.*

This clearly shows, after all their plausible reasonings in support of exclusive immersion, how intimidated men are at the terrible sequences of that theory. And well may they be. But it is far less responsible, in our estimation, to hold that baptism may be administered by sprinkling or pouring, than to hold fellowship, at the Lord's table, with persons we do not believe have received Christian baptism.

We now proceed to arrange and bring forward the main arguments which may be adduced in support of the position that baptism should precede the act of communion at the Lord's table. It has been urged by Baptist writers who have plead for strict communion, that the institution of baptism was prior to the institution of the Lord's supper, and that, therefore, the administration of the former should always take place prior to the participation of the latter. This argument, however, is built entirely upon the hypothesis that Christian baptism originated with John the Baptist. We trust it has already been satisfactorily shown that the baptism of John was not identical with that which was administered by the apostles after the resurrection. The argument, therefore, cannot be relied on. Besides, we cannot perceive what force an argument can embody, which is deduced merely from the chronological order of institution.

1. The first argument under this head is based upon the order of the apostolic commission.

* Works, vol. i, p. 401.

The words of the commission, as given by Matthew, (chap. xxviii, 19, 20,) run thus: "Go ye therefore, and teach all nations, baptizing them in the name of the Father, and of the Son, and of the Holy Ghost: teaching them to observe all things whatsoever I have commanded you," &c. It is well known that our English version does not give a satisfactory view of this passage. The word rendered *teach*, in the nineteenth verse, is altogether a different word, in the Greek text, from that which is rendered *teach*, in verse 20. It should read: "Go ye therefore and *disciple*, i. e., *make converts to Christianity*, of (μαθητευσατε) all nations, baptizing them, &c.... *teaching* (διδασκοντες) them to observe," &c. Here it is to be observed, first, certain *things* are enjoined; viz., to disciple, to baptize, and to teach; secondly, these things are enjoined in a certain *order;* viz., the order in which they stand in the divine commission. The apostles were first required to persuade the people to forsake heathenism and Judaism, and embrace Christianity. This being done, the next injunction in order, in their commission, was to baptize them. Being thus brought into a church relationship with one another, and to a visible relation to Christ, they were to be taught to observe all things whatsoever Christ had commanded. Of course the ordinance of the supper was one of the "all things whatsoever" alluded to. One thing further deserves particular notice. The participial form of the word baptize (βαπτιζοντες) indicates that the nations were to be discipled BY baptism; and this ordinance was certainly a public recognition of discipleship. If baptism was to be the public process of making disciples, or of recognising men as such, then, it is plain, it must precede communion.

Without adverting at large to the controversies which have been had on this passage, we may simply remark, that we cannot appreciate the difficulties that have been urged as attending the above mode of construing the divine commission of the apostles. It is true that the ordinance of the supper is not particularized as coming in either before or after baptism; but the reasonable, and, indeed, the necessary presumption is, that it is one of the things commanded to be taught *after* baptism. It is certain that baptism is enjoined as the first public duty after discipleship; or, it may be regarded as the very act itself, or process, of visible discipleship. The very position, therefore, that baptism is made to occupy, in relation to a course of Christian duty, viz., at the commencement, sufficiently establishes the conclusion that the ordinances of the supper, and all other observances which have an exclusive reference to the Christian profession, must come in as subsequent duties.

The reader will perceive that this argument is based entirely upon the ORDER of the apostolic commission. It may be questioned by some whether the argument is genuine, and whether it is entitled to any considerable force. But suppose we assume an opposite ground? Suppose we say that the *things* commanded are important to be done, but that the *order* observed in the commission is a subject of indifference. Now, what will be the consequence of this position? What, but total and irretrievable confusion? The apostles go forth; they are intent upon doing *all* that Christ commanded them, but the *order* of the duties is a subject of indifference. The consequence is that some are baptized before they are converted from heathenism; some receive the holy supper before either baptism or conversion; others are engaged in a course of instruction before they are discipled; and the most incoherent and unsuitable practices everywhere prevail. Improper persons are baptized, or baptism is improperly delayed; the holy supper is approached before the candidate has been duly prepared, and it is therefore desecrated, or it is unduly withheld from rightful communicants. Is not the prescribed ORDER, therefore, in the administration of the ordinances, and the duties of the apostolic commission, all important? And thus we hold that Christ *enjoined* the *order* as well as the *duties* themselves; and, in this order of Christ, baptism precedes communion at the Lord's table.

2. Our second argument is drawn from apostolic precedent.

It will be more satisfactory to inquire, How did the apostles understand their commission with respect to the relative order of the Christian institutes? The argument from apostolic precedent is undeniably important. They were commissioned to teach the converted nations "to observe all things whatsoever" Christ had commanded. This was the extent, and this the limit of their authority. Hence, Paul says to the Corinthians: "*I have received of the Lord* THAT *which I delivered unto you.*" Hence he says,—"I praise you, brethren, *that ye .... keep the ordinances* AS *I delivered them unto you.*" "Stand fast and hold the traditions which ye have been taught, whether by word or our epistle." Their teaching, also, was uniform. The order of one church was the order of all the churches: "as I teach everywhere in every church," says Paul. 1 Cor. iv, 17, and xi, 2, 23; 2 Thess. ii, 15. Whatever, therefore, was the practice of the apostles, we must suppose that that practice was founded upon the command and instructions of Christ. We speak now, not of forms of church government, or any other accident of the apostolic churches; but we speak particularly of what concerns the doctrines, ordinances, and spiritual order of the churches; and we need hardly say that apostólic precedent is, therefore, endued with the same authority over our faith and practice, as any of the commands of Christ. They received ample instructions from Christ, and those instructions were faithfully carried out. And though they did not adduce, in each particular instance, the express command authorizing them thus to act, still, we must suppose them to be endued with such authority. The act must necessarily imply the specific instruction from Christ, unless we suppose (which no consistent believer in revelation will suppose) the apostles were left, on important occasions, to act at option, without any divine authority or instruction. But their commission utterly forbade such a discretion on their part. They were strictly charged, not, to act their own private judgment or discretion; not, to teach the doctrines of their fancy, or administer the ordinances at haphazard, but, to teach "all things whatsoever" Christ commanded them. To teach more or less than was commanded, or to establish precedents unauthorized by Christ, would be plainly transcending their commission, or betraying their trust.

What. then, did the apostles *teach* and *practise*, with respect to the time and relative order of baptism? On the day of Pentecost, when the people inquired of the apostles, "Men and brethren, what shall we do?" Peter answered, "Repent and be baptized every one of you." Luke sums up the glorious results of that memorable day, thus: "Then they that gladly received the word were baptized: and the same day were added to the church about three thousand souls. And they continued steadfastly in the apostles' doctrine and fellowship, and in breaking of bread and in prayers," Acts ii, 41, 42. This was the first occasion on which the apostles were called upon to exercise their high commission. It was only ten days after they had received that commission, and the freshness of that event, and the plenary inspiration of the Holy Spirit now received, all combined to render it certain that on this occasion they would not act under the influence of any mistaken views as to their duty, or the powers of their office. And here, indeed, we are called upon to notice particularly the *order* in which they enforced the divine precepts. Upon their adult, penitent hearers, they enjoined, first repentance, then baptism, then the duty of church fellowship, then "breaking of bread," or the Lord's supper. Comparing the order here observed with the order of the words of their original commission, we are struck with admiration at the prompt fidelity of the apostles.

A few examples more must suffice to illustrate the uniform practice of the apostles:

Acts viii, 12: When the Samaritans believed Philip, "they were baptized, both men and women."

Ver. 13: Simon believed and was baptized.

Verses 36–38: The eunuch was baptized immediately after professing faith in Christ.

Acts ix, 18: Saul received his sight, and arose and was baptized.

Although Saul was evidently weak through long fasting, as appears from the next verse, still he was baptized before he took meat. It is worthy of notice that Paul, in rehearsing the matter afterward before a large and tumultuous concourse of Jews, represents Ananias as chiding a little delay in coming to baptism, after his conversion: "And now, *why tarriest thou?* Arise and be baptized."

Acts x, 47, 48: After the Holy Spirit had descended upon Cornelius and his household, Peter "commanded them to be baptized" on the spot.

Acts xvi, 14, 15: "The Lord opened Lydia's heart that she attended unto the things which were spoken by Paul. And when she was baptized, she besought us," &c.

Ver. 33: When the jailer believed, "he was baptized, he and all his *straightway*."

Acts xviii, 8: "And many of the Corinthians hearing, believed, and were baptized."

The above quotations need no comment to make them plainer in their teaching, respecting the relative order of baptism. They bear an unequivocal testimony to the point, that baptism was commanded and administered as the next act of religious duty after conversion. This was apostolic practice; and, if we suppose them not to have transcended, nor to have fallen short of the instructions of Christ, and the powers of their commission, but, on the contrary, to have acted upon divine authority in all those important matters which relate to the administration and order of the Christian institutes, we must admit the authority of their practice to be valid ground of action for us, and that, to depart from their practice, is, to say the least, a doubtful and dangerous policy. It will not be doubted that what the apostles enjoined upon their converts is equally binding upon the disciples of Jesus in all ages. Peter commands Cornelius to be baptized; and this command, originally addressed to the centurion, is admitted, under all similar circumstances, to have the same authority over us that it had over the faith and practice of the Roman. On this ground, we shall have no controversy with any person who admits the obligation of external ordinances. But why may we not suppose, also, that the same *order* of duty is now binding on every adult candidate for baptism? Is not baptism binding upon us, as the next duty in order after conversion, as much as it was upon Cornelius, or the converts on the day of Pentecost? Suppose Cornelius had withstood Peter on the question of the order of baptism? Suppose he had desired Peter to defer baptism till after he had communed at the Lord's table, or to some indefinite period? Would he not, in this instance, have arrayed himself against a positive command of God? The command was, to be baptized. This was enjoined as the next act of religious duty after conversion. The time and relative order of the institution were points of palpable and direct obligation, as well as the ordinance itself in the abstract; and to invert this order, or defer baptism, would have been to oppose the divine arrangement.

We readily admit, the obligation of the eucharist rests "on the precept that enjoins it," and not "on the previous reception of baptism." But the *order* of the eucharist in relation to baptism is a distinct question from that of primary obligation, and a question that rests upon other ground. It is asked, "Where is it asserted in the New Testament, that no unbaptized person shall partake of the eucharist?"* We answer, It is nowhere so asserted. But what then? Is the controversy settled? Far from it. The argument does not necessarily hinge on that kind of evidence; and yet, the evidence which the Bible affords is scarcely a shade inferior to that of positive declaration, and certainly is sufficient to decide the controversy. But if men are not satisfied with the light in which the Bible has left the question, still, there is no higher source of evidence to which they may carry their appeals—the case is without remedy. The argument from apostolic precedent we consider fairly deduced, and of sufficient authority to decide this controversy. We readily admit that such arguments are often, from their very nature, somewhat liable to objection. The difficulty lies in determining what constitutes a precedent; and also, whether the particular conduct appealed to is of such a nature. The apostles felt themselves at times impelled, from the force of local circumstances, to act in a particular way. In such cases their conduct could not be proposed as a universal model. But no such restrictive circumstances can be supposed to impart a local aspect to their uniform practice with respect to the time and relative order of baptism. Herein their conduct was evidently regulated by the high and authoritative tenor of their commission. Herein their practice was the same in all countries, among all nations and classes of men, in all climates, and at all times. So universal a practice can be regarded in no other light than as forming an apostolic precedent, and if so, it furnishes an authoritative rule

* Rev. R. Hall's Works, vol. i, p. 306.

of faith and practice to the Christian church in all ages of the world.

3. Our third argument is deduced from the *nature* and relative import of the Christian ordinances.

That eloquent and incomparable polemic, the Rev. Robert Hall, was the great champion of the rights of open communion. Himself a Baptist, and at the same time a strenuous advocate of what Mr. Benedict, the Baptist historian, calls "the embarrassing practice of open communion;" surrounded by great spirits of the antagonistic party, of whom not the least were the gigantic Fullers, he gave unlimited range to his mighty genius, and left no weapons untried—no resources unexplored—that might aid in establishing his own favourite theory, or in confounding his numerous and powerful opponents. His writings have produced, as might have been expected, a deep and abiding impression upon many minds. Those who wish to find an answer to Mr. Hall, from a member of his own order, will find it in the work of J. G. Fuller on communion. We can give no more than the general weight of the argument here, leaving the reader to follow out the minuter bearings at will.

Among the subtle and plausible arguments of Mr. Hall is the following:—"To justify the exclusion of such [i. e., unbaptized persons] from the Lord's table, it is not sufficient to allege the prescribed *order* of the institutions; it is necessary also to evince such a *dependance* of one upon the other, that a neglect of the first, from involuntary mistake, annuls the obligation of the second.... But we affirm, that in no part of Scripture is it [baptism] calculated as a *preparative to the Lord's table*."*

In all positive institutes it is sufficient for us to know the authority on which they are founded, and the order in which they are enjoined; for our obligation to observe them rests, primarily, not so much on the force of our perceptions of their abstract reasonableness and propriety, as upon the clear dictates of that divine authority which first erected them into the forms of law. The Bible has certainly left the question of the order of the Christian institutions in an obvious, intelligible light. It is true,

* Works, vol. i, p. 306–7.

the practice of the apostles rather establishes the simple, yet invariable, *priority* of baptism than asserts any correlative dependance of the two ordinances. But, pausing here, let us inquire, Is not this sufficient? If the invariable *priority* of baptism can be maintained by all the evidence which the sacred history furnishes, what more need be done? Are we to reject this evidence, and appeal to the fitness of things on a question respecting a positive institute? Such a procedure, we hesitate not to pronounce, is wholly unwarrantable, and the principle dangerous to adopt. We cannot suspend this question on such a pivot. It would be rejecting the palpable testimony of God, and flying to our own fallible, partial perceptions of abstract truth. It would be to exalt our own deductions from abstract principles, not merely to a level with, but above the level of apostolic practice and precedent. We cannot rest any great stress of argument upon the intrinsic character, the abstract fitness, or the natural dependance of these rites. This is a mode of arguing that should, to say the least, be admitted with caution on subjects of this nature, and should never be allowed to rise higher in its authority than the positive light of revelation. Positive duties are not like moral precepts: they do not, like the latter, arise in the order of a natural series, where each succeeding duty flows as a consequence of the pre-existent state of the mind. That we are often able to trace an abstract fitness and propriety in them, is true. But their authority, as rules of action for us, does not rest on our perceptions of that fitness and propriety. All that we may hope to know clearly and perfectly, in general, is, that by an adequate authority they are enjoined upon us.

Yet we do not wholly refuse to meet the objector on this ground. Nay, we here erect one of our most satisfactory arguments, next to the apostolic commission and the apostolic precedent.

1. Can any person of intelligence persuade himself that the uniform practice of the apostles, in relation to the order of the Christian institutions, was the result of any loose, unsettled notions with respect to their proper order? Does not the perfect *harmony* of their conduct, in this case, clearly indicate in them established principles, clear and intelligent views of the nature and relative dependance

of the ordinances, and also unity of sentiment? Now, this is not begging the question. This is not reasoning in a circle. We say, the apostles did administer the ordinances in a certain *order*. We hold that the *uniformity* of their practice, herein, can be accounted for only on the supposition of *settled views* of the ordinances, and these views originated in divine authority, and in the perceptions of reason; not in chance, or fortuitous circumstances. Here, then, we argue the necessity of a certain *theory* from the certainty and uniformity of given *facts*. We argue that there is, and must be, a *fitness* in this order of the Christian institutes, or the apostles would not have so uniformly adopted and practised it. If it had been otherwise—if the ordinances have no natural dependance—if it may be a matter of perfect indifference which is attended to first—if the apostles had no reason *in the nature of the case* for their uniform practice—why have they left us no exceptions to their general conduct? If chance, or circumstances, control the question, why has it not assumed a more equivocal aspect? We are willing these suggestions should pass for what they may be worth.

2. Although the obligation and order of positive precepts rest on the annunciations of legislative authority, and not on the nature and fitness of things; still, there *is* a fitness, either relative or absolute, in their existence and their order, and this fitness we may generally trace to a considerable extent. For instance, baptism, from its nature, stands at the opening of the visible career. It is a badge of the Christian profession—the seal of the gospel covenant—the ordinance of admission into the visible church of Christ. Previously to baptism, the individual has no rights in the visible church. Setting aside, for the present, communion at the Lord's table as a mooted right of the unbaptized, they have no privileges as the members of Christ's mystical body. No society of Christians would receive an unbaptized person into their community, and tender to him the privileges of their body. So far as proper church rights and privileges are concerned, he is regarded in the same light as any unconverted man. The converts on the day of Pentecost were first baptized, and then added to the church. The concurrent voice of

the Christian world excludes an unbaptized person from fellowship in the visible church of God. On the contrary, the eucharist, from its very nature, is a church ordinance, and as such can be properly participated in only by church members. As a church ordinance, it never can be carried out of the church. This is so evident that no words can make it more plain, or add to its force. And here lies the relative dependance of the ordinances. Baptism is the ordinance of initiation into the church; it is therefore applied, not to church members, but to persons without, in order to bring them within the pale and fellowship of visible Christianity. But the eucharist is not an initiatory ordinance; it belongs to those who have been brought into the church by baptism; to recognised and acknowledged members. Hence it has a retrospective relation to baptism. It is not our business here to give a treatise on the nature of the eucharist, but we cannot withhold from the reader a few further remarks.

3. According to the true, Oriental notion of a feast, this eucharistic feast is a token of *fellowship*. Those who meet at the Lord's table signify thereby that they have mutual fellowship in the faith, experience, and practice of the gospel. Hence, Paul calls it the "*communion* of the body and blood of Christ;" "for we, being many, are one bread and one body; for we are all partakers of that one bread." Or, says Dr. A. Clarke, "The original would be better translated thus: *Because there is one bread*, or *loaf*, *we*, *who are many*, *are one body*," 1 Cor. x, 16, 17. This feasting together declares a community of interest in the merits of the same Jesus whose sacrificial death is exhibited in the distributed elements, and proves the disciples of Christ to be "ONE BODY." How, then, can an ordinance which manifestly declares its recipients, though "*many*" individuals, to be "ONE BODY," be administered to those who are *not of that* "*body?*" If the celebration of the Lord's supper be a recognition and acknowledgment of church fellowship among the communicants, I know not how it is to be extended to those who hold no such fellowship with Christians.

From the above view of the case, therefore, we are warranted in concluding that there is a natural fitness in the order of the Christian ordinances, as exhibited in apostolic practice. We are able to trace a relative dependance, and we perceive a reason for giving the priority of order to baptism.

4. But we take the ground that, if unbaptized persons are to be admitted to the Lord's table because their exclusion is not expressly required by any prohibitive law, so also, by parity of reasoning, their admission is not to be allowed, because it is not expressly enjoined in the word of God.

If it be a responsible act to reject them, in the absence of an express interdict; certainly it is not less responsible to admit them in the absence of an express command. If, in rejecting them, there is danger of offending a "little one that believes" in Christ; so also, in receiving them, there is danger of diverting the ordinance from its intended application, and profaning its sanctity. If express precept is what the advocates of mixed communion demand, certainly they are in no better case than we are. And we have the same authority for rejecting, as they have for receiving unbaptized persons to the table of the Lord; and, so far as we can now judge, they incur a responsibility of no less magnitude than we ourselves. The truth is, that the preponderance of Scripture evidence is against mixed communion; and yet our opponents think it far less hazardous, in a matter which they think the Bible has not directly decided, to neglect this preponderating testimony, the best evidence the case affords. "There is no position," says Robert Hall, "in the whole compass of theology, of the truth of which I feel a stronger persuasion than that no man, or set of men, are entitled to prescribe, as an indispensable condition of communion, what the New Testament has not enjoined as a condition of salvation."* So then, either baptism is necessary to salvation, or it is not necessary to communion at the Lord's table. But if baptism be not necessary to communion, it is not necessary to church fellowship, and to a union with Christ's mystical body, for feasting together at the communion table is an outward expression of our being "*one body*," and hence a person can belong to the visible church, or, which is the

* Preface to "Terms of Communion," Works, vol. i, p. 285.

same, enjoy all the immunities of the visible church, without baptism. Yes, this is the sequence of the charitable position of that eloquent and admirable writer; this is the bearing of his argument, when stripped of its cumbersome verbosity, and dismantled of the charms of its diction. It is true, much may be said on the subject of "Christian toleration," "brotherly love," "involuntary ignorance," in lefence of mixed communion; but, specious as are all such pleas, they are wholly inadmissible in a controversy like this. In admitting persons to church fellowship we do not act upon a discretionary power, as to the terms to be dictated. Those terms are already settled by the great Head of the church. All our discretion in the premises consists in judging of the conformity of the candidate to the terms already prescribed,—whether he comes within the provisions of the charter, and may claim its rich and heavenly immunities.

"Men will, ere long, tremble," says Robert Hall, "at the thought of being more strict than Christ, more fastidious in the selection of members to the church militant, than he is in choosing the members of the church triumphant:" to which Mr. J. G. Fuller has replied in the following forcible and sensible manner: "You take it for granted," says he, "that the rule of admission into the church militant and the church triumphant *is one and the same rule;* a position perpetually asserted and assumed, but totally incapable of proof. In the admission of members into the celestial church, Christ acts as a *sovereign:* in the admission of members to Christian churches on earth, we must act as *servants*, yielding implicit, undeviating obedience to the direction of our sovereign Lord. To reproach us with being 'more fastidious in the selection of the members of the church militant, than Christ is in choosing the members of the church triumphant,' may be applauded as an unanswerable argument by those who are less attentive to sense than to sound, to reason than to the charms of eloquence. Could you reproach us with being more strict, more fastidious, in the selection of our members, than the commission of Christ requires us to be, there would be some justice in the rebuke: at present there is none; and it may better become those to 'tremble' who are *less* strict, *less* fastidious, than their Lord's commission, and who wish to receive members [to their communion] in a way which Christ *never authorized.*"*

To these sensible remarks there can be no rejoinder. If Christ has left us directions for the formation and spiritual order of his church, we are concerned no further than to understand and apply those rules. And although in moral purity the militant church should be an image of the heavenly family; still, to assert that the external ordinances are no more necessary to fellowship in the former than in the latter, or that a strict analogy obtains here between the two great branches of God's redeemed offspring, is to transcend the powers of the divine commission, and treat the authoritative injunctions of Christ with unlimited discretion.

5. We argue from the analogy of Jewish and Christian rites.

Baptism and the Lord's supper bear the same relation to the Christian church, that circumcision and the passover did to the Jewish church. It does not become necessary for us here to enter into the proof of this statement. The proof is abundant, and the case is clear. Among the Jews the passover was celebrated only by those who had been previously circumcised. Circumcision was an indispensable prerequisite to a seat at the paschal feast, not so much on account of any natural dependance between the two rites, as of the relative positions they were made to occupy, and the peculiar ends they were destined to serve. Circumcision was the ceremony of initiation into the Jewish church, as baptism is to the Christian church. The passover of the old dispensation is revived under the new, in the ordinance of the Lord's supper; "Christ our passover is sacrificed for us." The passover could not be carried out of the church to uncircumcised persons, neither can the eucharist be carried to unbaptized persons; we have as much authority for the former as for the latter. It is true the latter is not prohibited in so explicit terms as was the former; but, where analogy diffuses so great light, it is not to be supposed that positive prescription must necessarily be superadded. The preponderance of

* Conversations on Communion, pp. 106, 107.

the argument, we repeat it, is in favour of admitting those only to the Lord's table who have been baptized. Baptism may be attended to at any time; no inconvenience need result from giving it always the priority, or, if it do result, it must be chargeable to the theory of exclusive immersion, and for it that theory must be responsible. But to adopt the opposite custom could be productive only of confusion, embarrassment, and disorder, in the church of God. The line of church distinction would soon be obscured, procrastination and delay of baptism would be engendered, and loose practices be encouraged in young converts, while a sense of propriety, order, and discipline would be effaced from the conscience. Let all the pastors of Christ's flock, and the appointed guardians of his church look well to this important subject, and relax not the rule which the Scriptures have so plainly laid down for their guide.

APPENDIX.

NOTE A. Referred to page 13.

THAT the words πολλα ὑδατα *polla hudata, many waters*, convey the idea of *plurality*, I think, is clearly demonstrable. The idea is sometimes that of a large mass, or collection of water, but generally, that of distinct, separate or broken masses. We adduce a few instances:

2 Sam. xxii, 17: "He sent from above, he took me, he drew me out of ὑδατων πολλω *many waters*."

David here celebrates his providential deliverance from the power of strong enemies; as he says in verse 18th, "He delivered me from my strong enemy AND from THEM that hated me." Many waters, then, here stands for numerous and powerful enemies, viz., Saul and his minions.

Psa. xviii, 16: (Same words in the same sense.)

Psa. xciii, 4: "The Lord on high is mightier than the noise of ὑδατων πολλων *many waters*, yea, than the mighty waves of the sea."

The idea here is, that of broken and separate masses of water in a state of agitation, like the "waves of the sea." The idea is evidently that of a plurality of waters. See also Rev. i, 15, and xiv, 2, and xix, 6.

Jer. li, 13: "O thou that dwellest ἐφ' ὑδασι πολλοις *upon*, or *among many waters*."

This address was made to Babylon; and because that city was situated on the Euphrates, therefore it is urged that *many waters* means only that river. But, that the idea is plural and not singular, will appear, if we attend to the following facts. The plain around Babylon, being in many places marshy, and being also subject to the inundations of the Euphrates, was intersected by numerous artificial canals, dykes, lakes, &c. These were for the purposes of irrigation, the regulation of the overflow of the Euphrates, and the draining of the marshes. The city itself was traversed by many of these canals and artificial rivers, by whose banks, as well as in the extensive gardens which they watered, sprang up a heavy growth of willow. Some of these artificial canals united the waters of the Euphrates and Tigris. It was here that the Jews, while exiles in Babylon, sitting by the sunny banks of these pleasant waters, recalling to mind their own Jordan, and the sweet murmurs of their native streamlets, took up that beautiful and pathetic lamentation recorded Psa. cxxxvii: "By the RIVERS of Babylon there we sat down; yea, we wept while we remembered Zion." These 'rivers of Babylon" were the "many waters" upon, or among which, the city was situated. "Babylonia," says Professor Robinson, "was a land abounding in water; and Jeremiah might, therefore, well say of it, that it dwelt *upon many waters.*"

Rev. xvii, 1: The mystical Babylon "sitteth επι ὑδατων πολλων *upon many waters.*"

As Babylon here is supposed to be mystically put for Rome; and, as this city is situated on the Tiber, therefore Mr. Robinson, the Baptist historian, and others, have supposed that the phrase *many waters*, in this text, means the Tiber. A little attention to facts, however, will show to the contrary. Rome, or the Roman power, was literally upon "many waters," while she commanded the maritime resources of the world. Her "sitting upon many waters" denoted her extensive commercial intercourse with the nations of the earth; and hence, her merchants are represented in the apocalyptic vision as the chief mourners of her catastrophe. Chap. xviii, 11–19. Also, mystical Babylon's "sitting upon many waters," denotes, in the strongly Hebraistic style of St. John, her dominion over "peoples, and multitudes, and nations, and tongues," chap. xvii, 15. These descriptions may also apply to ancient Babylon literally.

Psa. lxxvii, 19: "Thy way is in the sea, and thy path in ὑδασι πολλοις *great waters.*"

Psa. cvii, 23: "They that go down to the sea in ships, that do business in ὑδασι πολλοις *great waters.*"

The phrase *great waters*, in these passages, is equivalent to our phrase, *high seas.* The idea is that of *vast* and *various* collections of water.

These citations and remarks may suffice to show that πολλα ὑδατα *polla hudata* properly has a *plural* signification, and may mean *many waters*, in John iii, 23, in distinction from *one body* of water. This, then, being a lawful, and, indeed, a common signification of the phrase, and agreeing so much better with all the circumstances of the case than the common reading, ought to be adopted in the above passage. But as this rendering destroys that seeming countenance to the doctrine of immersion that our English version has been supposed to give, our Baptist brethren have contended hardly against it.

Mr. Robinson, after remarking upon the meaning of *polla hudata,* says, "How it comes to pass that a mode of speaking, which on every other occasion signifies *much,* in the case of baptism signifies *little,* is a question easy to answer." (History of Baptism, p. 27.) The meaning of this insinuation lies upon the surface. We have taken *polla hudata* in John iii, 23, in a *plural* sense, to mean *many waters;* that is, *many living springs* or *streams* of water; and Mr. Robinson covertly charges us with disingenuity in so doing, because the Greek πολλα *polla,* in other places, may mean *much* instead of *many.* Our translation, and the reasons for it, are before the reader. We only wish here to say, that immediately after the above ungenerous insinuation of Mr. R,, he proceeds to prove, by elaborate arguments, that Enon was a celebrated "cavernous spring," and that John probably baptized in a small basin of clean water supplied by a little stream, like a "spring issuing from the fissures of a rock, gurg ling through the chinks as water out of a bottle, falling from crag to crag, murmuring from bed to basin, and from basin to bed, fretting along the ragged sides of a rocky channel, and echoing through rude and spacious caverns." (History of Baptism, p. 30.) And this, gentle reader, is what our veritable author would have us believe is the *much water* spoken of John iii, 23. And this, too, is HIS opinion, after castigating us for translating πολλα *polla* by *many,* instead of *much,* as he would have it!

NOTE B.—Referred to page 14.

The passion of the Jews for a numerous offspring was a trait of character worthy of remark. It was the maxim of the Jewish state, which lay at the foundation of all their politics, that "in the multitude of people is the king's honour; but in the want of people is the destruction of the prince," Prov. xiv, 28. "Lo," says David, "children are a heritage of the Lord . . . happy is the man that hath his quiver full of them," Psa. cxxvii, 3, 5. To have many children was regarded as a peculiar mark of divine favour. Eccl. vi, 3. Thus, the prayer of Balaam (which is not always rightly understood) was in perfect keeping with the spirit of those ages. After alluding, prophetically, to the numerous posterity of Israel, he intimates it as his highest ambition, and his dearest earthly desire, to be in this respect like them: "Let me die the death of the righteous, and let my *posterity* be like his." (*Vide* Dr. A. Clarke, *in loc.*) So the Septuagint understood it: *Και γενοιτο το σπερμα μου ὡς το σπερμα τουτων, and may my* SEED (*posterity*) *be made like his* SEED (*posterity*.)

NOTE C.—Referred to page 15.

On the populousness of ancient cities and states it may be proper to submit to the reader some statements, with a view to show that we have not transcended probable bounds of correctness in our estimate of the population of Palestine.

In the most flourishing period of Rome, at the close of the republic and beginning of the imperial monarchy, the population was very great. The number of citizens may be estimated at three hundred thousand, and the whole number of residents at two millions, and upward.

Lipsius computes the inhabitants of Rome, at its most flourishing period, at *four millions;* and Tacitus states, that by a census in the reign of Claudius, the number of Roman citizens amounted to nearly *seven millions*, (including, probably, all who had attained Roman citizenship throughout the world.)—*Eschenburg's Man. of Class. Lit.*, edited by Professor N. W. Fiske, 2d edition, p. 482.

Gibbon computes the total amount of the population of the Roman empire at about *one hundred and twenty millions.*

Attica was a small province of Greece, of a triangular shape. Its base, which was northward, was not thirty miles wide; and its vertex, which penetrated into the Saronicus Sinus, (gulf of Engia,) was not removed above thirty geographical miles from its base. Yet Attica was estimated to contain five hundred thousand inhabitants, while the county of Rensselaer, (N. Y.,) which may compare with Attica in geographical limits, contained, in 1830, only forty-nine thousand seven hundred and thirty inhabitants.

Sparta, which did not embrace more than *one-fifth* of the territory of the Peloponnesus, (modern Morea,) was reckoned to contain more than three millions one hundred and twenty thousand inhabitants. This immense population was confined within a territory about *one half* as large as that of Palestine.

The city of Corinth is said to have once contained four hundred and sixty thousand slaves, and Egina four hundred and seventy thousand.

Julius Cesar was said to have encountered four millions of Gauls, to have killed *one* million, and to have taken another million prisoners. The whole nation of Gauls was supposed to number two hundred millions.

The city of Agrigentum (Sicily) is computed by Fleury to have contained not less than two millions.

The city of Nineveh contained one hundred and twenty thousand infants. Jonah iv, 11. The population was, indeed, great. Ninus, the founder of this city, led an army of one million seven hundred thousand foot, two hundred thousand horse, and about sixteen thousand chariots, against the Bactrians.

Italy, a little before Hannibal's time, could send into the field (including citizens and allies) near *one million* men.

The city of Syracuse alone, in the time of Dionysius the tyrant, furnished one hundred and twenty thousand foot and twelve thousand horse, besides four hundred vessels manned.

Semiramis employed two millions of men in building Babylon. The same queen, in her expedition into India, headed an army of *three millions* foot, and five hundred thousand horse.

Xerxes, in his Grecian expedition, commanded an army of *two and a half millions.* The whole number that followed this vain monarch on this rash enterprise is supposed to be not less than five millions. See Fleury's Manners of the Israelites, edited by Dr. A. Clarke, pages 48, 49; and Rollin's History.

NOTE D.—Referred to page 17.

I say, the Pharisees and Sadducees, *in general*, submitted to his baptism. And so, it appears to me, we are to understand the sacred historians. Mr. Robinson, however, says, "It doth not appear that John baptized any persons of rank and fortune. No great names were seen among his converts. The Pharisees, in reputation for piety, and the lawyers, famous for their knowledge of the law, rejected the counsel of God by John, and were not baptized by him."—*History of Baptism*, p. 32.

I think it appears from the account, that John did baptize many of the Pharisees and Sadducees who came to him, of which notice is given in Matt., chap. iii. On that occasion John says, "Who hath warned you to flee from the wrath to come? Bring forth, THEREFORE, fruits meet for repentance." The force of the conjunction ὄυν *therefore,* leads us directly to suppose that John proceeded without loss of time to baptize them. As if he had said, "Inasmuch, then, as you submit yourselves to my baptism on profession of your repentance, exhibit that conduct that is suitable to this profession."

In the eleventh verse, John says, "I truly baptize YOU with water," &c. This was a continuation of his address to the Pharisees, in the audience of the people, and designed also for their general instruction.

In Luke vii, 30, it is said, "The Pharisees and lawyers rejected the counsel of God against themselves, being *not* baptized of John." I take these words, together with the twenty-ninth verse, to be those of the evangelist, and not of Christ. The attentive reader will easily discern the difference. Consequently, the Pharisees and lawyers spoken of refer only to those who were present at that time, and not to those of the whole nation. Other passages might be noticed, but it is not important. The truth seems to be, that many of the Pharisees and great men received John's baptism, but still the number of baptized among them was disproportionate to that among the common people.

Note E.—Referred to page 17.

Mr. Robinson, the author of the History of Baptism, pp. 32, 33, holds the following statements respecting the numbers baptized by John :—"It is generally supposed John baptized great multitudes. His converts were, indeed, of the multitude, but it is far from being clear that they were numerous. All Jerusalem, all Judea, and all the region round about, *went out to him*, many of the Pharisees and Sadducees *came to his baptism*, but they went out only as spectators—they *went out*, as our Lord expresses it, *for to see*; and this will appear most worthy of belief to such as consider the general character of the Jewish populace, and their blind guides and the prerequisites necessary to John's baptism, especially when it is observed, that after the resurrection (and it is supposed all Christians saw him) the greatest number of believers assembled together at any one time were not many above five hundred."

This, to be sure, is a very extraordinary passage, and is an indirect effort to convey the impression that John did not baptize much above five hundred persons. It seems, too, that the author leans largely upon the doctrine of final perseverance for the force and conclusiveness of his arguments. For unless we suppose all John's converts to have persevered and embraced the doctrine of Christ, the argument in question falls to the ground. This is the more unaccountable, as the author was not a Calvinist, but a Unitarian.

But are we at liberty to pass the accounts of John's baptism to the score of hyperboles and Hebraisms, and explain away their force and natural meaning? If a plain, common sense man, unaffected by party bias, could read the accounts given of John's ministry without being impressed with the belief that he baptized the major part of the nation, we very much mistake the sincerity of our impressions. That the reader may more fully appreciate the conclusion to which we have arrived, we request his attention,

1. To the prophetic descriptions of John's ministry, and its effects upon the Jewish nation.

Isaiah says (chap. xl, 3) of John Baptist, that he should be a crier in the desert, saying, "Prepare ye the way of the Lord, make straight in the desert a highway for our God." Now, the duty and office of John are here described. Can any man, who understands the force and interpretation of these figures, suppose, in sobriety of speech, that they fitly apply to the actual repentance of only about five hundred, as Mr. Robinson supposes? The prophet further says, speaking of the *effect* which John's ministry was to have on the moral condition of the nation, "Every valley shall be exalted, and every mountain and hill shall be made low; and the crooked shall be made straight, and the rough places plain," verse 4. That the prophet here alludes to John Baptist is evident by comparing Luke iii, 4, 5, and Matt. iii, 3.

That Isaiah is here speaking of the great moral change that should be effected in the feelings, expectations, and conduct of the Jews, through John's preaching, none will doubt. And I apprehend we must allow, that either John did, in fact, baptize immense multitudes, or the vivid and strong imagery of the prophet must be ascribed to a mythic inspiration. See also Mal. iv, 6; comp. Luke i, 16, 17.

2. The incidental notices of John's reputation go to establish, upon higher grounds of probability, the hypothesis that John baptized the major part of the Jewish population.

Luke iii, 15: "And as the people were in expectation, all men wondered in their hearts of John, whether he were the Christ."

"So general was the reformation produced by the Baptist's preaching, that the people were ready to consider *him* as the promised Messiah."—*Dr. A. Clarke.* The people were *suspending* (προδοκωντος) their judgment respecting the real character of John. In this state "all men," that is, the nation generally, inclined to the opinion that "he was the Christ."

Matt. xiv, 5: "And when Herod would have put John to death, he feared the multitude, because they counted him as a prophet."

It was the force of political, not moral motives, that swayed the mind of this profligate governor. He feared, not the opinions of the virtuous, but the indignation of his people. He feared an insurrection, and summary vengeance on his own head. This clearly and most strongly proves the firm attachment of the people of his province to the Baptist.

Matt. xxi, 26: If we say the baptism of John was of men, "we fear the people; for all hold John as a prophet."

Here, indeed, is a remarkable instance, illustrative of John's popularity. The proud persecutors of Christ—the dignitaries of the Jewish church—the men who enacted, in the chief council of their nation, "that if any man confessed Christ, he should be put out of the synagogue"—these very men, I say, feared to attack the reputation of John, being awed by public opinion; for, said they, "ALL THE PEOPLE WILL STONE US," Luke xx, 6.

John v, 35: "John was a burning and a shining light, and ye [that is, 'ye as a nation, generally'] were willing, for a season, to rejoice in his light."

Our Saviour addressed these words to no particular class of Jews, but to the multitudes, assembled from all parts of Palestine, to celebrate one of their religious feasts. His words on this occasion prove two things:—1. That the Jews generally rejoiced at, and gladly received, the word of John at first; but, 2, when they afterward found John's dispensation linked to the humiliating doctrines of the cross, unwilling to embrace the latter, they thenceforward receded from the light of John's ministry. This fickleness of mind, and defection from John's dispensation, the Saviour rebukes in the parable of the sower. Matt. xiii, 5, 6, 20, 21.

Such, then, are some of the notices given of John's reputation and influence among the Jewish people. We find the enemies and calumniators (for such there were, Matt. xi, 18) of John always in the minority, and that minority always awed by "the people." Now, can any man believe that such a state of opinion respecting John could have subsisted with a common consent to reject his baptism? Believe it who can. All the reason in the case, all right interpretation of Scripture, go to establish the conviction that John baptized the major part of the Jewish population. And adding to the presumptive proofs here adduced those positive declarations of Scripture which have been considered in the body of this work, and also the reason of the case deduced from the design of John's ministry, I know not how any person can escape from the force of the conclusion we have adopted, unless he do it in defiance of all the proper evidence of the case.

Note F.—Referred to page 19.

We are bound to understand the words of the evangelists either in a narrative, natural sense, or else hyperbolically. But where is the necessity of resorting to the hyperbole to explain these descriptions? The hyperbole is a figure of speech frequently employed in the Scriptures, and consists in magnifying or diminishing an object beyond its natural limits. "Hyperbole," says Dr. Gerard, "whether consisting in bold tropes, exaggerated comparisons, or impossible suppositions, gives an appearance of falsehood; to avoid which the *sense*, not the *expression*, must be regarded." (Bib. Crit., p. 362.) But in general there is not the least difficulty in determining the sense. We are not to take every statement, which may chance to out-step our former notions or prejudices, as an hyperbole. When God says to Abram, "I will make thy seed as the dust of the earth; so that if a man can number the dust of the earth, so also shall thy seed be numbered," (Gen. xiii, 16,) there being a manifest absurdity in the literal sense, we must take it as an hyperbole. So Job says, (vi, 3,) if his grief were "thoroughly weighed," "it would be heavier than the sand of the sea."

The Pharisees, in a rage of jealousy and malice at the popularity of Christ, exclaimed, "The world is gone after him," John xii, 19. So John supposes that if all the acts of Christ were written, "the world itself could not contain the books that should be written," John xxi, 25. But in these, and similar instances, there is no danger of misconception.

The statements of the evangelists, however, in regard to the numbers baptized by John, are wholly of another character. They involve, necessarily, no exaggerated statements, no impossible suppositions. The attempt to fix upon them an hyperbolical construction is uncalled for, and forbidden by the laws of Biblical interpretation. No necessity exists for such a construction, and therefore such a construction is inadmissible.

We cannot forbear noticing how improbable it is that the evangelists intended an hyperbole here, considering their usual mode of speaking on similar subjects. When they speak of the numbers that followed Christ, they are far from using exaggerated comparisons. When Mark speaks of the five thousand who were fed in the desert, he simply says, "multitude," "much people." Matthew also calls the four thousand a "multitude;" and Luke holds the same language. Mark vi, 33, 34, 44; Matt. xv, 32, 38. This is certainly a chastened mode of speaking. No extravagant terms are employed; nor do we find, in the New Testament, any tendency to extravagant, hyperbolical descriptions, where multitudes are spoken of. We cannot, therefore, suppose any departure, in the cases in question, to be made from a plain, narrative style.

Note FF.—Referred to page 53.

Since writing this work an article has appeared in the American Biblical Repository for April, 1841, on "the Bible and its Literature," from the pen of Edward Robinson, professor of Biblical literature in the Union Theological Seminary, New-York. It cannot fail to be acceptable to the reader to find the remarks of Professor Robinson, on the New Testament dialect, appended to this work in this place. After enumerating the chief difficulties attending the exegesis of the Hebrew Scriptures, and remarking upon the mere fragmentary form of Hebrew literature as possessed by us, he says, "Nor is the case very dissimilar with the Greek language of the New Testament.

This, too, is but the fragment of a peculiar dialect in the wide field of Greek philology. True, we have here the aid of all the branches of the classic Grecian language and literature, in their poetic youth, their Attic manliness and vigour, and their later decline. We have, too, all the results of ancient and modern research in regard to Greek philology; while the idiom and character of the language are far more accordant than the Hebrew with our own. The Greek, too, in an altered form, is to this day a spoken language. Yet all this neither suffices for the illustration of the idiom of the New Testament, nor does it supersede, even here, the necessity of an acquaintance with the Hebrew tongue of the earlier Scriptures.

"The language of the New Testament is *the later Greek, as spoken by foreigners of the Hebrew stock, and applied by them to subjects on which it had never before been employed by native Greeks.* After the disuse of the ancient Hebrew in Palestine, and the irruption of western conquerors, the Jews adopted the Greek language from necessity; partly as a conquered people, and partly from the intercourse of life, of commerce, in colonies, in cities, founded like Alexandria and others, which were peopled with throngs of Jews. It was, therefore, the spoken language of ordinary life which they learned; not the classic style of books which has elsewhere come down to us. But they spoke it as foreigners, whose native tongue was the later Aramaean; and it therefore could not fail to acquire upon their lips a strong Semitic character and colouring. When to this we add, that they spoke in Greek on the things of the true God, and the relations of mankind to Jehovah and to a Saviour,—subjects to which no native Greek had ever then applied his beautiful language,—it will be obvious that an appeal merely to classic Greek and its philology will not suffice for the interpreter of the New Testament. The Jewish-Greek idiom must be studied almost as an independent dialect; and its most important illustrations will be derived from the idiom of the Old Testament, especially as exhibited in the version of the Seventy and the Apocrypha, and from the contemporary writings of Philo and Josephus.

"The volumes of controversy which have been written in former centuries upon the character of the idiom of the

New Testament, may at the present day be safely left out of view in a theological education, except as matters of history. Even in this view, they are important chiefly as showing by what crude theories and slow advances the human mind and human learning often arrive at truth.

"The principle virtually laid down was, that as God spoke to man in Greek, he could employ only the most pure and perfect Greek; and therefore the idiom of the New Testament must be accounted as one of the purest models of the Greek language. It was here overlooked that God spoke to man only in the language of those whom he addressed; and that therefore to judge of this language, we must look to the character and circumstances of those who spoke it. These were at the time a conquered, and, in some respects, already an abject people; and their dialect of the Greek, in comparison of the Greek itself, was much like the dialect of the Jews at the present day in modern lands, unpolished, and corrupted by foreign words, idioms, and forms."

Note FFF.—Referred to p. 54.

It is unaccountable that philologists and divines should have ever consented to argue, or concede any force to the reasonings of others who did argue, upon the principle here condemned. Yet it has been the practice, time out of mind, to urge that, because the primitive meaning of a word was so and so, therefore its meaning in a given connection was the same; whereas, nothing can be more fallacious and absurd.

I wish the reader to attend to one general principle, or law, governing or modifying the change of words from their primary to their secondary sense. Words which, in their primary use, signified a particular act, or thing, are also used to express some general consequence, or adjunct, of that particular act, or thing. It is on this principle that we say βαπτιζω *baptizo*, which primarily means *to immerse*, is used in the sense of *purify*, without any allusion to the mode, because *purification* is a very general *consequence* of immersion. Now, to illustrate this principle further we subjoin the following examples :—

The word καταλυω *kataluo*, primarily signified, *to ungird, to unloose*. Afterward it was used to signify, *to lodge, to rest, to halt, refresh*, &c. But where is the natural connection between the primary and secondary senses? By what principle did the mind take its transit from the first to the second? Modern customs and ideas would not readily suggest the true answer. The ancients wore long and loose, flowing garments. When they travelled, walked, or laboured, &c., it became necessary to "*gird* their garments about them." When they *rested*, they *ungirded* themselves. Now, it is very easy to perceive how καταλυω *kataluo* took its change of signification. The ancients had to *ungird* themselves *in order to rest;* therefore, the word which primarily signified *to ungird*, came at length to signify *to rest, lodge*, &c.

The word שָׂם *sham* means, primarily, *to place, put, set, adjust*, &c. Now, it would be impossible for a person, unacquainted with the philosophy of the formation of words, to account for the fact, that this same Hebrew word is used to signify the *aerial regions, the celestial expanse, heaven*, as the abode of God and holy beings; and, which is still more paradoxical, an *onion*. But let the reader start with the primary idea, and then follow its occult operations in the formation of other words. For instance, nothing appeared so *immovable* as the *firmament*, or *expanse*. Therefore, the word which primarily signified *to put, place, set*, &c., was used to denote the *celestial expanse*, as being *fixed* and *immutable*. And because the abode of Jehovah was located above the stars, in the opinion of the Jews, therefore, they invented still another שָׂם *sham*, called the *third heavens*. Now, by this process, the attentive reader will perceive how the word that at first only signified *to put*, came at length to signify *heaven*, as the abode of the glorious Creator.

But how could the same word come to signify a species of *onion?* All analogy seems here to fail, on first view. But look again. When you cut an onion diagonally, you find it composed of concentric layers, arranged in great order and regularity, apparently around a common nucleus. Now, the Hebrew word *sham* means, *to put, place, arrange, adjust*, &c., and it hence denotes the onion, because its layers are *arranged*, or *placed* with such care and regularity.

But, how can the same word denote *astonishment*, *amazement*, &c.? Because *astonishment* denotes a kind of *fixedness*, or *immobility* of mind.

So also the English word *heaven* comes from the Saxon *heofon*. But *heofon* primarily means, the *place* or *region overhead*, without any reference to a place of happiness, or to any religious notion whatever. The *region overhead* was called *heofon*, merely because it was *heaved*, or, as it was anciently written, *hoven*, that is, *raised up*, *elevated*. Now, how could such a word come to signify a *place of holy delight*, without any reference to its being *up*, or *down*, or *horizontal* to us, in its *position?* How can it come to drop the idea of relative *position* altogether, and assume another meaning, viz., that of *happiness?* Is not this as great a change of signification as that which we claim for βαπτιζω *baptizo?* But the reader is requested to mark the process by which the word *heaven* has acquired its present use and meaning. It first signified the *place overhead*, the region of the stars, because they seemed to be *lifted* or *raised up* above the earth. But as all idolatrous nations consider the stars, planets, and sun, to be the abode of the gods; and as they conceive the gods to be happy, so *heaven*, the place overhead, the region of the stars, the abode of the gods, was at length considered as a place of *happiness;* and now, the primary sense is wholly lost, and this new sense is the exclusive idea imparted by the word.

The word *charity* formerly denoted *the principle of benevolence*, *love*, without including the idea of any outward act; but now, it means the *outward act* of giving to the needy, without any reference to the *principle*. Here is an exact inversion of the sense. Paul says: "Though I bestow all my goods to feed the poor, ... and have not charity, I am nothing." This clearly shows that charity was a *principle*, and not an *act*, formerly; but if a man should bestow all his goods to feed the poor now, that very act would define him as a person of the most extensive charity, according to the modern sense of the term.

It were easy to extend examples of this kind, but

enough have been adduced. Let the reader, then, understand, that it is according to the general analogy of language that a word which signifies a particular act or thing, afterward may come to signify some attribute, consequence, adjunct, or circumstance of that act or thing. All this clearly applies to the case in hand, and proves that βαπτιζω *baptizo* may take the sense of *purify*, without the least departure from the analogy of language.

The importance of the subject will be a sufficient apology for subjoining to these remarks others from the pen of President Beecher:—

"On the other hand," says he, "even if I were to admit that its original and primitive idea was to immerse, and that, when it denotes an external act, it never departs from this sense; still the question would arise, Is there not another meaning derived from the *effects* of this act, and in which the mind contemplates the effect alone, entirely irrespective of the mode in which it is produced? I contend that there is—and that, as thorough purification, or cleansing, is often the result of submerging in water, so the word βαπτιζω *baptizo* has come to signify to purify, or cleanse thoroughly, without any reference to the mode in which it is done.

"There is not, *a priori*, the least improbability of such a change of meaning, from the laws of the mind, or of language.

"It may, at first sight, seem an improbable position to some, that if a word originally signifies 'to immerse,' it can assume a meaning so remote from its primitive sense as '*to purify*,' and entirely drop all reference to the mode. Yet the slightest attention to the laws of the mind, and to well-known facts, will show that not the least improbability of such a result exists.

"No principle is more universally admitted by all sound philologists, than that to establish the original and primitive meaning of a word is not at all decisive as to its subsequent usages. It often aids only as giving a clew by which we can trace the progress of the imagination, or the association of ideas in leading the mind from meaning to meaning, on some ground of relative similitude, or connection of cause and effect.

"But to multiply words on a point so plain would be

needless, had not so much stress been laid on the supposed original meaning of this word. It is therefore too plain to be denied, that words do so often depart from their primitive meaning, as entirely to leave out the original idea—and that the secondary senses of a word are often by far the most numerous and important.

" Moreover, to establish such secondary meanings, it is not necessary that we should be able to trace the course of the mind, though it is pleasant to be able to do it. A secondary meaning, however unlike it may seem to the primitive, may yet be established like any other fact in the usage of language, that is, by appropriate testimony.

" But while such transitions are common in all words, they are particularly common in words of the class of βαπτιζω *baptizo*, denoting action by, or with reference to, a fluid. This is owing to the fact that the effects produced by the action depend not on the action alone, but on the action and fluid combined—and, of course, may be varied as the fluid or its application varies.

" Let us now take the general idea of enveloping, or immersing in a fluid, and see how unlike [to each other are] the effects to which it may give rise.

" If the envelopment is produced by a flood, a torrent, or waves, the effect may be to overwhelm, to oppress, to destroy.

" If by taking up an object and immersing it into a colouring fluid, it is to impart a new colour, or to dye.

" If by taking up an object and immersing it into a cleansing fluid—or by going into the fluid—or by pouring the fluid copiously over the object—the effect is to purify or cleanse. And on these natural, or material senses, may be founded the same number of spiritual or moral senses, by transferring the ideas to the mind. . . ."

" . . . But what secondary sense shall be adopted cannot be told *a priori*, but must be decided by the habits, manners, customs, and general ideas of a people, and sometimes by peculiar usages for which no reason can be given. For example, no reason exists in the nature of things why βαπτω *bapto* rather than βαπτιζω *baptizo* should pass from the sense of *immerse* to the sense *to dye*—yet there is evidence that it did. On the other hand, it could not be certainly foretold that βαπτιζω *baptizo* would pass to the sense *to cleanse*, and yet that it did so pass may still be true, and, if true, can be proved like any other fact. And the existence of manners and customs tending to such a result renders such a result probable."—*Biblical Repository*, January, 1840.

Not only does the meaning of words vary from their primitive use, so as often to come to signify entirely a different thing, but the same word, in all languages, is differently used in different places. Let the reader observe the Scripture use of *conversation*, *thought*, (Matt. vi, 31,) *deacon*, *everlasting*, *flesh*, &c. Now, who would admit it as valid argument that, because either of these words had a particular meaning in a given place, therefore it has the same meaning in another particular place? Yet this is the mode of reasoning that has been adopted in the case of βαπτιζω *baptizo*—a method which is at war with sound philology, and will never fail to land its abettors in perplexity, confusion, and error.

NOTE G.—Referred to p. 73.

Some noun must necessarily be understood after βαπτισωνται *baptisontai*. Now, as the subject of washing hands was the principal subject before the mind of the writer, and as the verb νιψωνται *nipsontai*, *wash*, in the third verse, has for its object the noun χειρας *hands*, so also it would seem justifiable and necessary, according to all just rules of grammar, to supply the same noun (χειρας *hands*) after βαπτισωνται *baptisontai*, in the fourth verse. It must be remembered, that the washing, or purification, or baptism, here spoken of, is of that character that fitly applies before eating. This sufficiently suggests, that it is the purification of the hands and arms, or, as Theophylact has it, "*up to the elbows*," that is intended. Besides, why should they immerse *before* eating any more than *after* eating? Their hands and arms alone might be supposed to come in contact with the food, so as to defile it.

Some may urge, that as βαπτισωνται *baptisontai* is in the middle voice, the action is *reflexive*, turning back and terminating upon the actor, and that, therefore, *themselves* should be understood after the verb; as, "*except they bap-*

tize themselves," &c. This, however, is an argument that cannot be relied on. The middle voice is elsewhere used in an active sense, taking a noun expressed, after it, as in Job ix, 30; Matt. xxvii, 24. This, indeed, is a frequent use of the middle voice in Greek. (See Valpy's Greek Grammar.) Besides, where the phrase *wash myself* occurs, as in Job ix, 30, the meaning is simply *wash my hands*. Thus: "Though I *wash myself* in snow water, (απολουσωμαι χιονι,) and *purify my hands* (αποκαθαρωμαι χερσι) *thoroughly*." The last member of the sentence is evidently added, merely as an *intensive* of the former. We see no valid objection, therefore, to the following reading of Mark vii, 3, 4: "For the Pharisees, and all the Jews, except they wash their hands oft, eat not, *particularly* (και) on returning from market, except they purify their hands, (or themselves, as the case requires,) they eat not." We only add, that the above use of the conjunction και is somewhat frequent; as, "Go view the land, και *particularly* Jericho." "Tell his disciples, και *especially* Peter." Josh. ii, 1; Matt. xvi, 7.

Let not the reader misunderstand me. I do not mean to say that βαπτιζω, in Mark vii, 4, simply means *washing* of hands. I hold it to mean *purify*, and it may apply to the purifying of *hands* only, or of some other part of the body, or of the *whole* body, without itself determining the mode. But I think the purifying of hands, in Luke xi, 38, and Mark vii, 4, was the subject emphatically alluded to by βαπτιζω in those places, as it was *that kind* of purification, or baptism, which the superstitions of the Jews required always before eating. They at such times expected it, as a matter of course; but they did not expect an immersion, as a matter of course, before eating.

NOTE GG.—Referred to p. 73.

On the custom of washing hands among the Pharisees, the following remarks will not be unacceptable to the reader. They are taken from the works of Thomas Godwin, B. D., published in London, 1641. The writings of Godwin have been long held in high estimation. They were formerly used as a standard of reference, but are now scarce, and are superseded by works of more modern date and style. Speaking of the Pharisees, he says: "They would not eat until they washed their hands. Why do thy disciples transgress the tradition of the elders? for they wash not their hands when they eat bread. Matt. xv, 2. This washing is said to have been done πυγμη *pugme*, (Mark vii, 3,) that is, *often*, as some translate it, taking πυγμη *pugme*, in this place, to signify the same as πυχα *pucha*, in Homer, *frequenter*. Others translated the word, *accurate*, *diligenter*, intimating the great care and diligence they used in washing. With this the Syriac text agrees. Others think that there is in that phrase allusion to that rite or manner of washing, in use among the Jews, termed by them *netilah ziddim*, the *lifting up of their hands*. The Greek word πυγμη *pugme* is thought to express this rite, because in this kind of washing they used to join the tops of the fingers of each hand together with the thumb, so that each hand did, after a sort, resemble a *fist*. This ceremony was thus performed: First, they washed their hands clean; secondly, they composed them into the forementioned form; thirdly, they lifted them up, so that the water ran down to the very elbows; lastly, they let down their hands again, so that the water ran from off their hands upon the earth. And that there might be store of water running up and down, they poured fresh water on them when they lifted up their hands, and poured water twice upon them when they hung them down. Unto this kind of washing Theophylact seems to have reference, when he saith that the Pharisees did *cubitaliter lavare*, *wash up to their elbows*. Lastly, others interpret πυγμη *pugme* to be the fist, or hand closed, and the manner of washing hereby denoted to be *by rubbing one hand closed in the palm* or *hollow of the other*. All imply a diligent and accurate care in washing: the ceremonial washing, by lifting up the hands and hanging them down, best expresseth the superstition, which openly was aimed at in the reproof; though all these sorts of washing, to the Pharisees, were superstitious, because they made it not a matter of *decency* and *civility*, but of *religion*, to eat with washed or unwashed hands, urging such a necessity hereof, that in case a man may come to some water, but not enough both to wash and to drink, he should rather choose to wash than to drink, though he die with thirst. And it was deemed among them as great a sin to eat with unwashed hands as to commit fornication. This tradition of washing hands, though it were chiefly urged by the Pharisees, yet all the Jews maintained it, as appeareth by the places quoted."—*Civ. et Ecclesiast. Rites, &c.*, pp. 39, 40.

Note GGG.—Referred to p. 75.

It will be impossible for the reader to appreciate the argument fully, unless he have the true Oriental idea of a bed, or couch. European or American notions are inadmissible, although they might sufficiently serve the argument.

The tables of the ancients were constructed in the form of a hollow square, or else in the form of a crescent, or semicircle. As they reclined (upon the left elbow) while eating, their beds, couches, or divans were arranged around upon the outside of their tables. The servants entered the inside of the hollow square, or crescent, while serving the table. Upon their couches were arranged quilts and bolsters, for the ease and luxury of their occupants while eating. The beds were much larger, more ponderous and clumsily constructed, in reference to moving, washing, &c., than their tables. Yet these are said to have been *baptized*. But were they *immersed?*

Note GGGG.—Referred to p. 89.

For the sake of those readers who may not be able to consult the original Hebrew and the Septuagint version, we subjoin here a list of citations from the Old Testament, illustrative of the sense of רָחַץ *rahats*, and λουω *louo*. The ground we take, in reference to the meaning of these words, is this,—that they denote *the application of water to the person* or *thing*, and *not* of the thing or person to the water, as in the case of immersion: that they denote an *indefinite* use of water, that is, they do not define the *quan-*

tity of water used, or the *mode* of using it, or the *extent of its application* to the person or thing on whom, or on which, it is used. They are used, as nearly as can be defined, synonymously with the English *wash*, but they are not synonymous with *bathe*.

Gen. xviii, 4: "Let a little water be fetched, and *wash* your feet." (רָחַץ *rahats*, νιπτω *nipto.*)

Gen. xix, 2, and xxiv, 32: (The same words, in the same sense.)

Gen. xliii, 24: (Same words, in same sense.) Verse 31: "And Joseph *washed* his face." (רָחַץ *rahats*, νιπτω *nipto.*)

Ex. ii, 5: "And the daughter of Pharaoh came down to *wash* herself." (רָחַץ *rahats*, λουω *louo.*)

It is possible that the Egyptian princess did, as a matter of fact, *bathe;* but the original is unadapted to convey such an idea, if we look merely at the structure of the sentence. It says, "The daughter of Pharaoh came to wash herself עַל־הַיְאֹר, επι τον ποταμον, BY OR AT *the river*."

Ex. xxix, 4: "And Aaron and his sons thou shalt bring to the door of the tabernacle, and *wash* them." (רָחַץ *rahats*, λουω *louo.*)

Ex. xxx, 19: "For Aaron and his sons shall *wash* their hands and feet thereat." (רָחַץ *rahats*, νιπτω *nipto.*)

Ex. xxx, 20, 21: (Same words, used in the same sense.)

Ex. xl, 12, 32: (Same words, used in same sense of chap. xxix, 4.)

Lev. xiv, 8: "And he that is to be cleansed shall *wash* himself in water." (רָחַץ *rahats*, λουω *louo.*)

The same words occur in the same sense Lev. viii, 6, and xv, 5, 6, 7, 8, 10, 11, 13, 16, 18, 21, 22, 27, and xvi, 4, 24, 26, 28, and xvii, 15, 16, and xxii, 6; Deut. xxiii, 11; Num. xix, 7, 19.

Deut. xxi, 6: "And all the elders of that city shall *wash* their hands over the heifer." (רָחַץ *rahats*, νιπτω *nipto.*)

Judges xix, 21: The Levite and concubine "*washed* their feet." (רָחַץ *rahats*, νιπτω *nipto.*)

Ruth iii, 3: Naomi said unto Ruth, "*Wash* thyself and anoint thee." (רָחַץ *rahats*, λουω *louo.*)

The words also occur, 2 Sam. xi, 2, and xii 20; 1 Kings xxii, 38, (and they *washed* his armour;) Job ix, 30; Isa. i, 16; Ezek. xvi, 4, 9, and xxii, 40; 2 Kings v, 10, 12, 13.

1 Sam. xxv, 41: "Behold, let thy handmaid be a servant to *wash* the feet of the servants of my lord." (רָחַץ *rahats*, νιπτω *nipto.*) The same words occur, in same sense, 2 Sam. xi, 8; Cant. v, 3.

2 Chron. iv, 6: "Such things as they offered for the burnt-offerings they *washed* (רָחַץ *rahats*, πλυνω *pluno*) in the lavers; but the sea was for the priests to *wash* in." (רָחַץ *rahats*, νιπτω *nipto.*)

Job xxix, 6: "When I *washed* (רָחַץ *rahats*) my steps in butter, and the rock poured me out rivers of oil." The Septuagint render it thus: "When my paths *were flowed* (εχεοντο) with butter, and my mountains *poured forth* (εχεοντο) milk." The reader will observe that the Hebrew *rahats* is translated into Greek by χεω *cheo, to pour out, diffuse, to shed.*

Psa. xxvi, 6: "I will *wash* my hands in innocency." (רָחַץ *rahats*, νιπτω *nipto.*) The same words occur, in same sense, Psa. lxxiii, 13.

Psa. lviii, 10: "The righteous shall *wash* his feet in the blood of the wicked." (רָחַץ *rahats*, νιπτω *nipto.*) The sense of this text, and the force of the words, seem evidently to be synonymous with Psa. lxviii, 23. The sense is that of *staining* or *wetting*, by having the blood *gush out* upon the feet. See this last text explained, chap. iii of this work.

Cant. v, 12: "His eyes are ... *washed* in milk." (רָחַץ *rahats*, λουω *louo.*)

Isa. iv, 4: "When the Lord shall have *washed* away the filth of the daughter of Zion." (רָחַץ *rahats*, πλυνω *pluno.*)

The above are all the places, save one or two, in the Old Testament, in which רָחַץ *rahats* occurs. We wish the reader to observe,—1. The latitude of its meaning is indicated by the fact that it is sometimes translated into Greek by λουω *louo*, which means *wash*, and is generally used to denote the washing of the body; sometimes by νιπτω *nipto*, which means also *wash*, and is used to denote washing of hands or feet; sometimes by πλυνω *pluno*, *wash*, which is used to denote the washing of clothes; and once it is translated by χεω *cheo*, *to flow*, *to pour forth*, *to shed*.

2. It is never used as a synonyme of *bathe*. It properly denotes *wash*. The washing, it is true, might be performed by *bathing;* but then it might be performed equally well without it, and where bathing might have been practised it was not of itself sufficient. The force of the word implies some effort made to cleanse, as by rubbing with the hand. And, as President Beecher has well said, bathing fulfilled the command, not because it was a bathing, but solely because it was a washing. Besides, in many cases, as in the washing of hands, the water was poured. At other times it was simply taken out of the vase or vessel by one hand, and applied to the body. This was *washing*, and this mode was included in the βαπτισμων *baptisms* of Heb. ix, 10.

The word used to enjoin the washing of clothes, in the Old Testament, is כָּבַס *kabas*, which primarily means, *to tread*, *to trample with the feet;* and hence, *to wash*, *to cleanse*, &c., as garments, by treading them in a trough; and finally, *to wash* in any way. (Vide Gesenius's Lexicon.) It is sometimes used in a figurative sense, as in Psa. li, 4, 9; (Eng. version;) li, 2, 7; Jer. iv, 14, and ii, 22; Mal. iii, 2. It may shed a ray of light upon this subject to add, that πλυνω, *pluno*, *to wash*, (clothes,) in the Septuagint, sometimes answers to שָׁטַף *shatap*, *to gush*, *to pour out*, *to rush*, *to overflow;* hence, to *wash*, *rinse;* as Ezek. xvi, 9: "Yea, I thoroughly *washed* away thy blood." The same word is used in Job xxxviii, 25, to signify an "*outpouring*" of waters. See also Prov. xxvii, 4, where it should read, "Anger is an *outpouring*," Eng. "outrageous." This word is generally translated *rinse* in English, where it denotes *washing* of *hands*, or *vessels*, as in Lev. xv, 11, 12.

Such, then, is the force of some of the words employed in the Mosaic ritual, to set forth the duty of external washings. I trust the reader is satisfied that *bathing* or *immersion* was never *enjoined* by the law of Moses, although it was practised on different occasions. In view of all this, is it not astonishing that Mr. Judd (p. 40) should render διαφοροις βαπτισμοις (Heb. ix, 10) *different* or *diverse immersions?* Did not that author know that different modes of purification were required? such as washing, sprinkling, rinsing, and, in the case of inanimate things only, they were sometimes required to be *put in* the water? Now, the apostle says the Levitical institutes consisted μονον *monon*, "ONLY of meats and drinks, and diverse baptisms." But did the lustrations consist ONLY of *immersion?* Besides, the adjective διαφοροις *different*, qualifies the noun *baptisms*. This makes good sense, if we suppose the noun to be *generic*, as *purifications*, but it is absurd if we take the noun as *specific*, like *immersion*. The Baptists are wont to argue that the words ἑν βαπτισμα *hen baptisma*, ONE *baptism*, (Eph. iv, 5,) proves their doctrine of one *mode* of baptism. This they think good logic. But what, then, does the phrase DIFFERENT *baptisms* import? Does it not prove *different* MODES? Will they not allow us to argue upon their own principles?

NOTE H.—Referred to p. 109.

The following statements of President Beecher, in the Biblical Repository, for January, 1841, are clear and cogent. "What, then," says that author, "are the facts, as it regards the earlier ages of the church? I am willing freely and fully to concede, that, in the primitive church, from the earliest period of which we have any historical accounts, immersion was the mode generally practised, and, except in extraordinary cases, the only mode. I do not mean that these remarks shall apply to the *apostolic age*, but to the earliest historical ages of the uninspired primitive church. The practice of the apostolic age, I shall consider by itself. After all that has been said upon this point by learned men, it will not be deemed necessary for me to advance proof of the position, that, in the primitive church, immersion was the general mode of baptism. . . . . . But, admitting these things to be facts, what then? Does it follow of course that the fathers were led to adopt this form, by a belief that the import of the word βαπτιζω is to immerse? This I know seems very generally to have been taken for granted on both sides of the question. For example, Professor Stuart, after an able and clear exhibition of the proof that the early churches did baptize by immersion, says: "In what manner, then, did the churches of Christ, from a very early period, to say the least, understand the word βαπτιζω in the New Testament? Plainly, they construed it as meaning immersion." "That the Greek fathers, and the Latin ones, who were familiar with the Greek, *understood* the general import of the word βαπτιζω, would hardly seem to be capable of a denial."—*Biblical Repository*, vol. iii, p. 362.

Now, all this is manifestly based on the assumption, that the practice of the fathers, in this case, is an infallible index of their authority; i. e., if they did, in fact, immerse, they must of course believe that βαπτιζω means to immerse. Indeed, this seems generally to have been regarded as a first principle, an indisputable truth. As long as it is so regarded, the facts already stated, as to early practice, will exert a strong, disturbing influence on the mind. The scholar, in the region of philology and logic, finds all plain; but he enters the dizzy and bewildering region of early practice, and his brain reels, his energy is dissolved, and some unseen power seems to be wresting his previous philological conclusions from his grasp. Indeed, if it is a sound principle, that we must infer the principles of the fathers, as to the import of βαπτιζω, from their practice, I see not how we can avoid letting them go; for, of the facts there can be no doubt. But it is high time to ask, Is the principle sound? Is it logical? Has it any force at all? It may seem adventurous to call in question a principle so generally received and so firmly believed. Nevertheless, I am compelled to say, that I cannot perceive that the position is based on any sound principle of philology or logic; nay, it seems to me that there is abundant evidence that it is entirely illogical and unsound: 1. Because, where a given result may have been produced by many causes, it is never logical to assume, without proof, that it is the result of any one of them alone. The proper course is, to inquire which of the possible causes was, in fact, the real and efficient cause of the result in question. 2. Because, on making the inquiry, it appears manifest to me that the practice in question did not originate in the belief that the word βαπτιζω means immerse, but in entirely different and independent causes. Suppose, now, the word to mean *to purify*, it is neither impossible nor improbable that certain local and peculiar causes may have led to some one mode of purifying rather than another, and that this mode may have been immersion; and if all these things may have been so, who has a right to assume, without proof, that they were not so? I believe that they were. If it is inquired, what causes they were? I answer: 1. Oriental usages, and the habits of warmer regions. 2. A false interpretation of Rom. vi, 3, 4, and Col. ii, 12. 3. A very early habit of ascribing peculiar virtue to external forms. The first is sufficient to begin the practice; the other two to extend, perpetuate, and confirm it. Now, if it can be shown that these causes did exist, and did operate, and had great power, then a sufficient account of the origin and progress of the usage *may be given by these alone;* and thus, all presumption against the meaning I have assigned to βαπτιζω, or in favour of the sense to immerse, will be taken away; and thus, the way will be prepared to resume the direct philological proof, that in the earlier ages the word βαπτιζω did mean *purify*. But of their existence, or their power, can there be a doubt? Did not Christianity begin in the warm regions of the East, and in the midst of a people whose climate, habits, costume, and mode of life, were all adapted to bathing? And was not the practice nearly universal? Hence, nothing could be more natural than its use on *convenient occasions*, as a mode of religious purifying; and if, as some maintain, the form had been previously used as a religious rite, nothing could be more natural than its adoption, as a mode of purifying, in the church. As to the interpretation of Rom. vi, 3, 4, and Col. ii, 12, as referring to the external form, all may not be ready to concede that it was false; yet that it was early prevalent and powerful, no one, I think, at all acquainted with the facts of the case, will deny. But of this, more in another place. As to a superstitious attachment to forms—who can deny it? nay, who that is a Protestant does? Evidence of it throngs on every page that records the early history of the church. To omit all else, the history of this rite alone would furnish volumes of proof. Let the holy water—the baptismal chrism, to symbolize and bestow the Holy Spirit—the putting on of white robes after baptism, to symbolize the putting on of Christ—the baptism of men and women perfectly naked, to denote their entire moral nakedness before putting on Christ—let the anointing of the eyes and ears, to denote the sanctification of the senses—let the eating of honey and milk—the sign of the cross; and finally, let baptismal regeneration—the sum and completion of all these formal tendencies—bear witness to the mournful truth. Now, when the tendencies to formalism and superstition were so all-pervading and almost omnipotent, what could avert a blind and superstitious devotion to an early form—one especially in which so much was supposed to be involved, both of emblematical import and of sanctifying power?

Note I.—Referred to page 110.

Mr. Judd gives another turn to this passage, which certainly appears plausible, and we insert it for the information of the reader.

"The expression, '*Can any man forbid water?*' &c., can mean neither more nor less than, *Can any man forbid that these should be baptized in water, who have received the Holy Ghost as well as we?* The Jewish believers who accompanied Peter from Joppa were the only persons present who could be supposed to have objections to any of the proceedings; and their objections would not lie against the use of a *river*, or a *bath;* nor yet against water *being brought into the house.* Their only possible objection must be against these Gentiles being baptized into the church. The Jews had hitherto scrupulously avoided all religious association with the Gentiles; and the brethren of the circumcision would have trembled at the thought of their being admitted, without further ceremony, into the church, unless they had the most explicit intimations that such was the divine pleasure. The apostle, being already informed by a vision that the partition wall between Jews and Gentiles was now removed, therefore exclaims, "Since God hath shed down upon these Gentiles the abundant influences of his grace, baptizing them with the Holy Ghost, as he did us at the beginning, thus evincing that he puts no difference between us and them, *can any one forbid that they should be baptized in water*, and thus be incorporated into the Christian church?"—*Review of Stuart*, pp. 67, 68.

THE END.

www.ingramcontent.com/pod-product-compliance
Lightning Source LLC
LaVergne TN
LVHW021258110826
845150LV00003B/420

* 9 7 8 1 4 2 5 5 6 0 4 4 7 *